P.8

CAMPAIGNING WITH THE DUKE OF WELLINGTON & FEATHERSTONE

A Guide to the Battles in Spain & Portugal, with Donald Featherstone, the Duke of Wellington, and All the Others, 1808-1814 & 1973-1992

by

Donald Featherstone

EMPEROR'S PRESS
Chicago, Illinois

CAMPAIGNING WITH THE DUKE OF WELLINGTON & FEATHERSTONE

©Emperor's Press

Original Edition; Published in 1993

Printed and Bound in the United States of America

ISBN 0-9626655-9-2

THE EMPEROR'S PRESS
5744 West Irving Park Road
Chicago, Il. 60634 U.S.A.
Toll Free, if calling in U.S.A: 1.800.59.EAGLE
Calling from outside U.S.A: 312.777.7307

• •

CARTOGRAPHY
Yonan "Tony" Badal

TABLE OF CONTENTS

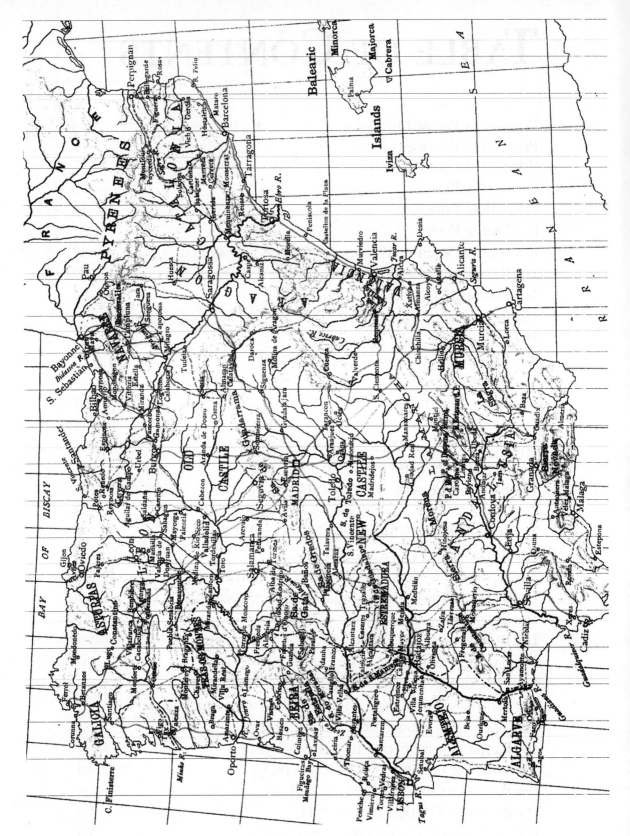

THE THEATRE OF WAR

Peninsular Preamble

In no way claiming to be an academic or definitive work, this book aims at being both interesting and instructive, by transforming the reader into a fly on the wall of history. This is achieved by maximum quotation and minimal interpretation, the battles and sieges being described through the extensive use of accounts written by soldiers who actually took part in the actions, embellished by that generation of military historians and writers whose prolific literary output stimulated the jingoistic Empire conscious patriots of late 19th century Britain. Long out of print, their florid, sometimes emotional accounts of this colourful Napoleonic War have been resurrected and marched again into battle.

Those Victorian writers, along with those 'saucy fellows' of the Light Division: Johnny Kincaid, George Simmons, Riflemen Costello, Harris and Surtees, as well as the ebullient Sir Harry Smith and the doyen of them all, William Napier, would no doubt find great satisfaction in knowing that their accounts of the actions in which they fought are stimulating their descendants 180 years later. It could be said that their full blooded stories bestow a certain aura of glamour to the war they fought, perhaps bringing it more in line with the desired fun element of this book.

Walking the battlefields in Portugal and Spain, where Wellington achieved his greatest victories, on at least ten separate occasions, the author, who has similarly traversed more than 200 such fields in Europe, Africa and America, believes these Peninsular fields to be among the most interesting. Perhaps this is because of the pride engendered by knowing himself to be a descendant of these incomparable soldiers. Or is it an affinity born of being one of an army which, after 1940, proved just as much of an ulcer to Hitler as the Peninsular War did to Napoleon.

Whatever the reasons for this pre-occupation, the author continues to nurture fond memories of Peninsular fields and they are continually being refought on our wargames tables, despite hot competition from those many other historic battles in which the soldiers of many nations displayed courage and dignity. It is hoped what is written in this book will arouse ardour and inspiration among American comrades-in-arms so that they will not only research and wargame these battles, but be encouraged to venture forth and actually explore these fields in Portugal and Spain. To have walked a battlefield makes it incomparably easier to reproduce an accurate and enjoyable wargame.

Looking at it from the other end of the picture, when comfortably cruising along endless dusty roads under a blazing sun, the wargamer will find his mind immensely concentrated on the awesome realisation that these soldiers of the Napoleonic Wars marched every mile, carrying heavy musket and ammunition, a pack containing all their meagre possessions, foot sore and muscles aching. No wargamer can ever realistically recreate the heights of Sorauren or Busaco, the Rhunes in the Pyrenees, without knowing what it is like to scale them on hands and knees.

Can a preface of a book with our aims be better concluded than by quoting William Shakespeare's stirring Agincourt words?

Now, soldiers, march away!
And how thou pleasest, God, dispose the day.

PENINSULAR PANORAMA

A BRIEF SURVEY OF THE COURSE OF THE PENINSULAR WAR 1808-1814

In 1808, just as in 1940, Britain was facing the greatest threat since the Spanish Armada of 1588. It was a time when another despot found Britain to be the last stumbling block in his plans of conquest. By force of arms, annexation and alliance on terms of submission, Napoleon had systematically taken over the continent of Europe, which had resigned itself to acceptance of French domination: nothing it seemed could check the onward march of Napoleon. In a manner strangely akin to the events of 1939, the French ruler and Czar Alexander of Russia had met and divided the world between them, like two children sharing out a bag of sweets. Only the British Isles, "this precious stone set in a silver sea, Which serves it in the office of a wall, Or as a most defensive to a house, Against the envy of less happier lands" remained defiant and determined to bring down the tyrant.

Napoleon, pursuing his ambitions, decided he required control of Portugal and her South American dependencies. So Junot was sent to conquer that country and, on a pretext, French armies moved into strategic positions in friendly Spain. But Bonaparte, by forcing the Spanish King to abdicate and proclaiming his own brother Joseph King of Spain, alienated the Spanish people. The peasants rose in anger against French garrisons throughout the country. Believing this to be a turning point, Britain seized the chance for which she had been waiting.

Napoleon called the Peninsular War the Spanish Ulcer and there is little doubt that it played a big part in his downfall. A classic example of guerilla warfare, the war also emphasized the value of British seapower. In December 1807, a French army under Junot invaded Portugal and, in March 1808, Murat led an army of 100,000 into Spain; Napoleon's brother Joseph was placed on the throne.

The French army in Spain largely consisted of recent conscripts completing their training under service conditions, and in July 1808, 20,000 of these raw troops under Dupont stunned Europe by surrendering at Baylen to a force of Spanish regulars and guerillas.

The British sent arms, equipment and money to the Portuguese and Spanish people, and an expeditionary force under Sir Arthur Wellesley landed in Portugal. On 1 August 1808 Wellesley's army landed north of Lisbon; Junot marched out to meet him with 14,000 men. On 17 August, Wellesley skilfully manoeuvred a smaller French force from a strong position at Rolica. It was a small but significant battle because Delaborde's force of veterans fought stubbornly and for sixteen years the French had rarely been defeated in the field even when fewer in number. On 20 August, Wellesley positioned his 16,500 on two long hills at Vimeiro, where they were attacked by 13,000 French in two columns shielded by tirailleurs, supported by mobile field artillery and with cavalry protecting their flanks. The tirailleurs were so troubled by the riflemen that they were unable to adequately protect the columns and the French gunners were so harassed that their fire was light and ineffective. The British line were using all their muskets as their flanks wrapped round the columns, who found it impossible to deploy into line under fire, finally breaking and fleeing, taking artillerymen with them so that the guns were stranded and captured. Similar events occurred on at least five more occasions during the battle, forming a pattern to be repeated in every British success in the Peninsula. This defeat amazed the French army and astonished the rest of Europe, unaccustomed to a veteran French army, even outnumbered 13 to 17, using the invariably successful Napoleonic tactics in the open field and being beaten.

In September 1808, Sit John Moore with 22,000 men marched from Portugal to aid the Spanish armies, hoping to join up with Sir David Baird's 18,000 at Corunna, but he had to change his plans because of Spanish defeats and the fall of Madrid, together with the fact that Napoleon himself, disgusted with the showing of his generals, had arrived in Spain and with 194,000 men was advancing towards him. Sir John Moore skilfully retreated, outwitting and outmarching three French armies under Napoleon, Soult and Junot, fighting rearguard actions under appalling winter conditions in the mountains of Galicia, until his decimated, exhausted and ragged army of 15,000 men reached Corunna on 11 January 1809 with Soult and 20,000 men at their heels.

Moor's force of about 15,000 infantry, nine 6 pounder guns, but no cavalry. They were positioned on high ground with the village of Elvira on their right centre repeatedly changing hands. After Sir John Moore was mortally wounded, the battle tailed off to a quiet end with both armies occupying their original positions, having lost about 1,000 men each. The British forces were able to embark without leaving a man behind.

After Corunna, the French overran the Peninsula and beat the Spanish armies in four battles until, on 12 May, Wellesley, after days of marching, feinting and manoeuvring, made a daring, crossing of the River Douro and threw the French out of Oporto with surprising ease; retreating into the mountains, the French lost several thousand men. In June 1809, Wellesley invaded Spain, hoping to unite with some 100,000 Spanish regulars and guerillas, but found them poor allies.

One tactical formula brought continued success to wellesley in the Peninsula, the pattern being set at Talavera on 28 July, when he was attacked by 46,000 men under Victor and King Joseph Bonaparte. His Spanish allies were so ineffectual that Wellesley placed them behind fortifications, supported by both British and their own cavalry while he able to take on 46,000 French with more or less 20,000 British and King's German Legion positioned behind and protected from artillery fire by a low ridge. On the forward slopes a screen of British riflemen engaged enemy skirmishers and harassed the French columns, steadily advancing up the hill, while shrapnel* shells burst over and amongst them. When the columns neared the crest of the ridge, the riflemen fell back and the two lines of British infantry went forward to the crest where they met the French with platoon volleys fired at fifty to hundred yards range. In less than three minutes they fired ten platoon volleys before the French broke and ran. Successive column attacks met the same fate.

Even so, after one attack had broken down, the pursuing British infantry, including the Guards and two King's German Legion brigades, went out of control and, with unloaded muskets, came up against overwhelming numbers of French infantry who roughly handled them before pursuing them back to their own lines. There, four British battalions, about three thousand men, opened out to let their comrades through and then closed to beat the French back. The British cavalry took unnecessary punishment when the 23rd Light Dragoons and K.G.L. Hussars hit a small ravine at speed, causing losses and disordering them so that the 23rd lost half their strength when they encountered a brigade of chasseurs a cheval.

At Talavera, Wellesley lost 5,365 men, a quarter of his entire force while the French loss of 7,268 represented only 18% of theirs. His rear menaced by Soult and Ney, Wellesley withdrew back into Portugal.

During the winter of 1809-1810, the Spanish, defeated in the filed, carried on a most effective guerilla campaign, while Wellington (Made Viscount Wellington after Talavera) constructed north of Lisbon, the Lines of Torres Vedras, stretching for 30 miles mounting some 600 guns. French troops crossed the Pyrenees and poured into Spain throughout the winter. Wellington reorganised his army by allocating a brigade of Portuguese infantry, armed and organised in the British style, to each infantry division, giving the local troops experienced backing so that by Busaco they had become first class soldiers. In May, when Massena was ordered to take Portugal, there was 300,000 French soldiers in the country. By mid July he had taken Ciudad Rodrigo, but on 27 August at Busaco, his 65,000 strong army was soundly beaten by Wellington's 46,000 (including 46,000 Portuguese) by the same tactical methods of line versus column that h̲ ̲umphed at Talavera. The French fought so courageously as they had ever done but their artillery and cavalry could accomplish nothing and the tirailleurs, far from disordering the Allied line, were not even capable of defending their own columns. French casualties of nearly 5,000, including four generals, provided the highest casualty rate of officers to men suffered by the French in the entire war. The allies lost 1,250. At Busaco, Wellington avoided any massive concentration of fire, siting his guns in small numbers in line with his infantry and used them at effective ranges. The ratio of artillery to infantry in the Allied army seldom exceeded one gun per thousand men while the French armies in central Europe had three guns per thousand men, and four in Spain.

In October 1810, Wellington withdrew into the Lines of Torres Vedras and Massena, after fruitlessly probing the defenders, settled down to blockade the lines, living so precariously in a devastated area that 25,000 French were lost through wounds, malnutrition and hunger. He found blockade would not work against a seapower. In early March 1811, the French withdrew to Spain, harassed by Wellington and by guerillas, reaching their base at Salamanca in early April after Massena had skilfully extricated his army from a number of critical situations.

In March 1811, Soult attempted to advance into Portugal and captured Badajoz, but was prevented from further when a detached force under Victor was well beaten at Barrosa on 5 March 1811 by a smaller force under Sir Thomas Graham. On 3 May, Massena, marching with 48,268 men to relieve Almeida, came up with Wellington's 37,000 positioned behind the village of Fuentes d'Onoro. There two days of hard fighting with desperate hand to hand fighting in the village; at one stage the Light Division with Cotton's cavalry were isolated on an open plain surrounded by large numbers of French cavalry, three divisions of infantry and several batteries of artillery. Craufurd handled his command with great skill, keeping the line battalion in mobile squares while using his riflemen as skirmishers, not allowing himself to be pinned down by enemy cavalry, so that infantry and artillery could pour their fire into his formations. Slowly retiring, the riflemen, behind cover of low stone outcrops, kept up a galling fire on the enemy cavalry and artillery at about 250 yards range, running to the cover of the squares whenever cavalry the cavalry approached too near. When the French artillery came too near, the danger of being charged by Cotton's cavalry forced them back; Bull's horse artillery positioned themselves between the formations and kept off the French cavalry, artillery and infantry. In their two mile withdrawal the Light Division, showing the highest discipline, courage and confidence, lost only 35 men. A British Army legend began here when Captain Norman Ramsay's two guns of Bull's troop, completely enveloped by French cavalry, cut their way through the encircling mass at a gallop, with mounted gunners surrounding their limbered pieces and caissons.

At Fuentes, the British open order fighting was more effective than French mass system, even within the confines of the village, where the light companies and riflemen showed more aptitude for street fighting than the French, accustomed to attacking in column. The British cavalry surpassed themselves and working in small units, did not get out of hand in charges.

Soult advanced to relieve Badajoz, besieged by Beresford, who marched to meet him at Albuera on 16 May with 20,000 men, including British, German and Portuguese brigades and a Spanish force of 14,650. After early skirmishing, the French made the most massive single attack of the entire war, against four battalions of Spanish infantry on the Allied southern flank. There were 8,500 men , two full infantry divisions, in an almost solid column with only a light skirmish line in front; artillery accompanied the mass, whose left flank was protected by 3,500 cavalry and more guns. The Spanish infantry fought unusually well but would have been broken had not a British division come up on their right flank, with Colborne's brigade attacking the flank of the French column. A sudden thunder storm with sheets of rain swept across the field, allowing a regiment of Polish Lancers to approach unseen and hit one end of the of the British line, whose muskets had been put out of action by the sudden downpour. The first three of Colborne's battalions were practically annihilated under the lances wielded by skilled horsemen in tight formation. Breaking into the Spanish rear, the French cavalry almost caught Beresford and his staff besides sweeping over a battery of K.G.L. guns. Rallying, the Spanish infantry came back to the front, reinforced by two British brigades and the remaining battalion of Colborne's brigade; muskets were now effective as the rain had ceased. Seven British battalions, about 3,700 men, in a two deep line, now began a close range fire fight with about 8,000 French formed in one huge column about 200 men wide and 40 ranks deep. Occupying an area about the size of a cricket field, this contest dragged on for nearly an hour, with several French batteries, less than 300 yards back from the head of the column, enfilading and cross-firing through the centre of the British line with grape and canister. Losses would have been astronomical but for the smoke and heavy clouds which obscured targets.

Torrents of rain brought the fighting to an end; armies remained in position until late on the following day when the French retired covered by horse artillery and cavalry. The Allies lost nearly 6,000; the French about 7,000. The British, German and Portuguese soldiers missed Wellington and did not have the same confidence in Beresford, who, although brave, loyal and talented, did not employ Wellington's successful tactics, and if Soult outmanouvred him, then he would have done so to any other British commander in the Peninsula, bar Wellington himself.

Wellington stormed Ciudad Rodrigo on 19 January, where Craufurd was killed, and Badajoz in April, where he lost more men than in any major battle except Talavera and Albuera. Then Wellington thrust boldly into northern Spain with an allied army of some 48,000 British, Portuguese and Spanish troops, with 54 guns. In mid-July Wellington and Marmont, who had taken over form Massena, at the head of a similar sized armies, marched parallel for several days with each commander his army well in hand, seeking tactical; advantage. At midday on 22 July, at Salamanca, Marmont extended his left flank, and Packenham's 3rd Division with Portuguese cavalry, hidden behind a range of hills, were able to drive into the leading French column before they were knew what had hit them. A second French division formed into square but were slaughtered in three volleys by a two deep infantry line, and the survivors broke and fled. Le Marchant's cavalry charged the disintegrating French infantry and smashed five battalions, then charged into a third French division, who had double-timed for a mile and, although in square, were unable to withstand the heavy dragoons and were scattered. A French counterstroke of 12,000 men in columns lacking artillery and with less skirmishers than the Allies, was stopped in its tracks and was completely broken in five minutes. Five of the original eight French divisions were now dispersed; Marmont and General Bonnet were among the casualties. To cover their retreat Clausel, for the first time in the Peninsular War, formed the seven battalions of a complete French division in a continuous, three deep line with a single battalion at either end in square, but these were dispersed by artillery fire. The French army, having lost 14,000 men, was now in full retreat, but the physically exhausted British army was unable to pursue.

During the winter of 1812-1813 Wellington trained his army hard and every battalion was capable, even in rough country, of moving from line to open column or square in thirty seconds. Some veteran French units were withdrawn from Spain to rebuild Napoleon's armies in Germany, but their conscript replacements were good soldiers and did all that was asked of them. The total French force south of the Pyrenees still exceeded 200,000 men. Moving with great speed and secrecy, Wellington had his entire force north of the Douro by 3 June, and the outmanoeuvred French streamed north in disorder, constantly harassed by Spanish guerillas.

On 21 June 1815 the French, 66,000 men under Joseph and Jourdan, took up defensive positions around Vitoria, formed in three lines with artillery and cavalry support. Wellington divided his force of 27,000 British, 27,000 Portuguese and 9,000 Spanish, into four columns that came into the valley of Vitoria at various points, cutting the French line of retreat. All went as planned and by late afternoon the French, outfought and outmanoeuvred, were streaming away in small groups. Although suffering fewer casualties than at Salamanca, the French abandoned everything and saved only two guns so that they required complete reorganisation and re-arming before returning as a fighting force.

Joseph retired across the Pyrenees; the Allies did not pursue because Napoleon had signed an armistice with Russia and Prussia and might well bring an army of overwhelming strength against them. Soult, replacing Joseph and Jourdan, reorganised the French forces which were more numerous than the Allies, who had less than 60,000 Anglo-Portuguese on a front of 40 miles, positioned in depth to take advantage of the road system. On 25 July, with Wellington away, Soult sent strong forces strong forces to partially force the passes at Maya and Roncesvalles, where 13,000 British troops held 40,000 French until withdrawing at nightfall; four Portuguese guns were lost, the first and only guns ever taken from Wellington in any action. It was said that British soldiers had rarely fought so courageously but had seldom been worse commanded. With Wellington back in control, the Allied army took up defensive positions on ridges at Sorauren, to be attacked on 28 July by Soult, with a considerable numerical advantage, when Spanish troops backed by British infantry fought well to beat Soult back, causing 4,000 casualties. The Allies lost 2,650. On 30 July the numerically weaker Allied columns stormed down from the ridges with all the precision and impetuosity of Salamanca against strong enemy positions, but French morale was low and the second battle of Sorauren was soon over. The French streamed back over the border into France, more disorganised and defeated than they had been after Vitoria.

In October 1813 Wellington attacked at San Sebastian where the French, immobilised in static field fortifications, were outflanked by the Light Division and forced to retreat when the 5th Division, after crossing the River Bidassoa by little known fords, appeared on their other flank. Thus, the line of the Pyrenees was broken. Along the Nivelle, Soult had some 63,000 men in naturally strong positions, heavily fortified with numerous artillery in redoubts. Wellington's army totalled 80,000, including some doubtful Spanish units. His attack on 10 November 1813 included some excellent work by the Light Division in capturing the Lesser Rhune, an area so rugged that only three mountain guns could move up to support them. By the end of the day, the French had lost all their positions and 50 guns, and Soult had been forced back.

All the Spanish, with the exception of Morillo's experienced division, were sent home following atrocities committed on French civilians in looting a village, so that Wellington was left with a command in France of 36,000 British, 23,000 Portuguese and 4,000 Spaniards, in all 63,000 men exclusive of cavalry. Soult had about the same number less cavalry, National guards and the garrison of Bayonne. Crossing the River Nive at dawn on 9 December Hill's corps, formed of troops from three nations with 12 guns, was cut off when the river suddenly rose, and were attacked by a concentration of French at odds of five to one. After fighting for four hours Hill, unaided, defeated Soult and caused him 3,300 casualties as against 1,775 of his own. On the same day, three whole German battalions, complete with officers, colours and baggage, defected from the French army and came over to the Allies.

In the early days of 1814 Soult, with a total force of 62,500 men, still held Bayonne with his field army of 36,000 in position on a ridge at Orthez. Wellington divided the Allied army into a siege force of 18,000 men under Hope around Bayonne, and a field force of 48,000 under Hill, Beresford and himself. In an amphibious operation, Hope got a force across the Adour to completely surround Bayonne. On 27 February Wellington, with 31,000 men attacked in five columns and drove the French from strong positions at Orthez largely because of the decline in French morale following an unbroken series of defeats.

By mid-March, Wellington had driven Soult halfway across southwestern France and on April 10th made a strong assault on Toulouse which, although not apparently successful at the time, forced Soult to abandon the city. A few hours later it was learned that Napoleon had abdicated and after almost six years the fighting was over. British cavalry and artillery proceeded across France to Calais, while Anglo-Portuguese divisions marched to Bordeaux, both conscious that they had been partners in many hard fought battles.

10

PENINSULAR PROMENADING

SEEING IT FOR YOURSELF - WALKING THE BATTLEFIELDS OF THE PENINSULA WAR.

This section of the book is all about assorted groups of Englishmen, some of who have been under fire themselves and heard shots fired in anger, who find an evocative pleasure in venturing to far-flung corners of the world to contemplate and walk those fields of conflict hallowed by their ancestors. For nearly a quarter of a century, their bonds of comradeship has been forged by 'Services-style' mucking-in and living amicably with fellow enthusiasts while walking some 200 battlefields, of 21 wars spread over 7 centuries, in 11 countries and 3 continents. Here we consider some 28 battles of the Peninsular War, fought in Portugal and Spain from August 1808 until April 1814., the fields of which have been visited and walked on no less than ten occasions!

Not only do these enthusiasts know their way around these historic fields, but they are also highly experienced in bringing to life and simulating - in miniature - the stirring events of the long-dead warriors who bestrode these fields. On tabletop reconstructions of Talavera, Vitoria, Salamanca and the like, all authentically scaled and realistically assembled, armies of meticulously painted model soldiers, under 1 inch in height, manoeuvre and fight in the manner of their day - advancing, retreating, firing, charging so as to cause the result to be in realistic doubt to the very last shot. On these mini-fields, Wellington does not always win at Vimeiro, nor does Marmont invariably lose at Salamanca!

So, the walking and the wargaming are synonymous, the former providing not only the background knowledge but - more important - the sheer inspiration to return home and be one - in miniature - with our ancestors who fought on these fields and whose courage and steadfastness we attempt to rekindle. All without any fear of causing grief to tiny metal or plastic widows and orphans!

In what it is hoped is a stimulating manner, these pages tell of truly memorable visits to the area of this Napoleonic Campaign that raged and smouldered for six years in Portugal and Spain and which, through articles and books, paintings, films and television, has gripped the imagination of nearly ten succeeding generations. The Peninsular War of 1808 to 1814 had all the 'highs' and perhaps more than its share of the 'lows' than most military campaigns, yet it has been sanitised through wargames so as to emphasize the colour and courage more than the fears and misery of Briton, Frenchman, Portuguese or Spaniard. Perhaps this presents the complete answer to those who believe that these tabletop games encourage participants to be aggressive and warlike.

In fact, the objective throughout has been to write a dual-purpose book that will be of interest to both wargamer and he who reads it out of sheer historical interest, for both will discover within its pages descriptions of the battles and the battlefields, the soldiers and their weapons, along with a deep undercurrent of comradeship revealed by both the long-dead combatants and those who retrace not only their footsteps but also their actions. Hopefully, the book might stimulate the general reader to enquire about the hobby of wargaming, through the inspiration of basically simple rules and suggestions that are sufficiently comprehensive to allow a realistic simulation of the battles of the Peninsular War. It is noteworthy that those already-wargamers who walked these fields for the first time, have been aware of being part of a 'time-warp' through being privileged participants in historical reconstructions of battles and battlefields all agreed to be among the inspiring of all they have visited and walked.

Speaking for himself and his immediate circle of friends - all enthusiastic and experienced wargamers - the Author can testify to the sheer excitement and pleasure of re-living our Peninsular Promenades by re-creating on tabletop terrains those battles whose fields we had actually walked. Far more than the majority of people who tread the fields of war, the wargamer truly dredges the last ounce out of his activities, viewing the topography of these now peaceful fields with all the clinical interest of the military historian, considering those tactical features that must be realistically reproduced on miniature terrains by scaled-down armies of authentically uniformed model soldiers. This alliance between fact and our all-pervasive practical interest has been among the most stimulating aspects during the quarter-century most of us have spent travelling to areas of conflict in eleven countries. So much have we learned from our battlefield-walking that our yearning for authenticity and realism persuades us to leave on the shelf those armies whose battlefields we have yet to tread!

One of the great drawbacks to Peninsular War battlefields lies in the fact that they lack the superb signposting and organisation of American battlefields of the Revolution or War Between the States -such immortal sites as Albuera, Busaco, Fuentes D'Onoro, Salamanca and Vitoria, all lay peacefully basking in relative anonymity - and the Spaniards, seemingly untouched by the patriotic pride and tourist awareness so marked in America, have built a motorway through the field of Talavera! Perhaps this worldwide habit of 'hiding' battlefields is not totally disadvantageous in that it forces the 'walker' to delve more deeply into local topography.

This is borne-out by leading British travel writer Elizabeth de Stroumillo who, in an article in the London Sunday Telegraph, reveals that she too is a Peninsular War buff!

Just back from Spain and the Peninsular War, I am still thanking whichever fate it was that first turned me on to battlefields. When time has greened over bloodstained furrows and transmuted grief into pride, nothing brings a landscape into sharper focus than picturing some bygone conflict that took place there. For the thoughtful traveller, it's a stimulating alternative to museums, churches and ancient streets—and old battlefields make far better picnic spots.

It was a picnic we had in mind as we left Salamanca one morning a couple of weeks ago; on the very spot, we hoped, where Wellington was lunching 175 years ago (on July 22) near the village of Torres, some five miles south of the city.

After a month of fruitless skirmishing, trying to manoeuvre Marmont's French army into a favourable battle position, Wellington had reached a crucial decision point: Napoleon was sending heavy reinforcements, and if a fight couldn't be forced immediately, the British would have to retreat to Portugal or be hopelessly outnumbered.

Wellington ordered the sick and wounded to be evacuated from Salamanca and waited just a little longer, his army concealed in the hollows of the rolling country just north of two little hills called the Arapiles. Marmont, grouped to the south and east, saw the dust rising from the moving column and, believing Wellington to be retreating and leaving only a rear guard, quickly started to loop south-westwards to cut him off.

Lookouts dashed back to Wellington, by now halfway through his lunch, and told him that Marmont's army had strung itself out, leaving two fatal gaps in his line. "By God! That will do!" Wellington is said to have cried, flinging away his chicken bone, and off he galloped to order his divisions into the gaps, thus perpetrating his first truly offensive battle and probably his greatest tactical one.

Clearly we wanted to picnic off cold chicken, but we had forgotten it was Sunday, with most food shops shut, so we changed plans and hoped at least for a bar that served Tapas, those delicious Spanish snacks, somewhere near Torres. First, though, we climbed a hill to the east of the hamlet of Calvarrasa de Arriba, raising the scent of wild thyme with every footstep, and surveyed from the summit the patchwork of green, gold and tawny fields that was once the battlefield, with the twin Arapiles punctuating it.

Then we set off for Torres, but missed a turning and came to a main road junction—and a restaurant. By now hunger, not history, was uppermost in our minds and, although it looked packed to the rafters, we went in and in rudimentary Spanish explained our plight. "But this is where your Wellington was lunching," said the proprietor, waving his arms at a tiny back garden. "We are in Torres, and this is the spot."

Chicken was not on the menu, but asparagus mayonnaise was, and so was a delicious paella (with bits of chicken in it) and salad and fruit and lots of wine and laughter and hours of fractured-Spanish chat. At the end of it all the patron, balding and rotund, his huge smile framed by a drooping moustache, presented us with a comic-book children's history of Salamanca. In it was proof of his assertions: a cartoon showing him leaning from the window of his restaurant saying to a sturdy band of British soldiery: "Well thrashed, Wellington, be my guests!"

For the record: the restaurant is Meson de los Arapiles, on the N630 seven kilometres south of Salamanca, and the Wellington Society of Madrid will lunch there on July 22. Our lunch, which cost less than 11 pounds a head, put paid to our plans to climb the Greater Arapile, but even the most dedicated military history buff can't do everything.

We hadn't done too badly. One day, we crossed the nearby Portuguese border to visit Almeida, a fairly forlorn but picturesque walled village that was formerly a key fort on the so-called "northern corridor" from Portugal into Spain, and came back via Ciudad Rodrigo, the corresponding fortress on the Spanish side, which Wellington stormed in 1812 on his way to Salamanca. Today it is a beautifully-preserved little walled city bristling with storks' nests, its watch-tower converted to a state-run parador hotel.

We had been to Alba de Tormes, better known now as the burial-place of St Teresa of Avila, to look at the bridge that a Spanish force should have held but didn't, thus allowing the remnants of Marmont's army to escape after Salamanca, and we had taken in a few other Peninsular War battlefields for good measure.

We had also been distracted more than once by the wild flowers along the roadsides, as rich in colour and variety as cottage gardens by contrast with our own barren verges, and we had spent a good deal of time prowling about Salamanca itself. Street upon street of noble buildings and a Plaza Mayor that must be one of Europe's most beautiful make it worth a few days of anyone's time

From my bedroom window at the Parador, the green and gold of the plateau, spiked with clumps of trees, village church towers and the far outline of the city of Vitoria, seemed to swell and dip away forever, so distant was the horizon. It was an archetypal view of tranquil rural Spain; only in the evenings, when the setting sun fractured the huge, bland sky into fiery splinters, did it acquire a hint of drama.

Yet on a June night 177 years ago, dramas of the utmost intensity had been played out there. The Marquess of Wellington (his dukedom was still to come) had just beaten the French on the plain of Vitoria in the last major battle of the Peninsular War. The French retreat towards the Pyrenees was hampered by their hordes of camp followers and, above all, by the wagon-loads of looted Spanish treasure in the baggage train of Napoleon's brother Joseph, puppet king of Spain. When the desperate French eventually abandoned the wagons, barely a mile from my window, British soldiers and their allies fell upon the cornucopia of spilled jewels, gold, silver, paintings and other treasures with a rapacity which prompted Wellington's famous "scum of the earth" phrase.

Retracing the Peninsular War, one of my favourite pastimes, animates many another otherwise unremarkable scene. In the case of Vitoria and the lesser battles that followed it, the trail is punctuated by low hills and old stone bridges and starts some 12 miles south-west of Vitoria.

The main road from Miranda de Ebro still runs alongside the Zadorra river, through the Puebla de Arganzon defile, from whose heights the French hoped to slaughter the advancing British, and you can well imagine how it must have been, pounding up those scrubby slopes to dislodge them.

A truncated watchtower still stands on the hillock above the village of Nanclares, just off the road slightly nearer to Vitoria. Today, it affords a fine view of the local prison; on June 21, 1813, it gave Wellington an equally fine view of the progress his forces were making along the Puebla heights, of the French guns on the nearby Arinez hill and of the Vitoria plain. Here it was that a peasant came to inform him that the French had failed to put a guard on the bridge of Trespuentes, further along the Zadorra, and over lunch we thought of that luckless man, who lost his life in the subsequent advance.

If you follow the minor road that roughly parallels the Zadorra, you will find no fewer than three ancient bridges: at the hamlets of Villodas and Mendoza as well as at Trespuentes itself - and the fenced-off but still impressive remains of Roman Iruna to boot. Only one bridge crucial to that battle fails to charm - at Gamarra, on the opposite edge of Vitoria, where the main line of

13

French retreat was cut: its replacement is new and traffic-choked. But Vitoria itself, a sparkling and handsome city, is unique in Spain in having a memorial to the part Wellington and the British played in its liberation.

There are more once-embattled hills and bridges to see to the east, by the sea and up in the Pyrenees. Take the creaky funicular to the summit of Monte Igueldo, on the western edge of San Sebastian, and you get a wonderful view, across that elegant resort, of the ruined castle on the hill opposite and of the old town at its foot. Here the French put up a heroic two-month resistance to a British and allied siege in the summer of 1813, at the end of which the town was, disgracefully sacked.

Turn into the hinterland along the French border and you come first to San Marcial and then to pretty Vera de Bidasoa, at both of which French attempts to relieve San Sebastian were defeated. The bridge at Vera bears a plaque in memory of the British captain who died holding it. A short way further south, just off the Pamplona road, is the enchanting unspoiled village of Lesaca, with a stout little stone castle that Wellington made his HQ.

An odd incident occurred on the bridge at Sorauren, a minute hamlet, not even marked on my map, astride the main N121 road just outside Pamplona. Wellington's forces had been pushed back in the high Pyrenees by Marshal Soult's French and Wellington had paused briefly to scribble orders to them to fall back on Sorauren when he was surprised by French Cavalry scouts. Leaping to his horse, he galloped across the bridge and up the hill above the village, where Portuguese soldiers loudly cheered him. The knowledge that Wellington himself was in charge there made the cautious Soult put off a further attack until the following day—by which time the British had been reinforced.

An inquisitive ancient in a large black beret accosted us as we were visualising the scene. Grasping what we were up to was beyond him but, when the word "war" got through, he repeated it scornfully and spat on the cobbles before stumping off. Well yes, quite so — but memories of past wars can greatly enrich present travels.

Long experience has taught we battlefield walkers to do our homework, so that we contemplate and study each individual site before proceeding to it; once on the spot we seek out, in order of priority, those places where we know significant events occurred. We endeavor to shut from our minds 20th century attitudes and beliefs in our efforts to become one with our marching forebears, sharing their apprehensions, deeds and sacrifices. Occasionally, this causes conflict with accepted and publicised accounts which, all too often in the manner of written history, tend to be perpetuations of an initial error or misjudgment. Seeing it for oneself, on the ground, backed by experience in reading military history and, for some of us, the personal experience of soldiering and being under fire (we also know that the emotion of fear is timeless) arouses a controversial or different assumption or conclusion - this is well argued out!

But rest assured, none of us ever walks a battlefield, least of all one fought upon by our own countrymen, without an awareness of that inestimable factor common to all fields of war - that they are hallowed by the courage and self-sacrifice of the soldiers who fought upon them.

There can be little doubt that all Peninsular War battlefield walks pale into insignificance when compared with the epic Expedition Corunna Walk performed in 1984 by a part of serving soldiers of the British Royal Green Jackets, descendants of those same Riflemen who, in 1808, blazed the path. What follows is the official report of their enviable expedition.

Background

This Christmas marks the 175th Anniversary of Sir John Moore's strategic withdrawal to Corunna. It as made in appalling weather conditions, across difficult terrain and under constant pressure from the advancing French.

Moore formed a Reserve Division from battalions of the 43rd, 52nd and 95th Regiments to cover the rear and flanks of his main army. This Division left Sahagun on 24 December 1808 and reached the heights above Corunna on 13 January 1809. It was evacuated on 18 January after the

Battle of Corunna.

The 1st and 3rd Battalions of today's Royal Green Jackets are the direct descendents of the old 43rd, 52nd and 95th Regiments.

The Aim

To commemorate this Anniversary it is hoped to send a party of 10 officers and men, drawn from the 1st and 3rd Battalions of The Royal Green Jackets, to march the route taken by the Reserve Division. It will keep, as near as possible to the same timings and halts, and will wear the uniforms of the period.

The Expedition

The expedition, consisting of 10 officers and soldiers drawn from the 1st and 3rd Battalions. The Royal Green Jackets will form up at Tidworth and move, via the Plymouth ferry to Santander. It will drive to Sahagun, arriving on 22 December.

The march, following the same route and timings as the Reserve Division, will take place between 23 December and 13 January. Marchers will be preceded each day by administrative advance party travelling by minibus. Marchers will wear contemporary uniform of Riflemen of the 95th Rifles Circa 1808.

On completion of the march, the party will spend 2 days in Corunna, before returning to England on 16 January, arriving back in Tidworth on 18 January.

Political Clearance

The approval of the Spanish Government has been sought, through the British Embassy in Madrid, for this project. The Embassy are confident that it will be forthcoming, but much depends on local reaction over the proposals to dump nuclear waste off the coast of Galicia.

Brief Outline of Route Schedule

Date	Event	Distance	Remarks
24 Dec 1808	Leave Sahagun in A.M.		
Evening	Reach convent near Majorga	32 kms	
25 Dec	Arrive St Miguel	29 kms	At midnight
26 Dec	Arrive Castro Gonzalo	13 kms	Defend bridge
27 Dec	Arrive Benevente	6 kms	
28 Dec	Remain Benevente	-	
29 Dec	Arrive La Beneza	42 kms	Sleep in convent
30 Dec	Arrive Astorga	23 kms	Leave at dawn
31 Dec	Arrive Fuencebadon	28 kms	Galician mtns.
01 Jan 1809	Arrive Ponferrada	23 kms	Army splits (Light Bde to Vigo)
02 Jan	Arrive Cacabelos	14 kms	
03 Jan	Battle in hills near Cacabelos	-	Night withdrawal
04 Jan	Arrive Hererias	42 kms	At 0400 hrs. Rest until 1000 hrs.
04 Jan	Arrive Los Nogales	19 kms	At 2200 hrs.
05 Jan	Arrive San Marie de Constantino	24 kms	Defend bridge
06 Jan	Arrive near Lugo	28 kms	In early morning
06 Jan	British army all concentrated at Lugo		
07 Jan	Remain Lugo	-	Outpost skirmishes
08 Jan	Night march north	-	Loss of many from weather, etc.
09 Jan	Arrive Astariz	42 kms	
10 Jan	Arrive Batangos	47 kms	Defend bridge
11 Jan	Arrive El Burgo	23 kms	French cavalry attack 95th
12 Jan	Remain El Burgo	-	Heavy infantry attacks
13 Jan	Arrive at heights over Corunna	13 kms	Defences dug
14 Jan	Royal Navy commences the evacuation of the army Reserve Division evacuated 17 Jan.		Battle of Corunna Sir John Moore killed 16 Jan.

The modern British Army do not let the grass grow under their feet and, to schedule, the show duly got on the road, in every sense of the word! In command was Captain Charles Blackmore RGJ who wrote the following report to his Commanding Officer, Lieutenant-Colonel Kit Owen RGJ :

Dear Colonel,   11 January 1984

A brief letter to bring you up to date with our movements, and at this stage to apologise if it is scruffy but writing in the confines of a tent by the small glow of a lantern prevents otherwise.

On arrival at Santander we had to disembark wearing our uniforms for the Spanish press and military reception. The Commander of the Spanish Army Unit at Santander welcomed us with an official speech and reception of wine and a standing buffet. There were plenty of handshakes and mutual exchanges of how excellent this all was for Anglo Spanish relations.

We have camped all the time less one night to date as the weather has been very favourable. Far from the snow blizzards and rain of 1808 we have walked in good sunshine although the evenings have been extremely cold with heavy frosts in the mornings. On Christmas Eve we camped inside the walls of the ruined convent where the rearguard slept in 1808, sat around a bonfire under the stars and had a small celebration. At 0600 hrs we filed out of the oak doors and down a muddy lane to cover the first 45 km to Mayorga, our uniforms silhouetted in the first rays of dawn made an impressive sight.

We have covered the route exactly and slept in the same places, as near as possible, as the rearguard did 175 years previously. All the men are thoroughly enjoying the novelty of this event and morale is extremely high. Every evening I hold a briefing for the next 24 hours and cover the historical aspects of the campaign in great detail from some books that I am carrying, and they are all feeling a great sense of achievement to study the map and see how far we have already gone.

Many of them are communicating well in Spanish as no one here speaks any English, and Jamie Bowden has been invaluable as our interpreter.

At Benavente the President of the British Chamber of Commerce drove to see us and spent a day watching our progress. He was extremely keen on the entire project and has been of great help. I have already presented him with a plaque. At Benavente the Mayor gave us a small reception and we did some press and radio interviews. We also enjoyed a small reception at Astorga and a large coverage in their local paper plus pictures.

The Spanish generally seem well informed of this, and as the eight uniformed men are going along we receive endless waves and honking of car horns (to such an extent that on one occasion I had to change the files over to rest their arms from waving!).

The Spanish press and radio have given us good coverage and we are expecting more. On one day we did a two hour long press session as we were walking along which rather distracted from the walk but made it worthwhile though. We have also left a steady trail of RGJ plaques with prominent people and in the inns of small villages where we have been well received, and the men have been excellent diplomats and are behaving extremely well. We realise that we are very much on a razors' edge until we leave, but to date it has been far better than I ever anticipated.

We are now halfway and the uniforms are holding out well; our sincere thanks to all who helped us fit the bill so well. Feet are becoming a problem as they have taken quite a severe pounding up to now, and the distances and route become harsher from now onwards. We have left the plain (which was dull to walk across) and are now in the mountains which are capped in snow in places. Last night we celebrated NY by leaving a small village at 0015 hours and walking 25 miles across the hills to reach this town at 0930 this morning. It was a cold and gruelling march but everyone stayed together and remained in good humour. Were it not for the fact that the rearguard halted for 12 to 24 hours to fight battles and sort out the stragglers of the main body, I think we would be very tired indeed!

I have been instructed to contact the consul of Galicia over the outline arrangements for the reception, etc in Corunna later this week. If wreaths are to be laid, then do you not think that they should have our insignia on them and therefore made in UK and brought out by you? The other aspect that slightly concerns me is that we cannot possibly, at this pace, keep smart in our uniforms with all the mud and general wear and tear. So either we should arrive in Corunna looking as though we have just walked 500 kms across Spain, or we should pop them into a dry cleaners prior to any official viewing (?). I feel the rough look would be more suitable but I shall check in with the Embassy nearer the time for your decision on that.

I trust you had a good Christmas and NY. As I said, everyone is in extremely good form and it has been a great success. The men are loving the attraction they are creating and have unstinted admiration for the fortitude of the men of our Regiment in 1808.

Your sincerely, Charles Blackmore

Seemingly all continued to go well, and the party completed their tribute to Sir John Moore and the Riflemen who marched with him in 1808. A newspaper report told of the satisfactory conclusion :

A party of soldiers who retraced the footsteps of Sir John Moore's retreat to Corunna 175 years ago were praised by their commanding officer on their return to Tidworth yesterday.

The 10-strong party from the Royal Greenjackets spent three weeks on the grueling 350 mile march during which they were given a rapturous reception by the Spaniards.

Said Lt. Col. Kit Owen: "The country can be proud of them. They have been magnificent representatives of the regiment and Britain. I do not believe it is fully appreciated in this country the interest, enthusiasm and excitement which this march created in Spain. The British have not been too popular recently in Spain - and Galicia - for various reasons. There's no doubt this march has done a great deal to restore some of the harmonious relations. That has been largely due to the impeccable behavior of all our men".

He said that Spanish businesses had donated a considerable sum of money to fund the march. "The Spanish have been most generous".

The march took the Greenjackets - wearing period uniform - over the rugged and wild Galician mountains.

In 1808 thousands of British troops died as Napoleon tried to cut off Moore's men from their main base at Corunna.

When the Greenjackets - descendants of Moore's Reserve Division -reached Corunna they were given a civic reception attended by the Mayor and military and civilian governors.

Large, cheering crowds lined the streets as the party were escorted into town.

General Napier, writing his account of the withdrawal, said of the Reserve Division:

For twenty one days these hardy warriors had covered the retreat, during which time they had traversed hundreds of miles of road, passed several nights under arms in the snow on the mountains, were seven times engaged with the enemy, and had assembled at the outposts having fewer men missing, including those who had fallen in battle, than any other Division of the army.

Perhaps going from the sublime to the ridiculous, the author fondly recalls his first-ever tour of Peninsular War battlefields - in 1973 with a British Military Historical Society party, under the able leadership of that amiable and knowledgeable British military historian - David Chandler (of the Royal Military Academy, Sandhurst) who subsequently penned this account of the tour :

Our nine-day visit started inauspiciously enough with our coach throbbing its way out of the grim and rain-sodden industrial dockland of Bilbao - incidentally the only wet weather we were destined to encounter - and then we were on our way through wonderful snow-clad vistas of the coastal mountain range heading for the highland plain of Vitoria.

Our visit to this famous battlefield of 21 June 1813, where Wellington defeated the relics of four of King Joseph's armies and once and for all established Allied paramountcy over the Spanish mainland, was necessarily curtailed by our need to reach Madrid that evening. Nevertheless, Napier's immortal flamboyant prose came into its own for the first time on our journey in support of my analysis of the great encounter's salient points. In his ghostly company, we examined the place where the Spaniard Longa sited his guns to sweep the French line of retreat, visited the bridges at Gamara Major (where General La Martiniere fought so gallant an action against Graham's stronger forces) and at Tres Puentes (where the Light Division infiltrated a passage over the River Zadora unseen by the French to turn the right flank of their main battle position). Finally, as we passed out of the valley of the Puebla Defile, we wondered at the staying power of General Hill's brigades which stormed and held the steep heights guarding the pass, and above all at Wellington's skill at controlling - in continuous rain - a diffuse and complex battle over a nine-mile front without benefit of any radio or telegraphy. At the same time we could but deplore (although with some sympathy) the plundering of the rich spoils left by the fleeing French which gravely hampered the pursuit, and had the result, as Napier noted, '...that of five millions and a half of dollars...a fiftieth part only came to the public.' Marshal Jourdan lost his baton, and more significantly, all but two of his 145 cannon.

Our road to Madrid lay across the bleak and barren plains of North Castille, periodically interrupted by steep lateral mountain ranges affording ideal positions for guerrilla ambushes; we could well appreciate the huge logistical problems faced by the under-administered French armies, used as they were to 'living off the country' in the far more fertile areas of central Europe. Shortly before the capital we crossed over the Somosierra Pass, scene of Napoleon's rash order for the charge by the Polish Light Horse against 12 positioned guns holding the head. The main road follows the old route almost exactly, and every stage of the operation (November 1808) could readily be identified and set in its natural context. As on the other fields we visited, the basic topography is unchanged; there are less trees than in the 1800s, and the roads and tracks have sometimes been replaced, but it proved relatively easy to reconcile 19th century maps with the modern sheets, and both with the actual ground.

A day in Madrid included visits to the Prado and the Military Museum, but then we were en route for Talavera de la Reina, some 60 miles south-west of the capital. With Napier in hand, we identified and visited the Casa das Salinas - scene of the surprise of Donkin's brigade and the near capture of Wellington on 27 July 1809. The building stands dilapidated by unchanged, but once again the woods through which the French Light Infantry stealthily approached their prey have been greatly thinned. Thence, after some frustrating false starts, we moved on to the main battlefield of the 27th and 28th, and climbed up the Medellin Hill - anchor of the Anglo-Spanish left where much bitter fighting took place. The view from the summit was impressive, but 'progress' is wreaking changes up here. The plain to the north where the 23rd Light Dragoons made their ill-fated charge into a hidden ravine is now a reservoir. Atop the Medellin itself stands a new, spacious modern villa, and the slopes of the Medellin have all been terraced ready to receive coniferous trees which, one day, will effectively obliterate the view. However the friendly owner, not at all put out by our unannounced arrival in his garden, could show us cannon and musket balls of every calibre, brought to light by the recent excavations. The events of late July 1809 seemed suddenly very close as we handled these evocative relics.

An evening and night in Toledo enabled us to savour some of the special medieval flavour of this famous city, and to visit the Alcazar, scene of the heroic siege in 1936. But early next day we were on the move again and reached the scene of possibly Wellington's greatest battle in time for a three-hour evening visit. We found the rebuilt Chapel of Nuestra Senora de la Pena, which the King's German Legion eventually lost to Foy's light infantry early on the 22 July 1812. From there we travelled round the battlefield and climbed the Lesser Arapiles, which (like the Medellin at Talavera) provided a near-perfect view over the afternoon battlefield, scene of Wellington's bold decision to attack Marmont's over-extended army, whose leading divisions, attempting to turn the whole British position, had become detached from the main body. 'By God! That will do!' exclaimed the Peer, who proceeded to build up almost a two-to-one advantage over the isolated French formations. Careful examination of the ground from this vantage point enabled us to identify almost every feature: the cliff-edged Greater Arapiles some 600 yards away from which the French guns blazed at Wellington's centre; the Heights of Azan to the South-West, scene of Pakenham's famous outflanking attack with Third Division which routed Thomieres and began the escalation of the French disaster; the southern plain, where General Le Marchant led the celebrated British cavalry charge by the Heavy Brigade, and found a glorious death; and the route followed by General Clausel's hard-pressed counter-attack, which came near to reversing the fortunes of the day. Once again we marvelled at Wellington's superb battle control - his unfailing knack for being near the critical point; his skilful deployment of his reserves. This victory finally established his reputation as a great tactical commander, and brought him, in the opinion of the enemy General Foy, 'almost to the height of the Duke of Marlborough'. It was a fair judgement, and later that night a number of us sought out Wellington's headquarters in a side-street of the old city to salute 'le grand chef'.

Our visit to North Spain was now almost over, but en route for Bilbao we were able to spend an hour around the Castle of Burgos, scene of the gallant but futile British siege of September 1812, and the abrupt capture of the place after Vitoria the next year in just two days. From the summit of the Napoleon battery we were able, through Napier's narrative and Fortescue's maps, to trace every major development of the operation. We walked the route followed by Major Somers Cock of the 79th which unexpectedly led to the capture of the Great Hornwork. From the castle we could identify the line of practically every sap and parallel trench driven by Wellington's under-gunned and under-engineered troops in their vain attempts to become masters of the fortress; the mines and breaches in the successive lines of defence are also identifiable, and we came away with a very real appreciation of the problems faced by the British troops in the over-looked and water-logged siege lines. General Dubreton had certainly fought a doughty defence. For some of us, this visit was the highlight of the tour.

The whole party left Spain with regret. In addition to our avowed historical objectives we had gained a fleeting impression of modern Spain: and, more to our point, we had seen for ourselves the mountains, the arid plains and the fertile river valleys with their vineyards and olive orchards which remain much as Wellington and Napier saw them. We had talked to numerous Spaniards, but found only one (the owner of the Medellin villa) who knew anything whatsoever about what Spanish history books term the 'War of Liberation'; memories of the Civil War, however, we found very fresh in people's minds, but little talked about; the scars are still too recent. In the country districts we had seen many pack-mules and ox-carts which might have stepped straight out of Wellington's triple system of supply convoys, and during our 700 mile tour we had come to appreciate the distances involved in some of his major campaigns. All this (the first morning excepted) had been in warm, sunlit Spanish springtime, surely the most pleasant and rewarding time of year to visit this proud and fascinating land, there to sample part of its rich historical heritage in which Great Britain had played a vital role.

PENINSULAR PASTIME

How to Re-fight, as Wargames, the Battles of the Peninsular War.

The wargamer attempting this is fortunate, because almost every battle of the War lends itself to practical and realistic reconstruction, both from a terrain and numbers point of view. This is important because if the wargame is to represent the battle in anything but name, the armies must represent a reasonable scaled-down proportion of the original formations, both in numbers and types, must be simulated in a tactically accurate manner, and governed by its historical and military backgrounds. And, of course, the miniature tabletop battlefield over which they are fighting, must be an accurate topographically-scaled representation of the true historical site.

The wargamer should never overlook that he is attempting authentically to re-create a period battle on a grossly under-scaled battlefield, using similarly under-scale numbers of inanimate miniature figures. He manoeuvres his armies in a style and manner much influenced by his temperament, military knowledge and any peculiar concept of historical tactics he may have derived from research. His little warriors cannot march and fight of their own volition so they have to be tactically directed by their wargamer/commander. But he possesses military knowledge of a much later date than the period in which he is specialising so that the tactics employed by his armies are those of leaders in far more advanced periods of military history, well beyond the military knowledge of their historical commanders. Consequently, although researching and painting armies to represent a reasonable scaled-down simulation of specific armies, those forces are performing tactical manoeuvres and evolutions arising from a military hindsight denied to their commander in those far off days. A well conceived set of rules, by formulating conditions and rulings that reflect the particular attributes of specific armies, can do much to correct this anomaly.

It is at this point that one encounters perhaps the greatest obstacle to wargaming becoming a majority-hobby. Wargamers, usually lacking professional military training or actual battlefield experience, acquire from reading and research widely differing concepts of tactics and warfare that are almost irreconcilable. They laboriously formulate rules that emphasise their accurate or possibly misguided concepts while viewing with ill-conceived disgust and frustration other people's rules that do not agree with their own concepts. In such company, wargamers have been known to be reluctant to perform some rather brilliant and quite authentic tactical manoeuvre simply because of an awareness that fierce arguments will be required to support their legality!

The greatest error into which a wargamer can fall is to select an army and then tactically manoeuvre them in a manner that bears little relation to their historically recorded tactics. For example, when re-fighting the Peninsular War of 1808-1814, it must be accepted that one of the predominant tactical reasons for the Duke of Wellington's success lay in his chosen method of forming the well-trained and confident infantry that formed his army into double-lines on the back slopes of a ridge. This tactic enabled them either to advance to the crest or wait until the advancing French columns came into view, before pouring a superior volume of musketry into their packed ranks prior to charging the discomforted column. And, equally important, his valuable infantry, behind the ridge-crest, were sheltered from enemy artillery fire. This was something of a precedent in an age when few commanders - not even Napoleon - drew up their formations so that they were out of enemy artillery fire.

The majority of tactics have historical precedents and those described above resemble the style of fighting of the Hundred Years War (1346-1453)., when consistently the French were devastated by advancing on foot into English archery volleys. To fight the Peninsular War in any other way is to prostitute History, and to create a situation completely lacking in authenticity.

Broadly speaking, so far as the Napoleonic period is concerned the main tactical concept was for infantry to be forced into square formation because of the threatening presence of enemy cavalry; then their tightly packed formations were flayed with close-range artillery fire from batteries that were themselves out of the range of the infantry muskets. Eventually the infantry ranks were so disordered by this artillery fire to become vulnerable to the attacks of cavalry or even more likely to succeed, infantry in column. Therefore, authentic rules for this period must be so designed that they give cavalry little chance of success against infantry in square, and that foot soldiers in the open and not in square have little or no chance of remaining unbroken in the face of a cavalry attack.

Similarly, when re-creating the Peninsular War, British infantry should be given some benefit for their known solidarity in line formation but French infantry, not only in the Peninsular but at all times, must be given benefits when authentically attacking in column. If any battle is to be realistically reconstructed with both armies employed in the authentic tactics of the period, then rules must be so devised as to force those tactics to be used on the table-top, even though the wargamer/commander may be conversant with differing tactics of another period that are likely to be more successful. The information on armies and their leaders, their equipment and their morale state, together with adequate background knowledge are sufficient to enable the wargamer to compile rules that reasonably reflect the strength and weaknesses of the armies of this period.

There are certain essentials which must be considered when formulating any set of rules to control a wargame, these include the reflection of an army's strength and weaknesses which, taken in comparison with the opposing army produce a reasonable simulation of the events of the time.

The rules must set out definitions that accurately reflect the speed and accuracy of an army's movement and manoeuvering, together with a means of simulating their ability or otherwise to maintain a rate of small arms and artillery fire that is known to be historically correct. For instance, under favourable conditions an artillery battery during the Napoleonic period took a minute to come into action and from one to three minutes to limber and move off from a firing position whilst a single gun could unlimber and fire in thirty seconds. A trained British soldier took between twelve and fifteen seconds to reload and fire his Brown Bess musket; French authorities believed that two shots per minute could be fired from the musket of the period. The musket itself was inaccurate over ranges from more than about 60 yards and there are recorded instances of volleys fired by entire battalions only hitting four men at ranges of 100 yards. It took an army of 30,000 men two hours to form line of battle if not under fire but longer if some of them were already engaged; infantry charges took 60 seconds to cover 180 yards while cavalry was said to be able to charge 700 yards in the same time - in either case the infantry being attacked, would be lucky if, under stress, they could fire more than one round before the enemy were upon them.

It is essential to bear in mind that these movement speeds and rates of fire were recorded during practice or drill when no one, including both the men and the recorder, were under any stress. The times are for trained veterans whose morale was steady; nervous troops, conscripts or inexperienced soldiers were inferior in every respect and took much longer to move and fire. Herein lies one of the great pit-falls for the inexperienced wargamer in that he accept these claims and figures to formulate rules that allow unjust powers to favoured forces; it must be realised (and rules must so reflect) that under the stress and strain of battle soldiers did not perform so creditably.

All wars, whether they be real-life conflicts or miniature affairs on tabletop battlefields, are fought to rules, and those used to control the tactical manoeuvering of model soldiers, far from being standardised as for Chess, usually reflect the character, temperament and knowledge of their devisor. There are almost as many sets of rules as there are wargamers, all optimistically formulated to give the game the greatest possible realism, which often results in bulky folders requiring reference taking up more time than the actual game! This is quite unnecessary and an equally realistic game - certainly a faster and more enjoyable battle - can be played by concentrating on the key word - Morale. Accepted from a military point of view to be the psychological condition of soldiers as it concerns confidence and discipline, success in battle being achieved by the winners possessing higher standards of both than the losers. However, regardless of the standards of morale at the start of a battle, it can be materially reduced through casualties and the reactions caused by combat. This positively implies that the principle object of fighting an enemy, both by missile-fire and by hand-to-hand fighting is to reduce his morale until it is lower than your own, causing him to react in a manner that is detrimental to him.

This inevitably leads to the proposition that, when wargaming, it is expeditious to formulate rules so that they achieve their ends by being balanced on the State of Morale of the respective armies. There is little mileage in calculating numerically the precise effects of taking fire, whether it be artillery or small-arms, or being charged and meleed - all that is required is an awareness of a unit suffering a lowering in their morale through these eventualities. Or conversely, whether their morale has risen through elation at having lived through fire or a change - in both cases the rules should reflect these situations by enforcing a reaction, adverse or beneficial respectively, upon the affected unit. Eventually, in this way, one side wins and the other loses.

It is achieved simply by combining effects of receiving missile-fire or taking a charge - giving both the overall title of Combat, with the chances of success of a specific type of Combat being represented by odds, as a percentage which has to be exceeded when throwing dice if the affected unit is to avoid an adverse morale-reaction. Perhaps the classic example is one peculiarly suited to the Napoleonic period and warfare in the Peninsular, where infantry were easy prey to cavalry when in loose or open order; a little safer when in line; but almost completely safe when in square formation. Thus, infantry caught in the open, in loose or open order need to throw a pair of percentage-dice (20-sided dice, black are 100's and red are 10's, capable of producing a combined score of from 1 to 100; the two 0's together representing the latter) and score 80 percent or more to be safe. When in line they need to score 75 percent; but when in the comforting formation of a square they only require 15 percent - while the opposing cavalry have to throw 85 or over to break the square.

Each army or force is listed on a chart in columnar form, extending from each unit is a series of squares, five for ordinary run-of-the-mill units and perhaps six or seven for elite, veteran or Guard units. When a unit fails to make their required score when throwing the dice, they are considered to be momentarily shaken, so one attrition-point (represented by a tick in the first square) is marked against them; subsequently, they have to throw again - this time a single dice -which, if falling 1 or 2 means that their morale is rock-bottom, they have been routed in disorder and - next game-move - they are pulled back their respective move-distance and they stand in disorder until such time as their owner - throwing dice at the beginning of each move - scores 50 or over, when they are considered to have rallied. Each failure to score 50 means a further attrition-point, and the initial dice score of 1 or 2 has already marked-in two more ticks. If, when throwing the single dice after an initial 'shaking', scores of 3 or 4 are secured, then one more attrition-point goes in the chart and the unit - next move - goes back its move-distance in good order; they may come forward again on the following move. When all five squares are filled with attrition-points, then the unit is removed from the wargames table. The chart given here as an example is that of Craufurd's famed Light Division, Wellington's 'crack' infantry force in the Peninsular; as they are an elite formation the chart is marked into six squares, giving them one more 'life' than an ordinary line-regiment.

This is the basic idea, the foundation upon which this rules system works, and it can be modified to suit any period, any army, or type of troops. This means that a club or group of wargamers can move rapidly from one period or type of warfare to another, knowing that the basic rules are the same with percentages and attrition-points devised to simulate the specific weapons and fighting-styles of the period in use. The system bears the merit of not having to assess individual casualties nor to remove them singly from the table, leaving a unit with perhaps two or three men; all reactions and results concern units as a whole. This is a great comfort when thoughtfully considered, because all those precious little model soldiers, so painstakingly painted, do not spend much of their time in casualty boxes under the table, but can be permanently fixed in groups (say three's) on cards. Because units are never broken up during a game, they can be of any manageable size - from ten to fifty, they fight as a unit irrespective of their numbers.

Recalling what is sometimes forgotten in the stress of wargaming - that it is a game played for amusement and relaxation - the wargamer can be happy in the knowledge that these rules banish calculations and the need to remember anything - one just gazes at the chart on the wall! This is what will be seen:

MOVEMENT:

		Infantry	Light Infantry
	In column	7 inches	When deployed in open order
	In line	6 inches	9 inches

	Cavalry				
Light	In column	9 inches	Heavy	In column	8 inches
	In line	12 inches		In line	10 inches
	Field Gun	6 inches		Horse Gun	12 inches

Changing formation takes up half a move. Form or unform infantry square takes a full move

UNIT FORMATION
a.   Both infantry and cavalry advance in Column forming line on confronting enemy.
b.   British infantry fight in Line.
        All cavalry fight in Line.
        French infantry fight in Column but may fire-fight in Line.
        Spanish infantry fight only in Column.
c.   Movement & Firing.
        Field-guns cannot move and fire in the same move.
        Infantry can half-move and fire muskets
        Light infantry cannot move and fire Baker rifles in the same move.
        Horse-guns: 2 inches to limber; 2 inches to unlimber; 2 inches to load. Remaining distance may be moved.
d.   Movement in woods. Light infantry move 1/2 rate.
        Impassable to artillery
        Infantry/Cavalry 1/2 move and are in disorder.

Disordered troops cannot initiate aggressive action; may defend themselves if attacked by seeking to make their required score before enemy, who only need to try if disordered troops are successful. If fired upon when in disorder, target-unit takes a mandatory attrition point (1 tick) for being disordered, then throw single dice to check their reaction i.e. score 1 or 2 they are routed (2 ticks); score 3 or 4 go back move-distance in good order (1 tick)

RANGES

		Short Range	Long Range
	Musket	4 inches	9 inches
	Baker Rifle	6 inches	12 inches
	Field Gun	10 inches	40 inches
	Horse Gun	10 inches	30 inches

Effects of Artillery and Small Arms Fire

Target Unit	Fired Upon by Infantry In:												Guns	
	Line		Column		Open Order		Square		Hard Cover		Soft Cover			
Infantry Line	30	45	20	30	20	30	20	30	35	50	30	45	40	60
Infantry Column	35	50	25	35	25	35	25	35	40	60	35	50	45	70
Infantry Open Order	25	35	15	25	15	25	15	25	30	45	25	35	35	55
Infantry Square	35	50	25	35	25	35	25	35	40	60	35	50	50	75
Hard Cover	20	30	10	15	10	15	10	15	15	25	20	30	30	50
Soft Cover	25	35	15	25	15	25	15	25	30	45	25	35	35	55
Cavalry	30	45	20	30	25	35	35	50	40	60	35	50	45	70
Gunners	25	35	20	30	25	30	20	30	35	50	30	45	45	70

First (lower) figure is score required at long range
Second (higher) Figure is score required at short range
Guard or Elite units deduct 5 from all the above scores
Target unit must throw % dice and equal or beat these scores for them to be O.K. If it fails, mark 1 attrition point and throw a six sided dice. A score of 1 or 2 means the unit is routed; a score of 3 or 4 the unit moves back its move distance in good order and resume next move.

Effects of Melees (Hand to Hand Combat)

Target Unit	Line	Column	Open Order	Square	Hard Cover	Soft Cover	Light Cavalry	Heavy Cavalry	Guns
Infantry Line	50	60	30	40	70	60	65	75	30
Infantry Column	40	50	30	35	70	65	65	75	25
Infantry Open Order	70	75	50	50	75	50	75	80	20
Infantry Square	60	65	50	—	—	—	20	15	—
Infantry Hard Cover	30	35	25	—	—	—	20	20	—
Infantry Soft Cover	40	35	50	—	—	—	30	30	—
Light Cavalry	30	35	25	80	80	70	50	60	20
Heavy Cavalry	25	30	25	85	80	70	40	50	20
Gunners	70	70	60	—	—	—	80	80	—

The unit in the first column on the left, when opposed by one of the opponents listed at the top of the chart, needs to to throw a pair of % dice and equal or beat the number shown in the chart to be safe. Thus, infantry in square facing heavy cavalry need to score 15 or over to be safe. Guard or elite units add 5 to the dice roll.

If it fails to equal or beat the stipulated score, the unit marks 1 attrition point on its record for being shaken. Then throw a six sided dice. A score of 1 or 2 means the unit is routed back its move distance in disorder (2 more attrition points); a score of 3 or 4 means the unit goes back its move distance in good order and may resume moving next game move (but mark one more attrition point for going back,)

Unit Reaction to Effects of Combat (Missile Fire or Melee)

Failing to make the require score:

a. the unit is Shaken and marks 1 attrition-point on its chart.

b. throws a single six sided dice -

c. Score of 1 or 2 means the unit has been routed; they move back (on the following Game-Move) their move distance in Disorder. Mark 2 more attrition-marks on their chart. While disordered, they may be fired upon or attacked - then they mark another 1 attrition-point, and then throw a single dice, trying to avoid scoring 1, 2, 3 or 4 (the penalty scores). If they fail, then they move back in rout or good order, depending upon the score thrown, marking more attrition points on their chart. To revive from rout, the unit requires to throw 50 on two % dice, which may be thrown at the start of every move subsequent to their rout. Each failure means another attrition-point and a further move back. Scoring over 50, the unit takes that move to rally, and may then resume action on the following move.

d. Score of 3 or 4 means the unit moves back its move distance, but in good order, on the following move. On the move after that, they may resume action. Withdrawal in good order costs another attrition-point.

e. Every Line unit has Five squares on its chart, Guard and Elite units have Six. An attrition point (a tick) fills one square, so that when a unit has its entire quota of Five squares filled with attrition points, that unit is considered to be Shattered and is removed from the field.

At the beginning of the wargame, total the number of units & guns that form an army; each of them will have a potential destruction-point of Five attrition-points. Thus, ten units have a collective destruction-point of 50. Assess the acceptable percentage of casualties your army can sustain - an optimistic view might be 50%., which amounts to a figure of 25 attrition-points which, when reached, means that your army has taken all the casualties it can handle, and has lost the battle.

The Peninsular War is a very convenient campaign to reconstruct on the wargames table because Wellington's unbroken victorious trend makes it possible to follow the historical sequence of battles in correct chronological order. This is difficult to achieve when wargaming a real-life campaign because if the enemy - on the wargames table -reverse the historical result of a battle, then the whole campaign is thrown out of sequence. This is because it makes it impossible to fight the action historically following on the authentic site or under the known historic conditions, such a course being affected by the 'wargaming losers' being perhaps driven to a distant area, or suffering losses negating the known background to the battle. Thus, instead of an army conveniently progressing to the next historical field as they did in the Past, in a tabletop re-enactment, they will be pushed back to another area on the campaign-map, ostensibly to fight a battle that never took place on an unknown field.

Fortunately, there is a method that obviates such painfully unrealistic courses of events - the Campaign League Table. The campaign is re-fought in exactly the same sequence as historically occurred, each battle of History following the other, regardless of which side wins on the tabletop fields. The trick is to give the winner 2 points, the loser nothing, with 1 point each for a drawn battle; the points being totalled as the campaign progresses with a perfectly clear and

Foy's 1st Division of Marmont's French Army (at Salamanca)						
Chemineau's Brigade	1	2	3	4	5	
1st Battalion 6th Leger						
2nd Battalion 6th Leger						
1st Battaion 69th Line						
2nd Battalion 69th Line						
Desgravier-Berthelot's Brigade	1	2	3	4	5	
1st Battalion 39th Line						
2nd Battalion 39th Line						
1st Battalion 76th Line						
2nd Battalion 76th Line						
The Light Division (commanded by C. Alten, at Salamanca) Elite Formation						
Barnard's Brigade	1	2	3	4	5	6
1/43 Regiment of Foot						
2nd 95th Rifles (part)						
3rd 95th Rifles						
1st Cacadores						
Vandeleur's Brigade	1	2	3	4	5	6
1/52nd Regiment of Foot						
1/95th Rifles						
3rd Cacadores						

obvious state of affairs at all times. For example, at Rolica it is necessary for the smaller French force in their strong hilltop position, to hold-off the considerably stronger British force, and to be able to make their getaway before the arrival of the flanking British detachment under Ferguson. During the wargame, if the French are able to do this, then the British will gain 2 points for the victory, while the French will gain 1 point for holding-off the British for a pre-agreed number of game-moves.

One of the least authentic facets of wargaming is the quite unrealistic proportion of losses suffered by scaled-down units. History records that battles in this period resulted in 10 to 15% losses sustained by the winner and 20 to 35% losses for the defeated army. Recording losses (in the form of morale) by means of attrition-marks on regimental charts (as described in the suggested rules herewith) usually results in units that have been heavily engaged reflecting that fact in their chart-standing. As in real-life, only their commander (i.e. the wargamer holding the chart) will be aware of the true combat-effectiveness of a unit and, as in real-life, will be able to nurse and shelter them. The tactical effect of the smoke and dust of battle is realistically simulated, as the opposing commander is unlikely to be able to assess the state of opposing units, as none of their casualties are removed from the table to give him any hint. Thus, the strength of the unit is recorded but not revealed, until a low-point is reached when their attrition-squares each carry a tick, and they are removed from battle.

It is doubtful whether wargames will ever provide a profound military insight, but the wargamer can hope to achieve an understanding of the problems of the commanders in the field and a glimpse of the military thinking of the time by re-fighting a battle in the correct tactical manner, using scaled down formations and weapon effects and reactions of the day.

On a completely different note, there have been - and will be occasions with the ethics of wargaming, of simulating warfare by possibly young people, will be brought-up in challenging manner. Throughout the ages, bitter experience has taught man that war, despite its aura of courage and comradeship, is not all fun. Rather than condoning or encouraging real war, wargaming must be stressed as an historical project which encourages unique social contacts and friendships. Back in 1913., Briton H. G. Wells a man of immense intelligence and standing in the community of his day, wrote:

And if I might for a moment trumpet! How much better is this amiable miniature than the Real Thing! Here is a homeopathic remedy for the imaginative strategist. Here is the premeditation, the thrill, the strain of accumulating victory or disaster—and no smashed nor sanguinary bodies, no shattered fine buildings nor devastated countrysides, no petty cruelties, none of that awful universal boredom and embitterment, that tiresome delay or stoppage or embarrassment of every gracious, bold, sweet, and charming thing, that we who are old enough to remember a real modern war know to be the reality of belligerence. This world is for ample living; we want security and freedom; all of us in every country, except a few dull-witted, energetic bores, want to see the manhood of the world at something better than aping the little lead toys our children buy in boxes. We want fine things made for mankind—splendid cities, open ways, more knowledge and power, and more and more and more,—and so I offer my game, for a particular as well as a general end; and let us put this prancing monarch and that silly scaremonger, and these excitable "patriots," and those adventurers, and all the practitioners of Welt Politik, into one vast Temple of War, with cork carpets everywhere, and plenty of little trees and little houses to knock down, and cities and fortresses, and unlimited soldiers—tons, cellars-full,—and let them lead their own lives there away from us.

My game is just as good as their game, and saner by reason of its size. Here is War, done down to rational proportions, and yet out of the way of mankind, even as our fathers turned human sacrifices into the eating of little images and symbolic mouthfuls. For my own part, I am prepared. I have nearly five hundred men, more than a score of guns, and I twirl my moustache and hurl defiance eastward from my home in Essex across the narrow seas. Not only eastward. I would conclude this little discourse with one other disconcerting and exasperating sentence for the admirers and practitioners of Big War. I have never yet met in the little battle any military gentleman, any captain, major, colonel, general, or eminent commander, who did not presently get into difficulties and confusions among even the elementary rules of the battle. You have only to play at Little Wars three or four times to realize just what a blundering thing Great War must be.

In 1778, the English philosopher Samuel Johnson said: "Every man thinks meanly of himself for not having been a soldier." He may have had a point in that, perforce, all wargamers don the mantle of commanders, that being about the lowest identifiable rank possible when faced with a tabletop battlefield crammed with ranks of miniature soldiers. A few wargamers have heard shots fired in anger, have taken part in wars and battles - although perhaps only Captain Pete Panzeri, an infantry officer in the American Army, actually fought in a battle (Ghazlani, in the Gulf War of 1991) and then came home to wargame it at a Convention! Another singular character was Brigadier Peter Young, famed and much-decorated British Commando leader of World War Two, who became impatient with manhandling armies of model soldiers, so formed the Sealed Knot, an English Civil War Re-enactment group, who fought their battles to his orders as a spectacle.

However, there is another point at which the wargamer can assuage latent militaristic desires in perfect safety, while reflecting character, personality and temperament in a role-playing guise - his alter ego being an inanimate metal or plastic model-soldier 25, 30 or 54mm in height. The term persona or personae can be said to cover this, as it means one's assumed character in an imaginary world, or an aspect of their personality shown to, or perceived by, others. In the parlance of the tabletop battlefield - Individualised Wargaming.

It cannot be denied that the best known of all formations in the Peninsular from 1808 to 1814 was the Light Division; and of that elite formation, the 95th Rifles stand high in the esteem of both historian and wargamer. So, it is not surprising that wargamers should seek to immortalize such Riflemen as Costello, Harris, Surtees, and Plunket, who shot French General Colbert at the Bridge of Cacabelos, during the retreat to Corunna. They do this through role-playing games, usually known as Individual Skirmishes, from the incomparable system devised by Mike Blake, Ian Colwill, and the late Steve Curtis, all from Great Britain.

Ian Colwill is a schoolmaster whose boys must love him if this is the sort of lesson he teaches! So, illustrated with an excellent map in the incomparable style of Mike Blake, another of the gifted triumvirate, here is -

CAPTURE THE 95TH RIFLEMAN! BY IAN COLWILL

The game, as I saw it, would go like this. A six foot by four foot table, with terrain as shown on the map; one experienced player to be the Rifleman (who would start the game at point A). Ten French players, one per figure, with experienced players as veterans, not so experienced players as averages and totally inexperienced players as novices (who would start on the road at B). The latter idea is a real possibility for those idiots like myself who run wargames clubs in schools! To add to the confusion, or rather realism, the ten French players sat at the south end of the table and the height of the slope plus the ridiculously low level of school chairs combined to render visibility of the area beyond the slope, impossible. (Of course, you then have to keep them sat down and being a schoolmaster helps there too!) Finally, we used 25mm figures.

The game began with a talk from 'Sir' outlining the situation; the Retreat to Corunna, French on the heels of the British, British stragglers, as well as an hostile indigenous population.

The French were told that they were a group of new recruits being sent up to the front to join their regiment (as in C. S. Forrester's tale, Death to the French). The Rifleman, and there was only one, was told he had been cut off and now saw his duty as delaying the French until he could rejoin his regiment. The French players were given no indication that their enemy comprised one man, indeed they were led to believe the one player controlled a similar force to theirs.

So much for the briefing. The game started with the French plodding along the road for two phases. Then a shot rang out and the officer was thrown over clutching his arm. The French

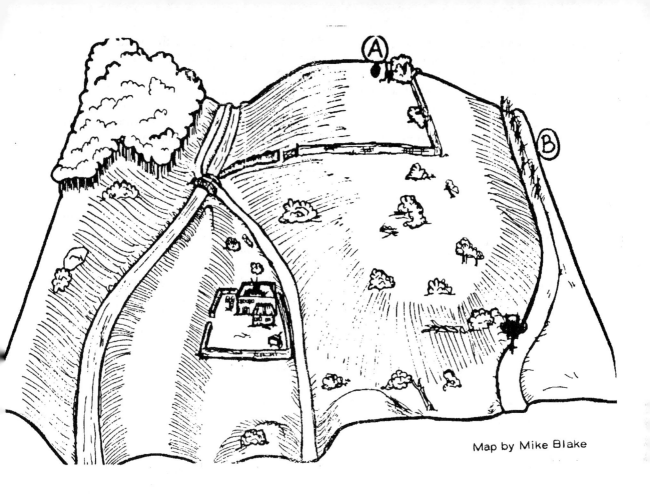

Map by Mike Blake

CAPTURE THE RIFLEMAN

novices and averages were told they had heard a shot but the veterans were told it was a rifle shot. A ball of cotton wool 'smoke' betrayed the firer's position.

The reaction of the French at this point was perhaps excusable. With the officer wounded the Sergeant yelled, 'Avec moi', and rushed to the lee of the slope where he was soon joined by all the novices. However, two averages decided to get medals, or court martialled and ran off up the road to an overturned wagon. It is sad to record that no one risked his life to give solace to the wounded Captain.

The French were, of course, expecting a full scale ambush by Spanish guerillas, but now there was nothing but silence, The rifleman had left his position and was running across the fields to the stream. He reached it, ducked behind a bush and began to reload. Meanwhile he was puzzled - where were the damned Frogs? The lay of the land combined with the French players' low eye level meant that they were unable to see the Rifleman's movements, of course.

Not surprisingly the French were still in the lee of yon slope with the novices waiting for the Sergeant to tell them what to do and the Sergeant wishing the Officer would tell him. Finally the Sergeant sent two men forward to 'Advance on the wall'. One novice stealthily stalked the hostile bush while the other stood up and charged it in a truly heroic French fashion. Both shot at the bush, so emptying their muskets and were somewhat annoyed to find that no one was there. The Sergeant's force now advanced to the wall at the top of the slope.

Meanwhile the two intrepid averages were creeping around all and sundry, dashing from cover to cover and slowly converging on the ruined cottage. Surely the green jacket was here! He wasn't!

He was, in fact, taking careful aim at the group of French at the wall. The group waited while the Officer, now back in action, rejoined them. He formed a skirmish line of sorts and the French

29

advanced. One man climbed over the wall and began an advance across the pasture. No finer target could have been presented to the Rifleman. The rifle cracked, the man fell with a leg wound, and the Rifleman raced off over the bridge into the woods.

The skirmish line dissolved. The French, like an exhausted pack of dogs who finally see their prey, went off into a run and raced towards the bridge. The French Officer's protest was in vain. The two averages joined the chase. One of the novices was the first man to cross the stream. He had an empty musket (which no one had reminded him to reload) and hadn't thought about fixing his bayonet. He broke into the forest with great determination only to receive a fatal wound from the fixed sword of the Rifleman. He had fixed his sword bayonet once he had got into the cover of the woods.

Having dealt with three Frenchmen the Rifleman now decided that discretion was the better part of valour and headed off into the depths of the forest. The French stumbled across their dead comrade and suddenly appreciated the danger of a pell mell chase through a dense forest. The pursuit was called off. They had not caught the 95th Rifleman.

The game ably demonstrated the difference in play when neither side is able to monitor the table with a bird's eye view and therefore have knowledge of what is happening on other parts of the terrain, even if nothing is done to directly affect this other activity. It also reflected the much more cautious play which results from neither side having any clear idea of how many men the enemy has deployed, which is much more in line with real skirmish situations.

Even more simple, is the derivation devised by the author for those occasions when audience-participation is desired, as at Wargames Club meetings or Conventions. Given the title Individualised Wargaming, it can involve up to about 15 players a side, each taking a name if desired - this led to Maurice Chevalier and Napoleon Bonaparte appearing as private soldiers in one French force!

Basically, the idea consisted of two small forces—one British and one French each consisting of a lieutenant, a sergeant, a bugler and ten riflemen. One of the riflemen was a 'strong man'! In other words, he was one of those exceptional men one occasionally finds in platoons who are not only bigger and stronger than their comrades but they are also better shots, bayonet fighters, etc., etc. Each figure had a small number painted in white on its base and at the commencement of the game all persons present were divided into two equal parties, a responsible and experienced war-gamer was nominated as the lieutenant and given the figure of the lieutenant. The lieutenant nominated his sergeant and his bugler to whom numbered figures were given and then each of the rifleman was given a figure. This meant that every person in the room was actually represented individually on the war-games table. A terrain was laid on a trestle table 6 ft. long by 2 ft. wide—it consisted of a river running right down the middle of the table from one end to the other lengthways which ended in a bridge at the furthest end. On either side of the river were small clumps of trees, mounds of earth, fallen trees etc., to give cover to the riflemen.

As this game proceeded very smoothly everyone appeared to readily understand the typed instruction sheet they were given (together with a 12 in. strip of stiff card marked off in inches like a ruler, plus a dice). It is considered adequate to give an exact copy herewith of that instruction sheet.

INDIVIDUALISED WARGAMING

Narrative

It is in the Peninsula in 1810. A small detachment of British Riflemen, formed of a lieutenant, a sergeant, a bugler and riflemen are making their way back from the French side of a river, over which there is only one bridge. By a strange coincidence, a force of French tirailleurs of the same strength have been trapped on British side of the river and are seeking to cross and gain their own lines. Both forces will need to cross by the same bridge.

Each man is worth 1 point. The lieutenant and the 'Strong man' are worth 2 points.

Movement: 9 in. normal. 12 in. running (only alternate moves). If a man is wounded, he deducts 3 in. from his move-distance, i.e. 6 in. When a wounded man is aided by a comrade, both together, they move 9 in. but neither can fire whilst moving. 'Strong man' always moves 12 in.

Firing: Range 12 in. It takes a man 4 1/2 in. of his move to load and fire. He can fire and them move or move and then fire. He may stand still and fire twice. To fire—the firer throws a dice and adds it score to his personal points value. Thus, a score of 5 + 1 (personal point) will equal 6 which is a hit. The firer does not add his personal points value if: (a) The firer is himself under fire, without being behind cover. (b) If the target is behind cover. (c) If the firer is himself wounded.

When a man is hit, he throws a dice and adds his personal points value to the score:
Total 5 or 6—it is a minor wound of no effect.
Total 3 or 4—he is wounded so that he loses his personal points value and takes 3 in. off his move-distance. Figure laid down until next move. Total 1 or 2—he is killed—figure laid down rest of battle.

Melees: Man fights man—each throwing a dice and adding personal points value and highest score wins. Loser throws hidden dice to see if he is (a) slightly wounded: (b) badly wounded and (c) killed. If (a) he fights on; (b) fights on less personal points value and 1 more point. If there are 2 men fighting 1—the 2 each throw a dice plus their personal points value—and the single man throws his dice plus personal points value. He can beat one of his two enemies if his total beats either of them. He is beaten if one of them totals more than him.

Orders: (1) The bugler can be heard by anyone within 18 in. of him. (2) A shout can be heard by anyone within 9 in. of the shouter. The first allows the officer can give a general order (by telling his men the same order). With the second he can call out orders to anyone within 9 in. of him.

Otherwise, everyone writes down what he is going to do before each move.

Perhaps outside the scope of this book, as seemingly it encroaches upon the realms of psychology, man-management, human character and temperament, etc., is the question of which war-gamers are selected to represent the 'Lieutenant', the 'Sergeant' and the 'Strong man'. Because this 'Individualised War-gaming' really is an individual, personalised affair, the war-gamers are really 'on their own' on the war-games table, just as much as the riflemen and tirailleurs would have been in 1810. Similarly, the Lieutenant and the Sergeant really do have to command, make decisions, use their judgement and give orders that will bring purpose to whatever individual actions the solitary rifleman pursues through his own reasoning or personal initiative. When re-enacting this interesting little charade as a Club project, try to select someone with known powers of command as the Lieutenant; let the Sergeant be a steady, mature man (as indeed most Sergeants are!) and for the 'Strong man' select a war-gamer who is noted more for brawn than brains! It all makes for a highly interesting exercise in noting what makes a man tick!

PENINSULAR PLUS'S

Heaven forbid that any self-respecting military historian and wargamer will ever tire of walking historical battlefields, his mind agog with ideas for reproducing the action on a tabletop terrain, on returning home. And yet! It gets dark, or it rains, or one gets tired, or it is too far to reach the next field that day, or one arrives (or departs) from say Lisbon or Madrid and has half-a-day's wait before taking-off time - there are innumerable reasons why even the most avid battlefield-walker should cast the eyes at some of the proliferation of interesting places that exist in Spain and Portugal. And, each and everyone of those offerings represent a bonus, a big plus to our Peninsular Promenading! Take another scenario - the historian/wargamer announces his intention of taking-off for Portugal and Spain to look at battlefields, at a not inconsiderable expense. His Wife, without any incredulity - having been married long enough to an ardent wargamer to know the breed - thinks this over, reflects that she has never been to either country, that they are warm, and different, perhaps with nice shops - and then drops the bombshell of announcing that she will go with him! Well, one cannot expect one's Wife to trudge over hill and dale, looking-at empty and peaceful fields and slopes, without being able to conjure-up a vivid picture of a battle fought nearly two hundred years ago, and about which she knows nothing. Obviously, some other attractions have to be discovered and offered, either in the company of the sullen deprived wargamer or with the Wives of other wargamers, who have jumped on the bandwagon.

Peninsular Plus's are the answer to this problem, possibly best in the form of the two fascinating capital cities - Lisbon and Madrid. Here even the wargamer, once over the frustration of being within a few miles of an historic field and not going to it, will more than likely find much of interest - and both cities offer fine military museums! That in Madrid is full of treasures from the time of El Cid, the Gran Capitan, and Cortes as well of many from the period of the Peninsular War. There is also a room containing military miniatures, both in wood and in tin, which has approximately 16,000 figures.

In Lisbon, the National Army Museum vies with the Maritime Museum at Belem - both are good, the former being one of those archaic, crowded places which house a multitude of interesting items.

When considering Continental museums - any museums, not only those dealing military items, always bear in mind that none of them are open on monday - keeping this in mind avoids a lot of disappointment and fruitless pre-planning.

And on the subject of which days to utilise visiting museums and galleries - the famed Prado in Madrid, contains the incomparable works of Goya depicting the horrors of the Peninsular War and his painting of the Duke of Wellington, among many other masterpieces - if you don't like queueing-up, then don't go there on a Sunday!

Outlying visits can often be embodied in the battlefield tour itinerary - for example, El Escorial is on the road to the walled city of Avila, and thence to Salamanca. It is a beautiful and historic town in the Guadarrama Range about 30 miles from Madrid on the A4, and is most adequately signposted. Without detouring, one can take in Valle de los Caidos - the Valley of the Fallen - a monument to the dead of the Civil War 1936-9, in a wild valley of the mountain range, it displays an unmistakable silhouette of its granite cross, 500 feet high and 150 feet across the arms. Then we came to Avila, enthroned on a hilltop like a castle carved out of the rock and, if you have never seen a completely walled-in town, then one finds oneself in an unreal, fantastic world, like an enormous Medieval stage. Its walls are the oldest and best preserved in Spain and rise to an impressive height. They take the shape of an equilateral hexagon, strengthened by 88 bastions and towers, and crowned by 2,500 embrasures; there are nine gateways.

At the northeastern end of the Guadarrama Range, about 50 miles from Madrid on N1 E25 lies the Somosierra Pass where, on 22 November 1808, Napoleon himself at the head of 45,000 troops marching to Madrid, came upon an extemporised Spanish force 9,000 strong, entrenched at the head of the Pass. Impatient at the halt, Napoleon ordered his personal escort squadron of 87 Polish lancers to charge the Pass and clear it. Bravely, they attempted to do so and were almost wiped out; quickly outflanking forces drove the Spanish from their position, and Napoleon's march to Madrid was resumed. Even today, on the modern road, with a little imagination, it is possible to picture this sanguinary action.

The author's usual battlefield-walking gang are neither too blase or lacking in finer feelings to occasionally indulge themselves with some detour to a place with only remote - or none at all - affiliations with military history or wargaming. In 1990, when but a single night remained before returning to Madrid and the homeward flight, it was agreed to spend it in a place about which it has been said "... a traveller who can only spend one night in Spain ought to spend it seeing Toledo." Approaching, the silhouette of this historic city stands out in sharp relief against a background formed by the crests of encircling hills and more distant mountains, sprawling over a vast crag surrounded by the River Tagus, it looks - and is - historic. Yet, possibly it is best known today through the dramatic 20th century events which pulverised the walls of its ancient Alcazar, rebuilt and standing guard over the picturesque town nestling around it.

The Alcazar is famous for the siege it endured during the Spanish Civil War. It was reduced to ruins, but now rebuilt, which gives it a disturbingly modern look. Still remembered as if yesterday is the final conversation between the garrison commander, Colonel Moscardo, and his son, Luis, captured by the Red militia. The militia commander telephoned to say unless the Alcazar was surrendered at once, Luis would be executed, and then put Luis on the line to confirm that plans were in hand to shoot him. "If that is true," said his father, "commend your soul to God, shout Viva Espana and die like a hero."

Colonel Moscardo then told the militia commander to forget about the ultimatum; "The Alcazer will never surrender," he said. It did not, but Luis was indeed shot. He was not the only victim of the siege, and the garrison suffered greatly in what was by any standards a heroic stand. That gives the Alcazer the grim fascination it has today.

Since the beginnings of Time, it has been noteworthy that Whoever controls these things has a knack of balancing bad with good, and the Alcazar siege in 1936 was no exception. Down in the stifling hospital beneath the citadel a Spanish surgeon, Trueta, lacking drugs and medical supplies to treat the many wounded, despairingly devised a revolutionary treatment for gunshot wounds which, by any accepted line of reasoning, could only culminate in gangrene and death. Incredibly, it did the reverse, the immobilised wounds healing successfully; during World War Two which shortly followed, this method of treatment saved countless lives of soldiers of many nationalities.

With some regret we left our Toledo hotel, the King Alphonse VII, an old and beautiful building where panelled corridors were lined with suits of armour and weapons, as befits a town noted throughout the Ages for its skill in making those artifacts. Madrid, on yet another Sunday, was as busy as it was when we left it on the previous Sabbath and, much as we had all enjoyed our Peninsular Promenade, we were glad to be returning to our normal lives in Britain.

Still in Spain. On more than one occasion we have driven over the area that lays between Salamanca and Badajoz - those milestones of Peninsular War history - through the wild countryside of Extramadura, Spain's 'Wild West' and the ancient land of the Conquistadors. The following article by travel-writer Adam Hopkins of the London Sunday Telegraph newspaper, paints a colourful and enticing picture. Everything he writes can be endorsed by the author, who shares his enthusiasm for the old town of Caceres, made even more memorable by being the only place in Spain where credit-cards are unacceptable!

Hawks hang overhead unswerving. Lean black cattle, bred for the bullfight, shift restlessly in the shadow of oak and cork oak. Nearby, hard mountains rise from the cattle-lands; towns tell of lost splendours and half-forgotten struggles.

The place is that far western edge of Spain, descending in a southerly direction along the Portuguese border. Once it nurtured the pitiless men who conquered South America, choking a continent with blood. Today, the wheel has turned full circle; local papers complain it is neglected by the centre, in danger of becoming "an Indian reserve". No part of Spain is less developed or less visited, more full of ancient echoes, ancient ways.

In the centuries before the Conquistadors set sail for the New World, Moors and Christians made it a battle ground. Fighting their way downwards from the north coast, the Christians reached the fertile grainlands of the Duero River, setting up a castle for almost every kilometre they captured. Even today the land here looks like a chessboard ready for a game. All this is part of the modern region of Castile and Leon—the name derived from its many castles.

Then as the Christians rolled southwards, they gave the obvious name to the land they conquered next, Extremadura, the country beyond the Duero, the rough and ready-made pasturelands bordered by rougher mountains, home now of free-range herds of grey-black pigs—they gain a special savour from the acorns—as well as the fighting cattle.

It is this southern part of Castile and Leon and the whole of Extremadura which make up the raw material for a visit to Spain's wild west. There are few finer tracts of country in Europe and few if any which will leave the visitor with a stronger, tangier set of memories.

It is possible to take a standard tourist trip, confining oneself entire to Salamanca, a sandstone city famous for its ancient university and fine cathedrals, one Romanesque, one Gothic-Renaissance.

Equally, one could aim further south, for the rugged town of Trujillo and the elegant monastery of Guadalupe, also much patronised by the Conquistadors.

But far more satisfactory in my view, and taking the visitor to places altogether wilder and less known, is to begin in the north as the Christians did in the Reconquest.

Zamora could make a good place to start. I came in this way, buzzing along in a little hire car on a trip that left me feeling I had shaken hands with an older Spain.

The town sits on a bluff above the Duero, ringed like so many Spanish towns with ugly apartment blocks but sleepily and satisfyingly monumental when you penetrate its centre. Here, as always, there are castles and cathedral. But the real joy of the town is its pure and ancient Romanesque churches—and add to this shops selling local sheeps' cheese and the quite outstanding tapas in the Bar Antonio in Pablo Morillo St (Calle de Pablo Morillo).

Thus to Salamanca and its heraldic splendours. But Ciudad Rodrigo just nearby is in its own way equally remarkable. Economic growth has passed it by so firmly that it remains in a state of virtually perfect preservation, still ringed by unbroken city walls. I strolled around them late one evening, admiring the sunset light that slants across Portugal to strike the Spanish mountains with spindly rays.

After Ciudad Rodrigo, it is mountains rather than towns that are the next excitement. Two groups mark the border between Castile and Leon in the north and Extremadura to the south. To reach the Pena de Francia, highest point of one of these two ranges, you take a road which circles round and round the mountain like John Donne's seeker after the truth. There are vistas back over the broad plains of the Duero basin, across into rolling Portugal, due east to snow-capped mountains closer to Spain's centre and southwards into the shaggy land of Extremadura, the next goal.

Crossing by the Sierra de Gata, closer to Portugal, there is an even greater feeling of remoteness. It was still late spring when I came over, the wildflowers standing in great profusion. On the lower slopes, farmers were ploughing with oxen, while sowers walked behind scattering seed from sacks suspended at their waists. The EEC might have been worlds away.

Jerez de los Caballeros, off the beaten track in a wild terrain of ruined castles, gave birth to the gentler adventurer Vasco Nunez de Balboa "discoverer of the Pacific". Though there is more to see in Trujillo, both places are eminently worth visiting—as are the monastery of Guadalupe and Merida, one capital of Roman Lusitania, with Roman bridge, amphitheatre and the museum of

34

Roman art.

My own particular favourite, though, has to be Caceres. As in Cuidad Rodrigo, but on a larger scale, the old walled centre is almost perfectly preserved, a stone-built city well-equipped with storks on every belfry. Little white-washed streets lead down towards the newer town or straight out into the sierra. There is an excellent restaurant, El Figon de Eustaquio, serving mountain-cured ham from Montanchez and village wines from Pitarra. Students from the new University of Extremadura lend a genial presence to main square.

Almost everywhere was wild lavender, in one spot traversed by a flock of goats, crushing the flowers as they went, their bells ringing out like an extra element of scent in the astonishing fragrance that enveloped the hillside. Higher came heather, with pale green lichen on the trees, and the strong-smelling cistus.

Once down off the mountains into the Extremadura heartland one is truly in Conquistador country. Here no one particular sequence is better than another in terms of historical logic; it is merely a matter of picking off objectives as they come within range.

Trujillo produced Francisco Pizarro, one-time swineherd, later conqueror of Peru and ruin of the Inca civilisation. He was murdered in South America, but many of his companions came back. Their palaces range round the town's main square.

And on to Lisbon, capital of Portugal, Britain's oldest ally and staunch fighters by the side of British infantrymen throughout the long war. Lisbon is the ideal jumping-off place from which to proceed north, first to the Lines of Torres Vedras, then to Vimiero, Rolica, over ground traversed by both the Allies and, briefly the French army. It is a colorful pleasing place in its own right, bordered on north and south by the two intriguing suburbs of Alfama and Belem, both containing so much of interest - even to the reluctant wargamer!

Quite different from our preoccupation with the Napoleonic Wars of the early 19th century, but equally fascinating, were the occasions when we slipped into another gear and forsook British Riflemen, Baker rifles and the Brown Bess musket for their equally renowned forbears, the English archer and his longbow, the man-at-arms and armoured knight of the 100 Years War. It is well known that long before Wellington and Soult battled amid Pyrenean Passes, the famed warrior-king Charlemagne fought in these parts and, in 778, his lieutenant Roland died in a glorious rearguard action against the Saracens, immortalized in the Song of Roland. That field, although open to conjecture, is said to be in the area of the Altabiscar (also fought over in the 1813 battle of Roncesvalles) between the Lepeder Pass and the Valcarlos road, above Roncesvalles.

Hardly realised however, is the fact that a notable and colourful English hero also passed this way - in February 1367 the Black Prince and his army marched from St. Jean-Pied-de-Port, to Arneguy and Valcarlos before crossing the Pass of Roncesvalles, snow-bound in the depth of Winter. Thirty thousand heavily accoutred soldiers and servants with countless wagons, mules and spare horses, clambered and slithered over snow and ice-encrusted rocky tracks on their way to a victory over the Castilians at Najera. Surprisingly they suffered little loss, largely due to the excellent staff-work by Sir John Chandos - even the great Hannibal in his famous march from the Ebro over the Alps to the Po lost 50,000 out of a total strength of 76,000!

Today, despite the modern road, it is an awe-inspiring area and must have been even more so on 15 February 1367 when the three corps of the Black Prince's army, on successive days, crossed the stream at Arneguy and began to mount the westward flank of the precipitous gorge. On all sides are scenes of gigantic grandeur - grey lichened crags, soaring peaks seeming to pierce the infinity of the sky, huge boulders poised deathly still atop sheer falls, and roaring torrents striking silver and white in the sad light of the Winter morn; far below, the flat meadows of the valley's floor with the glistening Nive threading its way as puny as a child's toy, while all around shimmered the exquisite brilliance of untrodden snows. That great soldier Sir John Chandos planned the march and his Herald wrote of it:

"....Since the just God suffered death for us on the cross, there was no such painful passage, for one saw men and horses, that suffered many ills, stumble on the mountain; there was no fellowship, the father made no tarrying for the son; there was cold so great, snow and frost also, that each one was dismayed, but by the grace of God, all passed in due time, ten thousand horses or more, and the men on them, and camped in Navarre."

The march to Pamplona and subsequently to victory at Najera on 3rd April 1367 is really beyond the terms of reference of this book, because the field was not among those visited; however there are certain singular aspects worthy of note. The Black Prince soon discovered campaigning in Spain was a vastly different affair to his usual chevauchee's in Languedoc and Poitou; his Spanish allies were a trial and the enemy, led by the Bastard Enrique, were in no hurry to come to grips and often failed to appear when the English were drawn up for battle.

At Najera, the Bastard Enrique had about 38,000 men - 8,000 men-at-arms; 4,000 genitors; 3,000 other horsemen; 20,000 foot and some crossbowmen and slingers; also a French mercenary contingent led by the famed Bertrand du Guesclin (he whose statue adorns the square at Dinant in Brittany). Although the Black Prince's experience at Crecy and Poitiers were of defensive battles against vastly superior forces, at Najera he proved equally skilful on the attack. As ever, the hails of arrows from English archers broke the cohesion and morale of the enemy who were soon in full flight, losing 5-6,000 dead in the pursuit and 2,000 ransom-worthy prisoners; English loses were 4 knights, 40 men-at-arms, and 20 archers. It is interesting to note that among the Prince's commanders was the Gascon Captal de Buch, who led the flanking cavalry charge that brought victory at Poitiers 11 years before. Fought on a bare featureless plain lacking trees or undergrowth, the Battle of Najera makes an interesting Medieval Wargame, with all the features of the period - characteristic formations, spirited cavalry charges, dour hand-to-hand fighting between dismounted knights and men-at-arms, and the power of the English longbow in the hands of archers on the flanks, channelling attackers into 'killing grounds' and holding off the genitors (light horsemen).

Last but not least, are the 'spin-off's' which can, with careful planning, be reasonably considered as Peninsular Plus's, certainly for those driving from the Channel Coast ferries, south through France to the Pyrenees - or, conversely returning home by that route. The author has innumerable cherished memories of long hauls of over 600 miles to pick-up the ferry at Le Havre or Cherbourg, after battlefield-walking in Spain as far south as Pamplona, when the three/four day drive was enlivened by visiting the fields of numerous other wars of past centuries.

Driving through France en route to or from Spain, it is possible to plan routes that take-in the following well-known battlefields, given in their historic chronological order .

The 100 Years War (1336-1453): Agincourt 1415; Auberoche 1345; Castillon 1453; Cravant 1423;
Crecy 1346; Formigny 1450; Mauron 1352; Patay 1429; Poitiers 1356; Verneuil 1424.
French Wars of Religion: Arques 1589.
Napoleonic Wars: Craonne 7 March 1814; Laon 9/10 March 1814.
World War One: The Argonne 1918; Arras 1917; Cambrai 1917; Chemin-des-Dames 1918;
Somme 1916.
World War Two: Caen and St. Lo 1944; D-Day (Normandy) 1944; Dieppe 1942; Dunkirk 1940.

Then there are the 'off-beat' places of interest, far too numerous to list, but fondly recalled by the author are such places as - Chateau Gaillard, at Les Andelys on the Seine (Richard the Lionheart's 'Saucy Castle'): Compiegne, where the 1918 Armistice was signed in a still-existent railway coach, where Hitler danced a jig of joy in 1941, and where the Hotel de Ville (townhall) has a remarkable display of model soldiers in a huge diorama of a French Army parade: Brouage, a medieval walled town, south of Rochefort; the Naval Museum in La Rochelle. Each place conjures up recollections of another one - the list could be interminable, and is perhaps far removed from our Peninsular War terms of reference.

PENINSULAR PRELUDE - WELLINGTON ARRIVES IN PORTUGAL

In 1808, on the basis that 'your enemy is our enemy', Britain sent arms, equipment and money to aid the Portuguese and Spanish peoples in their fight against the French invaders. In mid-July an expeditionary force under Sir Arthur Wellesley sailed from Cork and arrived in Montego Bay on 30 July to begin disembarking. On 5 August they were reinforced by a small army under General Spencer who, without orders, feeling his presence in the south was unnecessary after the astonishing Spanish victor over Dupont at Baylen on 20 July, sailed from Andalucia. The combined forces were as follows:

	Infantry	Cavalry	Artillery
(1) Division embarked at Cork:			
20th Light Dragoons (only 180 with horses)		394	
Artillery			226
5th Regiment (1st batt.)	990		
9th Regiment (1st batt.)	833		
36th Regiment (1st batt.)	591		
38th Regiment (1st batt.)	957		
40th Regiment (1st batt.)	926		
45th Regiment (1st batt.)	670		
60th Rifles (5th batt.)	936		
71st Regiment (1st batt.)	903		
91st Regiment (1st batt.)	917		
95th Rifles (2nd batt., four companies)	400		
	8,123		
(2) Spencer's troops from Andalusia:			
Artillery			245
6th Regiment (1st batt.)	946		
29th Regiment (1st batt.)	806		
32nd Regiment (1st batt.)	874		
50th Regiment (1st batt.)	948		
82nd Regiment (1st batt.)	929		
	4,503	394	471

A total of 12,626 infantry, 394 cavalry, 471 artillery = 13,491; adding forty-five men of the Staff Corps we get 13,536. (Oman)

Soon after arriving in Montego Bay, the young Lieutenant-General Wellesley had received a despatch from Castlereagh telling him that three commanders had been placed over his head. Despite his unbounded ambition, strong opinion of his own merits, allied to his well-marked tendency to take offence, Wellesley did not resign or ask to be recalled, believing that it would be an unsoldierly act. His dignified despatch to Castlereagh stated: "whether he was to command the army or quit it, he would do his best to ensure its success, and would not hurry operations one moment in order to acquire credit before the arrival of his superiors."

Except for two troops of the Irish Wagon Train brought with him, Wellesley had no transport, but managed to raise his mounted men from 180 to 240 and give some horses to the artillery; he purchased 500 mules and 300 bullocks, but Spencer's two batteries brought from Andalusia had to be left behind for want of draught-horses. A small Portuguese force commanded by

Colonel Trant, a British officer in Portuguese service, were placed at his disposal; they consisted of 258 sabres of the 6th, 11th and 12th Regiments of Cavalry, the 6th battalion of Cacadores comprising 562 bayonets, and 1,514 men of the 12th, 21st and 24th Line Battalions. The British did not think much of their looks, being described by Colonel Leslie thus: "The poor fellows had little or no uniform, but were merely in white jackets, and large broad-brimmed hats turned up at one side, some having feathers and others none, so that they cut a rather grotesque figure."

Beginning his march on Lisbon with just over 15,000 men, Wellesley reached Alcobaca on 14 August to learn that a French brigade under Thomieres had occupied the village until the previous day, and that General Delaborde, with a weak division, was somewhere to his front, in the direction of Obidos and Rolica. Junot, the French Commander-in-Chief soon learned of the landing at Montego Bay and on the same day it commenced had sent orders to Loison to march from Badajoz and join the main army. Meanwhile, Delaborde was sent out from Lisbon to contain Wellesley until Junot could concentrate his whole field-army and be ready to fight; Delaborde was told to expect Loison from the direction of Thomar and Santarem and they were to join forces. Delaborde had five battalions of infantry and a single regiment of Chasseurs a Cheval, with five guns, made up of:

Two battalions of the 70th of the Line;
the 2nd Leger,
the 4th Leger and
the 4th Swiss -
totalling about 4,350 men.

DELABORDE'S POSITION WAS ON TOP OF THIS HILL. THE RIGHT AND LEFT GAPS UP WHICH THE BRITISH ATTACKED CAN BE SEEN. WE CLIMBED DIAGONALLY UP THE RIGHTHAND DEFILE, ALONG A NARROW BRAMBLE STREWN PATH TO ARRIVE AT THE FRENCH POSITION ON TOP.

THE BATTLE OF ROLICA—17 AUGUST 1808

"Rolica was one of our most important affairs; it was terrible hard work to drive off the French. When we had got possession of the heights, they attacked us, and I had only 3 battalions to stand firm against them. Our men fought monstrous well. Junot was not there; the French were commanded by Laborde, a very good officer. We were nearly twice as numerous as they were; at Vimiera, on the contrary, they had rather more men than we had. Laborde was expecting Loison with about as many more troops as himself, and Junot had a third body about as strong at Lisbon. My movements at Rolica prevented Loison from joining, and obliged him to make a large circuit through the mountains."
Conversations with the Duke of Wellington. Earl of Stanhope.

More than one hundred years ago, James Grant, a noted military historian and a prolific writer, set down a record of Wellesley's first engagement of the Peninsular War:

On the 14th Sir Arthur reached the small town of Alcobaca, from which the French had fallen back on the preceding night. The next day he arrived at Caldos. The enemy's advanced posts were at Brilos, within a league of that place, and from it orders were given to drive them. On this duty four rifle companies marched; they were tempted into an incautious pursuit as the French retired. A superior force attempted to cut them off, and would have succeeded had not General Spencer come to their support. A trifling loss was sustained in this affair; but the village was won, and the French retired from the neighbourhood, their pickets having been driven from Obidos.

These were first shots fired in the great War of the Peninsula, and there the troops of France and Britain were face to face for the first time.

The companies engaged consisted of two of the 60th and two of the 95th Regiments. One officer was killed—Lieutenant Bunting, of the latter corps.

Two days later saw the French in position near the little town of Rolica, on the coast road leading from the North to Lisbon. It stands at the entrance to the mountainous country, and there General Laborde has posted himself strongly on the heights and in the passes, with such judicious care that superior numbers could not be brought against him.

In front of Rolica lies a fertile plain, overlooked by the green eminence on which the little town stands. At the end of the plain is a valley which commences at Caldas de Rainha. In its centre, and eight miles from Rolica, is the town and Moorish castle of Obidos, from whence the enemy's pickets had been driven on the 15th, "and from that time," says Sir Arthur in his despatch, "he had posts on the hills on both sides of the valley, as well as in the plain in front of his army, which was posted on the heights in front of Rolica, its right resting upon the hills, its left upon an eminence on which was a windmill, and the whole covering four or five passes into the mountains in his rear."

Laborde (or De Laborde) was at the head of 5,550 infantry and 500 cavalry, with five field-pieces; and as there was reason to believe that General Loison, who was the preceding day at Rio Major, would come in on Laborde's right flank in the night, it was resolved to attack the latter at once, and force the passes.

Sir Arthur having formed his plan of attack, broke up from Caldos on the 17th of August, and advanced upon Rolica with his army in three columns.

The right, which consisted of 1,200 Portuguese infantry, with fifty cavalry, was destined to turn the enemy's left, and penetrate into the mountains in his rear. The left column, consisting of the infantry brigades of Major-Generals Fergusson and Bowes, three companies of Rifles, a brigade of light artillery, and forty dragoons, had orders to ascend the hill at Obidos, turn all the enemy's posts on the left of the valleys, and watch for the approach of General Loison's corps.

The centre column, consisting of the brigades of the gallant Sir Rowland Hill, Nightingale, Crawford, and Fane, with 400 Portuguese caçadores (or rifles), a brigade of nine-pounders, and another of six-pounders, had orders to attack Laborde's position straight in front.

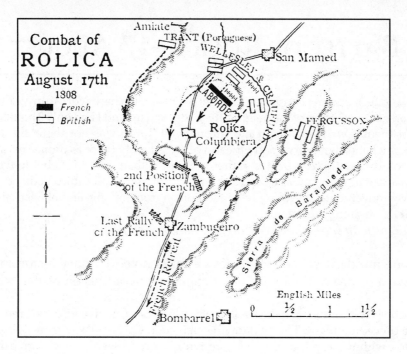

Combat of
ROLICA
August 17th
1808
■ French
□ British

At seven o'clock in the morning the troops moved off from Obidos, through a level country, interspersed here and there with pine woods; but though the distance between Caldas de Rainha and Rolica is not more than three leagues, much time elapsed before our troops were within musket-shot of the French outposts. Nothing, says the Marquis of Londonderry, in his "Story of the Peninsular War," could exceed the orderly and gallant style in which they traversed the intervening space. The day was clear, bright, and beautiful, and the woody scenery through which the marching columns passed was varied and striking, "but they were themselves by far the most striking feature in the panorama."

Whenever any broken piece of ground or other natural obstacle came in the way, the leading sections of the column having passed it, they stepped short till the rear had recovered its order; and then the whole pressed forward, with the same attention to distance and dressing which is usually preserved at a review. At last the enemy's line came in sight, all dark and sombre, save where the sunshine was reflected by their bayonets and polished musket-barrels. In a few minutes afterwards, light puffs of smoke and the report of scattered firing announced that the skirmishers were engaged.

Anon the regiments comprising the four brigades at the centre division broke into columns of battalions, with bayonets fixed and colours flying. The left continued to press on rapidly, while our rifles on the right drove in the tirailleurs who were opposed to them. At the same moment Ferguson's brigade, with its light artillery and little squadron of horse, was seen moving swiftly down the green slope of the hills, to cut off the retreat of De Laborde, who was too wary a soldier to permit that.

On finding that the posts which covered his position on the plain were carried, he withdrew his troops with great readiness into the rocky passes or gorges in the hills; and it now became evident that on these narrow ravines he had looked all along as affording him advantageous battle-ground. The new position he thus assumed became more formidable than ever, owing to the cover afforded to his musketry by the inequalities of the ground.

Sir Arthur Wellesley quite as quickly altered his plan of attack.

Five columns were formed, and to each of these was assigned the desperate task of carrying a pass; but as the ground was rough and steep, and the ravines extremely narrow, no more than five British battalions, a few companies of our light infantry, and the Portuguese brigade, could be brought into action. The latter, says Sir Arthur's despatch, were ordered to move up a pass on the right of the whole; the light companies of Rowland Hill's brigade moved into the pass; next on the right, the 9th and 29th Regiments, under Brigadier Nightingale, were to assail a third pass, and the 45th and 82nd Regiments the passes on the left. These ravines were all difficult of approach to the assailants, and were most defensible to the enemy. Impending rocks and dense dark groves overhung them, affording sure and secret cover to the crouching French tirailleurs; and as our troops advanced, their order became broken by clumps of wild myrtle and other shrubs.

Most particularly was this the case in that pass which the 9th and 29th were ordered to attack. Permitting the column to advance without molestation till the leading companies were within a few yards of a myrtle grove, the French suddenly opened a deadly fire from the front and both flanks, which only the most resolute bravery could have withstood. In a moment the ravine was full of smoke; the roar of the musketry was echoed by the hills and rocks with incessant reverberations, and the killed and wounded fell fast on every side. The advance was checked for a moment–but a moment only.

Lieutenant-Colonel Lake, of the 29th (son of Lord Lake of Delhi and Leswarree), who led the attack, waving his hat and sword, called on his men to follow him, and with loud cheers they dashed on. Full of confidence in their position and in themselves, the French fought valiantly, disputing every rock, and bush, and inch of ground, nor was it till after great loss had been sustained, including the gallant Lake, that the 29th succeeded in gaining the plateau.

That splendid regiment had not yet formed line, and the 9th were still entangled in the pass, when a French battalion had the temerity to advance to the charge. They were met with equal spirit, and the slaughter by the bayonet was great on both sides; but the French were repulsed. Again they attempted to charge with increasing numbers; but the 9th were now in line to aid their comrades, and again the French were beaten back before the hedge of British steel with renewed slaughter.

They had no opportunity given them to repeat these sanguinary efforts; for now the heads of the different columns, pressing onward and pouring their fire through the different passes, began to show themselves, and from that moment the position was carried on every point.

De Laborde at once drew off his troops by beat of drum, and they began to retire in excellent order, though many efforts were made to harass them by cavalry and light infantry; but his great superiority in the former force, and the nature of the wild country through which they retreated, rendered these attempts of little avail. In the passes the French left three pieces of cannon, and

ONE OF THE DEFILES UP WHICH THE BRITISH TROOPS ATTACKED.

more than a thousand officers and men killed or wounded.

Our total loss in killed, wounded, and missing amounted to 474 of all ranks. Among the latter were four officers and sixty-eight rank and file, most of whom were probably shot, or bled to death of their wounds unseen in lonely places.

Sir Arthur Wellesley, with his victorious troops, followed the enemy as far as Villa Verde, on the road to Torres Vedras, and halted for the night. The enemy retired behind that place, which is ten miles distant from the field of Rolica; and near there the junction was formed by the arrival of Loison's division.

On the following morning the advance of our army was about to be renewed; and it appeared, states Lord Londonderry, "as if no check would be given to the ardour of the troops till they should have won a second victory, and established themselves in Lisbon, when the arrival of a messenger at head-quarters caused a suspension of orders already issued."

This messenger was an officer bearing despatches from General Anstruther, to the effect that, with a large fleet of store-ships and a reinforcement of troops, he was now at anchor off the fortified town of Peniche, seventeen miles west of Obidos; and as it was a matter of the first importance to bring up these troops and stores without delay, Sir Arthur resolved to march in such a direction as would ensure a ready junction.

With this view, he directed the route of his troops towards Lourinha. He reached that place in the evening, and on the following day took up a position near the village of Vimiera.

Prior to General de Laborde retiring from Rolica, his situation had become most critical. He was severely wounded, but, with unyielding resolution, he had made a movement along the table-land leading from his position to the mountains in his rear, checking pursuit by partial charges with his cavalry, until he reached the village of Zambugeira.

There the ground opened, and the danger from the flanking force being fended off, he had made another stand ere he finally took to flight, and ultimately reached Torres Vedras.

In this ultimately indecisive action, Wellesley achieved his aim of defeating Delaborde's force before they could be reinforced and, although the French retreated in good order, Allied morale was encouraged and the advance towards Lisbon able to be continued. From it, certain significant lessons could be learned in this first "blooding" of the British forces in the Peninsular.

It proved that the much vaunted French forces were not supermen while establishing the effectiveness of British skirmishing tactics. At the same time as it demonstrated Wellesley's ability to coordinate an offensive action with an army divided into three attacking groups, it also demonstrated the cool efficiency of General Delaborde, who was a typical Napoleonic divisional commander of the type Wellesley was to frequently encounter. He displayed particular skill in his initial withdrawal to a better position and his ultimate retreat, while his outnumbered and outgunned troops offered a fierce resistance.

Official casualty figures differ from those given by Grant—the Anglo-Portuguese Army lost 485, including 35 P.O.W's; the French 700, including approximately 100 P.O.W's.

BATTLE HONOURS FOR ROLICA
1st Bn. 5th (Northumberland) Regt. of Foot
1st Bn. 6th (1st Warwickshire) Regt. of Foot
1st Bn. 9th (East Norfolk) Regt. of Foot
1st Bn. 29th (Worcestershire) Regt. of Foot
1st Bn. 36th (Herefordshire) Regt. of Foot
1st Bn. 32nd (Cornwall) Regt. of Foot
1st Bn. 38th (1st Staffordshire) Regt. of Foot
1st Bn. 40th (2nd Somersetshire) Regt. of Foot
1st Bn. 82nd Regt. of Foot (Prince of Wales's Volunteers)
1st Bn. 45th (Nottinghamshire) Regt. of Foot
5th Bn. 60th (Royal American) Regt. of Foot

1st Bn. 71st (Highland) Regt. of Foot
1st Bn. 91st (Argyllshire Highlanders) Regt. of Foot
2nd Bn. 95th Regt. of Foot (Rifle Corps)

Originally awarded as Roleia, Army Order 216 of 1911 directed that the award should read Rolica.

During the Peninsular War, certain officers one night at dinner were observed by their General to decline the soup. On questioning them, it was revealed that a dead French soldier had been discovered in the well the same day. The General is said to have ordered another basin of soup, remarking, "It would taste even sweeter if the whole French army, including Napoleon, were in it."

WALKING THE BATTLEFIELD OF ROLICA

The effort of finding and climbing this field bears a bonus, because it lays near the exquisite walled town of Obidos with its Pousada (State-run hotel) situated in an old castle. A night there is a memorable experience, but if its few rooms are booked, then there is a fine 'modern' hotel on the left-hand side of the narrow street leading up to the castle; one can stay there and dine in unique style in the stone-alcoved restaurant of the Pousada.

The hills on which the Battle of Rolica was fought can be seen from the ramparts of Obidos, and a short drive brings one to the roads bordering the position. After that, it is out of the car and, map in hand, either a climb up one of the gullies, or a less arduous path from the rear of the position. As the area is quite unchanged, one can adequately employ a contemporary map of the actual battle to locate salient points. It is possible to get right up behind Delaborde's second position, where one comes upon a mouldering stone memorial half hidden in relatively dense undergrowth, dedicated in British to Colonel Lake, who fell there when leading part of the 1/29th too far into the French lines. To find it, seek the village of Columbeira and go through it up the ravine, on the road, to the village of Zambugeira; go past an ancient tree and the church, take road to the left until reaching a dirt-track; then proceed through orchards through the rear of the French positions, until arriving at the memorial at the head of Lake's galley.

WARGAMING THE BATTLE OF ROLICA

The confined nature of the scene of operations allows one to cover the entire scene of the action, which will provide the greatest inspiration for a fine wargame requiring small numbers of figures. Such a game has been fought by the author's "team" on more than one occasion-the description given here is of a battle forming part of a chronological series embracing many of the actions of the Peninsular War, employing the "league-table" method of scoring described in the section *Peninsular Pastime.*

Because they are relatively diagramatic and readily available, the maps from Jac Weller's fine book *Wellington in the Peninsular* were used for this campaign. From them a diagramatic terrain was drawn which fitted the size of the wargames table-the report compiled at the time details the manner in which the project was tackled.

If the battle contains more than one "part" (i.e. two or more events of a major nature) then it may either be fought by splitting your table-top terrain so that each part takes the form of a separate battle or by "coming into the battle" just prior to what you consider to be the major or most interesting facet of the engagement. For example, when fighting Rolica, we decided on the second part of the battle when the French under Delaborde had fallen back from their first position because of a British out-flanking movement, and had taken up a second and stronger position on a ridge some two miles further back.

In order to obtain a reasonable accurate scaled-down force, we decided to let 1 man on the wargames table equal 40 men in the actual battle, which for Rolica gave the British a force of

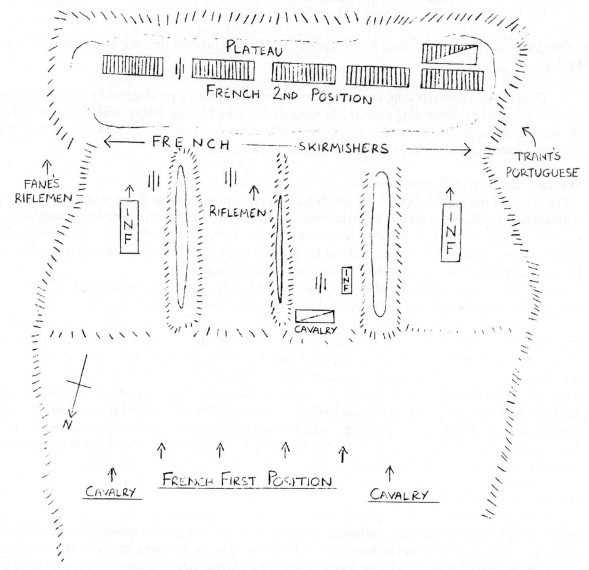

DONALD'S VERSION OF ROLICA

about 350 men and the French 115 men. The French of course had the advantage of a very strong position, they also had more cavalry than the British.

In re-fighting the battle of Rolica we deemed it necessary for the smaller French force in their strong hilltop position to have to hold off the considerable stronger British force advancing up the slopes and at the same time be able to make their getaway before the arrival on their flank of the strong British force. In the event, the French were able to do this and it was decided that the British had gained two points for the victory whilst the French had gained one point for holding off the British throughout 14 or 15 game-moves.

THE BATTLE OF ROLICA FOUGHT AS A WARGAME

This battle was begun at the stage where Delaborde had retreated back and was strongly in position on the top of the ridge approached by four boulder-strewn gullies and very steep slopes. The terrain was laid out on an 8'x4' table as shown in the accompanying map.

From his force of 350 men, Wellesley had to detach two flanking columns, leaving him with a force of about 200 men, all infantry plus three guns. The French behind a convenient rocky breastwork had 115 infantry, 15 cavalry and one gun.

Delaborde was aware that a strong flanking column was approaching him from the east but he did not know when to expect its arrival, on the other hand, neither did Wellesley know when his column would arrive, being unaware of any difficulties they might encounter on route. To represent this on the wargames table, an impartial umpire threw three dice and added the totals together, this total represented the number of game-moves at which Ferguson's flanking column would arrive on Delaborde's right flank. The proviso was made that Delaborde would be told three moves before the column actually arrived as it was considered likely that he would have seen them approaching from his lofty position.

The battle opened by a strong British column advancing up the western most gully with a smaller column advancing up the eastern gully. The centre/eastern gully was rapidly traversed by a force of riflemen whilst the centre/western gully held a reserve force of two battalions of infantry whilst a gun was thrown forward halfway up the gully and brought into action. A gun also accompanied the riflemen up the centre/eastern gully.

When within range a sharp fire fight ensued between the two eastern columns and the far western column. The latter struggled to deploy on emerging from the top of the gully, their numbers impeding them and making this manoeuvre difficult. They were charged by the French cavalry and similarly engaged by a battalion of French infantry, the resulting melee continuing for a number of game-moves. The British eastern flank came under fire from the French artillery and the riflemen, emerging from the top of the gully deployed into skirmishing lines and engaged similar lines of French Tiraillereurs. After about four moves the French gun was knocked out by artillery fire, a very severe blow to the French as they now had no artillery whatsoever. A French infantry regiment, taking severe losses, found their morale to be insufficient to stand the strain and retreated back out of line.

Delaborde was becoming a little apprehensive as the battle went on, wondering when Ferguson's flanking column were going to approach. They were coming from the British left on which flank the British forces were doing the most damage and making the greatest advances. On the 11th game-move, Delaborde could stand the strain no longer and disengaged his cavalry and began a withdrawal. He was close enough to the rear end of the table to be able to successfully evacuate his forces without them being engaged by the British, who lacked cavalry.

It transpired that the three dice thrown to indicated the time of arrival of the flanking force had turned up two sixes and a four so that Delaborde had two more moves before he would have been told that the British were approaching and then three more moves to get off the table. Under the circumstances it was considered that although this was undoubtedly a British victory, the French had earned themselves one point so that the final score was Wellesley two points, Delaborde one point.

THE BATTLE OF VIMIERO–21 AUGUST 1808

At the age of 15, Colin Campbell, later Field Marshal Lord Clyde, took part in his first battle–at Vimiero. In his life of Lord Clyde, General Shadwell wrote: "It was at the commencement of this battle that a circumstance occurred to the young subaltern, to which in after years he was wont to refer with the deepest feelings of gratitude. Colin Campbell was with the rear company of his battalion, which was halted in open column of companies. His Captain, an officer of years and experience, called … him to his side, took him by the hand, and leading him by the flank of the battalion to its front, walked with him up and down the front of the leading company for several minutes, in full view of the enemy's artillery, which had begun to open fire on our troops whilst covering his attack. He then let go of the boy's hand and told him to join his company. Many years later Lord Clyde commented: 'It was the greatest kindness that could have been shown me at such a time, and through life I have felt grateful for it.' "

On the day following the Battle of Rolica, the Allied Army marched south to Vimiero, some fifteen miles southwest of Rolica and inland of Maceira Bay. Receiving despatches telling of a convoy of transports laying off-shore awaiting to land reinforcements, Wellesley selected the crescent-shaped beach and enveloping headlands that would afford the transports some protection from the heavy surf. Subsequently, Anstruther's brigade were brought ashore on 19th and Acland's followed next day, giving Wellesley command of nearly 17,000 British soldiers. But it was to be a short-lived command, for with the transports came Sir Harry Burrard to take command of the army. Wellesley heard that he had been superseded as he was busily arranging his line of battle, having expected to be attacked from the south, up the valley of the Maceira.

Wellesley was taken out in a boat to greet Sir Harry on board the sloop Brazen; Sir Harry listened to the course of events to date before placing a strong embargo on any further offensive movement, as he was resolved not to stir until the arrival of Sir John Moore with a division from the Baltic. Wellesley went back to the army, leaving Sir Harry Burrard to sleep on board ship for one more night, a decision that cost him the enviable chance of commanding a British Army in a pitched battle!

Meanwhile, Junot had marched out of Lisbon with his army to support Delaborde and Loison but, alarmed by reports of a convoy of troop transports off the mouth of the Tagus (it was the 3rd Regiment [The Buffs] being brought from Madeira) he left no less than seven battalions (about 6,500 men) in Lisbon and neighbouring forts.

Hearing that Wellesley had been stationary at Vimiero since the morning of the 19th, Junot determined to attack him as quickly as possible.

Wellesley's order of battle reveals his expectation of being attacked from the south, up the valley of the Maceira; little or no provision had been made against the tactics actually adopted by Junot–of assaulting the British left-centre while simultaneously turning their extreme left-flank, while leaving the right unmolested. As Junot had plenty of cavalry there was no reason for anything less than a thorough reconnaissance of the British position, but meaning his attack to be a surprise, he possibly felt that time thus lost would give Wellesley more time to prepare. The Allies held a good position with the bulk of the army occupying the heights between Vimiero and the sea; the heights are intersected by a steep pass formed by the valley of the Maceira, covered by the hill of Vimiero to the south-east, a round and broad elevation. The whole position was less than three miles in length, so short that there was no difficulty in moving troops rapidly from one end to the other and, as events showed, without the slightest risk.

Although made under cover of darkness, Junot's approach-march and arrival was no surprise; delayed by bad roads and heard crossing a wooden bridge during the night, the dust of his march gave away his position inevitably. In the event he did make contact until well after daybreak, at about 8 A.M., and even then he had only the haziest idea of the exact Allied position, so masterful was Wellesley's use of ground. On the other hand, Wellesley could easily discern Junot's right hook and, as always, handled his troops very quickly and surely; he reinforced his centre and left with four brigades from under cover of the central hill, practically unobserved by the French.

James Grant continues the story from the point where Delaborde retreated from Rolica:

Calms prevented the fleet with Anstruther's reinforcement from standing in from the Berlings till the evening of the 19th of August; and the brigade was landed on the following day on the sandy beach at the mouth of the Maciera, but amidst difficulties of no ordinary nature. Foaming and white, the surf ran there with great fury, and flying parties of French cavalry hovered about, carbine in hand, with the intention of cutting off each detachment as it landed. One or two boats were swamped, and some six soldiers were drowned. After marching three leagues, as far as Lourinha, they found a detachment under General Spencer waiting to receive them, and took their position in the advanced guard.

Meanwhile the French army had assembled about Torres Vedras; the advanced guard, under Marshal Junot, the Duc d'Abrantes, having taken up a strong position in front of the town, and the main body, under De Laborde, being strongly posted in rear of it. During this and the preceding day their cavalry were very active. They covered the whole country, hence Sir Arthur Wellesley could gain no exact information concerning the enemy, save that their post was one of great strength.

About noon on the 20th, news arrived that General Auckland was off the coast; and in the evening of the same day Sir Harry Burrard arrived in the roadstead of Maciera, with orders to assume the command of the army. The plan of Sir Arthur had been to march on the following day, to send on his advanced posts as far as the town of Mafra, in Portuguese Estramadura, and halt the main body five miles from that place, and thus outflank the French position at Torres Vedras. He possessed an excellent map of the country, and topographical accounts of it, which had been prepared for Sir Charles Stewart, during his command in Portugal. He thus anticipated that the battle would be fought in a district of which he had complete knowledge, and that ere long he should be in Lisbon, with the foe flying before him. The arrival of a new commander disconcerted all these plans. Sir Harry Burrard would sanction no rash movement, as he called it, with a force as yet incomplete; and, as senior officer, his will could not be disputed. Sir Arthur, with keen emotions of disappointment, returned to the camp that night: and the next day afforded proof that he had erred in what he had anticipated the enemy would do; for Junot, who had procured better intelligence than his antagonist, was leaving nothing undone to bring into the field a force capable of sustaining a battle with the British army.

Every man fit for service was drawn from the garrisons of Lisbon and the forts near it; and the corps of Loison, Thomieres, Kellerman, and De Laborde were concentrated without delay at the position of Torres Vedras. By the 20th this was all fully effected. One division was assigned to De Laborde, another to Loison; while Kellerman assumed the command of the reserve, which was entirely composed of grenadiers. Marshal Junot, then advanced in all his strength towards Vimiera, where he knew the British troops were encamped.

The town of Vimiera stands in a lovely valley, through which the Maciera winds towards the sea, about three miles distant. On each side the hills rise to a considerable height, especially on the north, where a chain of detached peaks start with striking abruptness out of the fertile plain. The western termination of these mountains reaches the shore, while the eastern in separated by a deep ravine from the heights over which the road passes from Lourinha. On the north-east of Vimiera there is a piece of table-land covered with laurels and other shrubs; this commands all the approaches from Torres Vedras, and is, in turn, commanded by the mass of mountains that rise between the left bank of the river and the sea.

With eight pieces of cannon, the great portion of our infantry were posted on these mountains;

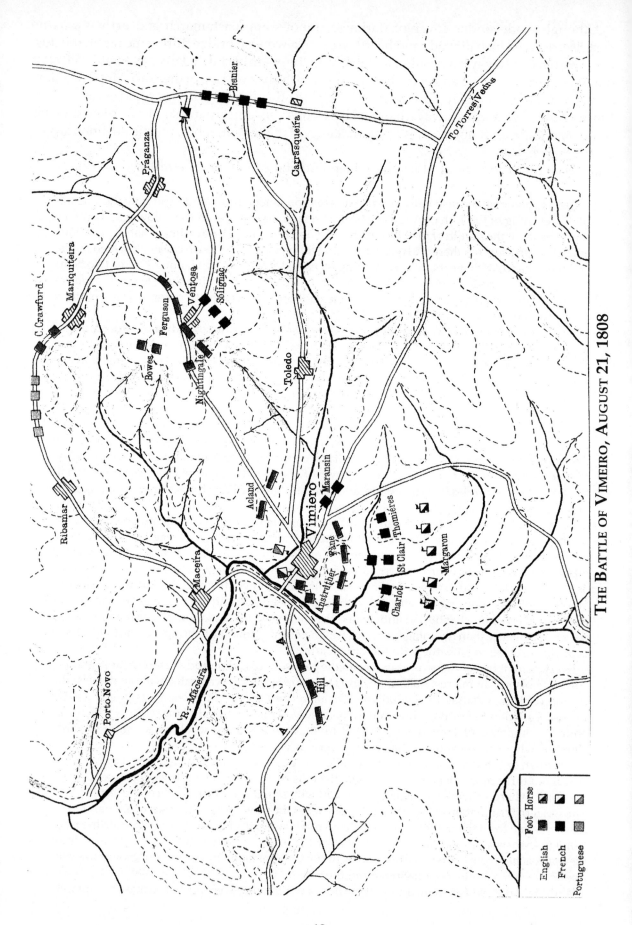

THE BATTLE OF VIMEIRO, AUGUST 21, 1808

Foot Horse

English

French

Portuguese

Hill's brigade being on the right and Fergusson's on the left, having one battalion on the heights above the ravine. A hill on the south-east of Vimiera was occupied by the corps of Fane and Anstruther—the former with his riflemen and the 50th Foot; and the latter were supported by two half brigades of nine and six-pounders. The high road to Lourinha, and the heights which it crosses, were occupied only by an out-picket, because, as there was no spring water in the neighbourhood, Sir Arthur Wellesley had intended to shift his camp at sunrise. In the village last named were stationed our reserves of artillery and cavalry.

Marshal Junot began his march about nightfall; and, after a tedious and difficult route, through narrow defiles and mountain passes, about seven o'clock next morning the head of his leading column was within four miles and a half of our outposts. As the ground he occupied was completely hidden from these, he was enabled to form, unseen, his columns of attack; nor was it until the helmets and sabres of a considerable mass of cavalry were seen to glitter in the sunshine, as they deployed immediately in front of the picket on the Lourinha road, that Sir Arthur anticipated there would be action.

Full of grand decision, and never for a moment taken by surprise, his eagle eye perceived in a moment that the principal assault would be made exactly where he had most cause to apprehend it—on the weakest portion of his line—he therefore ordered the brigades of Generals Nightingale, Fergusson, Auckland, and Bowes to cross the ravine with all speed; and thus, long before the first shots were exchanged by the advanced posts, his left flank was secure.

The enemy came on in two great columns, supported and flanked by a cloud of skirmishers. They were dressed in long white linen coats and trousers. Their muskets were six inches longer in the barrel than ours, but their bayonets were three inches shorter; and the locks of their pieces were better constructed, the priming not being so liable to fall out of the pans—an accident that often happened then in our service.

The right column, which consisted of 6,000 men, poured along the Lourinha road; while the left, 5,000 strong, turned its efforts against the table-land. As the French troops are always impetuous, and usually go into action uttering yells and cries, the first onset of both these masses was made with great fury; hence, on the left of the table-land the skirmishers were swept away, and the head of the column, as it came surging on, appeared almost unchecked in front of the 50th Regiment, or West Kent.

Veterans of Egypt, this fine old regiment—long popularly known from the then colour of its facings as "The Black Half Hundred"—drawn up in line, permitted this oblong mass to approach till scarcely twenty yards divided them. Then, after pouring in a steady and most destructive volley, the corps prepared to charge. For a moment—but a moment only—the enemy stood as if resolved to meet the shock. But the bayonets of the 50th were barely crossing theirs when they began to pause; and ere the final rush was made they wavered, broke, and, with wild halloos, ran down the slope in confusion and with precipitation.

About the same time that this was occurring, the 2nd battalion of the 43rd Light Infantry was attacked with singular determination in the town of Vimiera, by the lesser column. The 43rd were posted partly in the houses, and along the churchyard wall, from both of which points they opened a fire upon the road, and resolutely repelled every attempt to dislodge them; and the same result attended the attack which was made on the British left. Though led on with singular gallantry by General de Laborde, the enemy were repulsed with great slaughter by the exertions chiefly of the 52nd Light Infantry and the old 97th or Queen's German Regiment.

Meantime the roar of musketry was elsewhere heard among the echoing hills that overhung the Lourinha road on the British right. On this quarter the French had forced their way, as they had done on the other flank, through the line of skirmishers; and coming on with all their usual élan, they never paused until they saw before them the solid array of the 36th, the 40th, and 71st Highlanders; "and several searching discharges of musketry," says Lord Londonderry, "were exchanged at a distance which hardly allowed a single bullet to miss its mark."

One loud and ringing cheer that burst along the line warned the French of what they had to expect; but this column was composed of well-tried troops, the flower of Junot's army, and they stood to the last. The onset was awful. The entire front rank of the enemy perished to a man; and after the action the men who composed it were found lying dead on the very spot where, during its formation, each had stood.

"They came up to the charge like men accustomed to victory," records the "Edinburgh Register" for 1808; "but no troops, however disciplined, however brave, however accustomed to victory, have ever withstood the charge of the British bayonet. In one moment their foremost rank fell, like a line of grass beneath the scythes of the mowers. The very men whose superiority was thus so decidedly proved could not speak without an involuntary emotion of awe or so complete and instantaneous a destruction, produced as it was, not by artillery or explosions, but by their own act and deed, and the strength of their own hands."

The French gave way, and six pieces of cannon were taken from them in the pursuit.

They made a resolute attempt, under General Kellerman, to recover them, at a moment when the 71st Highlanders and 82nd Regiment, who had halted in the valley, were lying down to rest. These fine corps only fell back to a little rising ground, from whence their fire could be given with greater effect. It was given, and once more bringing the bayonet to the charge, they swept all before them, repulsing the French with renewed loss.

When the 71st Highlanders were advancing, Stewart, the piper of their grenadier company fell; his thigh had been broken by a musket-shot. Yet he refused to quit the field, says a note to Londonderry's narrative; and sitting on a knapsack, continued to inspire this comrades by a pibroch, crying:

"Deil hae me, lads, if ye shall want music!"

For this he received a handsome stand of pipes from the Highland Society of Scotland.

In the attempt to recover the guns, the French General Bernier was wounded, and would have been bayoneted by those into whose hands he had fallen, but for the intervention of Corporal Mackay, of the 71st, to whom, in gratitude, he offered his watch and purse. These Mackay positively declined to accept. When he delivered his prisoner in safety to Colonel (afterwards Sir Dennis) Pack, the general said, with astonishment:

"What sort of man can this be? He has done me the greatest service, and yet refuses to take from me the only reward I can present him!"

"Sir," replied Colonel Pack, "we are British soldiers, not plunderers."

By the request of Sir Arthur Wellesley, Mackay was immediately made a sergeant; and the Highland Society presented him with a gold medal

Gallantly did the French fight in this action; they had been long accustomed to conquer, and were slow to learn what defeat was. The grenadiers of their reserve, under Kellerman, advancing under a cross fire of cannon and musketry, never paused or gave way till the levelled bayonets of the British hurled them in total disorder down the descent. They were thus routed at every point, with a slaughter greater than usually occurs in armies of similar magnitude. Between three and four thousand of them perished on the field. A large proportion of prisoners fell into our hands; many of these were officers of rank. There were also captured six pieces of cannon, six field howitzers, 23 ammunition carts, and 20,000 rounds of ball cartridge. Generals Foy and Thiebault insist that the French loss was under 2,000 men.

Our total loss of all ranks, killed, wounded, and missing, was 740 men and 43 horses.

In the first of these casualties is found the name of Lieutenant-Colonel Charles Taylor, commanding the 20th Light Dragoons. He was shot through the heart while leading his troopers in a brilliant charge, during which they were suddenly beset by an entire brigade of the enemy's cavalry.

The battle had hardly begun when Sir Harry Burrard, with his staff, arrived upon the field. As bound in duty, Sir Arthur Wellesley offered to resign all further responsibility; but Sir Harry "possessed too much judgment not to perceive that the execution of plans could not be left in safer hands than in those of the man who had formed them. He accordingly declined to interfere in any way till the result of the struggle should be known; and took upon himself the direction of future operations only when the defeat of the enemy had been ascertained."

Most of the wounded French who fell into our hands were young men, and of delicate appearance; apparently men whose lot would not have been in the ranks but for the new system of conscription which forced them into the service. Mr. Ormsby, the chaplain of the staff, as he was endeavouring to render assistance to some of them, addressed one whose appearance interested him in language of commiseration, and expressed at the same time a regret for the horrors of war.

"Monsieur, I glory in my wounds," replied the prisoner, "and I consider war the greatest happiness of life!"

During the whole day the armed Portuguese peasantry were prowling about the field, barbarously murdering every wounded or struggling Frenchman whom they could find, in revenge as they alleged, "For the manifold wrongs of their country, and the aggravated injuries which they had endured."

So conscious, indeed, were the prisoners of the little mercy they would meet with at the hands of the Portuguese, that they expressed dread lest a massacre should take place, and a strong guard was posted for their protection. The peasantry, however, passed the night on the field, carousing round large fires, and recounting to each other exultingly the bloody work they had severally done with the musket or stiletto.

So vacillating were the Ministry of the day, that on the morning subsequent to this great victory of Vimiera, Sir Hugh Dalrymple arrived to supersede Sir Harry Burrard; so that the British army, with an enemy in front, had no less than three commanders-in-chief within four-and-twenty hours.

Shortly after his arrival, General Kellerman came in with a flag of truce from the Duc d'Abrantes, to propose a cessation of hostilities, during which a convention might be concluded for the final evacuation of Portugal by the French.

Various points arise as a postscript to the Battle of Vimiero. History tells that Junot had afterthoughts about his right-hook, originally made by Solignac's Brigade, and sent Brennier's Brigade to support it. But these two formations were from different divisions and with no General present to coordinate their efforts, their bolts were shot separately and disastrously. Also, their absence left the main thrust against Vimiero itself far too weak, with only eight battalions launched piecemeal into the assault. The traditional French tactics of heavy columns preceded by clouds of skirmishers came unstuck–as it was to do so often in succeeding years– against the British "thin red line." As one came to expect from British cavalry in the Peninsular, the cavalry charge towards the end of the day went much too far; luckily the French were by then semi-demoralized so that the Light Dragoons lost only half their number.

All in all, the French were guilty of: bad reconnaissance; ill-coordinated attacks; and faulty minor infantry tactics. On the other hand, the Allies must be praised for–good use of ground; excellent handling of reserves; above average use of the characteristics of the weapons of the day; but earn a minus point for their uncontrollable cavalry.

Wellesley's Order of Battle at Vimiero

Cavalry, 20th Light Dragoons	240	6th Brigade, Fane:	2,005
Artillery, three batteries	226	50th (1st batt.)	
1st Brigade, Hill:	2,658	60th (5th batt.)	
5th (1st batt.)		95th (2nd batt. four companies)	
9th (1st batt.)		7th Brigade, Anstruther:	2,703
38th (1st batt.)		9th (2nd batt.)	
2nd Brigade, Ferguson:	2,449	43rd (2nd batt.)	
36th		52nd (2nd batt.)	
40th (1st batt.)		97th (2nd batt.)	
71st (1st batt.)		8th Brigade, Acland:	1,332
3rd Brigade, Nightingale:	1,520	2nd	
29th		20th (seven and a half companies)	
82nd (1st batt.)		95th (1st batt., two companies	
4th Brigade, Bowes:	1,813		
6th (1st batt.)		Total British present	16,778
32nd (1st batt.)			
5th Brigade, C. Crawfurd:	1,832	Plus Trant's Portuguese	2,100
45th (1st batt.)		Total force approximately	18,800
91st			

JUNOT'S ORDER OF BATTLE OF VIMIERO

Division Delaborde:		Cavalry Division Margaron:		2,251
Brigade Brennier:	4,531	1st Provisional Chasseurs		
2nd Léger (3rd batt.)		3rd Provisional Dragoons		
4th Léger (3rd batt.)		4th Provisional Dragoons		
70th of the Line (1st and 2nd batts.)		5th Provisional Dragoons		
Brigade Thomieres:	2,191	Squadron of volunteer cavalry		
86th of the Line (1st and 2nd batts.)				
(minus four companies left at Elvas)		Artillerymen for 23 guns,		
4th Swiss (two companies)		engineers, train, &c.		700
Division Loison:				
Brigade Solignac:	3,986	Total		15,656
12th Léger (3rd batt.)				
15th Léger (3rd batt.)				
58th of the Line (3rd batt.)				
Brigade Charlot:	1,997			
32nd of the Line (3rd batt.)				
82nd of the Line (3rd batt.)				
Infantry	12,705			

Towards the end of the Battle of Vimiero, when the French could attack no more and would suffer a complete defeat if pursued industriously, Wellesley put spurs to his thoroughbred and galloped a mile along the eastern ridge to where Sir Harry Burrard was watching the battle.

"Sir Harry," Wellesley urged, "now is your chance. The French are completely beaten; we have a large body of troops that have not yet been in action. Let us move on Torres Vedras. You take the force here straight forward: I will bring round the left with the troops already there. We shall be in Lisbon in three days!"

A direct quotation from Wellesley, given by Fortescue VI.231

BATTLE HONOURS FOR VIMEIRO
20th Regt. of (Light) Dragoons
2nd (the Queen's Royal) Regt. of Foot
1st Bn. 5th (Northumberland) Regt. of Foot
1st Bn. 6th (1st Warwickshire) Regt. of Foot
1st & 2nd Bns. 9th (East Norfolk) Regt. of Foot
1st Bn. 20th (East Devonshire) Regt. of Foot
1st Bn. 29th (Worcestershire) Regt. of Foot
1st Bn. 36th (Herefordshire) Regt. of Foot
1st Bn. 32nd (Cornwall) Regt. of Foot
1st Bn. 38th (1st Staffordshire) Regt. of Foot
1st Bn. 40th (2nd Somersetshire) Regt. of Foot
1st Bn. 82nd Regt. of Foot (Prince of Wales's Volunteers)
2nd Bn. 43rd (Monmouthshire Light Infantry) Regt.
2nd Bn. 52nd (Oxfordshire Light Infantry) Regt.
1st Bn. 45th (Nottinghamshire) Regt. of Foot
1st Bn. 50th (West Kent) Regt. of Foot
5th Bn. 60th (Royal American) Regt. of Foot
1st Bn. 71st (Glasgow Highland) Regt. of Foot
91st (Argyllshire Highlander) Regt. of Foot
1st and 2nd Bns. 95th Regt. of Foot (Rifle Corps)

Sir Arthur Wellesley was laying among the mountains of Rolica and in the valley of Vimiera "the foundations of that renown which received its consummation on the plains of Waterloo."

WALKING THE BATTLEFIELD OF VIMIERO

Ideally, when visiting the fields of Vimiero or Rolica, one should first take-in Montego Bay, where Wellington disembarked his troops after their transports had brought them laboriously and uncomfortably from Cork. On viewing the turbulent surging surf one can understand how 80 men and their arms and equipment were lost when boats capsized bringing them ashore. David Chandler insisted in paddling in the ice-cold sea, but it is not recommended to less hardy souls, like the average wargamer!

Make for the monument on Vimiero Hill-considerably "tarted-up" in recent years. From this commanding elevation it is easily possible to identify East and West Ridges. This is another relatively unchanged field so far as its topography goes, and it is possible to discover all salient points if one is working from a detailed map of the battle. It is only a short drive from the monument to where, for the first but not the last time in this War, British Riflemen destroyed French columns.

As with most of these Peninsular fields, it is impossible to view it without becoming overawed at the sheer size of the area-Vimiero was a battle involving much tactical manouvering over a succession of hills, providing a lasting impression of the sense of ground shown by the respective commanders, and feeling for the unfortunate soldiers who had to march every yard of it.

This was another battle fought in the Peninsular Series, as was Rolica, and provided a fine and close-fought wargame of a battle admirably suited to be reproduced in miniature.

THE BATTLE OF VIMEIRO AS A WARGAME

The map that accompanies this report shows the actual ground on the wargames table with the ground "off the table." This included the western ridge on which was posted one British battalion and the broken country to the north where Trant and Craufurd were posted. Thus these three forces took no part whatsoever in the wargame. It was decided to scale down the numbers so that a battalion (45 men) on the wargames table equalled a brigade in real life. This meant that the British dispositions were as shown on the map; they had one horse gun on Vimiero Hill and three field guns on the eastern slopes of the eastern ridge. Thus the British were formed up at the start of the battle, although with proportionately reduced numbers, as they were in real life in 1808.

The French force consisted of six battalions of infantry plus tirailleurs; 60 cavalry; four field guns; four horse guns and two howitzers. They were to be divided into three columns-column A composed of 80 infantry with tirailleurs, 20 cavalry and 3 guns, column B the same, column C 100 infantry, 20 cavalry and four guns. Column A was to go north and come in on the north-eastern end of the eastern ridge; column B was to go north-west towards Ventosa and column C, the largest column, was to approach Vimiero Hill from the front. It was decided when any one of the three columns became engaged, the others could be disengaged or used to reinforce it in case of success of failure.

As soon as the battle commenced the French cavalry moved out on their left flank to come on to the southern side of Vimiero Hill. The French column A moved forward and deployed with two cavalry squadrons on their right flank between Ventosa and the edge of the board. Column B kept to the south of the river and moved directly forward towards Vimiero village. On Vimiero Hill there was a battalion of Highlanders and a rifle battalion. The Highlanders took up a defensive formation while the rifle battalion sent a third of its numbers into the flat ground south of Vimiero Hill, another third went forward to the lower slopes of Vimiero Hill while a left hand group moved down into Vimiero village and occupied all four houses. The horse gun went with them and posted itself between Vimiero village and the hill. The French had four guns in position firing upon the Highland battalion who steadily moved towards the rear of Vimiero Hill. The French sent their cavalry forward in a sweeping movement to the south of Vimiero Hill where they caught the British riflemen in the open. Attempting to ride them down, they were met with a fierce volley of fire which caused them sufficient losses for their morale to be shaken and for them to turn back. The French infantry slowly advanced westwards towards Vimiero Hill being under fire from the horse gun although the Highland battalion was never within musket range. French tirailleurs and infantry attacked the village but were easily held off by the riflemen in the houses. A French gun to the south of the river and five French guns in Ventosa village were at once successful against the four British guns on the forward slopes of the eastern ridge and very soon three of the four were out of action. Here the British had two battalions stretched across the ridge whilst a third battalion moved northwards down the slopes to the northern side of the ridge accompanies by the 12 cavalry, Wellesley's entire force of horsemen. The British reserve battalion with the cavalry and the other battalion moving down from the eastern ridge moved steadily forward through trees and the cavalry soon engaged in a melee with the French cavalry, causing them to break.

On this flank, the British were completely successful, a French infantry battalion turning and running from the field when their colonel was killed and soon the British were threatening the guns in Ventosa, a threat which multiplied when the Light Companies of the two battalions on the hills moved down and came into Ventosa from its south-western side.

It was apparent that the French right flank was completely broken and that the Highlanders who had now moved down from Vimiero Hill and were in the rear of Vimiero village would be very hard to dislodge if they reinforced the riflemen in the village. At this stage the French decided not to continue the battle (which had lasted two nights) and began to withdraw from the field.

It was decided that the British had been successful on all counts and that they had gained two points while the French had no points whatsoever. It was an interesting battle and one that the British were pleased to win as they had a rather alarming inferiority in artillery and cavalry. The inability or reluctance of the French to move forward on their right flank together with the stubbornness of the riflemen and the light companies swung the battle, which in the early stages looked a "damned close run thing" when three-quarters of the British artillery were out of action.

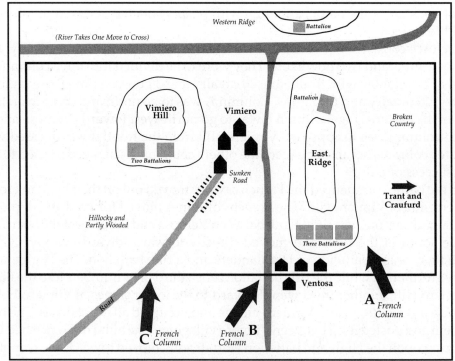

The Battle of Vimiero Fought as a Wargame
The Inner Table is the Table

54

THE RETREAT TO CORUNNA 1808/9
THE BATTLE OF CORUNNA—16 JANUARY 1809

"Christmas Day fell on a Sunday in the Year of our Lord 1808. Thus was happily combined a day of grace with a day of traditional good cheer; roast meat, beer, and children playing in the white snow. Reality for the British Army in Spain was somewhat different. There was only enough bread for two days, rain fell monotonously from grey skies and in the vineyards east of Sahagun the half-naked corpses of French dragoons, stripped by the peasants, lay in brown slush whilst the town dogs sidled closer."
Robert W. Gould

In the autumn of 1808 Napoleon had 250,000 soldiers in Spain, and he took possession of Madrid on 4 December, remaining there until 22 December, being chiefly employed in reorganising the Civil administration of the country. He had sent Marshal Soult westward in the valley of the Douro with 16,000 infantry and 2,000 horse.

When the terms of the infamous Convention of Cintra became known in England, a violent outcry arose against the generals who had signed it and effigies of Sir Hew Dalrymple, Sir Harry Burrard and Sir Arthur Wellesley were hung and burned. This was a little unfair to Wellesley, who had strongly argued against the timid inaction of his two senior generals that allowed Junot to escape after Vimiero.

Two days after his defeat at Vimiero, Junot had asked for terms, and an agreement was made in Lisbon in August, termed the "Convention of Cintra" by which the French evacuated the fortresses they held; kept their own property and equipment (tacitly taken by the French to include the valuable items looted from Portuguese churches and public buildings); and they were to be conveyed back to France by the British Navy.

Chronology of the Corunna Campaign 1808-1809

31st July 1808	Bore sails for the Peninsula from the Isle of Wight U.K.
20th Aug. 1808	Arrives Mondego Bay.
6th Oct. 1808	Moore received news of his appointment as C-in-C of Army in Spain.
13th Oct. 1808	General Baird arrives at Corunna. (10,000 men; no arrangements made for his landing: cavalry and artillery arrive three weeks after the main body.)
	Moore decides to join Baird by land marches and not by sea. Little knowledge of roads; little transport; inadequate feeding arrangements; lack of bullion. Need to be out of Portugal before the rains. Concentrate his forces at either Valladolid or Burgos.
27th Oct. 1808	March to Spain begins.
30th Oct. 1808	Moore at Abrantes.
4th Nov. 1808	At Castello Branco.
8th Nov. 1808	Almeida.
13th Nov. 1808	Moore at Salamanca—receives news of capture of Burgos by the French.
15th Nov. 1808	At Salamanca—receives news of French capture of Valladolid on 13th Nov. Reactions of Spaniards completely neutral.
26th Nov. 1808	Moore's letter to Castlereagh re-appreciating the situation. Deplores lack of collaboration with Spanish, but realises something must be done.

28th–30th Nov. 1808	Moore receives news of General Castanos' defeat near Tudela and decides to withdraw. British Army from Spain. Baird instructed to retire on Corunna and Hope on Lisbon via Cuidad Rodrigo.
6th Dec. 1808	News of Spanish resistance in Madrid makes Moore decide to cancel orders for retreat and to do all he can to help Spain while Napoleon is busy in Madrid.
11th Dec. 1808	Moore's army less Baird's forces, concentrated at Valladolid. Decision to threaten French lines of communication through N.E. Spain by attacking Marshal Soult.
13th Dec. 1808	Receives the captured dispatches from Berthier to Marshal Soult. New appreciation of situation. Decision to retreat not made yet as French ignorant of his whereabouts.
15th Dec. 1808	To Toro instead of Valladolid.
19th Dec. 1808	Moore's H.Q. at Valderas.
20th Dec. 1808	At Mayorga.
21st Dec. 1808	At Sahagun.
23rd Dec. 1808	Receives news that Napoleon was aware of Moore's whereabouts, and was about to attack him. Decision to retreat taken.
26th–30th Dec. 1808	Moore at Benevente.
31st Dec. 1808	Moore at Astorga–Moore decides not to fight, as that would be Napoleon's game.
Jan. 1–3 1809	Villa Franca–Scenes of appalling indiscipline.
Jan. 4th 1809	La Herrerias.
Jan. 6-8 1809	Lugo: Hoped for battle did not materialise.
Jan. 10-11 1809	Betanzos.
Jan. 16 1809	Battle of Corunna–Death of Sir John Moore.

The three Generals returned to England, Burrard and Dalrymple to face a court of enquiry, and command of the troops in Portugal devolved upon Sir John Moore, who had arrived soon after Vimiero. For some weeks he was fully occupied trying to create an army out of what was merely a collection of battalions, without any of the essential auxiliary departments. Sir Hew Dalrymple had reported to Lord Castlereagh on 27 September 1808: "The army is in high order and fit to move when required." This would indicate that the General was singularly inept, for there was no army, neither was there any divisional, brigade or regimental transport.

At the turn of the 20th century, Field Marshal Sir Evelyn Wood (1834-1919) who achieved unique fame by rising from being a midshipman in the Royal Navy to the highest rank in the British Army, and won a Victoria Cross during the Indian Mutiny, wrote a series of books entitled *British Battles on Land and Sea*. What follows is taken from them:

Sir John Moore (1761-1809), the only British General who had ever won lasting fame by conducting a retreat, was the most cultivated soldier of his epoch. He joined the 51st (Yorkshire Light Infantry) in 1777; was Member of Parliament for a pocket borough at 23 years of age, and became a Lieutenant-Colonel in 1790, when he resigned his seat in Parliament. He distinguished himself in Corsica, in the West Indies, and in Egypt, where he was severely wounded, but he is best known in the Army for the system which he adopted in training our infantry when in command of the camp at Shorncliffe, where he laid the foundation of our series of successes during the six years of the Peninsular War. He had great difficulty in overcoming the prejudices of the senior officers of the Army, who clung at that time, and for at least three generations afterwards, to the spirit and drill formations of Frederick the Great.

Moore's influence on our Army can scarcely be overstated, and it is remarkable that without exception the men who rose to eminence under Wellington's command all acknowledged Moore as their instructor and example.

On 18 October Moore marched out, his army wearing the red cockade of Spain in their caps to conciliate the people, and on 13 November reached Salamanca where he halted to concentrate his forces.

In the General's views he had been induced to advance to Salamanca by inaccurate statements: (a) That his concentration would be covered by large Spanish armies; (b) That he would be received by an enthusiastic population and their rulers, who would provide supplies and transport. In the result:

(a) When the wings of Moore's force were at Astorga, 120 miles north-north-west of Salamanca, and at El Escorial, 90 miles south-south-east of his head-quarters, he had no Spanish armies in front of him, but merely fugitives flying after the disastrous routs at Espinosa and Gamonal, after the victories gained by Soult and Victor ten days earlier.

(b) The General could get neither supplies nor transport, and the Spanish people were at that moment profoundly apathetic.

Sir John Moore reported to Lord Castlereagh November 25th, and again November 26th, on the critical situation, Spain being without armies, government, or generals. He predicted that General Castaños, from whom the Spaniards hoped great things, would either retreat from Tudela, on the Ebro, or be beaten there. Moore, in spite of the adverse circumstances of his position, determined to try by an advance to draw Napoleon's pressure off the Spaniards, and on November 28th issued orders for a march forward on the following day.

Sir John Moore now heard that the Spaniards were resolved to defend Madrid. He therefore recalled Sir David Baird, who had retreated 50 miles towards Corunna, and on December 6th countermanded the retreat on Lisbon.

Moore learnt, December 9th, that the garrison had capitulated the day after its chiefs had urged Moore to make a diversion in its favour. He heard at the same time that General the Marquis Romana had 15,000 men under arms, though badly equipped and supplied, and who asked to cooperate in Moore's advance to Valladolid to threaten the French lines of communication.

The General sent his sick and his heavy baggage back to Lisbon, and moved to Sahagun, December 22nd.

Romana wrote two days later to Sir David Baird that he meant to retire into Galicia, but this did not alter Moore's resolve to advance with or without Romana's aid.

Sir John Moore was personally at Alaejos, Segovia, December 13th, where he received an intercepted dispatch from Marshal Berthier, Napoleon's Chief of the Staff, addressed to Marshal Soult, which had been taken from the body of a French Staff officer, who was murdered by Spanish peasants near Segovia. The dispatch showed clearly the Emperor's intentions. Soult with his corps, and Fransechi's cavalry division, in all 16,000 strong, was to move westwards from Saldana and Carrion to subdue Leon, taking Zamora and Benevente. It is stated that the last news of the English rear-guard showed it to be at Salamanca and El Escorial, retreating to Lisbon. The "Grand Army," headed by Lefebvre's corps, was moving from Talavera to Badajos. Bessieres was chasing Castaños to the southward on the Valencia road, Mortier's and Junot's corps had reached Spain.

Moore at once determined to fall on Marshal Soult, who had no supports nearer to him than the corps of Junot, who was marching from the frontier to Burgos. The heads of the British column which had been marching eastwards were turned northwards, crossing the Douro, with the cavalry acting as a screen to the eastward at Tordesillas, the infantry at Toro and Zamora.

The Salamanca and Corunna columns concentrated at Mayorga, December 20th. Soult had not received any duplicate of the intercepted dispatch and was still at Saldana and Carrion, his front being covered by Debelle's Light Cavalry Brigade, with its head-quarters at Sahagun.

It was at this place that, on the following day, Lord Paget dashingly defeated Debelle's cavalry force.

The leading battalions of British Infantry reached Sahagun that evening. Moore halted December 22nd to allow the rear to close up. Marshal Soult, guessing from the way Debelle's brigade had been crushed, that Moore must be near at hand, brought his right column of infantry from Saldana to Carrion, and sent orders to Burgos and Palencia for all supports to hurry up to his assistance. His direct line with Madrid by Valladolid being now cut he could communicate only with the Emperor by the circuitous route of Burgos.

Sir John Moore had issued orders for the troops to advance in order to attack Soult. Romana had moved to Mansilla Bridge with 8,000 men and a battery, 18 miles northwest of Sahagun, December 22nd. The report of this march was received at 8 P.M., but two hours earlier Moore heard from Romana that he had been advised by a friend living near Madrid that all the French armies except a small garrison had left the capital, and were moving in a north-westerly direction.

When Sir John Moore heard this news his leading brigade had already marched off in an easterly direction to attack Soult at Carrion, tramping over frozen snow, but it was now recalled to its previous bivouac. The troops were bitterly disappointed, and Moore had been criticised for not fighting Marshal Soult, and then afterwards falling back; but so far as we have read no soldiers of repute have endorsed this criticism, and the best known military writers of recent days scouted the suggestion.

The General wrote in his diary, Sahagun, December 24th: "To draw off the enemy's attention from the Spanish armies in the south I have risked infinitely too much." His success is shown clearly by Napoleon's orders issued on December 21st, wherein the subjugation of Spain was abandoned for a time. The Emperor marched his troops to crush Moore with such relentless vigour that some of his soldiers, unable to keep in the ranks, committed suicide to avoid falling into the hands of the Spanish peasantry. As Napoleon said later of the immediate result of Moore's advance, "it was the only move which could have checked the victorious southward progress of the French Army," Ultimately "it was the spirit and example of Moore which made possible the victories of Wellington." Sir John Moore's difficulties of transport were very great, for many of the drivers of the hired vehicles deserted the moment that the columns turned towards the coast, preferring the certain loss of their animals to the risk of being killed. The strategical and tactical skill of the British General may be to some extent realised when we reflect that with 30,000 troops he upset all Napoleon's plans for the strategical employment of 300,000.

Moore commenced his retreat on Christmas Day, moving off his troops by successive brigades, so as to utilise the few houses on the road for shelter for his men in the inclement weather, and arrived at Benevente on December 26th, leaving that town with the last of the infantry on December 29th. He transferred all the stores for which he had transport from Benevente to Astorga, moving those at Astorga to Villafranca.

For the next 72 hours after the long retreat left Sahagun on Christmas Day, it rained by day and froze by night, as the sullen soldiers retired by roads ice-covered at dawn and ankle-deep in mud at noon. The men in the ranks, having been led to believe that all Spain was up in arms against Napoleon, looked in vain for such an uprising and, exasperated at having to run from an enemy he knew he could beat, his discipline began to suffer.

WOOD:

When Sir John Moore ordered his infantry to retreat towards Corunna he sent Lord Paget with five cavalry regiments to demonstrate against Marshal Soult, who was thus kept inactive, anticipating an attack until December 26th. The French Marshal then sent Lorge's Dragoons towards Mayorga, marching himself with the infantry and Franceschi's Cavalry Division by Mansilla on Astorga.

Napoleon's columns were now approaching, and on December 27th Marshal Ney's advance brigade, and Lahoussaye's Dragoons, numbering 2,400 sabres, strove to push back Lord Paget's five cavalry regiments who were covering the retreat on a frontage of 30 miles. How well these five regiments were handled, and with what determination they fought is shown by the Emperor's estimate of their numbers, which he calculated to be between four and five thousand sabres. The 18th Light Dragoons (now Hussars) charged six times, December 26th, each time riding over opposing squadrons and thereby securing further unmolested retirement. One troop of 38 sabres, near Valencia de Don Juan, charging a squadron of 105 men, killed 12, and captured and carried off 20 Dragoons. As Sir John Moore noted December 28th, "they obtained an ascendancy over the French."

The 10th Hussars, after holding back General Lorge's Dragoons, December 27th, near Mayorga, were retiring when they found one of Ney's Light cavalry regiments drawn up behind them on rising ground. Without hesitation the 10th charged up the hill, and though the soil was deep in the slush of half-melted snow, they rode over the French cavalry regiment, and retired to a safe position, carrying off with them 100 prisoners. All the five cavalry regiments had plenty of hand to hand fighting December 26th and 27th. In twelve days' operations from Salamanca out they captured 500 prisoners, suffering themselves comparatively but little loss.

The divisions of General Hope and Fraser moving by the main road, and that of Baird marching by cross-roads, reached Astorga on December 29th unmolested, while the rear-guard division under General Lord Edward Paget, and cavalry under Lord Paget, held back the enemy until the infantry had left Benevente, when the cavalry crossed to the western bank of the river. (Esla)

General Lefebvre-Desnouettes spent some time in searching for a ford, as Lord Paget had blown up the bridge. Having found one near the ruined structure and seeing apparently only pickets, for the supports were in Benevente, forded the river with four squadrons of the cavalry of the Guard, numbering from five to six hundred sabres. The pickets found by the 18th Light Dragoons (Hussars) galloped in from the north and south flanks, and when about 130 sabres had collected, Colonel Otway charged with them but was beaten back. They rallied on a troop, 3rd King's German Legion under Major Burgwedel, and then charging once more rode through the French leading squadron, and again retired. Brigadier Charles Stewart withdrew the squadron towards the 10th Hussars, which Lord Paget had formed behind the eastern suburb of Benevente. When Lefebvre's leading squadrons were close up to the town the 10th Hussars and those of the 18th, which had already been engaged under Otway, charged, and routing the Frenchmen after a hard fight, pursued them for two miles down to the ford, where Private Grisdale made Marshal Lefebvre a prisoner. The 10th captured 70 wounded prisoners, killing or wounding 55 Frenchmen who were left on the ground, the British casualties being 50. Captain Downman's Horse Battery now galloped up from Benevente, and dispersed the rest of the cavalry of the Guard, who were about to cross the ford.

Moore reached Astorga on 29 December and left on 31st, to begin "…a rapid march towards the coast, through the mountainous region of Galicia, and one of the most splendid and masterly yet harassing and disastrous retreats in the annals of British warfare, pursued by a swift and active enemy, through defiles deep with snow, across rivers that were bridgeless, for…250 miles, amid sufferings that were unparalleled, without the loss of a single standard, a piece of cannon, or any military trophy whatsoever…" (James Grant)

WOOD:

When the Emperor left Madrid on December 22nd the weather was fine, but just as he overtook the Imperial Guard at the foot of the Guadarama Mountains, the whole column had been stopped by a terrible blizzard from the north which had made deep snowdrifts in large heaps. Batteries and train were stuck in the pass, and further progress seemed to be impossible. The Emperor, dismounting his cavalry, ordered them to lead their horses. He set to work every available pioneer to cut tracks in the snow, and then put on the Guard to trample it down. He carried his point, but at the loss of several men who died from exposure and over-exertion.

The gale blowing in the faces of the troops obliged the Emperor to dismount, but he struggled forward on foot, until halfway up the mountain he could go no farther unassisted, when he linked either arm in those of Marshals Duroc and Lannes. When the three leaders were overcome by fatigue from marching through the snow in jack-boots, they rode astride of the guns, and in that manner reached the top of the pass. When the army got into the plain of Leon the Emperor pressed on his troops without pity, insisting on their trying to accomplish on a short winter's day 30 miles in deep snow, but on reaching Benevente Napoleon learnt that the British troops were already across the Esla.

The Emperor, who was on the east bank of the Esla during the brilliant encounters between Lefebvre's and Paget's horsemen, wrote to King Joseph, his brother: "Lefebvre's affair was disgusting." Napoleon had instructed his brother from Benevente: "Put in your newspapers that

36,000 English are surrounded. Soult is in their front, I am in their rear, and you may expect to hear of great events."

The Emperor ordered Joseph to publish accounts also in the newspapers of outrages committed by the English troops at Leon, but as a matter of fact no British soldier had ever been within thirty miles of that town. They had, however, done much damage and some plundering at Mayorga, Valderas, and Benevente. The soldiers were generally half-frozen and exhausted by hunger, often unwilling to wait for food, and in order to sustain life they pulled down and burnt gates and doors for their bivouacs in the snow.

Napoleon took possession of Astorga on January 1st, 1809, and then, despite the losses sustained during forced marches from Madrid, succeeded in concentrating an army of 70,000 infantry, 10,000 cavalry, and 200 guns.

The astonishing speed with which this powerful force had been moved thither, in the face of every obstacle that badness of roads and weather could present, attests conclusively the ability and energy of the Emperor.

But, for all this, the great effort proved fruitless. Napoleon failed to overtake Sir John Moore. The main body of the British army left Astorga thirty-six hours before the French arrived, and, having reached the mountains of Galicia, no longer stood in danger of being cut off from its line of retreat upon the coast.

Such a contingency Napoleon had never for one moment regarded as being possible; and its accomplishment came as a very rude shock to him. He had pledged himself publicly to overthrow and crush the army of Moore. In these circumstances, to make his appearance in France without having fulfilled that pledge would be, as he clearly saw, an admission of defeat.

Now, at this time, political consideration forbade the Emperor to lay himself open to such a charge. Feeling, therefore, that he could not afford further to court failure, he set about to find some good pretext for his immediate return to Paris. By leaving the direction of the pursuit in other hands, he hoped to be able to create the impression that it was merely the fact of his recall which had saved the British from disaster–that is, of course, if Moore should be able to escape from the large armies following him.

Hence the dramatic scene enacted on January 1st. At Astorga a courier, riding at speed, overtook the pursuing army, and, before the eyes of the troops, handed dispatches to the Emperor.

These dispatches Napoleon read, evidently in a state of great excitement. Then he gave orders for the return of the Guards and other detachments of his army, at the same time allowing the rumour to be spread abroad that intrigues in Paris and the threat of an Austrian war necessitated his immediate presence in France. And that very day he set out for Paris, entrusting to Marshal Soult "the glorious Mission of destroying the British–of pursuing them to the point of embarkation, and driving them into the sea."

Professor Oman, who has studied all the records of that period, states that "there was absolutely nothing in the state of European affairs to make an instant departure from Spain necessary." The intrigues in Paris were not so serious as to be beyond the Emperor's control; the coming war with Austria was a war of his own creation!

Napoleon returned to Paris, therefore, in order to save his reputation from the indignity which failure would have cast upon it. This can be the only valid explanation to his movements; and, when viewed in the light of this knowledge, Moore's campaign stands out in history not merely as a memorable act of daring, but as one of the most important campaigns of modern times.

At Astorga there was but little food for Sir John Moore's soldiers, but unfortunately there were vast quantities of rum; and there were also stores of muskets, ammunition, and entrenching tools, boots, wagons, and carts, the draught animals of which had died, and in the town was stored the heavy baggage of Baird's division. There must inevitably have been much confusion under the circumstances even with effective Commissariat and Ordnance establishments, which in those days did not exist. Thus much valuable property was necessarily abandoned, and also 400 invalids, who, being too ill to be carried on in open carts, fell with all the stores into the hands of the enemy.

Both at Astorga and especially at Bembibre and down to near Corunna there were many scenes of indiscipline amongst the infantry, both officers and men in that branch being irritated by continual retreats, and, except those in the rear division, without the satisfaction of fighting. Sir

John Moore had reorganised his army at Salamanca, apparently mixing among the divisions battalions which had and had not seen fighting. The division commanded by his friend, Lord Edward Paget, alongside whom he generally rode throughout the Retreat, was called the reserve. Its officers and men were probably encouraged by the presence of two determined generals riding with them, but it is remarkable that, although they had had all the fighting that was done on the Retreat, their casualties were but a fraction of those who never fired a shot.

In the other divisions men often robbed the inhabitants, and pillaged stores they know must be abandoned. Many men who broke into the stores of rum, stupefied with drink, were left behind, some being indeed saved by the cavalry rear-guard, who hustled them on to their feet.

At Bembibre there were huge wine-vaults as this place was the centre of the local wine trade; hundreds of British soldiers drank themselves insensible and when, on New Year's Day 1809, the rearguard marched into the town they found the streets literally strewn with prostrate bodies. Those who had not frozen to death were dragged to their feet and driven forward by men of the reserve or the cavalry. But when Lahoussaye's Dragoons rode in later that day there were still hundreds of them staggering about or standing stupefied, to be cut down by the slashing sabres of the exultant French cavalrymen. Only a handful escaped to rejoin the main army, each hideously mangled and disfigured, to be paraded as an example and dire warning to the rest.

WOOD:

The enemy's cavalry never, however, ventured to close on Lord Edward Paget's division, composed of 20th (1st Lancashire Fusiliers), 28th (1st Gloucestershire), 52nd (2nd Oxfordshire and Bucks Light Infantry), 91st (1st Argyll and Sutherland Highlanders), and 95th (Rifle Brigade).

At Villafranca there were similar scenes of indiscipline and consequent suffering and loss of life. The number of men who quitted the ranks was in direct proportion to the discipline of the regiments. The 43rd (1st Oxfordshire and Bucks) and 95th throughout the Retreat lost less than 100 men each, whilst other battalions in the same brigade lost nearly four times that number of stragglers.

James Grant tells of another occasion:

...The French cavalry came up with a long string of half-frozen and footsore stragglers, through whom they galloped, slashing right and left with their sabres; many were trod under foot and 2,000 were taken prisoners between Astorga and Lugo. "I looked round," says an officer in one of his letters, "when we had gained the highest point of those slippery precipices (towards Castro-Gonzalo), and saw the rear of the army winding along the narrow road. I saw the way marked by the wretched people, who lay on all sides expiring from fatigue and the severity of the cold; their bodies reddened in spots the white surface of the ground."

Moore's tender and compassionate heart bled for the misery he beheld on this most miserable retreat, and he deplored the relaxation of discipline it produced. He never ceased to issue orders, exhortations, and cheering addresses; but rage or sullen apathy were in many instances too apparent while the movement lasted.

In despatch to England, Moore wrote: "The people run away, the villages are deserted, and I have been obliged to destroy a great part of the ammunition and military stores. For that same reason I am obliged to leave the sick. In short, my whole object is to save the Army."

WOOD:

Lord Edward Paget's division between Villafranca and Nogales, 18 miles, passed through a continuous line of abandoned equipment and dead horses, the cavalry shooting every horse which could not carry its rider. Sir John Moore, January 5th, marched the troops for 36 hours, and with fatal results. Now it was not only the faint heart who fell out of the ranks but good soldiers who, short of food and sleep and starved with cold, succumbed. An eyewitness, standing on Monte Cebrero, describes the painful scene as looking down from the highest point of the hills, he saw the army winding along the road. The oxen pulling the wagons loaded with sick and wounded in many cases died in their yokes, and the soldiers in the wagons necessarily perished. The track was dotted for miles with dead and dying men and women, who had struggled on till they fell unable to rise again. In some cases on the women's breasts their babies, still alive, were seen trying to draw sustenance from the corpse. The conduct of some of the French soldiers was deplorable; according to one of their own writers, several young English women fell a prey to the French cavalry advanced corps, and were put up to auction in the same way as were the horses.

The wives and children of married soldiers had accompanied their husband's regiments to Portugal, and at the time of marching out of Lisbon in early October, Sir John Moore had offered them passages to England but had not insisted on their embarkation. Nor did he prevent their marching with their regiment into Spain, a cruel kindness fraught with indescribable misery during the retreat to Corunna.

WOOD:
Owing to the rugged nature of the ground between Villa Franca and Lugo, Sir John Moore sent on the cavalry in advance, but he himself accompanied Lord Edward Paget, and on the morning of January 5th arrived with the reserve at Herrerias.

Here he received from his Staff officers the reports about the harbours. Corunna, it appeared, offered better cover for an embarkation than did Vigo. Accordingly, abandoning his original idea of retreating to the latter port, the General decided to make for Corunna, and issued instructions for the transports to be sent thither immediately from Vigo.

Having done this, he sent one of his aides-de-camp to Sir David Baird, who was then at Nogales, with orders that the 1st Division was to halt at Lugo, explaining that he intended to rally his army there and offer battle to the enemy. This order he requested Baird to forward to Hope and Fraser, whose divisions were then approaching Lugo.

But Baird, although he had received the order from an aide-de-camp, sent it forward by a private dragoon, who got drunk on the way and lost the dispatch. In consequence of this, Fraser, instead of resting at Lugo, marched on a track towards Compostela; and when he returned, not only were his troops greatly in need of food and rest, but he had lost by this unnecessary exertion more than 400 stragglers.

Meanwhile Moore, hastening forward with the reserve, through a continuous line of dead horses and of equipment abandoned by the columns that had gone before, marched his troops 36 miles in one day, and arrived at Nogales on the evening of the 5th, having gained twelve hours on the enemy.

On the following day the French succeeded in gaining some of the distance they had lost, and on passing Nogales were able to gall the rear-guard persistently.

So closely did the enemy press that Sir John Moore found it necessary to abandon wagons containing silver dollars to the value of £25,000. Seeing that he could not save the money without risking an ill-timed engagement, the General ordered it to be hurled down the mountain-side into the valley, where it fell in a silver cascade–to be gathered later, some by the enemy, but the greater part by the local peasantry, when the snow melted in the spring.

While the money was being pitched over the rocks, an officer stood near, pistol in hand, with orders to shoot anyone who might attempt to help himself to the booty. Nevertheless, the wife of Sergeant Maloney, of the 52nd, succeeded in amassing quite a considerable fortune. But, luckless woman, she did not live to enjoy it, for later, while stepping from a small boat into a transport in Corunna harbour, she slipped, fell into the sea, and, overburdened by the weight of the stolen treasure concealed about her, never rose again to the surface.

The road from Nogales onwards presented a terrible spectacle. The camp-followers of the army were dying daily from cold and hunger; whilst the soldiers, barefooted and weakened by their recent excesses, were falling to the rear in hundreds. Oxen, pulling the wagons loaded with sick and wounded, in many cases died in their yokes; and their hapless burdens were left, of necessity, also to perish.

By nightfall on January 6th, Sir John Moore succeeded in assembling the main body of his army at Lugo; and on the following morning issued a general order in which he sternly rebuked officers and men for their recent indiscipline, and intimated his intention of offering battle to the enemy.

The effect of this order was immediate. Men who only a short while before had been riotous, insubordinate, and drunken, in a moment became orderly and eager for the fray. The thought of battle was the very stimulus they needed.

Since the time of his departure from Salamanca Sir John Moore had lost 1,500 men who had either dropped to the rear or been killed in action; but, counting the three battalions which Sir David Baird had left behind when he made his advance to Astorga, and which joined the army between Villa Franca and Lugo, he still had 19,000 troops under arms.

These he drew up in a strong position; then waited for the enemy to attack.

Towards midday, Marshal Soult approached Lugo with 10,000 or 12,000 men–the rest of his army straggling in the rear–and drew up his columns in order of battle along a ridge facing the British position. However, having satisfied himself that he was opposed by more than a rear-guard, the French General decided to await the arrival of reinforcements, and made no serious endeavour to dislodge our troops that day.

The following morning found the two armies still in position. But Soult, although he had now 17,000 infantry, 4,000 cavalry, and 50 guns in line, still deferred his attack, and when darkness fell not a shot had been fired.

This delay proved fatal to Moore's hopes. Despite the eagerness of his soldiers, he dared not attack the enemy, for only two marches in the rear Soult had 20,000 more troops drawing up, and the British army had sufficient ammunition for one battle only; whilst, owing to the scarcity of food in the stores at Lugo, Moore could not afford to wait longer for the enemy's attack.

Accordingly he prepared to retreat during the night, hoping thereby to steal a march on Soult. He gave orders for the fires to be kept burning brightly so as to deceive the enemy; then appealed to his troops to make what he hoped would be the last great exertion required of them.

Silently and in good order, the army moved off at 10 P.M.; and everything seemed to indicate that the General's stratagem would prove successful. But ill-fortune ordained otherwise. Barely had the columns got under way when a terrific storm broke over them–wind and rain, mixed with sleet–in consequence of which the guides lost the direction, and the troops again became demoralised.

One division gained the main road, but the other two, bewildered by the storm and darkness, strayed from their course, and, when day broke, were still near Lugo. Fatigued, drenched by rain, and shoeless, the troops lost all sense of discipline, and stragglers became more numerous than during any other period of the retreat.

The officer commanding the leading division allowed his men, during the halt in the night, to take refuge in some houses near the road. This well-meant act had a disastrous result, for when the time came for the march to be resumed the troops refused to keep their ranks; and the infection soon spread through the other divisions. Thus the main body of the army, after bivouacking for six hours in the rain, reach Betanzos on the evening of the 9th "in a state," writes Napier, "very discreditable to its discipline."

Sir John Moore, with Lord Edward Paget and the reserve, covered the march, and, thanks to their exertions, the French cavalry were held in check, otherwise a large number of stragglers must inevitably have fallen into the enemy's hands. Even as things were, more men were lost between Lugo and Betanzos than in all the other stages of the retreat.

Seeing that the enemy were unable to collect in strength, the British General made no endeavour to move forward on the 10th, but spent the day rallying his troops; and, on the morning of the 11th, having reassembled the army in one mass, he personally directed the march to Corunna.

Victorian military historian and writer D. H. Parry tells of the final miles into Corunna:

The last halt was made Betanzos, and while the rear-guard covered the partial destruction of the bridge there, the army marched in column to Corunna, only to find the Atlantic roaring on the rocks, but not a sail in sight!

The French were in great force at Betanzos, and furious at our continued escape. Our sergeant charged alone in advance of his squadron, to the centre of the bridge, but a private of the 28th, named Thomas Savage, stepped out and shot him securing his cloak before the others came up.

The Engineers bungled the bridge, and blew up one of their officers with it, while we had to fall back on Corunna before it was properly destroyed.

And James Grant wrote of their disappointing arrival:

To reach our shipping and abandon the country by sea, without the slaughter of a useless battle with a foe whose numbers were overwhelming, was, for a time, the sole object of the British general. By his energy he massed the army, now reduced to about 14,000 men, and fell back on Corunna. This was on the 11th of January. On reaching the heights that commanded a view of the coast and the picturesque citadel of La Corunna, with all its towers, not a ship was visible in the bays of Orsan or Betanzos; the roads of Ferrol and all the expanse of sea were, save some fisher boats with lateen sails, open and empty. Fate was against him and against his army, for contrary winds detained the fleet of men-of-war and transports at Vigo, a hundred and twenty miles distant by sea; so there was no other resource now but to defend the position in front of the town, and fight till the fleet should come round.

It was not only the cavalry who distinguished themselves during these terrible days–Craufurd's Light Brigade earned immortal fame under a hard commander who told them:

"You think because you are Riflemen, you may do whatever you think proper, but I'll teach you the difference before I have done with you!" And no less an authority than the almost legendary Sir Harry Smith said of them:

"The Light Division Gentlemen were proper saucy fellows!"

In order to deny the French the Castro Gonzalo bridge over the River Esla, the greater part of the army marched via Benevente: 1st Battalion 95th Rifles (about 700 strong) were with Paget in the Reserve Division, while the 2nd battalion (about 750 strong) formed part of Craufurd's 1st Light Brigade. Reaching Benevente, the army rested for a day, during which a party of Light infantrymen drowned a fat abbot in one of his own wine-vats, "… to teach him not to be so damned stingy with it!" On New Year's Eve the army divided, the 1st and 2nd Light Brigades turning westwards towards Vigo, to guard the southern flank. It may well have been General "Black" Bob Craufurd's iron discipline that brought his Brigade into Vigo; Robert C. Young (in an article in Tradition) tells of it:

"No man but one formed of stuff like General Craufurd could have saved the brigade from perishing altogether. I detest the sight of the lash; but I am convinced the British Army can never go on without it," so wrote Rifleman Harris in his memoirs. The route taken by the Light Brigades was even more appalling than that of the main army and Craufurd was determined to keep his men together. At Ponferrada, an officer being carried across the river on the back of one of his men was "dropped … like a hot potato into the stream" when Craufurd bellowed to the bearer "Put him down, sir! Put him down, instantly". Some riflemen, trying to find a bridge in order to avoid wading waist high through the river, were flogged and then made to cross in the deepest water that Craufurd could find. Later in the retreat, two men caught straying were given an immediate drum head court martial and each sentenced to 100 lashes. Rifleman Dan Howans turned to two of his comrades, Harris and Jagger, and in an undertone damned Craufurd's eyes, adding that he would do better to find them something to eat. "Black Bob" overheard the comment and snatching one of their rifles laid the butt across Jagger's head. Howans then admitted that it was he who had spoken, whereupon he was promptly tried and awarded 300 lashes. At the time, the enemy was too close for the sentence to be carried out and the brigade moved on. At dawn next day, Howans received his punishment "without a murmur" and his wife, a strapping Irish-woman, covered his lacerated back with a greatcoat and marched with him, carrying his knapsack and accoutrements. An hour later Craufurd again halted the men and said: "Bring out the two men of the 95th who were tried last night." At this point their commanding officer, Lieut. Colonel Hamilton Wade, asked pardon for his men on the ground they had fought well in all the battles of Portugal. Craufurd's concession was to allow them to draw lots "… and the winner shall escape but one of the two I am determined to make an example of."

The measure of this incredible commander is reflected by an anecdote related by one of his descendants:

> General Craufurd threatened to hang a commissary if the rations for his Division were not produced at a certain time. Whereupon the commissary went to Lord Wellington and complained greatly, and also asked his advice as to what he had better do. Apparently Wellington seemed sympathetic at first; for he said, "Did General Craufurd go as far as that? Did he actually say he would hang you?" "Yes, my lord, he did," said the commissary. To which Wellington then answered, "Then I should strongly advise you to get the rations ready; for if General Craufurd said he would hang you, by G-d, he'll do it."
> *The Rev. Alexander Craufurd*

Linked arm-in-arm to keep themselves moving, the Light Brigades staggered into Vigo on 12 January 1809; one of the survivors recalled:

"Almost all were without shoes and stockings, many had their clothes and accoutrements in fragments, while not a few had now become quite blind from toil and fatigue."

On the road from Astorga, at Cacabellos where the road passed over the little River Cua, there occurred an incident which is immortally enshrined in the annals of the Light Division, featuring Rifleman Tom Plunkett of the 95th. He was a notable marksman who, during the expedition to Monte Video in 1807, had killed about 20 Spaniards during the battle of Buenos Aires when, hoisted to the roof of an outbuilding, he had "… killed everyone of the enemy imprudent enough to come within range."

To allow time for stores at Villafranca to be destroyed, Moore fought a rearguard action at Cacabellos, with five battalions of Paget's reserve; the 15th Hussars and a Horse Artillery battery. Half the 95th and a cavalry squadron were posted along the road to Bembibre, beyond the river; the guns commanded the road up from the bridge from the western side of the river, with the 28th as their escort. The other three battalions were hidden behind a line of vineyards and stone walls parallel with the winding stream. About one o'clock in the afternoon, French cavalry began pushing cautiously forward, led by Colbert's brigade of Ney's Corps, with Lahoussaye's division of dragoons in support. A young and very dashing officer, Colbert had never before met the British but, through the drunkards and stragglers he had seen on the road, had a very poor opinion of them; thus he felt that the defile might be forced with little loss if enough pressure was placed upon the rearguard. So he placed himself at the head of the 15th Chasseurs and 3rd Hussars and dashed forward, scattering a squadron of the 15th Hussars and, coming suddenly to the bridge, rode into and over the last two companies of the 95th Rifles, yet to cross the stream. Sweeping down on them, he took 48 prisoners before the riflemen could escape over the stream. However, he now saw the 28th and the guns holding the slope above, and halted to consider the situation.

He decided to try and "bounce" the bridge by a furious cavalry charge; so ranged his leading regiment four abreast and led them to the bridge. The head of the column was torn to pieces by the six British guns, but enough cavalrymen got across to attempt to dash uphill and capture the position. But they were in a deadly position, for the guns and the muskets of the 28th lay ahead blocking the road, while the 52nd and 95th poured in an accurate flanking fire from the vineyard walls on either side–it was quite impossible to get forward, and then Colbert himself fell. He had been shot, at long range, by Rifleman Tom Plunkett, laying on his back, propped up on left elbow with the rifle supported by his foot through the sling; a few seconds later, he similarly shot Latour-Maubourg, his aide-de-camp riding at the General's side.

It was too much for the horsemen to bear, turning rein they plunged back across the bridge, leaving behind scores of dead and wounded. Lahoussaye's Dragoons came forward, some squadrons fording the river at different points but, unable to charge through the rocks and vines, dismounted to skirmish, but found themselves no match at this against the practised 52nd. The leading infantry of Merle's division came up just before dusk, their voltigeurs bickering with the 52nd and 95th for about an hour, but when their formed columns tried to cross the bridge they were swept away by the guns on the slope above. The firing ceased after dark and Moore ordered a withdrawal, which was carried out without interference.

Sir John Moore, in Corunna awaiting transports, quartered his army, posted the Reserve at El Burgo on the Mero (after blowing the bridge). From the extensive stores of arms and ammunition, his infantry were issued with new muskets which, when the time came for battle, gave them a great advantage over the enemy whose weapons had become battered and rusty during the long pursuit. Unlimited supplies of fresh ammunition caused the British fire to be superior in range and accuracy during the battle.

D. H. PARRY:

Fine weather now dried our rags. On the 11th January the Guards were quartered in the town, the Reserve near St. Lucia, and the other regiments posted in strong positions. Vast stores were meanwhile destroyed in Corunna, and two hundred and ninety horses of the German Legion shot in the arsénal square at St. Lucia, amid the tears of the brave troopers.

The 12th proved damp and foggy, and no trace of the fleet could be seen. The French still held back, our officers exchanging potshots with them until Paget put a stop to it; and on the 13th a terrific explosion from 4,000 powder-barrels caused something very like a panic in both armies. Corunna was shaken, its windows smashed, and a rain of white ashes fell for a considerable time.

At last, on the afternoon of the 14th, the transports hove in sight, and as soon as they were anchored we began to embark the wounded and the guns, the cavalry being ordered to ship thirty horses per regiment and shoot the rest, as there was not time to get them on board with a heavy sea running. The 15th Hussars brought four hundred to Corunna, and landed in England with thirty-one! The 10th—the Prince of Wales's particular regiment, and the first in our service to wear the showy Hungarian dress, which its Hussar troop had adopted in 1803 and the entire corps two years later—began the campaign with six hundred handsome chargers and took thirty home again.

The greatest confusion took place among the camp-followers, but by degrees the embarkation proceeded, our gallant tars going in some cases two days without food in their noble efforts to help us.

There was a little skirmishing, but no very decided movement, until the 16th—in fact, French officers were seen picking up shells on the sands at low water within range of our muskets—but at last the infantry alone remained on shore.

JAMES GRANT:

All had been prepared for the withdrawal of the fighting men as soon as darkness set in, and four O'CLOCK on the afternoon of the 16th was the time fixed upon by Moore for embarking; but about noon, a messenger came from Sir John Hope with tidings that the enemy were in position on the heights above Corunna, and getting under arms, and that a general movement was taking place along the line.

A range of heights or swelling knolls forms an amphitheatre round the village of Elvina, at the distance of a mile or more from Corunna, and on these Sir John Moore drew up his army; for although there was a much more formidable range farther in advance, his numbers were inadequate for its occupation. General Hope's division he stationed on the left, posting it along a ridge commanding the Betanzos road, and sloping away with an inclination rearward in the direction of Elvina. There the division of Sir David Baird took up the line, covering the hills which bend inward and extend to a green valley dividing this range from another on the opposite side

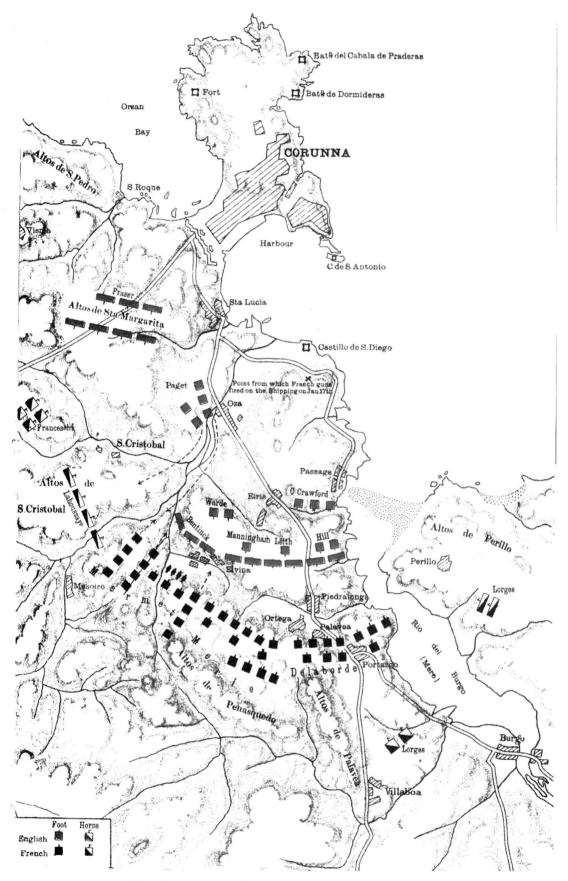

THE BATTLE OF CORUNNA, JANUARY 16, 1809

of the road to Vigo.

Across the valley the dark figures of the Rifle Corps were seen in extended order, supported by the division of General Fraser, which covered the road to Vigo, and protected the principal approach to Corunna. Under Lord Paget, the reserve took post at a village half a mile in rear of General Hope. But all the advantage, in strength of position, of horse, foot, and artillery, was in favour of the enemy. The only cavalry in the field with Moore were forty hussars of the 15th Regiment.

Opposed to the slender red lines of Hope and Baird were the dark and heavy divisions of De Laborde, Merle, and Mermet; while the cavalry of the French left, under Lahousaye, Lorge, Franceschi, and others, were thrown forward, almost in échelon, in heavy columns along the whole British right, hemming them in between the waters of the Mero and the harbour of Corunna, and menacing the rear even so far as San Christoval. Moore's was lit with animation as he rode along the line at the head of his staff; and to Colonel Graham, of Balgowan, he expressed his regret that "the shortness of the evening would prevent them from profiting by the victory which he confidently anticipated."

Thus, then, about two in the afternoon, began this trial of strength between 20,000 French veterans and 14,000 British, who had but nine six-pound guns to oppose to a numerous and well-served light artillery, and were also galled by eleven pieces of heavy cannon on a clump of rocks on the French left, from whence their bullets could be sent even to rake Moore's centre; and soon that formidable battery opened the bloody game with a slaughtering cannonade.

Then the columns of infantry, throwing to the front clouds of skirmishers, descended from their grassy ridges to the fray. Those coming from Palavia and Portosa, having some distance to march, did not immediately engage; but the third poured all its strength against Elvina, with bayonets flashing, eagles brandished, and tricolours waving. These were the columns of De Laborde, Neale, and Merniet.

To the Black Watch, with the 4th and 50th Regiments, was entrusted the defence of the extreme right, the weakest point of the line; and on their maintenance of it rested the safety and honour of the army. From his master in the art of war, Sir John Moore had learned that the presence of a leader is always most necessary near that point at which the most desperate struggle is likely to be made; thus he remained near Lord Bentinck's brigade, and, perhaps through some national preference, close to the 42nd Highlanders.

Famed historian of the Peninsular War, Sir William Napier was present at the Battle of Corunna and later wrote of the inspiring presence of Sir John Moore:

Our line was under arms, silent, motionless, yet all were anxious for the appearance of Sir John Moore. There was a feeling that under him we could not be beaten, and this was so strong at all times as to be a great cause of discontent during the retreat wherever he was not. "Where is the General?" was now heard along that part of the line where I was, for only of what my eyes saw and my ears heard do I speak. I stood in front of my left wing, on a knoll, from whence the greatest part of the field could be seen, and my picquets were fifty yards below, disputing the ground with the French skirmishers; but a heavy French column, which had descended the mountain at a run, was coming on behind with great rapidity, and shouting "En avant, tue, tue, en avant, tue!" Their cannon at the same time, plunging from above, ploughed the ground and tore our ranks. Suddenly I heard the gallop of horses, and turning saw Moore. He came at speed, and pulled up so sharp and close he seemed to have alighted from the air, man and horse looking at the approaching foe with an intenseness that seemed to concentrate all feeling in their eyes.

Thrown on its haunches the animal came, sliding and dashing the dirt up with its forefeet, thus bending the General forward almost to its neck; but his head was thrown back and his look more keenly piercing than I ever before saw it. He glanced to the right and left, and then fixed his eye intently on the enemy's advancing column, at the same time grasping the reins with both his hands, and pressing the horse firmly with his knees. His body thus seemed to deal with the animal, while his mind was intent on the enemy, and his aspect was one of searching intenseness beyond the power of words to describe. For a while he looked, and then galloped to the left without uttering a word.

Again Sir John Moore returned, and was talking to me when a round shot struck the ground between his horse's feet and mine. The horse leaped round, and I also turned mechanically, but Moore forced the animal back, and asked me if I was hurt. "No, sir." Meanwhile a second shot had torn off the leg of a 42nd man, who screamed horribly, and rolled about so as to excite agitation and alarm with others. The General said, "This is nothing, my lads; keep your ranks; take that man away; my good fellow, don't make such a noise; we must bear these things better." He spoke sharply, but it had a good effect, for this man's cries had made an opening in the ranks, and the men shrunk from the spot, although they had not done so when others had been hit who did not cry out. But again Moore went off, and I saw him no more.

JAMES GRANT:

At Elvina was the crash of the battle. Our pickets were driven pell-mell out of the village; and when it was taken, the French mass divided with yells of triumph. One portion turned their fire and steel against Sir David Baird's command; the other turned his right flank by advancing up the valley, driving in his fringe of skirmishers, who fell back on the main body, firing and reloading with all speed.

Against the half column at Elvina, Sir John dispatched the 42nd and 50th Regiments; and wheeling back the 4th on the extremity of his right, poured a steady stream of musketry into the flank of the troops penetrating up the valley, where it was also sturdily met by the light infantry. At that instant Moore saw the whole plan of Marshal Soult's attack. No infantry were seen to menace the valley from where the French cavalry were posted, and the number in front showed that a body strong enough to do much mischief was placed in rear of the heights; and it was hence evident that the Marshal offered a close, rough trial of arms, without stratagem, trusting to the valour of his veterans of the Austrian and Italian wars.

The moment for Moore's counter-stroke was come. He ordered the division of Fraser to support that of Paget, and gave the later an order to descend into the valley. The French column on his flank being amply provided with work cut out for them, he turned to watch the progress of recapturing Elvina.

The Highlanders and the 50th had driven the enemy back into the village with such spirit, that Moore exclaimed, exultingly–

"Well done, 50th–well done, my majors!" But in the struggle one of these, Major Charles Napier (afterwards the Conqueror of Scinde), was taken prisoner; and the other, the Hon. Major Stanhope, was mortally wounded. Surrounded by a hundred bayonets, the former was denied quarter; but he fought like a lion, till five pierced him, and he was rescued at last by a gallant French drummer. Entering the streets of Elvina with the routed and disordered masses of the French, without giving them a moment of respite, the two victorious regiments drove them out, still fighting, on the other side. To support them, Moore sent forward a battalion of the Guards; upon which the 42nd, thinking they came as a relief, and not as a reinforcement, halted, all save their grenadiers, who went on with the 50th, then fighting without support in the open ground beyond all the houses, among which they were once more driven by the French, when the latter were reinforced.

The struggle here was terrific, and the killed and wounded lay in ghastly and gory piles in every little thoroughfare and garden of Elvina. General Baird had already quitted the field, his left arm being shattered by a grape shot.

At this crisis Sir John Moore observed the error committed by the 42nd, and galloped to them in person; but now their pouches were empty.

"My brave Highlanders," he exclaimed, "you have still your bayonets! Remember Egypt!"

Responding by a hearty cheer, the regiment rushed once more to the attack at Elvina, now the centre of battle and the pivot on which every movement hinged; though far away on the left there were the roar and carnage of a general and furious conflict, with Hope's division holding the enemy in check.

On the right and in the valley, the attacking column was at bay, says Napier, wavering under a double fire in front and flank; everywhere the signs of coming victory were bright; when the gallant man, the consummate commander who had brought the battle to a crisis, was dashed from his horse by a cannon-shot.

It came from the battery on the rocks, and had torn away all the flesh from his left breast and shoulder, "and broken the ribs over a heart undaunted even by this terrible–this ghastly mortal hurt."

With an anxiety and impulse that rose superior to the pangs of pain or terror of death, he struggled into a sitting posture, and, with fixed look and unchanged countenance, continued to watch the struggle at Elvina; and when he saw the black and crimson plumes of the 42nd appear in the village again, something like a smile of gratification spread over his face. He then sank back and accepted succour. On being placed in a blanket for removal, an entanglement of his belt caused the hilt of his sword to enter the wound. (Captain, afterwards Viscount) Hardinge proposed to take the weapon away, but Moore said:

"I would rather it went out of the field with me."

Or, as Napier has it, "With martial pride, the stricken man forbade the alleviation–he would not part with his sword in the field! Epaminondas, mortally wounded at Mantinea, was anxious for the recovery of his shield; Moore, mortally wounded at Corunna, sustained additional torture rather than part with his sword."

Six soldiers–42nd men and Guardsmen–now bore him slowly away in a blanket; and when a wagon came up, and it was proposed to place him beside Colonel Wynch, of the 4th Regiment, who lay in it wounded, the poor fellows objected with tears in their eyes.

"We will all keep step, and carry him more easily," they urged.

As Moore was borne from the field of his glory, he frequently made the bearers halt and turn him round, that he might behold it, and be assured that everywhere the French were already falling back.

In the town of Corunna it was soon found that all hope was over; yet he lingered for a time, talking feebly but collectedly to those about him, and in many ways evincing the gentleness and kindliness of his heart.

"Anderson," said he to the colonel so named, an old and valued friend, "you know I have always wished to die in this way."

After a pause.

"Are the French beaten?" he asked; and on being assured that they were so, and retiring fast, he added, with touching earnestness, "I hope the people of England will be satisfied; I hope my dear country will do me justice. Oh, Anderson, you will see my friends at home! Tell them everything–my mother—" Here his voice completely failed him, till he inquired if all his aides-de-camp were safe. To one of these, the son of Earl Stanhope, he said, faintly–

"Remember me, Stanhope, to–to your sister."

It was to the brilliant and famous Lady Hester Stanhope, of Djouna celebrity, who died in Syria in 1839, he referred, and whom he is said to have loved with great tenderness. Pressing to his breast the hand of Colonel Anderson, who had saved his life at the capture of St. Lucia, he expired without a struggle, in his forty-eighth year, having been born in the Trongate of Glasgow, in 1761.

On the fall of Sir John Moore, and the removal of Sir David Baird, the command devolved upon a third Scottish officer, General Hope (afterwards Earl of Hopetoun), who led the army with great judgment and coolness.

Though the battle was won, he resolved to carry out the plans of his then dying leader, by embarking, and quitting the country. The French had no sooner fallen back than, the boats being all in readiness, about ten o'clock at night brigade after brigade filed silently down to the beach in the dark, and went off to the fleet. This final movement was covered by General Beresford, who held the land front of Corunna with 2,000 men, while Hill's brigade kept the promontory in rear of the town.

The embarkation went on with great celerity, and without interruption from the French; but on the following morning they pushed a corps of light infantry towards the town, and seized the heights of St. Lucia, which command the harbour; but the covering brigades were unmolested, and by three in the afternoon the last man was safely on board, and the fleet stood out to sea. Thus, without other interruption than a somewhat feeble cannonade directed against the transports, was the whole British army including its sick, wounded, and artillery, and even its prisoners, conveyed from the coast.

The losses of every regiment were great; as an example, those of the 1st Royal Scots alone, in killed, wounded, and missing, were 250 men.

The general, with his dead comrades, alone remained at Corunna; and, though disastrously, yet gloriously, thus ended our first campaign in the Spanish peninsula.

The 23rd Royal Welsh Fusiliers was the last regiment which quitted the shore.

Moore had been buried in the citadel by the soldiers of the 9th Regiment, in the night. "The lantern dimly burning," was held by Sergeant Rollo, of the Artillery, who died lately at Teignmouth, in his eighty-second year. Near Moore's hasty and coffinless grave–for he was literally buried with "his martial cloak around him"–lay that of General Anstruther, who had died of his sufferings on the march.

"Full justice has not been done, because malignant faction has striven hard to sully his reputation as a general. But this died, and the record of his worth will be as a beacon to posterity, so long as heroic virtue, combined with great capacity, is reverenced; for in any age, any nation, any conjuncture, Sir John Moore would have been a leading man." (Napier)

In the evening, as the fleet stood seaward, the tricolour was seen half hoisted on the citadel of Corunna, where, in the old spirit of French chivalry, the French artillery fired a funeral salute over the grave of him who had won alike the praises of Napoleon, of Wellington, and of Soult, who raised a tomb to his memory. It still stands in the citadel of Corunna, and bears the simple inscription:

John Moore,
Leader of the English Armies in Spain;
Slain in Battle, 1809

D. H. PARRY:

Great confusion existed on board the vessels, and an attempt to transfer the men to their respective ships was prevented by the enemy opening fire from St. Lucia. The cables were cut, and the three hundred transports put to sea on the 17th, convoyed by several men-of-war, the old Victory amongst them, and after cruising about in the offing for two days, they put helm up for England, where the army landed in a wretched condition.

All the clothing of the Rifles was burned behind Hythe barracks, in a state that spoke volumes for the misery undergone.

The Smallbridge went ashore near Ushant, and over two hundred of the German Legion were drowned. Then the newspapers began to raise a disgraceful outcry against the whole expedition, and the good name of Sir John Moore was placed under a cloud by men whose information was false, and whose opinion was of no more value than a spent cartridge.

We have learned the true state of things since then, and ample justice has been rendered to Moore's noble character in the subsequent histories of that glorious period.

The last survivor of Corunna, Thomas Palmer, of the 23rd, died at the great age of a hundred, and was buried at Weston-super-Mare, with full military honours, in April, 1889–eighty years after his chief was laid to rest "with his martial cloak around him."

BRITISH ARMY IN CORUNNA CAMPAIGN

	Total strength in Oct. 1808	Losses
Cavalry (Lord Paget):		
7th Hussars	672	97
10th Hussars	675	24
15th Hussars	674	24
18th Light Dragoons	624	77
3rd Light Dragoons K.G.L.	433	56
	3,078	278
1st Division (Sir D. Baird):		
Warde's Brigade:		
1st Foot Guards, 1st batt	1,340	74
1st Foot Guards, 2nd batt.	1,102	66
Bentinck's Brigade:		
4th Foot, 1st batt.	889	149
42nd Foot, 1st batt.	918	161
50th Foot, 1st batt.	863	264
Manningham's Brigade:		
1st foot, 3rd batt.	723	216
26th Foot, 1st batt.	870	208
81st Foot, 2nd batt.	719	241
	7,424	1,379
2nd Division (Sir J. Hope):		
Leith's Brigade:		
51st Foot	613	107
59th Foot, 2nd batt.	640	143
76th Foot	784	170
Hill's Brigade:		
2nd Foot	666	205
5th Foot, 1st batt.	893	239
14th Foot, 2nd batt.	630	138
32nd Foot, 1st batt.	806	187
	5,032	1,189

Catlin Crawford's Brigade:		
56th Foot, 1st batt.	804	243
71st Foot, 1st batt.	764	138
92nd Foot, 1st batt.	912	129
	2,480	510

3rd Division (Lt. Gen. Fraser):
Beresford's Brigade:

6th Foot, 1st batt.	882	391
9th Foot, 1st batt.	945	373
23rd Foot, 2nd batt.	590	172
43rd Foot, 2nd batt.	598	230

Fane's Brigade:

38th Foot, 1st batt.	900	143
79th Foot, 1st batt.	932	155
82nd Foot, 1st batt.	830	228
	5,677	1,692

Reserve Division (Maj. Gen. E. Paget):
Anstruther's Brigade:

20th Foot	541	113
52nd Foot, 1st batt.	862	143
95th Foot, 1st batt.	863	157

Disney's Brigade:

28th Foot, 1st batt.	926	302
91st Foot, 1st batt.	746	212
	3,938	927

1st Flank-Brigade (Col. R. Crawfurd):

43rd Foot, 1st batt.	895	85
52nd Foot, 2nd batt.	623	161
95th Foot, 2nd batt.	744	96
	2,262	342

2nd Flank-Brigade (Brig. Gen. C. Alten):

1st Lt. Batt. K.G.L.	871	163
2nd Lt. Batt. K.G.L.	880	262
	1,751	425
Artillery, &c.	1,455	255
Staff Corps.	137	38
Total	33,234	7,035

MARSHAL SOULT'S FRENCH ARMY AT CORUNNA:

Infantry
  1st Division, Merle
(Brigades Reynaud, Sarrut, Thomieres)
2nd Léger (three batts.)
4th Léger (four batts.)
15th of the Line (three batts.)
36th of the Line (three batts.)
  2nd Division, Mermet
(Brigades Gaulois, Jardon, Lefebvre)
31st Léger (four batts.)
47th of the Line (four batts.)
122nd of the Line (four batts.)
2nd Swiss Regiment (two batts.)
3rd Swiss Regiment (one batt.)
  3rd Division, Delaborde
(Brigades Foy and Arnaud)
17th Léger (three batts.)
70th of the Line (four batts.)
86th of the Line (three batts.)
4th Swiss Regiment (one batt.)

Cavalry
  Lahoussaye's Division of Dragoons
(Brigades Marisy and Caulaincourt)
17th, 18th, 19th, and 27th Dragoons
  Lorges's Division of Dragoons
(Brigades Vialannes and Fournier)
13th, 15th, 22nd, and 25th Dragoons
  Franceschi's Mixed Division
(Brigades Debelle and Girardin [?]
1st Hussars, 8th Dragoons,
22nd Chasseurs, and Hanoverian Chasseurs

Artillery
600 men (?): exact figures not available.

Details of French casualties do not appear to be available, but, at the time, they admitted to about 3,000 killed, wounded, and missing at the Battle of Corunna.

BRITISH BATTLE HONOURS AWARDED FOR CORUNNA
1st & 3rd Bns. 1st Regt. of Food Guards
3rd Bn. 1st (Royal) Regt. of Foot
To 1st and 2nd Bns. 2nd (Queen's Royal) Regt. of Foot
1st Bn. 4th (King's Own) Regt. of Foot
1st Bn. 5th (Northumberland) Regt. of Foot
1st Bn. 6th (1st Warwickshire) Regt. of Foot
1st Bn. 9th (East Norfolk) Regt. of Foot
2nd Bn. 14th (Buckinghamshire) Regt. of Foot
20th (East Devonshire) Regt. of Foot
2nd Bn. 23rd Regt. of Foot (Royal Welsh Fuzileers)
1st Bn. 26th (Cameronian) Regt. of Foot
1st Bn. 28th (North Gloucestershire) Regt. of Foot

1st Bn. 36th (Herefordshire) Regt. of Foot
2nd Bn. 59th (2nd Nottinghamshire) Regt. of Foot
1st Bn. 32nd (Cornwall) Regt. of Foot
2nd Bn. 76th (Hindoostan) Regt. of Foot
1st Bn. 38th (1st Staffordshire) Regt. of Foot
1st Bn. 82nd Regt. of Foot (Prince of Wales's Volunteers)
1st Bn. 42nd (Royal Highland) Regt. of Foot
1st Bn. 50th (West Kent) Regt. of Foot
51st (2nd Yorkshire West Riding) Regt. of Foot
2nd Bn. 43rd (Monmouthshire Light Infantry) Regt.
1st Bn. 52nd (Oxfordshire Light Infantry) Regt.
2nd Bn. 81st Regt. of Foot
DISTINCTION TO REGIMENT
1st Bn. 71st (Highland) Regt. of Foot
1st Bn. 92nd (Highland) Regt. of Foot
1st Bn. 79th Regt. of Foot (Cameron Highlanders)
1st Bn. 91st Regt. of Foot
95th Regt. of Foot (or Rifle Corps)

Soult, with generous admiration, ordered a monument to be set over Moore's grave at Corunna; and the Spanish Government ... raised another with a laudatory inscription in his honour, but his memory is more safely enshrined in the verses of Charles Wolfe and in the eloquent prose of William Napier. Nevertheless, if not a stone had been raised nor a line written, his work would remain with us; for no man, not Cromwell, nor Marlborough, nor Wellington has set so strong a mark for good upon the British Army as John Moore. Fortescue:

THE BURIAL OF SIR JOHN MOORE AT CORUNNA

Not a drum was heard, not a funeral note,
As his corpse to the rampart we hurried;
Not a soldier discharged his farewell shot
O'er the grave where our hero we buried.

We buried him darkly at dead of night,
The sods with our bayonets turning;
By the struggling moonbeam's misty light
And the lantern dimly burning.

No useless coffin enclosed his breast,
Not in sheet nor in shroud we wound him;
But he lay like a warrior taking his rest
With his martial cloak around him.

Few and short were the prayers we said,
And we spoke not a word of sorrow;
But we steadfastly gazed on the face that was dead,
And we bitterly thought of the morrow.

We thought, as we hollow'd his narrow bed
And smoothed down his lonely pillow,
That the foe and the stranger would tread o'er his head,
And we far away on the billow!

73

Lightly they'll talk of the spirit that's gone
And o'er his cold ashes upbraid him,–
But little he'll reck, if they let him sleep on
In the grave where a Briton has laid him.

But half of our heavy task was done
When the clock struck the hour for retiring:
And we heard the distant and random gun
That the foe was sullenly firing.

Slowly and sadly we laid him down,
From the field of his fame fresh and gory;
We carved not a line, and we raised not a stone–
But we left him alone with his glory.

C. Wolfe

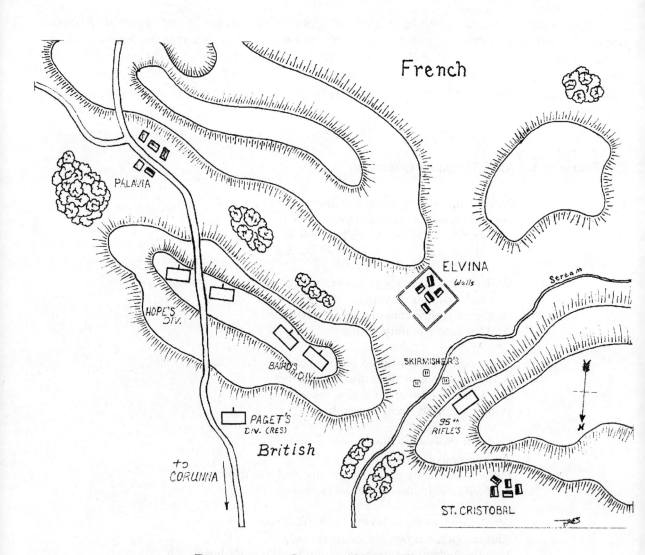

THE BATTLEFIELD OF CORUNNA ON THE WARGAMES TABLE

WALKING (OR NOT WALKING) THE BATTLEFIELD OF CORUNNA.

Not without a little shame, the author admits to never having walked the immortal field of Corunna-the only battlefield of the entire Peninsular War thus neglected. As a fervent admirer of American military historian Jac Weller (have I not carried his definitive work *Wellington in the Peninsular* on every one of my ten trips to that area?) I doubt if he will object to a quotation from his fine book on the subject of the field of Corunna, as he saw and described it in the early 1960's-here it is:

"The actual battlefield of Corunna is much as it was at the time of the conflict; the hamlet of Elvina can have changed hardly at all. The place where Moore fell may be established to within a few yards. Corunna itself has grown considerably; the old walls have been mostly demolished and the entire area built over.

"The modern main road from Madrid to Corunna, passing through dreary and inhospitable country, seldom follows the old roadbed along which the retreat from Benavente to Lugo was made. There are stretches, particularly in and out of villages, where the original road can be identified without difficulty."

from Wellington in the Peninsular *by Jac Weller, Nicholas Vane Ltd (1962)*

THE BATTLE OF CORUNNA, 16TH JANUARY 1809, FOUGHT AS A WARGAME.

The forces were scaled down so that one man on the wargames table equalled 50 in the actual battle. Thus the British had-the Fusiliers; the Royals; the Seaforths; the Buffs; the Black Watch; the Rifles; and Guards, with two field guns and one howitzer.

The French were formed in three Divisions-under Laborde, Merle and Mermet. They had more infantry than the British and three squadrons of Cavalry, with nine guns.

The British began the battle in position as shown on the map. The French were required to act somewhat similarly to the actual battle, with Laborde's division advancing in columns in the area of Palavia; Merles' division advancing against the British left-centre and Mermet's division advancing on Elvina. The cavalry were kept in a body on the extreme French left. The French artillery were formed in a large battery on the hilltop immediately facing the British centre with howitzers behind the wood on the French left.

Hope's division on the British left commenced the battle by advancing down the road and occupied Palavia, where they put up a spirited resistance against three times their number. The British howitzer was posted on the hill with Baird's division, whose right hand battalion moved down the hill and attacked Elvina, supported by Paget's division. The Guards Battalion moved to the right, west of Elvina to attack the French left flank. Earlier, the British riflemen of the 95th had moved slowly back under fire up the slopes of the hill on the immediate British right flank covering their two artillery pieces. The French cavalry massed and attacked this sprinkle of riflemen and the guns, but were severely repulsed with the loss of one complete squadron. For the remainder of the battle the riflemen and the cavalry watched each other without taking any offensive action.

A very severe fight took place in Elvina, the buildings being occupied and lost in rapid succession by the riflemen of the 95th and French Tirailleurs. The Buffs and the Seaforths went into the village but were both forced to withdraw after heavy losses. Bairds' division and Paget's reserve forces were strong enough at this point to prevent any serious penetration by the French. On the British left, Hope's division had been steadily forced back from Palavia by vastly superior numbers. Eventually, they did not adequately cover the road to Corunna. With all their cavalry on their left flank, the French were unable to take advantage of this uncovering of the British line of communication and the battle ended in stalemate at the close of the day with both sides sharing the two points given for victory.

Sir John Moore was actually hit during the battle but saved by a fortuitous throw of the dice! Lord Paget, however, was not so lucky and was killed. This poses problems for future battles, such as Waterloo!

Evidently the rules in use at the time involved writing Order-Sheets, as part of one for Moore's Army was clipped among the Game-Notes:

Unit	Move 1	Move 2	Move 3	Move 4	Move 5	Move 6
Fusiliers	Downhill to village	into houses	Stay	2 Coys on road rest stay.	Back	Back
Royals	Back/rt 6 ins	6" right	Stay	Column right	Right 6"	Stay
Seaforths	Back/rt 6 ins	6" right	Into Elvina	Into Elvina	Re-form	Forward 4"
Buffs	Downhill to Elvina	6" right	Into Elvina	6" fwd into Elvina	Stay	Back 4"
Guards	Right 6 ins	6" right	6" forward	6" forward	6" forward	Extend lt.wheel
42nd	Right 6"	6" right	6" forward	6" forward	forward up hill	wheel right on slope
Howitzer	Stay	Stay	Stay	Stay	Stay	Stay
Right Gun	Stay	Stay	Stay	Stay	Stay	Stay
Left Gun	Stay	Stay	Stay	Stay	Stay	Turn left

Also included in the Notes was a pertinent query, for which no answer was appended! It says "Should allowances be made for Sir John Moore being killed? Could he be kept well forward and given some additional advantage of morale and fighting-power to the area in his immediate vicinity, with morale-drop if, and when, he is killed?

THE ACTION AT SAHAGUN–21 DECEMBER 1808

There was however another side to the coin and whilst part of the army became a rabble, Lord Paget's cavalry, the 7th, 10th and 15th Hussars, plus the 18th Light Dragoons and the 3rd L.D. K.G.L., gained fresh laurels and battle honours. For three days after Christmas the British and German horsemen had held their own against triple forces, including cavalry of the Imperial Guard, on a front of thirty miles. Dozens of brilliant little actions had engendered in the French a healthy respect for their opponents' steel. Near Valencia de Don Juan a troop (38 sabres) of the 18th L.D. charged a French squadron of 105 officers and men and broke them, killing twelve and capturing twenty. The 10th Hussars, while fending off Lorge's dragoons near Mayorga, found that one of Ney's light cavalry regiments was drawn up on high ground to their rear and preparing to attack. Charging up the slope, made slippery by slush and mud, the 10th stormed through the enemy lines and got off safely with 100 prisoners. Paget's five cavalry regiments, in twelve days hard fighting, had taken no less than 500 prisoners and inflicted heavy losses in killed and wounded on the French. There was still one more success in front of them before they were condemned to comparative uselessness in the Galician mountains.

ROBERT W. GOULD

In 1913 in London, a book by Colonel H. C. Wylly was published, entitled "The Journal of a Cavalry Officer in the Corunna Campaign," being the daily diary kept by Captain Alexander Gordon of the 15th Light Dragoons (Hussars). In matter-of-fact way, it tells of the operations of this distinguished British cavalry regiment during the crucial days of Winter 1808/9, when Sir John Moore and his army were retreating through Galicia in Northern Spain, to be taken off by the Royal Navy at Corunna:

Captain Thornhill of the Seventh, who attended Lord Paget, with ten or twelve orderlies of his regiment, rode beside me during part of the night, and told me the object of our movement was to surprise a body of cavalry and artillery posted in a convent at Sahagun, a large town on the Cea, five leagues from Melgar de Abaxo. I afterwards learned that General Slade was directed to attack the convent with the Tenth and Horse Artillery, whilst the Fifteenth was to make a circuit and form on the opposite side of the town, in order to intercept their retreat.

Our march was disagreeable, and even dangerous, owing to the slippery state of the roads; there was seldom an interval of many minutes without two or three horses falling, but fortunately few of their riders were hurt by these falls. The snow was drifted in many places to a considerable depth, and the frost was extremely keen. We left Melgar in the midst of a heavy fall of snow, and when that ceased I observed several vivid flashes of lightning.

On our arrival at Sahagun we made a detour, to avoid passing through the streets, and discovered the enemy formed in a close column of squadrons near the road to Carrion de los Condes; but, owing to the darkness of the morning and a thin mist, we could neither distinguish the number nor the description of the force opposed to us, further than to ascertain it consisted of cavalry.

Lord Paget immediately ordered us to form open column of divisions and trot, as the French, upon our coming in sight, made a flank movement, apparently with the intention of getting away; but the rapidity of our advance soon convinced them of the futility of such an attempt. They therefore halted, deployed from column of squadrons, and formed a close column of regiments, which as it is their custom to tell off in three ranks, made their formation six deep. During the time the two corps were moving in a parallel direction, the enemy's flankers, who came within twenty or thirty yards of our column, repeatedly challenged, "Qui vive?" but did not fire, although they received no answer. As soon as the enemy's order of battle was formed, they cheered in a very gallant manner, and immediately began firing. The Fifteenth then halted, wheeled into line, huzzaed, and advanced. The interval between us was perhaps 400 yards, but it was so quickly passed that they had only time to fire a few shots before we came upon them, shouting: "Emsdorf and victory!" The shock was terrible; horses and men were overthrown, and a shriek of terror, intermixed with oaths, groans, and prayers for mercy, issued from the whole extent of their front.

Our men, although surprised at the depth of the ranks, pressed forward until they had cut their way quite through the column. In many places the bodies of the fallen formed a complete mound of men and horses, but very few of our people were hurt. Colonel Grant, who led the right centre squadron, and the Adjutant who attended him, were amongst the foremost who penetrated the enemy's mass; they were both wounded–the former slightly on the forehead, the latter severely in the face. It is probable neither of them would have hurt if our fur caps had been hooped with iron like those of the French Chasseurs, instead of being stiffened with pasteboard.

It was allowed, by everyone who witnessed the advance of the fifteenth, that more correct movements, both in column and in line, were never performed at a review; every interval was accurately kept, and the dressing admirably preserved, notwithstanding the disadvantages under which we laboured. The attack was made just before daybreak, when our hands were so benumbed with the intense cold that we could scarcely feel the reins or hold our swords. The ground was laid out in vineyards intersected by deep ditches and covered with snow. Our horses, which had suffered from confinement on shipboard, change of forage, and the fatigues of incessant marches in inclement weather, were not in their usual condition; and, as the commanding officer had neglected to halt the regiment during the march for the purpose of tightening their girths, they had become so slack that when we began to gallop several of the blankets slipped from under the saddles.

My post being on the left of the line, I found nothing opposed to my troop, and therefore ordered, "Left shoulders forward!" with the intention of taking the French column in flank; but when we reached the ground they had occupied, we found them broken and flying in all directions, and so intermixed with our hussars that, in the uncertain twilight of a misty morning, it was difficult to distinguish friend from foe. Notwithstanding this there was a smart firing of pistols, and our lads were making good use of their sabres. Upon reaching the spot where the French column had stood, I observed an officer withdrawn from the melee. I followed, and having overtaken him, was in the act of making a cut at him which must have cleft the skull, when I thought I distinguished the features of Lieutenant Hancox; and, as I then remarked that he wore a black fur cap and a cloak which in the dim light of the morning looked like blue, I was confirmed in the idea that he belonged to our regiment. Under this impression, although his conduct in quitting the field at such a period struck me as very extraordinary, I sloped my sword, and merely exclaiming: "What, Hancox! is it you? I took you for a Frenchman!" turned my horse and galloped back to the scene of action. The shock I felt from the idea that I had been on the point of destroying a brother officer instead of an enemy deprived me of all inclination to use my sword except in defence of my life; and the hostility I had cherished against the French only a few minutes before was converted into pity for them. When I met with Hancox after the action, I found that he wore an oilskin cover on his cap, and was not the person I had followed, who, I conclude, was an officer of the grenadiers-a-cheval or compagnie d'elite, which is attached to each regiment of dragoons in the French service, and doubtless was much astonished at my sudden appearance and abrupt departure. For my own part, I shall always consider it a most fortunate circumstance that I was thus deceived, since I have escaped the feeling of remorse, to which I should have been exposed had I taken that man's life.

Many mistakes of the same kind must have occurred in the confusion after the charge. One of our men told me that I had a narrow escape myself, for that during the melee he had his sword raised to cut me down, but luckily recognised his officer in time to withhold the stroke.

At this time I witnessed an occurrence which afforded a good deal of amusement to those who were near the place. Hearing the report of a pistol close behind me, I looked round and saw one of the Fifteenth fall. I concluded the man was killed, but was quickly undeceived by a burst of laughter from his comrades, who exclaimed that the awkward fellow had shot his own horse, and many good jokes passed at his expense.

The melee lasted about ten minutes, the enemy always endeavouring to gain the Carrion road. The appearance of their heavy dragoons was extremely martial and imposing; they wore brass helmets of the ancient Roman form, and the long black horsehair streaming from their crests as they galloped had a very fine effect.

Having rode together nearly a mile, pell-mell, cutting and slashing each other, it appeared to me indispensable that order should be reestablished, as the men were quite wild and their horses almost blown; therefore, seeing no superior officer near, I pressed through the throng until I overtook and halted those who were farthest advanced in pursuit. As soon as I had accomplished this object, the bugles sounded the "rally." Whilst we were re-forming our squadrons, the enemy also rallied and continued their flight by different routes. Our left centre squadrons were detached in pursuit of the chasseurs a cheval, who took the road to Carrion; the other two squadrons followed the dragoons, who retired in the direction of Saldana.

There was not a single man of the Fifteenth killed in the field. The actual losses were, four men died of wounds, two officers and nineteen other ranks wounded; four horses killed, four wounded, and ten missing. We had about thirty wounded, five or six severely, two of whom died the next day; most of the others were so slightly hurt that they returned to their duty within a week. The French had considerable numbers of killed and wounded, but numbers unascertainable; 13 officers and 150 men were taken prisoner together with all baggage.

Thus, Debelle's brigade, which rallied at Saldana, lost about half its strength in this action made notable by Paget's boldness of conception and flexibility once the alarm was raised. It was an action which emphasized the disadvantages of cavalry receiving a well-pressed charge at the halt.

Robert W. Gould tells of a further famous success near Benevente:

On 29th December the Chasseurs of the Imperial Guard, led by General Lefebvre-Desnouettes, forced the River Esla. Pickets of the 18th L.D., supported by a troop of 3rd L.D., K.G.L., made a fighting withdrawal to where Lord Paget had drawn out the 10th Hussars under cover of houses in the southern suburb of Benavente. Suddenly, the 10th swooped down whilst the pickets wheeled about, cheered and charged the enemy flank. During the melee the French general was taken prisoner by Johann Bergmann, a lad of 18 serving in the K.G.L. Not recognizing the worth of his capture he handed the man to Private Grisdale of the 10th, who was promoted to sergeant for his valuable prize! Lefebvre-Desnouettes lived in Cheltenham until 1811 when he broke his parole and escaped to France. The imprudent French lost two captains and 70 unwounded men as prisoners and over a hundred killed and wounded.

FORCES IN ACTION AT SAHAGUN:
British: 15th Hussars–approximately 400 cavalrymen–with some belated help from General Slade with the 10th Hussars; 2 guns.
French: 8th Dragoons and 1st Provisional Chasseurs (who were Hanoverians) variously estimated at about 500 men.

Battle Honour
15th (the King's) Regiment of Light Dragoons (Hussars).

In a summing-up David Chandler defines the Lessons and the Military Significance of the action at Sahagun:
1) A good example of bold, and successful, handling of British cavalry in a small-scale action.
2) The failure of the surprise element owing to good French security.
3) The disadvantages of cavalry receiving a well-pressed charge at the halt; this caused by inaccurate intelligence.
4) Paget's boldness of conception, and flexibility once the alarm was raised.

THE BATTLE OF TALAVERA—27/28 JULY 1809

On the morning of the 28th a heavy and constant cannonade was commenced, and the battle was renewed with more vigour. The French columns came on boldly and tried again and again to walk over us and break our lines, but we defied them, and at every assault they were driven back with fearful slaughter; then they advanced with fresh troops, cheering and shouting "Vive l'Empereur!" The others, disheartened by our determined resistance, faced about with the altered cry "Sauve qui ... peut." The slaughter on both sides was fearful butchering work, and was continued by both armies the whole of that memorable day. Our loss in men was unusually great, and the French loss was said to be greater than ours. When the morning of the 29th dawned, not a Frenchman was to be seen! Their whole army had retired during the night of the 28th! leaving us the victors and masters of the field of battle.

Recollections of a Peninsular Veteran, Lt. Col. Joseph Anderson

SIR EVELYN WOOD:

The main object of Sir John Moore's retreat to Corunna had been to delay the intended French invasion of Portugal.

This object it fully attained. In his eagerness to crush Moore, Napoleon temporarily abandoned all other projects, and, with the exception of the troops in the eastern provinces of Catalonia and Aragon, hurried all his available forces into the mountains of Galicia in pursuit of the British. The French were not ready to begin the conquest of Portugal until March, 1809.

In the meanwhile the Portuguese had been arming. At the request of their Government, British officers were appointed to the higher commands in the Regular Army; and General Beresford, who arrived at Lisbon, in February, 1809, soon made it into a fair fighting force, which he took into the field with a British officer in command of each battalion.

At the same time Sir Robert Wilson landed at Oporto, and organised a band of adventurers whom he named the "Loyal Lusitanian Legion." Numerous other volunteer corps were enrolled; the local Militia was called out and partially armed. The Spaniards, moreover, encouraged by the British Government, began again to reorganise the wrecks of their armies which had been driven south of the Tagus.

Sir Arthur Wellesley therefore found a force at his disposal when, on April 22nd, he landed in Portugal and assumed command of the Allies in the place of Sir John Cradock, who he superseded. At Leiria, just north of Lisbon, was a British force which, with German auxiliaries, numbered 25,000 men. At Tomar, Beresford had 16,000 Portuguese. In Estremadura and Andalusia, Spanish troops were assembling—under General Cuesta south of Merida, and under General Venegas at Carolina.

The Portuguese levies were mainly in the north of the country, one force, under General Silveira, being posted at Amarante, on the River Tamega, whence it could observe Soult, who had marched southwards from Corunna, and who, after a series of bloody battles, captured Oporto, March 29th.

This movement was part of a scheme of triple invasion planned by Napoleon; the Emperor's idea being that Soult should advance from the north, and that two other corps, respectively under the command of Marshal Victor and General Lapisse, should move forward from the east and co-operate with him; while King Joseph, Napoleon's brother, remained at Madrid with a force ready to strengthen whichever of the three armies might be in need of assistance.

Had this combined movement been carried out rapidly and successfully, nothing could have saved Portugal. The French Marshals, however, acted without concert, each being too ambitious of personal distinction to serve for the common good under either of the others; and when Wellesley arrived in April, Soult with 20,000 men was still at Oporto; while Victor and Lapisse, who at the former's insistence had united forces, had moved no further than Merida, where, with 30,000 men, they awaited news from the Douro.

The problem which confronted Wellesley was against which of these armies he should

80

advance–Victor's or Soult's. Victor, on account of his strength and position, was the more serious menace to Lisbon, and an immediate success over him might be attended by greater results. Still, Wellesley thought that the recovery of Oporto would serve to raise the spirits of the Portuguese. So he decided, as a preliminary to attacking Victor, to advance against Soult and drive him from the northern frontier. He calculated that he could reach the Douro before Victor heard of his march, and that, even if Victor then made a forward movement, he would be able to fight Soult, retrace his footsteps, and still arrive before Lisbon in time to protect the capital.

Wellesley's advance against Soult–one of the most remarkable and brilliant of all his achievements–proved more successful than he had hoped. Soult was taken completely by surprise; and the British, having effected a daring passage of the Douro, drove the French army in confusion into the rugged mountains called Sierra Catilina.

At one time it seemed impossible that the army could avoid capture. In some measure, however, fortune favoured the French commander; and although he was compelled to destroy his artillery and a large part of his baggage and ammunition, he contrived on May 18th to reach Montalegre with the bulk of his men–just in time to escape disaster from Beresford, who, in command of Wellesley's flanking division, arrived on the 17th at Chavres, only one march distant.

From Montalegre Soult marched to Lugo, where he was joined by Ney, "being at this time," writes the French historian, Jomini, "in a far worse condition than General Moore six months earlier."

Wellesley now conceived the bold plan of directing a great movement against Madrid, in concert with Cuesta and Venegas. The moment seemed an opportune one, since, owing to the completeness of his victory over Soult, the British General felt that he could now safely advance eastwards without being in danger of a serious attack in flank from the north.

In its general idea the plan of operations advocated by Wellesley was that his own army and Cuesta's should unite, then together move up the Tagus against Victor; while Venegas, advancing from the south, directed his march on Toledo and Madrid. Sir Robert Wilson's force he proposed to use as a flank guard to the invading army when it entered Spain; and he hoped that Wilson, by moving on Madrid through the Escurial Pass, would serve to distract Joseph's attention from the main line of advance of the Allies.

Before Wellesley could come to a final decision he had first to consult with Cuesta, and secure from the Spanish General a promise to accept his advance as part of a joint campaign. This entailed a considerable delay, for Cuesta was jealous of Wellesley, being a perverse old man whose pride and sense of self-importance made him hesitate to adopt any of his colleague's suggestions.

Whenever the British commander proposed a course of action, Cuesta made counter-proposals; and to such an extreme did he carry these purposeless arguments that Wellesley almost despaired. "The obstinacy of this old gentleman," he wrote, "is throwing out of our hands the finest game that any army's ever had."

The head of the British army arrived at Abrantes early in June, but it did not move to the Spanish frontier until the 28th of the month. Many of the regiments had been constantly on the march from May 9th to June 14th, with the result that their shoes were worn out and their baggage animals had dropped far to the rear. The transport of the army was not organised, money was lacking, and reinforcements long overdue had not yet arrived.

While waiting at Abrantes, Wellesley arranged his army in divisions, and gave to it the organisation which it maintained throughout the operations now being considered.

The cavalry, which numbered 3,047 sabres, was formed into one division, consisting of one heavy (Fane) and two light brigades (Cotton and Anson), the whole being under the command of Lieutenant-General Payne.

The infantry was divided into four divisions of unequal strength, commanded as follows: 1st division (6,023 bayonets), Lieutenant-General Sherbrooke; 2nd Division (3,957 bayonets), Major-General Hill; 3rd Division (3,736 bayonets), Major-General Mackenzie; 4th Division (2,957 bayonet), Brigadier-General Campbell.

The six brigades of artillery, comprising 30 guns, he placed under the command of Major-General Howorth.

At this time his whole force amounted approximately to 21,000 men.

On July 3rd the leading brigades passed the frontier river, and bivouacked that night on Spanish soil. At the same time Sir Robert Wilson's "Lusitanian Legion" of 1,500 Portuguese crossed the border farther to the north.

On July 10th the British force reached Placencia. Cuesta was then at Almaraz; whilst Victor, still ignorant of the impending storm, had been compelled by lack of provisions to fall back, and had taken up a position behind the River Alberche.

At Placencia Wellesley halted his army, and rode over with his staff to Almaraz to confer with Cuesta.

The main principles of the campaign were simple, the enemy's strength and position being fairly well known. Victor lay behind the Alberche with some 22,000 men, and King Joseph, with a force estimated at 12,000 men, was at Madrid.

Sebastiani, who, with the 4th Corps of the French army, had been detailed off to operate against Venegas, was supposed to be at Madridejos with a force somewhat smaller than Victor's. Thus, assuming that Venegas would be able to keep Sebastiani occupied, there were at the most 34,000 French soldiers to oppose the advance of Wellesley and Cuesta, whose combined armies numbered 55,000 men.

The British commander was eager to push forward. Victory seemed sure; but he had yet to learn the incompetence of Cuesta, and the true value of Spanish troops.

The British General did not anticipate having to fight the King's, Victor's, and Sebastiani's concentrated armies, which, owing to the negligence of Venegas, he had eventually to do at Talavera on July 28th.

Wellesley, on July 12th, having settled the plan of campaign with his colleague, returned to Placencia, and on the 18th gave orders for a general advance.

Wellesley, on learning that up to the present Victor had not received reinforcements either from Joseph or Sebastiani, was anxious to engage him at once, but the afternoon (July 22nd) was too far advanced. Accordingly the British General decided to postpone his attack until the following day, and, having left the 3rd Division and Anson's Light Horse in front of the right wing of Victor's position, encamped with the rest of his army some distance to the rear. Cuesta occupied the town of Talavera, having posted Zaya and Albuquerque near to the river opposite the French left.

Wellesley spent the evening trying to persuade Cuesta to consent to attack at dawn, and by midnight succeeded in obtaining a reluctant approval of his plans.

At 3 A.M. on July 23rd the British troops were opposite the fords. But in the Spanish lines on their right there was no movement, and Wellesley rode over in person to learn the cause of the delay. Eventually he found Cuesta resting on cushions taken from the coach in which he had driven to the outposts.

In reply to Wellesley's protests, the aged Spaniard calmly announced that the attack most be postponed until the following day. It would be quite impossible, he said, for him to get his army in battle order that morning. Wellesley tried to persuade him to deliver the attack in the afternoon; but Cuesta remained obdurate; and when, on July 24th, he at last consented to move forward, Victor had disappeared.

Cuesta, sorely wounded by Wellesley's disgust allowed pride to master his judgment, and announced his intention of pursuing Victor unaided. He would pursue him, he declared, to the very walls of Madrid; and disregarding his colleague's advice, recklessly pushed forward.

Wellesley's warnings were amply justified, for, on the morning of the 25th, Cuesta, who had taken no steps to ascertain Victor's intentions, learned, to his dismay, that he had in front of him not 23,000 of the enemy but 46,000 – Victor's corps, Sebastiani's corps, and the King's reserves from Madrid.

Venegas had not only failed to contain Sebastiani, but had made no effort to threaten Madrid; and the result was that the whole French force in New Castile was now concentrated, and within a few miles of Cuesta.

Victor–including Latour-Maubourg's Dragoons (3,279 sabres)–had in all 23,000 men, the infantry being divided into three divisions, respectively under Ruffin, Lapisse, and Villatte.

Sebastiani brought up 17,800 men: 14,300 infantry and 3,500 horse–Merlin's Light Cavalry (1,200 sabres) and Milhaud's Dragoons (2,300 sabres).

Finding themselves opposed only by Spaniards, the French took the offensive. But Cuesta, when he discovered the strength of the enemy, beat a hurried retreat, and reached the Alberche unmolested.

Near the river he found the divisions of Sherbrooke and Mackenzie, which Wellesley had sent forward to cover the Spaniards' retreat. The British General now rode over to meet Cuesta and to beg the Spaniard to hasten his retirement.

This Cuesta declined to do. His troops, he declared, were too exhausted; he would encamp on the eastern side of the river. And no arguments of Wellesley could convince him of his folly.

Fortunately, the enemy did not make an appearance during the night. Hence the Spaniards were spared the disaster which otherwise must have overtaken them; and in the morning their leader consented to occupy the position which Wellesley had selected in front of Talavera.

THE COMBAT AT SALINAS

At daybreak on the 27th the French advanced–Latour-Maubourg's cavalry leading; Victor, Sebastiani, and the reserve following in succession.

At 1 P.M. Victor, from the Heights of Salinas, on the east side of the Alberche, saw the Allies then taking up their position. Mackenzie's division, however, with Anson's Light Horse, was still near to the ruined Casa de Salinas, a mile to the west of the Alberche.

The ground here is thickly wooded, a fact which, owing to the insufficient precautions taken by the pickets, enabled the enemy to approach without being observed; and at 3 P.M. the divisions of Lapisse and Ruffin, having forded the river, advancing briskly, took the British by surprise. Wellesley, who at the time was standing on the roof of the Casa making observations on the surrounding country, was fortunate in escaping capture, for he barely had time to mount his charger before the enemy was upon him.

The construction of the battlefield bypass was not the only 20th century aberration to be inflicted upon the battle of Talavera. In 1981 there arose hints impinging upon the sacrosanct character of the Great Duke of Wellington himself, when under the heading "Eagle-eyed," the London Daily Telegraph of 10 February 1981 reported as follows:

> While Bernard Cornwell was researching his historical novel "Sharpe's Eagle" he thinks he may have shed new light on a fabled close escape from death by the Duke of Wellington. On the eve of the battle of Talavera, Wellington was staying at the Casa de Salinas and was watching the approach of the French battalions through a spyglass so intently that he failed to notice that skirmishing troops were already in the courtyard. According to Lady Longford's biography, the Duke made a hasty escape with his staff and narrowly escaped a volley of French fire.
>
> But five independent sources in Talavera told Cornwell that the Duke was actually engaged in the house in a conquest of a distinctly unmilitary kind.

As might be expected, there is not the slightest hint in a single one of the accounts of the battle contained in books both old and more recently published. But then, if such an event *did* actually occur it would be conducted in conditions of utmost secrecy and hardly likely to be recorded in official military papers or books likely to be researched by later historians. Wellesley was in the area of Talavera for some days prior to the battle as indicated by his meeting with Cuesta in the town on the evening of 22 July. On the other hand, no less an authority than Sir John Fortescue, historian of the British Army, wrote when describing the battle:

> Returning now to the Alberche, the French columns began to appear about noon, whereupon the British cavalry and Mackenzie's division fell back from their position at Cazalegas, setting fire to the French huts before they moved. Crossing the river at a ford, the British infantry made its way through a wood to an old ruined house called the Casa de Salinas, which stood in a cleared space by the road that leads from Talavera north-eastward to the village of Cardiel. Here the division halted, with Donkin's brigade in advance and Mackenzie's in rear, but, as the sequel proved, without taking any proper precautions for its security. The men of Donkin's brigade were lying down comfortably in the shade when they were suddenly startled by a volley which

killed several before they could rise from the ground; Lapisse's division, which led the march of Victor's corps, having passed the ford unobserved under cover of the smoke from the burning huts, and stolen in upon the British before their presence was even suspected. For a time there was wild confusion amounting to panic in part of the surprised brigade. The Eighty-seventh and Eighty-eighth ran back, firing wildly at each other; though the Sixtieth, which seems to have been a little isolated from them, stood firm. An aide-de-camp flew to Wellesley to report the mishap; and the General, galloping with all speed to the spot, scrambled up the ruined walls of the Casa de Salinas to see what was going forward. He had hardly done so before the enemy's sharp-shooters came swarming round the building, and he barely escaped capture by jumping down and remounting his horse in all haste. He now made his way to Mackenzie's brigade ...

"The History of the British Army" by Sir John Fortescue, Book XIII, Ch. XXX, pp. 226/7.

THE CASA DE SALINAS

There are a number of points to be considered, in addition to Fortescue's clear assertion that "...the General, galloping with all speed to the spot, scrambled up the ruined walls of the Case de Salinas ..." First, Wellesley was in the process of deploying his army on the Medellin and other points; second, Casa de Salinas was, in a straight line, three and a half to four miles from that position and it seems unlikely that a commander so singleminded and talented would have decided to frolic at such a time. And, as is stressed more than once, the place was in ruins and hardly likely to be the residence of a Spanish lady of the status likely to entice the patrician Wellesley!

So, from late 20th century spice back to early 19th century drama, with:

EVELYN WOOD:

The attack fell mainly on Donkin's brigade, 60th (King's Royal Rifles), 87th (the Royal Irish Fusiliers), and 88th (the Connaught Rangers) Regiments, and on the 31st (the East Surrey) Regiment in Mackenzie's brigade. These battalions were broken and driven to the rear, losing 80 prisoners.

Disaster seemed imminent, but Wellesley in person succeeded in restoring the fight, rallying the fugitives round the 45th (the Sherwood Foresters) and 60th. The steadiness of these troops saved the situation; and, although the French still pressed vigorously forward, Mackenzie's men retired in good order, and took up their assigned positions.

The country between the Alberche and Talavera in a plain covered with cork and olive trees; bounded on the north by a round, steep hill, the Cerro de Medellin, which runs parallel with the Tagus at a distance of two miles. This hill is separated by a deep valley, about half a mile in width, from the range of mountains which divide the Alberche and the Tietar.

Wellesley's front extended from Talavera to the Cerro de Medellin. The Spaniards were posted in and in front of the town in a very strong position, concealed by woods, and covered by walls, ditches, and enclosures, which rendered it almost unassailable. Their left rested on a mound where a large field redoubt had been constructed.

To the north and in rear of the mound Campbell's division took up position. The centre of the Allies' front, which was exposed and devoid of cover, was held by Sherbrooke's division, drawn up in single line, the Guards Brigade (1st Coldstreams and 1st Scots) being on flat and open ground, Cameron's two battalions, the 61st (Gloucestershire) Regiment and 83rd (Royal Irish Rifles), occupying the spurs of the Cerro de Medellin, below which the Portiña stream flows through a deep ravine, and Langwerth's and Low's brigades of the King's German Legion continuing the line to the foot of the hill.

Behind Sherbrooke, Wellesley placed Mackenzie's division and all his cavalry, Cotton's Light Dragoons being in rear of Campbell, and the cavalry of Fane, and Anson's Light brigade massed behind Cameron.

To Hill, the most experienced of his divisional Generals, Wellesley entrusted the defence of the Cerro de Medellin, the vital point of the position. Yet, for some unexplained reason, Hill neglected to occupy the summit on the evening of the 27th, but halted his men in the rear, Stewart's battalions on the left, Tilson's on the right flank of the reverse slope.

Sir Evelyn Wood, appointed Field-Marshal in 1903, has set the scene up to the rising of the curtain on the drama of the two-day battle of Talavera. Now Victorian military historian D.H. Parry will relate, in somewhat florid prose, the events which cost Wellesley 22% of his total British force:

D. H. PARRY:

Dense woods drooped under the burning heat of a Spanish July afternoon; the grass of the plain was scorched to a dull brown, and white dust lay thick on the roads that led to Talavera. The one-storied, red-tiled houses of the squalid town on the banks of the Tagus were reflected in the broad river, but the habitual siesta of its inhabitants was for once interrupted as, from the shadow of the ancient ramparts, they watched a British army drawn up in line of battle–a line stretching, with here and there a gap, until it rested on a steep hill, two miles away, beyond which again a chain of blue mountains rose against a cloudless sky.

It was a tattered line–patched, torn, and campaign-stained, and the dust of the roads had sullied it, dimming the scarlet of its coats. It was, moreover, a hungry half-starved line, having lived for many days on a handful of raw wheat and a draught of water, or a species of field-pea called corovanzen, by way of rations. There were rough detachments and undrilled lads among its regiments, some still wearing militia badges on their appointments, as many of our men did afterwards at Waterloo; but nevertheless they were waiting for the French, who were somewhere across a little river hidden by the woods in their front, beyond the Casa de Salinas, where Sir Arthur Wellesley lay with the outposts, 10,000 Spaniards under Cuesta being strongly posted on the skirt of the forest, nearer to the town itself.

The plain that stretched before the line was level, and well grown with olives and handsome cork-trees; and on the 27th July, 1809, it was baked and dry, the passage of a single horseman being sufficient to raise a great cloud as the sun beat fiercely down.

King Joseph Bonaparte, brother of the great Emperor, was marching to oppose our further progress into Spain, and when the clocks of Talavera were striking three the divisions of Ruffin and Lapisse, having forded the Alberche, came through the forest, with their cartouche-belts and red epaulettes worn outside long white linen overcoats, and debouched so suddenly that our leader was nearly captured in the Casa, and the outpost was thrown into momentary confusion.

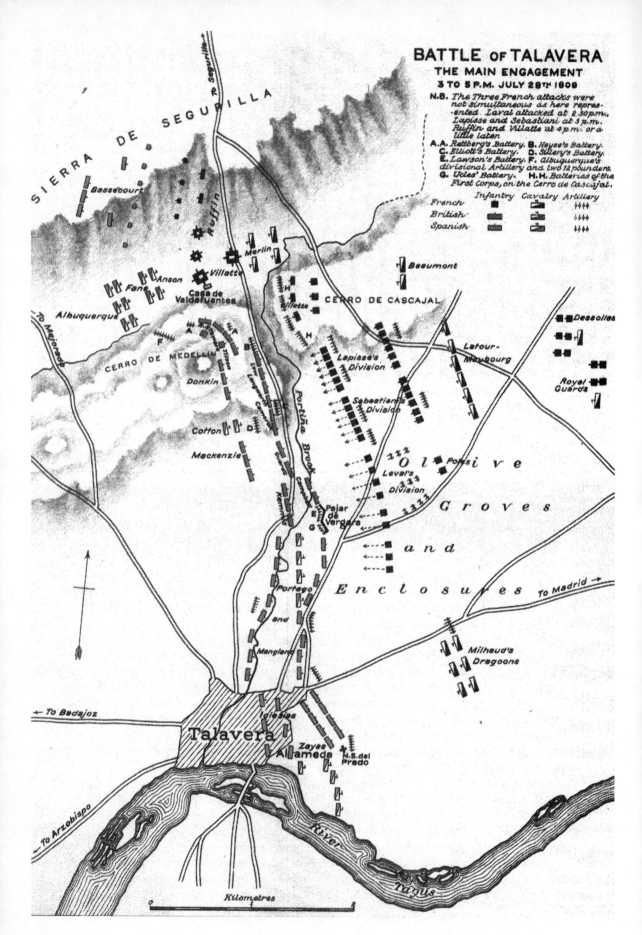

BATTLE of TALAVERA
THE MAIN ENGAGEMENT
3 TO 5 P.M. JULY 28TH 1809

N.B. The Three French attacks were not simultaneous as here represented. Laval attacked at 2.30 p.m. Lapisse and Sebastiani at 3 p.m. Ruffin and Villatte at 4 p.m. or a little later.

A.A. Rettberg's Battery. B. Heyse's Battery.
C. Elliott's Battery. D. Sillery's Battery.
E. Lawson's Battery. F. Albuquerque's divisional Artillery and two 12 pounders.
G. Ucles' Battery. H.H. Batteries of the First Corps, on the Cerro de Cascajal.

	Infantry	Cavalry	Artillery
French			
British			
Spanish			

SIERRA DE SEGURILLA

To Segurilla

Basecourt

Ruffin

Merlin

Villatte

Casa de Valdefuentes

Anson

Fane

Albuquerque

Beaumont

Villatte

CERRO DE CASCAJAL

Deasolles

F

A

C

Tilson

B

Low German Legion

Donkin

CERRO DE MEDELLIN

Lapisse's Division

H

H

Latour-Maubourg

Royal Guards

Sebastiani's Division

Portiña Brook

Cotton

D

Meckenzie

Olive

Passive

Leval's Division

Groves

and

Sherbrooke's Guards

Pajar de Vergara

G

Enclosures

To Madrid →

Portego

and

Milhaud's Dragoons

Mangiana

Talavera

To Badajoz ←

Iglesias

Zayas

Allameda

N.S. del Prado

← To Arzobispo

River

Tagus

To Majorada

To Mejorada

Kilometres

86

The young, untrained troops lost their heads, fired on each other, and were driven into the open, the gallant "Old Stubborns"–as the 45th was nicknamed–and the 5th Battalion of the 60th Regiment alone remaining firm, and receiving the French with a heavy fire from the well-known "Brown Bess" and the Baker rifle.

After 400 of our men had fallen, and a goodly number of the enemy, the French paused, and our two brigades retired step by step, under cover of our light dragoons, to take up their position in the main line, which had eagerly listened to the rattle of the musketry and watched the smoke drifting slowly away above the tree-tops.

With drums beating, and the sun pouring on them until the brass eagles on their shako-plates glowed like gold–with the bold assurance of men whose colours bore the magic names of a score of battles won beyond the Rhine against Germany, Austria, and Russia–the veteran soldiery of the Empire came proudly on, their artillery unlimbering to open a cannonade against our left wing, while their green Chasseurs trotted forward to discover the position of the Spaniards.

Sir Arthur Wellesley had taken great precautions in posting our allies, who were placed behind mud walls and high banks between our right and the town, screened still further by the cork woods and barriers of felled timber and the buildings of a large convent, whose musical chime went unheeded amid the strife; but he had no confidence in them.

The Chasseurs soon discovered the Spaniards through the screen of leaves, and, cocking their carbines and pistols, sent some balls whistling among them.

For a moment there was a returning fire, but the next instant, without warning, ten thousand able-bodied cowards turned tail and fled helter-skelter to the rear, carrying with them artillery, stores, and baggage-waggons.

In point of fact, this is something of an exaggeration! More sober accounts relate how the Spanish line, stretching from the British right to Talavera itself, suddenly opened fire although the French cavalry were far out of range. Then, four battalions of Spanish infantry broke and ran to the rear in disorder, without being attacked or even threatened! Wellesley, who witnessed the occurrence, could explain their conduct only on the ground that they were "… frightened by the noise of their own gunfire …" The fugitives were eventually rounded-up by Spanish cavalry, and on the morning after the battle (20 July) Cuesta determined to decimate the battalions which had fled. Wellesley dissuaded him from taking such drastic measures, but none the less, the Spanish commander insisted on executing between 25 and 30 men, chosen by drawing lots!

D. H. PARRY:

Close to a large field redoubt the Oporto road bisected our position, and Brigadier-General Campbell's division stood there in two lines, on their left being Sherbrooke's division–the 1st Battalion of the Coldstreams and 3rd Guards–with Mackenzie's men behind them, panting from their recent skirmish at the Casa.

To the left of the Guards were the King's German Legion, their artillery posted on the slope of the height that bounded our line, and which was also occupied by Rowland Hill's 2nd Division, with our cavalry in their rear – 19,846 men only on whom we could depend, to oppose 50,000 veterans under Marshals Jourdan and Victor, with such well-known generals as Villatte, Lapisse, Ruffin, Sebastiani, Latour-Maubourg, and Milhaud to execute their commands.

The last gleam of the setting sun was fading from the spires of the town, and twilight had already begun to shroud the two hostile armies, when they came at us again, making a desperate attempt to seize the hill, Ruffin's division rushing forward with great rolling of drums on Colonel Donkin's brigade posted there.

Luckily, two regiments lost their way in a ravine, and the 9th arrived alone, thus giving us time to bring up reinforcements before Villatte and Lapisse reached our line; but as it was, some of the bold fellows got round in the dusk and climbed the height, from which they fired down on to Donkin's men, who were taken in front and rear.

Rowland Hill was ordering on the 48th when bullets began to rain round him, and thinking that some of our lads were aiming in the wrong direction, he rode up the rising ground with his brigade-major, Fordyce, to find himself instantly surrounded by the enemy.

A grenadier wounded his horse and grabbed at the bridle, but the general spurred so violently that he broke away, and, leaving Fordyce dead, galloped down again to meet the 29th, which he led back at the charge.

The Worcestershires, with bayonets lowered, made short work of the daring 9th, and pitched them over into the valley; but red flashes came from the darkness as two other French columns advanced. The whole of our line stood to arms, cartridges were bitten and ranks dressed, while the brass drums kept up their dull roar, amid cries of "En avant!" "Steady there!" "Make ready, present, fire!" and all the jumble of sounds and shouting that told of a deadly combat.

Villatte–who, to his immortal honour, refused in after years to sit in judgment on Marshal Ney– urged his horse forward and brandished his sword in vain; in vain the gallant Lapisse–formerly colonel of the famous 57th Demi-brigade–pushed his men on against the German Legion until his feint attack became a real one. The British kept their ground, cheering as they reloaded, and closing up the ranks as man after man sank bleeding on the withered herbage, until Victor drew off and silence fell over the plain. The wounded crawled towards their own lines, where bright bivouac fires were soon blazing; but 1,000 Frenchmen and 800 of the allies lay stark and stiff in the starlight.

During the short summer night there were several alarms that kept us on the alert, though they arose principally from our Spanish friends, who suddenly began firing at nothing at all, with no object whatever; but with the dawn of the 28th the serious business of war recommenced. The French beat the pas-de-charge–known as "old trousers" by our men–and Ruffin again advanced to turn the coveted hill, followed by Villatte, and heralded by a cannonade that mowed us down by sections.

From the openness of the plain in front of our position–for the Spaniards had all the cover to themselves–we could see the enemy's masses and the French officers flying from one division to another. They, on the other hand, had a precipitous hill before them, dotted here and there with patches of dingy red above which the grey smoke floated–dangerous patches which resolved themselves into companies and battalions as they approached them at a quick step. There is something grim and soldierly in the clean-shaven faces of our Peninsular infantry, with the little tufts of side-whisker then in vogue as we see them in the prints of the time; and grim they must have looked to the enemy on that Talavera morning, with the sunrise lighting up their bayonets and the pikes of the sergeants, as they awaited the attack unflinching under the fire of the guns.

As the grenadiers and light infantry neared our position, the cannoniers turned their pieces on the centre and right of the British, leaving the hill to the stormers, who approached at a run on two sides, shouting loudly.

Rocks and ridges, grassy dips and hollows, broke the compact columns as they got within arm's length, and the attack became a series of little struggles where all formation was lost, and each man fought for himself.

Kentish Buffs clubbed their muskets and hewed at the moustached veterans of Jéna and Austerlitz; the Connaught Ranger and the *enfant de Paris* grappled with each other and rolled down the slope strewn with ammunition-paper and cartridge-cases.

The vicious little curved briquet of the French officer flashed in the sunlight and met the regulation sword of our subaltern, generally in favour of the former; for we were behind them in the use of small arms, as in many other things. Some of their men mounted the height, and were dislodged with difficulty. Hill was wounded, and many of our best and bravest met a soldier's death with the hurrahs of their comrades ringing in their ears. But inch by inch, we forced them back, and after a fiendish forty minutes they retired in disorder, with the loss of no less than fifteen hundred, to the shelter of their batteries.

King Joseph now reconnoitred our line with a glittering Staff, and held a council of war at which Jourdan and Victor violently opposed each other in a way that seriously embarrassed poor Joseph, at heart an amiable, good-natured fellow, but a mere cat's-paw in the hands of his ambitious brother.

Marshal Jourdan, who had been so frequently beaten in battle that the soldiers christened him "the anvil," was in favour of taking up a position and waiting for Soult to arrive; but Victor, smarting under his three repulses, urged the king to reopen the conflict, promising to carry the hill if they would attack along our whole line simultaneously. The greatest indecision prevailed, but the king eventually gave in to Victor against his own better judgment, afraid lest Napoleon should rebuke him for neglecting an opportunity. Sir Arthur Wellesley sat on the summit of the hill, calm and cool under a fearful weight of responsibility.

Our "General of Sepoys," as he was contemptuously called in some quarters, had full confidence in his own powers, and continued to gaze across the plain, where our thirsty men mingled with the enemy at the stream, forgetting for a time their mutual animosity.

This may seem a strange statement, but the history of that war is full of generous instances on the part of both armies. Many courtesies were exchanged between brave fellows who, perhaps, next day met in mortal combat; sentries would often chat, and obtain a light for their pipes from each other, or the French bands give concerts for the benefit of our men.

The British cavalry, which had gone some distance to water their horses, had now returned and drew up behind the hill. Several hundred infantry came back from their duty of bearing the wounded to a place of safety, and were mistaken by the enemy for Sir Robert Wilson's corps; and now the drums and bugles recalled each army to its ranks, as the French eagles were uncased about half-past one.

The day was intensely hot; a blue sky stretched in unclouded brilliancy overhead, and every feature of the landscape showed with great distinctness, except where the dust rose round the mustering men, whose accoutrements and flashing bayonets scintillated in the glare.

Eighty pieces of cannon stood ominously silent, waiting the touch of the dark-blue uniformed artillerymen to vomit death among us. Three strong brigades of infantry with mounted officers were drawn up in columns, the silk tri-colours drooping in the breathless air, each ensign flanked by two sergents-porte-aigles, chosen from the most valiant in the ranks who could neither read nor write, and hence could not hope for promotion, and whose honourable duty it was to guard the eagle with their lives, carrying a formidable halbert and a brace of pistols for that purpose.

Behind the infantry were long lines of horsemen, the tall yellow-and-black plumes of the 5th French Chasseurs–whose first colonel, D'Andigeau, was a romantic Spanish brigand far back in the seventeenth century–and the crimson facings of the 10th, lending a touch of bright colour to the array, further increased by the brass helmets of the 1st and 4th Dragoons, with gay scarlet revers to their green coats.

In rear of Villatte a bunch of red-and-white pennons showed where the Polish Lancers stood, stern troopers from the Vistula with light yellow plastrons and blue uniforms, and a great cloud of the ubiquitous dust betrayed King Joseph's Guards marching up in reserve.

The people of Talavera, once more on the ramparts, saw a movement agitate the four French columns; eighty tongues of flame darted from the cannon behind them; eighty puffs of white smoke mingled into a dense pall which threw its shadow along the plain, followed by a mighty crash that set the horses rearing and made the Spaniards tremble in their security. Marshal Victor had given the signal, the enemy sprang forward, and the battle proper, to which the other affairs had been merely preludes, began.

The 4th Corps was the first to reach us, the active little fantassins scouring over the ground and flinging themselves upon our 4th Division, only to be impaled on the bayonets of the 7th Fusiliers and the "Old Five-and-Threepennies," which was the cant name of the 53rd Shropshire; while the 5th Battalion of the 60th, in whose ranks were many Germans, emptied their rifles into them again and again. The universal practice of Napoleon's armies was to send a cloud of light infantry against the enemy, preceded by a cannonade and followed by the line. It was the light infantry that Campbell's regiments had repulsed, and as the column behind came through the dust General Mackenzie's men and some Spaniards stepped out to help the 4th Division, reserving their fire until they came to close quarters.

Sir Arthur watched the combat from the hill, and seeing Ruffin creeping round to turn our left, and Villatte advancing at the double in front, he sent orders to Anson's cavalry to charge down the valley which lay between the mountains and our friendly eminence.

"Squadrons, march!" rang the trumpets, and two gallant corps–the 1st King's German Legion Hussars and our 23rd Light Dragoons–moved off and trotted towards Villatte.

The 23rd, in blue with crimson facings and huge bearskin crests surmounting their helmets, rode on the right of the Hussars, whose yellow-braided pelisses and scarlet busby bags floated gracefully out when they got under way and the trot merged into a canter.

Villatte threw his men into three squares and began firing; steel scabbard and black sabretache clashed and jingled as the canter became a hand-gallop and the trumpets sounded "Charge!"–

Hill's division cheering lustily as they thundered past the height.

Within thirty yards of the squares there lay a hidden gully, quite concealed by the long grass until you came close on to it, and which history has exalted into alarming proportions, like the very much overrated "sunken road of Ohain"; but, although it was only eight feet deep by from twelve to eighteen in width at its worst part, it was still an obstacle bound to disorder a charging squadron, and the watchers on the hill saw the Germans rein up, as Arentschild pulled his horse on to the crupper and cried, "Halt! I will not kill my young mens!"

Some of the Hussars, nevertheless, jumped it and continued their way, and the 23rd, who arrived at a spot where the hollow was broader but much more shallow, dipped into it at full speed, lost their formation as some of the horses fell, and scrambled up the opposite bank in twos and threes, having lost their impetus and order, but not their hearts, for they rode right through the intervals of the squares before them, and laid about them gallantly with their half-moon sabres on the green Chasseurs.

Their triumph was short. Colonel Seymour was hurt, and Major Frederick Ponsonby led, gallantly as was his wont; but down came the Polish Lancers and the Westphalian Chevaux-Légers; the 23rd were outnumbered, cut down, and ridden over; and although a few got back, amid the redoubled cheering of our infantry, 207 lay under their horses, the loss of the 1st Hussars being also heavy – 37 men and 64 mounts.

While this incident was enacted, Campbell and Mackenzie had closed with the main body of the 4th Corps, under the brave Corsican general, Count Porta Horace Sebastiani, and a furious struggle took place, the carnage on both sides being horrible.

At Talavera French and English fought hand to hand, the French having the advantage of length in their musket-barrels, although our Brown Bess bayonets were longer than theirs. We were half-starved into the bargain, but we possessed that historic characteristic of never knowing when we were beaten.

The huge silk colours were riddled with balls; writhing groups of mutilated wounded screamed piteously as they were trampled under foot. It was more like a melee of the Middle Ages than a nineteenth-century battle; for men got at each other and hit hard, the blood spurting right and left until the musket-butts, and the trodden grass, and every bayonet in the division was red with it, while the cannon-balls came whanging and tearing into the throng, and we smashed and smote blindly through the smoke and sand.

"Forward, forward!" was the cry, and with tremendous cheering we sent Sebastiani's veterans back and captured ten guns, a regiment of Spanish horse cutting in as they tried to rally, and driving the 4th Corps to the rear.

Sir Arthur thanked the 2nd Battalion of the Fusiliers; but Lapisse's drums turned all eyes on the hill again, and the German Legion, who were assailed with fury in their turn.

Magnificent as the Hanoverians always proved themselves while they were in our service– equal, and in some points superior even, to our troops, whose uniform they wore–the impetuosity of this attack shook them. Sherbrooke's Guards were shattered at the same moment by the French artillery, and the very centre of our line was broken.

The Guards charged valiantly, and were for an instant successful, but they advanced too far and there was great confusion. Von Rettberg's battery pounded steadily, and Bombardier Dierking won the notice of Sir Arthur Wellesley, who exclaimed, "Very well, my boy!" clapping him on the back as shot after shot fell into the middle of the enemy; but the situation was most critical.

Our leader ordered Stapleton Cotton up with his cavalry, sending to Colonel Donellan to bring the 48th from the hill; and soon the broad buff regimental banner was seen approaching side by side with the king's colour, as the Northamptons marched proudly into the disorder, wheeling back by companies to let the retiring jumble through and then resuming their steady line, shoulder to shoulder.

Gallant Lapisse lay dying on the grass, his life-blood welling out over the general's gold aiguilette; but his column, hot with victory, had penetrated our centre, and were making the most of a triumph destined to be short.

The sun had got behind us, for it was afternoon, and the band of purple shadow that preceded the scarlet line of the 48th was ominous of the disaster about to fall on the Frenchmen.

Taking the column on its right, the Northamptonshire poured a tremendous volley into it and closed with the bayonet.

Colonel Donellan fell mortally wounded near the gruesome masses of dead guardsmen, 600 of whom were slaughtered there; but even in his agony the fine old man remembered his regiment, and raising his three-cornered Nivernois hat–the last seen in our service–he desired Major Middlemore to take command, sinking back with dimmed eyes as the stout fellows faded from his sight for ever.

Like an avalanche the 48th fell on the column and checked its progress, giving the Guards and the Germans time to rally; then another hand-to-hand struggle began, fiercer if possible than the last, for we were fighting desperately to recover lost ground, and two of the bravest nations in the world strove for mastery, loud and long.

Those who could not get to the front held aloof, and fired shot after shot wherever they saw an enemy; men wrestled and rolled over, clutching at each other; fists were used when weapons were broken; bearded Sapeurs in bearskin caps and white leather aprons hewed with their axes as though our men had been the walls of a fortress; officers in topboots shouted themselves hoarse; and Dermoncourt's 1st Dragoons slashed and pointed in the most frantic attempt to break us; but our order was restored by the example of the Northamptonshire, and our cavalry came up at a trot with sabres in hand.

Nearly all the Staff were either unhorsed or wounded, and Sir Arthur was hit on the shoulder, but not seriously. Ruffin hesitated beyond the valley, and was lost; Lapisse lay dead, and Sebastiani was in disorder. King Joseph's reserves and his Guard had not been engaged, but the French morale was shaken and we began to cheer–a pretty usual sign that we were conquering.

The artillery still continued; but little by little the enemy retreated to their own side of the plain, an about six o'clock the battle was over.

Towards the end, while the shot was plunging around Von Rettberg's battery, a distinguished act of heroism was performed by Sergeant Bostelmann, who was bringing ammunition up from the waggons in the rear. The dry grass caught fire, scorching the wounded and burning some of them to death, and it threatened the powder as the flames ran rapidly across the heath.

With four brave gunners named Luttermann, Zingreve, Warnecke, and Lind, the sergeant dragged each waggon, four in all, to a place of safety behind a trench, heedless of the fact that they might all be blown to atoms in an instant should one of the tempest of balls strike their dangerous charge; and after superhuman efforts all the waggons were saved and galloped down the road beyond, when the limber teams arrived, Bostelmann being publicly thanked, and afterwards receiving a commission.

Fearful was the slaughter when men found time to look around them.

Generals Mackenzie and Von Langwerth of the Legion were killed, and 31 other officers, with 767 rank and file; 3 generals, 92 officers, 3,718 sergeants and men wounded, and 652 of all ranks missing; or a total on our side of 6,268 during the two days. Of these the 7th Fusiliers lost 65, and the German Legion nearly 1,500 and 88 horses; while other corps counted their casualties in varying proportion.

One strange incident reaches us from the private journal of an English officer to whose friend it occurred: the enemy, seeing him to be badly wounded and in great pain, requested his permission to put him out of his misery. Needless to say, he declined with thanks!

The French are reported to have lost 10,000 men, 2 generals, and 17 guns, the prudent Napier giving the number at between 7,000 and 8,000. Truly an awful feast of blood and woe!.

Again the bivouac fires flared up in the darkness, and the surgeons were busy on each side. We were too weary and too weakened to press in pursuit, and both armies remained all night within range of each other, ours suffering in addition from hunger–the commissariat, as usual, unequal to its duties, and death threatening any who attempted to plunder.

In the morning the search parties of the German Legion discovered three blue standard-poles among their dead, and after a ghastly hunt Captain von Düring, of the 5th Battalion, found the brass eagles belonging to them.

A burst of military music rose unexpectedly, and shading their eyes from the sun which again beat down on the now corpse-covered plain, our army saw Craufurd's light division march proudly in, too late to take part in the battle, although their efforts to arrive in time have made their march historic. The iron warrior, whose stern discipline rivalled that of Martinet, the celebrated colonel of the Regiment du Roi under Louis XIV, had halted his men, after a twenty-mile tramp, near Malpartida de Placencia, and they were cooking their meagre rations when Spanish fugitives hurried up with a report of our defeat.

"Buglers, sound the 'fall in!' " cried Craufurd, buckling on his sword-belt; and there and then, after selecting fifty of the weakest to remain behind, he marched off with his three regiments–the 43rd, 52nd, and 95th Light Infantry–covering sixty-two English miles in twenty-six hours, every man carrying sixty pounds on his shoulders.

Although it was the hottest season of the year, only seventeen stragglers dropped behind–a glorious record of British endurance and eagerness for the fray, the division taking over the outpost duty immediately on its arrival.

Before this, however, with the first gleam of daylight, the French army left its gory bivouac.

For the last time the dust floated along the edge of the forest, and whitened the foliage of the cork trees; regiment after regiment, squadron after squadron gazed with sullen anger at the tattered British line, now sadly thinned, which had maintained its position in spite of them, and which still stood to arms in the pearly haze of the morning. The dull tap of the drums grew fainter; the rumble of caissons, and waggons heavy with the wounded, died away; the Lancers wheeled in a cloud and followed, and the sunshine burned in a dazzling blaze on the brass helmets of the vanquished Dragoons. Then the woods hid them; the crows and the vultures settled undisturbed as the dust subsided–the French army was gone!

EVELYN WOOD:

A distressing calamity occurred during the final cannonade on the evening of the 28th. The grass on the Cerro de Medellin took fire, and the flames, fanned by the wind, spread so quickly over the lower slopes of the hill that many of the wounded on both sides were badly scorched, several being burned to death.

Lack of water and supplies, moreover, occasioned a good deal of suffering to the wounded.

"It is positively a fact," wrote Wellesley on July 31st, "that during the last seven days the British army have not received one-third of their provisions, and that at this moment there are nearly 4,000 wounded soldiers dying in hospital from want of common assistance and necessaries, which any other country in the world would have given even to its enemies."

While the British General waited, uncertain as to what course of action next to pursue–whether to return to Portugal, advance on Madrid, or join Venegas–he heard that Soult had forced his way over the Baños Pass and had arrived at Placencia.

This changed the situation. Leaving the Spaniards at Talavera. Wellesley immediately turned about to face the new menace in his rear.

On August 3rd he reached Oropesa, and there learned from captured dispatches that he had in front of him not only Soult's but Ney's and Mortier's corps. He heard further that Joseph had again advanced, and that Cuesta was retiring in haste from Talavera.

His position was serious. Naval Moral being in the hands of the enemy, his line of retreat on Abrantes by the bridge of Almaraz was cut off. Two alternatives only remained–to stand his ground and fight, or to retire across the Tagus to Arzobispo, and so try to reach the main road to Badajoz before the French could intercept him.

To fight was too hazardous. Soult had with him 50,000 men. It would have been madness to assail such a force with 18,000 hungry troops; and, Napier tells us, "the peril was apparent to every soldier in the British ranks.

Accordingly Wellesley fell back, crossed the Tagus at Arzobispo on August 4th, and moved towards Jaracejo. Cuesta followed the same route, whilst Sir Robert Wilson, who had done everything that was possible to harass King Joseph, fought his way back into Portugal by the Baños Pass

Thus the Allied army avoided the trap set by the enemy for its destruction. But the escape was a narrow one. Sir Arthur Wellesley had fought a great battle, won a great victory; and, if the material effects of that victory were small, the moral effects were immense.

The British General, now created Baron Douro and Viscount Wellington, had learned the difficulties of conducting a campaign in Spain, and the necessity of being so provided with supplies and transports as to be independent of the civil authorities.

THE BRITISH FORCE AT TALAVERA

From the Morning State of July 25, 1809
Present and fit for duty
Cavalry Division (Lieut.-Gen. Payne)
Fane's Brigade

3rd Dragoon Guards	525
4th Dragoons	545

Cotton's Brigade:

14th Light Dragoons	464
16th Light Dragoons	525

Anson's Brigade:

23rd Light Dragoons	459
1st Light Dragoons K.G.L.	451
Total Cavalry	2,969

Infantry
1st (Sherbrooke's) Division
H. Campbell's Brigade:

1st batt. Coldstream Guards	970
1st batt. 3rd Guards	1,019
One company 5/60th Foot	56

Cameron's Brigade:

1/61st Foot	778
2/83rd Foot	535
One company 5/60th Foot	51

Langwerth's Brigade:

1st Line batt. K.G.L.	604
2nd Line batt. K.G.L.	678
Light Companies K.G.L.	106

Low's Brigade:

5th Line batt. K.G.L.	610
7th Line batt. K.G.L.	557
Total of the 1st Division	5,964

2nd (Hill's) Division
Tilson's Brigade

1/3rd Foot	746
2/48th Foot	567
2/66th Foot	526
One company 5/60th	52

R. Stewart's Brigade:

29th Foot	598
1/48th Foot	807
1st batt. of Detachments	609
Total of the 2nd Division	3,905

3rd (Mackenzie's) Division
Mackenzie's Brigade:

2/24th Foot	787
2/31st Foot	733
1/45th Foot	756

Donkin's Brigade:

2/87th Foot	599
1/88th Foot	599
Five companies 5/60th	273
Total of the 3rd Division	3,747

4th (Campbell's) Division
A. Campbell's Brigade

2/7th Foot	431
2/53rd Foot	537
One company 5/60th	64

Kemmis's Brigade:

1/40th Foot	745
97th Foot	502
2nd batt. of Detachments	625
One company 5/60th Foot	56
Total of the 4th Division	2,960

Artillery

British: Three batteries, Lawson, Sillery, Elliot	681
German: Two batteries, Rettberg and Heyse	330
Total of Artillery	1,011
Engineers,	22
Staff Corps,	63
Total Present	20,641

TALAVERA–BRITISH LOSSES ON JULY 27, 1809

(1) In the Combat of Casa De Salinas
RegimentsKilled, wounded and missing
Cavalry:

14th Light Dragoons	1
1st Light Dragoons K.G.L.	4

3rd Division
Mackenzie's Brigade:

2/24th Foot	9
2/31st Foot	119
1/45th Foot	25

Donkin's Brigade:

5/60th Foot	27
2/87th Foot	198
1/88th Foot	64
Total	447

(2) Combat in Front of Talavera at 9 A.M.

Staff	1

1st Division
H. Campbell's Brigade:

1st Coldstream Guards	3

Cameron's Brigade:

1/61st Foot	7

Langwerth's Brigade:

1st Line batt. K.G.L.	9
2nd Line batt. K.G.L.	3
Light Companies, K.G.L.	36

Low's Brigade:

5th Line batt. K.G.L.	41
7th Line batt. K.G.L.	146

2nd Division
Tilson's Brigade:

2/48th Foot	3

R. Stewart's Brigade:

29th Foot	55
1/48th Foot	8
1st batt. Detachments	70
Artillery	2
Engineers	1
Total	385

BRITISH LOSSES AT TALAVERA ON JULY 28, 1809
Killed, wounded and missing

Staff	13
Cavalry	
Fane's Brigade	
3rd Dragoon Guards	3
4th Dragoons	12
	15
Cotton's Brigade:	
14th Light Dragoons	15
16th Light Dragoons	14
	29
Anson's Brigade:	
1st Light Dragoons K.G.L.	37
23rd Light Dragoons	207
	244
Infantry	
1st Division (General Sherbrooke):	
H. Campbell's Brigade:	
1st Coldstream Guards	293
1st 3rd Guards	322
	615
Cameron's Brigade:	
1/61st Foot	265
2/83rd Foot	283
	548
Langwerth's Brigade:	
1st Line batt. K.G.L.	291
2nd Line batt. K.G.L.	387
Light Companies, K.G.L.	43
	721
Low's Brigade:	
5th Line batt. K.G.L.	255
7th Line batt. K.G.L.	110
	365
2nd Division (General Hill):	
Tilson's Brigade:	
1/3rd Foot	142
2/48th Foot	68
2/66th Foot	126
	336
R. Stewart's Brigade:	
29th Foot	132
1st batt. Detachments	203
1/48th Foot	168
	503

3rd Division (General Mackenzie):	
Mackenzie's Brigade:	
2/24th Foot	343
2/31st Foot	131
1/4th Foot	158
	632
Donkin's Brigade:	
5/60th Foot	50
2/87th Foot	60
1/88th Foot	85
	195
4th Division (General A. Campbell):	
Campbell's Brigade:	
2/7th Foot	65
2/53rd Foot	39
	104
Kemmis's Brigade:	
1/40th Foot	58
97th Foot	53
2nd batt. Detachments	21
	132
Artillery	
British	32
German	34
Engineers	1
Staff Corps	2
Total	4,521

STRENGTH OF THE FRENCH ARMY AT TALAVERA
(Figures of July 15,
excluding sick and men detached.)
Strength

1st Corps, Marshal Victor:
1st Division (Ruffin), 9th Léger, 24th and 96th of the Line, three batts. each
2nd Division (Lapisse), 16th Léger, 8th, 45th, 54th of the Line, three batts. each
3rd Division (Villatte), 27th Léger, 63rd, 94th, 95th of the Line, three batts. each
Corps-Cavalry (Beaumont), 2nd Hussars, 5th Chasseurs

19,310

4th Corps, General Sebastiani:
1st Division (Sebastiani), 28th, 32nd, 58th, 75th of the Line, three batts. each
2nd Division (Valence), one regiment only, 4th Polish, two batts.
3rd Division (Leval), Nassau, Baden, Hesse-Darmstadt, Holland, two batts. each: Frankfort, one batt.
Merlin's Light Cavalry, 10th and 26th Chasseurs, Polish Lancers, Westphalian Chevaux-Légers

15,456

Reserve Cavalry:
1st Dragoon Division (Latour-Maubourg),
1st, 2nd, 4th, 9th, 14th, 26th Dragoons
2nd Dragoon Division (Milhaud), 5th, 12th,
16th, 20th, 21st Dragoons, and 3rd Dutch
Hussars

                  5,635

From Madrid:
One Brigade of Dessolles' Division, 12th
Léger, 51st Line, three batts. each
King's Guards, infantry
King's Guards, cavalry
27th Chasseurs (two squadrons)

                  5,737
Total   46,138

FRENCH KILLED, WOUNDED AND MISSING

1st Corps (Marshal Victor):	
État-Major Général	1
1st Division (Ruffin)	
9th Léger	457
24th Line	567
96th Line	606
État-Major	2
	1,632
2nd Division (Lapisse)	
16th Léger	407
8th Line	437
45th Line	388
54th Line	532
État-Major	3
	1,767
3rd Division (Vilatte)	
27th Léger	189
63rd Line	40
94th Line	145
95th Line	27

	401
Corps-Cavalry (Beaumont):	
2nd Hussars	16
5th Chasseurs	23
	39
Artillery and Engineers	64
Total of 1st Corps	3,904
4th Corps (General Sebastiani):	
1st Division (Sebastiani):	
28th, 32nd, 58th, 75th Line	2,180
2nd Division (Leval):	
Baden, Hesse, Nassau,	
Holland, Frankfort	1,007
3rd Division (Valence):	
4th Polish Regiment	40
Total of 4th Corps	3,227
Cavalry Divisions	
1st Division of Dragoons	
(Latour-Maubourg):	
1st, 2nd, 4th, 9th, 14th,	
26th Dragoons	83
2nd Division of Dragoons (Milhaud):	
5th, 12th, 16th, 20th, 21st Dragoons	3
Milhaud's Artillery	3
Merlin's Light Cavalry Division:	
10th, 26th Chasseurs, Polish Lancers,	
Westphalian Chevaux-Légers	48
Total of Cavalry Divisions	137

General Totals: 45 officers, 716 rank and file killed; 220 officers, 6,081 rank and file wounded: 1 officer, 205 rank and file missing = 7,268

BRITISH BATTLE HONOURS FOR TALAVERA
3rd (Prince of Wales's) Regt. of Dragoon Guards
4th (Queen's Own) Regt. of Dragoons
14th (Duchess of York's Own) Regt. of (Light) Dragoons
16th (the Queen's) Regt. of (Light) Dragoons
1st Bn. Coldstream Regt. of Foot Guards
1st Bn. 3rd Regt. of Foot Guards
1st Bn 3rd (East Kent) Regt. of Foot (or the Buffs)
2nd Bn. 7th Regt. of Foot (Royal Fusiliers)
2nd Bn. 24th (2nd Warwickshire) Regt. of Foot
1st Bn. 61st (South Gloucestershire) Regt. of Foot
29th (Worcestershire) Regt. of Foot
2nd Bn. 31st (Huntingdonshire) Regt. of Foot
1st Bn. 40th (2nd Somersetshire) Regt. of Foot
1st Bn. 45th (Nottinghamshire) Regt. of Foot
1st Bn. 48th (Northamptonshire) Regt. of Foot
2nd Bn. 53rd (Shropshire) Regt. of Foot
5th Bn. 60th (Royal American) Regt. of Foot

2nd Bn. 66th (Berkshire) Regt. of Foot
2nd Bn. 83rd Regt. of Foot
2nd Bn. 87th (Prince of Wales's Irish) Regt. of Foot
1st Bn. 88th Regt. of Foot (Or Connaught Rangers)

THE MEDELLIN. I TOOK THIS PHOTOGRAPH HALFWAY UP THE THE SLOPES OF THE MEDELLIN, OR MORE LIKE AT THE FOOT OF THE SLOPE COMING DOWN FROM THE CASCAJAL. THIS IS THE RIGHT HAND END CLOSEST TO THE RESERVOIR.

WALKING THE BATTLEFIELD OF TALAVERA

Memories abound from the hours, days and weeks spent rushing across Spain and Portugal seeking battlefields, museums and, last but by no means least, hotels (although on two tours we took a tent and achieved a high degree of pleasure sleeping on the fields of Roncesvalles, Sorauren, Vitoria and the Nivelle, among other places-there is nothing like it for bringing one truly close to the men who did the fighting on that hallowed ground). High among those nostalgic recollections is the long haul north-east across Spain, moving from Badajoz to Talavera de la Reina, on the E4 a good road, running through the southern part of the ancient land of the Conquistadors, Estremadura, Spain's "Wild West," littered with splendid castles and elegant cathedrals, set in an atmosphere steeped in ancient echoes and ways. Coming upon the very old and intriguing town of Merida, we chanced upon perhaps the most extraordinary hotel in our experience-the Emperatriz, an incredible building of great antiquity, its interior mounting skywards in an open, chandelier-hung space, encircled by great railed galleries from which led the bedrooms. A very old town, founded in 25 B.C.., called Emeritus Augustas and known as "the Rome of Spain," today it proudly displays a Roman theatre in remarkably good state of preservation, together with sculpture, statues, columns and arches, and bearing witness to Merida's glorious past.

Further along the road to Talavera, one passes through the old town of Trujillo, its remarkable colonnaded plaza proudly surmounted by a large mounted statue of the town's famous son, the

Conquistador Pizarro, conqueror of Peru, born there in 1471. Then the eye is caught by a magnificent skyline landmark, the 16th century monastery towering over the sleepy town of Guadalupe below. Truly these picturesque Spanish towns must be counted among one's "Peninsular Pluses"!

And so to the historic battlefield of Talavera de la Reina, and today perhaps the greatest disappointment of all Peninsular fields. If Wellington himself was moved to ask what had they done to his field of Waterloo, then he would surely be brought to the verge of apoplexy by Talavera field today! On the first occasions, about twenty years past, when Talavera was visited, notes taken at the time reveal certain reservations even then:

> We moved onto the Medellin, where reality confounded minds set in patterns by reading and wargaming, as we endeavoured to identify the well-defined ridges behind which Wellington hid his troops, and noted that the reverse slopes were very gentle. On an artificial mound topping the Medellin a luxury bungalow has been built; its owner showed us an old map of the field and made mouths water with a collection of cannon-balls ploughed-up when building his house. Our respect for the Duke increased as we contemplated positions by no means as perfect as expected, showing that he had made the best out of very little. The valley over which the 23rd Light Dragoons charged is now a lake or reservoir with a dam.

Later trips were made in the knowledge that a well publicised national scandal had been caused in Spain (and to a lesser extent in Britain) when it was revealed that a motorway had been built through the centre of the battlefield, disturbing gravepits and the general topography. In 1988, after 180 years, the battlefield of Talavera again made the headlines when British newspapers carried stories heralded by "Battlefield Graves Dug Up For Motorway," and "Spain to Mark Battlefield Threatened By Motorway."

The Daily Telegraph's Tim Brown, writing from Madrid on 8 September 1988, said:

> Spain's Ministry of Defence yesterday started an urgent investigation onto why a major by-pass is being constructed through the heart of a major battlefield. Earth-moving machines and bulldozers are digging up the communal graves of thousands of British, French and Spanish soldiers at the site of the by-pass which is a year from completion. It is being built to take traffic around the town of Talavera on the main route from Madrid to Portugal. But the planned motorway cuts a wide swathe through a small valley and the higher ground, where on July 28 1809 British and Spanish troops, under General Arthur Wellesley-later the Duke of Wellington-won the battle of Talavera, forcing Napoleon's troops to retreat to Madrid.
>
> The bloody day and night battle in which more than 100,000 soldiers took part, saw the British suffer 5,500 casualties, the French more than 7,000 and the Spanish 1,500. In the few days that followed the major battle in the Peninsular War, soldiers buried the dead of all three armies in mass communal graves. Now, after 179 years, the remains of the soldiers are being unearthed and ploughed back into the ground as the valley is filled in and smoothed out to await the asphalting of the new highway. A British military historian, tells me: "When I visited the battlefield a few weeks ago there were piles of yellowing bones being shifted around by earth-diggers."
>
> The Madrid-based Wellington Society has launched a campaign calling for a monument or at least a plaque on the site, and their chairman has had a three-hour meeting with Señor Leopoldo Stampa, the Spanish Defence Ministry's Foreign Liaison Advisor and Official Historian. "He was horrified when I showed him the photographs and told him of the thousands of bones of the fallen being dug up. Señor Stampa knew about the by-pass but was unaware that the mass-graves had been dug up. He agreed that the planners had moved in on what should have been consecrated ground and that the by-pass could have been pushed a little to the north. The most we can hope for now is a little bit of land to be consecrated and on it there be a small plaque or monument to tell travellers that they are motoring over the spot where so many brave men died."
>
> The present Duke of Wellington is adding his weight to the growing campaign to prevent the battlefield being obliterated without some recognition of the men who died, and has said: "If they find relics of any sort I hope something will be done to preserve them.

In a later report, Tim Brown wrote:

> "Spain's embarrassed Ministry of Defence yesterday announced plans to save the historic battlefield of Talavera from being obliterated by a motorway bypass. Señor Stampa said the Minister for the project had give him "...the green light to mark the battlefield"
>
> Señor Stampa said, after an urgent meeting with top Ministry officials: "There will be a monument erected, possibly on the hill from where the Duke of Wellington commanded the British and Spanish troops. A small area will be consecrated around it and we will invite detachments from regiments involved in the battle. Besides British, French and Spanish troops there were also German and Dutch soldiers on both sides. We want representatives from all those countries to attend a ceremony once the motorway is finished next year."

When walking the battlefield in May 1990, the author was unable to find any trace of such a monument, although the bypass was in full use; perhaps it will have been erected, with all the promised ceremony, by the time this book is published.

On the left flank now there is a sheet of shining water held in check by an impressive dam at the foot of the Medellin. That hill still exists but can only be ascended for a small part of its height, the high railings of a private dwelling on its summit bar further access. The whole area is a mass of wheel-tracks and dumps of road-making materiel; so, after studying maps and reading notes, we gained what could only be a sketchy impression, before crossing the busy motorway and walking the flat area by the Portina, between the Medellin and the town itself, accepting that it was something to even be in the general area of one of Wellington's great triumphs.

Of course, one never visits Talavera without taking-in the Casa de Salinas from the towers of which Wellington was watching through a spyglass the approach of the French columns, so intent was he that he failed to realise that enemy skirmishers were in the courtyard below. The Duke made a hasty retreat with his Staff, narrowly escaping from a volley of French fire. Partly in ruins, the house had not changed since last visited, indeed probably not over the past 180 years, still looking peaceful and serene, a valuable piece of property.

RE-FIGHTING THE BATTLE OF TALAVERA AS A WARGAME

As no action took place in the actual battle in the area south of the Pajar down to the River Tagus, where the Spanish troops were almost impregnably positioned, it was decided to omit this area completely from the map and subsequent battle. The terrain, laid out on a 8'x4' table, was as shown on the map. The opposing forces were as follows:

The British: 1st, 2nd, 3rd, 4th Divisions. Total 164 infantry (including 12 riflemen), 29 cavalry and 3 guns. The Spanish portion of Wellesley's forces not being concerned in this section of the battle, were not represented on the table.

The French: 1st Corps (183 infantry), 4th Corps (142 infantry), Reserve infantry (51), Cavalry (22), Reserve cavalry (63), and 8 guns.

For a change, it was decided in this battle not to blindly follow what actually transpired at the Battle of the Talavera on the 28th July, 1809. The British, with the smaller force, were to defend the area west of the Portina stream whilst the French attacked with their superior numbers. Thus the British laid out in defensive positions as shown on the map. The Black Watch were on the rear slopes of the Medellin with a gun forward of them; to their left rear behind the hill were two trays of Hussars, the plain west of the river between the Medellin and the Pajar was occupied by the Fusiliers and Seaforths in double rank with a gun between them; two companies of the Dorsets garrisoned the walled farm on the Pajar whilst two Troops of Light Dragoons were behind the hill with a Howitzer. The French had a grand battery of four guns on the Cascajal north of which was their entire cavalry force together with two Regiments of infantry and a screen of Tirailleurs. Left of the Cascajal was another screen of Tirailleurs together with four infantry regiments advancing in columns with two guns. Another infantry regiment moved forward into the enclosures and were supported by two pieces of artillery.

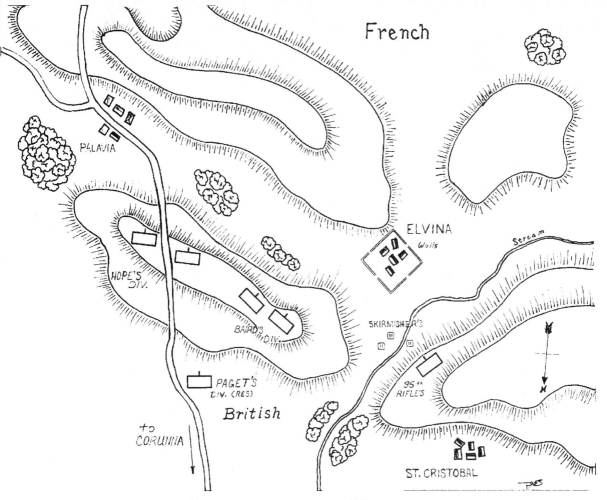

TALAVERA FOUGHT AS A WARGAME

The French made little more than threatening noises at the Pajar, engaging in a fire-fight from the western-most wall of the enclosure with the Dorsets snugly positioned behind the walls of the farm. The two Troops of Light Dragoons moved round south of the Pajar, through the trees to appear in the left/rear of the French artillery. These guns turned and fired grape at the cavalry without very great effect but it was sufficient to force the cavalry to withdraw to the shelter of the trees where they remained until the end of the battle, compelling the French infantry and artillery to watch that area rather than to advance towards the Pajar.

In the centre the French columns advanced forward to the Portina stream to be met by heavy fire from the Fusiliers and Seaforths who had stolidly awaited their arrival. The effects of this fire together with grape shot from the British gun caused three of the six French columns to withdraw, some in disorder and some under control. But the effects of this repulse were sufficient to prevent any further threat from the French in this sector. The French grand battery on the Cascajal had been firing on the solitary British gun forward on the Medellin and on the British Riflemen who had advanced across the Portina and had begun to scale the Cascajal towards the unprotected French artillery. South of the Cascajal some French Tirailleurs fired into the flank of the Rifles and this desultory action of Riflemen moving backwards and forwards across the stream continued almost throughout the battle. The solid British gun on the Medellin was so disdainful of the fire being placed upon it by the French grand battery that it turned right and poured flanking fire into the advancing French columns in the centre sector- with considerable effect!

If the French had any success at all it could be claimed to be on their right wing where two battalions of infantry came steadily across the Portina with a very large cavalry force on their right flank. The Black Watch on the rear of the Medellin, out of sight of the grand battery, turned their left flanks to face the threat coming from the north and the two lone Troops of British Hussars charged valiantly forward into the mass of French cavalry causing a melee which lasted for almost a third of the battle. Finally, however, the overwhelming strength of the French cavalry prevailed and the Hussars were either wiped out or captured.

Ten game-moves had taken place at this stage and it was decided that nightfall had arrived to put an end to any further fighting (actually, this game rather dragged over a period of three nights interspersed over six weeks!) It was clear that the French had not obtained their objectives nor were likely to except possibly in the area of the Medellin where they still had to face a completely unbroken Black Watch in their laborious climb up the steep slopes. Therefore, it was decided that the honours of battle should go to the British, as in real life. Two points were awarded to the British for retaining possession of the Medellin and one point for retaining possession of the Pajar farm whilst the French took one point for being still in possession of the Cascajal.

At this stage in the campaign the British were well ahead on points-having a total of $9^1/2$ points ($2^1/2$ for Rolica; 3 for Vimiero; 1 for Corunna and 3 for Talavera). The French had a total of $4^1/2$ points($1^1/2$ for Rolica; 1 for Vimiero; 1 for Corunna and 1 for Talavera).

The Game-Notes for the refought Talavera contain "local" rules used for both British and French:

Local Rules for British Army at Talavera.
    The blue "formation-blocks" on the British right represent the Spanish Army, which will not take part in the battle under any circumstances-but the French do not know this.
    Infantry will always fight in line
    Infantry on the Medellin, when defending against troops coming up the hill to attack them, will have 50% points bonus.
    The Artillery Battery in the right-hand farm is behind earthworks and will have 50% points bonus at all times.
    <u>Objective</u>: To defend and defeat French force from you chosen position.

Local Rules for the French Army at Talavera.
    The blue "formation-blocks" on the British right represent the Spanish Army, which will not be attacked, but will be watched in case they decide to take action.
    The Spanish on the British left-beyond the valley and behind the Medellin-will not take offensive action unless you attack them, but your tactics must take their presence into account.
    French infantry move up the actual (denoted) slopes of the Medellin at half-speed.
    British infantry on the Medellin (providing they do not move in any specified Game-Move) will fight at 50% points bonus, when defending against French coming up the hill to attack them.
    The British battery in the farm on the right flank is behind earthworks, and fights at 50% points bonus at all times.
    French heavy cavalry on your left watching the Spanish to the left of and in front of Talavera will not move until after midday (Note -Time Charts were always used) or until there is some positive change in the British formation or deployment.
    The same applies to the five heavy batteries on the Cascajal.
    French infantry will attack in column at all times.
    At the start of the battle, it is deemed that the French have deployed under cover of darkness, and they will be laid-out where they are to commence attacking from, but <u>not</u> further forward than gun-batteries on Cascajal.
    <u>Objective</u>: To attack and defeat British in their chosen position.

THE COMBAT ON THE COA–23 JULY 1810

23rd July 1810 General Craufurd's Light Division was engaged in an action usually referred to as the "Combat on the Coa." The British force numbering less than 5,000 horse, foot and guns held off French troops six times their number. Suffering some 3,000 casualties they inflicted twice that number on the enemy. It was a most gallant and successful action, and when in 1848 a medal was granted to survivors of the Peninsular War, Lt. Frederick, who lost a leg in the affair, put in a claim to it. However, he was refused the medal on the grounds that he had not been present in a "general action."

JAMES GRANT:

Sir Arthur Wellesley's position on the Guadiana, subsequent to the victory at Talavera, though somewhat to the disadvantage of his own army, checked the advance of the French into Andalusia; but the destruction of the best of the Spanish troops at the battle of Ocana, in November, 1809, together with the contemptuous neglect of Cuesta and the Junta, compelled him at last to give up for the present the prosecution of the war in Spain, to retire into Portugal, and confine his efforts to the defence of that country. The army, in consequence, crossed the Tagus.

The confident expectation of the Emperor, that "the Leopard would fly into the sea," seemed as if it was about to be realized. The withdrawal of Sir Arthur–now created Viscount Wellington– was an immediate signal for King Joseph's rapid advance upon the South; and everything seemed to indicate that the entire peninsula would become the prey of the invader.

Wellington foresaw the forthcoming invasion of Portugal and intended countering it by reorganising the Portuguese forces and the construction of massive field-works, a place of refuge for his army and the population of the land before it which, as an essential part of his plans, he intended devastating to the extent that a French army could not survive there. On 20 October 1809 he directed Colonel Fletcher, his commanding engineer in Lisbon, to draw up immediate plans for the construction of two successive lines of trenches and redoubts, stretching right across the country above Lisbon, from the Atlantic a point on the estuary of the Tagus, twenty miles north of the capital.

During the months that followed there was extensive maneuvering but little fighting, save for two disastrous Spanish defeats at Ocana and Alba de Tormes in late 1809. Wellington's army wintered in North Portugal, save for Robert Craufurd's Light Division (their new title from 1 March 1810) pushed forward to lay amid the villages around Almeida on the Spanish frontier. Here he was in contact with Ney's Corps along the line of the River Agueda, a dangerous and solitary position forty miles in advance of the main army; his orders were to retain communications with the fortress/town of Cuidad Rodrigo (Spanish garrisoned) until it fell, to cover the smaller walled town of Almeida as long as was prudent, and to keep Wellington informed of every enemy move. Here, from March to July 1810, Craufurd, in charge of the Army's whole outpost system, guarded a front of forty miles in the face of a force six times stronger than his own, without once having his line pierced or allowing Ney any indications of events to his rear.

"Since you have joined the army, I have always wished that you should command our outposts, for many reasons into which it was unnecessary to enter."
Wellington to Brigadier Craufurd Commanding the Light Division. 9th April, 1810.

Meanwhile, Ney had begun besieging Cuidad Rodrigo in late May where, despite its garrison of 5,000 being poor quality inexperienced troops under a brave elderly commander, the town

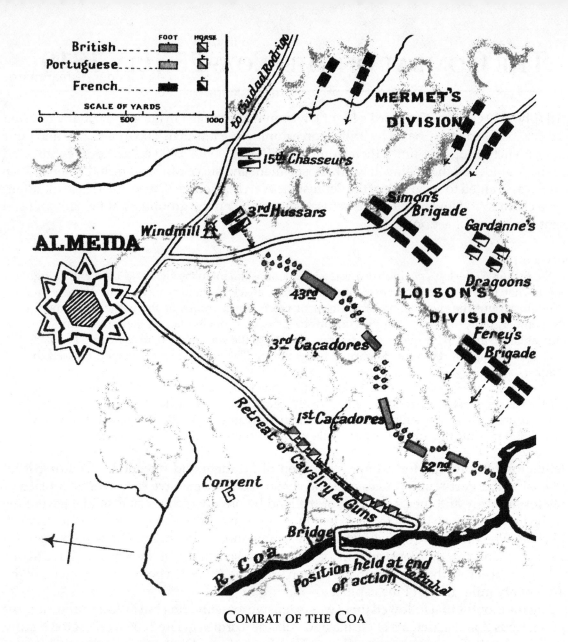

British ------ FOOT ▨ HORSE ▨
Portuguese ------ ▨ ▨
French ------ ■ ▨

SCALE OF YARDS
0 ———— 500 ———— 1000

to Ciudad Rodrigo

MERMET'S DIVISION

15th Chasseurs

3rd Hussars

ALMEIDA

Windmill

Simon's Brigade

Gardanne's

43rd

Dragoons

LOISON'S DIVISION

3rd Caçadores

Ferey's Brigade

1st Caçadores

52nd

Convent

Retreat of Cavalry & Guns

Bridge

R. Coa

Position held at end of action *to Pinhel*

COMBAT OF THE COA

held out until 10 July. Their gallant resistance cost the French about 1,200 casualties, and considerable bitterness was aroused at the failure of Wellington to make any attempt at relieving the place–rightly, he judged the odds against him and the risks of failure were too great.

Massena now wished to besiege Almeida, twenty-one miles from Cuidad Rodrigo and ordered Ney to drive Craufurd back onto that area. In the face of overwhelming numbers, Craufurd reluctantly blew-up Fort Concepcion, the isolated Spanish fortress on the frontier facing Almeida, where he had been established, and withdrew to a position on the River Coa, with his left flank on Almeida. On 22 July Wellington sent Craufurd a "strong suggestion" (not an order) that he bring his force back behind the Coa.

> "I am not desirous of engaging an affair beyond the Coa. Under these circumstances, if you are not covered from the sun where you are, would it not be better that you should come to this side of it, with your infantry at least?"
> *Wellington to Craufurd, from Alverca, 16 July 1810.*

But Craufurd, confident of his own judgment and ability, aware that the French had never attacked him with more than a division, and never at a very brisk rate, believed it would be possible, under stress, to make an orderly retreat properly covered by a moderate rearguard. So, he hung on two days longer by the glacis of Almeida, with what could have been disastrous results.

General Craufurd Commanding the Light Division was not an easy subordinate. On one occasion, Lord Wellington said, "Craufurd, you are going into a delicate situation; what orders do you wish for? I will write what you think best." Craufurd told him his own plan and went away. Whilst Lord Wellington was writing them out, and acting accordingly, Craufurd sent him word that he had done something else.
Biographical Quote

The ridge upon which Almeida stands forms the western boundary of the great upraised plain of Leon, the altitude of the town above the sea exceeding two thousand feet. The summit is broad, flat, and sound, an ideal country for cavalry, and to eastward the upland rolls away in broad billows which are furrowed by little rapid streams. But on the westward side of the fortress the ground plunges down rapidly to the gorge of the Coa; the distance from the walls to the river in a direct line being almost three thousand yards, and the difference in height over three hundred feet. The whole of its hillside is seamed by hollows, about three in every mile of ground, each carrying its trickle of water to the sea. From the southern face of the fortification there descends to the Coa a road, narrow and fairly steep indeed, but by no means bad, being for the most part paved and enclosed between fairly high stone walls. It would, however, be too slippery for horses to descend it safely at high speed, particularly after rain. This road follows a leading spur very nearly to its foot; and the final descent to the bridge, upon which Craufurd's salvation depended, is a comparatively easy slope. The ridges immediately to right and left of the leading spur both tend to converge upon the bridge. The ground along the upper part of the declivity is broken by countless vineyards, high walls, and little enclosures, but the soil steadily becomes poorer as the water is approached. The rock crops up more and more thickly through the heather and broom, the enclosures become less frequent, and for the last few hundred yards the ground is open and the rock is everywhere. At a short distance from the water the road for wheeled traffic is forced aside by many obstacles, and after turning for a little way up-stream doubles back to its final access to the bridge. But for men and pack-animals the track leads perfectly straight down, and upon each flank of this final descent to the bridge rise two rocky knolls, covered with heather and broom. The Coa itself is a boiling torrent which, at the point where the road touches it, has cleft its way through the rock and turned the valley into a chasm. The bridge consists of two lofty arches, and the roadway runs nearly forty feet above the highest flood mark. The left or western bank offers above the bridge a fairly easy slope, which becomes far steeper below; immediately opposite to the bridge itself it presents a sheer cliff over one hundred feet high.
From "History of the British Army" by Sir John Fortescue Book XIII, Ch. XXXVII

Around Almeida the vast Plains of Leon lay in a low and rolling, treeless expanse, strangely contrasting with the wild, rocky and picturesque ground where it falls away to the gorge of the River Coa, only a mile or so away, where rushing water swirls under the old curved bridge set amid rocks and fir trees. This was the stage Nature set for Craufurd's combat on the Coa, claimed by no less an authority than Fortescue to be as sharp a fight, on its own scale, as was seen in the entire course of the War.

With his left based on one of the many windmills in the area, Craufurd had his line formed across the slope of the hill, facing roughly east, his left 500/700 yards south of the town of Almeida, where half a company of the 52nd with two of Ross's guns held the windmill, then came the 43rd, followed in succession by the 95th; 1st Cacadores; 3rd Cacadores, and the remainder of the 52nd nearest to the river-the whole line in convex formation covering a front of about a mile and a half, with cavalry picquets dispersed out in front. Ney believed Craufurd's position, with the defile to its rear and only a single narrow bridge for retreat, to be faulty. Before dawn on 24th July 1810, he arranged his whole corps of 24,000 men in a broad and deep column, fronted by the two cavalry brigades of Lamotte (3rd Hussars and 15th Chasseurs) and Gardanne (15th and 25th Dragoons). Then came the thirteen battalions of Loison's Division in line of columns, behind them Mermet with eleven battalions while three regiments of Marchand's Division formed the reserve. After taking over an hour deploying for action, the French infantry then came forward rapidly as the French cavalry in line of fifteen squadrons bore down on the much smaller British mounted force to send them and Ross's advanced guns flying back over the plain. Then came the overwhelming infantry assault with Craufurd's line of three British and two Portuguese battalions being suddenly hit by Loison's thirteen battalions, coming on at the pas-de-charge, their loud cries and shouts rising above the monotonous beating of numerous drums. Their first rush was momentarily halted by rolling volleys, then the French 3rd Hussars, in bearskin caps and light-coloured pelisses, braved the gunfire from the ramparts of Almeida to sweep across the interval between Craufurd's left and the fortress walls down onto the flank of the Light Division. Flurried by this sudden charge, the gunners in Almeida fired so wildly as to cause few casualties so that the cavalry were able to fall upon a company of the 95th and then sweep along the rear of Craufurd's line, rolling it up until checked by volleys from the 43rd and from riflemen behind stone walls.

Seeing he was turned on what he thought to be his safest flank, Craufurd realised he must retreat at once, so ordered cavalry and guns to gallop to the bridge, followed by the Cacadores. The rest of the British infantry were to fall back in echelon from the left, defending each enclosure and hillock, with the 52nd holding fast on the right flank. Marching westward straight upon the British line, the French, due to the smoke and the nature of the ground, were unable to see Craufurd's enforced change of front more or less to the south. Preserving their direction they struck the British line in an oblique grazing blow. This was fortunate for Craufurd, because had the French fully hit his right at the same time as they closed with his left, they would have overwhelmed the 52nd and reached the bridge before the main body of the retreating force. Coming successively into action, Loison's battalions struck first and hardest against the British left, nearest the top of the hill; a wing of the 43rd, hotly pressed, found themselves trapped within the ten feet high stone walls of an enclosure and were only able to escape by throwing down the wall by the sheer strength of many desperate hands.

It is hard to make a fighting retreat when pressed by an overwhelming foe. The British companies dared not stand too long in a position for fear of turned flanks cutting off retreat to the bridge, besides having to watch for French cavalry who were cantering down the paved road, sabreing everyone encountered. Delayed by the sharp turn in the road near the bridge, the guns and cavalry were further impeded when an artillery caisson overturned at the bend and had to be righted by hand. At the same time they were harried by French artillery unlimbering in the rest of the ridge to pour shot down on them. They were still choking the passage of the bridge when Craufurd's left was gradually forced down upon them and the Cacadores. The situation was eased when Major McLeod of the 43rd rallied four companies on one of the pine-covered knolls which lay above the bridge, while two companies of the 95th positioned themselves on a corresponding hillock on the other side of the track. Holding firm, they allowed Craufurd to range the guns and Cacadores on the slopes on the far side of the bridge, in order to command the passage when all had crossed. Then it was seen that the five companies of the 52nd holding the right wing were still making their way along the river bank. Hoping to cut them off, the French made a supreme effort and dislodged McLeod from his knoll, but he rallied and, aided by everyone within reach, threw the French from the hillock which was held until the 52nd had reached safety. Then the rearguard dropped down from the knolls, ran swiftly across the bridge and allowed the French infantry to reoccupy the wooden eminences.

Contours at 5 metre intervals, scale 1:20,000

1 Kilometre

1 Mile

On the far bank the British infantry strung themselves out behind rocks and walls on the lower slopes commanding the bridge, with Ross's guns unlimbered on upper slopes to sweep the passage. The cavalry were sent off to watch the fords six miles south in case of an attempted enemy crossing that would cut them off. Just as a wargamer might, in the full flush of triumph, Ney decided to force the bridge, but the wargamer only loses metal figures whereas the impetuous French general was playing with flesh and blood, and first sacrificed a mounted officer in a vain attempt to find a shallow crossing of the river. French skirmishers came down to the water's edge and took cover behind rocks, engaging in a lively musketry duel with the riflemen across the river, while guns thundered at each other across the valley. Next, Ney ordered the 66th, a leading regiment of Loison's Division, to carry the bridge. Quickly they formed, and let by grenadiers the column rushed gallantly forward, to be mown down until bodies rose almost as high as the top of the bridge's parapets, before they fell back. But the blood of the fiery red-headed Ney was up and he ordered an elite battalion of picked marksmen to take the bridge, but they only added to the heaps of dead until the bridge was quite blocked. Out of 300 men, 90 were killed and 147 wounded in less than ten minutes, and a third attack by the 66th, delivered with little dash or enthusiasm, was easily beaten back.

The duel of artillery and musketry across the valley was resumed, until at four o'clock a rainstorm of tropical intensity caused it to cease. Craufurd remained in position until midnight before retiring on Pinhel, having lost 36 killed, 206 wounded, and 75 missing in an action he had handled very badly. Ney, had he been wise and contented himself with driving in the Light Division for small loss, would not have lost 527 men, mostly in mad attempts to rush the bridge.

George Simmons was 25 years of age and a Lieutenant in the 1st Battalion 95th Regiment (Rifle Corps), part of Craufurd's Light Division on the Coa in July 1810. Arriving at Lisbon on 1 July, he served with the regiment throughout the Peninsular War, arriving back in England on 22 July 1814, and was subsequently severely wounded at the Battle of Waterloo on 8 June 1815. During his entire service, George Simmons kept a journal, described by Lieutenant Colonel Willoughby Verner in his book "A British Rifleman," published in 1899 and containing Simmons' journals and his letters to his parents, written during the wars.

As regards compilation of this volume, the original journals are contained in three small pocket-books, in paper covers, measuring only a few inches square and weighing $3/4$ ounce, one ounce, and two ounces respectively. These were carried by George Simmons in his headdress throughout the wars, and hence he was always able to make notes from day to day of the events as they occurred. These small books form the framework, so to speak, of the more voluminous journals, which were evidently written subsequently, when more time was available for such a purpose.

The journal which is now published is chiefly taken from the latter, but all dates, etc. have been verified from the smaller books. Concurrently with the journal, a series of letters to his parents from the seat of war, covering the whole period between May 809 and September 1815, are here reproduced without alteration.

George Simmons wrote graphically of the Combat on the Coa on 24 July 1810, both in his Journals and in a letter to his parents:

> 23rd July 1810. Spent a jovial evening with Lieutenants Pratt and Beckwith in Almeida. About eight o'clock an officer told us that he had orders to clear the town of every person that was not to be employed in the siege, and regretted that we could not be allowed to remain longer within its walls. We drank success to their defence of the fortress, and that many Frenchmen might bite the dust before the place, shook him by the hand, and departed. We had scarcely left the town when the rain began to fall in torrents; the thunder and lightning of that night was the most tremendously grand I ever beheld either before or since. The Division, officers and man, had no

shelter from this inclement night; as to lying down, it was nearly impossible, for the water ran in gutters amongst the rocks. I sat upon a stone like a drowned rat, looking at the heavens and amusing myself with their brilliancy and longing for the morning, which came at last, and the rain ceased. Our next consideration was to set the men to work to clean their arms and look after their ammunition. Our cavalry outposts since the fall of Fort Concepcion had been on the Turon.

COMBAT OF THE COA

A little after daybreak the enemy advanced against our piquets and drove them in. The Division was put into position, the left upon Almeida and the right in rugged ground upon the Coa, which river was running furiously in its course; several companies of Rifle Men and the 43rd Light Infantry were placed behind stone walls. The enemy now advanced in vast bodies. The whole plain in our front was covered with horse and foot advancing towards us. The enemy's infantry formed line and, with an innumerable multitude of skirmishers, attacked us fiercely; we repulsed them; they came on again, yelling, with drums beating, frequently the drummers leading, often in front of the line, French officers like mountebanks running forward and placing their hats upon their swords, and capering about like madmen, saying, as they turned to their men, "Come on, children of our country. The first that advances, Napoleon will recompense him." Numbers returned to the attack. We kept up a very brisk fire. Several guns began to play upon us, and as the force kept increasing every moment in our front, and columns of infantry were also moving upon our right flank, we were ordered to retire half the company. Captain O'Hare's retired, and the remainder, under Lieutenant Johnston, still remained fighting for a few moments longer. I was with this party. We moved from the field into the road, our men falling all round us, when the body of Hussars in bearskin caps and light-coloured pelisses got amongst the few remaining Rifle Men and began to sabre them. Several attempted to cut me down, but I avoided their kind intentions by stepping on one side. I had a large cloak rolled up and strapped across my body; my haversack was filled with little necessary articles for immediate use; thus I got clear off. A volley was now fired by a party of the 43rd under Captain Wells, which brought several of the Hussars to the ground. In the scuffle I took to my heels and ran to the 43rd, Wells calling out, "Mind the Rifle Man! Do not hit him, for heaven's sake." As I was compelled to run into their fire to escape, he seized me by the hand and was delighted beyond measure at my escape. The road to a small bridge across the Coa, which the Division would have to retire over, was very bad and rocky. Our gallant fellows disputed manfully every inch of ground and retired towards the river. Every place we left was covered with the enemy's Light Infantry in ten times our number. As we got near the river the enemy made several attempts to cut us off. General Craufurd ordered a number of Rifle Men who had occupied a place that prevented the French from stopping our retreat over the bridge to evacuate it before half the 52nd, who were on the right, had filed over. The enemy directly brought up their infantry to this hill, which commanded the bridge, and kept up a terrible fire. Colonel Beckwith, a most gallant and clever soldier, saw this frightful mistake and ordered us to retake the wall and hill instantly, which we did in good style, but suffered severely in men and offices. Lieutenant Harry Smith, Lieutenant Thomas Smith, and Lieutenant Pratt were wounded, and I was shot through the thigh close to the wall, which caused me to fall with great force. Being wounded in this way was quite a new thing to me. For a few moments I could not collect my ideas, and was feeling about my arms and body for a wound, until my eye caught the stream of blood rushing through the hole in my trousers, and my leg and thigh appeared so heavy that I could not move it. Captain Napier took off his neckerchief and gave it to a sergeant, who put it round my thigh and twisted it tight with a ramrod, to stop the bleeding. The firing was so severe that the sergeant, on finishing the job for me, fell with a shot through the head. Captain Napier [William Napier, 43rd Light Infantry, the author of History of the War in the Peninsula. Ed.] was also about the same time wounded in the side. The Division had now nearly got over the bridge; some men put me into a blanket and carried me off. Our General had placed himself some distance from the fight to observe the enemy's movements. I passed him in the blanket. The General had still in his remembrance the loss of his light cart. He told the men this was no time to be taking away wounded officers, and ordered them back. They observed, "This is an officer of ours, and we must see him in safety before we leave him." The last party of our men retired over the bridge and occupied it. The ground was very rugged and rocky close to the bridge, so that Rifle Men were placed behind every stone, and two companies of the 43rd hid themselves and were ready to support our men. Several Frenchmen held up calabashes as much as to say, "Let us get some water to drink." Our men allowed some of the enemy to get water, and did not fire upon them, but the cunning rogues made lodgments between the stones, and when their party was ready to storm the bridge, they commenced firing upon our men.

A number of French officers and other drummers headed the storming party. Our fellows allowed them to come close to the bridge. Some officers got over before they fell, but few went back to tell the tale, either men or officers. They attempted to force the bridge several times before the evening, and finding it impossible to effect their purpose, they made a signal to cease firing. An officer came forward waving a white handkerchief and requested to be allowed to remove their wounded, as the bridge and its vicinity were covered with their killed and wounded. This request was granted. The officer said he had heard of the English fighting well, but he could not have supposed men would have fought against such fearful odds. He complimented our men much upon their gallantry, and observed what a pity it was we were enemies. During this day it rained occasionally, and towards evening more so, which made the arms frequently miss fire. After dark the Light Division marched to Carvalha.

A part of the 1st Hussars, under Colonel Arentschildt [Colonel Arentschildt, of the 1st German Hussars, was very kind to me and put me upon a horse, sending two Hussars to accompany me. He thought I was dying. The tears trickled down the veteran's face. God bless his memory. G.S.] was upon the road. He paid me the most kind attention and ordered a Hussar to dismount. I was placed upon the horse, and was taken on it to the church of Alverca, where I found a number of poor fellows as bad, and some worse wounded, laid in every direction upon the stone floors. A poor fellow, who died some time after I entered, begged of me to lie upon a paillasse beside him as I was upon the bare stones; he divided it with me [This soldier belonged to the 43rd Light Infantry. I was on the ground, and very ill from loss of blood; he had been placed on a paillasse of straw and was dying, but his noble nature would not allow him to die in peace when he saw an officer so humbled as to be laid near him on the bare stones. I have experienced many such kindnesses from soldiers, and indeed if I had not, I should not be alive to tell the tale. G.S.]. In the evening I was put upon a car drawn by bullocks–the most clumsy machine possible. Here now commenced my misfortunes. The car proceeded, with me upon it, to Pinhel, suffering the most severe torture from the jolting motion to my poor limb, sustained at almost every movement. I was lodged in the Bishop's house, and Colonel Pakenham behaved very kindly to me. I now became anxious to know the nature of my wounds. My trousers and drawers were cut up the side; the latter article of dress was literally glued to my thigh; in fact, I had bled so profusely that it had steeped my shirt, which stuck to my skin most unpleasantly. I found the ball had passed through the sartorius muscle and close to the main artery, directly through my thigh, partially injuring the bone. The surgeon who visited me shook his head and looked serious, recommending a tourniquet to be put round my thigh, and in case of a sudden effusion of blood to stop it by tightening the ligature until assistance was procured. A spent ball had also hit the calf of my leg, but the skin was not broken.

LISBON, 10TH AUGUST 1810

My Dear Parents–When this letter comes to hand, which I hope no unforeseen accident may prevent, it will be a means of quieting your troubles on my account. I am out of danger. I know my dear mother's affection for her graceless son. An earlier opportunity did not present itself, which you will be convinced of in the sequel.

For some time, as usual, the Light Brigade had been continually in sight of the army under the command of General Massena, numbering about 80,000, frequently partially engaged in skirmishing, which we took little notice of, being so much in the habit of it.

About the 14th of July the enemy advanced, feeling their way toward Almeida. We retired, fighting, to the right of Almeida, and took up a position, having the town on our left flank, or rather in front, and here we waited the further advance of the enemy.

On the evening of the 23rd of July, on coming off piquet, and having a mind to go once more into Almeida, a friend of mine accompanied me. After taking coffee we returned to our encampment. It began to rain most violently, attended with the most vivid lightning I ever beheld, thundering also most terrible. This would have been of little consequence, but having to sleep among the rocks without any covering from the weather, we of course were soon wet through.

On the appearance of day (about 4 o'clock A.M.) the enemy began to advance and fight with our piquets. Our Brigade immediately took up their position in the grape gardens behind walls and rocks, ready to receive them. After smoking two pipes I damned them to my Captain for not coming on faster, who laughingly said, "Stop, my boy, do not let us be in a hurry; there is time enough before night to get a broken head." Soon after this observation the French appeared in great numbers, some singing, others screaming and howling like wild beasts, their drums also beating in every direction. Our company was ordered to advance with three companies of the 43rd Light Infantry. We soon came very near the enemy, who kept up a most desperate fire. We returned a steady fire. They now advanced very near, then retired a little, and came on again several times, until our ranks became much thinned, and in our return we retired, moving more to the left, our company being ordered to protect the left of our line, as the enemy were now moving round and menacing our flank in that quarter. Our Rifle Boys brought them down like wild ducks. At this moment a shot passed through the side of a brother officer in the same company with me. He exclaimed, "Oh! Simmons, I am wounded." A horse being near, we luckily got him away; he is likely to recover. In passing a road the fire was excessively hot from their cannons, their shells bursting continually above our heads in every direction. I was coming over with the rear section of the company when suddenly 300 or more French Dragoons dashed in among us, knocked down my sergeant, and cut down three or four men. A fellow brandished his sword in the air, and was going to bring it down upon my head. I dropped mine, seeing it was useless to make resistance. He saw I was an officer, and did not cut me. I looked round me to see if I had the least chance of escaping, and pulled my boat cloak off, which was buckled round me, when fortune favoured me: some of the 43rd and our own men gave them a volley. I took advantage of their confusion, rushed through them, and got through the breach in a wall our men were firing from, pleased enough at my good fortune. We were soon engaged in every direction, retiring very slowly, until about five o'clock most of the Brigade had passed the bridge. The French now endeavoured to cut off the remainder; every place was lined with them. They now got possession of a hill near the bridge in great numbers. We were ordered to advance up the hill and drive them from the place. A party of the 43rd, with Major M'Leod at their head and several of their officers, as well as our men and officers, ran up the hill, exposed to a desperate fire, as the enemy had a strong wall to fire over. They did us much mischief before we got at them. It was a grand sight. Our brave boys would face anything. They shouted. The French became panic-struck. At this moment I had nearly come to the wall. A musket ball hit me in the middle of my left thigh, and passed through a little upwards; being so near the man that favoured me with the shot, it luckily went directly through, and took a small piece of my cloth trousers with it, at the same time I was also slightly hit in the leg. I staggered on a little, but fell; the blood spouted out on both sides. I put my hand into my pocket for my tourniquet, but fainted. Captain Napier of the 43rd, being near, twitched his handkerchief round my thigh. A sergeant of the 43rd, with three of their men, carried me off. By the time I got to the bridge I came to myself; there was a desperate fire at it. A sergeant and three of my company came to my assistance and relieved the other men. They dragged me up the hill, which was nearly a mile, up a very rocky and steep place. The blood kept pouring from my wounds. I fainted several times. The Colonel of the German Hussars gave me some wine and put me on a horse, an Hussar also with me. I sent my men back. In this way I was conveyed about a league, and put into a church, where I met with numbers of men and officers in the same plight. I was anxious to see my wound, and on examining it I thought directly I should soon want a billet in another world, but fortune has since favoured me. The large artery in my thigh is not injured. After being dressed I was put upon a car drawn by bullocks, and got into Pinhel about 10 o'clock at night, having had nothing to eat all day except some wine; it rained frequently, which made me uncomfortable.

In this way we travelled over rugged rocks and mountains until the 31st of July, about 100

English miles at least; we encamped on the river-side near a small village. The next morning we sailed down the river Mondego about seven leagues to Coimbra. Moved to Figueira next day, a seaport, and embarked on board the Nestor transport for Lisbon, at which place I arrived on the 7th of August. I have, after some trouble, got into an empty house; there is a mattress and sheets, things I have seldom of late been used to. My Colonel sent my servant after me. He is a trusty and good fellow. I have him here. As I have the house to myself, I have no one to disturb me. The people are not worthy of notice. I met with great barbarity all the way. They would let you die in the streets before they would assist you. Lisbon seems like every other place. If any of them come near to pity, it is only to rob you, if possible. I have several times on the road been robbed of the bread I was going to make a poultice of, and not had an opportunity of buying more. My thigh is much better; this day I have got a crutch made.

THE BRIDGE OVER THE RIVER COA, WITH THE ROUGH TRACK STRETCHING UPWARDS BETWEEN THE TWO KNOLLS THAT PLAYED SUCH A BIG PART IN THE COMBAT.

Fortescue provides the epilogue to Craufurd's Combat on the Coa:

Wellington was extremely and rightly annoyed at his subordinate's escapade, but he accepted his report of it and transmitted it to England without comment. Only to his brother, Wellesley Pole, did he reveal the full measure of his vexation not only over the combat of the Coa but over the other "foolish affairs in which Craufurd had involved his outposts." Yet he added, "If I am to be hanged for it, I cannot accuse a man who, I believe, has meant well, and whose error is one of judgment and not of intention; and indeed I must add that, although my errors and those of others also are visited heavily upon me, that is not the way in which any, much less a British, army can be commanded." There spoke a true ruler of men, who knows–what representative assemblies can rarely grasp–that a chief must not be extreme to mark what is done amiss by an honest and zealous subordinate. With all this faults Craufurd was a really good soldier; and it behoved a wise commander to make the best of him.

From "History of the British Army" Book XIII, Ch. XXXVII

FORCES ENGAGED:
  British, under Brigadier-General Robert Craufurd
  Cavalry: 1st Hussars King's German Legion
  16th Light Dragoons
  Infantry: 1/43rd Regiment
  1/52nd Regiment
  1/95th Regiment
  1st Portuguese Cacadores
  3rd Portuguese Cacadores
  Artillery: Captain Hew. D. Ross's Battery R.H.A.
  French, 6th Corps under command Marshal Ney

Cavalry: Lamotte's Brigade	3rd Hussars
	15th Chasseurs
Gardanne's Brigade	15th Dragoons
	20th Dragoons

  Infantry: Loison's 3rd Division

Brigade Simon	5th,6th, and 7th Battalions of 26th Ligne
	Legion du Midi
	2 bns Legion Hanoverienne
Brigade Ferey	2nd Bn of 32nd Leger
	4th, 5th, 6th Bns of 66th Ligne
	4th and 6th Bns of 82nd Ligne

  Mermet's 2nd Division

Brigade Bardet	1st and 2nd Bns 26th Leger
	1st, 2nd, 3rd Bns of 27th Ligne
Brigade Labassee	1st, 2nd, 3rd Bns of 50th Ligne
	1st, 2nd, 3rd Bns of 59th Ligne

  Reserve: Marchand's 1st Division

Brigade Maucune	1st and 2nd Bns of 8th Leger
	1st, 2nd, 3rd Bns of 69th Ligne
Brigade Marcognet	1st, 2nd, 3rd Bns 39th Ligne
	1st, 2nd, 3rd Bns. 76th Ligne

(It is known that one regiment of Marchand's Division was detached, garrisoning Cuidad Rodrigo, but it is not known which one.)
Plus Corps Artillery–details not known

Casualties:

British	Officers	Men	killed, wounded and missing
1/43rd	13	116	
1/52nd	2	20	
1/95th	10	119	
Portuguese (2 Bns)	1	44	
Cavalry	1	6	

Total: 4 Officers killed; 23 wounded; 1 missing; 32 men killed; 191 wounded; 82 missing = 333
French: Not known in detail. Said to have been 117 killed and 410 wounded, which includes 7 officers killed and 7 wounded.

AFTERMATH OF THE COMBAT ON THE COA

Craufurd's enforced retirement left the fortress of Almeida completely isolated and, on 15 August 1810, Ney's Corps began the investment, setting-up his siege-train and beginning the digging of parallels–made very difficult by thin soil and rocky ground. Almeida was a neat little fortress of six bastions, a covered way, a dry ditch cut out of solid rock, and six lunettes; nearly circular, it had a diameter of 700 yards. Its weak points were a glacis that was too low and an inadequately protected magazine situated in a dilapidated medieval castle set in the middle of the little town. The commandant was British Brigadier Cox, a capable man in the Portuguese service, who had a garrison of 5,000, half of whom were regular troops; its fortifications mounted more than 100 guns, and it was abundantly supplied. In better material condition than Cuidad Rodrigo, there seemed to be every chance of Almeida holding out for at least two months; circumstances and the nature of the ground for an approach made it almost certain that Wellington would not make any attempt to relieve the besieged town. After ten days the first parallel had been completed and eleven batteries mounted, which opened fire on 26th August and seemingly did little damage in twelve hours of firing. However, Fate stepped in and on the following morning a falling shell kindled a train of powder leaked from a barrel in its passage from the magazine to the ramparts, practically destroying the town, killing 500 men including more than half the gunners, and leaving little if any powder for the remaining guns.

Brigadier Cox had little alternative but to surrender which, after attempting to brazen things out, he did on 28 August.

> When the last of the retreating troops had passed over the bridge (of the Coa), an Irishman of the 43rd named Pigot–a bold turbulent fellow–leaned on his firelock, regarded the advancing enemy for some time, and then in the author's hearing [At that time serving in the 43rd Regiment] thus delivered his opinion of the action: "General Craufurd wanted glory, so he stopped on the wrong side of the river, and now he is knocked over to the right side. The French general won't be content until his men try to get on the wrong side also, and then they will be knocked back. Well! Both will claim a victory, which is neither here nor there, but just in the middle of the river!"
>
> Then, firing his musket he fell into the ranks. Even to the letter was his prediction verified, for General Craufurd published a contradiction of General Massena's Despatch.
>
> *From "English Battles and Sieges in the Peninsular" by Sir William Napier, at that time serving in the 43rd Regiment*

WALKING THE FIELD OF CRAUFURD'S COMBAT ON THE COA.

This is an absolute joy, to be pursued in an unhurried fashion (taking at least a very full day) and savoured like drinking a good wine because it bestows upon the industrious battlefield-walker a host of bonuses! It is known that, prior to moving onto the area outside Almeida, Craufurd's Light Division had positioned themselves in and around an isolated 18th century Spanish fortress Fort Concepcion, just inside the Spanish border facing the Portuguese fortress-town of Almeida, with the River Turonnes between them. Jac Weller had been there and photographs of the ruins adorned his book *Wellington on the Peninsular* but the author knew of no one else who had set foot in the area, which is not shown in a modern map. However, it was discovered and pinpointed in a very small-scale map in vol.VII of Fortescue's *History of the British Army*, but this lacked any of today's roads, so guesswork had to be employed to find this huge heap of military ruins we knew lay somewhere to our right as we drove up to Fuentes D'Onoro on the frontier, after an enthralling day in Cuidad Rodrigo.

Within sight of the Custom-house and barriers at the frontier, there is a small signpost pointing to the right, labelled Aldea de Obispo, some ten kilometres away-Fort Concepcion *had* to be somewhere to the left of that road or village! On our first visit two false trails over rough tracks proved useless until, working in a field, we encountered a labourer who spoke French (we spoke no Spanish) who directed us into the village of Aldea del Obispo, turn left on a track marked "Private" and the fort lay ahead on the ridge! Last time there it had been made easier by a direction sign showing the route to the Fort, which we approached in some awe! It is an extensive desolate place, massive outworks and main buildings, a huge gate still surmounted by the Spanish royal crest carved in its stonework, now in ruins through Craufurd blowing it up on 21 July 1810, on Wellington's orders as it was too remote to defend and it had to be denied to the French.

Back at Fuentes D'Onoro (to be walked later) and over the frontier into Portugal, to visit the fortress-town of Almeida, compact and picturesque, completely surrounded by low fortifications and earthworks. Seemingly it has changed little since being levelled by the vast gunpowder-magazine explosion of 1810, the ruins of the cathedral (Oman says it was a castle) wherein was situated the magazine can be walked, and around it the ramparts and embrasures are being repaired and dummy guns point threateningly from them. A State-run Pousada, a modern, comfortable place, has been conjured-up from a building of great antiquity. Visiting Almeida with a party led by David Chandler, our party was taken to an underground casemate, filled with cannon-balls of all sizes and weights, and a 6pdr ball rests proudly in the author's study to prove this!

So we walked through the gates of this pleasant historical town to find that windmill on which Craufurd's left flank was anchored, which forms perhaps the best way of orientation the whole affair. On previous occasions we had been straight to the low white windmill but, on this occasion for a while we were confused by a multiplicity of similar buildings-however, we found it in the end. Craufurd's position on the exposed ridge was not a good one, the river defile and only a single narrow bridge to his rear meant that, if attacked, he risked either being hustled down to the bridge and forced to pass the whole Light Division across it in dangerous haste, or to be thrown into Almeida and became part of the trapped garrison. Wellington would not have liked that at all, and was also conscious of the other risk so he had repeatedly warned Craufurd against becoming involved in the area. But the commander of the Light Division did not consider he was being imprudent, as his only peril lay in being attacked by overwhelming numbers without warning; this had not happened to him during the four and a half months he had defied the French 6th and 8th Corps along the banks of the Agueda when they had never attacked with much more than a division, and never at headlong speed so as to prevent an orderly withdrawal covered by a moderate rearguard. So, if he should be attacked on the Coa, Craufurd resolved to treat himself to a skillful rearguard action, not going until pushed. In all fairness, walking the ground certainly leads to the belief that it would be hard to find a more suitable battlefield for a detaining force-providing the enemy were in no more than moderate strength. There are numerous successive points to be held one after the other, and the many stone-walled enclosures dotting the area give good cover for skirmishers. So, with his left covered by the guns mounted on the walls of Almeida and his right "refused" down by the river bank, Craufurd waited to be attacked and to give the leading French brigade a sharp lesson.

On inspection, the ground on the westward side of Almeida plunges down rapidly to the gorge of the Coa, from the walls to the river is about 3,000 yards and the difference in height is over 300 feet; the town is not visible after the first mile of the descent towards the deepsunk gorge through which the river cuts its way. The whole of this hillside is seamed with hollows while the ground along the upper part is broken into small fields by walled vineyards, high walls and small enclosures; the last few hundred yards down to the river are covered with heather and broom and are plentifully rock-strewn. From the southern face of the town a narrow and steep road descended down to the bridge over the river. Enclosed within high banks and stone walls it was partly paved which made the surface, after rain, hazardous for horses. Nearing the river, the nature of the ground forced the road to turn sharply a little way upstream before doubling back to the bridge, a factor likely to present further difficulties to cavalry and guns retreating in a hurry. Descending to the river, the bridge is not visible until reaching water-level, being masked by a pine-tree covered knoll covering the bridge from attack or fire from above. These details, still almost completely applicable today, reveal that it is a difficult terrain for fighting over and one likely to hinder both attacked and defender, as it did on the day. Also, such precise and vivid details provide the wargamer with a mouthwatering project when converting his table top to this arid area.

Crossing the Coa diagonally in a gorge where the rocks on both sides are nearest top each other, the 70 yard long bridge has a curious twist in its middle where the battlefield-walker will find a little monument. Hastening to read and figure out from the Portuguese what has been said about Craufurd's fight, prepare for disappointment because it commemorates repairs made to the bridge long after the war by order of the Portuguese King John VI! Though the narrowness of the gorge causes the river to run fiercely between rocks and boulders upstream where the channel is broader, it is much less formidable-although on this visit it seemed to us to be a pretty languid, dried-up stream. However, this is no doubt caused by a startling innovation since last I was there in that the road has been diverted and a huge modern motor-bridge stretches across the Coa, completely dwarfing and overshadowing the quaint old stone bridge which, thankfully, has been allowed to remain in place.

This relatively minor engagement is stressed for wargaming purposes because it is the author's conviction, after numerous reconstructions of it, that in the whole history of warfare there can be few engagements that better lend themselves to tabletop re-creation. And what a gloss of perfection can be brought to it by first walking the field, surveying the contours, studying those spots where brisk action occurred, pin-pointing down to the actual bridge whose parapets were levelled by the bodies of dead French infantrymen.

WARGAMING THE ACTION ON THE COA

The material that follows has been extracted from the Game Notes of one of the author's Coa wargames, and it is not unreasonable to believe that the charts and diagrams are sufficiently self-explanatory to require too much explanation.

The action makes a quite superb table top battle taxing the tactical abilities of both Craufurd and Ney-the latter having knowledge of all facts including the full British strength, the former best represented by a wargamer unfamiliar with the battle so that he does not know what is going to hit him! Craufurd should be given a map and told to defend the line of the Coa with force positioned off the glacis of Almeida, if necessary making a fighting retreat over the bridge. He will have the same force as on the day, while Ney will be given Loison's thirteen battalions. Only the 3rd Hussars seem to have got among the British infantry but as both cavalry brigade (of four separate units) initially swept the British cavalry and Ross's guns before them, allow them all to be present to oppose two units of British cavalry. Ross's guns were horse artillery represented by a battery of three with the French having six battalion guns.

To avoid the French striking immediately at the British right by the river, which would quite alter the historical aspects of the battle, make an initial condition that Loison advances directly westward until making contact, then he can change his direction within two game moves.

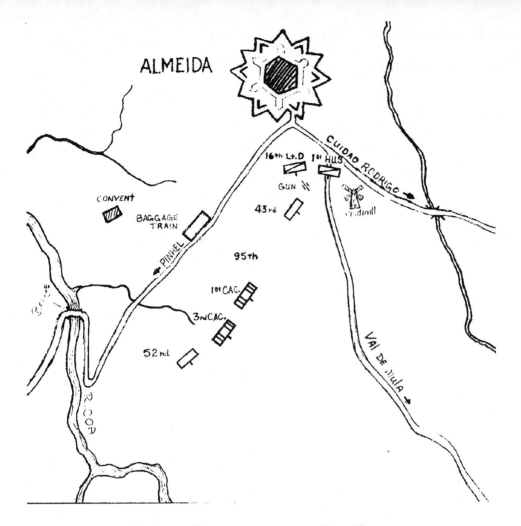

ALMEIDA

CONVENT

BAGGAGE
TRAIN

PINHEL

16th Lt.D 1st HUS

GUN

43rd

95th

1st CAC.

3rd CAC.

52nd

CUIDAD RODRIGO

Windmill

VAL DE MULA

R. COA

INITIAL DISPOSITIONS FOR COA GAME.

The ground should be littered with rocks and small enclosures.
The remaining two guns of Ross's battery can be deployed where required.
The French enter on the left.

The centre rectangle is the actual wargames table.

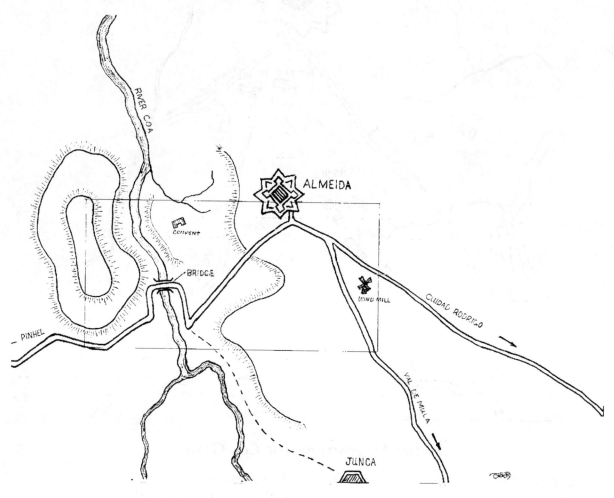

Forces: British Light Division.
Composition: See attached sheet.
Dispositions: See attached sheet.
Intention: To defend line of the Coa, positioned of the glacis of the fortress of
                     Almeida. If attacked by grossly superior numbers, to make fighting
                     retreat over bridge on Pinhel Road.
Line of Communication: Bridge over the Coa on the Pinhel Road.
Action if victorious: To hold ground.
Action if defeated: To withdraw to Pinhel.
Information on the Enemy: Ney is is the area with strong forces. He may attack and will
                     undoubtedly be in greater strength, but not by much. His intention
                     is to beseige Almeida.

General Craufurd's Force:
Light Division   95th Rifles
                     43rd Foot
                     52nd Foot
                     1st & 3rd Cacadores
                     16th Light Dragoons & 1st K.G.L. Hussars
                     Ross's Battery R.H.A. (3 guns)

The centre rectangle is the actual wargames table.

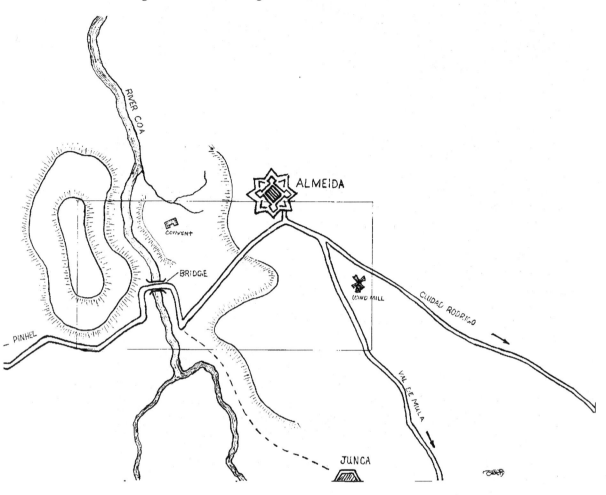

Forces:	Ney's Corps.
Composition:	See attached sheet.
	Simon's Division is beseiging Almeida on north and east.
Intention:	To attack Light Division, badly positioned in front of Almeida with only a single bridge over the Coa as line of retreat.
	On their left flank, the enemy are supported by the guns of Almeida.
Line of Communication:	To Cuidad Rodrigo.
Action if victorious:	To destroy Light Division and press on to Pinhel. Beseieg Almeida.
Action if defeated:	To withdraw to Cuidad Rodrigo.
Information on the Enemy:	The strength of the Light Division is known to be 5 battalions (3 British, 2 Poruguese), with attached cavalry and horse artillery. He will not expect an attack in such overwhelming force and will probably try a fighting withdrawal.
French forces:	Ferey's Brigade: 66th Line (3 bns), 82nd Line (3 bns), 32nd Legere (2 bns), Legion Hanoverienne (2 bns), Field Artillery (3 guns).
	Lamotte's Cavalry Brigade: 3rd Hussars, 15th Chasseurs
	Gardanne's Cavalry Brigade: 15th Dragoons, 25th Dragoons
	Horse Artillery (2 guns).

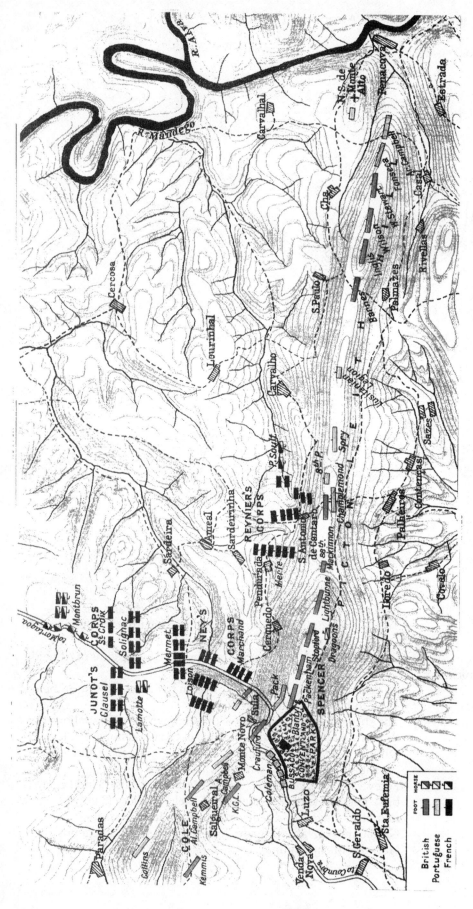

THE BATTLE OF BUSSACO. THE COMMENCEMENT OF THE FRENCH ATTACK.

THE BATTLE OF BUSACO–27 SEPTEMBER 1810

General Craufurd himself stood on the brow of the hill watching every movement of the attacking column; and when all our skirmishers had passed by and joined their respective corps, and the head of the enemy's column was within a very few yards of him, he turned round, came up to the 52nd, and called out, "Now, 52nd, revenge the death of Sir John Moore! Charge! Charge! Huzza!"; and waving his hat in the air, he was answered by a shout that appalled the enemy, and in one instant the brow of the hill bristled with 2,000 British bayonets wielded by steady English hands, which soon buried them in the bodies of the fiery Gaul!

from The Battle of Busaco, Sir George Napier

JAMES GRANT

Massena led his French armies into Portugal on 16 September 1810, in three columns led by Junot, Ney and Regnier; at the same time the Allies retreated in the finest order by the road on the left bank of the Mondego River, leaving the other road through Vizen to Coimbra open. When, after delays awaiting his artillery, Massena again advanced he found "…the rocks of the Sierra de Busaco bristling with British bayonets, and their colours waving in defiance on the summit…"

Wellington had taken up a strong position on the Sierra with the intention of fighting a spoiling action against the French Army of Portugal, in the hope of delaying their advance. This he achieved, gaining the Allies valuable time in what was said to be "a triumph of forethought and planning." Numerous salient points emerge from the action, many extremely favourable to Wellington, such as:

1. He concealed his infantry well and used the terrain with great skill.

2. His Light Infantry intercepted the French Tirailleurs on the forward slopes very effectively.

3. In what was a classic example of line versus column, the French showed they had learned few lessons from the defeats at Vimiero and Talavera.

4. Wellington's guns were said to have been placed with considerable skill, doing great damage to the advancing French. This was later disputed by an historian of the Royal Regiment, but Wellington's relations with his artillery were not always harmonious!

5. Wellington's construction of a lateral track gave him great flexibility.

6. His selection of the position rendered French guns and cavalry ineffective.

7. On the other hand, the French chose assault-routes that were dauntingly steep despite the fact that the position was one that could have been turned. Their attacks were launched without proper reconnaissance and too hastily.

8. The French continued to underestimate the worth of the new Portuguese Army, which drew great confidence from this battle. Similarly, the hand of the Home Government was greatly strengthened by the victory.

Further to 7 above. It is significant that it was Massena's outflanking movement on the following day that compelled Wellington to evacuate the position and continue his withdrawal towards the Lines of Torres Vedras..

More than 80 years ago, British Field Marshal Sir Evelyn Wood V.C., wrote a graphic description of the Battle of Busaco:

Although of no strategic importance in the Peninsular campaign, the Battle of Busaco provides many points of interest not associated with the greater and more sanguinary conflicts which had already taken place during these operations. Directly preceding, as it did, Wellington's defence of Torres Vedras, it has been described as the turning-point in the campaign which culminated in the crushing of the French power in the Peninsula.

Massena, arrogant and boastful as he was, pressed into Portugal on the heels of the Allies. Wellington ascribed his invasion of this country to the necessity for the better provisioning of his troops, and rest from the exigencies of the Spanish operations. Eleven days before the Battle of Busaco, Massena crossed the border from Spain, declaring that he would plant the Eagle upon the towers of Lisbon. Had his knowledge of the fighting powers of the British and Portuguese troops been more exhaustive, the probabilities are that he would never have offered battle at Busaco. The nature of the terrain was entirely in favour of the allies, and Massena had sustained a further handicap by having to wait two days for his artillery, which, owing to faulty maps and want of local information, had been sent a long way round. This afforded Wellington ample opportunities for strengthening his position on the wooded heights of Busaco.

All things considered, there can be little question that, had Massena hustled forward and given battle without delay, he might have pressed Wellington more than he did; but at the end of the battle, out of 52,000 Allies 33,000 had not been engaged. Hill's division had not arrived, nor would Wellington have been able, harassed by the enemy, to have occupied the splendid positions he took up, and the points of vantage for his guns. As it was, the French, on arrival at the foot of the Heights of Busaco, were met by a foe stretched in a line of nine miles across the road to Coimbra, Massena's objective, and occupying a position which no commander, save one with a poor opinion of his enemy's fighting power, would have dared to attack.

"They will never dare to attack," said one of Wellington's generals.

"If they do I shall beat them," was the response.

The position of Busaco offered no scope for the action of mounted troops. It is one of the highest points in Portugal, and from the summit of the ridge one can see for a distance of nearly fifty miles over some of the most wonderful valleys in southern Europe. On the southern and western sides the ridge is clothed with dense woods, which at that time provided ample screen for the English forces, and misled Massena as to their strength.

To the east and the north is broken ground, with deep ravines and rocky spurs, stretching away to the river Mondego on the right; and it was from this point that the French attacked. Indeed, so precipitous is the country that the employment of cavalry at any stage was almost impossible, although Wellington took six squadrons of Dragoons through the woods to the tableland at the summit in case occasion arose for their use. Moreover, both English and French artillery were prevented repeatedly during the engagement from using their fire with any effect owing to the nature of the ground.

When, late in the afternoon of September 25th, 1810, the heads of the French columns under Reynier pushed up from the banks of the Mondego and began to skirmish with Wellington's pickets, Hill had just come in from Alva, and had taken up his position on the extreme right, with Leith–who was also late in coming up with the main force–on his left, and next to him Picton, Spencer, Pack with the Portuguese regiments, and Craufurd, then Cole on the extreme left. Massena had sent Ney and Reynier forward with their army corps–Reynier leading–and held Junot's corps in reserve together with Montbrun's cavalry. At this point Massena seems to have displayed lack of initiative in attempting to gauge the extent of the Allies' forces and the nature of their position. It was left to Ney to undertake this duty. After a brief reconnaissance he consulted with Reynier, and, seeing the allied troops moving about on the heights as they took up their positions, the two Generals decided to urge Massena to attack at once. A messenger was dispatched with a letter; but Massena was ten miles to the rear, and it is said that when the messenger arrived he was in bed, and spoke to him through the door. This was on the night of the 26th. Be this as it may, Massena made no haste in response to the request of his Generals, and it was not until many hours later that, arriving at the front, he ordered Reynier to attack.

Meanwhile, on the wood-clad heights of Busaco, the Allies waited for the dawn. It was a clear night, and from points and spurs came the glow of camp fires, while Wellington passed through the woods on foot and visited the principal points of defence. A remarkable incident is recorded by Napier as having taken place in these woods that night, and, as it is borne out by other historians, there is no doubt that it contains a certain amount of truth.

In the woods on the hills the Light Division was encamped, and just before dawn these troops were seized with sudden fright, and declared that Massena's cavalry were upon them. Panic of this kind is impossible to explain, and is apt to occur even in the best-trained troops. Quite recently the writer visited this wood by night. It is an eerie spot, full of strange noises made by the rasping of aged trees and the sweep of the wind through the cavities of the hill-side. It is possible that the troops coming late into position had not realised what is at once apparent to anyone by daylight, and to trained troops in particular—that it is practically an impossibility for cavalry to attack such a position.

At daybreak on the 27th Reynier began his move in column against Picton's and Leith's positions. Ney, in the rear, was facing Wellington's centre, composed of Spencer, Packenham, Pack and Coleman's commands with Portuguese troops, and Craufurd.

Victorian military historian and writer James Grant describes the scene:

...the enemy was seen approaching from the direction of Martiago.

Nothing could be more varied, more interesting or enlivening, than the scene then viewed by our troops from the lofty heights of Busaco. As these commanded a vast prospect eastward, the movements of the French army were distinctly visible; it was impossible to conceal them from the troops stationed on the whole range of the mountain, nor did this seem to be the care of the enemy.

The rising grounds, says Leith Hay, were covered with marching troops and cannon or equipages; the wide extent of country seemed to contain a host gradually condensing into many solid masses, that were partially checked in their progress only by the base of the grand natural barrier on which the Allies were posted. It was not alone an army that was pouring forward to that base, but a multitude—cavalry, infantry, artillery, country cars, horses and mules laden with baggage, their attendants, sutlers, and camp-followers of every description.

As they drew nearer, the different uniforms of corps could be seen, the waving of the unfurled tricolors; and that peculiar cadence on the drum to which the French usually march came floating upward on the morning wind.

In the centre of the position, awaiting Reynier's assault, in McKinnon's Brigade of Picton's Division, was the 88th Regiment—the Connaught Rangers—in whose Records is this passage:

The weather was calm and fine, and the dark mountains rising on either side were crowned by innumerable fires. The French were apparently all bustle and gaiety, and following their usual avocations with as much sang-froid as if preparing for a review, not a battle. Along the whole British line, the soldiers in stern silence examined their flints, cleaned their locks and barrels, and then stretched themselves on the ground to rest, each with his firelock within his grasp. In their rear, unsheltered by any covering but his cloak, lay their distinguished leader. An hour before day on the 27th of September, Lord Wellington passed through the ranks on foot. He passed in comparative silence, for British soldiers seldom indulge in those boisterous demonstrations of joy so common with the troops of other nations, and, indeed, are rarely known to huzza except when closing with the enemy; but wherever he was recognised, his presence was felt as a sure presage of another victory, to be gained by the men whom he had already led in so many fields of triumph. To be beaten when he commanded seemed, in the opinion of his soldiers, next to impossible.

EVELYN WOOD:

Reynier opened the battle with an attack so impetuous that his riflemen reached the brow of the hill in half an hour, and several Portuguese regiments were decimated while bravely resisting the onset. In front of Picton and Leith was a vast expanse of heather-covered ground, boulder-strewn; but Craufurd and Pack had deep gullies before them which hid the French as they advanced by the steep slope. The position was commanded by 60 guns, and Reynier was ordered to choose his points of attack, but to force his way through the British position at all cost. Massena's reason in sending him first is clear. He believed that the position in front of Reynier was easier to climb than that opposite to Ney, and that the success of the former would enable him to re-form his men in the woods, and then press the Allies from the rear and crumple them up against Ney. It was a bold conception, but impracticable, for Massena was reckoning without any possibility of Reynier being defeated. Had this belief been well founded, the Allies would have been cut in half, and the direct road to Coimbra would have been in his hands. Meanwhile the only precaution Massena took against repulse was to station Junot behind Ney, with his guns laid on the intervening ground between Ney and the British position so that any British advance would necessarily be under heavy fire.

At daybreak, while thick patches of fog still clung to the woods, Reynier's fifteen battalions moved to the attack, supported by Merle's division of eleven battalions on the right.

This was said to be an elite corps, headed by three of the most distinguished regiments in the French Army–the 32nd, 36th, and 70th, and Merle himself had won the highest reputation at Austerlitz in the previous December. A writer of the day said that "…they pressed forward with such gallantry as to draw hearty plaudits from the British soldiers…"

WOOD:

Immediately the 88th (1st Connaught Rangers)–a regiment which, under the command of Colonel Wallace, later executed the most brilliant maneuver of the day–the 74th (2nd Highland Light Infantry) and the 45th (1st Sherwood Foresters) Regiments opened a heavy fire on the advancing columns, but owing to the fog its effects were not serious. Directly the fog lifted, however, the situation was rendered desperate for the French, inasmuch as they had come well within range of Arentschildt's guns, which swept away whole companies. The French thereupon bore to the right in search of shelter, and succeeded in forcing their way to the summit of the hill, scrambling up among the boulders to the plateau.

The situation at once became serious for the Allies, and had the French been in force, sufficiently under control, and physically able to push ahead after the harassing climb in the face of a murderous fire, they might have cut into Wellington's position for a time, but could never have forced it. For a moment they halted, gasping. Behind them, down the hill, was a pathway of dead and dying. It was a critical moment, and Wallace of the 88th, seeing it, decided to attack. He threw out skirmishers, called the 45th to his assistance, and, with a few hundred bayonets in line, bore down furiously upon the enemy as they were in the act of re-forming.

An account of the action, written in the mid-19th century, claims that even in the stress of the moment, Colonel Wallace found time to make a typically Victorian exhortation:

"Now, mind what I tell you! When you arrive at the spot I shall charge; and I have only to add the rest must be done by yourselves. Press on them to the muzzle; I say, Connaught Rangers, press on to the rascals!"

This animated address was said to have been received by the men with silence and a deep attention that indicated decisions and firmness.

WOOD:

The French, surprised by the determined onslaught, recoiled, gave way, and were flung back, a broken wave, against the 2nd Léger, which in its turn fell back upon the 4th Léger, and the whole in a confused mass went headlong down the slope–British, French and Portuguese mixed in a shambles of dead and dying men. It was Wallace's hour, and the quick brain of the brilliant leader averted in a few minutes of time what might have become a situation requiring some hard fighting to bring to a satisfactory conclusion.

The Regimental Record of the 88th records: "Twenty minutes sufficed to decide the question and to teach the heroes of Marengo and Austerlitz that, with every advantage of position on their side, they must yield to the Rangers of Connaught."

Lord Wellington galloped up to the 88th and, taking its Colonel by the hand, said, "Wallace, I never saw a more gallant charge than that just made by your regiment!"

VIEW OF SULA ACROSS THE VALLEY, SHOWING SLOPES UP WHICH LOISON AND
MAUCUNE ATTACKED TOWARDS SULA AND THEN UP TO THE HEIGHTS ABOVE THE
VILLAGE. THE HEIGHTS ON THE TOP LEFT WOODED SKYLINE ARE WHERE CRAUFURD WAS
POSITIONED. YOU MIGHT GET AN IMPRESSION OF THE VERY DIFFICULT TERRAIN,
ALTHOUGH IT WAS FAR LESS WOODED THEN THAN NOW.

WOOD:

Nevertheless the battle on this side was not yet over. Reynier had Foy with his seven battalions in reserve, and as Wallace pursued the broken French regiments down the hill Foy advanced. Meanwhile, on the side of the Allies, Leith was moving to the left to fill the gap that lay between his position and that of Picton, in case of any fresh attack from Reynier, although out of the regiments which Reynier was commanding there was only one which had not suffered severely.

But there yet remained Ney to be reckoned with, and Wellington had expected that he would attack the Allies' centre, hence his reason for moving Leith to the support of Picton. As a matter of fact, the attack eventually took place in very much the manner Wellington anticipated.

It is generally conceded that Massena made a grave error of judgment in waiting to see the result of Reynier's attack before ordering Ney to move. Had the Allies' centre been attacked as vehemently by Ney as was their right by Reynier, the French might have reached the summit; but they must have been beaten back by superior numbers available on the spot. Three miles separated Reynier and Ney, and the English position was so dominating that it was possible to detect every tactical move of the French as soon as it was begun.

Thus it came about that, while Leith was moving to the support of Picton, Foy with his seven fresh battalions advanced up the hill, covering the disaster which threatened Reynier, and actually making his way to the summit, where he drove in the two Portuguese regiments–the 8th and 9th. Fortunately, Leith observed Foy's advance in time to deploy the 9th (Norfolk) Regiment, which charged down the hill-side, and with the aid of the 38th (1st Staffordshire) Regiment, rolled back the French attack.

The battle of the Allies' right was now virtually over. Reynier's guns had been silenced, his regiments were broken up and in confusion, and over 2,000 dead and dying Frenchmen lay on the ground they had tried to cross; while the British casualties on this side numbered something under 700. Seeing that Reynier had failed, Massena ordered Ney to advance at once. But the order was given too late; the British regiments had reformed, and reinforcements had been brought up to the very point from which it was most difficult to dislodge them. Ney had Loison and Marchand commanding his right and left respectively, while Mermet was in command of the reserves. Marchand's orders were to advance up the hill to where the Busaco Carmelite convent stood among the trees on the summit; but at the fringe of the woods he was met by a hot fusillade from Pack's Portuguese, and was beaten back again and again. Never once did he gain footing in the woods, and he left long heaps of dead and wounded after each attack.

The brunt of the fighting now fell upon Loison. He was ordered to make his way through the village of Sula, which lies in the valley to the north-west of Busaco. This village was commanded by British artillery, well screened on the rising ground above, and in addition Craufurd had the 95th (Rifle Brigade), the 43rd (1st Oxfordshire Light Infantry), and 52nd (2nd Oxfordshire Light Infantry), and a regiment of Portuguese rifles.

JAMES GRANT:

...Crawford had made masterly arrangements. He concealed the 43rd and 52nd Regiments on a scooped platform, when the Germans, on higher ground, could support them, and some rocks overhanging the ravine he had to defend furnished natural embrasures for his cannon.

While the morning was still dark, or at least obscure, three heavy French columns entered the woods. One, led by General Marchand, on emerging from a gloomy chasm, wheeled to its left, with intent to turn the right of the division; another, under Loison, rushed straight up the face of the mountain by the road that led to the convent gate; the third remained in reserve.

WOOD:

The French, knowing that the Allies were strong at this point, did not hesitate. Directly they passed through Sula they were mown down in scores by the artillery; but they pressed on, drove in the skirmishers, crossed the sunken road, and began to climb up the side of the hill, which was unbroken save for a mule track. At this point the hill is one of the steepest inclines in the whole Busaco heights; it is strewn with slabs of rock not sufficiently high to afford cover, but extremely difficult to walk over. The writer found it trying enough to climb it at leisure; but for men carrying packs, and under artillery and rifle fire, the task must have been sufficient to test the courage of the best-trained and most courageous troops.

Loison's objective was to rush the British guns, and though the fire to which he was subjected grew hotter every yard of the way, it seemed at one time that he might accomplish his mission. He had with him two of the picked regiments of France, besides other regiments of war-hardened men, and these two alone—the 66th and the 26th—lost over 400 killed and wounded in the grim ascent.

What followed resembled very much Wallace's attack on Merle's brigade of a few hours before, only it was on a larger and grander scale.

JAMES GRANT:

...the head of the French column, all breathless and blown, and with faces begrimed by biting their cartridges, came swarming up the steep with cries of triumph.

Standing on a rock, Crawford, who had watched their approach, waved his sword, and cried, "Forty-third and Fifty-second, charge!"

Then, we are told, a "horrid shout" startled the French column, and eighteen hundred British bayonets went flashing over the brow of the hill; yet so resolute were the enemy, that each man of the first section raised his musket, and two officers and ten soldiers of the 52nd fell. But they could do no more. Unable alike to retreat or resist, they were hurled back in dreadful confusion; and, with their knapsacks and kettles, muskets and bayonets, they were rolled like a torrent of hailstones down the steep; and not the weapons only, but the very hands of our soldiers became in an instant reddened with their blood. All down the face of the hill, as day stole in, could be seen the dead and dying of Ney's attacking column, as it retired a shattered and wavering mass.

With the destruction of Ney's corps the battle was won and lost, although this latter half of the conflict lasted no more than half an hour, it was said. Reynier was crushed, and Ney's forces in such a state of demoralisation that it was hopeless to expect them to return to the conflict.

JAMES GRANT:

....The French fell back and drew off. The desultory firing of the light troops ceased; and by two o'clock in the afternoon, parties from both armies, during a brief interval of truce, were seen amicably intermingled and assisting each other in the search after the wounded, and their conveyance from a field which Massena fought unnecessarily and Wellington reluctantly.

WOOD:

Massena now realised that the capture of Busaco was almost an impossibility, and he did not even order Junot and his 13,000 fresh troops forward. He decided to withdraw and make a detour for Coimbra, and this he began to do on the 28th, masking his movement with some sharp skirmishing.

The capture of the position of Busaco was essential if Massena insisted on using the direct road to Coimbra, but his cavalry found an alternative route, which he used to turn the Allied flank. Massena's first experience in attacking English troops had taught him his lesson–so severe a lesson that, so the story goes, had it not been for a peasant who told him of the road over Caramula towards Coimbra, he would have returned to Spain.

THE ALLIED ARMY AT BUSACO

First Division. Spencer.

Stopford's Brigade.	1/Coldstream, 1/3rd Guards, 1 Co. 5/60th
Blantyre's Brigade.	2/24th, 2/42nd, 1/61st, 1 Co. 5/60th
Löwe's Brigade.	1st, 2nd, 5th, 7th Line batts., detachment L.I., K.G.L
Pakenham's Brigade.	1/7th, 1/79th
	Total 7,053

Second Division. Hill.

W. Stewart's Brigade (Colborne in command).	1/3rd, 2/31st, 2/48th, 2/66th, 1 Co. 5/60th
Inglis's Brigade.	29th, 1/48th, 1/57th, 1 Co. 5/60th
Wilson's Brigade.	2/28th, 2/34th, 2/39th, 1 Co. 5/60th
	Total 5,737

Hamilton's Portuguese Division (attached to Hill's)

Archibald Campbell's Brigade.	4th, 10th Line (each 2 batts.)
Fonseca's Brigade.	2nd and 14th Line (each 2 batts.)
	Total 4,940

Third Division. Picton.

Mackinnon's Brigade.	1/45th, 1/74th, 1/88th
Lightburne's Brigade.	2/5th, 2/83rd, 3 Cos. 5/60th
de Champlimaud's Portuguese Brigade.	9th Line (2 batts.), 21st Line (1 batt.)
	Total 4,743

Fourth Division. Cole.

Alex. Campbell's Brigade.	2/7th, 1/11th, 2/53rd, 1 Co. 5/60th
Kemmis's Brigade.	3/27th, 1/40th, old 97th, 1 Co. 5/60th
Collins's Portuguese Brigade.	11th and 23rd Line (each 2 batts.)
	Total 7,400

Fifth Division. Leith.

Barnes's Brigade.	3/1st, 1/9th, 2/38th
Spry's Portuguese.	3rd & 15th Line (each 2 batts.), Thomar Militia, 1 batt.
Eben's Portuguese.	3 batts. Lusitanian Legion
Douglas's Portuguese.	8th Line (2 batts.)
	Total 7,305

Light Division. Craufurd.
Beckwith's Brigade.   1/43rd, 4 Cos. 1/95th, 3rd Port. Caçadores
Barclay's Brigade.   1/52nd, 4 Cos. 1/95th, 1st Port. Caçadores
                                       Total 3,787

Independent Portuguese Brigades.
Pack.   1st and 6th Line (each 2 batts.),
                                       4th batt. Caçadores   2,769
H. Campbell.   6th and 18th Line (each 2 batts.),
                                       6th batt. Caçadores   3,249
Coleman.   7th and 19th Line (each 2 batts.),
                                       2nd batt. Caçadores   2,345
Cavalry.   2 squadrons 4th Dragoons   210
Artillery.   British.   Horse 332; Field 700; Total 1,032
                  K.G.L.   Field 318
                  Portuguese   (say) 600

	British	Portuguese	Total
Infantry	24,777	24,549	49,326
Cavalry	210	nil	210
Artillery	1,350	600	1,950
Total of all ranks			*51,486*

ANGLO-PORTUGUESE LOSSES AT BUSACO
(killed, wounded and missing)

1st Division (Spencer):
Stopford's Brigade:
1st Coldstream Guards   -
1/3rd Guards   2
Blantyre's Brigade:
24th Foot, 2nd Batt.   1
42nd Foot, 2nd Batt.   6
61st Foot, 1st Batt.   -
Löwe's Brigade:
1st Line batt. K.G.L.   9
2nd Line batt. K.G.L.   9
5th Line batt. K.G.L.   10
7th Line batt. K.G.L.   9
Light Companies   15
Pakenham's Brigade:
7th Foot, 1st batt.   24
79th Foot, 1st batt.   56
Divisional Loss   141
2nd Division (Hill).   No Losses
3rd Division (Picton):
Mackinnon's Brigade:
45th Foot, 1st batt.   150
74th Foot, 1st batt.   31
88th Foot, 1st batt.   134
Lightburne's Brigade:
5th Foot, 2nd batt.   8
60th Foot, 5th batt.   29
83rd Foot, 2nd batt.   5
Champlemond's Portuguese Brigade:
9th Line (two batts.)   29
21st Line (one batt.)   87
Divisional Loss   473

4th Division (Cole).   No Losses
5th Division (Leith):
Barnes's Brigade:
1st Foot, 3rd batt.   -
9th Foot, 1st batt.   24
38th Foot, 2nd batt.   23
Spry's Portuguese Brigade:
3rd and 15th Line   No Losses
Lusitanian Legion   No Losses
Portuguese 8th Line: two batts.   144
Divisional Loss   191
Light Division (Craufurd):
43rd Foot, 1st batt.   8
52nd Foot, 1st batt.   16
95th Foot, 1st batt.   41
1st Caçadores   23
3rd Caçadores   89
Divisional Loss   177
Pack's Portuguese Brigade:
1st Line (two batts.)   39
16th Line (two batts.)   33
4th Caçadores   66
Coleman's Portuguese Brigade:
7th Line (two batts.)   3
19th Line (two batts.)   37
2nd Caçadores   43
A. Campbell's Portuguese Brigade:
6th Line (two batts.)   -
18th Line (two batts.)   -
6th Caçadores   23
Total   244

Artillery:		6th Corps.	
British	8	Marchand's Division:	
K.G.L.	3	Maucune's Brigade:	
Portuguese	9	6th Léger	365
Total	*20*	69th Ligne	480
General Staff		Marcognet's Brigade:	
Grand Total	1,252	39th Ligne	235
of whom British	626	76th Ligne	93
of whom Portuguese	626	Divisional Total	1,173

an extraordinary coincidence that the two nation's loss would be the same.

FRENCH LOSSES AT BUSACO

(killed, wounded, missing/prisoners)		Mermet's Division:	
2nd Corps.		Bardet's Brigade:	
Merle's Division		25th Léger	23
Sarrut's Brigade:		27th Ligne	1
2nd Léger	308	Labassées Brigade:	
36th Ligne	483	(50th, 59th) no losses	
Graindorge's Brigade:		*Divisional Total*	*24*
4th Léger	248	Loison's Division:	
Artillery	2	Simon's Brigade:	
Divisional Total	1,041	26th Ligne	283
Heudelet's Division:		Légion du Midi	311
Foy's Brigade:		Légion Hanoverienne	217
17th Léger	353	Ferey's Brigade:	
70th Ligne	317	32nd Léger	113
Arnaud's Brigade:		66th Ligne	158
31st Léger	296	82nd Ligne	170
47th Ligne	6	*Divisional Total*	*1,252*
Artillery	6	État-Major:	7
Divisional Total	978	*Grand Total*	*2,456*

BRITISH BATTLES HONOURS FOR BUSACO
3rd Bn. 1st (or Royal) Regt. of Foot
2nd Bn. 5th (Northumberland) Regt. of Foot
1st Bn. 7th Regt. of Foot (or Royal Fuzileers)
1st Bn. 9th (East Norfolk) Regt. of Foot
2nd Bn. 24th (2nd Warwickshire) Regt. of Foot
1st Bn. 61st (South Gloucestershire) Regt. of Foot
2nd Bn. 38th (1st Staffordshire) Regt. of Foot
42nd (or Royal Highland) Regt. of Foot
1st Bn. 43rd (Monmouthshire Light Infantry) Regt.
1st Bn. 52nd (Oxfordshire Light Infantry) Regt.
1st Bn. 45th (Nottinghamshire) Regt. of Foot
5th Bn. 60th (Royal American) Regt. of Foot
1st Bn. 74th (Highland) Regt. of Foot
1st Bn. 79th Regt. of Foot (or Cameron Highlanders)
2nd Bn. 83rd Regt. of Foot
1st Bn. 88th Regt. of Foot (or Connaught Rangers)
1st Bn. 95th Regt. of Foot (or Rifle Corps)

...the French leaders were unfair to their troops. There can be no doubt that they hurried their men far to fast up the ascent. Napier says that Reynier's first attacking columns were close to the summit of the hill within half an hour after they started. This is almost incredible [I speak with some confidence, having climbed the hill of Busaco myself, over rock and heather, as did the French troops. I am not a slow mover, and I was not carrying a heavy musket, ammunition, and pack, but I should have been sorry to undertake to accomplish the ascent in much less than forty-five minutes], yet it is certain that the French infantry scaled the height with great rapidity, probably for two reasons. First, the men were mostly young soldiers [Foy wrote a fortnight before the battle, "Before the Revolution our armies were composed of men commanded by children; now they are composed of children commanded by men." Girod de l'Ain, Vie du General Foy, p. 95], eager to show themselves worthy of the famous names of their regiments; and secondly, the sharp-shooters of the Allies, pursuant to Wellington's practice, were in great strength, overmastering the French skirmishers and galling the advancing columns severely. The officers naturally hastened the men forward to end this annoyance the more quickly; and, being themselves encumbered with no heavy weights, probably set an example of speed which the men strained themselves to follow. No doubt the mounted officers, until their horse were shot–and only one horse on the French side reached the plateau–aggravated the evil.

Sir John Fortescue
"History of the British Army", Book XIII, Chap. XXXVIII

Walking the Battlefield of Busaco

Among the easiest of all Peninsular War fields to visit, Busaco is probably more forested than it was at the time of the battle. The village of Sula lays under the hot sun, and it does not need too much imagination to people it with fighting soldiers; indeed, it is possible to still find walls pockmarked by missiles fired in 1810. The Convent, later a Royal Palace, is now a luxury hotel and its imposing baroque appearance is reflected in its charges for accommodation, food and drink! Using a battle map, it is easy to find the exact spot where Craufurd stood, in solitary splendour, awaiting the French onslaught before ordering his infantry to come forward; Wellington's command post at the southern end of the ridge is market by a memorial stone (in Portuguese) and Massena's command-post is signposted and similarly marked (on the squat circular stone building). There is a small but interesting museum (closed on Mondays); a monument to the battle on the hill overlooking the ridge (near the museum) and one can see the cell in the convent where Wellington is said to have slept on the night of the battle.

It is a steep and awe-inspiring terrain and any sensible wargamer would far rather be the defending British and Portuguese than the French infantryman plodding upwards in his columns, bearing heavy pack and equipment under the undoubtedly hot sun of the late September day.

Refighting the Battle of Busaco as a Wargame

In the actual battle, the French had about 65,000 men, of whom about 50,000 were infantry, with about 6,700 cavalry strength "not known" but thought to be superior to Allies. Wellington had 24,000 British and about the same number of Portuguese infantry, with two squadrons of cavalry which took no part in the battle. Respective losses were 4,600 to the French and 1,252 Allied. For the table-top battle, the French were given 507 infantry, 84 cavalry and 16 guns; the British having 488 infantry and 9 guns.

Rather than slavishly follow the actual sequence of the original battle, with French columns blindly attacking semi-impregnable Allied lines in defensive positions, it was decided to allow each general a certain degree of initiative. A map was drawn and divided into three-a southern section stretching from the farm to the river, a middle section upwards from the farm to just below the centre field, and a northern section from that point upwards, past the crossroads. Each map constituted a separate wargames table and was to take an individual battle, the three results to be assessed in deciding the whole result. Each general was permitted to dispose of his troops as he wished on the three maps, but could only use in each battle those troops he had actually allocated to that sector. Knowing each others methods, Messrs. Dickinson and Featherstone (the Allies) showed a remarkable insight into each others tactics! In the southernmost sector, the British did not position a single man, whilst the French had only a single infantry brigade there!

This meant that the Allied southern flank rested on the Palmeiros crossroads, halfway up the middle sector, with a scattering of Rifles south of the crossroads. The Allied force for the battle in the centre sector consisted of 16 trays of infantry (12 men per try) with three guns; the French had 24 trays of infantry, 84 cavalry with seven guns under Junot and Reynier. The Allies were under Picton and Hill here. The Allied guns were placed one forward of the crossroads and one actually at that point, with the other gun at the northernmost tip of the woods on the road. The Light Companies (24 men) were in the woods and south of the crossroads. The infantry in double-lines were placed behind the crest of the ridge.

The French attacked the woods strongly, so that the 42nd were sent forward to add to the Lights; a strong attack was put in diagonally up the slopes towards the northern side of the wood and the ridge above whilst a force of infantry preceded by cavalry attacked the crossroads from the south. The British Rifles, aided by the two guns performed marvels here, throwing back two brigades of cavalry by firepower alone. In the woods, the 42nd were forced back but concentrated fire together with that of the single gun, forced the French to retire. On the extreme Allied left, a strong French cavalry attack went up the slopes to be first repulsed by the fire of Inglis's brigade but later to break through when a second Cuirassier brigade renewed the attack.

The French attacking forces seemed to have moved forward more rapidly than expected in their abortive attacks, so that when they were repulsed there was a big gap between them and the forces in support. Hence, the French did not manage to keep up a continuous assault and by judicious moving of the Seaforths and the Connaught Rangers, the Allies were able to keep an intact line until nightfall. The cavalry breakthrough on the Allied left came to nothing as a long-drawn out melee sapped both sides until nightfall brought hostilities to a close.

The last battle, as only two were fought although three 'tables' were covered by the map, brought an Allied superiority in numbers. The French put into the field 18 trays of infantry and 7 guns against the Allied 21 trays of Line infantry, 3 trays of Lights and 6 guns - neither side had any cavalry. General Massena (Neville Dickinson) whose troops were being used, had not needed much acumen to figure out he was outnumbered and expected to attack well positioned infantry, with artillery parity, on the crest of a steep ridge possessing lateral road that enabled rapid reinforcement of threatened points. The French massed in the Petit Valley area and around the field and wood at the southern end of the field. Finding the French unwilling to attack, Wellington impetuously flung two thirds of his infantry downhill at this last French grouping. A stubborn and prolonged melee ebbed and flowed for the last part of the day until nightfall brought a - not - very interesting battle to a close. Busaco as a wargame had been about as successful to the French as the actual battle of 1810.

The 'local rules' accompanying the Game Notes are as follows:

French.
Must always attack in column.
Guns cannot go up slopes, except by road, then one abreast.
Cavalry ditto; one unit abreast by road.
French come by road from Mortagoa; deploying when in sight of Busaco positions. Their cavalry are already scouting ahead and on flanks, and will be on wargames table at start.
Apart from odd movements on ridges, the British positions cannot be seen.
The French are shielded by the fog of early morning and it is an hour and a half after dawn, when they are beginning to ascend slopes, that they come into British view.
Slopes marked in red can only be climbed at half speed.

British

Wellington has troops in position and under arms by 4 a.m. (Note - Time chart essential) From the moment of seeing the French at 5.30 a.m., units may be placed on table and revealed - if units want to move from designated positions, then they have to be revealed.

French cannot move guns up slopes except by road, and then only one gun abreast; the same applies to cavalry.

Slopes marked red mean only half speed in ascending.

GENERAL CRAUFURD TELLING THE 43RD AND 52ND REGIMENTS TO CHARGE NEY'S TROOPS BELOW AS THEY NEAR THE CREST OF THE RIDGE AT BUSACO.

THE LINES OF TORRES VEDRAS—AUTUMN 1810

Finding himself outflanked at Busaco, Wellington began a slow retreat into Portugal, an act which outraged the politicians in London and his Spanish Allies. But he knew what they did not, that he had performed an extraordinary act of foresight from which neither his masters in London nor local pressure could deflect him.

In the Autumn of 1809 he had ridden secretly over a large part of Portugal to plan a huge fortress of natural geography reinforced by strategic planning. This he designed to halt the French, preserve a part of Portugal as England's bridgehead and continental base, and to provide a strongpoint for a later attack or a back door for the escape of the British Army. For he had in his control the best if not the whole of the British Army, which Britain could not afford to lose.

He rode with Colonel Fletcher of the Sappers. And then he sent him a memorandum consisting of an introduction and 21 paragraphs. Its turgid military prose and repetitions conceal a cool and clear plan.

Colonel Fletcher was left to get on with it. Fascines and timbers were ordered. Some 7,000 Portuguese peasants were employed and paid and there was local labour conscription. The British engineering staff was about 18 strong.

The lines cost the British £100,000. They protected Lisbon, cutting off a peninsular 18 miles wide. Wellesley gave orders that the rest of the country must be devastated, scorched, made impossible for the French, who made a habit of living off the country. Valleys were blocked with debris, streams damned to make swamps. The large part of a poor country was sacrificed to its survival as a nation.

Even the olive trees came down. Villages were put to the flame. This devastation was assisted by the British soldiers who, if steady in battle, were a sort of rapacious and uniformed riot when let loose in a countryside where there was wine for the broaching. Only the rich seriously protested. Once the lines were manned, Lisbon and its enclave were fed by the British Navy. Even so, 50,000 Portuguese died of starvation.

In October 1810 Wellington entered his vast fortress. Colonel Fletcher was thanked for his work and that was all. Later he got a bullet in his brain at the attack on San Sebastian.

All this 500 square miles of fortification was built in secrecy so that even the British diplomats in Lisbon knew nothing about it. Marshal Massena, the French commander, knew of it only four days before he saw it. Then it is said that his embarrassed staff excused themselves by saying that Wellington had built it. "Que diable," said the Marshal, "Wellington n'a pas construit ces montagnes."

EVELYN WOOD:

> ...Massena came, October 10th, in sight of those vast works, of which he had never heard, although he had a score of Portuguese officers and grandees on his Staff, one of whom was the principal land-owner of the country around Coimbra. The French Marshal for a whole month looked, but looked in vain, for an opening by which he might penetrate the girdle of forts. In the meantime the Portuguese Militia and Ordenanza captured his supply convoys, and his men must have starved even early in the winter had he not dispersed them widely. He sent General Foy to see the Emperor at Paris and to beg him to send reinforcements, and after a fruitless attempt to cross the Tagus, cantoned his troops at Thomar, Santarem and Punhete, where the Zerere flows into the Tagus.

Throughout these pages the recorded descriptions of the many battles and events of the Peninsular War were written by a conglomeration of military writers and historians putting pen to paper at the turn of the 19th/20th centuries. In marked contrast, the notes that follow concerning the Lines of Torres Vedras were written by a hero of World War Two, a man almost a legend in his own lifetime as a famed Commando leader and perhaps the most decorated soldier of his day. More than that–and likely to tickle the palates of the readers of this book–the late Brigadier Peter Young DSO MC MA FSA was one of the earliest of British wargamers, battling with such "tabletop" immortals as the late Charles Grant under the auspices of the British Model Soldier Society in London. In the 1960's Peter Young achieved the wargamers ambition of fighting bloodless battles with armies of soldiers moving under their own volition, by forming the first of the re-enactment societies–the 17th century Sealed Knot. At that time he was Reader in Military History and Director of War Studies at the Royal Military Academy Sandhurst in Camberley, Surrey, England, and these notes were written for a party of officer-cadets about to embark upon a tour of Peninsular War battlefields in Portugal and Spain.

So, with pride and pleasure at being able to put before the world the words written by an old friend of the author's; here is:

THE LINES OF TORRES VEDRAS
BY BRIGADIER PETER YOUNG, DSO MC MA FSA

In 1810 the French, under Massena, made their third, and last, attempt to invade Portugal. Repulsed with loss at Busaco (27 September, 1810) Massena did not reach the Lines until the 11 October, when French cavalry discovered that there was a continuous range of entrenchments from the Tagus to the Zizandre. Massena is said to have heard vaguely of the existence of the Lines as early as the 5 October, when he may have got some idea of them from prisoners. In fact, however, there great strength was a surprise to the French. Wellington had been preparing this "surprise" for about a year.

The country between Torres Vedras and Lisbon is mountainous, with abrupt peaks, deep gullies and ravines–its whole nature is rugged and inhospitable.

The front Line runs from Alhandra on the east to Rio Sao Lourenco on the west, its advanced works at Torres Vedras itself (where we hope to see the fort of Sao Vincente, which is being restored by Portuguese engineers) and Monte de Agraca. The latter, which covers the important road from Sobral to Lisbon, is also in our itinerary. The right of the Line rests on the Tagus, where Wellington had arranged for the support of a strong flotilla of gun-boats. Twenty-three redoubts, mounting ninety-six guns, had been constructed on the five-mile front between Alhandra and Arruda. Towards the Tagus a mile of the front had been flooded. For another mile the mountain had been turned into a precipice. Gullies running into the position were blocked by abatis–trees with their tops towards the enemy, their branches sharpened.

From Arruda to the west of Monte Agraca ran the second section of the Line. Monte Agraca (which was to be held by Pack's brigade, with Leith's division in reserve behind it) was crowned by a large redoubt, mounting 25 guns.

The third section, eight miles long, contained Wellington's Headquarters, at Poro Negro. There were not so many redoubts in this area as it was very rugged and contained most of the field army.

The fourth section of the first Line ran from the gorge of the Zizandre to the sea, about twelve miles, half of which had been flooded by damming the Zizandre. The fortress at Sao Vincente is the chief defence of this section of the Line. It is an entrenched camp, north of the town of Torres Vedras, covering the bridge over the Zizandre and dominating the paved road for Leiria to Lisbon. Picton's division was responsible for this sector.

The second line of defence was yet more formidable than the first, but the French never saw it and we are not going to see it either! It ran from Quintella on the Tagus to Bucellas, to Mafra, and thence to the sea – 22 miles.

A third line, two miles long, had been thrown up round Sao Juliao to cover an embarkation, should it ever become necessary. This line was manned by two battalions of the Royal Marines.

There was a similar line south of the Tagus, round Setubal.

Wellington had some 35,000 British and 24,000 Portuguese regulars, and about 12,000 Portuguese militia. In addition, there were 8000 Spaniards of La Romana's division in the lines about Mafra.

The redoubts of the first line required about 20,000 men to defend them, so that Wellington's field army was ready, and free, to act as a "mass of manoeuvre."

A chain of signal stations had been built from end to end of the lines, and lateral roads of communication had been made. The signal stations were manned by sailors, who employed the normal system then used at sea. Messages could pass all along the line in seven minutes in clear weather.

Hill's division occupied the right section of the first line. The Light Division was in the strong, but not completely fortified, country east of Monte Agraca. The 1st, 4th and 6th divisions were in the third sections.

The officer in charge of the work of building the Lines was Colonel Fletcher, RE, whose monument is still to be seen in the town of Alhandra.

The lines are an excellent illustration of Wellington's character—his foresight, patience and reticence. He had long anticipated Massena's invasion and, knowing that the French, with their almost unlimited resources, might well improve on their normally rather haphazard administrative arrangements if they learned in good time of the existence of the Lines, he issued his orders to Fletcher alone. Meanwhile, he arranged that transports should remain permanently stationed on the Tagus in case anything should go wrong, not that he ever expected that it would. His was the genius which is shown by the infinite capacity for taking pains.

The actual work in the Lines was done by gangs of Portuguese labourers and militiamen, strengthened by engineers, some of whom were Germans and Portuguese. Altogether, the Lines, consisting of well over 100 different works, mounting hundreds of guns, did not cost more than £100,000 – a pretty good investment when it meant retaining a British foothold on the continent of Europe. It is amusing to note that the unfortunate engineers were at first compelled to spend a whole day each week paying out the labourers and getting their signatures in triplicate! The numerous guns, which were obtained largely through the energy of the Portuguese general in charge of the Lisbon arsenals, were for the most part mounted on carriages of the naval type, so that if any redoubt was captured the French would be unable to make use of them as field guns, even if they had had horses available to do so.

Massena pushed forward troops of his 8th Corps on the 12 October and they drove the British outposts from Sobral. That night Wellington concentrated five British divisions and three Portuguese brigades on the Serra de Agraca front. There was skirmishing on the next two days, in which both sides had several hundred casualties, and on the 14 October Massena himself reconnoitred Monte de Agraca. Massena did not at all like the look of the allied position. The Portuguese renegades on his staff excused themselves for misinforming the Marshal by saying that the allies had thrown up the various obstructions that barred his path. "Hang it all, they did not throw up these mountains," Massena replied. Massena and his numerous staff were observed reconnoitering the British position. He could be seen examining it through a telescope, no doubt purloined from the University of Coimbra (he had offered one from the same source to Marshal Ney, who had indignantly refused the present). The British had a number of guns bearing on the wall from which Massena was observing them and eventually thought he had had enough time to do his recce. They let off one piece as a warning: the cannon-ball hit the wall. The Marshal courteously raised his cocked-hat in acknowledgment of their gentle hint, mounted his horse and rode off to his Headquarters, where, no doubt, he recounted this adventure to his mistress, a lady who accompanied him on the campaign disguised in the attractive uniform of an Officer of Dragoons.

Junot asked to be allowed to take a division and storm Monte de Agraca one morning, in the early hours, but Massena, who had not forgotten his ugly experience at Busaco, would not permit anything of the sort, nor is it probable that such an attempt would have met with much of a success.

We are told that Wellington was observing the French from the forts above Sobral one day and said, "I could lick those fellows indeed, but it would cost me 10,000 men, and as this is the last army England has, we must take care of it."

Eventually the French moved, but it was backwards! On the 10 November Massena, whose army had been dispersed for some days in all directions, looking for food, gave orders for a general retreat to Santarem.

Massena advised Napoleon that the lines were impregnable and his near-starving army quietly and secretly withdrew. Wellington was aided by some of the fiercest and most unforgiving guerrillas in the world, the Portuguese and the Spanish. They made French retreats terrible things. Wellington's intelligence from these most angry men was excellent, aided oddly and bravely by the Irish clerics in the recusant colleges of the Peninsula.

The French probing of the lines had cost both sides a few hundred casualties. But that was a therapeutic bloodletting compared with what was to come. The lines were the cheapest and most effective of victories. No retreat could pay higher dividends, no defence so punish an enemy. The front of the lines marked the Napoleonic high tide in the south. Here a deterrent worked to perfection, but a terrible cost to Portugal.

Although every hilltop in the area of Torres Vedras bears signs of crumbling fortifications, it is only San Vincente to the north that has been restored so that it is now much as it must have been when Wellington's army moved into the famous lines. Work is continuing there, currently the roof of the magazine is being re-tiled. Recalling that San Vincente must have been one of many such forts, it is truly impressive to consider how much work must have been done in relatively short time, and how much military foresight was shown by Wellington and his chief engineer, Major Richard Fletcher (later killed in 1811 at San Sebastian.)

British travel writer Martin Symington described the area in an article in the London Daily Telegraph.

Motoring north from Lisbon you cannot avoid crossing Wellington's path at the Lines of Torres Vedras, but you can easily miss them. The "Lines" consist of three series, of 100 fortified hilltops, built in 1809-10 by the Anglo-Portuguese forces under Wellington, to defend Lisbon from Napoleon's armies.

Some of the walls, ditches and gun emplacements are still intact. Many can be identified from the nearest road and a scramble up guarantees a view over the bumpy hills to the next fortification in the line on either side, or across the plain towards Vimeiro battlefield, where the French were defeated in August 1808.

The small town of Torres Vedras itself is dominated by a sturdy Moorish castle, used by Wellington, and hour's drive more or less due north brings you to the hilltop fortifications of the town of Obidos, enclosed within massive ramparts quite out of proportion to the quaint, Lilliputian town.

Not a single modern building is here to be found; instead there are scaled down versions of typically Portuguese baroque churches, and villagers squat at the base of the 40 foot walls to weed diminutive cabbage patches.

Obidos castle, at the top of the town, has been made into a pousada (a government run inn), where twelve guests can be put up in comfort. At the bottom of the town, by a formidable arched gateway, is the other tiny inn - a converted convent.

The historically inclined might continue northwards for 17 miles through vineyards, orchards of peaches and fields of honeydew melons towards Alcobaca. Here a 12th century monastery and great abbey church dwarf the rest of the small market town.

Further north again, Batalha monastery comes startlingly into sight round a bend of the main road, its church a towering monument of pale, intricately carved stone. A short distance away are both the castle of Leiria and the university city of Coimbra.

EVELYN WOOD:
The French retreat from Portugal began March 5th, all but the daily essentials of existence having been previously sent back towards Spain. Lord Wellington had just dispatched part of his army to the southward to assist Badajoz, and not expecting Massena to give way quite so soon,

THE DITCH OF FORT ST. VINCENTE, ABOVE TORRES VEDRAS

was unprepared to advance, and did not move forward till four days after the French retired. When he followed them he soon outmarched his supplies, and had to wait near Foz d'Arouce until he could get rations brought up from the mouth of the Mondego.

The French suffered terribly in this retreat, their troops having been weakened from the effects of receiving short rations during the winter. Marshal Ney commanded the rear-guard, showing daily his superb qualities for that trying position. Lord Wellington might have driven his troops in on several occasions, in spite of his masterly dispositions, but the English general's main object was to drive the French out of Portugal with the smallest loss of life to his own troops. He was always looking ahead, and wrote at this time, "Almeida and Badajoz must be retaken."

As Massena and Ney, on two different roads, retired, they were obliged again and again to sacrifice baggage, and even their battery and ammunition wagons, in order to use the horses for the gun teams. Massena during the night, March 14th-15th, ordered the destruction of all his wheeled transport except a few ammunition wagons, Marshal Ney setting the example in his own corps, by burning the carts which conveyed his personal baggage.

The 2nd and 8th Corps left Miranda de Corvo at nightfall March 14th, Ney with the 6th Corps following at 1 A.M. March 15th. Massena had ordered Ney to cross the Ceira at Foz d'Arouce, and destroy the bridge of 100 feet in length over the river which was then in flood. The Marshal, instead of doing so, kept three brigades and a cavalry regiment on the west side of the river.

The morning was foggy and Wellington would not march until it lifted, and it was therefore late in the afternoon before the 1st and 3rd Divisions, which were in front, came in sight of Ney's rear-guard, and by order of their commanders, who did not imagine that any operation would be undertaken so late in the day, were encamping, when shortly before dusk Wellington, riding up, sent them forward and surprised Ney's rear-guard, some of whom were panic-stricken.

Some companies of the 95th (Rifle Brigade), passing down a ravine, got into position close to the bridge, and drove off the 39th French Regiment, which plunged into the river, losing several men by drowning, and an Eagle, which was found later when the waters subsided. Marshal Ney retrieved the situation at the bridge by personally leading a charge which drove out the companies of the 95th, and enabled all on the west bank to recross, but with a loss of 250 men.

When Marshal Massena arrived at Guarda he cancelled his orders for the retreat on Almeida, and directed his army to prepare to cross the mountains through a roadless, uninhabited country into the valley of the Tagus.

Marshal Massena deposed Marshal Ney, who had protested vehemently against the orders, from his command, and ordered him to proceed to Valladolid and there await the Emperor's decision, and put General Loison, the senior General, in command of the 6th Corps.

General Reynier a few days later wrote, also protesting against Massena's plans, and their remonstrances were followed up by protests from Marshal Junot and General Drouet. Then Massena gave way, and recrossed the frontier into Spain, having lost in Portugal 30,000 men and nearly all his cavalry and artillery horses.

A VIEW OF FUENTES DE ONORO. IN COMPANY WITH FRIENDS OF THE 1974 TOUR, WE ARE LOOKING FROM THE FRENCH SIDE OF THE STREAM AT THE OLD TOWN.

THE BATTLE OF FUENTES DE ONORO – 5 MAY 1811

EVELYN WOOD:

Wellington, having driven the French out of Portugal, invested Almeida April 9th, and having arranged for the handling of his troops for all possible contingencies in the event of their being attacked, rode rapidly to the southward to confer with General Beresford, meeting him just as he was about to undertake the investment of the fortress of Badajoz. The two Generals reconnoitred the fortress and discussed the plans for besieging it, and then Wellington, hearing that Massena was collecting a provision convoy for Almeida, rode rapidly back to Fuentes de Onoro, where he had left his troops in a selected position some twelve miles to the south of that fortress, where he arrived April 28th-29th.

Marshal Massena, advancing May 3rd from Ciudad Rodrigo, drove back the Light Division, which, with two regiments, was posted in advance of Fuentes de Onoro on the Aguada river. Massena who brought forward 48,000 men, halted the convoy at Gallegos, 12 miles to the east of Wellington's position. When Wellington fought May 3rd and 5th, he had 8,000 less infantry, and less cavalry than half of the French horsemen.

The British position extended from the village of Fuentes de Onoro five miles to the northward to a ruin called Fort Concepcion, facing generally south-south-east. In front was the river Dos Casas, and two miles in the rear a smaller stream, the De Turon, the Coa river running nearly parallel but five miles farther back.

The village of Fuentes de Onoro, with the exception of a farm and a few houses, stood on the west side, or behind the Dos Casas, which is there broad and shallow, but the water-bed deepens as it goes northward and, gradually becoming more rugged, is a ravine over a hundred feet deep near Fort Concepcion. Two miles south of the village there is a smaller hamlet, called Pozo Bello.

JAMES GRANT:

Fuentes Onoro is situated in a mountainous district, near the right bank of the Rio das Casas; it was then a beautiful village, hitherto, until these operations, untouched by the ravages of war. It is situated in a valley, having on one side a morass, bounded by a thick forest; on the other the ground is undulating and the surface rocky. A portion of the village crowns the summit of a ravine, and rises abruptly from the river, and there its picturesque old chapel and some houses, being difficult of access, formed points for making a resolute defence. Every family in Fuentes Onoro was known to the light division, "and it was with deep regret," says Napier, "they found the preceding troops had pillaged it, leaving shells of houses where three days before a friendly population had been living in comfort. This wanton act was felt so much by the whole army that 8,000 dollars were subscribed for the inhabitants; yet the injury sunk deeper than the atonement."

WOOD:

Massena reconnoitred May 3rd, but could not be certain how Wellington's position was occupied, for he, as usual, had concealed his troops as much as possible in folds of ground, so it was difficult for the Marshal to locate them.

Wellesley was the first general to conceal troops in folds of ground, or on the reverse slope of hills, until the last moment and then to meet the enemy's column by the fire of deployed lines. The determined resolution of the British troops enabled them to crush all the serried masses they encountered; it was the front companies only of the French which could use their muskets, and they were smitten to the ground by the line opposing them face to face, generally within 60 yards, while the unscathed flanks of the line wheeling inwards poured a leaden hail on the flank and rear of the dense column, which were soon decimated. Hampered by the dead and dying they withered away in consternation and confusion, and seldom awaited the charge of bayonets they saw impending, after the last destructive volleys had been poured in, when the combatants were near enough to see the whites of their opponents' eyes.

137

WOOD:

In the afternoon Massena attacked the village with two brigades and held for a time the farm and lower houses on the stream, but was then beaten back with 600 casualties. No further attack was made next day, as General Montbrun was trying to find out the best line of attack on Wellington's right flank.

Massena, at dawn, May 5th, had 14,000 troops ready to assault Fuentes de Onoro, then held by the 71st (Highland Light Infantry) Regiment, 79th (Cameron Highlanders) Regiment with 24th (South Wales Borderers) Regiment in support, and 20,000 were assembled to the east of Pozo Bello ready to turn the British right flank. A force of guerrillas, under Sanchez, posted on the hill of Nave de Aver, was surprised at dawn, and retreating rapidly to the southward, escaped without loss. Two squadrons 14th (Hussars) Light Dragoons had moved up to the guerrillas' to bivouac during the night, 4th-5th, and made a brilliant resistance to General Montbrun's advance, never giving ground until their flanks were threatened. They were joined by two other squadrons near Pozo Bello, and resisted strenuously for an hour, when two French infantry divisions stormed Pozo Bello and the wood standing to the south of it, then held by two battalions of the 7th Division. As the infantry were leaving the wood and village they were ridden over by a Light cavalry regiment, losing 150 men, and would have been destroyed but for a gallant and opportune charge made by two squadrons King's German Legion, who, with the 14th Light Dragoons, then covered the broken infantry until they rejoined their division under General Houston. Its position was perilous, for with only two British battalions, the 51st (King's Own Yorkshire Light Infantry) Regiment and 85th (King's Shropshire Light Infantry) Regiment, which had recently joined the army in Portugal, and other newly raised Continental battalions, it was being outflanked by Montbrun's masses of cavalry.

General Robert Craufurd had only resumed command of the Light Division the previous evening, when he returned from leave of absence in England. Though much disliked by officers, the men welcomed him warmly. Wellington now sent him from where the division was lying behind Fuentes de Onoro in reserve, to cover the retirement of the 7th Division.

JAMES GRANT:

…the French cavalry came on in masses; ours retired in rear of the light division, then formed in square; and the Chasseurs Britanniques, who were ranged behind an old wall, poured upon the foe a fire so steady and deadly that they retired in disorder, with many a riderless horse. Meanwhile the enemy had made great progress in the wood near , Poco Velho; and as our divisions were separated, and the right wing turned, there were chances that the battle might be lost if the original position above Fuentes Onoro was not regained with speed. To achieve this, Lord Wellington sent the 7th division to Frenada, and made other dispositions to secure the post.

Crawford, with his light division, covered the movement of the 7th towards Frenada, and then fell back slowly in squares of battalions. The French cavalry outflanked him, and surprising a post held by Colonel Hill, of the 3rd Scots Guards, took him and his party prisoners. Continuing their course towards the 42nd Highlanders, under Lord Blantyre, they were vigorously repulsed, and swept backwards in disorder. From the higher ground about Fuentes Onoro, at this crisis, the whole of the vast plain before it appeared to be covered by a confused multitude of armed men, and amidst the dust the infantry squares seemed to shimmer like glittering specks.

The French cavalry, however, only hovered about Crawford's steady squares, and the plain was soon clear of them. They formed a reserve to the 1st division; the Rifles occupying the rocks on its right; and connecting it with the 7th division, which arrived at Frenada, and was joined by the corps of the famous Don Julian Sanchez. On beholding this new front so deeply lined with troops, Massena halted and opened a cannonade, to which the British guns replied; while a body of his infantry, which attempted to steal down a ravine where the Turones flowed, was repulsed by the light companies of the Foot Guards.

WOOD:

…The confidence Craufurd felt in his men was fully reciprocated, and while he delayed the advance of the French masses of infantry, Wellington, pivoting on Fuentes de Onoro, in military

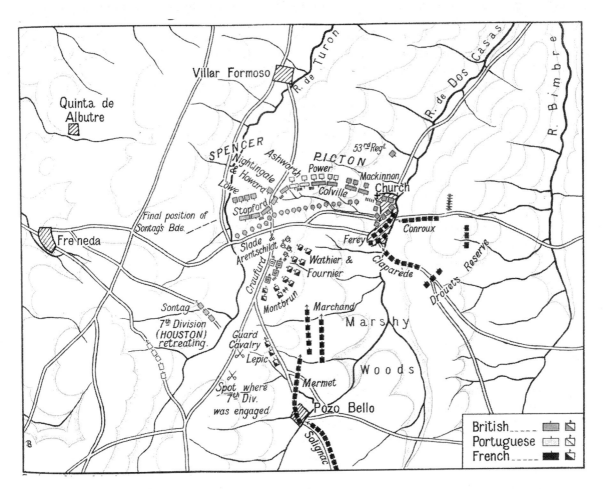

FUENTES DE ONORO. THE FRENCH ATTACK ON MAY 5TH

language, "changed front, right back," that is, he retired his right flank until it stood at almost a right angle to the troops holding Fuentes de Onoro. Craufurd's resistance was so steadfast that Wellington had ample time to occupy is new front while the Light and 7th Divisions were retiring, for the French advanced but slowly.

It is extraordinary to a cavalry student of war that Wellington should not have appreciated more highly than he did the work of his cavalry, and Major Bull's troop of Horse Artillery, at least, on May 5th. There is some dispute as to the exact numbers of sabres present, for our military authorities have for 200 years acted illogically as regards their mounted forces. We spend about three times the amount of money and time in training a horse solder more than is required to train infantry, and then, instead of utilising them all on the field of battle, we employ large numbers as messengers and attendants on general officers. At Fuentes de Onoro there should have been 1,500 cavalry soldiers in the saddle, but both Sir William Napier and Major Tomkinson give the number present as 1,000 sabres; on the other hand, there is no question but that Montbrun had 2,700 cavalry present.

French authorities have exhausted terms of eulogy in writing of this brilliant cavalry leader, calling him "le brave, l'intrépide, l'héroïque Montbrun," of whom Napoleon, writing November 3rd, 1806, says, "A cavalry leader of the first class."

General Montbrun tried again and again to ride over the British squadrons, which, assisted by Major Bull's troop, protected the 7th Division, which was retreating in squares over a sound galloping ground as Newmarket Heath, according to Sir Thomas Graham, who knew both places. The four cavalry regiments knew that they must be finally beaten, but that it was imperative for them to ride "home," especially in the earlier parts of the retreat, when it was necessary to gain time for a battalion, which had been ridden over, to re-form its ranks. The cavalry retired by alternate squadrons, and each squadron as it became in turn that nearest to the enemy, charged, and in every case drove back its opponents and pursued until its progress was arrested by the oncoming French reserves. The squadrons never got out of hand, and though they lost 157 of all ranks, only five men were taken prisoners.

Massena had, however, got 15 guns up to the front, but on the only occasion on which they unlimbered close to the retreating Light Division, Captain Knipe led his squadron, 14th Light Dragoons, directly up to the muzzles of the guns, and although he was killed in the charge and his squadron suffered terribly, the delay that the attack caused enabled the threatened squares to get away to the rear. Major Bull's troop of Horse Artillery co-operated closely with the British squadrons, continuously checking the advance of Montbrun's masses, remaining in action again and again until the attacking squadrons were close up to the guns, the detachment relying, and with good reason, on their cavalry comrades.

It was at this time the incident occurred which has been immortalised by Sir William Napier in his History. Just before the Light Division rejoined Wellington's main position. Lieutenant Ramsay, with a subdivision (section, two guns), remaining for a few last rounds of case-shot, was caught while limbering up by a regiment of French Light cavalry, which charged the section in flank.

James Grant:

The enemy, with one tremendous shock drove in all the out-guards, cut off Norman Ramsay's battery of Horse Artillery, and fell like a torrent upon the reserves and 7th division.

As their leading squadrons came somewhat confusedly on, with their horses loosely in hand, they were checked by the steady but slender band of British cavalry, and their files were seen closing in to one particular point, where tumult and disorder reigned supreme, and the flashing of sword-blades and the explosion of pistols at close quarter, and amid clouds of whirling dust, seemed to indicate some extraordinary occurrence.

Anon the British hurrah rang high in air–lances swayed to and fro–the mass of horsemen were burst asunder–and sword in hand from amid them came Norman Ramsay, at the head of his battery of flying artillery, "his horses, breathing fire, stretched like greyhounds along the plain, the guns bounding behind them like things of no weight, and the mounted gunners following close, with head bent and pointed weapons, in desperate career." (Napier)

On beholding this, Lieutenant-Colonel W. Brotherton, at the head of our 14th (or Duchess of York's Own) Light Dragoons, dashed forward to his aid, and with a single squadron checked the pursuers; while General Charles Stewart, afterwards Lord Londonderry, joining in the charge, after a hand-to-hand combat, took prisoner the French general, Lamotte.

Wood:

…Ramsay got through the French cavalry in safety, taking post in the main position amidst the cheers of the infantry.

When General Montbrun's cavalry were seen hustling the two battalions, 7th Division, out of Pozo Bello and the wood adjoining it, about two hours after daylight, General Ferey, sending several battalions at Fuentes de Onoro, drove the 71st and 79th out of the lower part of the village, but they rallied on the 24th, and with it retook the houses from which they had been driven. After this struggle, which had been severe, Ferey's leading battalions being exhausted, a pause in the operations in that quarter ensued.

General Drouet now sent in three crack battalions, composed of the Grenadier companies of all battalions of the 9th Corps. The fighting was obstinate, and the losses were heavy on both sides, but eventually the Grenadiers got up close to the top of the hill, where, however, the 24th, 71st, and 79th stood firm, and Lord Wellington now reinforced the brigade by sending to it in succession several Light companies, and later a battalion of Portuguese Riflemen.

At noon Drouet sent forward two fresh battalions, and although they were much impeded by the corpses strewn in the narrow streets of the village, and by the stern resistance of the remaining Highlanders in the houses, the French gradually pushed on, and carried the position at the church and the houses on the top slope of the hill, but there the advance was arrested.

Lord Wellington was close at hand waiting for the crisis, and now sent forward Brigadier-General McKinnon. He, leaving the 45th (1st Sherwood Foresters) in support, charged with the 74th (2nd Highland Light Infantry) and 88th (1st Connaught Rangers). The 88th, leading in column of sections, met the front of the 9th Léger at the church, and a severe struggle with the bayonet took place. While the 9th Léger, which was at the head of Conroux's division, was gradually pushed back, the 74th, charging down another lane, was followed by a cheering crowd of the remnants of the 71st, 79th, and part of the Light companies which had been supporting them. When the first backward impulse was given to the French they were driven tumultuously out of the village, some of the British troops pursuing them and being killed on the far side of the Dos Casas stream, and the French now retreated to their original position. In their attacks on the village Generals Ferey and Conroux had lost 1,300 men, while the British had 800 casualties, mainly amongst the 71st and 79th Regiments, who were engaged throughout the struggle.

JAMES GRANT:

The Highlanders, disputing every foot of ground, had been driven to the churchyard at the end of the village, where they fought hand to hand with the grenadiers of the Imperial Guard, over the tombs and graves; while the French 9th Voltigeurs had penetrated as far as the ancient chapel, and were preparing to debouch upon our centre.

Thus the enemy had actually possession of the village for a time, but their triumph was of short duration. Wellington was speedily on the spot, and, on inquiring what regiments were in reserve, on hearing the 88th named, "Is Wallace with the 88th?" he asked; and on being answered in the affirmative, he said, "Tell him to come down and drive these fellows back; he will do the thing properly."

In columns of sections, left in front, and in double-quick time, the 71st and 79th Highlanders and 88th Regiments came down the road leading to the chapel, and they were warmly cheered by the troops lying about the wall of the burying-ground. Forming line to the front, they rushed with wild cheers and levelled bayonets on the Voltigeurs and some hundreds of the Imperial Guard, casting in their fire as they advanced, and, totally overthrowing them, hurled them out of the village.

In their flight, about 150 of the Imperial Guard ran down a street the farther end of which had been barricaded by our troops on the preceding night. Shut up in a complete cul-de-sac, the result may be imagined–a frightful slaughter, but it was unavoidable. Some of the French Guards sought, vainly, a refuge by bursting into the houses, and ascending the chimneys; but they were pulled down by the heels and bayoneted. In his excitement, a lieutenant, named George Johnston, succeeded in climbing to the summit of a stone cross, in a square near the river, and taking off his cap, waved it in defiance of the enemy.

In his despatch of the battle, Wellington particularly praises the gallantry of the three regiments which cleared the village; and makes special mention of Colonel Mackinnon, who led the charge, and of Colonel Wallace and Adjutant John Stewart, of the 88th. In this affair Colonel Cameron, of the 79th, fell mortally wounded.

WOOD:

It was now 2 P.M., and the battle beginning at break of dawn, since the sun got up, had been fought during an oppressively hot day, and each time the French had assaulted they had suffered severely, while Wellington's men, with the exception of the 7th Division, being in a good position, had been more fortunate. Marshal Massena, attended by Major Pelet, his senior aide-de-camp, now dismounted, and walked up and down the whole of the front of the village of Fuentes de Onoro, looking for a spot where he might break through the defence, but found none.

General Reynier, to the north of the village, was faced by the ravine, and on its west bank stood 10,000 British troops, whom Wellington had not brought into action. The fire gradually petered out during the afternoon; the Allies had 1,800 men down, and the French 2,800. Wellington's position was strong in itself, but there can be no doubt the force of Montbrun's turning movement had been broken by Craufurd's superb handling of the Light Division and the steadfast courage of the men who, profiting by the instruction imparted by Sir John Moore, had gained in mobility

THE VILLAGE OF **F**UENTES DE **O**NORO HAS PROBABLY CHANGED LITTLE SINCE THE
BATTLE. **I**T IS STILL A MAZE OF STONE WALLS.

without losing one atom of their steadiness under fire.

When day broke, May 6th, the French were still in position, and the British troops had entrenched their front, putting the guns in pits. Marshal Massena remained on the ground he had occupied on May 4th until midnight May 7th-8th. He had realised that he could not re-provision Almeida, and was distributing the stores amongst his army, the convoy being still halted at Galleggos. He offered £240 to any soldier who would carry into Almeida instructions for the Governor. Three men came forward; two disguised themselves as Spanish peasants, and, being caught, were hanged as spies, but the third, wearing uniform, crawled down the Dos Casas ravine to the north of the ruined Fort Concepcion, and then, still on his hands and knees, he passed through standing crops into the fort, and delivered the letter to General Brennier.

The Governor was informed that he must evacuate the fort forthwith, but was directed to destroy all the guns and ammunition, and to blow up the works, firing salvoes at 10 P.M. as a sign that he understood his orders. This was done, and, at midnight Massena marched his troops back to Ciudad Rodrigo, and next day Lord Wellington sent his advanced troops to resume their position on the Agueda river, directing the 6th Division to watch Almeida, and warning the general officer in command that the French might probably try to escape. The General somewhat carelessly cantoned his division in villages three and four miles distant, and at midnight, May 10th-11th, Brennier, marching out with 1,300 men, broke through the cordon of 6,000 and escaped over the Barba del Puerco bridge. He had done well, for he had destroyed his cannon, and had blown up the fortifications.

Lord Wellington censured all concerned, describing the failure to capture the garrison, which was inevitable if his orders had been obeyed, as "a most disgraceful affair." It seems, so far as our records go, that the regimental and junior officers received censure which was more justly attributable to the two generals, and one of the lieutenant-colonels, when he learnt that his statements as to the non-receipt of orders was disbelieved, committed suicide.

The Allied Army at Fuentes D'Onoro

Slade's Brigade	
1st Dragoons	388
14th Light Dragoons	378
Arentschildt's Brigade	
16th Dragoons	362
1st Hussars K.G.L.	414
Portuguese Brigade, Barbacena	
4th Line	104
10th Line	208
Total Cavalry	*1,854*

Infantry

1st Division (Spencer)	
Stopford's Brigade	
3rd Guards, 1st batt.	959
Coldstream Guards, 1st batt.	940
1 comp. 5/60th Foot	44
Nightingale's Brigade	
24th Foot, 2nd batt.	371
42nd Foot, 2nd batt.	445
79th Foot, 1st batt.	922
1 comp. 5/60th Foot	36
Howard's Brigade	
50th Foot, 1st batt.	597
71st Foot, 1st batt.	497
92nd Foot, 1st batt.	764
3/95th Foot, 1 comp.	76
Löwe's Brigade	
1st Line Batt. K.G.L.	512
2nd Line Batt. K.G.L.	484
5th Line Bat. K.G.L.	422
7th Line Batt. K.G.L.	410
2 Light Comps. K.G.L.	86
Total 1st Division	*7,565*

3rd Division (Picton)	
Mackinnon's Brigade	
45th Foot, 1st batt.	508
74th Regiment	485
88th Foot, 2nd batt.	687
3 comps. 5/60th Foot	183
Colville's Brigade	
5th Foot, 2nd batt.	504
83rd Foot, 2nd batt.	460
88th Foot, 2nd batt.	467
94th Regiment	536
Power's Portuguese Brigade	
9th Line, 2 batts.	910
21st Line, 2 batts.	740
Total 3rd Division	*5,480*

5th Division (Erskine)	
Hay's Brigade	
1st Foot, 3rd batt.	672
9th Foot, 1st batt.	627
38th Foot, 2nd batt.	402
1 comp. Brunswick Oels	69
Dunlop's Brigade	
4th Foot, 1st batt.	612
30th Foot, 2nd batt.	507
44th Foot, 3rd batt.	437
1 comp. Brunswick Oels	68
Spry's Portuguese Brigade	
3rd Line, 2 batts.	724
15th Line, 2 batts.	556
8th Caçadores, 1 batt.	484
Total 5th Division	*5,158*

6th Division. (Campbell)	
Hulse's Brigade	
11th Foot, 1st batt.	837
53rd Foot, 2nd batt.	459
61st Foot, 1st batt.	697
1 comp. 5/60th Foot	48
Burne's Brigade	
2nd Foot	558
36th Foot, 1st batt.	514
Madden's Portuguese Brigade	
8th Line, 2 batts.	915
12th Line, 2 batts.	1,222
Total 6th Division	*5,250*

7th Division (Houston)	
Sontag's Brigade	
51st Foot, 2nd batt.	590
85th Foot	387
Chasseurs Britanniques	839
Brunswick Oels, 8 comps.	593
Doyle's (late Collins's) Brigade	
7th Line, 2 batts.	713
19th Line, 2 batts.	1,026
2nd Caçadores, 1 batt.	442
Total 7th Division	*4,590*

Light Division (Craufurd)	
Beckwith's Brigade	
43rd Foot, 1st batt.	754
95th Foot, 1st batt. (4 comps.)	354
95th Foot, 2nd batt. (1 comp.)	76
Drummond's Brigade	
52nd Foot, 1st batt.	835
52nd Foot, 2nd batt.	542
95th Foot, 4th batt. (4 comps.)	357
Portuguese	
1st Caçadores	450
3rd Caçadores	447
Total Light Division	*3,815*
Ashworth's Portuguese Brigade, unattached	
6th Line, 2 batts.	713
18th Line, 2 batts.	1,130
6th Caçadores	423

Artillery
Horse (Bull's and Ross's) 987
Field (Lawson's and Thompson's) 270
Portuguese (4 batteries) 550
Engineers 40
Train 226

Totals
Cavalry 1,854
1st Division 7,565
3rd Division 5,480
5th Division 5,158
6th Division 5,250
7th Division 4,590
Light Division 3,815
Ashworth's Portuguese 2,539
Artillery 987
Engineers 40
Train 226
Grand Total 37,504
(Total of Infantry, 34,397)

ALLIED LOSSES AT FUENTES D'ONORO

1ST DAY (Killed, wounded and missing)
1st Division. Spencer:
Nightingale's Brigade
24th Foot, 2nd batt. 2
42nd Foot, 2nd batt. 9
79th Foot, 1st batt. 25
Howard's Brigade
30th Foot, 1st batt. 5
71st Foot, 1st batt. 52
92nd Foot, 1st batt. 10
3/95th Foot, 1 comp. 10
Löwe's Brigade
1st Line batt. K.G.L. 4
2nd Line batt. K.G.L. 4
5th Line batt. K.G.L. 4
7th Line batt. K.G.L. 3
Light comps. 11
        Divisional Total 139
3rd Division. Picton:
Mackinnon's Brigade
45th Foot, 1st batt. 2
74th Foot, 1st batt. 10
88th Foot, 1st batt. 5
5/60th Foot, 3 comps. 22
Colville's Brigade
5th Foot, 2nd batt. 4
83rd Foot, 2nd batt. 12
88th Foot, 2nd batt. 6
94th Foot, 2nd batt. 3
        Divisional Total 64
Cavalry:
Slade's Brigade
1st Dragoons -

14th Light Dragoons 3
Arentschildt's Brigade
16th Light Dragoons -
1st Hussars K.G.L. 5
British General Total 211
Portuguese loss 48
(nearly all in 6th Caçadores of Ashworth's Brigade)
General Total of Allied Loss 259

SECOND DAY
1st Division. Spencer:
Stopford's Brigade
1st Coldstream Guards 63
1st Scots Fusilier Guards 72
Nightingale's Brigade
24th Foot, 2nd batt. 29
42nd Foot, 2nd batt. 25
79th Foot, 1st batt. 256
50th Foot, 1st batt. 24
Howard's Brigade
71st Foot, 1st batt. 127
92nd Foot, 1st batt. 42
3/95th Foot, 1 comp. 6
Löwe's Brigade
1st Line batt. K.G.L. 3
2nd Line batt. K.G.L. 17
5th Line batt. K.G.L. 11
7th Line batt. K.G.L. 9
Light comps. 5
Divisional Total 689
3rd Division. Picton:
Mackinnon's Brigade
45th Foot, 1st batt. 9
74th Foot, 1st batt. 59
88th Foot, 1st batt. 52
5/60th Foot, 3 comps. 14
Colville's Brigade
5th Foot, 2nd batt. 3
83rd Foot, 2nd batt. 35
88th Foot, 2nd batt. -
94th Foot, 2nd batt. 5
Divisional Total 177
5th Division. Erskine:
Hay's Brigade
1st Foot, 3rd batt. 9
9th Foot, 1st batt. 4
38th Foot, 2nd batt. -
Dunlop's Brigade
4th Foot, 1st batt. -
30th Foot, 2nd batt. 4
44th Foot, 2nd batt. 4
Divisional Total 21
6th Division. Campbell:
No losses whatever -

7th Division. Houston:
Sontag's Brigade

51st Foot, 2nd batt.	6
85th Foot, 2nd batt.	95
Chasseur's Britanniques	58
Brunswick Oels	18
Divisional Total	177

Light Division. Craufurd:
Beckwith's Brigade

43rd Foot, 1st batt.	9
1/95th Foot, 4 comps.	7

Drummond's Brigade

52nd Foot, 1st batt.	7
52nd Foot, 2nd batt.	14
2/95th Foot, 4 comps.	6
Divisional Total	43

Cavalry. Stapleton Cotton:
Slade's Brigade

1st Dragoons	41
14th Light Dragoons	38

Arentschildt's Brigade

16th Light Dragoons	27
1st Hussars K.G.L.	43
Cavalry Total	149

Artillery. Howarth:

Horse	2
Field	26
General Staff	2
British General Total of May 5th	1,286
Portuguese losses (mainly in the 2nd and 3rd Caçadores, and 6th and 21st Line)	259
Allied General Total of May 5th	1,545
Total of both days	1,804

FRENCH ARMY AT FUENTES DE OÑORO

A. ARMY OF PORTUGAL, State of May 1st
2nd Corps. Reynier
Division Merle:
Brigade Sarrut

2nd Léger (1st, 2nd, 3rd batts.)	1,867
36th Ligne (1st, 2nd, 3rd batts.)	1,650
4th Léger (1st, 2nd, 3rd batts.)	1,374
	4,891

Division Heudelet:
Brigade Godard

17th Léger (1st, 2nd, 3rd batts.)	1,224
70th Ligne (1st, 2nd, 3rd batts.)	1,073

Brigade Arnaud

31st Léger (1st, 2nd, 3rd batts.)	1,583
47th Ligne (1st, 2nd, 3rd batts.)	1,606
	5,491

Cavalry Brigade

1st Hussars	103

22nd Chasseurs	363
8th Dragoons	226
	682
Total of Corps	11,064

6th Corps. Loison
Division Marchand:
Brigade Maucune

6th Léger (1st, 2nd, 4th batts.)	1,245
69th Ligne (1st, 2nd, 4th batts.)	1,591

Brigade Chemineau

(39th Ligne (1st, 2nd, 4th batts.)	1,339
76th Ligne (1st, 2nd, 4th batts.)	1,697
	5,872

Division Mermet:
Brigade Menard

25th Léger (1st, 2nd, 4th batts.)	1,867
27th Ligne (1st, 2nd, 4th batts.)	1,820

Brigade Taupin

50th Ligne (1st, 2nd, 4th batts.)	1,413
59th Ligne (1st, 2nd, 4th batts.)	1,602
	6,702

Division Ferey:

26th Ligne (4th, 5th, 6th batts.)	1,015
Légion du Midi (1 batt.)	385
Légion Hanovrienne (1 batt.)	431
66th Ligne (4th, 5th, 6th batts.)	1,380
82nd Ligne (4th, 6th batts.)	1,031
	4,232

Light Cavalry Brigade Lamotte:

3rd Hussars	164
15th Chasseurs	170
	334
Total of Corps.	17,140

8th Corps. Junot.
[Clausel's Division absent, guarding Communications.]
Solignac's Division:

15th Ligne (1st, 2nd, 3rd batts.)	1,261
86th Ligne (1st, 2nd, 3rd batts.)	1,500
65th Ligne (1st, 2nd, 4th batts.)	1,563
Régiment Irlandais (1 batt.)	390
	4,714

9th Corps. Drouet.
Claparéde's Division:

54th Ligne (1 batt.)	284
21st Léger (1 batt.)	629
28th Léger (1 batt.)	474
40th Ligne (1 batt.)	519
63rd Ligne (1 batt.)	518
88th Ligne (1 batt.)	653
64th Ligne (1 batt.)	583
100th Ligne (1 batt.)	514
103rd Ligne (1 batt.)	542
	4,716

Conroux's Division:

16th Léger (1 batt.)	609
9th Léger (1 batt.)	760
27th Léger (1 batt.)	667
8th Ligne (1 batt.)	616
24th Ligne (1 batt.)	642
45th Ligne (1 batt.)	445
94th Ligne (1 batt.)	696
95th Ligne (1 batt.)	614
96th Ligne (1 batt.)	539
	5,588

Fournier's Cavalry Brigade:

7th Chasseurs	282
13th Chasseurs	270
20th Chasseurs	242
	794
Total of Corps	11,098

Montbrun's Reserve Cavalry:
Cavrois's Brigade

3rd Dragoons	93
10th Dragoons	138
15th Dragoons	230

Ornano's Brigade:

6th Dragoons	326
11th Dragoons	178
25th Dragoons	222
Total Reserve	1,187

Artillery

Twelve batteries with 31 officers and 931 men appear in the state of May 1 as totally destitute of horses, and were evidently left in cantonments. Five batteries were taken into the field, with 20 officers, 410 men, and 425 horses.

Total Army of Portugal:

2nd Corps, infantry and cavalry	11,064
6th Corps, infantry and cavalry	17,140
8th Corps, infantry	4,898
9th Corps, infantry and cavalry	11,098
Reserve Cavalry	1,187

Artillery	430
Sappers, Train, &c.	897
Total	46,714

B. Army of the North Marshal Bessieres
Lepic's Brigade of Guard-Cavalry

Lancers	370
Chasseurs	235
Mamelukes	79
Grenadiers a cheval	197
	881

Wathier's Light Cavalry Brigade:

11th Chasseurs	231
12th Chasseurs	181
24th Chasseurs	200
5th Hussars	172
	784
One battery of Artillery	73

Total Army of the North	1,738
Total Army of Portugal	46,714
General Total	48,452

FRENCH LOSSES AT FUENTES DE OÑORO

N.B.–I have been unable to find any detailed table by regiments in the Archives de la Guerre, or the Archives Nationales at Paris, and can only give the subjoined table of losses by corps.

Combat of May 3rd	
6th Corps	
(Divisions Ferey and Marchand)	652
Battle of May 5th	
2nd Corps (all in 31st Léger)	52
6th Corps (Divisions Ferey, Marchand, Mermet)	944
8th Corps (Division Solignac)	2
9th Corps (Divisions Conroux and Claparede)	835
Montbrun's Cavalry	359
Total	2,844

BRITISH BATTLE HONOURS FOR FUENTES D'ONORO
1st (Royal) Regt. of Dragoons
14th (Duchess of York's Own) Regt. of (Light) Dragoons
16th (the Queen's) Regt. of (Light) Dragoons
1st Bn. Coldstream Regt. of Foot Guards
1st Bn. 3rd Regt. of Foot Guards
2nd Bn. 24th (2nd Warwickshire) Regt. of Foot
2nd Bn. 42nd (Royal Highland) Regt. of Foot
1st Bn. 43rd (Monmouthshire Light Infantry) Regt.
1st & 2nd Bns. 52nd (Oxfordshire Light Infantry) Regt.

1st Bn. 45th (Nottinghamshire) Regt. of Foot
2nd Bn. 51st (2nd Yorkshire, West Riding) Regt. of Foot
85th (Bucks Volunteers) (Light Infantry) Regt.
5th Bn. (Royal American) Regt. of Foot
1st Bn. 71st (Highland) Light Infantry Regt.
74th (Highland) Regt. of Foot
92nd (Highland) Regt. of Foot
1st Bn. 79th Regt. of Foot (or Cameron Highlanders)
2nd Bn. 83rd Regt. of Foot
2nd Bn. 88th Regt. of Foot (or Connaught Rangers)
1st, 2nd & 4th Bns. 95th Regt. of Foot (or Rifle Corps)

I TOOK THIS PHOTOGRAPH NEAR THE VILLAGE OF POCO VELHO, SOUTH OF FUENTES DE ONORO, WHICH IS DIRECTLY AHEAD. THE PORTUGUESE-SPANISH BORDER IS ABOUT 50 YARDS TO MY LEFT. THIS IS ALMOST CERTAINLY THE GROUND OVER WHICH CRAUFURD AND HOUSTON WITH THEIR DIVISIONS, AND RAMSEY WITH HIS BATTERY, RETREATED IN THE FACE OF OF FIERCE FRENCH OPPOSITION.

"Lord Wellington the other day was again talking of the battle of Fuentes d'Onoro. He said that he was obliged to ride hard to escape, and thought at one time, as he was on a slow horse, that he should have been taken. The whole of head-quarters, general and all, he added, English dragoons and French dragoons, were all galloping away together across the plain, and he more than once saw a French dragoon in a green coat within 20 yards of him. One Frenchman got quite past them all, and they could not knock him off his horse. At last they caught his bridle and stopped him."
The Private Journal of Judge-Advocate Larpent

WALKING THE BATTLEFIELD OF FUENTES D'ONORO

In many ways the battlefield of Fuentes D'Onoro fully lives up to expectations, the village itself seems little changed over nearly two centuries, and if the tumbledown buildings, scattered stone walls and enclosures are not those which figured so significantly in the fierce fighting of 5 May 1811, then they must greatly resemble them. The churchyard in which the Highlanders fought hand-to-hand with the French Grenadiers has been vanquished by a modern road, but the church still stands ruminatively there, with a memorial for all to see. Imaginations working overtime, we wandered through the deserted streets, found the dried-up stream with its stone-slab footbridge, across which the French attacked, before moving up above the village to where Picton's 3rd Division and other allied formations had been positioned.

But of course, the aspect of the battle that tends to stick in the memory is the fighting retreat of the Light Division and Cotton's cavalry across two miles of open ground against greatly superior numbers, and where Norman Ramsay's troop of Horse Artillery performed their legendary charge. On the first occasion when seeking this area, we felt it necessary to cross the frontier and go into Portugal, which rather threw us because we seemed to lose the thread of the course of the battle as our coach trundled along dusty roads before passing through Portuguese and Spanish customs posts, with the mandatory passport examinations. Then we came to this rather featureless plain, where David Chandler told us was where it had all happened, and thoughts translated into transforming the area into a scene of galvanic activity. On the last occasion in the area, we drove slowly along rough tracks bordered by walled frontier signs, with the ground of Portugal within touching distance on our right hand. With three minds actively considering the problem, finally we agreed upon the area, and the car was halted while each of us painted a mental picture of green-clad riflemen in square and behind sparse cover, with the mounted General Craufurd exhorting and ordering, as fast moving Light Dragoons of Cotton's cavalry force swooped hither and thither, while Ramsay's guns and limber thundered on!

Not far from Fuentes D'Onoro is the small village of Freinada where in 1811, Wellington and his staff had their headquarters in a house that still stands and is lived-in. On one occasion a party of thirty Britons descended on the place, to create considerable tumult but also to be welcomed effusively! Taken into the house, we were invited to view the connected residences of three families and to crowd into Wellington's personal room. Discussions ensued between the local schoolmaster, who lived in part of the house, and those in the party connected officially with the British Military Historical Society, as to the chances of having a commemorative plaque installed. Revisiting Freinada some years later, the author was both gratified and proud to find just such a plaque set in the wall of the house!

FUENTES D'ONORO FOUGHT AS A WARGAME

To represent the British force of 34,000 British and British infantry, 987 cavalry and 48 guns, Don Featherstone had 348 infantry, 15 cavalry and 5 guns (1st Fusiliers, 42nd, Guards, Buffs, 88th, 43rd Light Infantry, Light Dragoons, 1 howitzer, 1 horse, and 3 field guns.) They were under Wellington, Hill, Picton and Craufurd. The French under Massena and four other generals, 422 infantry (42,206 in the battle), 46 cavalry (4,662) and 4 guns (38). They were formed of 72 Chasseurs, 4 companies Line Grenadiers, 2 battalions of Swiss Line, 2 battalions 10th, 3 battalions 11th, the Irish Legion, Hussars, Cuirassiers and Dragoons.

At first it was intended to split the battle and fight it in two parts - in and around Fuentes and, secondly, Craufurd's Lights and Cotton's cavalry on the plain. For various reasons this was abandoned and the game became more or less a straightforward battle for the village. Neville Dickinson, who had been French throughout this campaign, was now labouring under a pessimistic complex that the French just could not win if any sort of realistic representation of what actually took place in 1811 was attempted on the table-top! Perhaps he was right, because

THE HOUSE AT FRENADA USED BY WELLINGTON AS HIS HQ DURING THE LATER STAGES OF THE PENINSULAR WAR. ON THE RIGHTHAND WHITE WALL IS THE COMMEMORATIVE PLAQUE ERECTED AFTER A PARTY OF US, WITH DAVID CHANDLER, HAD VISITED THE PLACE IN VARIOUS YEARS BACK IN THE 1980s.

the results of most of these attempted re-creations were exactly as they were in real life - the British Line with Wellington's know-how dismissed the French column attacks as easily on the wargames table as they did in Spain and Portugal. This is an interesting finding but hardly conducive to good and competitive wargaming!

In the event the battle turned out to be a not particularly inspiring artillery duel across the river, with French attacks coming over the bridge (until it became blocked by a knocked-out horse gun) and across the knee-deep river. The French cavalry moved across the river and attacked a concentration of British cavalry (all of them in fact) by the side of the clump of trees on the British side of the river. Superior numbers were prevailing, but it was not going to be of much avail because British infantry were in strong defensive formations behind Fuentes with guns on the ridge and would have been a match for the reduced-strength French cavalry.

In Fuentes itself, the 42nd on the right of the road and the 88th on the left, moved forward to aid the Lights manning the front of the village. In the fire-fight that followed with the French infantry, units on both sides took casualties sufficient to cause them to momentarily break and withdraw but neither side established enough of a superiority to force a complete withdrawal of the enemy. The battle petered out more due to a lack of interest on the part of both contestants rather than on any results caused by good/bad dice or tactics!

Had it been possible to lay out a battlefield large enough to have included the plain on the Allied right and the village of Poco Velho and Nave de Haver realistically further out, then there would have been scope for better tactics. As it was, the filed was limited on one side by the gorge that forbade crossing the river and the siting of Fuentes, made it essential to fight in or around it. The hindsight that told us of results and events in the Peninsula plus creditable attempts to re-create battles as they occurred seemed to tie our hands and, if a lesson has been learned from what has gone on so far in this re-fought Peninsula Campaign, it is that considerable preliminary map moving is necessary to make it not only an interesting campaign but also for the French to be in with any sort of chance at winning even the occasional battle. Of course, this would have meant that it would have been a re-fought Peninsula War in nothing but name because only coincidentally would the actual battle sites have been used and both sides, particularly the French, would have avoided the mistakes and manoevres that did not pay off in real life.

Better to have laid out terrain similar to those used in the Peninsula and then attempted, by preliminary map moving, to 'winkle' out the enemy from strong defensive positions and, finally, to have a go in the way *you* think it should have been done on the day. But, I think it would be difficult to better Wellington's tactics in any battle!

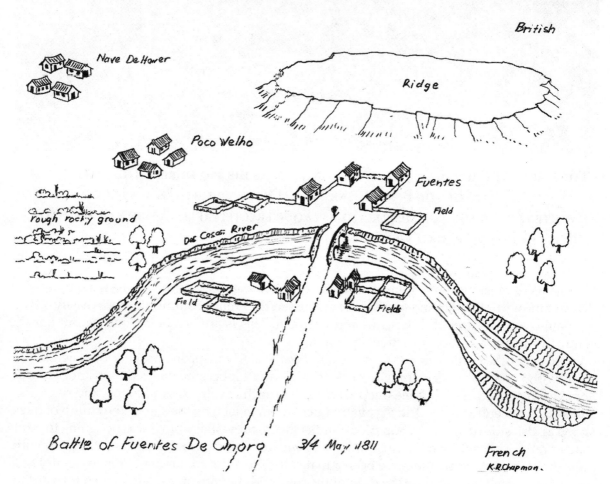

FUENTES DE ONORO AS IT APPEARED ON DONALD'S TABLETOP

THE BATTLE OF ALBUERA—16 MAY 1811

"Then was seen with what strength and majesty the British soldier fights ... nothing could stop that astonishing Infantry. No sudden burst of undisciplined valour, no nervous enthusiasm, weakened the stability of their order."
Sir William Napier's account of the Fusilier Brigade at Albuera on 16 May 1811

This is the story of what has been termed, "...a glorious yet gratuitously disastrous battle," where little tactical skill was shown by the generals in command, the British victory being won by the indomitable courage of the soldiers, who stood their ground for four hours, losing 50% of the British effectives. Beresford had more or less decided to retreat when the remonstrances of a young Staff Officer persuaded him to sanction the advance of Cole's Fusilier Brigade, who turned an impending defeat into victory. Soult, the defeated French commander, then abandoned all hope of raising the siege of Badajoz, and retired to Seville.

As told by yet another Victorian military historian/writer, Colonel W. W. Knollys, it is a colorful and inspiring tale:

We mentioned Lord Wellington's rapid ride between his northern and southern armies, just before the battle of Fuentes de Onoro, when he paid Beresford a flying visit, and then hurried northwards again to withstand Massena on the Agueda.

Soult, on May 10th, started from Seville with the view of relieving Badajoz, and on the 15th arrived at Santa Marta. Beresford at once suspended all operations against Badajoz, and on the following day, in spite of the remonstrances of his engineers, raised the siege, and after a conference with Blake at Valverde he decided on giving battle to Soult at Albuera, the Spanish commander promising to bring his army into line before noon on the 15th. That morning the British army occupied the left of the selected position, but there was no sign of Blake. About 3 P.M. the whole of the Allied cavalry was driven in hurriedly by the French Light cavalry, and General Long, who was in command, was replaced by Lumley, formerly a cavalry officer, but at this time in command of an infantry brigade.

Beresford sent to hasten Blake and his own detached troops. His main body did not reach the ground till 11 P.M., and his rear-guard not till 3 A.M. on the 16th. Colonel Kemmis's brigade of the 4th Division marched to join Beresford via Jerumenha, and consequently did not arrive till May 17th.

The position occupied by the Allies early in the forenoon of May 16th was on a line of undulating, bare, low hills varying from 50 feet to 150 feet above the Albuera stream facing east, and from one and a half to two miles west of it, covering from north to south about three and a half miles. The stream rises near Almendral twelve miles due south of Albuera and joins the Guadiana at Talavera Real 10 miles east of Badajoz. In front of the right of the position of the Allies was a wooded hill, lying in a fork formed by the junction of two streams with the Albuera river. These streams were easily passable above the village, but there was a bridge near Albuera in front of the left centre of the allies where the road to Valverde crossed.

The position was first occupied as follows: On the extreme left, a mile northwest of Albuera and one mile behind, stood Cole's, or the 4th Division, and General Hamilton's division of Portuguese. Next, a mile due west of the bridge, came the 2nd Division, under Major-General the Hon. W. Stewart, consisting of the brigades of Colonel Colborne, 1st Batt. 3rd (The Buffs) Regiment, 2nd Batt. 31st (East Surrey) Regiment, and 2nd Batt. 48th (Northamptonshire) Regiment, 2nd Batt. 66th (Royal Berkshire) Regiment, 2,000 strong; Major-General Houghton, 1st Batt. 29th (Worcestershire) Regiment, 1st Batt. 48th (Northamptonshire) Regiment, 1st Batt. 57th (Middlesex) Regiment, 1,600 strong; and Colonel the Hon. A. Abercrombie (late Lumley), 2nd Batt. 28th (Gloucestershire) Regiment, 2nd Batt. 34th (Border) Regiment, 2nd Batt. 39th (1st Dorsetshire) Regiment, 1,500 strong; Divisional Light Infantry, three companies of 5th Batt. 60th (King's Royal

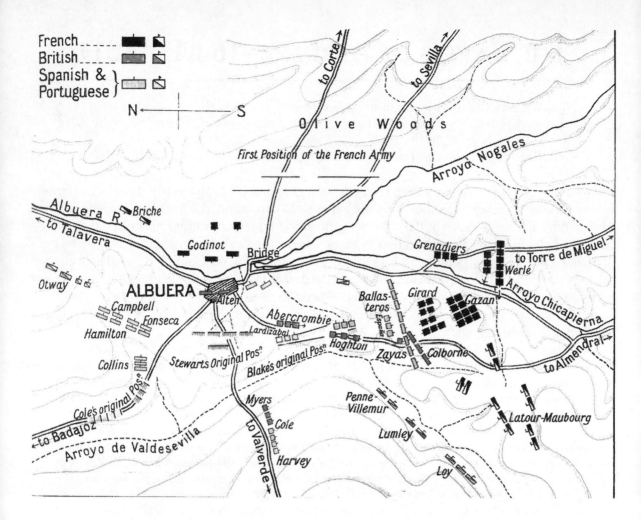

THE FIELD OF ALBUERA ABOUT 10 A.M. THE FRENCH ATTACK.

Rifle) Corps; 4th Division, General Cole; Myers's brigade, just coming up from Badajoz, 1st Batt. 7th (Royal Fusiliers) Regiment, 2nd Batt. 7th (Royal Fusiliers) Regiment, 1st Batt. 23rd (Royal Welsh Fusiliers) Regiment, 2,000 strong; Kemmis's detachment, 160 men; Alten's independent brigade (King's German Legion), 1,1000 strong. On the extreme right, on the highest, broadest, steepest part of the position, were the Spaniards under Blake. The Allied cavalry were drawn up, the main body across the Valverde road. The remainder of the cavalry were distributed along the front. Major-General Alten, with his brigade of Germans, held the village.

The numbers on both sides were approximately as follows: The allies at–Spaniards 14,700, Portuguese 10,000, British and Germans 10,400, guns 30; total, 35,100, French, total present all arms, 24,600 (21,000 infantry, 3,000 cavalry, and 40 guns).

Soult hoped, by fighting on May 16th, to separate the English and Spanish armies; but his main body had a march of 11 miles from Santa Marta, where they had bivouacked at nightfall, May 15th, and the rear of Werlé's division got up only at 8 A.M. Soult was then unaware of Blake's army having joined Beresford at midnight, May 15th - 16th. About 9 A.M. a force of French Light cavalry and Godinot's division of infantry attacked the bridge in front of the village of Albuera. This force was followed by Werlé's division. The assailants were stoutly resisted by Alten's Light Brigade and D Troop Royal Horse Artillery–under Captain Lefebvre. It soon became evident, however, that the real attack was on the right, for Werlé did not follow Godinot closely. Soon after 8 A.M., some French cavalry had issued from the ilex wood, opposite the prolongation of the Allies' right. Beresford therefore sent an order to Blake, to form his second and part of his first line on the broad elevated plateau facing to the south at right angles to the general direction of the Allies' position. He at the same time directed the 2nd Division to take ground to the right to support Blake. General Hamilton was ordered to move to his right and, while sending one brigade forward to support Alten at the village and bridge, to hold the other in readiness to go to any part of the field where it might be needed. The two Portuguese regiments of light infantry under Colonel Collins were attached to General Hamilton's division. The cavalry and 4th Division were moved a mile to the southward.

Advance of the French Infantry

While these changes of position were taking place, rain came down and helped to screen the advance of the French infantry through the wood on the right; but Beresford was soon shown clearly Soult's intentions; for Werlé, leaving only a battalion of Grenadiers, and a few squadrons to watch Otway, countermarched, and hastened to join the main body of the French army; while the Light cavalry, galloping along the bank of the Albuera, crossed it, forming up on the right of Latour-Maubourg's Heavy cavalry, Ley's Spanish cavalry falling back. Godinot, however, continued to demonstrate at the bridge. Beresford, as soon as he saw Werlé's countermarch, rode to Blake, who, vain and punctilious, had refused to obey the first order carried by Colonel Hardinge, whom he told with great heat that the real attack was at the village and bridge. He had similarly disregarded a second message, and, with the exception of Zaya's brigade, which had moved to the Albuera-Torre de Miguel road and was facing southwards when Beresford arrived in person, the Spaniards still occupied their original position facing westward. At this moment, however, a German officer on Blake's Staff pointed out to him that heavy French columns were appearing on his right. Yielding to the evidences of his eyesight, Blake proceeded to change front, but, to quote Napier's words, "with such pedantic slowness, that Beresford, impatient of his folly, took the direction in person." Unfortunately, the movement was too late, and, before the Spaniards could be drawn up in order on the summit of the beforementioned plateau, the French were upon it.

When Marshal Soult rode on to the wooded hill which stands between the Nogales and Chicapierna brooks, he could see none of his enemy's infantry; for General Blake, at the request of Beresford, who had profited by Wellington's experience, had put the Spanish troops in a fold of the ground, and the English troops were hidden by the higher part of the range of hills which stands at the south end of the Allied position.

Soult could, however, see Spanish cavalry three miles south-west of Albuera, and the fact that Godinot's division was engaged near the village, where the river is crossed by a bridge, led the Marshal to assume, and correctly, that his enemy's infantry was posted between those two points. The Marshal mistook Ley's cavalry for some of Castaños's squadrons, who, under Penne and Villemur had been for some days working under Beresford.

Soult directed General Girard to take his and Gazan's division, followed by Werlé's brigade, which was 6,000 strong, to move on to the south-west end of the elevated ground west of the Albuera stream.

The Marshal left the actual formation to be adopted to Girard, who went forward in une colonne serrée des bataillons. This, translated into our drill book, means "each division in a mass of brigades of battalions of double companies at quarter-column distance." Each battalion had four companies, varying from 400 to 500 men, who stood in three ranks. The front of each battalion was formed by two companies, and standing behind them were two more at quarter-column distance, i.e. the intervening space from front to rear of companies was equal to one-fourth of their frontage. The other battalions of the brigade were similarly formed, and standing behind the front battalion. Outside these two brigade columns a battalion marched in line on each flank, and outside these battalions in line marched either a regiment of three battalions, formed in columns like the centre columns, or a column of one battalion. The object of these outside flanking columns was to protect the deployed battalion from an attack of cavalry on their flanks. They varied in strength according to the units they had detached to serve in the garrison of Badajoz.

It was intended that Gazan's division should move forward as a separate support, but when Girard's division began to suffer loss, Gazan's regiments instinctively closed up.

The huge mass, some 8,400 men, ascended to the high ground on a frontage of about half a mile, accompanied by three batteries, two batteries being attached to Werlé's brigade, which advanced later in support.

While the French infantry columns were advancing, General Zaya had posted one of his brigades and a battery skilfully on the rising ground a mile south of Albuera. He and this brigade behaved very well throughout the day, standing steady even when the leading battalion of General Houghton's brigade on coming up mistook them for the French and, firing into their backs, killed many. Zaya's officers then remonstrated, but never offered to give ground, even though two divisions advanced on them on an equal frontage and with a four times greater depth.

As the French masses came within 60 yard, their skirmishers cleared the front, and the leading ranks of the column fired, and then advanced slowly after each volley.

Many French and Spaniards had fallen when General Stewart, commanding the 2nd Division, brought up his leading brigade. General Beresford had intended to form a line to the front on Colborne's brigade, in support of Zaya's brigade; but Stewart, seeing an opening to attack the flank of the French column then advancing slowly between each volley on Zaya, was unable to resist the opportunity of falling on the Frenchmen's unprotected flank.

The Buffs, the leading battalion of the brigade, passed to the right, that is to the west, of the Spaniards, the 48th and 66th moving through its right battalion, and all three came into action against the left flank of the French column, Cleave's battery of the King's German Legion pouring into the mass of Frenchmen case-shot at short range; while the infantry, with repeated volleys from their line, created terrible havoc in the mass. The two left columns of Girard's men facing to the left opened fire with their front rank men kneeling. The officers beat the men who, fearing the terrible slaughter, tried to run off to the rear, as the Buffs, 48th, and 66th, cheering, advanced closer to the mass.

While the three battalions were thus occupied, the 31st was still a little way behind, coming up to the highest part of the ridge in column.

The early morning had been fine, but later heavy clouds had been lowering, and just as Colborne's brigade was delivering its attack, there was a violent downpour of hail and rain. The three battalions were intent on crushing Girard's mass, and were themselves enveloped from time to time in the smoke of their own musketry. On the hill, 2,000 yards to the south-west, sat General Latour-Maubourg, who, seeing the breaking up of Girard's unwieldy masses under the attack of Colborne's brigade, sent down against their unprotected flank the 1st Vistula Lancers, followed by the 2nd Hussars.

Colborne's three battalions were absolutely surprised, for the few officers and men who felt the thud of the horse's feet and had momentarily looked round, mistook the Lancers for Spaniards.

The crash came, and in five minutes 58 out of 80 officers, and 1,200 out of 1,600 of other ranks, were speared or ridden over. The Polish Lancers killed the wounded lying on the ground, 212 of one heap being killed outright against 254 wounded. The officer commanding the 2nd Battalion 48th Regiment, who had surrendered, while being taken towards the French head-quarters by two infantry men, was attacked by a Lancer, who, having knocked him down, made his horse trample on him. These brave but savage Poles gave no quarter. The 66th, when surprised, formed groups, the officers snatching up muskets from men who had fallen, and offering a strenuous resistance.

A fierce hand to hand fight ensued, many of the French infantry taking advantage of the respite afforded by the intervention of the Lancers and joining the struggle. Some of the Poles galloped on down the rear of Zaya's brigade; one man alone attacked the brigade staff, rode over a man and horse, knocked down another with the butt of his lance, and fought all the head-quarter staff before, falling at last, "he literally bit the ground." Another Pole attacked Beresford, riding against his side, his spear passing under the General's arm. Beresford was a powerfully built man, and catching his adversary by the throat, brought him to the ground.

The havoc amongst the infantry was such as is seldom seen in brave troops. Ensign Thomas, carrying a colour of the 66th Regiment, refusing to give up the colours, was killed. When the battalion broke up, Ensign Walsh, carrying the King's Colour, after the sergeants of the colour party had been killed, attempted to carry the colours to the rear. He was pursued, wounded, and taken prisoner. At that moment, Lieutenant Latham seized the colour before the Lancers could carry it off, and was immediately attacked, but, fighting with his sword, although wounded in several places, refused to give it up. A French Hussar, grasping the colour staff, cut open Latham's head, severing one side of his face and nose. Several hussars, now surrounding him, tried to take the colour away, and one cut off his arm. He dropped his sword, but continued the struggle with the colour pole, but must have been killed outright but that his assailants got in each other's way. At last thrown down, wounded in many places, he tore the silk from the colour staff, and lay on top of it, while Lancers were trampling their horses on his prostrate body and spearing him. Two squadrons of the 4th Dragoon Guards, sent by General Lumley against the Lancers, arrived on the ground, but too late to save Colborne's brigade. They fought gallantly, losing both their squadron leaders, who were wounded and taken prisoner by a regiment of Hussars; but the attack created a diversion, and the 31st, standing in column, easily repulsed a wild attack of some of the Lancers as they galloped towards the river. When later in the day the Fusilier Brigade passed where Latham lay, apparently dead, Sergeant Gough, of the 7th fusiliers, seeing the colour, restored it to the remnant of the Buffs. Latham eventually recovered, though painfully disfigured, and Ensign Walsh, having told the story, the officers of the regiment, proud of their comrade, subscribed a hundred guineas to give him a gold medal.

The Poles themselves left 130 out of 580 men on the ground, and the Hussars 70 out of 300. They drove off, however, 480 prisoners from our three battalions, carrying away five out of six colours and a howitzer, being unable to remove three others they had taken for want of horses.

After these bloody scenes there was a pause, during which General Houghton's brigade came into action, its leading lines firing at first by mistake into the rear of Zaya's brigade. They and Girard's were still firing at each other, but the latter were so badly shaken that an endeavour was made to bring Gazan's brigade up through the shaken ranks, but without success, and the remnants of 8,000 men, still uninjured, remained immobile on the ground they held when Colborne's brigade was annihilated.

Colborne's brigade having been cut to pieces alike by the musketry and grape from their front as by the charge of cavalry on their flank and along their rear, the confusion was great. Beresford did his utmost to induce Carlos d'España's brigade to advance, but in vain; and it is stated in all accounts of the battle that Beresford, having appealed to the officers in vain, at length seized a Spanish ensign and dragged him with the colour he bore some distance to the front, but the fellow ran back as soon as released. Whilst this was going on the French cavalry had pretty well surrounded the remains of Colborne's brigade, which had broken up with the exception of the 31st, on the extreme left.

It was now that General Houghton's brigade came into action, accompanied by General Stewart, who, warned by the catastrophe which had just occurred, deployed the regiments before they advanced, the 29th being on the right, the 48th on the left, and the 57th in the centre. The weather, which had been wet and misty, cleared at this moment. Houghton's brigade established itself on the hill, and the 31st fought by its side. Stewart was twice wounded; Houghton, after having been several times wounded, at length, struck by three bullets, fell and died; Colonel Duckworth, of the 48th, was killed; Colonel White, of the 29th, was mortally wounded; Colonel Inglis, of the 57th, was severely wounded, and the 29th men fell in swathes. Two-thirds of each of the three regiments were on the ground; ammunition was beginning to run short. Werlé's division was seen coming up in support of the French.

Beresford thought that the battle was lost. He had ridden to the bridge of Albuera to ascertain why a brigade of General Hamilton's Portuguese division for which he had sent had not arrived, and found that it had been moved to the left of the line. He then ordered Colonel Collins to advance to the hill.

Major (later Sir Alexander) Dickson, commanding the Portuguese artillery, was ordered to retreat with his artillery towards Valverde, and Baron Alten, by order, withdrew from the village to support Houghton's brigade. Beresford intended the Spanish brigade to replace Alten, but Godinot got in before they arrived. Fortunately, Colonel Hardinge (afterwards Lord Hardinge), was at his elbow, and, gathering from his manner and orders what his intentions were, he said, "I think, sir, I ought to tell you that you have a peerage on the one hand and a court martial on the other," and Beresford, after a moment's reflection, said, "I will go for the peerage." Hardinge directed General Cole to attack with the 4th Division, and, as soon as he (Hardinge) saw the

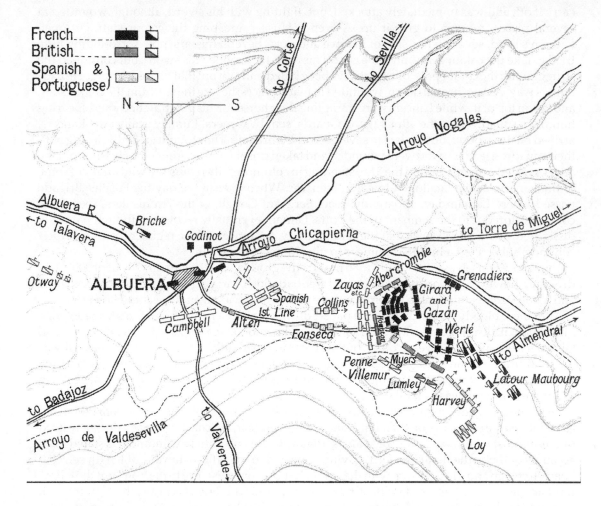

The Field of Albuera about 11.30 a.m. The British counterattack.

Fusilier Brigade approaching the left of Houghton's brigade he "went to Abercrombie," commanding Stewart's 3rd Brigade, "and authorised him to deploy and move past Houghton's left. While Houghton's brigade held the hill, Myers and Abercrombie passed the flanks on the right and left, and made a simultaneous attack on the enemy, who began to waver and then went off to the rear. Myers and Abercrombie, in my opinion, decided the fate of the day." The above is a literal extract from Lord Hardinge's own journal.

The Fusilier Brigade was on the left of Cole's division, and Hervey's Portuguese brigade on the right. Colonel Hawkshawe, with a battalion of the Lusitanian Legion, flanked the advance in column. Cole brought his division up somewhat obliquely. When the 4th Division advanced, 5,000 bayonets in line, with a battalion in column on each flank, Soult sent into the fight Werlé's 6,000 men to protect Gazan's left flank, and ordered Latour-Maubourg to charge Hervey's Portuguese, but they were perfectly steady and drove off the squadrons. They behaved very well, but the brunt of the fighting was borne by the Fusilier Brigade. It had deployed before it reached the crest of the hill, and 2,000 British and 600 Portuguese fought 5,600 Frenchmen under Werlé, who used Girard's formation. He had three columns on a front of two companies each and nine in depth, so he had in each case only about 120 men, firing against 500, for Myers's battalions had each a separate column for targets. The brigade advanced steadily in line under a heavy fire of musketry and artillery. As they neared the hill, the French charged some Spanish cavalry in front of the brigade. A volley fired into the mass of the combatants checked the French, and the Spaniards, galloping round the left flank of the brigade, took no further part in the action. The

156

brigade, continuing its progress, gained the summit of the hill, and then ensued a furious duel. The French guns vomited forth grape in a continuous stream, while under cover of their fire the heavy French columns strove to deploy, but the musketry of the brigade swept away the heads of their foes' formations, though not without suffering fearful loss themselves. Myers, the Brigadier, fell stricken to death. General Cole and Colonels Ellis, Blakeney, and Hawkshawe were all disabled, and many other officers, together with hundreds of men, were killed or wounded.

The brigade, indeed, seemed on the point of being vanquished by annihilation. To quote Napier's eloquent words, "The Fusilier battalions, struck by the iron tempest, reeled and staggered like sinking ships. But, suddenly and sternly recovering, they closed on their terrible enemies, and then was seen with what a strength and majesty the British soldier fights." Firing and advancing, the brigade pressed steadily but slowly onward, leaving behind it a constantly expanding field of dead and wounded men. In vain did Soult encourage his splendid troops; in vain did the latter fight with the historical gallantry of their race; in vain did the reserve, pushing to the front, strive to stem the ebbing tide. Our men were not to be denied, the French reserve was swept away by the fragments of the leading combatants, and again to quote Napier, the "mighty mass gave way, and like a loosened cliff went headlong down the steep. The river flowed after in streams discoloured with blood, and fifteen hundred unwounded men, the remnant of six thousand unconquerable British soldiers, stood triumphant on the fatal field." It is but common justice to record that the conduct of Abercrombie's brigade at the crisis was as gallant as that of the Fusiliers. Indeed, all the British, Portuguese, and German troops behaved splendidly. The battle began a little before 9 A.M. and ended about 2 P.M., the fighting during the remainder of the day being confined to a desultory distant cannonade and an occasional exchange of musket shots between the advanced troops. Beresford, though he had driven his adversary over the river, had suffered too heavily to permit of following up the victory. Indeed, he was in some apprehension of a renewed attack on the morrow.

The field of battle presented a dreadful sight. Major Dickson, writing of the scene, said that on the hill, where the battle chiefly ranged on a space of 1,000 by 1,200 yards, "there were certainly not less than 6,000 dead or wounded." In Houghton's brigade, as we have seen, the General was slain, as was also Colonel Duckworth; whilst Colonel White was mortally, and Colonel Inglis and Major Wray were severely, wounded. In fact, every field officer of the brigade was either killed or wounded, so that at the close of the action the brigade was commanded by Captain Cemétière, of the 48th Regiment. The 57th lost, out of 30 officers and 570 men, 20 officers and 420 men, and was brought out of action by the Adjutant, who in the morning had been fourteenth in seniority.

The last-named regiment received on this occasion the honourable name of "The Die-Hards," which has survived till this day. The battalion, when on the top of the fatal hill, was losing officers and men every second. The regimental colour had twenty-one holes in it, the Queen's colour seventeen, the latter also having its staff broken. Ensign Jackson, who carried it, being hit in three places, went to the rear to have his wounds dressed. On his return he found Ensign Kitch, who had succeeded him, severely wounded but obstinate in refusal to give up his charge. Many companies had all their officers killed or wounded, and owing to the heavy losses, the line presented the appearance of a chain of skirmishers. There is a tradition in the regiment that on the morning following the battle the rations of No. 2 company were drawn by a drummer, who carried them away in his hat. Captain Ralph Fawcett, a young officer of only twenty-three years of age, although mortally wounded, caused himself to be placed on a small hillock, whence he continued to command his company, calling out from time to time to the men to fire low and not to waste their cartridges. Colonel Inglis, commanding the regiment, being struck by a grape-shot, which penetrated his left breast and lodged in his back, refused to be carried to the rear, and remained where he had fallen in front of the colours, urging the men to keep up a steady fire and to "die hard."

James Grant, in his description of the battle, wrote:

"When Colonel Inglis fell, as his 57th men swept over him, he waved his cap and cried after them: Well done, my lads, you'll die hard, at any rate!

"No officer or man on this terrible day failed in doing his duty; and at the close of the action the dead and wounded men of our gallant 31st and 57th Regiments–the latter known ever since as 'The Die-Hards'–were found lying in two distinct lines on the very ground they occupied when fighting."

One of their officers, writing after the battle, said:

"They fought too in every imaginable order ... they resisted cavalry in square, deployed into line, and received and returned repeated volleys, while a few yards only divided them from their opponents. At last everything was carried by the bayonet. To add to the horror of the scene, at the close of the day our artillery were compelled to gallop over everything, as they came past with blood and brains and human hair upon their hooves and wheels. They were compelled to pass over the wounded, deaf to their cries, and averted their gaze from the brave fellows thus laid prostrate in the dust."

BERESFORD'S ARMY AT ALBUERA

I. British Troops

2nd Division (William Stewart):	Strength	Loss
Colborne's Brigade		
1/3rd Foot	755	643
2/31st Foot	418	155
2/48th Foot	452	343
2/66th Foot	441	272
Total of Brigade	*2,066*	*1,413*
Houghton's Brigade		
19th Foot	507	326
1/48th Foot	497	280
1/57th Foot	647	428
Total of Brigade	*1,651*	*1,044*
Abercrombie's Brigade		
2/28th Foot	519	164
2/34th Foot	596	128
2/39th Foot	482	98
Total of Brigade	*1,597*	*390*
Divisional Light Troops:		
3 comps. 5/60th Foot	146	21
Total 2nd Division	*5,460*	*2,868*
4th Division (Cole):		
Myers's Brigade		
1/7th Fusiliers	714	357
2/7th Fusiliers	568	349
1/23rd R. W. Fusiliers	733	339
Total of Brigade	*2,015*	*1,045*
Kemmis's Brigade, detachment of one company each of 2/27th, 1/40th, 97th Foot	165	20
Total 4th Division	*2,180*	*1,065*

Alten's Independent Brigade:		
1st Light Batt. K.G.L.	588	69
2nd ditto	510	37
Total of Brigade	*1,098*	*106*

Cavalry (Lumley):	Officers	Men
De Grey's Brigade		
3rd Dragoon Guards	374	20
4th Dragoons	387	27
13th Light Dragoons	403	1
Total Cavalry	*1,164*	*48*

Artillery:		
British (Lefebure and Hawker)	255	15
K.G.L. (Cleeves and Sympher)	292	45
Staff	?	5
Grand Total of British	*10,449*	*4,139*

II. Portuguese Troops

	Stregth	Loss
Harvey's Brigade (4th Division)		
11th Regt. (2 batts.)	1,154	13
23rd Regt. (2 batts.)	1,201	19
1st Batt. L.L.L. (1 batt.)	572	171
Hamilton's Division		
2nd Line (2 batts.)	1,225	8
14th Line (2 batts.)	1,204	2
4th Line (2 batts.)	1,271	60
10th Line (2 batts.)	1,119	11
Collins's Brigade		
5th Line (2 batts.)	985	60
5th Caçadores (1 batt.)	400	31

Left Column

Cavalry (Otway)		
1st Regt.	327	–
7th Regt.	314	2
5th Regt. (1 squad)	104	–
8th Regt. do.	104	–
Artillery (Arriaga and Braun)	221	10
Staff	?	2
Grand Total of Portuguese	*10,201*	*389*

Grand Total of Beresford's Army

	British	Portuguese	Total
Infantry	8,738	9,131	17,869
Cavalry	1,164	849	2,013
Artillery	255	221	476
Grand Total of all arms			*20,358*
Losses	*4,159*	*389*	*4,548*

III. Spanish Troops	Strength	Loss

(1) Blake's Army

	Strength	Loss
Vanguard Division (Lardizabal):		
Murcia (2 batts.), Canarias, 2nd of Leon, Campo Mayor	2,398	291
3rd Division (Ballasteros):		
1st of Catalonia, Barbastro, Pavia, Lena, Castropol, Cangas de Tineo, Infiesto	3,525	275
4th Division (Zayas):		
2nd & 4th Spanish Guards, Irlanda, Patria, Toledo, Legion Estranjera, 4th Walloon Guards, Ciudad Real	4,882	681
Cavalry (Loy):		
Santiago, Husares de Castilla, Granaderos, Escuadron de Instrucion	1,165	40
Artillery (1 battery)	103	9
Staff ?	11	
Total of Blake's troops	*12,073*	*1,307*

(2) Castaños's Army

	Strength	Loss
Carlos de España's Infantry:		
3 batts., Rey, Zamora, Voluntarios de Navarra, 1 company Sappers	1,778	33

Right Column

	Strength	Loss
Penne Villemur's Cavalry:		
Detachments of seven regiments, none over 1 squadron strong	721	28
Artillery (1 battery)	62	–
Total of Castaños's Troops	*2,561*	*61*
Grand Total of Spaniards	14,634	1,368

Grand Total of The Allied Army

	Present of all arms	Losses
British	10,449	4,159
Portuguese	10,201	389
Spaniards	14,634	1,368
Total	*35,284*	*5,916*

SOULT'S ARMY AT ALBUERA, AND ITS LOSSES

Infantry	Strength	Killed
5th Corps		
1st Division (Girard):		
34th Line (2nd & 3rd batts.)	953	419
40th Line (1st & 2nd batts.)	813	348
64th Line (1st, 2nd, & 3rd batts)	2,589	651
88th Line (2nd & 3rd batts.)	899	405
2nd Division (Gazan):		
21st Léger (2nd & 3rd batts.)	788	255
100th Line (1st & 2nd batts.)	738	267
28th Léger (1st, 2nd, & 3rd batts.)	1,367	496
103rd Line (1st, 2nd, & 3rd batts.)	1,290	287
Total 5th Corps	8,437	3,128
Werlé's Brigade:		
12th Léger (1st, 2nd, & 3rd batts.)	2,164	769
55th Line (1st, 2nd, & 3rd batts.)	1,815	351
58th Line (1st, 2nd, & 3rd batts.)	1,642	328
Brigade Total	5,621	1,448
Godinot's brigade:		
16th Léger (1st, 2nd, & 3rd batts.)	1,673	381
51st Line (1st, 2nd, & 3rd batts.)	2,251	3
Brigade Total	3,924	384
Grenadiers Reunis of 45th, 63rd, 95th Lineof 1st Corps, & 4th Poles of 4th Corps (11 comps.)	1,033	372
Total Infantry	19,015	5,332
Cavalry (Latour-Maubourg)		
Briche's Brigade:		
2nd Hussars	305	73
10th Hussars	262	32
21st Chasseurs	256	25
Bron's Brigade:		
4th Dragoons	406	70
20th Dragoons	266	25
26th Dragoons	421	21

Bouvier des Éclats's Brigade:			Artillery Génie Train:		
14th Dragoons	316	24	Of 5th Corps	608	95
17th Dragoons	314	45	Of other Units	625	?
27th Dragoons	249	19	État Major	?	13
Unattached Cavalry:			Total of Army	24,260	5,936
1st Lancers of the Vistula	591	130			
27th Chasseurs	431	26			
4th Spanish Chasseurs	195	6			
Cavalry Total	4,012	496			

BRITISH BATTLE HONOURS FOR ALBUERA
3rd (Prince of Wales's) Regt. of Dragoon Guards
4th (the Queen's Own) Regt. of Dragoons
13th Regt. of (Light) Dragoons
1st Bn. 3rd (East Kent) Regt. of Foot or The Buffs
1st & 2nd Bns. 7th Regt. of Foot (or Royal Fuzileers)
1st Bn 23rd Regt. of Foot (or Royal Welsh Fuzileers)
2nd Bn. 28th (North Gloucestershire) Regt. of Foot
29th (Worcestershire) Regt. of Foot
2nd Bn. 31st (Huntingdonshire) Regt. of Foot
2nd Bn. 34th (Cumberland) Regt. of Foot
Distinction to Regiment
2nd Bn. 39th (Dorsetshire) Regt. of Foot
1st & 2nd Bns. 48th (Northamptonshire) Regt. of Foot
2nd Bn. 66th (Berkshire) Regt. of Foot
1st Bn. 57th (West Middlesex) Regt. of Foot
5th Bn. 60th (Royal American) Regt. of Foot

Sir William Beresford, in his dispatch, said that the dead, particularly those of the 57th, were to be seen "lying as they had fought in the ranks, and every wound in front."

General Stewart was twice hit but would not quit the field. General Houghton, who had received several wounds without shrinking, at last fell dead, as we have mentioned, pierced by three bullets, whilst cheering on the men of his brigade.

From the account of the late Sergeant Cooper, of this regiment, we learn that when the Fusiliers had mounted the hill there were constant cries of "Close up!" "Close in!" "Forward!" Sergeant Cooper relates as an illustration of the great opinion which the army even then entertained of their leader, that when he (Cooper) was going into action, a comrade said to him, "'Where's Arthur?' meaning Wellington. I said, 'I don't know. I don't see him.' He replied, 'Aw wish he were here.' So did I."

Beresford was afterwards created Viscount Beresford, and from the Portuguese Government received the titles of Duke of Elvas, Marquis of Campo Mayo, and Count Trancoso. There can be no doubt that throughout the action Beresford exposed himself with a degree of intrepidity which could hardly fail to spread an example of heroism around him. He repeatedly dragged Spanish officers from their ranks and compelled them to lead on their men.

Both armies remained on the field, but during the night of the 18th Soult retired to Solano – much to Sir William Beresford's peace of mind.

In his Despatch, Beresford observed: "It is impossible to enumerate every instance of discipline and valour shown on this severely-contested day; but never troops more valiantly or more gloriously maintained the honour of their respective countries."

THE BRIDGE AT ALBUERA WITH THE VILLAGE BEYOND, AND FRIENDS OF THE 1974 PARTY IN FRONT.

WALKING THE BATTLEFIELD OF ALBUERA

Not a strong or well-marked position, the battlefield of Albuera was situated on a long rolling line of hills which extend for several miles along the Albuera stream. Fordable more or less anywhere by infantry or cavalry, here and there the banks drop ten or twelve feet, impassable to wheels. The French side slopes upwards and numerous olive groves prevent other than vague impressions of troop movements; on the north-west (British) bank the rolling slopes are completely bare of trees. There are many dips on the summit of the position and the main battle-spot was on the two slopes of one of these dips.

The Albuera stream is formed by two small brooks, the Nogales and the Chicaperna, which meet a little south of the village; there is a little wooded hill between them which conceals from an observer on the British position the upper course of the Nogales and part of the woods beyond. The French formed their order of battle in these woods and Soult hid his main attacking column behind this long low knoll, covered by the more distant woods Beresford drew up his army in the assumption that, by capturing Albuera village and storming the heights beyond Soult would attempt to penetrate his centre. The slopes are so gentle that nothing can be concealed, except by the woods on the French side; but a dip in the skyline of the British position meant that the French had an imperfect view of the British line near the village of Albuera.

The relatively featureless expanse over which Albuera was fought gives little help when attempting to picture the truly stirring events that took place there. But painstaking study on the ground and considerable map-reading acumen while pacing its deceptive undulations provided a pin-point of the spot where Colborne's battalions were smashed by French cavalry, and the attack area of what was claimed to be the biggest French column formation of the entire war.

The field is approached over the bridge beyond the town (village) of Albuera, marked by a huge rectangular building of some antiquity. The bridge lays unused, having been replaced by a more modern construction and a mini-bypass, but standing on the old bridge allows the battlefield to stretch out before the eyes. A road leading off at an angle to the right takes one to the Allied right flank area. A marked feature of the filed is how its shallow undulations must have been adequate to hide formations from each other, so a group in one hollow would have scant idea of what was befalling their comrades perhaps only 75 to 100 yards distant. To the author, the rolling agricultural countryside was so English in appearance that it required the widest stretch of imagination to adequately picture the stirring events that had taken place upon it.

Notes taken of a previous tour with David Chandler and the British Military History Society reveal an amusing reference to what occurred, "We found the battlefield to have changed little and the principal points to be easily recognisable as, like a horde of ravaging Tartars, we ploughed a path across a neatly sown field of crops, to arrive at a point well below the crest of the ridge from we would have gained a much better view. But as that area was densely covered with high waving corn, even David did not have the cheek to plough through it!

WARGAMING THE BATTLE OF ALBUERA

Despite being such an obviously suitable battle to be produced in miniature on a tabletop terrain, the author shamefacedly admits that he can only recall attempting it once, and then with mixed and unmemorable results. Fought at a Wargaming Holiday Centre with a host of players each handling small formations, the game was controlled by a single computer, using *Eaglebearer* software to arrive at casualties, morale, reactions and the like. Admittedly, there is a great atmosphere of realism generated by being unaware of the effects of combat on both the enemy's facing formation and one's own, and the highly desirable absence of the vagaries of the dice. However, certain practical difficulties marred proceedings and caused the running of the game to be aggravatingly slow, as each player, in turn, reported what he had done that move and the computer handler fed this into the apparatus, received results and subsequent reactions, then passing on to the next player and so on. As there were about a dozen players a side, this meant twenty-three of them had to hang about doing nothing while the activities of one of their number was recorded; it was worsened by the ruling that all players were self-contained entities beyond any communication with neighbouring units; in other words, all conversation was forbidden and even a simple whisper concerning the need for a beer aroused displeasure and penalties.

Undoubtedly, wargaming with computers can be carried out in a far more satisfactory manner and will achieve results of a standard of realism well beyond pre-silicon chip days, and the author looks forward to being part of such an up to date game. Meanwhile, he has promised himself the pleasure of setting up a miniature Battle of Albuera, using both 1:300 scale figures for optical realism and the old 25mm favorites for another spectacular, when a good time will be had by all!

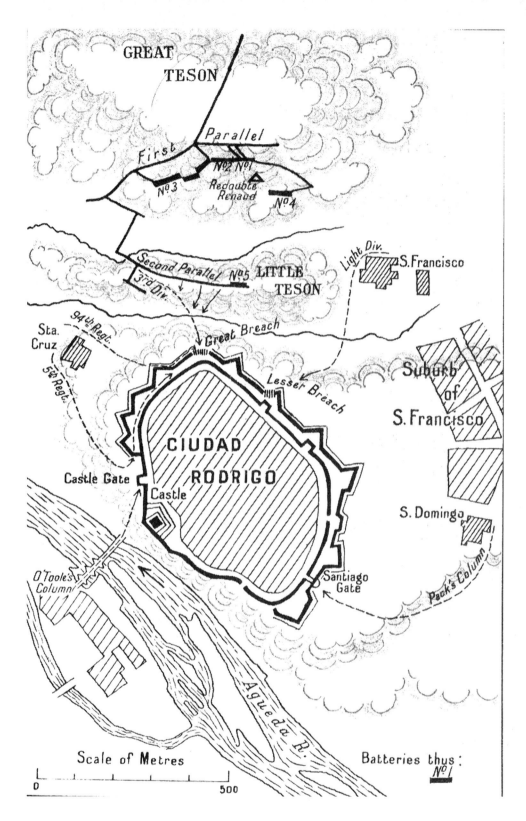

CUIDAD RODRIGO

"The campaign of 1812 commenced with the siege of Cuidad Rodrigo, which was invested by our division on the 8th of January. There was a smartish frost, with some snow on the ground; and when we arrived opposite the fortress, about midday, the garrison did not appear to think we were in earnest, for a number of their officers came out, under the shelter of a stone-wall, within half musket-shot, and mused themselves in saluting and bowing to us in ridicule; but, ere the day was done, some of them had reason to wear the laugh on the opposite side of their countenance."

Captain Sir John Kincaid of the 95th Rifles

Wellington had begun to draw in his widely dispersed regiments on New Year's Day 1812, and to prepare the heavy siege-train required for the investment of Cuidad Rodrigo. On 6 January, pontoons were thrown across the Agueda, and with 35,000 troops pouring over, next day the citizens of Cuidad Rodrigo once more found themselves under siege. Although not as formidable as those of Badajoz, the town's defences were reasonably strong, consisting of a medieval wall thirty-two feet high with masonry counterscarps rising to twelve feet, surrounding a network of narrow streets. The town was dominated by the San Francisco Convent, an outlying redoubt that had to be taken before any storming of the main fortress. On the evening of 8 January Colonel Colbourne led 300 men of the Light Division across the icy river and, in a brilliant twenty minute action without any preliminary bombardment, they carried the redoubt with only six men killed and 20 wounded. This was the action that Captain John Kincaid said took the smile off French faces!

This daring assault is described in some detail by Major Arthur Griffiths in an article written a hundred years ago:

The fortress of Ciudad Rodrigo stood on rising ground in a nearly open plain with a rocky surface, about 100 feet above it, but to the northward there were two hills respectively some 180 and 600 yards distant from the ramparts. The first of these, called the Lesser Tesson, was about on a level with the walls; the second, or Greater Tesson, rose a few feet above them.

Upon the Greater Tesson an enclosed and palisaded redoubt had been constructed, called San Francisco, and this prevented any siege operations on this side while it was in the enemy's hands. The town itself was defended by a double line of fortifications–one, the inner, an ancient wall of masonry; the second, outside it, intended to cover the inner wall. The latter is known in old-fashioned fortifications as a "fausse braie." It gave but little defence, being set so far down the slope of the hill. Besides the foregoing, the suburbs of the town were defended by an earthen entrenchment hastily thrown up by the Spaniards two years previously. Since the French had held Ciudad Rodrigo they had utilised three convents, large and substantial buildings, in the general defence, fortifying them and placing guns in battery upon their flat roofs.

Wellington, having decided to attack from the north side, assaulted the redoubt of San Francisco on the Greater Tesson. It was carried on January 8th in most gallant style by a portion of the Light Division, led by Lieutenant-Colonel Colborne, one of the most brilliant of the soldiers in the Peninsular War. Major Napier, of whom more later, had volunteered, but Wellington said the stormers should be commanded by the first field officer for duty. Colborne's orders were given so clearly and precisely that it was impossible to misunderstand them. The storming party was to descend into the ditch, cut away the palisades, and climb over into the redoubt. They moved forward about 9 P.M., the watchword being, "England and St. George"; and finding the palisades close to the outward side of the ditch, sprang on them without waiting to break them down. Then they rushed on "with so much fury that the assailants appeared to be at one and the same time in the ditch, mounting the parapets, fighting on the top of the ramparts, and forcing the gorge of the redoubt." Such undaunted courage was irresistible. The garrison of the redoubt were all killed or made prisoners, and with only trifling loss on our side.

The capture of the redoubt was the signal for "breaking ground," as it is called, the digging of the first trench or parallel–the first of the series of zigzags or approaches–under cover of which the assailants creep up to a fortress which is being besieged. A brigade covered this operation, and 700 men with pick and shovel laboured to such purpose that a trench 3 feet deep and 4 feet wide was dug by daylight. Once safely established at a height which gave a good view of the whole place, the English engineers proceeded to lay out batteries and improve the parallel. The work was continued the next night, 1,200 men being regularly employed in pushing it forward till a point was reached near enough to batter down the walls and make a breach in the place.

Two well-known soldiers of the Light Division who actually took part in these arduous operations wrote of their experiences–Rifleman Edward Costello of the 95th:

… suddenly ordered to break ground by commencing to throw up intrenchments in the face of the city. In executing this task, being unsheltered from the enemy's shot, their grape and canister occasionally played in among us, so that although it was freezing hard at the time, we had no reason to complain of not having a good fire.

Now was the time to cure a skulker, or teach a man to work for his "life". There we were, in twos, each provided with a pick-axe and shovel; now digging with a vengeance into the frozen mould, and then watching the glances of the shot and shell; and again sticking to work like devils, or perhaps pitching ourselves on our bellies to avoid their being "purged" with grape or canister.

And Lieutenant George Simmons of the same Regiment:

Began immediately to break ground, and before morning dawned we had commenced our first parallel and completely covered ourselves. The enemy kept up a most tremendous fire all night. I became perfectly familiar with the difference of sound between the two missiles, shot and shell, long before day. Returned to our quarters, and the 1st Division relieved us in the trenches.

Marched back and resumed our work in the trenches. The weather was keen and it froze sharply. Our poor fellows had to cross the river nearly up to their shoulders, and remain in this wet state until they returned to their quarters, some working and some covering the working parties by firing upon the works of this town; others were ordered to get as close as possible and dig holes sufficiently deep to cover themselves, and take deliberate aim at the enemy's embrasures, which a good marksman would easily do by observing the flashes of their cannon, although it was dark.

I had charge of a party to carry earth in gabions, and plant them upon the advanced saps in places where the ground was an entire rock and could not be penetrated. The enemy fired grape, and consequently numbers fell to rise no more from the effects of it. I ran the gauntlet here several times, and brought gabions of earth, always leaving some of my poor fellows behind, when I returned for more, and glad enough I was when the Engineer said "We have now sufficient."

Returned to quarters in a whole skin.

MAJOR ARTHUR GRIFFITHS:

Four Divisions were employed in the siege of the 1st, 3rd, 4th, and Light; but as the weather was bitterly cold and the army had no tents, there was no cover or protection to the troops on the north side. The regiments therefore occupied cantonments on the south bank among the villages, crossing over to their work from day to day as their turn of duty came round. In this way each division had one whole day in the trenches out of every four, taking with them cooked food and entrenching tools. The hardship of this service was great. It was necessary to cross the icy-cold river Agueda going to and fro, wading through water sometimes up to the waist. No fires could be lighted, and their wet clothes often froze on to the men during the night. One of those who went through this siege describes how pieces of ice were constantly brought down by the rapid current, and so bruised the troops in fording the river that cavalry were ordered to form across the ford, and under this equine barrier the men crossed unharmed.

Time was of vital importance. The French General Marmont, was collecting his strength for its relief. The best chance lay in attempting an assault, without waiting till the fortifications were ruined by bombardment. Heartless as it may sound the only solution was to sacrifice life rather than time. This is what Wellington had meant when he prefaced his final orders by the announcement that Ciudad Rodrigo must be taken on a particular day. His men knew what was expected of them, and, without hesitation, they answered: "We will do it!"

From the captured redoubt on the Greater Teson, twenty-four heavy siege-pieces roared night and day, pounding the curtain wall until, by the 19th, two breaches had been made and were considered practicable for an assault.

Griffiths writes of this:

The bombardment went on without intermission until January 18th. Then Wellington, ready to avoid unnecessary bloodshed, summoned the place to surrender. The French commandant, General Barrié, refused, declaring that his Emperor had entrusted him with the defence of the fortress, and that he could not give it up. "On the contrary," the message ran, "my brave garrison prefers to be buried with me under its ruins." Wellington at once issued his orders, prefacing them with the memorable words already quoted, that Ciudad Rodrigo must be attacked that evening.

There were to be two principal attacks, made by the two divisions on trench duty during the night of January 18th - 19th. These were the 3rd and Light Divisions. To the first was entrusted the assault upon the main breach, to the latter that on the lesser, or breach by the tower. The brigade of General Mackinnon was to lead the first, supported by Campbell's brigade; Vandaleur's led, and Andrew Barnard's brigade supported, the second. Both were to be preceded by forlorn hopes and storming parties, with others carrying wool-bags and ladders to facilitate descent into the ditch and the escalade of the walls. The eagerness, the emulation among British soldiers to be foremost in these, the most dangerous services in an assault, were well illustrated on this occasion. George Napier, who had obtained a promise from his General, the famous but ill-fated Craufurd, that he should lead the Light Division stormers, was directed to call for volunteers. The young Major, addressing the 43rd, 52nd, and Rifle Corps, said: " 'Soldiers, I want a hundred volunteers from each regiment: those who will go with me, step forward.' Instantly there rushed out nearly half the division, and we were obliged to take them at chance." Such is Napier's own account of the affair, written years afterwards.

Known to the French as "Les Enfants perdus" (Lost Children) the Forlorn Hope always led or made the first attack, usually consisting of two sergeants and twenty-five men, led by a junior officer. Officially unrewarded, survivors gained promotion, taking the places of NCO's and officers killed in the action.

Rifleman Edward Costello formed part of the Forlorn Hope at Cuidad Rodrigo on 19 January 1812, which makes him perhaps the ideal authority to explain the role of the Forlorn Hope, as he did in his memoirs after the War:

On the eve of the storming of a fortress, the breaches, etc., being all ready, captains of companies, on their private parade, give the men to understand that such and such a place is to be taken by storm. Every man then, who wishes to volunteer to head the stormers, steps forward to the front, and his name is immediately taken down by the officer; if none offer themselves the first men for duty are selected. With our regiment this latter alternative was never required, as a sufficient number were always ready.

In the same book he described his personal experiences at the time:

...we joined the 3rd division in the works, and then heard that the city was to be stormed.

166

Volunteers were immediately required from the different regiments of our division. Many of our men came forward with alacrity for their deadly service. With three others I had, as I then considered, the good fortune to be chosen from our company. This was an occasion, as may be believed, momentous and interesting enough in the life of a soldier, and so we seemed to consider it. We shook hands with a feeling of friendly sincerity, while we speculated as to the chances of outliving the assault. We were at this time in the trenches in front of the city, from whence proceeded a very smart fire of shot and shell, probably to give us an idea of the warm reception we might expect on our visit at night, and here the entire company gathered round our little party, each pressing to have a sup from his canteen. I gave my father's address to my comrade before starting, in case of accident.

Darkness had no sooner closed over the devoted city, and our imaginations awakened to the horrors of the coming scene, than the "stormers" were immediately ordered to "fall in" and "form". We were four or five from each company, and in all about a hundred and twenty men. The volunteers of our regiment were led by Captain Mitchell and Lieutenants Johnston and Kincaid; the whole of the storming division being commanded by Major George Napier of the 52nd regiment. The forlorn-hope, or stormers, moved to a convent, occupied by the 40th, the walls of which protected us from the enemy's shot.

Griffiths writes of the occasion:

Major George Napier, one of the three illustrious brothers whose names are now household words, stood at the head of his volunteer stormers, taking his instructions from Lord Wellington himself.

"Now, do you quite understand? Do you see the way you are to take so as to arrive at the breach without noise or confusion?"

"Yes, sir, perfectly," replied Napier.

Someone of the staff, who was standing by, then said:

"You are not loaded! Why don't you make your men load?"

"No," sturdily replied Napier; "I shall not load. If we cannot do the business with the bayonet and without firing, we shall not be able to do it at all."

"Let him alone; let him go his own way," remarked Wellington, interposing, and thus fully endorsing the view which Napier took of the work in hand.

A few minutes later Napier was shot down as he entered the breach at the head of his men. His arm was shattered, and hung helpless, but he disdained all assistance.

"Push on, lads, push on!" he cried undaunted, still cheering his men. "Never mind me; push on, the place is ours!"

And there he lay, till all had passed him, getting terribly bruised and trampled upon in the confusion in the darkness.

It was not till he heard the shouts of, "Victory! Old England for ever!" that he gave himself up to the surgeon for the amputation of his arm.

They were true heroes, these old Peninsular worthies; and there were few finer fellows than the Napiers–Charles, William, and George. But at Ciudad Rodrigo there were others who gained great fame: Generals Craufurd and Mackinnon, both killed at the breaches; Gurwood and Mackie, who led the forlorn hopes; Hardyman, a captain of the 45th, of whom it was said, so gallant was his demeanour, so noble his exploits, that although three generals and seventy other officers had fallen, "the soldiers fresh from the strife talked only of Hardyman." The taking of Ciudad Rodrigo was indeed a splendid feat of arms.

Later, Costello revealed that he experienced a silence and solemnity greater than ever before, encouraging gloomy speculations of his chances of survival. Even so, and despite the stress of the moment, he claimed to recall the words–among the last ever spoken–of their leader, General "Black Bob" Craufurd:

"Soldiers! The eyes of your country are upon you. Be steady–be cool–be firm in the assault. The town must be yours this night. Once masters of the wall, let your first duty be to clear the ramparts and in doing this, keep together!"

Costello said that his words sunk deep in his memory, "… and although the shock of many a battle has rolled over my grey locks since that period, I remember …"

Some three hundred yards from where the Light Division storming party was assembled the fortress walls loomed high in the gloom. Then the signal rocket traced its fiery arc through the night sky and Craufurd cried: "Now lads for the breach!" Through a hail of grapeshot the stormers rushed forward over the snow covered ground, the Forlorn Hope led by Lieutenants Johnson and Kincaid were driven by the weight of fire to the left of the breach, while Napier led the main body scrambling up the steep broken slope of the glacis, loose earth slipping from under foot. Nearing the breach, fire-balls illuminated their progress, bringing canister, grape, roundshot and shell crashing among them; then came hails of musket-balls and Craufurd was hurled, mortally wounded into the ditch.

GRIFFITHS:

The stormers raced for the breach, distant 300 yards, under heavy fire, and without waiting for the ladders, dropped down 11 feet into the ditch. The main body was checked at the breach because the opening was so narrow. This crushed the attacking column into a compact mass, upon which the enemy's fire told with terrible effect. Just now George Napier, its leader, was struck down. The men halted, irresolute, and, forgetting they were unloaded began to snap their muskets. Then their wounded chief, from where he lay disabled, shouted, "Push on with the bayonet!" and the stormers answered the inspiriting command with a loud "Hurrah!" and pressed forward. The breach was carried; the supporting regiments–Vandaleur's brigade–"coming up in sections abreast, gained the rampart, the 52nd wheeled to the left, the 43rd to the right, and the place was won."

The assault had been initiated by Pack's Portuguese at 7 P.M., when a regiment under Colonel O'Toole crossed the river by the bridge and attacked a work in front of the castle. Away to the right, the 3rd Division were attacking–before moving forward, Picton the Divisional Commander, addressed the 88th Foot:

"Rangers of Connaught … it is not my intention to expend any powder this evening, we'll do the business with the cold iron." It was a sentiment that delighted the wild Irishmen who formed the regiment!

The 5th and 94th Regiments of the Division, supported by the 77th, covered the attack of the main breach by Mackinnon's brigade, led by a party of sappers carrying hay-bags to fill the ditch, then the 500 strong storming-party under Major Manners, preceded by the forlorn hope, then the rest of the brigade. They had to scale an almost perpendicular mass of rubble while showers of grenades dropped among them and they were showered by grape from two field-pieces enfilading the breach. Stumbling forward, Private Donaldson remembered hearing General Mackinnon compliment the youngest officer in Donaldson's company on his bright new pelisse, saying:

"Come, Beresford, you look a fine lad, you and I will go forward together."

GRIFFITHS:

The whole space between the advanced parallel and the ramparts was alive with troops advancing reckless of the iron tempest that thinned their ranks. The column from Santa Cruz made good its entrance and scoured the opening between the two walls of defence, driving the French before them. This cleared the ground for Mackinnon's men, who pressed gallantly on; but from behind a retrenchment the defenders stubbornly resisted.

While the assailants were seeking to cross the ditch, a mine was sprung with an explosion which proved fatal to many, including the brave Mackinnon. The survivors held their ground; and now Mackie, who led the forlorn hope, clambered over the rampart wall and dropped inside, finding there an opening on one side of the main breach by which an entrance was possible.

Climbing back, he collected his men and led them by this road into the interior of the place. About this time they encountered and joined O'Toole's Portuguese regiment, and, these columns having made good their footing, established themselves strongly among the ruined fortifications, awaiting the vault of their comrades' attack.

All this had occupied but a few minutes in time. The assault was thus, practically, decided, but other successes contributed to the general result. The struggle at the great breach was still being maintained when three of the French magazines in this neighbourhood exploded, and then the 3rd Division broke through the last defences. The garrison still resisted, however, fighting as they fell back from street to street; but finally the castle, their last stronghold, was captured, and Lieutenant Gurwood, who had led the Light Division forlorn hope, received the Governor's sword. The attacks on all other sides had prospered equally, both O'Toole's and Pack's, the latter having entered without opposition on the southeastern front of the fortress.

It would be well if there were no more to be said of the successful attack on Ciudad Rodrigo.

But unhappily the glory of this great achievement was greatly tarnished by the shameful excesses of the victorious troops. The French garrison were spared, for out of a total garrison of 1,800 men, 1,500 were taken prisoners.

But the town itself was ruthlessly plundered. Houses were ransacked and burnt, churches desecrated and destroyed; the wine vaults and spirit stores were broken open, universal drunkenness prevailed, and every species of enormity were perpetrated.

It was said that order was finally restored in the streets by, among other stringent measures, Sir Thomas Picton laying about him with a broken musket-butt, roaring foul abuse so loudly that even the most drunken men were shocked into respectful silence.

Summing-up, British military historian David Chandler says that the lessons and military significance of the capture of Cuidad Rodrigo were:

1. A successful, short siege, based upon sufficient guns.
2. A thoroughly scientific plan.
3. The 3rd Division had been trained all summer in the arts of sapping.
4. Domination of the breach, once made, prevented the French from clearing the debris.
5. Correct proportion of besiegers to be besieged.
6. The length of time taken to establish the breaching batteries due to the narrow front and the hard earth.
7. French counter-fire very accurate.
8. The French took 24 days to capture the place in 1810; they lost it in 11 days in 1812.

British Losses at the Storm of Ciudad Rodrigo,

		3/95th	9
Staff	3	Barnard's Brigade	
Engineers	4	1/43rd	41
3rd Division:		1/95th	20
Mackinnon's Brigade		2/95th	6
1/45th	48	Divisional Total	113
5/60th	5	Portuguese	114
74th	21	Grand Total	560
1/88th	34		
Campbell's Brigade		**The French Garrison**	
2/5th	94	officers and men effective	
77th	50	34th Léger, one battalion	975
2/83rd	5	113th Ligne, one battalion	577
94th	69	Artillery, 2 companies	168
Divisional Total	326	Engineers	15
Light Division:		Non-combatants (Civil officers, &c.)	36
Vandeleur's Brigade		Sick in Hospital	163
1/52nd	28	Staff 3 officers and men effective	
2/52nd	9	Total	1,937

BRITISH BATTLE HONOURS FOR CUIDAD RODRIGO
2nd Bn. 5th (Northumberland) Regt. of Foot
1st Bn. 43rd (Monmouthshire Light Infantry) Regt.
1st & 2nd Bns. 52nd (Oxfordshire Light Infantry) Regt.
1st Bn. 45th (Nottinghamshire) Regt. of Foot
77th (East Middlesex) Regt. of Foot
5th Bn. 60th (Royal American) Regt. of Foot
74th (Highland) Regt. of Foot
2nd Bn. 83rd Regt. of Foot
1st Bn. 88th Regt. of Foot (Connaught Rangers)
94th Regt. of Foot
1st, 2nd & 3rd Bns. 95th Regt. of Foot (Rifle Corps)

In a small room, above the one in which George Napier lay recovering from the amputation of his arm, General Craufurd after suffering great agony for most of the day and night, succumbed to his wound and was buried where he had fallen at the foot of the breach. His coffin was borne by six veteran sergeants from the Light Division and was followed by Lord Wellington with a retinue of field officers, many of whom found it difficult to conceal their emotions.

"At Ciudad Rodrigo there was starvation: no corn, no hay, no straw, no bread, no rum, for three days, only beef and biscuit; at last we got some mouldy biscuit for the animals, which I mixed with carrot, cabbage, and potatoes; everything was devoured. Tea, 22s and 25s a pound; butter 4s; bread, 1/6d a pound, above 6s the loaf; no wine or brandy; gin, 12s the bottle; straw, a dollar for a small bundle, and all sold in a scramble. The truth was, the troops, poor fellows! came through the town quite starving; during retreat supplies had been mismanaged–regiments were 3 and 4 days without rations, and numbers died of absolute starvation, besides the sick. Lord Wellington is, I hear, very angry." November 1812.

The Private Journal of Judge-Advocate Larpent–Peninsular War.

WALKING THE AREA OF THE SIEGE OF CIUDAD RODRIGO

Unique and unchanged, Ciudad Rodrigo is a National Monument with a strict preservation order placed upon it that precludes any major work that might impair it retaining its original appearance. Passing over the bridge spanning the moat and through the heavily fortified gates set amid Vauban style defence works, it is not hard to believe that were both besiegers and besieged to return to Earth, they would readily recognise the ramparts and vaulted gateways, the narrow winding streets with overhanging buildings, and the dominating Moorish castle towering over this crowded walled enclave. we were fortunate to see this impressive building both from outside and in, as it is now a State-run Parador, where we spent nights on more than one occasion, and thoroughly recommend the lavish buffet breakfast. Standing on the ramparts near the castle, one can see to the left the bridge over the river, crossed by Colonel O'Toole's Portuguese, who met up with Mackinnon's Brigade inside the town.

Leaving the town by one of the many gates, one can walk around its outskirts, with the still existing deep moat and out works between one and the walls still rearing defiantly skywards. Then down into the ditch, gazing upwards at the church and city walls still pockmarked by the roundshot hurled at them by Wellington's siege-guns, and note the different masonry that indicates where the breaches were and later filled-in. Climb up onto the Tesons (not without difficulty as it is now a housing estate) and note the relation between the siting of the siege guns and the walls they were battering. From these parallels where the ground stood, it is possible to trace the flight of their shot to the Greater and Lesser Breaches, tracing grooves made by glancing shots and ricochets on the opposite wall to the original hit-mark. It is all as it must have been on that dreadful dark night in January 1812 and it is here, with the aid of a little imagination, that one can really catch the spirit of the stirring events that occurred here. Perhaps the greatest stimulus lays in standing in the Lesser Breach with the awareness that here Black Bob Craufurd was mortally wounded and later buried by a sorrowing party of his men. Alas, there is no indication of his grave and it has been suggested to the British Greenjackets Division, stationed in Winchester, Hampshire in England that they should erect a commemorative plaque here to one of their greatest forebears. The author picked a small piece of rock from the place which, suitably labelled, stands with other military treasures on the mantleshelf of his study.

If someone does not go to any other Peninsula War site, they *must* see Ciudad Rodrigo, which is satisfying, stimulating and an historical site one is proud to have visited.

REPRODUCING SIEGES AS WARGAMES.

Reproducing such a siege as Ciudad Rodrigo or Badajoz on a wargames table is far from easy, subsequently infrequently attempted by wargamers, who like their battle reconstructions to be sharp, snappy affairs, full of incident and clear cut opportunities. These are all things that a siege is definitely not, being essentially a long drawn out affair marked by patience on both sides, with both fighting off boredom, hunger, despair, and progressive casualties, while praying for the sight of relieving columns; attackers painstakingly go through the accepted formulae of establishing lines of circumvallation, digging parallels, setting up siege batteries, making and beating off forays and sorties, forcing breaches and then the deadly business of assaulting them and so on and so forth.

Eventually the code of conducting such events will prevail and, on being summoned, the garrison will surrender; or - to make a better wargame - they will fight on and there will be an assault. In their entirety, sieges are probably best fought on the wargames table as solo affairs, planned and conducted by the lonely wargamer who can set it up and then devote convenient periods to pursuing some small part of the operations. If fighting against a tangible opponent it might be best to extract from the traditionally lengthy process some salient aspect such as the storming of a breach, when the entire wargames table is taken up with the sections of wall on either side of it, plus that part of the town or castle immediately in the rear of the breach. Then the game can proceed along the lines of a standard wargame, with one side attacking and the other defending, employing devices such as feint attacks (on paper) at some other point of the perimeter, compelling defenders to be withdrawn from those on the table to cope with it. Now comes all the intriguing features of forlorn hopes, and storming columns mounting the glacis and descending into the ditch, climbing scaling ladders to ascend walls, or clambering up the mined and obstacle strewn rubble of the breach. Meanwhile the defenders line walls and hastily erected barricades in rear of the breach, eventually fighting in the streets and houses. Difficult and complicated to, perform, requiring understanding and friendly opponents - but stimulating and well worth the trouble of setting-up.

THE SIEGE OF BADAJOZ–16 MARCH 6 APRIL 1812

When Wellington read the casualty lists after the assault of Badajoz he is said to have burst into tears, and later wrote:

> *The capture of Badajoz affords as strong an instance of the gallantry of our troops as has ever been displayed, but I anxiously hope that I shall never again be the instrument of putting them to such a test.*

As long as the French retained their grip on the vital fortress towns of Almeida, Badajoz and Cuidad Rodrigo, on or near the frontier between Portugal and Spain, Wellington could not safely venture across the central and northern part of Spain to attack the enemy's Line of Communication with France. To do so would be to leave exposed his own links with the south and his base at Lisbon.

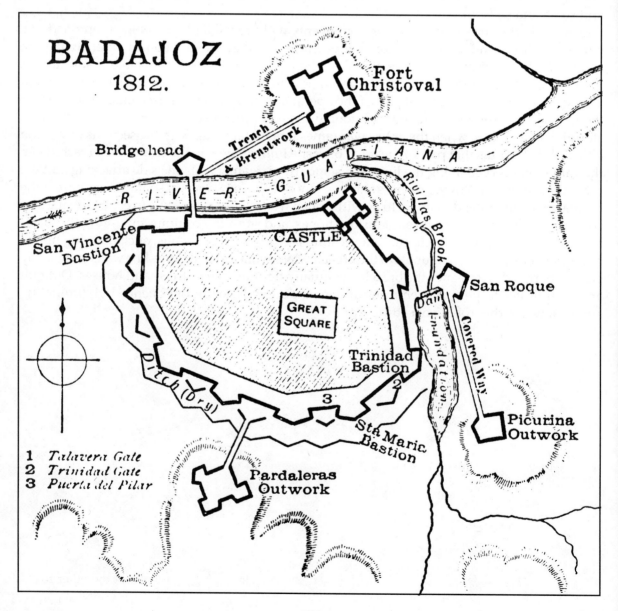

Late in April, 1811 part of Wellington's army under Beresford laid siege to Badajoz. But many of the guns were obsolete, the artillery resources were deplorably weak, the lack of proper material and trained engineers was marked–three sergeants, three corporals and 13 rank and file, the first company of "military artificers," did not arrive from England till later, and infantrymen had to be hurriedly trained as carpenters, sappers and miners. The engineer officers made some serious miscalculations and errors.

When Marshal Soult marched to the town's relief with 18,000 troops, Beresford had to raise the siege and block the Frenchman's path.

The fortified city of Badajoz had two distinctive features–three outworks–Fort Christoval 500 yards across the Guadiana River; and on the south, the Pardaleras fort and the Picurina fort. And at the north-eastern corner an ancient castle incorporated into the defences. Two attempts were made in May and June 1811 to capture Christoval, the first failing for want of an adequate siege-train, the second when breaches forced by a newly assembled siege-train of modern guns could not be stormed. On 10 June 1811 Wellington raised the siege because he was aware that strong French forces were about to relieve the fortress. Turning his attention to Cuidad Rodrigo, Wellington took it in January 1812 and then, in March of that year, returned to invest Badajoz.

On 6 March the Allies broke cantonments and marched towards Badajoz, crossing the Guadiana on 16 March; immediately three divisions began investing the town–the 3rd, 4th and Light divisions.

James Grant begins the epic story:

Badajoz, a strong and ancient city, in past ages many times taken and retaken by the Moors and Goths, stands upon an eminence at the union of the Rivollas with the Guadiana, a noble river, which there is 500 yards wide, and crossed by a bridge of twenty-eight arches. Its castle, built on calcareous rock, rises some hundred feet above the level of the river; and the town, from the angle formed by the confluence of the streams, spreads out like a fan, having eight regular bastions and curtains, with good counterscarps, a covered way and glacis.

A long promenade of poplar trees lies along the bank of the Guadiana, which, though fordable in summer, rolls in a deep and rapid flood during winter. Badajoz, though a fortress of the third order, is deemed the bulwark of Spain; and five gates give access to its narrow, crooked, but picturesque streets, over which towers the heavy mass of its cathedral. The precipitous rock on which its castle stands may be deemed the termination of the range of the Toledo mountains.

In this place was now a garrison composed of Frenchmen, Hessians, and some renegade Spaniards in the service of Joseph Bonaparte. They numbered in all about 5,000 men, and were commanded by Generals Phillipon and Vaillant. There were five French battalions, and two of the regiment of Hesse-Darmstadt–none of the former had eagles. The old castle was the extreme point of defence on their left; and from thence to the Trinidad bastion, terminating the eastern point of resistance, an inundation protected the ramparts, a short interval excepted, which was defended by an outwork beyond the steam, called the Lunette of San Roque.

On the right of this work, also beyond the Revollas, another outwork called the Picurina, was constructed, on an isolated hill about the same distance as San Roque from the castle; and these outworks had a covered communication with each other, and the San Roque had one with the town. But an inundation cut off the Picurina–which was an enclosed and palisaded work–from the latter. The right bank of the Guadiana was destitute of houses; but there, on a rocky height, stood Fort San Christoval, 300 feet square, and from its elevated position looking down upon the castle, which was exactly opposite to it, and only 500 yards distant.

The January of 1812 was cold and rainy; but, notwithstanding its inclemency, on the afternoon of the 17th we broke ground within 160 yards of Fort Picurina, a howling tempest of wind and rain stifling the sound of pick of shovel; and during all that night and the following day our troops, though seriously inconvenienced by the weather, and a terrible cannonade from the town, pushed forward the trenches, and achieved an opening 4,000 feet long, into a parallel of 600 yards, 3 feet deep, and 3 feet 6 inches wide. The 20th was spent in completing the parallel, and erecting two batteries; one to beat down the palisades of the Picurina, and the other to enfilade the space between it and the town. For five days the besiegers continued to push forward their trenches, harassed by an unceasing fire of shot and shell from the guns of Phillipon, and also by the elements. So stormy were the latter, that on the night of the 21st the waters of the Guadiana deepened with unlooked-for rapidity, and, with a mighty crash, swept away a pontoon bridge by which the troops employed in the siege communicated with their depots; but the disaster was speedily remedied by the skill and zeal of Lord Wellington, who substituted another.

The guns flashed nightly amid the misty gloom, and the sputtering port-fires gleamed with a weird effect on the parapets and in the parallels. The rain continued to fall in torrents; the trenches were flooded, and the ground became so soft and muddy that it was found almost impossible to work the guns with effect, or to drag them from place to place; so it was resolved to carry the Picurina by assault, and this was done in splendid style by 500 men of the 3rd division, with the loss of 4 officers and 50 men killed, 15 officers and 250 men wounded. In the attack on the Picurina, some of the ladders proved too short; but Captain Oates, of the 88th, observing that though the ditch was deep it was very narrow, called out–

"Come, my boys, though the ladders are too short to mount up the ditch, let us try our hand with them across it."

This was but a minor affair, yet the effect of the assault by night, the thousands of rockets that sparkled in the sky, the clamour of alarm-bells and drums in the city, the streams of fire that came from the Picurina, in the red light of which the dark figures of the combatants could be seen with bayonet and butt-end in close melee, all made by a startling scene; till the men of the 52nd and the Cameron Highlanders took Gaspar Thierry and eighty-six survivors prisoners–the rest being slain or hurled into the foaming Guadiana and drowned.

The celerity with which this outwork was carried alarmed Phillipon, who now began to stimulate the courage of his soldiers by urging them to prefer death to being immured in a British prison hulk, as so many of their comrades then were.

Of this, William Napier wrote: "An appeal which must have been deeply felt, for the annals of civilised nations furnish nothing more inhumane towards captives of war than the prison-ships of England."

Grant continues:

Throughout the whole of the 26th, working parties were employed in the Picurina; and against them the enemy from Badajoz directed a severe and unceasing fire. With their accustomed bravery our troops sustained it; and in the same night they not only established the second parallel, but formed two breaching batteries, which were armed and in full operation next morning. It was not a complete trial of skill between the besiegers and the besieged, for the latter, aware of the intended points of attack, busied themselves in counter-works. The fire was incessant of both sides, and more than once a desperate sortie was attempted.

At last the stones began to fall from the Trinidad bastion, amid cloud of dust, as ball after ball went home with terrific force; and the garrison commenced to form a retrenchment within the walls, by levelling houses behind the yawning breach. In place where the fortifications had not been completed the energetic Frenchman hung brown cloth which resembled earth, behind which his men were able to pass safely; they also made a raft with parapets and crossed the inundation to our side. But all their efforts were useless; the breaches became larger as masses of stone and rubbish fell into the fosse below, and, on the 6th, a tremendous gap showed in the masonry of the curtain between the two bastions which had not been renewed when the bastions themselves were rebuilt about 1757.

Wellington having at last brought up the 5th division from Beira, and thus strengthened a portion of his line which had been vulnerable, determined to bring matters to a crisis; and finding that three breaches were effected, he issued orders on the 6th of April for a general assault.

Wellington's commands were precise and to the point, but they are terribly eloquent to those who read them.

These paragraphs are from the original memorandum:

"1. The fort of Badajoz is to be attacked at 10 o'clock this night (April 6th). 2. The attack must be made on three points–the castle, the face of the bastion of La Trinidad, and the flank of the bastion of Santa Maria. 3. The attack of the castle to be by escalade; that of the two bastions, by the storm of the breaches … 20. The 4th Division must try and get open the gate of La Trinidad; the Light Division must do the same by the gate called the Puerta del Pilar. 21. The soldiers must leave their knapsacks in camp … 24. Twelve pioneers with axes, and ten miners with crowbars, must be with the Light, and ditto with the 4th Division."

Soult, Drouet, and Daricau were approaching; a battle was imminent which would need all our forces. In twenty-one days we had expended 2,523 barrels of gunpowder, and we had fired 35,346 rounds of ammunition. Badajoz must be taken at all risks.

GRANT:

Picton's division, on the right, was to quit the trenches and scale the walls of the castle, which varied from eighteen to twenty-four feet in height.

Sir James Leith's division, on the left, was to make a false attack on the Pardeleras; but the real assault was to be made on the Bastion de San Vincente, where the glacis was mined, the ditch deep, and the works filled with resolute Frenchmen, each of whom was armed with three loaded muskets.

Under Colville and Barnard, the 4th and light divisions were to advance against the breaches, furnished, like the 3rd and 5th divisions, with ladders and axes, and preceded by storming parties of 500 men, each led by their forlorn hopes, composed of volunteers, officers and men. The light division was to attack the Santa Maria quarter; the 4th division, the Trinidad; and, between these attacks, Major Wilson of the 48th, or Northamptonshire, was to storm the San Roque with the guards of the trenches; while, on the other side of the Guadiana, General Power was to make a feint at the bridge-head. Such were the plans of attack.

Darkness came down on Badajoz; the troops fell into their ranks, and in deep silence awaited the signal which was to send thousands into eternity.

The night of the 6th April, though cloudy and starless, was dry, and the air around the beleaguered city was dense with watery exhalations from the Guadiana on one side, the Rivollas on the other, and from the trenches. In the latter, a low murmur–the hum of subdued voices–rose at times from the deep, massed columns of the British. Along the dark walls of the city red lights were occasionally seen to flit, for the French were not unprepared.

D. H. PARRY:

The trench-guards and the forlorn hope fell in, and about nine o'clock four companies of the 95th Rifles crept forward and lay down, under the crest of the glacis, within a few yards of the French sentinels, whose heads could be seen quite distinctly against the sky.

Not a word was spoken as the riflemen crouched, unnoticed, in the mist that veiled their dark uniforms. They waited the arrival of the forlorn hope to begin the attack.

At length one of the sentries peered over the parapet; something had caught his quick ear, for he cried "Qui vive?" and there was a moment of keen suspense.

Not satisfied, he again challenged, and, receiving no reply, fired his musket into the darkness; it was the signal of alarm, and instantly the drums of Badajoz beat to arms.

Still, for ten minutes more the riflemen lay motionless, until the forlorn hope came up, and then, each man sighting carefully at the heads which showed above the rampart, poured in a volley, and the attack began.

This was unfortunate, for Wellington intended all our assaults to take place simultaneously; moreover the garrison threw a "carcass" from the walls, and by its powerful blaze they saw the 3rd Division drawn up under arms; so, "Stormers to the front!" was the order, and we rushed on in an uproar of cheers.

Overcoats were laid aside, and our men appeared in the well-worn scarlet coatee with white-tape lace, and the black knee-gaiter, which was the dress of a British infantry private at that time. Pigtails had been done away with four years previously, and the well-known grey trousers were not issued to the troops until the following September. The Rifle Corps wore dark green, and used a wooden mallet on the ramrod to drive the ball down the grooved barrel; Fusiliers and the Grenadier companies of the Line had bearskin caps, and Light infantry were distinguished by green tufts in their felt shakos, each man carrying–including knapsack, accoutrements, kit, weapons, etc.–a weight of seventy-five pounds twelve ounces, or ten pounds more than their opponents. The soldiers were enraged at the inhabitants of Badajoz for admitting the French, a feeling which boded ill to them if we took the town.

GRANT:

A blaze of light that broke upon the darkness, with the steady and continuous rattle of musketry, indicated the assault of the castle, where Kemp led the 3rd division, in the absence of Picton, who had been hurt by a fall in camp. Passing the Rivollas in single files, by a narrow bridge, under a terrible fire of musketry from the whole face of the works, he re-formed his men as fast as they came in, and led them impetuously up the rugged hill with great bravery, but only to fall at the foot of the castle wall, severely wounded. As he was borne to the rear he met Picton at the bridge, hurrying sword in hand to assume his place.

The fire from the walls never checked the soldiers of the 3rd division for a moment–they reached them in perfect order, and, rearing their ladders, began to escalade; but for that the foe were fully prepared. Enormous beams of timber, huge stones, loaded shell, cold shot launched from the hand, grenades, and missiles of every kind, were rained upon their devoted heads, crushing to death all who planted foot on the foremost ladders; while a murderous discharge of musketry dealt destruction on the centre and rear of the columns. Fresh ladders were reared, and other men mounted; but all who gained the summit were stabbed, shot, or roughly hurled over to die on the bayonets of their comrades below. In some instances the ladders, with their living freights, were hurled bodily from the wall, to fall with dreadful crashes, and amid deafening shouts, upon the armed crowds below.

Still swarming up the ladders that remained–ladders planted in some instances on the very bodies of the fallen–after being driven back to the edge of the hill, and once more led to the attack by Colonel Ridge, our intrepid soldiers still strove to reach the walls. By one ladder at last they were won.

A Grenadier officer named Canch reared it, and the two mounted together, followed by their men.

GRANT:

The garrison became terror-stricken; another ladder and another was reared; with pale faces, with flashing eyes, and mouths black with biting cartridges up rushed the desperate stormers– the ramparts were won; by bayonet and butt-end the garrison were driven off. Some were destroyed on the instant; others, in sullen despair, flung down their arms. The gallant Ridge fell, "and no man died that night with more glory–yet many died, and there was much glory."

While the attack against the castle by the 3rd Division was proceeding, a tremendous conflict was ensuing at the breaches between Santa Maria and Trinidad. William Napier said of it: "… they were such as if the earth had been rent asunder, and its central fires were bursting upwards uncontrolled …"

D. H. PARRY:

As the stormers of the Light Division moved off, Major Peter O'Hare–who had risen from the ranks to a commission in the 95th (a most unusual thing in those days), and who was, moreover, one of the ugliest men and one of the bravest in the army–shook hands with George Simmonds, of the Rifles, saying–"A lieutenant-colonel or cold meat in a few hours!" They found him next morning stone dead and stark naked, with nearly a dozen bullets in his gallant frame. Officers were divided into two categories by the Peninsular soldiers–the "Come on" and the "Go on." O'Hare was a "Come on."

As the troops approached the breaches, the latter seemed buried in darkness; save the explosion of a solitary musket, there came no sound from them. The hay-packs were flung into the ditch, and the stormers of the light division – 500 chosen men–leaped downward without opposition, when suddenly a bright flame that shot upward showed all the terrors of the scene. On one side the yawning breaches, and the ramparts on each side bristling with steel bayonets, and dark with French uniforms; on the other, the scarlet columns of the British, "deep and broad, and coming on like streams of burning lava."

A dreadful crash as of thunder followed, accompanied by a sudden blaze of light. Then all was dark again; and it became known that, by the explosion of hundreds of live shells and sunken powder-barrels, the stormers had been blown to pieces.

At the brink of the ditch, the veterans of the light division stood for a moment, as if amazed by this terrific catastrophe; then, with shouts of rage and defiance, they flew down the ladders, or, reckless of the depth, plunged like madmen into the dark gulf below; while, amid a blinding blaze of musketry, the men of the 4th division came on with similar fury, but only to get entangled in the counter-guard of the Trinidad, which was so full of mud and water that a hundred of the fusiliers, all men who had fought and conquered at Albuera, were smothered in it without a wound.

Those who followed them wheeled to the left, and came upon a rough and unfinished ravelin, which, in the dire confusion of the time, was mistaken for the breach, and instantly covered with brave fellows, whom a fire from the ramparts beyond it swept away in hundreds. Frightful was the disorder now; the ravelin was crowded with the men of both divisions, and while some fired at the ramparts, others rushed towards the breach, all cheering vehemently. "The enemy's shouts were also loud and terrible, and the bursting of shells and grenades, the roaring of guns from the flanks, answered by the iron howitzers from the parallel, the heavy roll and explosion of the powder-barrels, the whizzing flight of blazing splinters, the loud exhortations of the officers, and the continual clatter of the muskets, made up a maddening din."

Like leaves swept before a whirlwind, a multitude of soldiers rushed to the summit of the great breach; but lo! across that perilous gap glittered a dreadful and impassable chevaux-de-frise. It was composed of sword-blades, keenly edged, sharply-pointed, and fixed immovably in ponderous beams, chained together, and wedged deep in the shot-riven ruins. For ten feet in front of this dreadful barrier the ascent was covered with loose planks, studded with iron spikes, on which the feet of the foremost being set, the planks slipped, as they were intended to do, and the men rolled, torn and dying, to perish amid the ranks behind. Beyond the chevaux-de-frise were seen the dense dark ranks of the French, plying their volleys thick and fast, laughing, shouting, gesticulating, and exulting in their dreadful stratagem, their brass drums the while incessantly beating the pas de charge. They plied their shot with terrible rapidity, for every man had, as we have said, three loaded muskets, each of which, in addition to a ball cartridge, contained a cylinder of wood filled with slugs, which scattered like hail when they were discharged. Many officers and men who reached the summit grappled with the sharp blades of the chevaux-de-frise, and in striving to break them down were severely cut and bayoneted.

Again and again did the fierce stormers hurl their strength up the breaches, to be repelled by these barriers of bristling steel; while the bursting shells and the thundering powder-barrels shed tempests of iron splinters and blazing brands among them. Hundreds had fallen, and hundreds more were falling, wounded unto death by mutilations of every description. Blood and brains, torn corpses and dismembered fragments, made the ascent of the breaches and all the approaches thereto beyond description horrible and loathly. "Nevertheless, officers of all stations, followed more or less numerously by their men, were seen to start out, as if struck by a sudden madness, and rush into the breaches, which, yawning and glittering with steel, seemed like the mouth of some huge dragon, belching forth smoke and flame."

Barrels of flaming pitch, and bags of gunpowder that exploded on reaching the ground, were poured into the crowded ditches, where the bundles of hay that had been used to facilitate a descent took fire, and thus many of the helpless wounded were unhappily burned to death. Into these ditches the storming parties were ultimately driven, where, unable to advance, yet unwilling to retire, they remained, enduring with a degree of patience that was most marvellous

177

the weight of a fire to which even they had seen no parallel. Gathered in dark groups, they leaned on their muskets and looked with fierce desperation at the Trinidad; while the French, stepping out upon the ramparts, aimed shot after shot among them by the brilliant but ghastly light of the fire-balls, which they threw over from time to time.

"Why don't you come into Badajoz?" was ever and anon their mocking cry.

Ere the cathedral bells tolled midnight more than a thousand of our men had fallen.

Lord Wellington now gave orders to retire and re-form for a second assault. He had just heard that the castle was won; and, believing that the enemy would still defend the town, he was resolved to assail the breaches again.

The retreat from the ditch was not effected without fresh carnage and confusion. All this while the 3rd division was lying close in the captured castle, and, either from fear of risking the loss of a point which ensured the ultimate capture of the whole place, or that the egress was too difficult, made no attempt to scour the breaches on the inside.

In another quarter, the 5th division had commenced the false attack on the outwork called the Pardeleras; and on the right of the Guadiana, the Portuguese were sharply engaged at the end of the long bridge. Thus the town of Badajoz was literally zoned with fire, the flashes of which were reflected a thousand times in the waters around it.

The 3rd Division had taken the castle by about 11:30, and at about that time Leith's 5th Division came under the breastwork before San Vincente at the west end of the town. Together with a Portuguese Brigade, the regiments halted undiscovered, a few yards from a guardhouse where the French could be heard talking.

D. H. Parry describes what then occurred:

All was silent around them; the wash of the river rose on their left, the fortifications showed clearly before them as the moon came out; they knew that their comrades far off on the other side of the citadel were engaged, and an eager thrill went through the ranks. A sentinel discovered the mass of men from the glint of the moon-beams on the bayonets at the moment when our engineer guide exclaimed, "Now's the time!" and as he fired we ran forward against the gateway.

Seized by a sudden panic the Portuguese ladder-party bolted, but the Britons snatched up the heavy ladders and the axemen chopped fearlessly at the gate and wooden palings that fringed the covered way, while from the walls which towered 31 feet overhead, a tempest of beams, and shot, and bags of powder showered down on the heads of the division.

They cleared the paling and jumped into the ditch, crossing the cunette with difficulty and finding the ladders too short for the top of the escarp; the engineer was killed, and a small mine exploded in the ditch, but fortunately the ramparts at San Vincente had been thinned of their defenders, who had gone to fight Picton's men in the castle, and three ladders were placed under an embrasure where there was a gabion instead of a gun and where the scarp was only 20 feet high.

Hand over hand, the troops clambered up under a fire that struck down dozens, and the topmost stormers had to be pushed up by those behind in order to reach the embrasure; but as the leading men got a foothold, they pulled the others up, until the red-coated mass grew larger and larger, and then half the King's Own attacked the houses while the rest of the division charged along the ramparts, pushing the stubborn garrison out of three bastions in succession. Shouts mingled with the crash of grape-shot and the hum of shells; yells and curses were heard amid the boom of cannon and the incessant crack-crack of muskets fired at close quarters.

The awestruck watchers on the hill above our camp, spectators of the terrible struggle, stood in an agony of suspense; the entire citadel seemed full of flame and noise, as mine after mine exploded, and fireball after fireball was flung over the walls to enable the besieged to shoot their assailants. Napoleon's soldiers fought gallantly, officer and man vying with each other in their efforts to keep us out, and as we drove them from one defence they retired into another and stood once more at bay.

Philippon, and Vielland, the second in command, though both wounded, hurried, sword in hand, from rampart to rampart, encouraging their men, while the solemn chime of the cathedral rung out unnoticed hour after hour of that night of horrors.

Watching from a hill, Wellington exclaimed repeatedly: "What can be the matter?" sending one aide-de-camp after another to report progress, as the glare revealed faces on the ramparts, and the peculiar hollow booming reached his ears, caused by the defenders firing down into the cavernous depths of the ditch.

D. H. Parry:

A strange incident occurred at San Vincente when General Walker fell riddled with balls on the parapet. Either by accident or design, he made a masonic sign as he staggered backwards, and a brother-mason in the French ranks dashed aside the threatening bayonets of his countrymen and saved him; afterwards, it is said, the General found his preserver a prisoner-of-war in Scotland, and procured his exchange in remembrance of his chivalry on the ramparts of Badajoz.

James Grant:

During the feint on the Pardeleras, Walker's brigade, surmounting every obstacle–a mine that was sprung beneath the soldiers' feet, beams of wood and live shells rolled downward on their heads, showers of whistling grape from the flank of the ditch, and withering musketry–had won the ramparts of San Vincente, and, wheeling to the right, advanced in the direction of the breaches, where their presence was sorely needed.

By one of those strange accidents which occur in war, and for which there can be no accounting, an unexpected stand made by a body of the enemy, under General Vielland, paralysed their energies, and they were driven back to the very bastion over which they had found an entrance.

D.H. Parry explains what actually occurred:

The 5th Division had obtained firm hold, knowing nothing of what was happening at the castle or at the breaches, and as a portion of them were pursuing the enemy along the walls, in rounding an angle came upon a solitary gun with one artilleryman, who flung a port-fire down as they approached.

There arose a cry of "A mine! a mine!" and the men retired helter-skelter, followed by a fresh body of the French under Vielland, who drove them back to the parapet again, and pitched several over into the ditch. Now a reserve of the 38th, under Colonel Nugent, about two hundred strong, poured a volley into the French, and the men of the 5th Division rallied and charged along the wall toward the breaches.

Grant confirms this:

There, however, 200 men of the 38th, or Staffordshire, who had been kept well in hand by Colonel Nugent, checked the French by a volley, and made a rush at them with the bayonet. Walker's brigade then recovered its order, and advancing in a body towards the breaches, took their defenders in the rear of those dreadful chevaux-de-frise, and entirely dispersed them.

Parry:

The King's Own had entered the town at the first onslaught of Leith's division, and in strange contrast to the uproar of the bastions, with bayonets fixed and bugles blowing, they filed through the streets, silent and deserted as the tomb; every door shut, lamps alight in many of the windows, but not a soul abroad except some soldiers leading ammunition mules, who were promptly taken prisoners.

Sometimes a window opened and was immediately closed again; voices were heard, but the speakers were invisible; a few shots came from beneath the doors, but they were unheeded, and the battalion continued its march into the Great Square, where the same silence reigned, although the houses round it were brilliantly lighted.

The renewed fury at the breaches turned their steps in that direction, and they hurried off to take the garrison in rear: but they were met by a fire that repulsed them, and they continued their wandering down streets and lanes, unmolested, for the French began to be disheartened.

The Trinidad and Santa Maria were still wellnigh impregnable, in spite of their shattered condition, if the garrison had been able to concentrate there, but the capture of San Vincente had let us in behind them.

JAMES GRANT:

The 4th and light divisions, which Lord Wellington had withdrawn and re-formed, were led again to the front. The garrison offered no further resistance, and Badajoz was entered on all sides, for by this time the 3rd division had blown open the gates of the castle. With a few hundred men, Generals Phillipon and Vielland, both wounded, fled across the river into Fort San Christoval, where next day they hoisted a white flag, in token that they and their men, like those in the town, were prisoners of war, surrendering to Lord Fitzroy Somerset, the future leader of our armies in the Crimea. There were here taken, for transmission to London, the colours of the garrison, and those of the regiment of Hesse-Darmstadt.

With the capture of Badajoz the scene of horrors did not close, for others followed the wild fury of the assault and storm; and many a brave officer and many a good soldier strove in vain to check the madness that prevailed among their comrades. For hours ere the dawn came, shameless rapacity, brutal intemperance, cruelty, murder, and savage lust reigned supreme. The streets and squares resounded with shrieks and lamentations, with wild shouts and reckless oaths, the roar of flames bursting from windows, the smashing in of doors, the report of firearms; and for two days and nights this was the state of things in the picturesque old thoroughfares of Badajoz. On the third day discipline resumed its sway; the wounded were removed and the dead buried. There were expended during the siege 31,861 round shot, 1,826 shells, and 1,659 rounds of grape. There were captured 179 guns and mortars, and 6,000 stand of arms.

During the siege and storm, there fell 5,000 men and officers, including 700 Portuguese; of these, 3,500 perished on the night of the assault. Five generals were wounded, Kemp, Harvey, Bowes, Colville, and Picton; the first three severely. More than 2,000 officers and men perished in the breaches alone, and no regiments suffered more than the 43rd and 52nd Light Infantry.

It is perhaps appropriate that this bloody affair should be summed-up in the lyric prose of William Napier, historian-supreme of the Peninsular Wars:

Let it be remembered that this frightful carnage took place in a space of less than a hundred yards square; that the slain died not all suddenly, nor by one manner of death; that some perished by steel, some by shot, some by water; that some were crushed and mangled by heavy weights, some trampled upon, some dashed to atoms by the fiery explosions; that for hours this destruction was endured without shrinking, and that the town was won at last—these things considered, it must be admitted that a British army bears with it an awful power. And false would it be to say that the French were feeble men; the garrison fought manfully and with good discipline, behaving worthily. Shame there was none, on any side. Yet who shall do justice to the bravery of the British soldiers—the noble emulation of the officers? Who shall measure out the glory of Ridge, of Macleod, of Nicholas; of O'Hare, of the Rifles, who perished on the breach at the head of the stormers, and with him nearly all the volunteers for that desperate service? Who shall describe the valour of that Portuguese grenadier, who was killed, the first man at the Santa Maria; or the martial fury of that desperate rifleman who, in his resolution to win, thrust himself beneath the chained sword-blades, and there suffered the enemy to dash his head to pieces with the butt-ends of their muskets? Who can sufficiently honour the intrepidity of Walker, of Shaw, of Canch, or the resolution of Ferguson, of the 43rd, who, having at Rodrigo received two deep wounds, was here with all his hurts still open, leading the stormers of his regiment, the third time a volunteer, and the third time wounded? Nor are these selected as preeminent; many and signal were the other examples of unbounded devotion, some known, some that will never be known; for in such a tumult much passed unobserved, and often the observers fell themselves, ere they could bear testimony to what they saw; but no age, no nation ever sent forth braver troops to battle than those who stormed Badajoz! When the havoc of the night was told to Wellington, the pride of conquest sunk into a passionate burst of grief for the loss of his gallant soldiers.

The significance and lessons of the fall of Badajoz were many and varied; as summed up by British military Historian David Chandler, they included:

1. The Southern Corridor of the Peninsular War was placed firmly in Allied hands.
2. The tide of the war had turned. The French were now on the defensive as Wellington's 60,000 confounded and dominated 180,000 French troops.
3. This success inspired renewed efforts by Spanish guerillas.
4. In due course, the capture of Badajoz led indirectly to the victory at Salamanca.
5. However, in the long run, failure before Burgos in October 1812 was to lead to Wellington's retreat that winter into Portugal. Nevertheless, Badajoz never again changed hands during the Peninsular War and everything was regained in the following year 1813, at Vitoria.

BRITISH LOSSES AT THE STORMING OF BADAJOZ
Total Killed, Wounded & Missing

General Staff	17	Light Division:		
Royal Artillery	17	1/43rd Foot	341	
Royal Engineers	10	1/52nd Foot	320	
Assistant Engineers	3	1/95th Foot	194	
		3/95th Foot	64	
Third Division:		*Total Light Division*	*919*	
Kempt's Brigade:		Brunswick Oels, dispersed in companies		
1/45th Foot	97	in 4th and 5th Divisions	35	
3/60th Foot	35			
74th Foot	54	Total British loss	2,983	
1/88th Foot	144	Portuguese	730	
J. Campbell's brigade		*General Total*	*3,713*	
2/5th Foot	43			
77th Foot	14	Losses during		
2/83rd Foot	69	previous operations	957	
94th Foot	65			
Total 3rd Division	*521*	The total loss during the siege and storm		
		would therefore appear to been	4,670	
Fourth Division				
Kemmis's Brigade:		**STRENGTH OF THE FRENCH GARRISON, MARCH 15**		
3/27th Foot	185	Staff	25	
1/40th Foot	236	Infantry (officers & men):		
		3/9th Léger	580	
Bowes's Brigade:		1/28th Léger	597	
1/7th Foot	180	1/58th Ligne	450	
1/23rd Foot	151	3/88th Ligne	600	
1/48th Foot	173	3/103rd Ligne	540	
Total 4th Division	*925*	64th Ligne (2 companies)	130	
		Hesse-Darmstadt (2 batts.)	910	
Fifth Division:		Juramentados	54	
Hay's Brigade:			= 3,861 infantry	
3/1st Foot	–	Cavalry	42	
1/9th Foot	–	Artillery	261	
1/38th foot	42	Engineers and Sappers	260	
Walker's Brigade:		Sick in Hospital	300	
1/4th Foot	230	Civil Departments,		
2/30th Foot	130	non-combatants, &c.	254	
2/44th Foot	134		5,003	
Total 5th Division	*536*			

1st Bn. 4th (King's Own) Regt. of Foot
2nd Bn. 5th (Northumberland) Regt. of Foot
1st Bn. 7th Regt. of Foot (Royal Fuzileers)
1st Bn. 23rd Regt. of Foot (Royal Welsh Fuzileers)
3rd Bn. 27th (Inniskilling) Regt. of Foot
2nd Bn. 30th (Cambridgeshire) Regt. of Foot
2nd Bn. 38th (1st Straffordshire) Regt. of Foot
1st Bn. 40th (2nd Somersetshire) Regt. of Foot
1st Bn. 43rd (Monmouthshire Light Infantry) Regt.
1st Bn. 52nd (Oxfordshire Light Infantry) Regt.
2nd Bn. 44th (East Essex) Regt. of Foot
1st Bn. 45th (Nottinghamshire) Regt. of Foot
1st Bn. 48th (Northamptonshire) Regt. of Foot
77th (East Middlesex) Regt. of Foot
5th Bn. 60th (Royal American) Regt. of Foot
74th (Highland) Regt. of Foot
2nd Bn. 83rd Regt. of Foot
1st Bn. 88th Regt. of Foot (Connaught Rangers)
94th Regt. of Foot
95th Regt. of Foot (Rifle Corps)

"… the fire gradually slackened from the breach … I heard a cheering which I knew to proceed from within the town, and shortly afterwards a cry of 'Blood and 'ounds! Where's the Light Division? The town's our own! Hurrah!' This proceeds, no doubt, from some of the 3rd Division."
Edward Costello, 95th Rifles

THE APPROACH TO THE CASTLE STORMED BY THE 3RD DIVISION. THE WALLS ARE STILL IN GOOD CONDITION AND MUST BE MUCH AS THEY APPEARED DURING THE SIEGE.

'ON THE GROUND' IN BADAJOZ

We came into the city across the bridge over the River Guadiana, with Fort Christobal on our left, to the area where, behind the high city walls, the castle ruins loom over the area traversed by Picton's 3rd Division in their attack. We found rooms in the Hotel Cervantes, cool, clean and fascinatingly Spanish. In the heat of mid-morning we traversed the ramparts and into the castle area, found and studied the breaches, pausing to gaze sightlessly into the eye-narrowing bright sunlight as we imagined the turbulent events of the escalade in the fearful darkness of the night of 5/6 April 1812. Then a major study of the major breaches, identifiable by areas of obviously repaired wall, into which cannon-balls had been imbedded to spell out the year '1812.' On top of the walls in the area, we disturbed a pair of young lovers, or maybe worse if the evidence of many used syringes littering the ground was to be believed. It is a peaceful area of gardens bordering busy roads, and the imagination takes an awful pasting!

Next we walked right round the outside of the town walls, and studied that part of the defences where Picton's 3rd and Leith's 5th Divisions made their entrance, to take the breach in the rear and take the town. It was all so clear and so understandable on this unchanged ground, hallowed by the memory of the courage and fortitude of our ancestors, 180 years ago.

Back to the car and across the bridge again, over the River Guadiana and up to Fort Christobal, laying opposite Badajoz so that a panoramic view of the city walls could be seen - and duly photographed. Fort Christobal is in ruins yet sufficiently intact for one to get a pretty good idea of its size and importance, enough to resist Wellington's assaults twice, in May and June 1811 - it finally raised the white flag on the day following the fall of Badajoz.

In the cool of evening, along with seemingly most of the town's population, we walked the narrow streets, purposely thus to make difficult for invaders who might have breached the walls. It was all so bustling and colourful - and memorable.

THE PRACTICALITIES OF SIEGECRAFT

In considering that two previous attempts to take Badajoz had failed, it is worth studying some of the practical aspects of the sieges of both Badajoz and Cuidad Rodrigo, particularly so far as "breaching" is concerned. When studying sieges, it soon becomes obvious that even when an apparently practicable breach has been made there are many different ways by which the defender, comparatively easily and quickly, can make it impracticable. The most practicable breach was one where a gap has been caused in the curtain wall, the debris from it falling to form a slope up to the hole capable of being scaled by an active man. Adequate time and sufficient heavy guns employed intelligently could make it impossible for the defender to prevent the breaching of a curtain wall–but he could, in a few hours, render the breach impracticable for assault.

The simplest way was to shovel away the debris forming the slope or ramp up to the breach, so that when the attacker came up to it he found himself facing an unscalable vertical face. Or the defender could dig or erect effective defences (retrenchments) *inside* or behind the breach, out of sight of the attacker until confronted with this unexpected obstacle. Storming-parties, however courageous, could not physically surmount certain obstacles, such as a wall higher than eight or ten feet, or which was more than a few feet higher than the length of the scaling-ladders carried. When reading accounts of historical sieges it invariably seems that scaling-ladders were *always* four or five feet too short! Stormers could not cross ditches of more than a certain width without some means of bridging the gap–and, as in the case of the ladders, the bridging material invariably seems to have been too short. In the stress of battle, usually at night and in darkness, the storming party, unaware of what lay before them within the breach, were often held up or defeated by quite simple barriers that formed complete obstacles. When assaulting through a single breach, the entire defensive resources of the garrison can be concentrated on the clearly defined lone defile, so the besiegers were well advised to stretch the defenders by widening their breaching frontage.

THE BATTLE OF SALAMANCA–22 JULY 1812

Before Salamanca. The condition of the army was excellent, and the most exact discipline was preserved, while all unnecessary parades were dispensed with. The march ended, the soldier enjoyed all the comforts he could command. If foot-sore, he had rest to recruit; if untired, he had permission to amuse himself. His arms and appointments were rigidly inspected, his supper cooked, his bivouac formed, and at sunrise he rose with the reveille, to resume with light heart and "gallant hope" the march that was to lead to victory.
Maxwell

French General Maximilien Sebastien Foy fought with great distinction at Salamanca, covering the retreat of the routed French army with considerable skill. In his personal journal, under the date-line 28 July 1812 – six days after the battle–he wrote his own verdict of the contest:

> The battle of Salamanca is the most masterly in its management, the most considerable in the number of troops engaged, and the most important in results of all the victories that the English have gained in these latter days. It raises Lord Wellington almost to the level of Marlborough. Hitherto we had been aware of his prudence, his eye for choosing a position, and his skill in utilizing it. At Salamanca he has shown himself a great and able master of maneuvers. He kept his disposition concealed for almost the whole day, he waited till we were committed to our movement before he developed his own: he played a safe game: he fought in the oblique order, it was a battle in the style of Frederic the Great.

The fall of Cuidad Rodrigo and Badajoz reversed the previous position of the British and French armies. For whereas since Junot in 1808 first occupied Lisbon, the French had either been in possession of Portugal or of the frontier fortresses, and thus stood in the way of invasion. Now Wellington had the power of advancing on Madrid either by the valley of the Douro in the north, or by the Tagus in the south, dependent upon having sufficient men to justify such an invasion. Eventually, he determined to enter Spain according to the plan adopted by Sir John Moore in 1808, which he had himself suggested.

On 17 June Wellington crossed the Tormes River and captured some small forts at Salamanca on 27 June. Marmont, retiring north of the Douro (which was then in flood) guarded the river from the bridge at Toro on the west, that of Tordesillas in the centre, and Simancas to the east, on a front of 30 miles. British troops faced the French position on the south (or left) bank of the river, on a frontage of 22 miles from the Guarena river opposite the Toro on the west, to Rueda on the east. Wellington hoped that Marmont, for want of food, would be obliged to retire after a few days, but he held on. It was not possible to cross the river without incurring the risk of severe fighting, so Wellington waited and while he did so, Marmont moved on 15/16 July to Toro. Here he crossed and advanced a short distance southwards, then counter-marched his army throughout the night up the river bank, to make an unopposed crossing at Tordesillas, having covered between 40 and 50 miles without resting.

Wellington heard of the French being across the river on the night of the 17th at Toro, where he had gone on learning of the French advance in that part of the position. He drew in his right from Rueda, concentrating on the west bank of the Guarena which, like the Trabancos, runs due south to the Douro river. In falling back from the Trabancos, Wellington's right was closely followed by the French on 18 July, but when they attempted to cross the Guarena in the evening they were repulsed. Both armies were in the area of Canizal on 19 July and on the evening of that day Marmont marched southwards up the right bank of Guarena; moving up the opposite

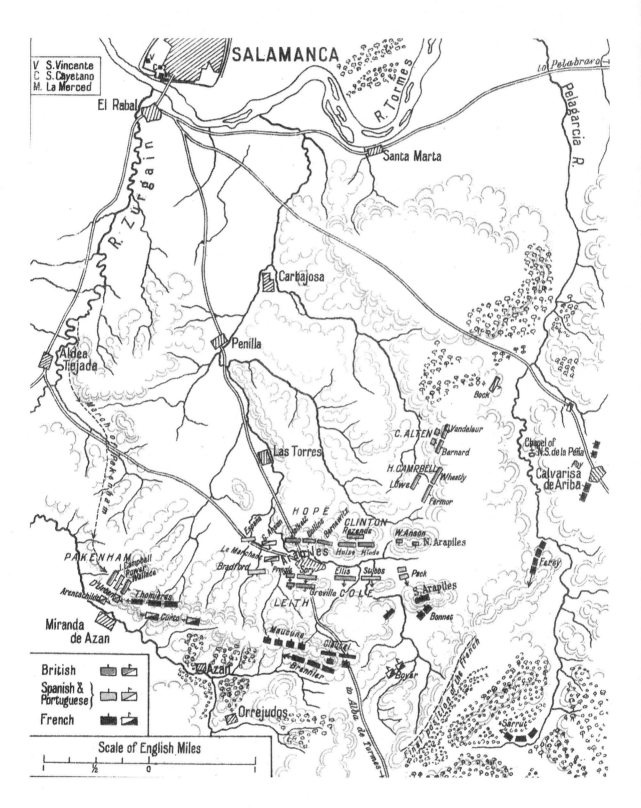

SALAMACA. At the time Packenham's 3rd Division started the battle.

bank, Wellington conformed. Both commanders wished to cross the Tormes river, which flows from the mountains southwards as far as Huerta, there bending sharply westwards, reaches Salamanca in ten miles, when it flows in a north-west direction to the Douro.

Wellington's object was to cover Salamanca and the high road leading to Cuidad Rodrigo 50 miles to its south-west; to threaten that town Marmont would have to cross the river.

Naming them from upstream, the fords were at Alba de Tormes, ten miles south of Huerta, where there was a good ford; and between Huerta there were fords at Aldea Lengua and Santa Marta, the last only four miles on the east side of Salamanca. Wellington had placed a garrison in Alba de Tormes and did not imagine that the ford would be attempted by Marmont, but the Spanish garrison abandoned the fort on the approach of the French, without informing Wellington. On 20 July, for some hours the opposing armies–horse, artillery, and foot–marched within musket-range of each other, over parallel ridges; occasionally the artillery fired a shot, and the officers of both armies saluted each other from time to time. Outmarching the Allies, the French reached the Huerta ford, to hold it along with that of Alba de Tormes, where they placed a garrison in the Spanish-abandoned fort. Next day, 21 July both armies crossed at the fords they were holding–the French at Alba de Tormes and Huerta; the British at Aldea Lengua and Santa Maria.

Now let us read the century-old account of Major Arthur Griffiths on what transpired:

In after years the Duke of Wellington told a friend that he looked upon Salamanca, Vittoria, and Waterloo as his three best battles. "Salamanca," he went on to say, "relieved the whole south of Spain, changed all the prospects of the war, and was felt even in Russia," where Napoleon was just then meeting his first great failure. Salamanca also showed Wellington, although strategically he had been outmaneuvred in a tactical sense, at his best: it displayed the finest qualities of his generalship, his quick unerring eye, his prompt detection of his enemy's mistakes, his consummate skill in turning them to his own advantage. For it was the serious error made by Marshal Marmont that led to Wellington's victory. "He wished to cut me off," said the Duke; "I saw that in attempting this he was spreading himself over more ground than he could defend; I resolved to attack him, and succeeded in my object very quickly. One of the French generals said I had beaten 40,000 men in forty minutes."

"Mon cher Alava, Marmont est perdu," was his remark to the Spanish General of that name as he shut his telescope with stern contentment, and gave the orders that resulted in victory.

Up to that moment, however, Wellington had been much disquieted. Matters had not gone well with him; he had been really out-maneuvred, out-generalled. Just when Marmont gave himself into his hands he had been on the point of retreating while there was yet time. How Wellington felt that morning may be gathered from a story told at Strathfieldsaye years afterwards in the Duke's presence by that very General Alava mentioned above. The Duke had been too busy, so the story ran, probably too anxious to think of breakfast on the morning of the battle. About two o'clock in the afternoon his Staff seized the opportunity of laying out a picnic lunch in the courtyard of the farmhouse. Wellington rode into the enclosure, but refused to dismount like the rest, declined to eat anything, and desired the others to make haste. At last someone persuaded him to take a bite of bread and the leg of a roast fowl, when, suddenly, on the arrival of an aide-de-camp with news, he threw away the leg and galloped out of the yard, calling upon the rest to follow him at once.

The news brought him was that of the French flank movement which so jeopardised them. "I knew something serious was going to happen," was Alava's comment on this episode, "when anything so precious as the leg of a fowl was thrown away." Food was scarce in those days.

Digressing, it is both amusing and interesting to note that as recently as January 1991 Elizabeth Ray, a journalist writing in the London daily Telegraph, went into print on the subject of the Duke's culinary tastes:

The first Duke of Wellington was certain no gourmet. His chef, Felix, one of the best in England at the time, departed his service in tears, saying: "I serve him a dinner that would make Ude or Francatelli burst with envy, and he says nothing; I serve him a dinner badly dressed by the cookmaid, and he says nothing. I cannot live with such a master, if he was a hundred times a hero."

So how does it come about that we have Beef Wellington, a fillet of beef covered by a layer of foie gras and mushrooms, then encased in rich pastry?

The duke seemed fond of beef (I have also read that he liked rice pudding); a devoted friend and comrade-in-arms, his Spanish liaison officer during the Peninsular War, General Avala, is quoted as saying that whenever he travelled with the duke and asked what time they would leave the next day the answer was usually "at daylight." To the question of what he wanted for dinner, the reply was invariably "cold meat" which, Avala said, had given him a horror of the words "daylight" and "cold meat."

The duke's lack of sophistication was obviously not due to a lack of adequate catering arrangements, as in those days the army would take wagon-loads of equipment, including furniture for the officers' tents. So it must have been the indifference to food that seems to affect great commanders.

Napoleon was apparently the same, eating immediately he felt hungry and without either comment or enjoyment–and he watered his wine. Field Marshal Montgomery was a teetotaller and there is no indication that he was particularly interested in what he ate either. Anyone aiming at high command had better be abstemious.

But to return to Beef Wellington, I think it might be an American version of a dish that started out on this side of the Atlantic as boeuf en croute and returned with a new name.

The present duke doesn't know either. He thinks it might be a clever device to cash in on the name, "Like the astute gum boot manufacturer". The first duke's boots were leather, worn for riding.

Miss Ray might be well informed on food but lacks a certain knowledge of military history– the Spanish liaison officer's name was actually Alava–General Miguel de, who served aboard the Spanish fleet at Trafalgar, was Spanish Commissioner on the Duke's staff during the Waterloo Campaign and, as such, attended the Duchess of Richmond's ball and was present at both the battles of Quatre Bras and Waterloo.

However, back to Salamanca and Major Arthur Griffith's account:

The position of the English and French forces in the Peninsula during the early summer of 1812 was briefly as follows:

Wellington was still in Portugal, although he had captured the two strongholds of Ciudad Rodrigo in Spain. These were to serve as advanced posts for his invasion of that country and the expulsion of the French, the main object of the Peninsular War. But there were 300,000 Frenchmen in Spain distributed nearly all over it, in five different armies. That immediately opposed to Wellington was under Marshal Marmont; it was said to be nominally 70,000 strong, and further reinforcements were expected from France. Moreover, Marmont was in touch with three other armies, one to the north of him, one behind him at Madrid, a third to the south in Andalusia.

Wellington had never more than 50,000, so it is obvious that while Marmont alone was quite equal to cope with him, he might be courting overwhelmingly superior concentration.

Again, Marshal Marmont's army was a fine fighting force in excellent condition, stronger in artillery, although inferior in cavalry; an army, moreover, composed entirely of Frenchmen, of men animated with one spirit, obeying one supreme leader, the great Emperor himself.

Wellington, on the other hand, commanded a mixed force: it was made up of four different nationalities–British, German, Spanish, and Portuguese. His cavalry was superior, the very flower of British horsemen, but he had fewer guns; his men were ill-found, pay was in arrears, for ready-money was desperately scarce through the niggardliness of the British Government, and the want of it, the real sinews of war, was severely felt in his matter of supplies–which had to be paid for cash down. Still, Wellington was nothing daunted. He hoped to achieve some signal success if only he moved against Marmont, taking him promptly, and before his supports could join him. There was at this time much friction between the French generals, and this was likely still further to delay concentration. Everything depended, therefore, upon immediate action.

It was now the month of July, and for the first fortnight the two Generals were like skilful chess players engaged in a closely contested game. Each tried to take advantage of the other and bring on a checkmate. Marmont had, if anything, the best of it. The very direction of his advance jeopardised the safety of the English army, and Wellington's only hope was in rapid retreat. The French now all but forestalled them at Salamanca, and it was a race between them for the River Tormes, behind which lay the English line of communications with Portugal and the rear. As the two armies hurried forward, the spectacle is described by eyewitnesses as almost unparalleled in war. "For there was seen," says Napier, the historian of the war, "the hostile columns of infantry at only half musket-shot from each other (not a hundred yards!) marching impetuously towards a common goal, the officers on each side pointing forwards with their swords, touching their hats and waving their hands in courtesy, while the German cavalry, huge men on huge horses, rode between in a compact body as if to prevent a collision. At times the loud word of command to hasten the march was heard passing from the front to the rear, and now and then the rushing sound of bullets came sweeping over the column, whose violent pace as continuously accelerated."

This neck-and-neck contest went on for ten miles, and in the most perfect order. The same strange maneuvre was repeated a couple of days later, and on a larger scale. In the end Wellington reached Salamanca safely, but none too soon. The French had the command of two fords on the Tormes river, and by threatening the road to Ciudad Rodrigo, could still force the English to retire.

At daybreak on July 22nd, the day of the battle, the positions of the two opposing armies were as follows:

The English were on both sides of the River Tormes; the bulk certainly on the left or southern shore, but one Division, the 3rd, was still on the right bank, as Wellington did not feel certain by which side Marmont would move. The left flank of the army rested about Santa Marta in the low ground; the right extended eastwards towards the village of Arapiles and the hills of that name.

The French at daylight were advancing into position; they had crossed the river by the fords of Huerta and Alba de Tormes, and had occupied the heights opposite the English from Calvariza Aniba to Nuestra Señora de la Pena.

The possession of these two last-named hills now became of consequence to both armies. They were called the Arapiles hills–sometimes Los Dos Hermanitos, "the two little brothers"–and they stood steep and rugged, rising like two small fortresses straight up out of the plain. Had the French gained them both, Wellington would have been obliged to throw back his right and fight with his back against the river–always a hazardous proceeding. But once more there was a race between the opponents, and the result may be called a dead-heat. Both sent off Light troops flying past to capture the hills, and each got the one nearest it. The twins were divided, and for the rest of the day one was known as the English Arapiles, or Hermanito, the other as the French.

This first small contest had an important bearing on coming events. It confirmed Wellington in his intention of retreating, but it obliged him to postpone his movement till after dark. For the French, in occupation of their Hermanito, could use it as a pivot around which to gather strongly and then swing a determined attack on Wellington's retrograding columns. So menacing was their possession of this hill that Wellington was half disposed to attack and try to capture it. For he forebore, preferring to wait on events, and knowing something of Marmont's impetuous character, hoping still that the Frenchman might commit himself to a general attack on the English position.

This was precisely what happened. Marmont was seized with a sudden fear that the English were about to escape him. He saw great columns of dust rising from the Ciudad Rodrigo road, and rashly concluded that the enemy was already in full retreat. These new dispositions amounted to a complete change of front. Till now the English line had faced north-east from the river at Santa Marta to the Arapiles hill; hereafter it faced south from Aldea Tejada on the right to the Arapiles village and hill, which became the left. This left was held by the 4th Division; the 6th and 7th Divisions were in a hollow, compact behind and below the Arapiles hill; the 3rd Division was brought across the river, and being posted at Aldea Tejada, became the right of the line.

Inspired by the groundless fear that Wellington was retreating, he directed General Thomière, supported by the Light cavalry, to march on Miranda and intercept the English in their supposed retreat; while he himself, if the English showed fight, would fall upon them with all his remaining force at about the Arapiles village and hills. Thomière's movement was a fatal mistake. By this hasty march the French advance–their left–was separated from their centre and their right; both the latter were still in the woods to the rear or crossing the river, and unable to support Thomière's division. Marmont had, in fact, as the Duke put it, spread himself out too far.

It must have been the report of Thomière's movement that was brought Wellington in the farmyard, and led to the sacrifice of the drumstick of a fowl. Napier says that the Duke was resting when the news reached him; but whether he was throwing away an untasted lunch or sleeping, he certainly rode straight to the English Arapiles hill, and from that high vantage ground fully realised what Marmont had done. It was then, no doubt, he told Alava that it was all over with Marmont. For Wellington no sooner saw the situation than he grasped it with the full and complete appreciation that marks true genius in war. His orders were few and precise; their object was to fall upon Marmont's advance, and crush it before it could be reinforced. He formed his troops in three lines: the first consisted of his 4th and 5th Divisions, with some Portuguese on their right, and beyond them the Heavy cavalry. In the second line were the 6th and 7th Divisions, with the Light cavalry on their right; and in reserve the third line, made up of the 1st and 8th Divisions, the rest of the Portuguese, and more cavalry. The right of the second line was closed by the 3rd Division, under General Pakenham, and to him was entrusted the honour of opening the ball. For as soon as the above-mentioned changes of position were completed, Pakenham was ordered to come up in four columns with 12 guns on his left or inner flank and cross the enemy's line of march. As soon as Pakenham attacked, the first line was also to advance and second his endeavour. Then, on the English left, which would thus become uncovered, an assault was to be made on the French Hermanito hill.

And here, at this the most critical juncture, on the very eve of joining issue with a determined enemy in a great and momentous struggle, Wellington gave a fresh proof of his iron nerve and strong character. Troops march slowly: three miles an hour is the average rate of infantry. There must therefore be a considerable interval of time before the orders first issued could take effect; the French division on the march under Thomière had a couple of miles or more to cover, and would hardly get within vulnerable distance under an hour. Wellington was tired; he had been at full stretch, mentally and physically, since daybreak, and it was now past three in the afternoon. "I am going to take a little sleep," he said to Lord Fitzroy Somerset, his military secretary, and the most favoured and confidential member of his Staff. "Watch with your glass. You see that large stone? Call me when the head of the French column reaches that point." Then, wrapping himself in his cloak, he lay down behind a bush and was soon sound asleep. Wellington had the faculty, like Napoleon and other great leaders, of sleeping at will, and he rose refreshed when Lord Fitzroy roused him presently with the information he needed.

This inspiring nonchalance, this studied and traditional affectation of the English aristocracy is further borne out by a story related by that renowned Light Division chronicler, Sir John Kincaid, who wrote:

Salamanca, 22 July 1812

Marmont came down upon us the first night with a thundering cannonade, and placed his army en masse on the plain before us, almost within gunshot. I was told that, while Lord Wellington was riding along the line, under a fire of artillery, and accompanied by a numerous staff, a brace of greyhounds in pursuit of a hare passed close to him. He was at the moment in earnest conversation with General Castanos; but the instant he observed them he gave the view hallo and went after them at full speed, to the utter astonishment of his foreign accompaniments. Nor did he stop until he saw the hare killed; when he returned and resumed the commander-in-chief as if nothing had occurred.

The time for action had arrived. Aides-de-camp and gallopers were dispatched with last orders, while Wellington himself rode to the 3rd Division, where Pakenham was waiting impatiently for the signal to commence the fight.

What passed between the two Generals (they were brothers-in-law) is historical. "Do you see those fellows on the hill, Pakenham?" said the Duke, pointing to the French columns as they straggled along, all unconscious of the impending attack. "Throw your division into columns; at them directly and drive them to the devil." Pakenham saluted, and then, as he passed on to the attack, stopped short to say, "Give me a hold of that conquering hand." His admiration for his chief was repaid by Wellington's warm approval, for as the 3rd Division went forward in grand order, a perfectly arrayed military body, the Duke, turning to his Staff, observed: "Did you ever see a man who understands so clearly what he has to do?" "Lord Wellington was right," says one who was present. "The attack of the 3rd Division was not only the most spirited, but the most perfect thing of its kind that modern times have witnessed."

Meanwhile, Marmont had fully realized his terrible error. The rapid movements of the English told him, too, that the mistake was patent to his enemy. He saw the country beneath him alive with their troops moving in combined and well-concerted strength, while his own army was scattered and in the midst of a difficult and half-completed manoeuvre. But still he had no knowledge of Pakenham's intended attack, for the 3rd Division was invisible, and he did not yet despair. He hoped he might yet reunite his army before the moment of collision; and with this object he dispatched messengers in all directions, one way to hurry up the centre and rear columns, the other to check Thomière in his overreaching advance. At the same time some of the troops in hand opened fire upon the central part of the battle-field, and others made a bold attack upon the Arapiles village and English hill of that name.

It was now, when hoping almost against hope, that Marmont caught sight of Pakenham and his division "shooting like a meteor across Maucune's path." Marmont was hastening to the spot most threatened when he was severely wounded by a bursting shell, and had to be carried off the field. General Bonnet, who succeeded him, was also disabled before he could take any steps to restore the right, and the command devolved upon General Clausel, an excellent soldier, who, in Napier's words, was "of a capacity equal to the crisis." But much delay ensued, many conflicting orders were issued before the French troops again benefited by their Commander-General's controlling hand.

It had fared badly with General Thomière, who led the first of Maucune's two divisions. Pakenham had come on, supported by cavalry and guns, and, while the artillery took the French in flank, the infantry formed line and charged furiously. The French guns at first essayed to answer, but were silenced and driven off the field; then the French formed a poor, disconnected line of battle upon two fronts, one to face Pakenham, the other opposed to the 5th Division and the Portuguese. At this time, too, the 4th Division had come into action, and had beaten back the attack made upon the Arapiles village and hill. Already within one short half-hour serious discomfiture had overtaken the French. It is true that General Clausel's own division, part of the centre, had come up through the wood, and had regained touch with Maucune's rear division. The latter made a gallant stand along the southern and eastern hills, but his line was loose and broken, without formation.

Writing at about the same time as Major Arthur Griffiths, James Grant adds colour to the inspiring scene:

Many French officers were seen rushing to the front to animate their men; and one, an officer of the 22nd Regiment, the leading corps of the French column, snatching up a musket, shot Major Murphy, of the 88th, through the heart. At the same moment a ball struck the pole of the king's colours of that regiment, nearly cutting it in two, and taking an epaulette off the shoulder of Lieutenant d'Arcy who carried it. The Irish cried out, "Revenge!" Then Pakenham cheered, and desiring Lieutenant-Colonel Wallace to "let them loose," the Connaught Rangers were plunging with their bayonets into a deep and ponderous mass of the enemy.

So close was the struggle, even when the infantry mingled, that in many instances the British colours were seen waving above the battalions of the enemy; while our dragoons at one time broke through square and line, taking deep vengeance for the fall of General le Marchant, by the havoc they made in the dark ranks of those who slew him.

By this brilliantly-executed maneuvre, the whole of the enemy's left was destroyed. Three thousand prisoners remained in our hands, with two eagles and eleven pieces of cannon; while the rest, broken and dispirited, fell back in utter dismay on their reserves, whom they swept away with them in their flight.

The complete overthrow of the French vanguard was greatly accelerated by another masterly tactic of Wellington, who had loosed Le Marchant's Heavy and Anson's and Arentschildt's Light Cavalry Brigades in what was one of the most brilliant charges ever made by British cavalry. In Homeric language, Napier tells how:

"…a whirling cloud of dust moved swiftly forward, carrying within it the trampling sound of a charging multitude"; how the horsemen rode down the French infantry "with a terrible clamour and disturbance. Bewildered and blinded, they cast away their arms, and crowded through the intervals of the squadrons, stooping and crying out for quarter, while the Dragoons, big men on big horses, rode onwards, smiting with their long, glittering swords in uncontrollable power." Le Marchant was killed, but others were there to lead his cavalry on. Pakenham, with his infantry, followed close, and after a struggle in which many were laid low, the French were completely defeated."
Griffiths

Let James Grant continue the colourful story:

From his post on the Arapiles, Marmont suddenly beheld with confusion the country beneath him covered thus by the masses of the enemy–the British in red, the Portuguese in blue–at a moment when he was in the act of executing a most complicated movement. Meanwhile, in the centre a fierce contest was going on, caused by an unsuccessful attempt made by General Pack, with his Portuguese, to capture that Hermanito, or Arapiles height, of which Marmont still retained a hold. Just as they gained the summit, when breathless and blown, they were charged by a line of 1,200 infantry. Unable to sustain the shock, they broke and fled in such confusion that the flank of our 4th division, with which they communicated, was left uncovered and exposed.

Against it all the efforts of the enemy were directed, and, General Cole having fallen wounded, a serious impression was made; till the steady advance of the 5th division speedily restored the battle, and from that moment our victory was never doubtful. Pouring into the enemy's lines a well-directed fire, steadily advancing, as they fell back stumbling and in disorder over their own dead and wounded, they won the crest of the position. A fatality was on the usually brilliant Marmont that day; he was hurrying in person, in the desperate hope of repairing the fatal errors already committed, when an exploding shell stretched him on the earth, with a broken arm and two deep wounds in his side. Confusion now reigned supreme in the French army; and the troops, distracted by ill-judged orders and counter-orders, knew not when to move, whom to fight, or whom to obey. All the skill exhibited by the maneuvres of the past week, one brief half-hour had compromised!

The advance of the 5th division, amid clouds of smoke, a stream of fire, and over a hill covered with the dark bodies of the fallen Portuguese, was the crisis of the battle, and it was evident that victory would remain with that general who had the strongest reserves; and Wellington, personally present that day at every point; when and where he was required, now brought up the 6th division, and turned the scale by a splendid and successful charge of bayonets. Yet the struggle was a terrible one. Hulse's brigade, which was on the left of the division, covered the turf in hundreds, while the 11th and 61st Regiments fought their way desperately to the front, through a dreadful and concentrated fire; and Boyer's dragoons, breaking in through a gap between the two divisions, cut down by their swords many men of the 53rd, or Shropshire Regiment; but that brave old corps never lost an inch, nor could the impetuous attack of General

Clausel, on whom the command of the French had devolved, after the successive fall of Marmont, Bonet, and Thomières, avail at any point, after the first burst, against the firmness of the Allies.

The annals of the British Army resound with stories such as this:

During the battle of Salamanca, after being driven from the slopes of the greater Arapiles, the 11th Regiment succeeded in forming square and repulsing the main attacks. When the French gave way in the evening, the 11th Regiment was ordered to retake a portion of the slopes of the hills. Fire was opened by the French at two hundred yards. In spite of the fact that at the first volley 80 men on the right wing fell, the Regiment advanced up the hill slopes as if on parade, closing in on the centre to fill the gaps. Before the battle, the 1st Battalion had a strength of 412 and when it concluded there were but four officers and 67 men, many of them wounded. To the officer commanding the remnant, their brigadier general said "Major Newman, it is impossible for me to find words to express my admiration of the glorious conduct of your Regiment this day." It was on this day that the Regiment earned the nickname of "The Bloody Eleventh".

James Grant again:

The southern Arapiles were re-won. The French generals, Menne and Ferey, were wounded, the first severely, the second mortally; Clausel was also hurt, and the fainting Marmont, borne on the shoulders of six grenadiers, was already far from the field. Again Boyer's dragoons came on at a canter with all their blades uplifted, but were swept away, as horse and rider went down in heaps before the withering fire of Hulse's grand brigade. The 3rd division continued steadily to outflank more and more the left of the failing foe. The slope of the Arapiles was abandoned, General Foy retired from the village of Calvarassa Ariba, "and the allied host, righting itself as a gallant ship after a sudden gust, again bore onwards, in blood and gloom; for though the air, purified by the storm of the night before, was peculiarly clear, one vast cloud of smoke and dust rolled along the basin, and within it was the battle with all its sights and sounds of terror."

Out of the cloud, the waving of a standard, a sudden line of caps and faces, or the gleam of a ridge of steel, with the incessant flashes of the red musketry, ever and anon broke forth. When Wellington, with the 6th division, had thus restored the combat in the centre, he ordered the 1st division, which up to this period had scarcely been under fire, to push on between Foy and the rest of the French army, which would have rendered it impossible for the latter to rally or escape. But the order failed in execution, and Foy, posted on undulating ground, and flanked by dragoons, covered the roads that led to the fords of Huerta and Encina; while General Maucune, after being driven from the Arapiles, on being reinforced by fifteen pieces of cannon, took post in front of a cork-tree forest, covering the road to Alba de Tormes; and in rear of this wooded ridge was all the rest of the French army, falling back in ruin and disorder before the advancing regiments of the 3rd, 5th, and 6th divisions.

In two lines, flanked by horse, the famous light division now hurried to the front, against Foy. These were supported by the 1st division in columns, flanked on the right by two brigades of infantry. The 7th division and the Spanish troops followed in reserve. The whole country was covered with soldiers pouring impetuously to the front, and a new army seemed to have arisen out of the earth.

Covering his rear by clouds of skirmishers, Foy fell back by wings in succession. From every rise in the ground these fronted about, and firing heavily into the light division, a pile of corpses and crawling wounded followed every fire, and for three miles this march under musketry went on. Occasionally it became more deadly, when a gun was unlimbered and discharged; but the French aim was often baffled by the rapid gliding of the lines, and by the twilight, for the last rays of the sun had already faded from the bloody summit of the Arapiles and the spires of Salamanca. On the last defensible ridge, he augmented his skirmishers at a place where a marshy stream was flowing. Next he redoubled his musketry, and made a menacing demonstration with his dragoons and lancers just as the night closed in. Then our British cannon opened once again, redly belching forth round shot and grape through the darkness and gloom, amid which the main body of the French army seemed to disappear, and their fringe of skirmishers also vanished.

Meanwhile one division, under Maucune, was still combating valiantly on very high ground. He was outflanked and outnumbered, yet he knew that with him lay the glory of covering the retreat of the beaten army; and Pakenham, who expected a fierce and prolonged resistance, advised Clinton not to assail him until our 3rd division should have completely turned his left. In spite of this, however, the gallant Clinton rushed with his troops into action under extreme disadvantage, for after having his ranks ploughed down by a brigade of French artillery, they advanced to a close attack.

Napier, riding at the head of the 43rd, could watch the final action and has given this description in his famous History of the Peninsular War:

> In the darkness of the night the fire showed from afar how the battle went. On the English side a sheet of flame was seen, sometimes advancing with an even front, sometimes pricking forth its spearheads, now falling back in wavy lines, anon darting upwards in one vast pyramid, the apex of which often approached but never gained the actual summit of the mountain (sic); but the French musketry, rapid as lightning, sparkled along the brow of the height with unvarying fulness, and with what destructive effects the dark gaps and changing shapes of the adverse fire showed too plainly; meanwhile Pakenham turned the left, Foy glided into the forest, and Maucune's task being then completed, the effulgent crest of the ridge became black and silent, and the whole French army vanished as it were in the darkness.

JAMES GRANT:

The field of Salamanca was won!

Till ten at night the light and 1st divisions continued the pursuit, marching fast, with their arms shouldered, save when an opportunity came to send in a volley with effect; and even at ten it would not have ceased, had not Wellington calculated on being able, when the next day came, of being able to dictate his own terms to the enemy. There were but two points at which the Tormes could be crossed, namely, at Huerta and Alba. Of the former he took command, by pushing on the light division towards it; while the latter he left, as he thought, in the safe keeping of a Spanish garrison. The latter, however, abandoned their post; and the consequence was, that when the morrow came, and the pursuit was resumed, it led only to a combat with the rear guard, as the whole main body was safe beyond the river.

Clausel had marched all night, and finding the ford at Alba de Tormes open, had passed through with all his troops. Save at La Serna, where three battalions of French infantry and a body of cavalry halted and faced about, there was no more fighting.

By gaining Salamanca, the allied leader had accomplished one part of his mighty plan. He had effectively cleared the northern frontier of Portugal, and rendered it impossible for the enemy to unite against him overwhelming numbers, save on a line entirely in the rear.

The results of the Salamanca operations were, according to Napier, as follows: Marmont's army, 42,000 strong, with 74 guns, passed the Douro on the 18th of July, to attack Wellington. On the 30th it re-passed the river in full retreat, having in twelve days marched two hundred miles, and fought three combats and one general action, in which one marshal of France, seven generals, and 12,500 men and regimental officers were killed, wounded, or taken, together with two eagles, several standards, and twelve pieces of cannon, exclusive of seventeen more taken at Valladolid.

The losses of the Allies were one marshal, four generals, and about 6,000 men and officers killed or wounded. Captain Lord Clinton conveyed to London the captured eagles and colours.

"It was a fine sight after the battle," wrote an officer to a paper of the time (the Edinburgh Star), "to see the whole people of Salamanca come out to welcome us, the women bringing wine and refreshments of every kind to the wounded. General Cole was struck by a ball, which entered near his shoulder, passed by the lungs, and came out at his back. If you had been at the Arapiles, you would have said there never was warmer work or a more glorious business."

The Portuguiz Telagrafo states that Marshal Beresford was wounded in the leg while leading on the 11th Light Dragoons, and again when charging with a brigade of Portuguese infantry; and it redounded but little to the credit of the people of Salamanca when, during the operations of subsequent months, after falling back from Burgos, when a position was taken up temporarily by the British on nearly the same ground, it was found to be strewed by the half-buried skeletons of those who had fallen in the battle of the 22nd of July.

Arthur Griffiths wrote:

> Other results, direct and indirect, followed from this great victory. One of the first was the occupation of the capital of Madrid, which King Joseph immediately left to join and strengthen the defeated and retreating Clausel. Of the indirect results the greatest was the clearance of southern Spain, for Soult was now obliged to abandon Andalusia, and, moving round by a circuitous route through the south-east, to regain touch with the road from France.
>
> Wellington's reputation, already high, was greatly enhanced by this brilliant feat of arms.
>
> It was his generalship that secured the victory. Not a fault was to be found with his conduct; from first to last, from the moment he caught his enemy tripping, through all the changing fortunes of the hard-fought day, until he smote him hip and thigh, true genius was displayed. "I saw him late in the evening of that great day," says Napier, "when the advancing flashes of cannon and musketry, stretching as far as the eye could command, showed in the darkness how well the field was won; he was alone, the flush of victory was on his brow, and his eyes were eager and watchful, but his voice was calm and even gentle. More than the rival of Marlborough, since he defeated greater generals than Marlborough ever encountered, with a prescient pride he seemed only to accept this glory as an earnest of greater things."

The British military historian and writer David Chandler sums up the significance and lessons of the victory at Salamanca:

(1) Proved superiority of properly-handled line attacking enemy in column.
(2) Illustrates Wellington's typical use of ground to achieve offensive surprise.
(3) Illustrates the use of the "oblique order" in the attack.
(4) Over confidence led Marmont to under-estimate his foe and over extend his two wings.
(5) Clausel's well devised counter attack had no effect thanks to Wellington's foresight.
(6) Wellington always managed to mass superior numbers of men at the critical points.
(7) The pursuit was disappointing–due to Spanish insubordination and overall tiredness.
(8) French shortage of cavalry had a dire effect on their divisional attacks.
(9) Note the French adoption of "linear" tactics at the end of the battle.
(10) Note Le Marchant's fine control over the Heavy Dragoons–a rare quality.
(11) The victory finally established "the Sepoy general's" reputation internationally, opened the road to Madrid, and consolidated the position of Liverpool's administration in U.K. More forces were consequently voted for the Peninsula, despite the new war with the U.S.A. Even the Parliamentary Opposition became Wellington's champion.

The Allied Forces at Salamanca

	Strength	Loss
Cavalry (Stapleton Cotton):		
Le Marchant's Brigade		
3rd Dragoons	339	20
4th Dragoons	358	29
5th Dragoon Guards	325	56
C. Anson's Brigade		
11th Light Dragoons	391	–
12th Light Dragoons	340	5
16th Light Dragoons	273	–
V. Alten's Brigade		
14th Light Dragoons	347	3
1st Hussars K.G.L.	399	23
Bock's Brigade		
1st Dragoons K.G.L.	364	–
2nd Dragoons K.G.L.	407	–
Total British Cavalry	3,543	136

Infantry

	Strength	Loss
Fermor's Brigade		
1st Coldstream Guards	954	38
1st Third Guards	961	24
1 comp. 5/60th Foot	57	–
Wheatley's Brigade		
2/24th Foot	421	5
1/42nd Foot	1,079	3

	Strength	Loss
2/58th Foot	400	4
1/79th Foot	674	4
1 comp. 5/60th	54	–
Löwe's Brigade		
1st Line Battalion K.G.L.	641	9
2nd Line Battalion K.G.L.	627	47
5th Line Battalion K.G.L.	555	19
Total 1st Division	6,423	153
3rd Division (Pakenham):		
Wallace's Brigade		
1/45th Foot	442	55
74th foot	443	49
1/88th Foot	663	135
3 comps. 5/60th Foot	254	36
J. Campbell's Brigade		
1/5th Foot	902	126
2/5th Foot	308	24
2/83rd Foot	319	34
94th Foot	347	28
Total 3rd Division	3,678	487
4th Division (Lowry Cole):		
W. Anson's Brigade		
3/27th Foot	633	8
1/40th Foot	582	132
1 comp. 5/60th	46	–
Ellis's Brigade		
1/7th Foot	495	195
1/23rd Foot	446	106
1/48th Foot	426	79
1 comp. Brunswick Oels`	54	–
Total 4th Division	2,682	520
5th Division (Leith):		
Greville's Brigade		
3/1st Foot	761	160
1/9th Foot	666	46
1/38th Foot	800	143
2/38th Foot	301	52
1 comp. Brunswick Oels	78	–
Pringle's Brigade		
1/4th Foot	457	18
2/4th Foot	654	31
2/30th Foot	349	27
2/44th Foot	251	29
1 comp. Brunswick Oels	69	–
Total 5th Division	4,386	506
6th Division (Clinton):		
Hulse's Brigade		
1/11th Foot	516	340
2/53rd Foot	341	142
1/61st Foot	546	366
1 comp. 5/60th	61	–

	Strength	Loss
Hinde's Brigade		
2nd Foot	408	109
1/32nd Foot	609	137
1/36th Foot	429	99
Total 6th Division	2,910	1,193
7th Division (Hope):		
Halkett's Brigade		
1st Light Batt. K.G.L.	569	9
2nd Light Batt. K.G.L.	494	16
Brunswick Oels (9 companies)	596	49
De Bernewitz's Brigade		
51st Foot	307	2
68th Foot	338	20
Chasseurs Britanniques	713	27
	3,017	125
Light Division (Chas. Alten):		
Barnard's Brigade		
1/43rd Foot	748	16
Detachments 2/95th & 3/95th Rifles	392	5
Vandeleur's Brigade		
1/52nd Foot	799	2
8 comps. 1/95th	542	4
Total Light Division	2,481	27
Royal Horse Artillery (troops of Ross, Macdonald, and Bull)	421	3
Field Artillery (companies of Lawson, Gardiner, Green, Douglas, May)	685	5
K. G. L. Artillery (Sympher)	80	6
Artillery Total	1,186	14
Engineers	21	–
Staff Corps	86	–
Wagon Train	139	–
British Total		
Infantry	25,577	2,968
Cavalry	3,553	136
Artillery	1,186	14
Engineers	21	–
Staff Corps	86	–
Train 24	–	
General Staff	?	11
Total	30,562	8,129
II. Portuguese Troops		
	Strength	Loss
Cavalry:		
D'Urban's brigade:		
1st and 11th Dragoons	482	37

Infantry:
Power's Brigade, 3rd Division:
9th and 21st Line,

12th Caçadores	2,197	76

Stubb's Brigade, 4th Division:
11th and 23rd Line,

7th Caçadores	2,554	476

Spry's Brigade, 5th Division:
3rd and 15th Line,

8th Caçadores	2,305	123

Rezende's Brigade, 6th Division:
8th and 12th Line,

9th Caçadores	2,631	487

Collins's Brigade, 7th Division:
7th and 19th Line,

2nd Caçadores	2,168	17

Pack's Independent Brigade:
1st and 16th Line,

4th Caçadores	2,605	376

Bradford's Independent Brigade:
13th and 14th Line,

5th Caçadores	1,894	17

Attached to Light Division:

1st and 3rd Caçadores	1,067	17
Artillery: Arriaga's battery	114	1
Total	18,017	1,627

III. Spanish Troops	Strength	Loss

Carlos de España's Division:
2nd of Princesa, Tiradores de Castilla,
2nd of Jaen, 3rd of 1st Seville,
Caçadores de Castilla,

Lanceros de Castilla	3,360	6

General Total	Strength	Loss
British	30,562	3,129
Portuguese	18,017	1,627
Spanish	3,360	6
Total	51,939	4,762

The Army of Portugal Before and After the Battle of Salamanca

	July 15	August 1

1st Division (Foy):
Brigade Chemineau

6th Léger (2 batts.)	1,101	725
69th Ligne (2 batts.)	1,458	1,369

Brigade Desgraviers-Berthelot

39th Ligne (2 bats.)	967	921
76th Ligne (2 batts.)	1,407	932
Artillery Train, &c.	214	214
Divisional Total	5,147	4,161

2nd Division (Clausel):
Brigade Berlier

25th Léger (3 batts.)	1,539	1,267
27th Ligne (2 batts.)	1,677	1,279

Brigade Barbot

50th Ligne (3 batts.)	1,542	1,223
59th Ligne (2 batts.)	1,578	1,316
Artillery Train, &c.	226	223
Divisional Total	6,562	5,306

3rd Division (Ferey):
Brigade Menne

31st Léger (2 batts.)	1,405	1,370
26th Ligne (2 batts.)	1,189	1,159

Brigade ?

47th Ligne (3 batts.)	1,625	1,712
70th Ligne (2 batts.)	1,163	1,097
Artillery Train, &c.	307	196
Divisional Total	5,689	5,534

4th division (Sarrut):
Brigade Fririon

2nd Léger (3 batts.)	1,838	1,770
36th Ligne (3 batts.)	1,639	1,585

Brigade ?

4th Léger (3 batts.)	1,282	1,052
130th Ligne (absent)	–	
Artillery Train, &c.	243	219
Divisional Total	5,002	4,626

5th Division (Maucune):
Brigade Arnaud

15th Ligne (3 batts.)	1,667	1,275
66th Ligne (2 batts.)	1,169	695

Brigade Montfort

82nd Ligne (2 batts.)	1,007	768
86th Ligne (2 batts.)	1,185	989
Artillery Train, &c.	216	216
Divisional Total	5,244	3,943

6th Division (Brennier):
Brigade Taupin

17th Léger (2 batts.)	1,120	897
65th Ligne (3 batts.)	1,586	1,354

Brigade ?

22nd Ligne (3 batts.)	1,547	756
Regiment de Prusse (remnant)	88	88
Artillery Train, &c.	217	217
Divisional Total	4,558	3,312

7th Division (Thomières):
Brigade Bonté

1st Line (3 batts.)	1,763	1,533
62nd Line (2 batts.)	1,123	1,093

Brigade ?		
23rd Léger (absent)	–	–
101st Line (3 batts.)	1,469	441
Artillery Train, &c.	208	nil
Divisional Total	4,543	3,067
8th Division (Bonnet):		
Brigade Gautier		
118th Line (3 batts.)	1,637	1,061
119th Line (3 batts.)	1,329	879
Brigade ?		
120th Line (3 bats.)	1,808	1,218
122nd Line (3 batts.)	1,635	1,040
Artillery Train, &c.	110	nil
Divisional Total	6,521	4,198
Light Cavalry Division (Curto):		
3rd Hussars (3 squadrons)	248	179
22nd Chasseurs (2 squadrons)	253	251
26th Chasseurs (2 squadrons)	294	243
28th Chasseurs (1 squadron)	94	42
13th Chasseurs (5 squadrons)	516	454
14th Chasseurs (4 squadrons)	322	350
Escadron de marche	152	61
Divisional Total	1,879	1,580

Heavy Cavalry Division (Boyer):		
Brigade ?		
6th Dragoons (2 squadrons)	395	351
11th Dragoons (2 squadrons)	430	377
Brigade Carrié		
15th Dragoons (2 squadrons)	343	300
25th Dragoons (2 squadrons)	332	300
Artillery attached to cavalry	196	151
Divisional Total	1,696	1,489
Total Cavalry Divisions	3,575	3,069
Artillery Reserve, Park, &c.	1,500	729
Engineers and Sappers	349	361
Gendarmerie	135	192
Équipages militaires	768	729
État-Major general	54	54
General Total		
Infantry Divisions	43,266	34,147
Cavalry Divisions	3,575	3,069
Auxiliary Arms	2,806	2,065
	49,646	39,281

N.B. Guns, July 15, 78; August 1, 58; lost 7 12-pounders, 3 8-pounders, 9 4-pounders, 1 3-pounder. Horses, July 15, 4,278; August 1, 8,231. Draught horses, July 15, 2,037; August 1, 1,847. Équipages militaires, horses, July 15, 800; August 1, 331.

BRITISH BATTLE HONOURS FOR SALAMANCA

5th (Princess Charlotte of Wales's) Regt. of Dragoon Guards
3rd (King's Own) Regt. of Dragoons
4th (Queen's Own) Regt. of Dragoons
11th Regt. of (Light) Dragoons
12th (Prince of Wales's) Regt. of (Light) Dragoons
14th (Duchess of York's Own) Regt. of (Light) Dragoons
16th (the Queen's) Regt. of (Light) Dragoons
Coldstream Regt. of Foot Guards
3rd Regt. of Foot Guards
3rd Bn. 1st (Royal Scots) Regt. of Foot
2nd (Queen's Royal) Regt. of Foot
1st & 2nd Bns. 4th (King's Own) Regt. of Foot
1st & 2nd Bns. 5th (Northumberland) Regt. of Foot
1st Bn. 7th Regt. of Foot (or Royal Fuzileers)
1st Bn. 9th (East Norfolk) Regt. of Foot
1st Bn. 11th (Devonshire) Regt. of Foot
1st Bn. 23rd Regt. of Foot (or Royal Welsh Fuzileers)
2nd Bn. 24th (2nd Warwickshire) Regt. of Foot
3rd Bn. 27th (Inniskilling) Regt. of Foot
1st Bn. 61st (South Gloucestershire) Regt. of Foot
1st Bn. 36th (Herefordshire) Regt. of Foot
2nd Bn. 30th (Cambridgeshire) Regt. of Foot
1st Bn. 32nd (Cornwall) Regt. of Foot

1st Bn. 38th (1st Staffordshire) Regt. of Foot
1st Bn. 40th (2nd Somersetshire) Regt. of Foot
1st Bn. 42nd (Royal Highland) Regt. of Foot
1st Bn. 43rd (Monmouthshire Light Infantry) Regt.
1st Bn. 52nd (Oxfordshire Light Infantry) Regt.
2nd Bn. 44th (East Essex) Regt. of Foot
1st Bn. 45th (Nottinghamshire) Regt. of Foot
1st Bn. 48th (Northamptonshire) Regt. of Foot
2nd Bn. 58th (Rutlandshire) Regt. of Foot
51st (2nd Yorkshire, West Riding) Regt. of Foot
2nd Bn. 53rd (Shropshire) Regt. of Foot
5th Bn. 60th (Royal American) Regt. of Foot
68th (Durham) Regt. of Foot (Light Infantry)
74th (Highland) Regt. of Foot
1st Bn. 79th Regt. of Foot (or Cameron Highlanders)
2nd Bn. 83rd Regt. of Foot
1st Bn. 88th Regt. of Foot (or Connaught Rangers)
94th Regt. of Foot
95th Regt. of Foot (or Rifle Corps)

"The English general, to use a French officer's expression, 'defeated forty-thousand men in forty minutes.' Yet he fought it as if his genius disdained such trial of its strength. Late in the evening of that great day I saw him behind my regiment, then marching toward the ford. He was alone, the flush of victory was on his brow, his eyes were eager and watchful, but his voice was calm and even gentle. More than the rival of Marlborough, for he had defeated greater generals than Marlborough ever encountered, he seemed with prescient pride only to accept the victory as an earnest of greater glory."
  William Napier

WALKING THE FIELD OF SALAMANCA

The tales of at least four visits to this incomparable field are a saga in themselves, arousing nostalgia and regret for days past - for this must truly be perhaps the best of all battlefields to explore and a delight to walk For the author it began about eighteen years ago, when visiting the area on perhaps the first of many tours with the British Military Historical Society, under the able and voluble guidance of my friend David Chandler (Head of War Studies Department, Royal Military Academy, Sandhurst). Notes taken at the time bring events back into the mind's eye.

1973. " Arriving in town of Salamanca in late afternoon, hastily checked bags into hotel and then rushed coach out to battlefield, where first surveys indicated enough dead ground to hide an army-as the French found out to their cost. Negotiating a barbed-wire fence, we climbed to the summit of the Lesser Arapile, where we encountered a bitterly cold gale-force wind as doggedly we turned binoculars in all direction. Sheltering in the lee of a clump of rocks, we listened to one of David's fascinating battlefield discourses and soon we had a pretty fair idea of the course of this somewhat complex battle. In the gathering dusk we began to imagine cavalry charging across the plain and columns of infantry pressing forward. It was almost dark as we drove on narrow dirt tracks to Aldea Tejada, but gave best to a truculent Spanish farmer driving a very big tractor. Re-entering the town of Salamanca, we were held up by a picturesque procession of candle-bearing penitents, garbed rather as one imagines the Klu Klux Klan; marching to the measured beat of drums, crosses held high above, it brought to mind tales we had heard of the Inquisition of the Middle Ages"

1974. " On first arriving in the town of Salamanca, a very pleasant civilised and colorful city, we lunched outdoors in the impressive colonnaded Plaza Mayor under a hot sun. Then we drove out to the battlefield where, last year on a much colder day, we had ascended the Lesser Arapile; this time we walked the area between the two Arapiles, halting to listen to David telling us a concise but colorful account of the events that had occurred over the ground on which we were standing."

1990 " On a hot day without a cloud in the sky, we were on the immortal field of Salamanca by nine of the clock and we stayed there until late afternoon, eating a picnic lunch on top of the Greater Arapile. Quite unchanged and unbuilt on, except for a wispy railway line and a minute halt, it is a field where everything falls into place, and from the summit of the Lesser Arapile it can all be placed in its chronological sequence, as the landscape's seeming flatness begins to reveal folds and dips in the ground that answer all the unspoken questions one might have on the battle. We left with reluctance, each of us ruminating on Wellington's incomparable military genius, the impressive tactical aspects and - as befits good wargamers - the mind filled with ideas for re-fighting this stimulating battle on the tabletop."

September 1991 " In the company of Todd Fisher and John Brewster of the Emperor's Headquarters in Chicago, a long drive was made from Badajoz, through Caceres, Plasencia and Beja laying somnolent in the wild regions of central Spain, to arrive in the region of Salamanca. Tired and thirsty, we stopped at a model hostel for a drink, and seeing from it an excellent view of both Lesser and Greater Arapiles, made a snap decision to book-in and begin exploring the area. Hardly pausing to dump baggage, we set off for the famed field and were soon cogitating on a series of grassy ridges, until deciding on which of them Packenham hit Thomiere's division, to put a match to the fuse that flared-up into the Battle of Salamanca, on 22 July 1812. Then onto the Lesser and Greater Arapiles, where imaginations were given full rein to people the bare and lonely grassland with the warring forces of Cole, Pack, Ferey, Bonnet and the rest. Seeking the scene of operations on the Allied left, we drove to Alba de Tormes, and determined where the Light Division were engaged, and the movements of Foy's force."

Following a visit to the battlefield, British military historian and wargamer Kenneth Brooks wrote what must be the model formula for getting most benefit from one's battlefield.

In April last year we left the coach at the foot of the Lesser Arapile, having already visited the village of Calvarrasa de Arriba where Foy's advance guard had arrived the night before the battle on July 22nd, 1812. Whilst there we had walked forward to the site of the convent of Nuestra Senors de la Pena around which skirmishing had taken place during the battle. It was both useful and very interesting to start by looking at the British position from a French viewpoint, and to see the reverse slope of the Greater Arapile.

Many accounts have been written about the battle and battlefield, but none have given a really living picture of it. Only a visit can do this. By coincidence we arrived at the time when the battle was in fact being fought, and I thought of this as I climbed the steep grassy side of the Lesser Arapile. Small rocks and outcrops both helped and hindered the ascent. I took a beeline to the top - arriving breathless and thankful I was not in full kit with musket.

The top of the hill is flat, harsh tussocks of grass and rock break the harsh outline - already yellowing and dry. After photographing the entire field I started to study the ground. One could imagine the tension of the day, caused by the frustration of retreating and impatience of waiting to see if a battle would be fought or not.

Half an hour earlier Wellington had galloped off to the north-east - to fetch Pakenham's 3rd division and D'Urban's cavalry. In the interval before his return I could look around and see what was going on.

The battleground can be described as two reversed L's formed by broken ridges and hills. The two Ls are anything from 1,200 to 1800 yards apart, with the western one fitting inside the eastern feature. The Lesser Arapile where I stood is at the south-eastern point of the British, or western feature. The Greater Arapile stands about 800 yards away from the Lesser in a south-westerly direction, and is forward of the main eastern ridges. Hot bright sun illuminates the area of rolling ridges, flat or gently sloping fields with woods visible in the distance.

Through my spyglass I can see to the north of me the Light division, the 1st division and Bock's heavy cavalry brigade. Some elements can doubtless be seen by the French, but most are in dead ground. All face east - where Foy bickers with the troops in the convent. Ferey's division can be

THE GREATER ARAPILE TAKEN FROM THE TOP OF THE LESSER ARAPILE. IT IS UP THOSE SLOPES THAT PACK'S PORTUGUESE ATTACKED AND WERE REPULSED.

seen in support of Foy and further round, nearer to the Greater Arapile can be seen another division. This turned out to be Sarrut's division. Although the Greater Arapile is in fact twenty feet higher than where I stand it is easy to see French guns and battalions on it. More French battalions are formed up behind it.

Sweeping my glass around until I am looking due south I can see the reason for Wellington's rapid exit. On the ridge opposite stands a solitary division facing us while to its left another division is striking out westwards. In the rear of these divisions are two more divisions - not yet in supporting distance. Later on we discovered it was Maucune facing us while Thomieres was busily trying to outflank our right.

Looking towards our right rear I can see the dust-clouds of our baggage-train moving from Salamanca to Ciudad Rodrigo. Nearer to us, however, can be seen the massed infantry of Leith's, Cole's, Clinton's and Hope's divisions. Their red and white contrasts with the blue of their Portuguese infantry, and the infantry of Pack's and Bradford's independent Portuguese brigades. Movement among them heralds Wellington's return! Shouted orders and movements taking shape indicate something is to happen shortly. Stirs of expectancy among the 40th and 27th Foot of Cole's division, who share the Lesser Arapile with me, gradually die down as no orders are received by them. Down on the plain to my right I can see Leith's division moving out and forming in two lines, with Hope forming to his rear. Nearer at hand Cole's two remaining brigades stand-to and Clinton's division appear in their rear. Something is certainly going to happen.

As though by pre-arranged signal a roar of cannon and musketry to our right announce the clash of Pakenham and Thomieres. It is now five o'clock in the afternoon and battle is to be joined at long last. Pakenham had advanced three miles from Aldea Tejada in our right rear and had approached unseen to within five hundred yards of Thomiere's leading column. Spirited action by Portuguese dragoons had halted them and Pakenham's leading brigade - the veteran 74th, 88th and 45th, are attacking without halting. The division is deploying for action on the march

200

before achieving overwhelming success. Thomieres' division has been destroyed before our eyes - it seemed almost in a flash.

In the meantime it is as though Leith had shouted "5th Division will advance in review order - by the, centre - quick march." As steadily as on the parade ground the front line of red coated bayonets advances, checking their dressing, while supported by the second line of Portuguese infantry. The village of Los Arapiles around British light companies had been skirmishing with French tirailleurs has been passed. After an advance over 1200 yards swept by French artillery the front line - still in perfect order - breasts the ridge and Maucune's division is lost to our right in clouds of smoke and dust.

Now here is a most stirring sight - in some ways the climax of the battle. Bradford's Portuguese brigade had been advancing on the right of Leith, while on their right again was Le Marchant's brigade of dragoons followed by Anson's light dragoons. Le Marchant is now breaking into a canter, riding up on to the ridge and the sound and milling dust - clouds tell us the great things are happening. Where Maucune had stood is now thronged with red coated figures - but beyond them billowing dust- clouds and fresh musket smoke suggest a further clash has occurred. This was in fact Brennier's division being destroyed by Le Marchant's cavalry before it could enter the battle effectively. The time is now 5:40 p. m. and three French divisions have been destroyed. The triumphant divisions of Leith and Pakenham have joined forces and can be seen reforming to sweep eastwards along the known ridge to our southern front.

It is difficult to choose between the spectacles claiming our attention. Cole has now been dispatched by Wellington to assault the eastern end of the ridge south of us - on which we can see a fresh French division forming. The 1,400 British bayonets form the right of the single two-deep line with 2,400 Portuguese on the left. Their job must be the toughest one so far. Advancing over 1,600 yards of reasonably flat, sun -parched glacis - enfiladed by artillery from both flanks and heavily outnumbered - the men of the 7th and 23rd Foot must surely be thinking this is Albuhera all over again. The divisions meet, muskets belch and the French front line recoils on their second line supports. The British stand firm until nine French battalions come out from behind the Greater Arapile and taking them in the left flank. The brazen helmets of a division of French dragoons can be seen gleaming dully through the smoke. Cole is down! Not even British Peninsular infantry can do more. They break and retire. The dragoons are charging in for the kill - but discipline and the will to survive triumph and ad hoc squares form as though by magic. Around me the 40th Foot are tumbling down the steep slope to re-form at the foot and advance as a bastion behind which the survivors of Cole's division can concentrate and retire to safety. Beaten but unbowed they return to fight again later that day.

The other competing spectacle is Pack's assault on the Greater Arapile with his Portuguese brigade. What a grandstand view we have! Pack has decided to attack as though assaulting a fortress - which in effect he is. There go his storming party of four grenadier companies followed by four line battalions in two columns. His approach is over clear ground, with no smoke to blind us, and I see his cacadores skirmishing forward and up the steep slope. Artillery fire has damaged but not stopped his columns. Our climb up the Lesser Arapile was difficult but theirs is worse. Up the go with bayonets flashing. But something has checked the cacadores! Ragged musketry continues as they spread out and start to climb some obstacle in company with the leading grenadiers. The scene is clouded by a sheet of smoke and the crash of musketry tells us the French battalions are counter-attacking. Through the smoke hurtle blue-clad figures and the French firing overthrows the grenadiers and the line battalions, tumbling them in a broken heap at the foot of the hill.

But more important events are taking place before us. The triumphant French battalions - 19 of them- who defeated Cole are now advancing to the centre. The dragoon division covers their right flank, eager to avenge the slaughter by Le Marchant's cavalry. A mounted staff officer clatters up to the 27th Foot and they are moving down to join the 40th already on the left of Clinton's division. 2,700 British bayonets form the first line with 2,500 Portuguese in close support. The rolling thunder of musketry is incessant, smoke and dust must be choking and blinding the fighting men. The French dragoons are threatening the British left, but the 40th and 27th are standing firm. A Portuguese brigade can be seen coming down from the far ridge and is taking the French in the left flank. They are still fighting, but swirling eddies of figures say the end is near - and off they go in a broken, stumbling mass.

Darkness is beginning to add its difficulties to smoke, dust, blood and fatigue. Clinton reforms his division and the battered remnants move after the French shattered masses. In the far distance to the south-east stands yet another ridge - wooded this time. Bitter fighting is taking place on the final ridge, but presently the last gun fires and it is all over. Small grass fires spring up over the fields and I fear that many wounded will suffer the same fate as many of their comrades at Talavera three years ago.

I wondered as I left the Lesser Arapile whether any survivors thought - as I did - that Wellington's iron resolve not to be tempted into doing something rash contrasted sharply with Marmont's overconfidence and underestimation of his adversary. I expect that their only wishes were for a drink and a chance to lie down in peace and quiet.

The Battle of Salamanca fought as a Wargame.

Because it was one of the major battles of the Peninsular War, considered by the Duke of Wellington to be his greatest and most satisfying triumph, and because it reveals a multitude of fascinating tactical movements and hard fighting in classical Napoleonic Wars style, wargamers will want to attempt the Battle of Salamanca, fought on 22nd July 1812. Not a big affair by the numerical standards of warfare, but conveniently situated as to make possible its simulation on a scaled replica of the ground, using exactly the same number of formations put into the field by Wellington in his Anglo-Portuguese Army and that of the French Commander, Marmont.

This was made possible by using 5mm Regimental blocks, allowing the 90 battalions of British and Portuguese infantry forming the 7 Divisions plus the Independent Portuguese Brigades; the five cavalry brigades of Stapleton Cotton, formed of 14 regiments; the 8 French divisions of 78 battalions of infantry, plus Boyer's Heavy and Curto's Light cavalry brigades. The only digression allowed was in artillery; Marmont's 78 guns being represented by 32, and the British 60 guns by 24; on the assumption that, even using the mildest wargaming concepts of the effects of artillery, would result in the full numbers of guns on the table exerting a certain over-emphasis which could unbalance the battle both as a wargame and a reconstruction.

Essentially, the terrain had to closely resemble both in scale and appearance the historical area and a map of the field was studied to find relative distances, to be scaled-down when building the tabletop terrain. For example, the Lesser and Greater Arapiles were 600 yards apart; 800 yards west of them was the lower ridge of Los Arapiles; south of it some 1,200 yards away was a low ridge about two miles long, wooded, along which Thomiere's column was marching when hit by Packenham's 3rd Division, who emerged unseen from woodland 500 yards away to the west; extending in a "L" shape from the north, the French columns were spread over 4 miles of front; the leading column (Thomieres's) strung - out in line of battalion-columns more than a mile long, imperfectly protected by Curto's cavalry. All these dispositions, scaled-down to an 8 feet by 5 feet table, at the opening stage when the British 3rd Division came into French view, set the scene for the Salamanca reconstruction that followed.

Such precise instructions, coupled with study of the map, provided the perfect jumping-off point for a memorable conflict, both commanders fought and manoeuvered in the manner of their historical counterparts and even thought the French were defeated on both occasions, it was, as on 22 July 1812, by no means a foregone conclusion.

The Battle of Salamanca began at 4:45 in the afternoon, carried on throughout the gathering dusk and was finally fought-out in the dark, ending at 9:30pm. So perhaps the French commander's greatest chance of victory is to slow-up the game to give himself time to extricate as much as possible under cover of night, living to fight again another day.

All historical movements were followed, their timing an essential feature of the battle, made possibly by a Time Chart that recorded off-table moves (or concealed moves) of different formations in outflanking or attacking movements that brings troops onto the table at some intermediate stage in the conflict. Not so marked in this game, a vital role of the Time Chart is to keep detached formations in touch with the Commander, perhaps unaware of their exact location, by means of gallopers whose progress is recorded on the Time Chart. Their non-arrival or delay provides Military Possibilities that can realistically affect the course of an historical battle.

No self-respecting wargamer likes to be saddled with an army in a battle they decisively lost, with few tangible alternatives to reverse the result, although the more spirited player may welcome the chance of revealing greater degrees of generalship than those shown by the vanquished commander, by turning defeat into victory. So he must be given some encouraging chance of changing military history, without making a 'dog's dinner' of the reconstruction. This is done by the use of Military Possibilities, controlled and logical alternative courses of action which, had they been taken at the appropriate moment during the battle, might well have caused a complete reversal of its result. Military Possibilities are courses of action followed by opposing wargamers with the agreement of both; they are not excuses for engaging in whims and fancies nor for diverting events merely to see what happens. In some cases the course of action indicate by a Military Possibility results in a more reasonable and credible result than actually occurred on the field of conflict. Some might depend upon Luck, represented by the throw of a dice or the turn of a Chance card, which is the simplest means of stimulating the ebb and flow of war. It has to be decided whether Military Possibilities are radically to alter the historical course of the battle or be restricted to relatively minor aspects of it, when they may result in a more interesting 'twist' in tactics, or even influence the eventual outcome.

So decisive was the nature and outcome of the Battle of Salamanca that credible Military Possibilities are few and far between; there was little chance of it being other than a British victory once Packenham's 3rd Division and Le Marchant's Heavy cavalry had routed their respective opponents. For the French to be in with a chance, one or both of these attacks must fail, and/or Clausel's counter-attack must succeed - three possibilities which, if allowed to occur, must take Salamanca into the realms of fantasy! It might be permissible to make Packenham less successful to make more of an even battle, or Clausel's counterstroke could be given a chance of success, which might make the battle a draw but an unlikely French victory. Rubbing it in, a Military Possibility could allow the Portuguese to reach and hold the Greater Arapile before the French arrive! Take heart, Military Possibilities abound in many of the battles described in this book! The interest and colour they will bring to the wargames table are proportionate to the experience and ingenuity of the wargamers.

Salamanca is the classic example of victory going to the better commander, which almost certainly occurs when both forces are equal in strength, morale, equipment, position, manoeuverability etc - as was the case on 22nd July 1812. In almost every battle described in this book a strong enemy force was beaten by a numerically weaker army solely because the victor's commander - Wellington - possessed outstanding tactical leadership and powers of command, being capable of inspiring his men to exceptional heights. Thus just as History dictates that one commander was 'Exceptional' while his opponent was only 'Average' or 'Below Average', so this fact has to be reflected on the wargames table.

The effect upon the battle of a commander's rating must be reflected by his troops, since those of an 'Exceptional' commander will possess a higher standard of morale and better fighting qualities - represented by adding any pre-decided figure to any dice affecting morale or fighting qualities. Conversely, a 'Below Average' commander would necessitate deducting a similar figure from dice scores; the troops of an 'Average' commander remain unaffected. If a system is in use where, at the start of the battle, orders are written for each army or group, the grading of commanders can be reflected by ruling that those armies or groups with 'Below Average' commanders must conform rigidly to their original orders until they are disorganised by a forced reaction (such as a low morale rating causing retreat or rout) 'Average' commanders can write orders to carry through three moves of the game; at the conclusion of the third move fresh orders may be written if circumstances have not altered the original instructions. "Exceptional' commanders may write orders at the beginning of each move of the game. In passing, it is fascinating to note that military history reveals many 'Below Average' commanders to be men of great personal courage, such as American Civil War General George B. McClellan, or British General Sir Hugh Gough, who commanded during the two Sikh Wars in India in the 1840's.

Akin to Military Possibilities but far more mundane in nature, Chance Cards introduce pleasant or unpleasant factors that materially affect aspects of a battle, perhaps even its result. They pose eventualities - tactical, physiological, or psychological - and the commander drawing such a card has to take practical steps to carry out the instructions it bears. Each historical battle can have its own set of cards designed to cover eventualities likely in the context of that battle; every real-life battle abounds with situations which, in a wargame, could give rise to the use of Chance Cards forming the 'human' element that may affect the purely tactical aspects of a Military Possibility. A chance card could declare that the horse of the galloper sent by Wellington to order Packenham to strike Thomiere's isolated division, has gone lame and the order is delayed- with possible consequences that could affect the whole battle. Or, when Le Marchant's Heavy Cavalry are charging forward on the right of the Allied 5th Division, they encounter a gully that delays them, or even halts the charge. Remembering Wellington's cavalry at Talavera, the card might decree that Le Marchant does not have his force under the rigid control that History indicates; or the columns of Sarrut's 4th French Infantry Division - the last to be encountered and destroyed by the Heavy Cavalry, have time to do what they could not do in 1812 - form square. Chance Cards are those major or minor everyday eventualities that can madden or delight, depending upon who is at the sticky end- but they certainly liven up, even revolutionise, a wargame!

"WELLINGTON GALLOPED OUT OF THE YARD, CALLING UPON THE REST TO FOLLOW HIM AT ONCE." SOME OF THEM ARE RELUCTANT TO LEAVE THEIR CHICKEN BEHIND.

THE ACTION AT GARCIA HERNANDEZ - 23 JULY 1812.

"la charge la plus audacieuse de la guerre d' Espagne"
General Comte Maximilien Sebastien Foy

This postscript to Salamanca would never have been fought had the Spanish commander at the ford of Alba de Tormes not abandoned his post without orders, allowing the disorganised French fugitives to pour across the bridge unhindered. And yet, had it not occurred, Military History would have been deprived of a classic instance - one of the few in the history of War - when cavalry succeeded in charging and breaking infantry squares drawn up on ground favourable to the foot soldiers.

The French withdrawal was covered by Foy's Division which alone had retained its discipline and confidence. Napier called this action 'The Combat of La Serna' from the heights and village of that name near to which the fighting took place -here is his account:-

During the few hours of darkness succeeding the battle of Salamanca, Clausel with a wonderful diligence passed the Tormes at Alba; but Wellington also crossed that river with his left wing at daylight, and moving up stream overtook the French on the Almar rivulet, near the village of La Serna, and launched his cavalry against them. Their squadrons fled from Anson's troopers, abandoning three battalions of infantry, who is separate columns were making up a hollow slope, hoping to gain the crest of some heights before the pursuing cavalry could fall on, and the two foremost did reach the higher ground and there formed square; the last, when half-way up, seeing Bock's heavy German dragoons galloping hard on, faced about and commenced a disorderly fire, and the squares above also plied their muskets on the Germans, who, after crossing the Almar, had to pass a turn of narrow road and clear rough ground before opening a charging front. They dropped fast under the fire. By twos, by threes, by tens, by twenties they fell, yet the mass, surmounting the difficulties of the ground, hurtled on the column and went clean through it: then the squares above retreated and several hundred prisoners were made by those able and daring horsemen.

This charge was successful even to wonder, and the victors standing in the midst of captives and admiring friends seemed invincible; yet those who witness the scene, nay the actors themselves remained with the conviction of the military truth, - that cavalry are not able to cope with veteran infantry, save by surprise.. The hill of La Serna offered a frightful spectacle of the power of the musket. The track of the Germans was marked by their huge bodies. A few minutes only had the combat lasted, and above a hundred had fallen - fifty one were killed outright. In several places man and horse had died simultaneously, and so suddenly, that falling together on their sides they appeared still alive, the horse's legs stretched out as in movement, the rider's feet in the stirrups, the bridle in hand, the sword raised to strike, and the large has fastened under the chin, giving to the grim yet undistorted countenance a supernatural and terrible expression.

When the French found their rear-guard attacked they turned to its succour, but seeing the light division coming up recommenced the retreat, and were soon joined by Caffarelli's horsemen and guns under General Chauvel: too late they joined for the battle, yet covered the retreat with a resolution that deterred the allied cavalry from meddling with them. Clausel then carried his army off with such celerity that his head-quarters were that night forty miles from the field of battle."

Far more detailed and explicit is the account written by a British cavalryman one-hundred and fifty years after von Bock's epic charges - Major General James Lunt, once Commanding -Officer and then Regimental Colonel of the 16th/5th Queen Royal Lancers (recently prominent as part of the British 7th Armoured Division in the Gulf War). General Lunt's book 'Charge to Glory - A Garland of Cavalry Exploits' (Heinemann, London 1961) contains a chapter on Garcia Hernandez which has accompanied the author of this book on each visit to that field. With General Lunt's permission, here it is:-

The 1st and 2nd Dragoons of the King's German Legion had been held in reserve over on the left flank during the battle. As night fell on 22 July they went into bivouac beside the village of Pelebravo, but shortly after midnight were roused by a galloper clattering through the streets and inquiring for the lodgings of Major-General Von Bock, who commanded the dragoon brigade. The galloper brought orders that the dragoons were to pursue the retreating French as soon as it was light. They were saddled up before dawn on 23 July and reached the Tormes about ninety minutes later. There they joined forces with Anson's brigade of light cavalry and waited for the infantry of the 1st and Light Divisions to catch up with them. At eight o'clock they forded the Tormes at Babilafuente and spurred on after the French.

The delay at the ford had given the French time to deploy two of Foy's regiments to cover their withdrawal. This was taking them along the narrow and marshy valley of the Garcia Caballero, a tributary of the Tormes by way of the rough and stony track leading through Garcia Hernandez to Peneranda. The banks of the stream were steep, and the ground was hopelessly rough for the proper employment of cavalry. For much of the way the track led through a defile and it was impossible to see very far ahead. The rolling nature of the terrain provided excellent positions for infantry, and the horses were tired after their forced marching since dawn. Anson's light cavalry led the advance with Von Bock's dragoons following close behind them Farther back were the weary British infantry, stumbling and falling over the broken ground as they tried to keep up with the trotting cavalry.

After about three miles the valley widened into a stony plain, crossed by the road running from Garcia Hernandez and flanked by rolling and stone-covered hills. As Anson's cavalry breasted the rise leading out of the valley they suddenly came upon the French rear-guard deployed in front of them. To the left there were several battalions of infantry drawn up in square formation on the hills. Beyond the infantry and out in the plain were some squadrons of enemy cavalry. It was these squadrons which first attracted Wellington's attention; he was unable to see the French infantry from his position. Lieutenant-Colonel May was immediately sent galloping forward with an order to Von Bock to charge the enemy cavalry with his dragoons, and May came up with Von Bock as his brigade was galloping through the defile. Von Bock, who was very short-sighted, could not see the French. "Perhaps you will be good enough to show us the enemy," he said to May, and the Englishman therefore found himself riding in the front rank of the leading German squadron. He was wounded later in the action, remarking afterwards, "This is what I get for leading Germans!"

Under normal conditions Von Bock would have wheeled his squadrons into line before charging, but the valley was so narrow that his leading three squadrons were compelled to advance echeloned back from the front. Every dragoon's attention was riveted on the French cavalry ahead of him, but the Frenchmen did not wait to receive the charge, and wheeled away to a flank. As they did so the leading squadron of the 1st Dragoons was taken in enfilade by the fire of the French infantry drawn up on the heights to their left.

The left squadron of the regiment was echeloned back some two or three hundred yards to the left rear of the leading squadron, and the first intimation it received of the presence of French infantry was the sudden burst of musketry and the thick black smoke drifting down from the heights. Captain Von der Decken, commanding the left squadron, could see the effect of the fire on the leading squadron and he knew that he must run the gauntlet of the same death-dealing musketry. He at once decided to charge the nearest French square, although the ground favoured infantry more than cavalry and despite the fact that there was no artillery available to redress the balance and clear a passage for his sabres. Wheeling his squadron into line, he led it headlong against the French, who greeted him with volley after volley. The dragoons enveloped two sides of the square but could not break into it. The two front ranks of the infantry were kneeling, and behind them were four more ranks standing. Fluttering over the centre of the square were the bullet-torn colours, and out in front were the lightly equipped skirmishers

206

picking off the leading dragoons. Von der Decken was one of the first of his squadron to fall.

In face of such a wall of musketry and steel, it seemed that the wave of horsemen must break and fall back, but at the crucial moment a shot killed one of the dragoon horses and it fell with its rider on top of the French ranks. The opening was made and with a wild yell the dragoons urged their terrified and snorting horses into the gap. It was like the flood which follows the bursting of a dam. The infantry disappeared under the onrush of slashing, yelling, thrusting horsemen, the confusion made a thousand times worse by the plunging and kicking of the fear maddened horses. By the time the dragoons were finished the entire battalion had either been cut down or taken as prisoners, and where the square had once stood lay the disemboweled carcasses of nearly forty horses.

Meanwhile the third squadron of the 1st Dragoons under Captain Von Reitzeuslen had followed Von der Decken's example and charged the second French square. This was drawn up on the edge of the heights and it was even better placed to drive back cavalry. But its morale was shaken by the fate of the other battalion. The cohesion essential if infantry was to withstand the shock action of cavalry was ruined by a number of soldiers who broke the ranks and took to their heels. The dragoons smashed their way into the gaps left by the fugitives and sabred their way through to the other side of the square; then rallying as one man to the trumpet-call, they rode back the way they had come and completed the rout.

A few unwounded French officers hastily rallied the survivors and attempted to form a third square. This in its turn was charged and destroyed by the two squadrons of the 2nd Dragoons which had been following behind their sister regiment. Foy's rear-guard had ceased to exist as an effective fighting force, and all who remained alive and untaken were withdrawn to some rising ground near the Peneranda road. The King's German Legion followed them, but by now their horses had been virtually ridden into the ground. The French held them off with the courage that is left by despair, picking up the stones which littered the ground and hurling them at the legs of the heaving and staggering horses. Wellington then sent orders for the dragoons to retire, and they made their way slowly back to the rear through the cheering ranks of the British infantry. They left behind them in the valley of Garcia Hernandez fifty-two dead dragoons and sixty-seven dead horses; their wounded totalled slightly more.

The charge of the 1st and 2nd Dragoons of the King's German Legion at Garcia Hernandez was probably the most brilliant cavalry action of the whole Peninsular War.

Inflicting 1,400 casualties, Von Bock lost 150 out of 445 engaged. Foy was forced into a defensive position with his Division, the sole French formation intact, but Wellington's infantry were too far back to exploit the opportunity, and the rapid French retreat was resumed. Wellington called off the pursuit at Arevalo three days later, heading for Madrid. Never lavish in praise, the Duke of Wellington, in his dispatch following the battle of Salamanca, wrote:

> I have never witnessed a more gallant charge than was made upon the enemy's infantry by the heavy brigade of the King's German Legion under Major General von Bock, which was completely successful and the whole body of infantry , consisting of three battalions of the enemy's 1st Division were made prisoners.

WALKING THE BATTLEFIELD.

It was not easy to transpose this rolling area of agricultural land into the battlefield it became on 23 July 1812, but to us, the rare military occurrence of the breaking of formed infantry squares by cavalry made it imperative that the exact site of such a phenomena be found. Inclement weather made the investigation of these bare hills and plains something of an ordeal but, despite the rain and biting wind, a broad and fairly accurate picture of this lesser-known action was obtained by means of intelligent map-reading, the application of tactical precepts, and repeated re-tracing of steps (both by car and on foot) - aided by a lot of imagination!

It is impossible to represent in adequate terms my sense of the conduct of the (Foot) Guards and German Legion upon this occasion 9 the 5th assault on 18 October, when a mine was exploded under the church of St. Roman) I am quite satisfied, that if it had been possible to maintain the posts they had gained with so much gallantry, these troops would have maintained them. Some of the men stormed even the third line, and even one of them was killed in one of the embrasures of the parapet.""
From Wellington's Official Despatch, dated Cabrecon 26 October 1812.

In 1808, Napoleon had ordered the modernisation of the fortifications of Burgos, for it controlled a vital part of the highway linking Madrid to France. After Salamanca, Wellington marched to Madrid, then on 1 September went north to besiege Burgos, leaving two divisions to garrison the Spanish capital. The story of the abortive siege of Burgos, Wellington's sole failure in Portugal and Spain, is graphically told by James Grant:

There was not much fighting in the progress of Wellington's march, which carried the British troops through the valley of Arlanzon to Burgos. Frequently the enemy appeared disposed to make a stand, at Cigales and Ducas, at Torquemada, Cellada del Camino, and elsewhere, for he showed 18,000 infantry and 2,000 cavalry in line; but their flanks were always turned, and as the French seemed more disposed to save their baggage - the plunder of churches and palaces - than to risk a battle, they always fell back; and on the 19th of September Wellington entered Burgos, one of the quaintest cities in Old Castile, which, with its gloomy houses and silent streets, is "like a city of the Middle Ages, a living page of the reign of Philip II.," as Blanqui describes it, in his "Voyage a Madrid."

It is situated on the right bank of the Arlanzon, at an altitude of nearly 3,000 feet above the level of the sea, on the high road from Madrid to Bayonne. It is an irregular and decaying town, of cruciform shape, surrounded by high walls, and was protected by a castle of considerable strength, of which the ruins alone remain. Its streets are sombre, narrow, and tortuous.

The Allies entered amid the greatest confusion. The garrison of the castle had set fire to several houses, the walls of which might impede their line of fire; and the partidas, " gathering like wolves round a carcass, entered the town for mischief."

In the castle there had been placed 1,800 infantry, besides a force of artillery; and Du Breton, the governor, " in courage and skill surpassed even the hoped of his most sanguine countrymen." The military works enclosed a rugged hill, between which and the Arlanzon the city was situated. An old wall, parapeted anew with planks, was the first line of defense; the second, within it, was of earth, a kind of field-work, but well palisaded. A third and inner line, similarly constructed, contained two elevated points, on one of which was an intrenched building called the White Church; on the other rose the ancient keep of the castle, an edifice old perhaps as the days of the Cid Rodrigo and his bride Ximena.

This last and loftiest point was intrenched and surrounded by a casemated work called the Napoleon Battery, which commanded every point save the north. There the hill of San Michael, only 300 yards distant, and quite as lofty as the castle, was crowned by a horn-work (i.e., two half-bastions and a curtain), with a sloping scarp, twenty-five, and a counterscarp, ten feet high. Nine heavy guns, eleven field-pieces, and six mortars armed the fortress; and , as the reserve artillery and stores of the army of Portugal were deposited in it, the armament could be greatly augmented. Such was the famous castle of Burgos.

It was formally invested on the night of the 19th of September, and the siege was entrusted to the 1st and 6th divisions. Wellington's train was quite inadequate to warrant hope of success. He had only eight battering guns, viz., three long eighteen pounders, five twenty-four pound

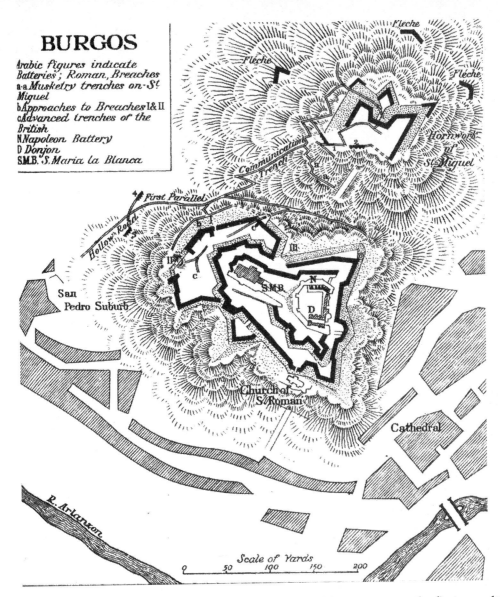

BURGOS

*Arabic figures indicate
Batteries; Roman, Breaches
a-a Musketry trenches on St
Miguel
b Approaches to Breaches I & II
c Advanced trenches of the
British
N. Napoleon Battery
D Donjon
S.M.B. S. Maria la Blanca*

Fleche

Fleche

Fleche

Hornwork of St Miguel

Communications Trench

First Parallel

Hollow Road

San Pedro Suburb

Church of St Roman

Cathedral

R. Arlanzon

Scale of Yards
0   50   100   150   200

howitzers, and scanty ammunition; but on the first night of the investment the first assault was made.

Major Cocks, with the 79th Highlanders supported by Pack's Portuguese, drove in the French outposts on the hill of San Michael; and in the night, when reinforced by the 42nd Highlanders, ladders were planted against the work, and the kilted men swarmed up its face with great gallantry, but the French were numerous in that quarter, and well prepared. A terrible fire opened upon the attacking troops; every Highlander who reached the top of a ladder was instantly bayoneted, and in his fall he knocked down several others. The attack was therefore attended with great loss. Major Somers Cocks, however, forced an entrance at the gorge, and the 42nd rushed into the works, which were immediately captured. The conduct of Major Dick, of the Royal Highlanders, was commended in the Marquis of Wellington's public dispatch.

The garrison was then cut off, but the stormers not being closely supported, the French broke through them with the loss of only 150, whereas ours was above 400 men and officers. Wellington's means for reducing the place were so small, that he relied on the contingencies of water becoming scarce and the magazines being destroyed, rather that on the result of shot and shell; thus it was that 12,000 men were set to the siege, while 20,000 formed the covering army.

From that night up to the 20th of October the siege dragged on; and brave hearts and strong arms had to accomplish with lead and steel much that should have been entrusted to the engineer. "Instead of battering in a breach," says Lord Londonderry, "mines were carried under the castle walls and exploded; while by escalade the troops won post after post, not without a terrible, though necessary, expenditure of human life; for the castle of Burgos was a place of commanding altitude, and, considering the process adopted for its reduction, one of prodigious strength."

Nothing could exceed the heroism of our officers and men. Though twice repulsed on the night of the 21st and subsequently on the 29th, the assailants won the outer line of defences on the 4th of October. Prior to these there had been no less than five assaults, all so much alike in their details of danger, suffering, and bloodshed, that to tell them would but weary the reader. In one of these, on the 8th of October, Major Cocks, the gallant leader of the assault on San Michael, was slain, with many more of his regiment.

In the last assault, the explosion of a mine under San Roman was to be the signal for advancing; and between these attacks the works covering an old breach which had been effected were to be escaladed.

Shedding a dull, red, smoky glare for a moment over everything the mine at San Roman exploded at half past four in the morning, doing but little injury to the church, which was resolutely attacked by some Spanish and Portuguese troops; and though the enemy sprang a counter-mine, which shook the whole edifice to ruins, the surviving assailants lodged themselves amidst them.

Meanwhile, 200 of the Foot Guards, with strong supports, pouring through the breach just referred to in the outer line of defences, scaled the second, but between it and the third were vigorously met by the French A similar number of Germans, under Major Wurmb, also well supported, simultaneously stormed the new breach, and some men mounting the hill actually gained the third line. Unfortunately, at neither of these points did the supports follow closely enough, and the Germans, cramped by a palisade on their left, extended their right towards the Guards.

At that moment the gallant Colonel Du Breton came dashing forward with a charge of bayonets from the high steep ground, and in an instant cleared the breaches of all but the dead and dying. Major Wurmb and many other brave men fell, and our Guards were driven beyond the outer line of works. More than 200 men and officers perished in this morning's conflict; and next night, by a sally, the enemy recovered the blood-stained ruins of San Roman.

The siege was now virtually drawing to a close; for though the French were beaten out of those ruins again, and a gallery was opened from then against the second line of works, these were mere demonstrations, for the fate of Burgos was to be decided outside. While the siege was in progress 44,000 good French troops, under General Souham, were preparing to raise it. The latter officer assumed the command in Spain, on the 3rd of October, and Wellington had now good cause for apprehension. Reinforced by every disposable man from the North, Souham was in full march to give battle should such be necessary, and to relieve Du Breton's beleaguered fortress. Elsewhere, too, all the movable columns of the enemy were pouring towards Burgos as to a common centre. Abandoning Seville, Soult was marching upon Granada; while Joseph Bonaparte and Marshal Jourdan hastened to join him with their troops. The whole, when united, moved upon Madrid; thus by the 21st of October no fewer than 70,000 men were in position about Aranjuez.

Burgos was still holding out; and with the defective means of attack at his disposal, its reduction to Wellington seemed hopeless. His real strength, exclusive of the British troops, was his Portuguese, chiefly led by British officers; for, besides those killed and wounded in the siege, the sick had gone to the rear faster than the recovered men came up. The odds were too much against him to commit his fortune to the chance of a battle there.

An order to raise the siege being given, the guns and stores were removed from the batteries; but as the greatest part of the draught animals had been sent to Santander for powder and artillery, the long eighteen pounders were abandoned.

Thus after five assaults, several sallies, and thirty-three days of close investment, during which the besiegers lost more than 2,000, and the besieged more than 600 men killed and wounded, the siege of Burgos was abandoned.

The French suffered greatly from continual labour, for their numbers were few; and want of water and bad weather had to be endured. The castle was too small to afford shelter for all, thus many had to bivouac between the lines of defence, and so were constantly in the open.

The valour of Colonel Du Breton was greatly extolled; and after the Restoration, in happier times, when a lieutenant-general commanding in Strasburg, he had the pleasure of paying the usual military honours to the Duke of Wellington , who was then inspecting the frontiers.

And now ensued the famous but miserable retreat from Burgos, which was commenced on the night of the 21st of October. After darkness was fairly in, the army left its position without beat of drum; the artillery, the wheels thickly muffled with straw, passed the bridge over the Arlanzon, immediately under the castle guns, with such silence and celerity that Du Breton, though ever alert and suspicious, knew nothing of the departure until some of the Spanish partidas, beginning to lose nerve, broke into a gallop. As the clatter of the hoofs went upward, the red flashes of the cannon broke from the castle walls, and a storm of round shop and grape was poured down at random till the range was lost.

On the 23rd our infantry crossed the Pisuerga; but while the main body made this long march, Souham, who had passed through Burgos on the preceding night, vigorously attacked the rear guard under Sir Stapleton Cotton, composed of cavalry and horse artillery, with two German battalions and partidas. On the 25th the bridges over the Carrion and Pisuerga were blown up, to arrest the progress of the enemy. Those on the Duero, at Tudela and Puente del Duero, shared the same fate; but many of the French swam the river at Tordesillas, so active were they in the firm pursuit that followed the abandonment of Burgos.

In the following year ,1813 there was a renewed Allied assault on Burgos, shortly before the battle of Vitoria; the garrison held out for two days only before surrendering on 12 June.

Wellington to Lord Liverpool. Dated Cuidad Rodrigo, 23 November 1812.

I see that a disposition already exists to blame the Government for the failure of the siege of Burgos. The Government had nothing to say to the siege. It was entirely my own act. In regard to means, there were ample means both at Madrid and at Santander for the siege of the strongest fortress. That which was wanting at both places was means of transporting ordnance and military stores to the place where it was desirable to use them. The people of England, so happy as they are in every respect, so rich in resources of every description, having the use of such excellent roads etc., will not readily believe that important results here frequently depend upon 50 or 60 mules more or less, or a few bundle of straw to feed them; but the fact is so, notwithstanding their incredulity, I could not find means of moving even one gun from Madrid.

ON THE GROUND AT BURGOS.

Driving here from Salamanca, through Old Castile, evoked thoughts of walking around on a wargames table bearing realistic scenic effects like mountain passes, precipitous roads, lakes, and forests of trees strongly resembling those we make for our tabletop battlefields. The steep slope of the Burgos castle were assaulted by our party and we found ourselves impressed by the strong defences of this site of Wellington's sole repulse throughout the entire Peninsular War. In ruined condition, the castle is still one of Burgos's sights along with the twice lifesize statue of El Cid on the bridge.

THE BATTLE OF VITORIA - 21 JUNE 1813

I look upon Salamanca, Vittoria , and Waterloo, as my three best battles; Those which had great and permanent consequences. Salamanca relieved the whole south of Spain, changed all the prospects of the war, and was felt even in Russia. Vittoria freed the Peninsula altogether, broke off the armistice at Dresden, and thus led to Leipsic, and the deliverance of Europe; and Waterloo did more than any other battle I know of, towards the true object of all battles- the peace of the world.
Duke of Wellington 1834.

The account of this decisive battle comes from the prolific pen of the ubiquitous James Grant, together with yet another late 19th century military historian and writer, Charles Lowe, whose words set the scene:-

The failure at Burgos, and the consequent retirement of Wellington into Portugal, gave the French a further respite from the fate that awaited them and their Emperor's brother, Joseph Bonaparte, whom Napoleon had forced upon the people of Spain as their King. Wellington retreated, but only to return after a brief space to repair his own reverses. It is only soldiers of the highest genius who can do this. Marshal Moltke was once in company where someone ventured to say that his name would rank in history with those of Marlborough, Turenne, the Great Frederick, Napoleon, and Wellington. "No," said the great German strategist, " I have nor right to be named with those great commanders for I have never in my life conducted a retreat."

Hitherto the French had vastly outnumbered Lord Wellington's troops (British and Portuguese) in the Peninsula, but in the winter of 1812-13, after his third retirement from Spain to Portugal, the scale was turned in his favour. For this winter had all but destroyed Napoleon's "Grand Army," and on returning to Paris the Emperor had to weaken his armies in the Peninsula to meet his allied foes in Germany. Soult, with 20,000 veteran troops, was recalled. Thus in the spring of 1813 the French had now only about 160,000 effective men with the Eagles in the Peninsula, while Wellington had the command of nearly 170,000 of which 44,000 only were British, 31,000 Portuguese, the rest being Spaniards and Sicilians. In May his Anglo-Portuguese army, numbering 75,000 men, lay cantoned from Lamego to the Banos Pass in the Salamanca province, and it is only this portion of his force that now concerns us.

Wellington did all he could, by the circulation of false reports, to encourage the French in their belief that he meant to re-invade Spain through the central provinces between the Tagus and the Douro.

But for various reasons Wellington resolved to make a flank march by the north, so as, if possible, to turn the French right and fall upon their rear. Dividing his forces into three armies- the left one under Sir Thomas Graham, the centre one commanded by himself, and that on the right led by Sir Rowland Hill- Wellington, by a series of movements which completely deceived the French, crossed the Ebro and fought his difficult way across the successive affluents of its right bank, pushing the outmanoeuvred Frenchmen ever before him through the fortress of Burgos, which they blew up in their retreat, and compelling them to transfer their main position from the line of the Douro to that of the Ebro.

The difficulties of these turning movements were great, the immensity of the operations were described by Judge-Advocate Larpent, in his 'Private Journal:

The brigade of heavy artillery, namely six eighteen pounders, were encamped about two miles from hence on Thursday, and I went over to see them. The difficulty of transport may be conceived when I tell you that there were above a hundred and sixty of the strongest oxen employed in getting these six pieces, with the appurtenances, along the road, besides spare animals." May 1813.

On 30th May 1813 the army under the Duke of Wellington reached the River Esla and at dawn on the 31st the 15th Hussars prepared to cross by the ford at Almendra. This ford was much swollen; the 51st Regiment (later the King's Own Yorkshire Light Infantry) crossed over with the 15th, many men and horses being swept away by the current. The men of the 15th were, however, able to rescue some of the 51st who, by clinging to the stirrups of the Hussars, were able to reach the bank in safety. For many years afterwards the two regiments, whenever possible, celebrated the occasion together."

Yesterday the Hussars again came up with the 16th French cavalry and some others; the latter had only a small bridge to pass which would only carry four abreast. Two squadrons of the 19th formed and charged; the French stood at first well, but were broken, and then formed again. The 10th formed, charged again, and again broke the French; the latter then still made another effort, but at last ran for the bridge. The 10th killed a few, and brought about a hundred and ninety prisoners in here : no horses were taken. : 3rd June 1813.

CHARLES LOWE:

Wellington, having executed his flank movement, which compelled his enemies to fall back on their lines of communication with France through the Pyrenees, transferred his own base of supplies, formed by his ships, from the Tagus to the Biscayan ports. Napier wrote of the entry by Wellington's troops into the Vittoria basin: "Neither gullies, nor ravines, nor the precipitate passes amongst the rocks, retarded even the march of the artillery. Where horses could not draw, men hauled; when the wheels would not roll, the guns were let down or lifted up with ropes" for six days in succession.

King Joseph Bonaparte concentrated about 60,000 men at Vittoria, together with all his stores and baggage , the pillage of five years, the artillery depots of Madrid, Valladolid, and Burgos, and a convoy of treasure from Bayonne.

It was within three miles of Vittoria that, in the year 1367, Edward the Black Prince had routed some of the finest troops of France under their famous leader Bertrand du Guesclin; and a prominent height in the region was still known as the "Englishmen's Hill " (Altura de los Ingleses), from the gallant stand which had been made by some English knights and their followers against a large body of Spaniards under Don Telo. Vittoria had previously to this derived its name from some ancient and forgotten victory.

Wellington intended to force Joseph Bonaparte's right and cut his main line of communication by the Bayonne road with France.

The position of the French could not have been stronger by nature. Their extreme left, under Maransin, rested on an elevated chain of craggy mountains; their right, under Reille, on a rapid river (the Zadora); while Gazan held the commanding heights in the centre, and a wide stretch of undulating ground afforded excellent situations for artillery. The French line extended for about eight miles, held by about 60,000 men with 152 guns; but, being obliged to scatter their troops widely in order to live on the country, they were much harassed by guerrilla bands. King Joseph allowed himself to be guided in all things by Marshal Jourdan, who on the 21st of June was suffering so acutely from fever that he was unable to mount his horse. The French army consisted of fair fighting material, but it was badly commanded, and the troops had no confidence in the King. In respect of position, cavalry, and artillery, King Joseph was decidedly superior to Wellington; but, on the other hand, Wellington had the advantage of being numerically stronger than his opponent by about 15,000 men, and enjoyed the thorough confidence of his troops.

After an early morning of mist the day broke in glorious sunshine, and then the British army began to move forward over very hilly and irregular ground from its bivouacs on the Bayas river, running almost parallel with the Zadora.

The French left extended from the heights overlooking the village of Puebla, past Arinez to Margarita, on the Zadora; an advanced post, with a battery, holding the spur between Tres Puentes and Villodar, d'Erlon in second line between Hermandad and Arinez.

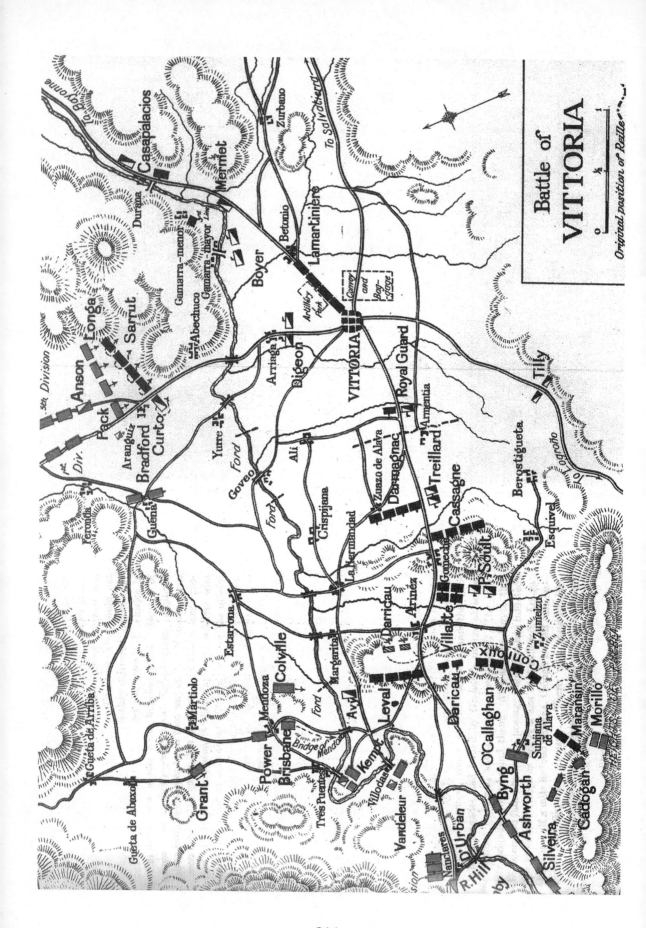

The French right, under Reille, guarded Abechuco and Gamara, north of Vittoria, and the heights beyond the river. A reserve was on the heights east of Arinez. The cavalry was massed near Ali, a mile west of Vittoria, and all the baggage was packed east of the town. All the country between the Bayas and Zadora rivers was broken, very rough, intersected by many streams and ravines, and in parts covered by woods. The river varied in width from 50 yards to a stream that in places was very deep. None of the stone bridges - six in number - from Puebla to Abechuco had been broken up.

Wellington's Attack. The right column (20,000 strong, under Hill) - second British division, a Portuguese division, and part of Morillo's Spanish division - with some cavalry, was to force the pass and seize the Puebla heights. The centre, 30,000 under Wellington, in two bodies, was to move on Nauclares and await orders. The left, under Graham - 1st and 5th Divisions, Portuguese, and Louga's Spaniards - was to move from Murgura on the Bayas River towards Abeclinco. Its support of 12,000 Spaniards made every effort, but did not get up in time for the battle.

James Grant takes up the story:-

The weather had been rainy and moist, and thus, amid clouds of thick vapour, on the eventful morning of the 21st the allied troops moved from their camp near the Bayas river, and slowly approached the Zadora; while Hill, on the other side of the ridge, commenced the passage of that river beyond the defile of the Puebla. As the morning mists dispersed and the sun shone out, the allied army as it moved to the front in three great masses must have presented a spectacle of unusual grandeur to the French in their fine position, as their dense masses came on in succession; the brilliantly polished barrels and bayonets shining steadily on the rays of the sun, the silk standards of so many varied colours - red, blue, white, or yellow - marking by pairs the various battalions; and the many different uniforms, the scarlet of the British, the blue of the Portuguese, the sombre brown of the Spaniards, and the still darker columns of the rifles and cacadores. Many warlike sounds added to the effect of the scene, for there were "the neighing of the cavalry horses, the roll of tumbrils and gun-carriages, the distant yet distinct words of command, the mingling music of many bands, the trumpets of the horse, the bugles of the rifles, and the hoarse wailing war-pipes of the Highland regiments, ever and anon swelling upon the breeze, pealing among the heights of Puebla, and dying away among the windings in the vale of Zadora.

On the other side, the lines of the French in position were perfectly motionless. They looked dark and sombre, save on their left, where stood some brigades attired in light green uniforms with white trousers.

CHARLES LOWE:

"The attack on the French position was begun by Sir Rowland Hill on the British right, where he sent forward a Spanish brigade under Morillo to seize the Puebla heights. With great difficulty, though unopposed, the Spaniards scrambled to the top of those heights. But presently they were sharply attacked by the French, who, perceiving the danger which thus threatened their left, detached a portion of their centre force to push the Spaniards down the hill again. And it would now have gone hard with Morillo's brigade had not General Hill been quick to perceive their peril and tell off the 71st Highland Light Infantry with another Light battalion, under Colonel Cadogan, to rush to their assistance.

This was General Murillo's corps: I went down to look at them. There were about ten regiments, I think, but most of them small ones, The men looked very well, though a great many were quite boys. They were singing, joking, and in good spirits; the artillery with them in good order, the draft mules quite fat. The clothing and equipments of some very good, though unequal to ours or to the Portuguese; others moderate only. They wore a sort of flannel jacket and trousers not at all alike, and some were ragged, here and there a man barefoot, - very few; all with good caps, in the French style, and the others more respectable than usual, and generally mounted; some very fierce-looking pioneers, fine grenadiers, and all with good

215

English muskets in good order, brighter than our own, being, most probable, nearly new: in short, the whole was respectable. If they will but fight as well as they look, it will do. 12th June 1813."
The Private Journal of Judge-Advocate Larpent - Peninsular War 1851.]

CHARLES LOWE:

The pipers of the Highlanders struck up Johnnie Cope, the regimental, march. As though inspired by all the memories associated with these stirring strains, the 71st rushed to the succour of the hard-pressed Spaniard, and soon reached the summit of the heights, though at a great sacrifice of life. Scorning the use of bullets, the Highlanders with levelled bayonets, swept up and upon the foe through clouds of smoke, and their attack was intensified by the sight of their idolised commander (Cadogan) falling mortally wounded from his horse. A few minutes later he died in the arms of Colonel Seaton, of the 92nd Highlanders. Nothing could now withstand their charge, and after a hand to hand conflict, Maransin's Frenchmen were hurled down the eastern side of the hill, which now began to resound with the sounds of the Highland war-pipe.

"We lay on the heights for some time," wrote a soldier of the 71st. "Our drought was excessive. There was no water there, save a small spring, which was rendered useless. One of our men stooped to drink. A ball pierced his head. He fell in the well, which was discoloured by brains and blood. Thirsty as we were, we could not drink of it. There were only three hundred of us on the height able to do duty out of one thousand who drew rations that morning. The cries of the wounded were most heartrending."

JAMES GRANT:

Encouraged by his good fortune, Sir Rowland Hill now ordered his 2nd and 3rd brigades to attack the heights of Subijana de Alava; and here the 92nd Gordon Highlanders took ground on the same spot where, after the battle of Najera, four hundred and forty-six years before, 200 gallant Englishmen, under Sir Thomas and Sir William Felton, were surrounded and cut to pieces by 6,000 Spaniards, under Don Tello. After a stern and severe conflict, these heights were also won, together with the village in front of General Count Gazan's portion of the French line; and then connecting his right with the troops on the mountain, Hill maintained that forward position, in spite of all the enemy's efforts until the central portion of the battle was begun by Wellington on his left.

In writing of the spirit with which our troops engaged at Vittoria, Sergeant Donaldson, of the Scots Brigade, in his "Eventful Life of a Soldier," says, "those who have not known it from experience can form no idea of the indifference with which our soldiers entered a battle, after being some time in the Peninsula. As an instance of this, when we were lying in front of the enemy in expectation of being engaged, one of our men, a Highlander, having lost a small piece of ornamented leather which is worn in front of the uniform cap, on taking it off the deficiency caught his eye, and looking at it for a few moments, he said, very seriously, "I wish there may be an engagement to-day, that I may get a rosette for my cap !'"

Keeping all his cavalry massed as a reserve, Wellington placed the 4th division opposite the bridge of Nanclares, and the light division at the bridge of Villadas, both being covered or concealed by rugged ground and woods; the light infantry were so close to the water that they could have shot down the French gunners as they stood beside their cannon at the loop of the stream. However, their skirmishers prolonged Hill's battle, by a sharp fire on those of the enemy. While waiting for the 3rd and 7th divisions, which had not yet reached the point for a combined attack, a Spanish peasant came in haste to Lord Wellington and told him that "the bridge of Tres Puentes had been left unguarded," and offered to guide the troops across it.

On this, General Kemp's brigade was at once ordered to that quarter, and being concealed by some rocks, passed the narrow bridge at double-quick pace, with their muskets at the trail; and mounting a steep piece of ground, lay close to his line of battle. Two cannon-shots were now fired by the enemy, and one of them cut in two the peasant who had acted as guide. The whole of our 15th Hussars, clad in blue, and then laced with silver, now defiled across the bridge, horseman after horseman; but still the French in that quarter remained motionless.

It was now long past noon. The assault by Hill on the village of Subijana was fully developed and successful; and the clouds of white smoke that rolled far up the green valley of the Zadora on the extreme left, together with the reverberated reports of cannon, announced that Graham's attack had begun on Reille's force, by the Bilbao road. Joseph and Jourdan, finding both flanks menaced thus, made their reserve move towards Vittoria, and gave Count Gazan orders to fall back by alternate masses; but at that critical moment our 3rd and 7th divisions were seen pouring down in successive regiments towards the bridge of Mendoza, so his cannon opened upon them at once, while his light troops commenced a heavy fire of musketry, and his cavalry drew near the bridge.

Some British cannon replied from the opposite bank; and now Barnard, springing to the front, led the rifles of the light division in a most daring manner between the French cavalry and the river, taking their light troops and cannon alike in flank, engaging them so closely that our artillerymen, taking his dark-green uniforms for those of the enemy, poured shot and shell upon them all.

CHARLES LOWE:

Meanwhile in the centre, where Wellington himself controlled the fight, General Picton, who commanded the impatient "Fighting Third" Division, was fretting under his enforce inaction. He had advanced from Anda, on the Bayas River, and was to work in connection with the Light and 4th Divisions, then on his right. His soldiers were eager, and their equally fiery leader had some difficulty in restraining them. As the day wore on, and the fight waxed ever warmer on his right, Picton became furious and observed to an officer, "D----n it ! Lord Wellington must have forgotten us."

When an officer galloped up from Lord Wellington Picton's face began to glow with animation at the prospect of being ordered into action; but it suddenly grew black again on the officer simply asking whether he had seen Lord Dalhousie. "No, sir," answered Picton sharply; "but have you any orders for me?" "None," replied the aide-de-camp. "Then pray , sir," continued the irritated General, " what are the orders you do bring ?" "That as soon as Lord Dalhousie, with the 7th Division, commences an attack on the bridge," (pointing to one on the left) "the 4th and 6th are to support him."

Picton could not understand the idea of any other division fighting in *his* front, so, drawing himself up to his full height, he said to the astonished aide-de-camp, with some heat: "You may tell Lord Wellington for me, sir, that the 3rd Division under my command shall, in less than ten minutes, attack the bridge and carry it, and the 4th and 6th Divisions may support me if the choose." Saying which, he turned from the aide-de-camp and put himself at the head of his eager men, with a wave of his hand towards the bridge and the cry of "come on, ye rascals ! Come on, ye fighting villains !"

He well fulfilled his promise. Under a heavy fire of artillery his "fighting" division moved steadily on, his leading companies rushing over the bridge, where they formed up in open columns . Then they moved to their left, so as to attack the enemy's centre. Still advancing in the same order, they pressed up the heights, where they quickly deployed into line. The foe hardly awaited the attack, for so rapidly were these manoeuvres carried out that the French for the moment were as if paralysed. Picton had gained the heights in front of him, but the divisions on his right had not yet made sufficient progress to come into line with and support him. Halting his impatient "rascals": he waited for the advance of the 7th Division (Lord Dalhousie's) and part of the "Lights," while the 4th (under General Cole) passed the Zadora a little farther to the right by the Nanclares bridge.

During the slower advance of these divisions the French made desperate attempts to roll Picton back, opening upon him with 50 guns and sending serried masses of infantry at his line. But the incessant fire which his men poured into their assailants made havoc in their ranks, completed by a charge with bayonets. When these were crossed with the enemy, the issue of the struggle in this part of the field was certain.

All this time "Picton's Division," as an eyewitness wrote, "acted in a manner which excited at once the surprise and admiration of the whole army. For nearly four hours did it alone sustain the unequal conflict, opposed to a vast superiority of force. From the nature of the ground, the rest of the army became witnesses of this animating scene; they beheld, with feelings more easily conceived than expressed, the truly heroic efforts of this gallant band. They saw the General - calm, collected, and determined- leading them on in the face of danger, amidst a shower of cannon and musket balls. Nothing could appall, nothing could resist, men so resolute and so led. They subdued every obstacle, bore down all opposition, and spread death, consternation, and dismay in the enemy's ranks."

The uneven and broken ground made Picton's advance difficult and his line irregular, but there was no confusion in his ranks. A second charge with the bayonet forced the enemy to retire, and so hasty was the French flight that they left 28 of their guns in the hands of Picton's irresistible men.

JAMES GRANT:

The 4th division passed the bridge of Nanclares; and now the whole vale of the Zadora, the heights of Gomecha, and those of La Puebla, the woodlands, the hedgerow, the bridges, were enveloped in smoke, streaked with incessant flashes of fire, In and about the hamlets, every cottage, garden, and vineyard-wall, became a breastwork, for the possession of which armed men contested desperately, often foot to foot and hand to hand.

Our 7th division and Colville's brigade of the 3rd, having forded the river with success, formed up on the left, and became immediately engaged with the French right; after which Wellington led Picton and the rest of the 3rd division at a swift run across the front of both armies, towards the central battle, or central point of attack, where Sir Andrew Barnard's rifles led the van. At the same time that the 4th division crossed the bridge of Nanclares, with all their arms flashing in the sun, our heavy cavalry, a splendid array of horse, galloped over also, squadron after squadron, and formed in the plain between the troops of Cole and Hill.

By this movement the French were caught in the midst of their dispositions for that retreat which King Joseph had already deemed it necessary to order. In clouds their skirmishers came rushing out, while fifty pieces of cannon loaded the air with the sound of thunder as they played on the Allies with increased activity. The guns of Wellington replied. The shot on each side sent up clouds of dust to mingle with the dense smoke of the battle; and when this veil cleared for a little, the French were seen retiring to a second range of heights, in front of Gomecha, yet still holding the village of Ariniz, on the main road.

Picton's troops, always headed by the riflemen of the light division, then plunged into that village, amidst a heavy fire of muskets and artillery, and three guns were captured. But the post was important; fresh French troops came down, and for some time the smoke, dust, and clamour, the flashing of the fire-arms, the shouts and cries of the combatants, mixed with the thundering of the guns, were terrible; but finally the British troops issued forth victoriously on the other side.

Ariniz was won! During this conflict, the 7th division, reinforced by Vandeleur's brigade, was heavily raked by a battery at the village of Margarita, until the Oxfordshire Light Infantry carried it by the bayonet; and in wild melee, the 87th Royal Irish Fusiliers carried the village of Hermandad; and thus fighting desperately from point to point, the whole British line continued to advance over ground that became exceedingly diversified with woods and plains, in some places covered with waving corn, intersected by watery ditches, vineyards, and little hamlets.

CHARLES LOWE:

On the British left Sir Thomas Graham brought his guns into action at 10 a.m., but as he was directed to conform to the left centre attack (3rd and 7th Divisions), his attack was not developed till noon, with the 1st and 5th Divisions, Pack's and Bradford's infantry brigades, a Spanish division under Longa, and Anson's brigade of horse-when it was equally successful in passing the Zadora and threatening the French right.

Some idea of the fighting on this flank may be gained from the terse account which was given of it by Lieutenant Campbell (afterwards to become Sir Colin, the hero of Lucknow, and Lord Clyde), who was then acting as orderly officer to Lieutenand-Colonel Crawford; "While we were halted the enemy occupied Gamara Mayor in considerable force, placed two guns at the principal entrance into the village, threw a cloud of skirmishers in front among the cornfields, and occupied with six pieces of artillery the heights immediately behind the village on the left bank. At 5P.M. an order arrived from Lord Wellington to press the enemy in our front. It was the

218

extreme right of their line, and the lower road to France, by which alone they could retire. Their artillery and baggage were close to Gamara Mayor. The left brigade moved down in contiguous columns of companies, and our Light companies were sent to cover the right flank of this attack.

The regiments, exposed to a heavy fire of musketry and artillery, did not take a musket from their shoulder until they had carried the village. The enemy brought forward his reserves and made many desperate attempts to retake the bridge, but could not succeed. This was repeated until the bridge became so heaped with dead and wounded that they were rolled over the parapet into the river below. Our Light companies were closed upon the 9th, and brought into the village to support the 2nd Brigade.

The battle now presented a magnificently imposing spectacle as the three divisions of Wellington's army, after having crossed the Zadora and beaten back their opponents from ridge to ridge, and from village to village moved forward to a grand general attack.

"Many guns," wrote Napier, "were taken as the army advanced, and at six o' clock the enemy reached the last defensible height, one mile in front of Vittoria. Behind them was the plain on which the city stood, and beyond the city thousands of carriages and animals and non-combatants, men, women, and children, were crowding together in all the madness of terror; and as the English shot went booming overhead, the vast crowd started and swerved with a convulsive movement, while a dull and horrid sound of distress arose. But there was no hope, no stay for army or multitude. It was the wreck of a nation. However, the courage of the French soldier was not yet quelled; Reille, on whom everything now depended, maintained his post on the upper Zadora; and the armies of the south and centre, drawing up on their last heights, between the villages of Ali and Armentier, made their muskets flash like lightning, while more than eighty pieces of artillery, massed together, pealed with such a horrid uproar that the hills laboured and shook, and streamed with fire and smoke, amidst which the dark figures of the gunners were seen bounding with a frantic energy."

James Grant:

On the 3rd division fell the brunt of that dreadful storm, and the French generals began to draw off their infantry from the right; while our 4th division, with a mighty and irresistible rush, carried the hill on the left of this, the last French position.

The heights were all abandoned then; and at that moment Joseph, finding the royal road so blocked up by carriages that the artillery could not pass, indicated that by Salvatierra as the line of retreat, and the troops went off at once in confused masses.

Over this plain, for the distance of six miles, the battle resolved itself in a running fight and cannonade-dust, smoke, tumult, death, and agony filling all the landscape-as the tide of war rolled on towards the low and half-ruined walls of Vittoria. Cannon were captured at every few yards;

Return of Ordnance, carriages and ammunition, captured from the enemy in the action at Vittoria on the 21st June, 1813:-151 Brass ordnance, on travelling carriages; 415 Caissons; 14,249 Rounds of Ammunition; 1,973,400 Musket ball cartridges; 40,668 Pounds of gunpowder; 56 Forage waggons; 44 Forge waggons.

A. Dicksom, Lieut-Colonel, Commanding the artillery.

Charles Lowe:

The French retirement was successively converted into retreat, flight, and headlong rout, followed by the scarlet masses of Wellington's victorious infantry from ridge to ridge, and from height to hollow. In the morning a superbly organised army, the French had by sunset become a wild mob. King Joseph himself had a very narrow escape. The 10th Hussars galloped into the town just as he was leaving it in his carriage, and when Captain Wyndham dashed after him with a squadron, His Majesty only escaped by quitting his vehicle and mounting a swift horse. But the Hussars were rewarded by the finding of the greater portion of the King's regalia in his carriage.

At the battle of Vittoria the baton of a Marshal of France, Marshal Jourdan, was captured by a soldier of the 87th Regiment. The baton was about fourteen inches long, covered with blue velvet, ornamented with the imperial eagle in rich embroidery, and tipped with gold. The case was of red morocco, clasped with silver, and adorned with eagles, having Marshal Jourdan's name inscribed at either end.

It was sent by General Lord Wellington to the Prince Regent. In July, 1813, the Prince wrote to Wellington as follows:-

My dear Lord,

Your glorious conduct is beyond all human praise, and far above my reward. I know no language the world affords worthy to express it. I feel I have nothing left to say, but devoutly to offer up my prayer of gratitude to Providence, that it has, in its omnipotent bounty, blessed by country and myself with such a General. You have sent me, among the trophies of your unrivalled fame, the staff of a French marshal, and I send you in return that of England.

The British army will hail it with enthusiasm, while the whole universe will acknowledge those valorous efforts which have so imperiously called for it.

That uninterrupted health and still increasing laurels may continue to crown you through a glorious and long career of life, are the never ceasing and most ardent wishes of, my dear Lord, your very sincere and faithful friend,

G.P.R.

JAMES GRANT:

"Spur, spur!" was now the cry, as our light cavalry swept, sword in hand, to the front, to intercept this new line of retreat, which passed a marsh now choked by wagons, carriages, and terrified fugitives. The greater part of the French guns were abandoned here; the artillerymen slashed through the traces with their swords, and fled with the horses, in many instances riding down their own infantry.

The French cavalry, however, preserved some order, and many were seen galloping to the rear with women and children on their holsters or cruppers, as they bore them out of the dreadful scene. Closely and vigorously did our dragoons pursue, and our horse artillery, also, with shot and shell; but neither the bravery of the French cavalry, which made some most splendid charges, nor the darkness of night, stopped their victorious career till the fugitive mobs were past Metanco.

Never was a rout and never was a victory more complete! The number of French slain was comparatively small; but, in the words of General Count Gazan, "they lost all their equipages, all their guns, all their treasure, all their stores, all their papers; no man could even prove how much pay was due to him. Generals and subordinate officers were alike reduced to the clothes on their backs, and most of them were barefooted."

From the field the French carried off only two pieces of cannon. Marshal Jourdan's baton, the colours of the 4th battalion of the Imperial 100th Regiment, 143 pieces of beautiful brass cannon, all the parks and depots from Madrid, Burgos, and Valladolid, carriages - many of them filled with ladies - baggage, ammunition, and the military chest, remained in the hands of the victors. Their loss in men did not exceed 6,000 while that of the Allies amounted to 5,176 killed, wounded, and missing. The British losses were more than double those of the Portuguese and Spaniards. "The spoil was immense," says Napier; "yet so plundered by the followers and non-combatants, that the fighting troops may be said to have marched upon gold and silver without stopping to pick it up; that of five millions and a half of dollars, indicated by the French accounts to be in the money-chests, not one dollar came to the public."

Many unfortunate women - some of them the wives of officers, and others ladies of the court - barefooted, almost naked, and in the most pitiable condition, were overtaken in wild and solitary places, and most barbarously used and then murdered by the merciless Spaniards.

All whom our cavalry found alive, and could secure, were carefully sent under escort to the rear. Among these was the Countess de Gazan.

In his 'Conversations with the Duke of Wellington', the Earl of Stanhope recorded: "The baggage and encumbrances of the French Army were immense at Vittoria. A great many ladies too ! One of their prisoners said to me after the battle: 'Le fait est, Monseigneur, que vous avez une armee mais nous sommes un bordel ambulant.' (The fact is, my lord, that you have an army and we have a travelling bordello.)"

JAMES GRANT:

" On the day after the battle," writes an officer who was engaged, " in company with another, I rode out to view the ground on which the armies had contended. It was strewed with dead and wounded, with accoutrements and arms, a great part of the latter broken. At those points where the more obstinate fighting took place, the ground was literally covered with bodies. A great number of wounded - French, British, and Portuguese - lay along the road, groaning and craving water, The village of Gamara Mayor was shattered by shot. The bridge was covered with dead, and its arches were choked up by bodies and accoutrements. A few straggling peasants could be seen at a distance, watching an opportunity for plunder. There was a dreadful silence over the scene. In our way back to the town, my companion's attention was attracted by a dead Portuguese. He raised up the body, and desired me to look through it. I did absolutely do so. A cannon-ball had passed into the breast and out at the back; and so rapid must have been its transit, from its forming such a clean aperture - in circumference about twelve inches - that the man must have been close to the cannon's mouth when he was shot. It spoke volumes for the courage of the troops."

Along the whole line of road from Vittoria to the Pyrenees, a distance of one hundred miles, the way was strewn with dead or abandoned horses, dilapidated carriages, clothing of every kind, uniforms, books, rich dresses, laces, veils, gloves, and bonnets, torn forth from mails and imperials, by the rude hands of guerillas, cacadores, and peasants; letters, orders, and French bank-notes in bundles, too, lay there.

From Vittoria to this place we have constantly passed at first stripped and unburied dead, then baggage and animals without number, but the French have got off to France, and march away like monkeys, scrambling over everything, consequently there are few prisoners. Lord Wellington is in the highest spirits. King Joseph was within 200 yards of our dragoons, and had a narrow escape. A few more cannon have been taken. June 1813.

The Private Journal of Judge-Advocate Larpent - Peninsular War.

JAMES GRANT:

At Pampeluna, the flying French army bivouacked on the glacis in front of the town; but in a state of such utter destitution and wild insubordination, that the governor would not suffer them to enter the gates.

Lord Wellington returned to Vittoria about nine in the evening, and found every door closed and every lattice darkened. A solitary oil lantern hung in front of each house gave the little city a mournful and melancholy aspect. Two nights before its streets had been one blaze of light , in honour of the presence of King Joseph !

After the Battle of Vittoria. I have been over the hospital, and the scene which I there witnessed was most terrible; 1700 or 1800 men, without legs or arms, etc, or with dreadful wounds, and having had nothing to eat for 2 or 3 days, the misery extreme, and not nearly hands sufficient to dress or take care of the men - English, Portuguese, Spaniards, and French all together, though the Spaniards and Portuguese had at first no provision at all for their people. Half the wounded have been scattered round the villages in the neighbourhood; and are lying in all the passages and spare places around the hospital. 23rd June 1813.

The Private Journal of Judge-Advocate Larpent - Peninsular War.

	Marching Strength May 25	Losses at Vitoria
1st Division, General Howard		
Stopford's Brigade	1,728	
1st Coldstream		–
1st Scots Guards		–
5/60th (1 comp.)		
Halkett's Brigade	3,126	
1st, 2nd, 5th Line K.G.L		2
1st Light K.G.L.		9
2nd Light K.G.L.		43
1st Division Total	*4,854*	*54*
2nd Division, General Sir Rowland Hill		
Cadogan's Brigade	2,777	
1/50th		104
1/71st		316
1/92nd		20
5/60th (1 comp.)		
Byng's Brigade	2,465	
1/3rd		110
1/57th		28
1st Prov. Batt. (2/31st & 2/66th)		40
5/60th (1 comp.)		
O'Callaghan's Brigade	2,530	
1/28th		199
2/34th		76
1/39th		215
5/60th (1 comp.)		
Ashworth's Portuguese	3,062	
6th Line		12
18th Line		1
6th Cacadores		9
2nd Division Total	*10,834*	*1,132*
3rd Division, General Sir Thomas Picton		
Brisbane's Brigade	2,723	
1/45th		74
74th		83
1/88th		215
5/60th (3 comp.)		51
Colville's Brigade	2,276	
1/5th		163
2/83rd		74
2/87th		244
94th		67
Power's Portuguese	2,460	
9th Line		212
21st Line		187
11th Cacadores		12
3rd Division Total	*7,437*	*1,382*
4th Division, General Sir G. Lowry Cole		
W. Anson's Brigade	2,935	
3/27th		42
1/40th		42
1/48th		19
2nd Prov. Batt (2nd & 2/53rd)		10
5/60th (1 comp.)		
Skerret's Brigade	2,049	
1/7th		4
20th		4
1/23rd		4
Brunswick (1 comp.)		
Stubb's Portuguese	2,842	
11th Line		153
23rd Line		58
7th Cacadores		35
4th Division Total	*7,816*	*371*
5th Division, General Oswald		
Hay's Brigade	2,292	
3/1st		111
1/9th		25
1/38th		8
Brunswick (1 comp.)		
Robinson's Brigade	2,061	
1/4th		91
2/47th		112
2/59th		149
Brunswick (1 comp.)		
Spry's Portuguese	2,372	
3rd Line		13
15th Line		28
8th Cacadores		40
5th Division Total	*6,725*	*577*
6th Division, General Pakenham		
Stirling's Brigade	2,454	
1/42nd		–
1/79th		–
1/91st		–
5/60th (1 comp.)		
Hinde's Brigade	2,418	
1/11th		–
1/32nd		–
1/36th		–
1/61st		–
Madden's Portuguese	2,475	
8th Line		–
12th Line		–
9th Cacadores		–
6th Division Total	*7,347*	*–*

	Marching Strength May 25	Losses at Vitoria
7th Division, General Lord Dalhousie		
Barnes's Brigade	2,322	
1/6th		–
3rd Prov. Batt. (2/24 & 2/58)		–
Brunswick-Oels (9 comp.s)		6[1]
Grant's Brigade	2,538	
51st		32
68th		125
1/82nd		31
Chasseurs Britanniques		140
Lecor's Portuguese	2,437	
7th Line		6
19th Line		–
2nd Cacadores		–
7th Division Total	7,227	340
Light Division, General Charles Alten		
Kempt's Brigade	2,077	
1/43rd		31
1st/95th		45
3rd/95th		24
Vandeleur's Brigade	1,462	
1/52nd		23
2/95th		9
Portuguese	1,943	
17th Line		28
1st Cacadores		4
3rd Cacadores		1
Light Division Total	5,484	165
Silveira's Portuguese Division		
Da Costa's Brigade	2,492	
2nd Line		–
14th Line		–
A. Campbell's Brigade	2,795	10
4th Line		
10th Line		
10th Cacadores		
Silveira's Division Total	5,287	10
Independent Portuguese Brigades		
Pack's Brigade	2,297	
1st Line		3
16th Line		37
4th Cacadores		35
Bradford's Brigade	2,392	
13th Line		17
24th Line		3
5th Cacadores		11
Independent Brigades	4689	106

	Marching Strength May 25	Losses at Vitoria
Cavalry		
R. Hill's Brigade	870	–
1st & 2nd Life Guards		
Horse Guards		
Ponsonby's Brigade	1,238	2
5th Dragoon Guards		
3rd & 4th Dragoons		
G. Anson's Brigade	819	
12th Light Dragoons		12
16th Light Dragoons		21
Long's Brigade		
13th Light Dragoons	394	1
V. Alten's Brigade	1,005	–
14th Light Dragoons		
1st Hussars K.G.L.		
Bock's Brigade	632	1
1st & 2nd Dragoons K.G.L.		
Fane's Brigade	842	8
3rd Dragoon Guards		
1st Royal Dragoons		
Grant's Brigade	1,624	
10th Hussars		16
15th Hussars		59
18th Hussars		84
D'Urban's Portuguese		
1st, 11th, 12th Cavalry	685	–
6th Portuguese Cavalry	208	2
Cavalry Total	8,317	157
R.H.A. and Drivers	803	40
Field artillery, Train, Ammunition Column, etc.	2,822	–
K.G.L. Artillery	352	28
Portuguese Artillery	330	7
Engineers & Sappers	345	1
Staff Corps	147	8
Wagon Train	202	–
Anglo-Portuguese	81,276	4,596
of which		
British	52,484	3,675
Portuguese	28,792	921
Add		
Morillo's & Longa's Spanish Divisions	7,681	562
Forces at Vitoria	88,957	5,158

[1] *These casualties were in the Brunswick Light Comps. attached to other divisions*

Army of the South, Return of May 29

1st Division, Leval:

Brigade Mocqery: 9th Leger, 24th Line	2,579
Brigade Morgan: 88th and 96th Line	2,099
Divisional battery and train	166
Divisional Total	4,844

2nd Division, *lent to Army of the Centre:*
3rd Division, Villatte:

Brigade Rignoux: 27th Leger, 63rd Line	2,579
Brigade Lefol: 94th and 95th Line	2,099
Divisional battery and train	166
Divisional Total	4,844

4th Division, Conroux:

Brigade Rey: 32nd and 43rd Line	3,669
Brigade Schwitter: 55th and 58th Line	2,717
Divisional battery and train	193
Divisional Total	6,589

5th Division, brigade Maransin only:

12th Leger, 45th Line	2,927

6th Division, Daricau:

Brigade St.Pol: 21st Leger, 100th Line	2,711
Brigade Remond:28th Leger,103rd Line	2,984
Divisional battery and train	240
Divisional Total	5,935

Total Infantry Divisions	26,169

Cavalry:
Pierre Soult's Division:

2nd Hussars, 5th, 10th, 21st Chasseurs	1,502
One battery H.A. and train	169

Tilly's Division:

2nd, 4th, 14th, 17th, 26th, & 27th Dragoons	1,502

Digeon's Division:

5th, 12th, 16th, 21st Dragoons	1,692
One battery H.A. and train	169
Total Cavalry	6,469

Artillery Reserve: two batteries & train	370

Artillery Park:

two companies Field Artillery, one comp. pontoniers, artificiers, train	713
Engineers: two companies sappers, two miners, and train	630
Gendarmerie	105
Wagon Train	65

Total Auxiliary Troops	1,883

Etat-major of the Army and divisions	115

Total of the Army of the South	34,636

Army of the Centre

1st Division, Darmagnac:

Brigade Chasse: 28th & 75th Line	1,794
Brigade Neuenstein: 2nd Nassau, 4th Baden, Frankfort Bn.	2,678
Divisional Total	4,472

2nd Division, Cassagne

Brigade Braun: 18th Leger, 8th Line	
Brigade Blondeau: 951st & 54th Line	
Divisional Total	5,209

Total Infantry	9,681

Cavalry:
Treillard's Division:

13th, 18th, 19th, 22nd Dragoons	1,038

Avy's Light Cavalry:

27th Chasseurs, Nassau Chasseurs	474

Total Cavalry	1,512

Artillery (3 batteries) & train	501
Engineers: one company sappers	131
Wagon Train, etc.	198

Total Auxiliary Troops	830

The King's Spanish Army:
Royal Guards, General Guy:

Grenadiers, tirailleurs, voltigeurs of the Guard	2,380
Hussars and Lancers of the Guard	425
Line: Regiments of Castile, Toledo, Royal Etranger	2,070
Cavalry: 1st & 2nd Chasseurs, Hussars of Guadalajara	670
Artillery: one battery	98

Total King's Army	5,638

Total of the Army of the Centre	17,691

4th Division, Sarrut:
Brigade Fririon: 2nd Leger, 36th Line
Brigade Menne: 4th Leger, 65th Line
Divisional battery and train
    Divisional Total   4,802
4th Division, Lamartiniere
Brigade Gauthier: 118th & 119th Line   2,567
Brigade Menne: 120th & 122nd Line   3,968
Divisional battery and train   176

Total Infantry   11,513

Cavalry:
Mermet's Division:
Brigade Curto: 13th & 22nd Chasseurs   902
3rd Hussars, 14th & 26th Chasseurs   899
Boyer's Division
6th, 11th, 15th, 25th Dragoons   1,471

Total Cavalry   8,472

Reserve Artillery:
One H.A., four filed batteries   890
One company pononiers, train, etc.   773
Engineers: two companies sappers   195
Gendarmerie   174
Wagon Train, mule train, etc.   933

Total Auxiliary Troops   2,455

Total of the Army of the Portugal   17,440

Total of the Army of the South   34,636
Total of the Army of the Centre   17,691

Grand Total of the French Army   69,767

Army of the South	
Leval's Division	759
Villatte's Division	291
Conroux's Division	1,087
Maransin's Division	681
Daricau's Division	833
Pierre Soult's Cavalry	6
Digeon's Dragoons	102
Tilly's Dragoons	25
Artillery	488
Engineers, etc.	28
Total	4,300

Army of the Centre	
Darmagnac's Division	1,346
Cassagne's Division	263
Treillard's Dragoons	80
Avy's Chasseurs	57
Artillery: no returns	?
Engineers, etc.	4
Casapalacios's Spaniards	358
Total	2,108

Army of Portugal	
Sarrut's Division	812
Lamartiniere's Division	586
Mermet's Light Cavalry	97
Boyer's Dragoons	105
Artillery, Engineers, etc.	?
Total	1,600

Grand Total of the Armies	8,008

BRITISH BATTLE HONOURS FOR VITORIA
3rd (Prince of Wales's) Regt. of Dragoon Guards
5th (Princess Charlotte of Wales's) Regt. of Dragoon Guards
3rd (King's Own) Regt. of Dragoons
4th (Queen's Own) Regt. of Dragoons
13th Regt. of (Light)Dragoons
14th (Duchess of York's Own) Regt. of (Light) Dragoons
15th (the King's) Regt. of (Light) Dragoons (Hussars)
16th (the Queen's) Regt. of (Light) Dragoons
3rd Bn. 1st (Royal Scots) Regt of Foot
2nd (Queen's Royal) Regt. of Foot
1st Bn. 3rd (East Kent) Regt of Foot or the Buffs
1st Bn. 4th (the King's Own) Regt. of Foot
1st Bn. 5th (Northumberland) Regt. of Foot
1st Bn. 6th (1st Warwickshire) Regt of Foot
1st Bn. 7th Regt. of Foot (or Royal Fuzileers)

1st Bn. 9th (East Norfolk) Regt. of Foot
20th (East Devonshire) Regt. of Foot
1st Bn. 23rd Regt. of Foot (or Royal Welsh Fuzileers)
2nd Bn. 24th (2nd Warwickshire) Regt of Foot
3rd Bn. 27th (Inniskilling) Regt of Foot
1st Bn. 28th (North Gloucestershire) Regt of Foot
2nd Bn. 59th (2nd Nottinghamshire) Regt. of Foot
2nd Bn. 31st (Huntingdonshire) Regt of Foot
2nd Bn. 34th (Cumberland) Regt of Foot
1st Bn. 38th (1st Staffordshire) Regt of Foot
1st Bn. 39th (Dorsetshire) Regt of Foot
1st Bn. 40th (2nd Somersetshire) Regt. of Foot
1st Bn. 82nd Regt. of Foot (Prince of Wales's Volunteers)
1st Bn. 43rd (Monmouthshire Light Infantry) Regt.
1st Bn. 52nd (Oxfordshire Light Infantry) Regt.
1st Bn. 45th (Nottinghamshire)   Regt. of Foot
2nd Bn 47th (Lancashire) Regt. of Root
1st Bn. 48th (Northamptonshire) Regt of Foot
2nd Bn. 58th (Rutlandshire) Regt of Foot
2nd Bn. 66th (Berkshire) Regt. of Foot
1st Bn. 50th (West Kent) Regt of Foot
51st (2nd Yorkshire, West Riding) Light Infantry Regt.
2nd Bn. 53rd (Shropshire) Regt. of Foot
1st Bn. 57th (West Middlesex) Regt of Foot
5th Bn. 60th (Royal American) Regt. of Foot
68th (Durham) Light Infantry Regt.
1st Bn. 71st (Highland) Light Infantry Regt.
74th (Highland) Regt. of Foot
1st Bn. 92nd (Highland) Regt. of Foot
2nd Bn. 83rd Regt. of Foot
2nd Bn. 87th (Prince of Wales's Own Irish) Regt. of Foot
1st Bn. 88th Regt. of Foot (or Connaught Rangers)
94th Regt of Foot
95th Regt. of Foot (or Rifle Corps)

William Napier, the chronicler of the Peninsular War, wrote the epitaph to the battle:

Joseph's reign was over; the crown had fallen from his head and, after years of toils and combats, which had rather been admired than understood, the English General emerging from the chaos of the Peninsular struggle, stood on the summit of the Pyrenees a recognised conqueror. From those lofty pinnacles the clangour of his trumpets pealed loud and clear, and the splendour of his genius appeared as a flaming beacon to warring nation.

Our contretemps arising from the battle of Vittoria was but one of the many connected with that field; another occurred soon after the conflict when, a thousand miles to the north-east, in Vienna, two gifted men prepared to celebrate the event in their own unusual way-

These were Ludwig van Beethoven and a man of rare and weird abilities named Johann Maelzel. Maelzel was an inventor with a pronounced Heath Robinson bias, who had, among other things, endeared himself to Beethoven by inventing an ear-trumpet. His latest creation was the Panharmonicum, a giant piece of mechanism designed to reproduce orchestral effects and incorporating flutes, trumpets, drums, cymbals, triangles, strings struck by hammers, violins, cellos and clarinets. In a moment of weakness, blindness or mischief, Beethoven agreed to write something for this juggernaut; and "Wellington's Victory" was hit upon as the composition.

Not unexpectedly, the project soon developed into one of the heavy public quarrels at which Beethoven was peculiarly adept. While the machine was being re-rigged to play 'Wellington's Victory", Beethoven rewrote the score for orchestra, gave two public concerts and made a tidy sum. Maelzel now stepped in and by claiming the score as his own on the grounds that he had paid for it, threw Beethoven into such a fury (never hard to do) that the composer gave yet another performance, devoting the substantial takings entirely to the aid-to-Beethoven fund. Maelzel, equally irate, tucked a copy of the score under his arm and made for London, a city which the collaborators had originally intended to visit together. Beethoven replied by addressing a letter to the musicians of London, in which he urged them to cold-shoulder Maelzel for the criminal he was; and by filing a law suit in Vienna. Finally, when Maelzel returned to Vienna without even having reached London, the two patched up the dispute, with Beethoven calling off the law-suit and Maelzel sharing the costs. Maelzel, characteristically, finished his life demonstrating a spectacular, animated set-piece called "The Burning of Moscow" to audiences in the United States. Musically, the standard of "Wellington's Victory" is not high, but it remains one of the most exciting attempts ever to re-create, by means of the orchestra augmented by muskets and cannons, the impression of a battle and the sense of elation after victory.

First, we hear from the English camp: faintly, as if out of nowhere, a drummer's tattoo pulsates in the distance; other drums join in and the sound grows in power and intensity until a thundering roar fills the air; then above the tumult of the drummers' steady roll, trumpets sound a battle cry; the English cap this brilliant fanfare with a rousing performance of "Rule Britannia". From their side, the French respond with their own trumpet-and-drum fanfare and the war song, "Malbrouck s'en va t'en guerre". Following these preliminaries, the French challenge the English to fight in a stirring trumpet call. The English accept, throwing back the original call with their higher-pitched E-flat trumpets. The battle commences.

Now the main orchestra takes over. Throughout the clamorous battle, the English and French trumpets may be heard distinctly from their respective sides, rallying the troops. Musket volleys and cannon shots punctuate the music. After a while, we notice that only the English cannon are firing. The British have gained the upper hand and the army of Bonaparte finally shudders to a halt in a pathetic, minor-key version of the Malbrouck tune. A victory finale, featuring a vigorous fugal treatment of "God Save the King" brings this festive piece d'occasion to a tremendous conclusion. Its form and patriotic musical content was certainly the starting point for Tchaikovsky's later inspiration in his "1812 Overture", but the Russian had other precedents, particularly with regard to orchestration, which no doubt contributed.

WALKING THE FIELD OF VITORIA.

The author has lodged in the pleasant town of Vitoria on more than one occasion, viewed the impressive Peninsular War monument and visited the Town Museum which displays a very large relief model of the battlefield, among many other military artifacts. The field has been driven over and around at least three times, and walked twice - there nearly was a third 'walk' but, as will be later seen, this proved abortive!

On the occasion of one visit, it snowed very hard over night, and we drove out to the field in a veritable blizzard and there was about a foot of snow underfoot when we recklessly decided to ascend the Knoll of Arinez, carried by the 3rd Division and two brigades under personal command of the Duke, at one stage of the battle. Arinez was no stranger to battle for, on that same hill on 22 March 1367, a small English force of about 100 knights, men-at-arms, and archers, under command of dark foppish Sir Thomas Felton and his stout brother William, fought almost to the last man against some 6,000 French and Aragonese, commanded by Don Tello and the French Marshal D'Andrehen. Today, the hill is known locally as Alture de los Ingleses - Englishman's Hill. In his wonderful book, The White Company, the writer Conan Doyle has his hero Sir Nigel Loring fight on the hill with the Feltons, being taken prisoner. However, back to the present, from the summit of the Knoll a good view of the field is obtained, and salient points can be orientated from the map.

The bridge at Nanclares is still there, presumably just as it was on 21 June 1813 when Wellington rode over it at the head of Lowry Cole's 4th Division: so is Trois Puntes, albeit in

THE 15TH HUSSARS CROSS THE BRIDGE AT TRES PUENTES

ruins and replaced by a more modern bridge, where the impatient Picton aggressively led his 3rd Division into the fray. The heights of Pueblo, where Hill's men performed wonders, and the hills north of the town of Vitoria from which Graham's flanking force came, are still there, unchanged and waiting to be walked.

In the section of this book entitled Peninsular Promenade there is a report of a visit to this area by British travel-writer Elizabeth de Stroumillo, in which she writes of "A truncated watchtower still stands on the hillock overlooking the village of Nanclares.... today it affords a fine view of the local prison."

The area is deeply etched in the author's memory for there occurred what could have become the third battle of Vitoria! In company with three comrades-in-arms, the author had left the ferry at Santander, skirted Bilbao on the motorway, going south and leaving it at Exit 5 marked Vitoria Gasteiz (today's name of the town). Eventually we arrived at the edge of the field of the Duke's great victory. We crossed the Zadorra River by that same bridge at Nanclares used by

TRES PUENTES BRIDGE, THE BRIDGE PICTON ATTACKED OVER, AS IT LOOKS TODAY.

the Duke himself and Cole's 4th Division, and carried on round to Tres Puntes, now a ruined stone bridge that Picton's 3rd Division stormed over on the fateful day. When photography was finished, the call of the flesh became apparent and we sought a congenial site for our midday picnic. Chris pointed in the direction of Nanclares: ' How about that hill with the ruined tower on it ?' He indicated Ms. Stroumillo's 'truncated watchtower.' All agreed it was just the place. "We can sit up there with the map and binoculars and work out a tour for after lunch !"

It seemed an ideal spot, facing the immortal Hill of Arinez, flanked on the right by the Heights of Pueblo - assailed by Hill in 1813., the Bridge of Nanclares at the foot of the hill behind us and, further over, a cluster of buildings which Ms. Stroumillo immediately recognised as the local prison, but we failed to do, despite the watchtowers at the corners of the walls. Binoculars flashed as the scene was surveyed, and the warm Spanish wine went well with the simple fare. Then, with all the breathtaking shock of a sudden bolt of lightning, a large and ferocious Alsatian dog leapt onto the rug between the four of us , its slavering jaws seizing from my grasp a piece of crusty bread liberally spread with meat-pate! Swinging round to see from whence this fearsome apparition had erupted, we were shaken to the core to see a group of soldiers, all armed with automatic rifles and with five more dogs on leashes. While his comrades held the straining dogs in check, their leader came forward and, after some linguistic difficulties, examined our passports which, after an age, he curtly handed back with an unmistakable hand-wave of dismissal; then they went back down the hill. Feverishly , we packed our picnic in the car and prepared to depart, but before we could so, two beige white police-cars arrived in a cloud of dust and blocked the track down from the hill. In their queer flat-fronted hats, the occupants poured out, pistol-holsters unbuttoned, barking incomprehensible works at us; in self-defense, we discovered that their Sergeant could also speak French, which most us could follow also.

'What are you doing up here?"

"We are looking at the battlefield"

229

"What battlefield?'

" Why, the battlefield of Vitoria, where the Duke of Wellington helped the Spanish armies to defeat the French, 21st of June 1813."

He seemed unconvinced; in the background two large young policemen eyed us balefully, barking out suggestions in Spanish, probably "Why don't we take them in and give them a good going over?" The Sergeant quietened them with a wave of the hand, eyeing us thoughtfully; then I had an idea and, with permission, extracted a copy of one of my own books from the car, pointed out the photo of myself on its rear cover, while Chris told him that I was writing a book on the glorious Spanish army at the battle, and that the three of them were my research assistants. Although the picture had been taken some 15 years before, it looked a bit like me and the Police sergeant appeared convinced. He ordered the cars to be moved and, in marked contrast to his hitherto calm demeanour, screamed:

"Allez, Allez, Go, Go !" simultaneously waving an arm in the direction of the road below. Wasting no time at all, we bustled into the car and bumped down the track in an enveloping cloud of dust. Once on the road, Roger put his foot down and we surged forward, towards distant Pamplona, all ideas and plans for in-depth viewing of the field of Vitoria gone from our minds. Then we noticed that one of the police-cars was following us, keeping a steady hundred yards of so behind us, and continued to do so for nearly twenty miles until, noticing it had dropped away, we pulled in at the first bar encountered for a much needed beer. In Spain a lot of people seem to speak French and the barman was one of them; we told him of our adventure, he relayed it in voluble Spanish to the bar's inhabitants and soon the place was rocking with laughter. Regaining control of his emotions, the barman told us that the building at the foot of the hill (which we had failed to recognise as a prison) held some of the top-level Basque terrorists, (in fact it was the equivalent of the Maze Prison in Northern Ireland) and of late there had been numerous break-out attempts, and our gang on the hilltop with maps and binoculars, well!

THE 71ST HIGHLANDERS AT VITTORIA

THE BATTLES OF MAYA AND RONCEVALLES - 25 JULY 1813

Our fatigue parties were out for forage and we were busy cooking when the signal was given on the 25th of July. The two rear companies moved to the heights, the rest of the regiment to the alarm post, where we had work enough upon our arrival. The French were in great force, moving up the heights in solid column. We killed great numbers of them in their advance; but they still moved on. We were forced to give way and continued thus to retire, maintaining every height to the last, contesting every foot of ground. At length we were forced to the height where our old quarter-guard used to be posted. We maintained our position against them a considerable time, during which we had the mortification to see the French making merry in our camp, eating the dinner we had prepared for ourselves. What could we do? They were so much superior in numbers.

By a 'Soldier of the Seventy-First' from 'The Journal of a Soldier of the Highland Light Infantry 1805-1815'

Writing in the 1890's, Major Arthur Griffiths painstakingly set out the situation in the high Summer months of 1813, after Wellington's classic victory at Vitoria and before the major battles began in the Pyrenees:

After the crushing defeat of Vittoria, Napoleon, although sorely pressed elsewhere, was resolved to make a last desperate stand on the frontiers of Spain and France. Unable to take command in person, he sent thither his most trusted lieutenant, Soult, the doughtiest antagonist - except Massena - that Wellington, in his own judgment, had ever encountered in Spain. Marshal Soult travelled post-haste, and reached Bayonne early in July, where, with characteristic energy, he strained every nerve to reorganise his shattered forces. He gathered up reinforcements as he went, hurrying troops forward by every kind of conveyance, and soon got together upwards of 100,000 men. Marshal Suchet, it must be remembered, was yet in the eastern province of Spain, so that the French could still make a good show. Wellington at this time was in about equal strength with Soult; but his army, as usual, was made up of three nationalities - English, Spanish, and Portuguese. Of the first-named he had little more than 30,000 infantry, with some 7,000 cavalry. According to the muster-rolls, the numbers actually facing each other, although not always available, in the Pyrenees were, roughly 82,000 under Wellington, against 78,000 under Soult. The latter could also count upon a number of foreign battalions and a large body of National Guards, all fierce and hardy mountaineers.

Soult, as has been said, was a man of indomitable and indefatigable activity. Within four days of his arrival at Bayonne he had worked out a new plan of operations on the boldest and most extensive scale. He was now resolved to take the offensive - that is to say, he meant to attack, not await attack - and his scheme was very admirably and elaborately devised. The initiative or first move gave him, as he knew, a very distinct advantage: he could chose his own line of advance, moving along it in strength, while his enemy, until fully alive to his direction and meaning, could not safely risk concentration to meet him. Wellington's position in the Pyrenees, it must be understood, was at this time defensive. He held all the passes along this long range of mountains, being obliged thus to cover the two sieges he had in progress - those of San Sebastian and of Pampelona, sixty miles apart. To hold passes in this way is considered the most hazardous undertaking in war. The only safe plan is to concentrate well to the rear of the passes, only leaving at them strong bodies to check the advancing enemy and give time to collect against him wherever he shows in strength. The run of the mountain ridges southward from the great central chain forbade this by cutting off lateral communication, or making it too tedious to be quickly effected. Soult believed, and rightly, that if he could throw his whole weight upon the centre or either end of the long line of English defence before he was expected, he would gain an early and

THE BATTLEFIELDS OF RONCESVALLES. THERE IS A TRACK RUNNING DOWN THE HILLSIDE (JUST ABOVE THE CENTRE WHITE PATCH). DOWN IT MARCHED REILLE'S THREE INFANTRY DIVISIONS, ADVANCING ON THE LINDUZ PEAK WEST OF RONCESVALLES. THE TRACK ENTERS THE CENTRE TREES WHERE THE FIGHTING TOOK PLACE. SO NARROW WAS THE TRACK THAT THEY MARCHED TWO ABREAST AND WHEN THE LEADING TROOPS WERE FIGHTING THE BRITISH, THE COLUMN'S REAR WAS 11 MILES BACK.

signal success. He could do this by good beaten roads. All he had to consider was the best line of advance - right, centre, or left.

He decided to move by the last-named, and he came to this conclusion partly because he feared for Pampelona on this side, and partly because he knew or hoped that San Sebastian upon the other could long hold its own. Moreover, he knew that Wellington's principal force was gathered towards San Sebastian, and held on that side singularly strong positions of defence. The English centre could also more quickly reinforce its left than its right: two marches would suffice for the first, three long days for the last. Again, the English right, although posted in the mountains, was in more or less isolated bodies; while, as has been said, the support of the centre and left could not be obtained for three or more days, and then much further to the rear. Wherefore Soult resolved to move with all his available force by his own left against Wellington's right, counting, and with reason, upon being much stronger there than his opponent. Great consequences would follow a first success. He expected to easily overbear all resistance, to succour Pampelona, then seize the great road that came from Bayonne through Irun, Tolosa, Lecumberri, and Irurzun. Here he would be firmly established directly in the rear of the English, and could operate with marked advantage against each British division piecemeal, as it came tumbling back from its now hazardous position in the advanced passes and foremost hills."

There is no one more fitted to tell of the struggles in the Pyrenean Passes than one who was there, nor better suited than William Napier, immortal chronicler of the War, able to confirm a

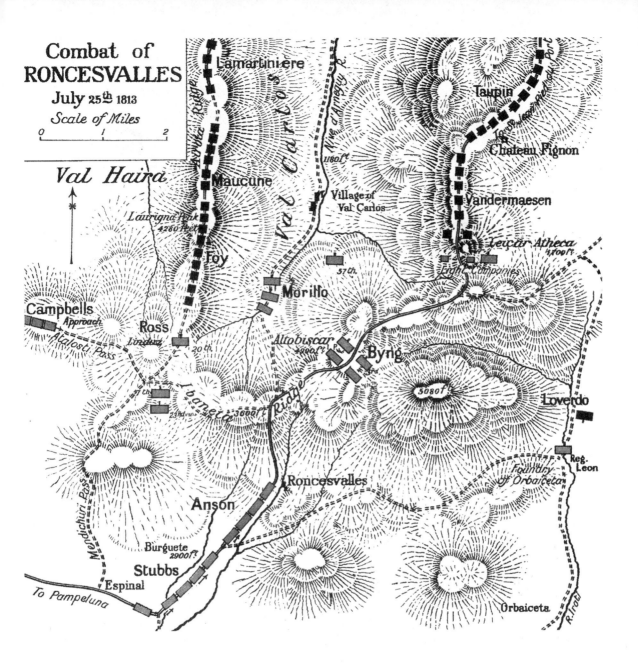

Combat of RONCESVALLES
July 25th 1813
Scale of Miles
0   1   2

Val Haira

Lamartiniere
Taupin
Château Fignon
Maucune
Vandermaesen
Laurigna Peak 4280 feet
Foy
Village of Val Carlos
1180 ft
Leucar Atheca 4100 ft
Light Companies
57th
Morillo
Campbells
Approach
Ross
Alosti Pass
Linduz
20th
Altobiscar 3900 ft
Byng
5080 ft
Loverdo
Ibaneta
Reg. Leon
4th
3600 ft
Ridge
2500 ft
Foundry of Orbaiceta
Anson
Roncesvalles
Mendichuri Pass
Burguete 2900 ft
Stubbs
Espinal
To Pampeluna
Orbaiceta
R. Irati

detail of the French Army by a casual footnote, saying that Marshal Soult told him! Here are the accounts given in his monumental work 'English Battles and Sieges in the Peninsular (1852) :-

"Soult thought no decisive result would attend a direct movement upon San Sebastian, and by his seaboard intercourse he knew that place was not in extremity; but he had no communication with Pampeluna, and feared its fall. Wherefore he resolved rapidly to concentrate on his left by means of the great French roads leading to St. Jean Pied de Port, covering his movement by the Nivelle and Nive rivers, and by the positions of his centre: thus he hoped to gather on Wellington's right quicker than that general could gather to oppose him, and, compensating by numbers the disadvantage of assailing mountain positions, force a way to Pampeluna.

The theatre of operations was quadrilateral, with sides from forty to sixty miles in length, having a fortress at each angle, namely, Bayonne, San Jean Pied de Port, San Sebastian and Pampeluna, all in possession of the French. The interior, broken and tormented by peaked mountains, narrow craggy passes, deep watercourses, dreadful precipices and forests, appeared a wilderness which no military combinations could embrace. The great spinal ridge of the

PHOTOGRAPH TAKEN FROM INSIDE THE EARTHWORKS AT THE TOP OF LINDUZ PEAK AT RONCESVALLES. BEYOND THE TREES IS THE GROUND WHERE COLE HELD OFF SOULT'S SUPERIOR NUMBERS COMING FROM BEYOND THE FAR HEIGHTS.

Pyrenees furnished a clue to the labyrinth. Running diagonally across the quadrilateral, it entirely separated Bayonne, St. Jean Pied de Port and San Sebastian from Pampeluna, and the troops blockading the latter were thus cut off from those besieging San Sebastian, the only direct communication between them being a great road running behind the mountains from Tolosa, by Irurzun, to Pampeluna.

Rapidity was of vital importance to the French marshal, but heavy rains swelled the streams and ruined the roads in the deep country between Bayonne and the mountains; the headquarters which should have arrived at St. Jean Pied de Port on the 20th, were a few miles short of that place the 21st, and Reille's troops were forced to go round by Bayonne to gain the causeway. The cavalry was also retarded, and the army, men and horses, worn down by severe marches. Two days were thus lost, yet the 24th more than sixty thousand fighting men, including cavalry, national guards, and gendarmes, with sixty-six pieces of artillery, were assembled to force the passes of Roncesvalles and Maya; the former being in the Great Spine, the latter giving entrance to the Bastan. The main road leading to Roncesvalles was repaired, and three hundred sets of bullocks were provided to drag the guns; the national guards of the frontier on the left, ordered to assemble in the night on the heights of Yropil, were reinforced with regular troops to vex and turn the right of the allies at the foundry of Orbaiceta.

At St. Jean Pied de Port Soult was almost in contact with the allies at the passes of the Roncesvalles, which were also the points of the defence nearest to Pampeluna. He had thirty thousand bayonets, the frontier national guards to aid, and his artillery and cavalry were massed behind his infantry; for here the great road from St. Jean Pied de Port to Pampeluna, the only one fit for cannon, entered the mountains: but to understand his movements a short description of the country is necessary, taking the point of departure from his camp.

Before him was the Val Carlos, formed by two descending shoots from the Great Spine of the

234

Pyrenees. That on his left hand separated this valley from the valley of Orbaiceta; that on his right hand separated it from several conjoint valleys, known as the Alduides and Baygorry, the latter name being given to the lower, the former to the upper parts.

The great road to Pampeluna led up the left hand tongue by the remarkable rocks of Chateau Pignon, near which narrow branches went off to the village of San Carlos on the right, and to the foundry of Orbaiceta on the left. The main line, after ascending to the summit of the Great Spine, turned to the right and run along the crest until it reached the pass of Ibaneta, where, turning to the left, it led down by the famous Roncesvalles into the valley of Urros.

A lateral continuation however run along the magistral crest, beyond the Ibaneta, to another pass called the Mendichuri, which also led down into the Val de Urros; and from Mendichuri there was a way into the Alduides valley through a side pass called the Atalosti.

On Soult's right hand the Val Carlos was bounded by the ridge and rock of Ayrola, from the summit of which there was a way directly to the Mendichuri and the lateral pass of Atalosti; and the ground between those defiles, called the Lindouz, was an accessible mountain knot, tying all the valleys together and consequently commanding them.

Continuing along the Great Spine, after passing the Atalosti, there would be on the right hand, descending towards the French frontier, the Val de Ayra, the Alduides and the Bastan. On the left hand, descending to Pampeluna, would be the Val de Zubiri and the valley of Lanz, separated from each other by a lofty wooded range. All these valleys on each side were, in their order, connected by roads leading over comparatively low portions of the Great Spine, called by the French cols, or necks, by the Spaniards puertos, or doors.

General Byng and Morillo, the first having sixteen hundred British troops, the second four thousand Spaniards, were in position before Soult. Byng, reinforced with two Spanish battalions, held the rocks of Altobiscar, just above Chateau Pignon. On his right a Spanish battalion was posted at the foundry of Orbaiceta; on his left Morillo's remaining Spaniards were near the village of Val Carlos on a minor height called the Iroulepe.

Behind the Great Spine, in the valley of Urros, General Cole held the fourth division in support of Byng; but he was twelve miles off, separated by the Ibaneta pass, and could not come up under four hours. General Campbell, having a Portuguese division two thousand strong, watched the Alduides; but he was eight miles off, and separated by the lateral pass of Atalosti. General Picton, with the third division, was at Olague in the valley of Lanz, on the Spanish side of the Spine; and both he and Campbell could at pleasure gain the valley of Zubiri - Picton by a cross communication, Campbell by the pass of Urtiaga, which was directly in his rear; he could also join Cole in the valley of Urros by the pass of Sahorgain.

In this state of affairs Soult placed twelve thousand infantry within two miles of the Chateau Pignon, against Byng, and directed the national guards at Yropil, reinforced with regulars, to move into the valley of Orbaiceta and turn the Spaniards at the foundry. A second column, four thousand strong, was placed in the Val Carlos to assail Morillo at Iroulepe. A third column of sixteen thousand, under Reille, assembled, in the night, at the foot of the Ayrola rock, with orders to ascend at daylight and move along the crest of the ridge to seize the culminant Lindouz. From that point detachments were to be pushed through the passes of Ibaneta, Mendichuri, and Sahorgain, into the Roncesvalles, while others extended to the right as far as the pass of Urtiaga, thus cutting off Byng and Morillo from Cole and Hamilton.

On the 25th at daylight he led up against the rocks of Altobiscar.

Byng, warned the evening before that danger was near, and jealous for the village of Val Carlos, had sent the 57th Regiment down there, yet kept his main body in hand and gave notice to Cole.

Soult, throwing out a multitude of skirmishers, pushed forward his supporting columns and guns as fast as the steepness of the road and difficult nature of the ground would permit; but the British fought strongly, the French fell fast among the rocks, and their musketry pealed in vain for hours along that cloudy field of battle, five thousand feet above the level of the plains. Their numbers however continually increased in front, and the national guards from Yropil, skirmishing with the Spaniards at the foundry of Orbaiceta, threatened to turn the right. Val Carlos was at the same time menaced by the central column, and Reille ascending the rock of Ayrola turned Morillo's left.

At mid-day Cole arrived in person at Altobiscar, but his troops were distant, and the French, renewing their attack, neglected the Val Carlos to gather more thickly against Byng. He resisted their efforts, yet Reille made progress along the summit of the Ayrola ridge, Morillo fell back towards Ibaneta, and the French were nearer that pass than Byng, when Ross's brigade, of Cole's division, coming up the Mendichuri pass, appeared on the Lindouz at the instant when the head of Reille's column was closing on the Atalosti to cut the communication with Campbell. This last-named had been early molested, according to Soult's plan, by the frontier guards of the Val de Baygorry, yet he soon detected the feint and moved by his right towards Atalosti when he heard the firing on that side. The Val d'Ayra separated him from the ridge of Ayrola, along which Reille was advancing, yet, noting that general's strength and seeing Ross's brigade labouring up the steep ridge of Mendichuri, he judged its commander to be ignorant of what was going on above, and, sending Cole notice of the enemy's proximity and strength, offered to pass the Atalosti and join battle, if he could be furnished afterwards with provisions and transport for his sick.

Before this message reached Cole, a wing of the 20th Regiment and a company of Brunswickers, forming the head of Ross's column, had gained the Lindouz, where suddenly they encountered Reille's advanced guard. The moment was critical, and Ross, an eager hardy soldier, called aloud to charge, whereupon Captain Tovey of the 20th run forward with a company, and full against the 6th French Light Infantry dashed with the bayonet. Brave men fell by that weapon on both sides, yet numbers prevailed and Tovey's soldiers were eventually pushed back. Ross however gained his object, the remainder of his brigade had time to come up and the pass of Atalosti was secured, with a loss of one hundred and forty men of the 20th Regiment and forty-one of the Brunswickers.

Previous to this vigorous action, Cole, seeing the French in the Val Carlos and the Orbaiceta valley, on both flanks of Byng, whose front was not the less pressed, had reinforced the Spaniards at the foundry, but now recalled his men to defend the Lindouz; and learning from Campbell how strong Reille was, caused Byng, with a view to a final retreat, to relinquish Altobiscar and approach Ibaneta. This movement uncovered the road leading down to the foundry of Orbaiceta, yet it concentrated all the troops; and Campbell, although he could not enter the line, Cole being unable to meet his demands, made such skilful dispositions as to impress Reille with a notion that his numbers were considerable.

During these operations the skirmishing never ceased, though a thick fog, coming up the valley, stopped a general attack which Soult was preparing; thus, when night fell Cole still held the Great Spine, having lost three hundred and eighty men killed and wounded. His right was however turned by Orbaiceta, he had only eleven thousand bayonets to oppose thirty thousand, and his line of retreat, five miles down hill and flanked by the Lindouz, was unfavourable; wherefore in the dark, silently threading the passes, he gained the valley of Urros, and his rear-guard followed in the morning. Campbell went off by Urtiaga into the Zubiri valley, and the Spanish battalion retreated from the foundry by a goat path. The great chain was thus abandoned, yet the result of the day's operation was unsatisfactory to Soult. He had lost four hundred men, he had not gained ten miles, and was still twenty-two miles from Pampeluna, with strong positions in the way, where increasing numbers of intrepid enemies were to be expected.

On the 26th Soult putting his left wing on Cole's track, ordered Reille to follow the crest of the mountains and seize the passes from the Bastan in Hill's rear, while D'Erlon pressed him in front. Hill would thus, Soult hoped, be crushed or thrown off from Pampeluna, and D'Erlon could thus reach the valley of Zubiri with his left, while his right, descending the valley of Lanz, would hinder Picton from joining Cole. A retreat by those generals, on separate lines, would then be inevitable, and the French army could issue in a compact order of battle from the mouths of the two valleys against Pampeluna.

Combat of Linzoain.

All the columns were in movement at daybreak, but every hour brought its obstacle. The fog still hung heavy on the mountain-tops. Reille's guides were bewildered, refused to lead the troops along the crests, and at ten o'clock, having no other resource, he marched down the Mendichuri pass and fell into the rear of Soult's column, the head of which, though retarded also by the fog and rough ground, had overtaken Cole's rear-guard. The leading infantry struck hotly upon some British light companies under Colonel Wilson, while a squadron, passing their flank, fell on the rear; but Wilson, facing about, drove them off, and thus fighting Cole reached the

**THE LITTLE PLATEAU WHERE ROSS'S MEN FOUGHT REILLE'S,
WITH THE LINDUZ IN THE BACKGROUND.**

heights of Linzoain. There Picton met him, with intelligence that Campbell had reached Eugui in the Val de Zubiri, and that the third division, having crossed the woody ridge, was also in that valley. The junction of all was thus secured, the loss of the day was less than two hundred, and neither wounded men nor baggage had been left behind; but at four o'clock the French seized some heights which endangered Cole's position, and he again fell back a mile, offering battle at a puerto, in the ridge separating the valley of Zubiri from that of Urros, which last, though descending on a parallel line, did not open on Pampeluna. During this skirmish, Campbell, coming from Eugui, showed his Portuguese on the ridge above the French right flank; he was however distant, Picton's troops were still further off, and there was light for an action if Soult had pressed one; but, disturbed with intelligence received from D'Erlon, and doubtful what Campbell's troops might be, he put off the attack until next morning, and after dark the junction of all the allies was effected.

This delay was an error. Cole was alone for five fours, and every action, by augmenting the wounded men and creating confusion, would have augmented the difficulties of a retreat for troops fatigued with incessant fighting and marching during two days and a night. Moreover Reille's failure from the fog, had reduced the primary combinations to D'Erlon's co-operation, and reports now brought the mortifying conviction that he also had gone wrong: by rough fighting only could Soult therefore attain his object, and, it is said, his manner discovered a secret anticipation of failure; yet his temper was too steadfast to yield, for he gave orders to advance next day, renewing his instructions to D'Erlon, whose operations must now be noticed.

That general, who had eighteen thousand fighting men, placed two divisions on the morning of the 25th near the passes of Maya, having previously caused the national guards of Val Baygorry to make demonstrations towards the lateral passes of Arriette, Yspeguy and Lorietta, on Hill's right. General William Stewart, commanding a division, and still the same daring but

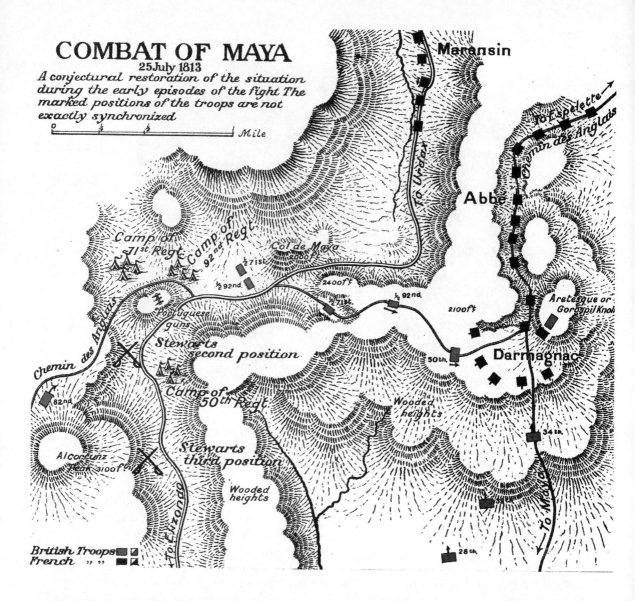

COMBAT OF MAYA
25 July 1813

A conjectural restoration of the situation during the early episodes of the fight The marked positions of the troops are not exactly synchronized

0   ¼   ½   Mile

Maransin

To Urdax

To Espelette

Chemin des Anglais

Abbé

Camp of 71st Regt.

Camp of 92nd Regt.

Col de Maya 2100ft

⅓ 71st

⅓ 92nd

2400ft

⅔ 71st

½ 92nd

2100ft

Aretesque or Gorospil Knoll

Portuguese guns

Stewarts second position

50th

Darmagnac

82nd

Camp of 50th Regt.

Wooded heights

34th

Chemin des Anglais

Stewarts third position

Wooded heights

Alcorrunz Peak 3100ft

To Elizondo

To Maya

British Troops
French   ,,   ,,

28th

imprudent man he had shown himself at Albuera, was deceived by these feints, and looked to that quarter which was guarded by Sylviera's Portuguese more than to his own front. His division, consisting of two British brigades, was consequently neither posted as it should be, nor otherwise prepared for an attack. His ground was strong, but however rugged a position may be, if it is too extensive and the troops are not disposed with judgment, the inequalities constituting its strength become advantageous to an assailant.

There were three passes over the Col de Maya to defend, Aretesque on the right, Lessessa in the centre, Maya on the left; and from these entrances two roads led to the Bastan in parallel directions; one down the valley through the town of Maya, the other along the Atchiola mountain. General Pringle's brigade guarded the Aretesque, Colonel Cameron's brigade the Maya and Lessessa passes. The Col itself was broad on the summit, three miles long, and on each flank lofty rocks and ridges rose one above another; those on the right blended with the Goramendi mountains, those on the left with the Atchiola mountain, near the summit of which the 82nd Regiment, belonging to the seventh division, was posted.

Cameron, encamped on the left, had a clear view of troops coming from Urdax, one of D'Erlon's camps; but at Aretesque a great round hill, one mile in front, masked the movements of an enemy coming from Esplette, the other French camp. This hill was not occupied at night, nor in the daytime, save by some Portuguese cavalry videttes, and the nearest guard was an infantry

THE BATTLEFIELD OF MAYA. THE HEATHER COVERED SLOPE OF MONT ALCORUNZ STRETCHING RIGHT, UP FROM THE LIGHT COLOURED AREA ON THE LEFT, IS THE CHEMIN DES ANGLAIS, WHERE A WING OF THE 92ND REGIMENT HELD OFF A FRENCH DIVISION.

picquet of eighty men posted on the French slope of the Col. Behind this picquet there was no immediate support, but four light companies were encamped one mile down the reverse slope, which was more rugged and difficult of access than that towards the enemy. The rest of Pringle's brigade was disposed at distances of two and three miles in the rear, and the signal for occupying the position was to be the fire of four Portuguese guns from the rocks above the Maya pass. Thus of six British regiments, furnishing more than three thousand fighting men, half only were in line, and chiefly massed on the left of a position, wide, open, and of an easy ascent from the Aretesque side. Stewart also, quite deceived as to the real state of affairs, was at Elisondo, several miles off, when at midday D'Erlon commenced the battle.

COMBAT OF MAYA .

From the Aretesque pass at dawn a glimpse had been obtained of cavalry and infantry in movement along the hills in front, and soon afterwards some peasants announced the approach of the French. At nine o'clock a staff officer, patrolling round the great hill in front, discovered sufficient to make him order up the light companies from the reverse slope, to support the picquet; and they formed on the ridge with their left at the rock of Aretesque, just as D'Armagnac's division, coming from Espelette, mounted the great hill in front; Abbe's division followed, while Maransin, with a third division, advanced from Ainhoa and Urdax against the Maya pass, seeking also to turn it by a narrow way leading up the Atchiola mountain.

D'Armagnac forced the picquet back with great loss upon the light companies, who sustained his assault with infinite difficulty; the alarm guns were then heard from the Maya pass, and Pringle hastened to the front; but his battalions, moving hurriedly from different camps, came up irregularly. The 34th arrived first at a running pace, yet by companies not in mass, and breathless from the length and ruggedness of the ascent; the 39th and 28th followed, but not immediately nor together, and meanwhile D'Armagnac, closely supported by Abbe, with domineering numbers and valour combined, maugre the desperate fighting of the light companies and the 34th, established his columns on the broad ridge of the position. Colonel Cameron sent the 50th from the left to the assistance of the overmatched troops, and that fierce and formidable old regiment, charging the head of an advancing column drove it clear out of the pass of Lessessa in the centre. But the French were many, and checked at one point assembled with increased force at another; nor could Pringle restore the battle with the 39th and 28th Regiments, which, cut off from the others, were, though fighting strongly, forced back to a second and lower ridge crossing the main road into the Bastan. They were followed by D'Armagnac, while Abbe pushed the 50th and 34th towards the Atchiola road to the left, upon Cameron's brigade. That officer, still holding the pass of Maya with the left wings of the 71st and 92nd Regiments, now brought their right wings and the Portuguese guns into action: yet so dreadful was the slaughter, especially of the 92nd, that the enemy was, it is said, actually stopped for a time by the heaped mass of dead and dying and then the left wing of that noble regiment, coming down from the higher ground, was forced to smite wounded friends and exulting foes alike, as mingled together they stood or crawled before its fire.

Such was the state of affairs when Stewart reached the field by the mountain road of Atchiola. The passes of Lessessa and Aretesque were lost; that of Maya was still held by the left wing of the 71st, but Stewart, seeing Maransin's men gathered thickly on one side, and Abbe's men on the other, abandoned it for a new position on the first rocky ridge covering the road over the Atchiola. He called down the 82nd from the highest part of that mountain, sent messengers to demand further aid from the seventh division, and meanwhile, though wounded, made a strenuous resistance, for he was a very gallant man. During this retrograde movement, Maransin suddenly thrust the head of his division across the front of the British line and connected his left with Abbe, throwing as he passed a destructive fire into the wasted remnant of the 92nd, which even then gave way but sullenly, and still fought, though two thirds had fallen: however, one after the other, all the regiments were forced back, the Portuguese guns were taken and the position lost.

Abbe now followed D'Armagnac on the road to the town of Maya, leaving Maransin to deal with Stewart's new position; and notwhitstanding its extreme strength the French gained ground until six o'clock; for the British, shrunk in numbers, wanted ammunition, and a part of the 82nd defended the rocks on which they were posted with stones. In this desperate condition Stewart was upon the point of abandoning the mountain entirely, when Barnes' brigade of the seventh division, arriving from Echallar, charged and drove the French back to the Maya ridge. Stewart was then master of the Atchiola, and D'Erlon thinking greater reinforcements had come up, recalled his other divisions from the Maya road and re-united his whole corps on the Col. He had lost fifteen hundred men and a general, but he took four guns, and fourteen hundred British soldiers and one general were killed or wounded.

Such was the commencement of Soult's operations to restore the fortunes of France. Three considerable actions fought on the same day had each ended in his favour. At San Sebastian the allies' assault was repulsed; at Roncesvalles they abandoned the passes; at Maya they were defeated—but the decisive blow was still to be struck.

FORCES ENGAGED:

AT RONCESVALLES

French:

six infantry divisions of Clausel's and Reille's 'lieutenancies', with two regiments of cavalry, approximately 40,000 men.

Allies:

Cole's 4th British Infantry division (formed of Anson's Brigade; Skerrett's Brigade and Stubb's Portugese Brigade)

Byng's Brigade (of Hill's 2nd Division)

Campbell's Portuguese Brigade

Morillo's Spanish Division

approximately 13,500 men.

Casualties:
French: around 200 killed, wounded and missing.
Allies: close to 345 killed, wounded and missing.

AT MAYA
French:
General Drouet D'Erlon, commanding a Corps or 'lieutenancy' of Soult's Army, formed of three infantry divisions, plus auxiliaries. 20,000 men.
Allies:
Cameron's 1st and Pringle's 3rd Brigades of Stewart's 2nd Division, reinforced by three battalions of Barnes's Brigade of Dalhousie's 7th Division. 6,000 men.

BRITISH LOSSES AT RONCESVALLES

Ross's Brigade	
1/7th Foot	31
20th Foot	139
1/23rd Foot	42
1 company Brunswick-Oels	4
Portuguese Brigade (A. Campbell)	29
11th Line	
23rd Line	
7th Cacdores	
Total	*245*

BRITISH LOSSES AT MAYA

2nd Division Staff	2
Cameron's Brigade	
1/50th Foot	249
1/71st Foot	196
1/92nd Foot	343
Pringle's Brigade	
1/28th Foot	159
2/34th Foot	168
1/39th Foot	186
Two companies 5/60th, attached to above brigades	44
Total	*1,347*

7TH DIVISION LOSSES IN THE PYRENEES

1/6th Foot	21
1/82nd Foot	79
Brunswick-Oels	41
Total	*141*

FRENCH LOSSES IN THE PYRENEES

I. Reille's Wing	
1st Division (Foy)	
7th Division (Maucune)	
9th Division (Lamartiniere)	
Total Reille's Wing	3,393
II. D'Erlon's Wing	
1st Division (Foy)	
7th Division (Maucune)	
9th Division (Lamartiniere)	
Total D'Erlon's Wing	4,034
III. Clausel's Wing	
1st Division (Foy)	
7th Division (Maucune)	
9th Division (Lamartiniere)	
Total Clausel's Wing	5,069

On the 23rd July Marshal Soult issued an Order of the Day remarkable for its force and frankness. Napier wrote: "Conscious of ability he avowed a feeling of his own worth; but he was too proud to deprecate brave adversaries on the eve of battle."

"Let us not." he said to his soldiers: *"defraud the enemy of the praise which is due to him. The dispositions of the General have been prompt, skilful, and consecutive; the valour and steadiness of his troops have been praiseworthy."*

WALKING THE FIELDS OF RONCESVALLES AND MAYA.

Marshal Soult personally accompanied Clausel's three divisions on the march over the Old Roman road from St. Jean Pied de Port to the Pass of Roncesvalles. Here the allies were outnumbered about seven to one but the terrain favoured them, as was discovered by the French near the Altobiscar Pass, where they were halted in their tracks by three light companies of Byng's Brigade plus a company of 5/60th Rifles and some Spanish Light Infantry. This force, not more than 500 strong, deployed on a front of 300 yards with deep flanking valleys falling away on either side, held them off. Small groups of riflemen securely sheltered amid clumps of rocks and behind rolling ridges, drove off repeated French assaults by the voltigeur companies of the three divisions. Clausel's entire corps was delayed for hours, until using infantry in columns to drive Byng's infantry back to an even stronger position on the slopes of the Altobiscar, where French attacks were easily held off until the battle petered out. The other flank lay west of the modern road and we struck off it by the chapel, to begin a steady climb on narrow rocky paths through what appeared to be a game reserve with shooting boxes concealed in the undergrowth. Eventually reaching the foot of the Linduz Peak (1065 metres at sea level) we began the climb until reaching the plateau atop the Linduz. Here, high above the Pass, lies a very well preserved and defined earthwork, with ditch, walls and entrance gates area; it does not seem to feature in any description of the battles of July 1813 and would seem to be off the track of events then. Three quite exhausting climbs up to this site and subsequent study on arrival, have led me to believe that, originally, this was a Roman 'marching fort' one of those overnight earthworks constructed at each halt when the legion was on the march. Later, the works were again dug out and made practical by possibly the French as part of a defence system during the Peninsular War. The Pass of Roncesvalles is indeed redolent with History!

On all sides, the terrain spread out until vanishing in mist, with the Bay of Biscay gleaming distantly to the west. We looked for and found the ridge-top mule-track running back towards France on which the 20,000 men of Reille's three divisions painfully worked their way forward on the narrow track, sometimes in single-file or two-abreast and so stretched that when the leading troops made contact with Ross's troops the rear of the French column was eleven miles back! At first fighting was confused, amid woods on a narrow ridge only 60 yards wide where both sides used the bayonet; there was only room for single battalions to fight so that when one ran out of ammunition it was replaced by another. The sprawling combat rolled onto a small plateau at the foot of the Linduz with neither side gaining any conclusive advantage. Then, between four and five o'clock in the afternoon, a thick mist began rolling in from the Bay of Biscay - just as it had done a few days previously to trap us high on the Rhunes - until forcing both sides to cease fighting. They bivouacked within hearing distance of each other.

Nostalgically, the author recalls visiting this area in April when the snow lay on the ground, so much so that the Spanish driver of the coach took one look at the snow-plough working on the icebound road, and refused to go any further! So, leaving the coach in the village at the foot of the Pass, we trudged up the slippery road to the mist-enshrouded summit where, nearly a thousand years before, Roland the Paladin had held the Pass for Charlemagne. In 1813 there was considerable action in the area, amid a countryside so rugged, torn and heavily wooded that one achieved an increased respect for the men who fought over it and for their commanders, who were able to keep a perhaps tenuous hold on operations far beyond their range of vision.

Returning to the Inn at the foot of the Pass near the monastery for warming drinks, we talked in execrable Spanish and sign-language with some conscript soldiers from the nearby barracks, and bought them wine when they told of earning less than one pound a month - in peseta's of course. So we crossed by the Pass of Maya some 20 miles south-west, briefly viewing the battlefield before thawing out in an inn at Urdax near the Spanish frontier; the tureens of fish soup and the omelettes we consumed remain vivid in the memory!

An area redolent with history, the fascination of the Pyrenees is derived not only from the militant activities of the Duke of Wellington and sundry French Marshals; such preoccupation with the Napoleonic Wars can easily be transferred from the British rifleman and the Baker rifle to his equally illustrious forbears - the English archer and his longbow, the man-at-arms and armoured knight of the 14th century Hundred Years War. Events in the Pyrenees are familiar through the stirring words written by medieval chronicler Jehan Froissart, actually present in person in 1367 when the Black Prince led thirty thousand heavily accoutred men from France into Spain through the Pass of Roncesvalles, snow-bound in the depth of Winter.

They set out from historic walled St. Jean Pied-de-Port, a small town set on a hill beneath the peaks of Jarra and Arradoy, where peasants still sell their produce in the market place amid a bustle that must have existed over the centuries when pilgrims passed through on their way to visit the grave of the decapitated St. James at Santiago de Compostela, one of the great shrines of the Middle Ages, along with Rome and Jerusalem. A carefully nurtured 9th century legend brought these pilgrims from all parts of Europe, through France to St. Jean, the Pass of Roncesvalles via the old Roman road, to Pamplona, Asturias, Galicia, along a route still marked by their seashell emblem carved in the stonework of churches where they rested their weary bones. The Black Prince in 1367 and French General Clausel in 1813 led their troops over the old Roman Road and we considered attempting to do so, but found the narrow rock-strewn track impassible even to a powerful 3.8 Mercedes; walking the 17 miles of precipitous mountain tracks was also considered but thankfully abandoned because of the crumbling vertigo-inducing chasm-bordered road.

So we used the modern road that relentlessly unrolled into the heart of the mountains until reaching the small frontier village Arneguy (named by Froissart) marked by twin frontier-posts. Beyond, the long steep-sided twisting Val Carlos climbed steadily along the right-hand wall of the ravine, following every ripple of the rock-encrusted hillside for nine miles, until emerging onto an open saddle between grassy summits at the top of the Pass of Roncesvalles 1057 metres above sea-level. It is marked by a small chapel and a monument, a rough-hewn granite pillar simply marked "Roland 778/1927" (the last date being when it was placed there). It was an artifact destined to carry us back 600 years before even the Black Prince breached the Pass.

Basque mountaineers believe that on stormy nights the sound of a horn echoes around the rocky crags, blown by Roland, hero of Charlemagne's army, as he lay dying at Roncesvalles where his small rearguard had held in check a huge army of Saracens. One of the world's great legends, sung by minstrels throughout the Ages, versions were collected into an epic poem 'The Song of Roland', translated into many languages. Based on authentic history of the period when Charlemagne was fighting the Saracens in Spain, it tells how when returning to France, the rearguard were cut-off in a narrow defile by savage Basque tribesmen of the mountains; poetic license transforms the Basques into a 40,000 strong Arab army, held at bay by Roland, Knight of Blaives, and the Twelve Peers of France. Oliver, a brother-in-arms, implored him to sound his horn and bring Charlemagne to their aid; but Roland refused until knight after dauntless knight had fallen when, too late, he blew upon the horn. Miles away, Charlemagne heard the horn's blast and turned back, to find the mighty hero of France dead among his faithful followers. The legend tells how, before dying, Roland wielded his mighty sword Darendal to clove in the solid rock a 300 foot fissure, known to this day as La Breche de Rolant.

In 1927 archeologists unearthed two huge skeletons in the vicinity of the chapel, not unnaturally they were claimed to be Roland and Oliver. The battlefield, if ever it existed outside legend, is said to be in the area of the Altobiscar Peak between the Lepeder Pass and the Val Carlos road; but it is far more likely to be in the Val Carlos itself where the rearguard would have been strung-out along the narrow track. Here the long column of heavily armoured cavalry would have been most vulnerable, with rocks and fallen trees blocking their path and huge stones hurtling down on them from above.

The Field of Maya is not easy to work out, at least we did not find it so, until orientating ourselves with the precipitous terrain around us by comparing it with photographs of the same area in Jac Weller's invaluable book *Wellington in the Peninsular*. Then it is possible to discover the area in which the two Portugese guns were lost (the only guns ever taken from Wellington); to stand and gaze with respect at the open heather-covered crest hardly 50 yards wide, where a wing of the 1/92nd (Gordon Highlanders) in two-deep line formed of less than 400 men, fought off an entire French division for twenty minutes. And the Chemin des Anglais, along which Barnes Brigade came from the west to save the day.

As did most of these mountainous fields, Maya surprised us by its overall area, considering that the battle was relatively minor and every man marched on his own two feet.

This now silent and solitary place resting under the midday sun, hallowed by our red-coated ancestors, brought the comforting assurance that long-held convictions had been right - that little takes place on a wargames table bearing more than a laboured resemblance between real-life warfare and a game. Nevertheless, it is possible through the detailed information imparted by military historians such as Jac Weller, Oman, Glover, Fortescue and others (whose books, or photocopied pages from them, accompanied us on every field) to achieve eminently satisfying re-creation of these exciting Napoleonic battles - but how difficult it is to reproduce realistic mountain scenery!

Walking the other battlefield at Roncesvalles is perhaps best remembered for the dramatic reappraisal of all personal concepts of wargaming in its revelation that battlefields are not always convenient flattish fields but can be precipitous areas, with fighting taking place on steep slopes and small plateaux. Laboriously clambering up and down these hills and mountains brought it home very forcibly that these soldiers were not carried to the spot in cars or coaches as we were, but tramped on their own feet every yard of the way during the heat of Spanish summer, carrying all they owned on their backs. It is difficult to reproduce such terrain on the tabletop, if only because model soldiers will not stand up on steep slopes, although it can be done by building small, almost symbolic, 'no-go' mountainous areas that do not occupy too much precious wargaming space, and battles being fought in detached areas on wide steps, terraces and plateaux. The unusual style of wargaming that results makes the trouble of setting up such terrain a worthwhile business.

Roland's epic battle, with his rearguard strung-out along a narrow track, blocked by rocks and fallen trees, can be fought as a wargame, taking the form of any ambush/action between disciplined troops and savage forces. Initially concealed amid rocks and undergrowth, the ambushers are represented by two coloured-headed pins for each group of them. The wargamer handling the ambushed force, on discovering a pin, challenges and is told whether or not it is an actual force if he is able to throw an agreed dice score; then the ambushers are placed in position and the battle fought-out. As in Individual Skirmish Wargaming, such Paladins as Roland and Oliver can be granted additional powers and strengths - such as higher dice scores before they are wounded or killed.

The Battle of Sorauren - 28 July 1813.

When the solitary horseman, Wellington, reached the summit of the ridge above the village of Sorauren, he was greeted by - "...that stern and appalling shout which the British soldier is wont to give upon the edge of battle, and which no enemy has ever heard unmoved. In a conspicuous place he stopped, desirous that both armies should know he was there. A spy who was present pointed out Soult, then so near that his features could be plainly distinguished. Finding his eyes attentively upon that formidable man, Wellington thus spoke: "Yonder is a great commander, but he is a cautious one and will delay his attack to ascertain the cause of these shouts; that will give time for the 6th Division to arrive and I shall beat him!"

William Napier, 'English Battles & Sieges in the Peninsular'

After the Battles of Maya and Roncesvalles, lacking Wellington's resolution, Cole and Picton became alarmed at these French incursions with superior numbers, and so they pulled back helter-skelter towards Pamplona. Here Picton actually intended taking position on ridges within artillery range of French guns on the walls of the blockaded town! Luckily Cole noticed the Sorauren-Zabaldica Ridge about 5kms from Pamplona and persuaded Picton to stand there, where Wellington found them at about midday on 27 July.

The Duke, accompanied by his Military Secretary Fitzroy Somerset and Murray his Quartermaster-General, travelled on the Pamplona road which they had been traversing since dawn looking for the army; at Velate they came up with the 6th Division moving south, and ordered them to hasten to join Cole and Picton - wherever they were. The QMG was left at the small village of Olague to hasten reinforcements - although at that moment the Duke knew the fastest reinforcements he could send Cole and Picton was himself! With only Fitzroy Somerset riding by his side, the Duke carried on until reaching the little village of Sorauren and saw his army massed on a ridge to the southeast; he also noted Reille's columns pouring onto a ridge in front of them, directly in the path of his reinforcements. Despite French Light troops coming through the village towards them, he halted on the stone bridge over the narrow river Ulzama and scribbled a message to QMG Murray telling him to detour the southwards marching 6th Division on a minor road through Lizaso.

Bearing the despatch, Fitzroy Somerset turned his horse and galloped back on the road to Olague - he was the same soldier who had his arm amputated at Waterloo and then sent for the limb to recover a ring he had left on a finger; forty years later he reappears in History as the kindly but bumbling Lord Raglan in command of the British Army in the Crimea, where he died

It would be difficult for any playwright or producer to stage-manage the dramatic entrance of the Duke of Wellington as, with the nearest enemy only about a hundred yards away, he turned his horse's head toward the steep slope of Cole's Ridge and galloped ostentatiously upwards - a solitary horseman unmistakable in a low hat, plain blue jacket and short white cape. The first to see him were men of Campbell's Portugese Brigade who set up the cry: "Douro! Douro!" -the name they knew him by since his feat across that river four years earlier; then British infantry joined in the cheering until every man knew Old Nosey had arrived - everything would be alright now! Putting his horse to the steep slope, the Duke knew he had done what had to be done - he had made his presence vividly felt by his Army - and by the French!

Soult sent five French divisions against the ridge, attacking with battalions formed one behind the other in columns of double companies; a brigade ascending from Sorauren by the Duke's path drove the Portugese from the chapel and with odds of three to one in their favor, the French succeeded in pushing back Ross and Campbell. Further to the right two battalions of Anson's brigade - the 3/27th and 1/48th - formed in the familiar two-deep line that gave them a musketry advantage of 1200 to 300, overthrew the columns of French battalions one after the other, sending them reeling back; then the victorious British infantry flung themselves down the slope into the flank of the French pressing Ross and Campbell. They smashed each enemy battalion first by firing rolling volleys, then followed by a bayonet charge - it has been said that never in the entire Peninsular War did two battalions achieve so much so quickly.

Pack's Division marched in from Lizaso and were in position by 11 o'clock under the left end of the ridge on the far side of the river below the bridge; an important round hill to the right, beyond the Zabaldica Peak, was held by Spanish troops. Wellington reinforced them with the 1/40th Regiment - wisely as it later turned out. The right, covered by Picton's Division was refused

Although outnumbered in the general area two to one, Wellington with remarkable tactical skill, managed to gain a two to one numerical advantage at each separate encounter. His foresight at Spanish hill was shown when, after the Spanish had gallantly withstood three French attacks, the 1/40th in a thin red line firing rolling battalion volleys, threw back an entire French infantry division. The battle terminated with four hours of daylight left; Wellington's 18,000 or so men had completely beaten Soult's 30,000, losing 2,652 against estimated French losses of about 4,000.

Both armies lay quiet next day and the Duke reinforced his left with Hill's forces from the Bastan Valley and had guns manhandled onto the ridge - the previous day's battle had involved hardly any artillery because of the nature of the terrain. Next day he took the offensive by attacking with all the precision and impetuosity of Salamanca and the French, whose morale was now very low, were sent reeling back into France. Facing Picton on the Allied right, Foy's 10,000 men made a noteworthy retreat over goat-paths running along ridges and mountain sides of this wild and frightening area.

There can be few writers more qualified to talk on a war or battle than one who was actually serving in it and, of course, William Napier was a much-wounded officer in the 43rd Regiment and present at most of the actions from 1808-1814. Furthermore, he possessed the superlative qualification of being a confidante (or at least having the ear) of Wellington himself, thus the passage that follows is marked by a bland footnote: "All these conjectures and proceedings are given on the Duke's personal authority."

Lord Wellington heard of the fight at Maya on his way back from San Sebastian, after the assault, but with the false addition that D'Erlon was beaten. As early as the 22nd he had known that Soult was preparing a great offensive movement; yet the impassive attitude of the French centre, the disposition of their reserve, twice as strong as he at first supposed, together with the bridges prepared by Reille, were calculated to mislead, and did mislead him. Soult's combinations to bring his centre finally into line on the crest of the great chain being impenetrable, the English general could not believe he would throw himself with only thirty thousand men into the valley of the Ebro, unless sure of aid from Suchet. But that general's movements indicated a determination to remain in Catalonia, and Wellington, in contrast to Soult, knew that Pampeluna was not in extremity, and thought, the assault not having been made, that San Sebastian was. Hence the operations against his right, their full extent not known, appeared a feint, and he judged the real effort would be to raise the siege of San Sebastian. But in the night of the 25th, correct intelligence of the Maya and Roncesvalles affairs arrived. Graham was then ordered to turn the siege into a blockade, to embark the guns and stores, and hold his spare troops ready to join Giron, on a position of battle marked out near the Bidassoa. Cotton was directed to move the cavalry up to Pampeluna, and Abispal was instructed to hold some of his Spanish troops ready to act in advance of that fortress. Meanwhile Wellington, having arranged his lines of correspondence, proceeded to San Esteban, which he reached early in the morning.

While the embarkation of the guns and stores was going on it was essential to hold the posts at Vera and Echallar, because D'Erlon's object was not pronounced; and an enemy in possession of those places could approach San Sebastian by the roads leading over the Pena de Haya, or by

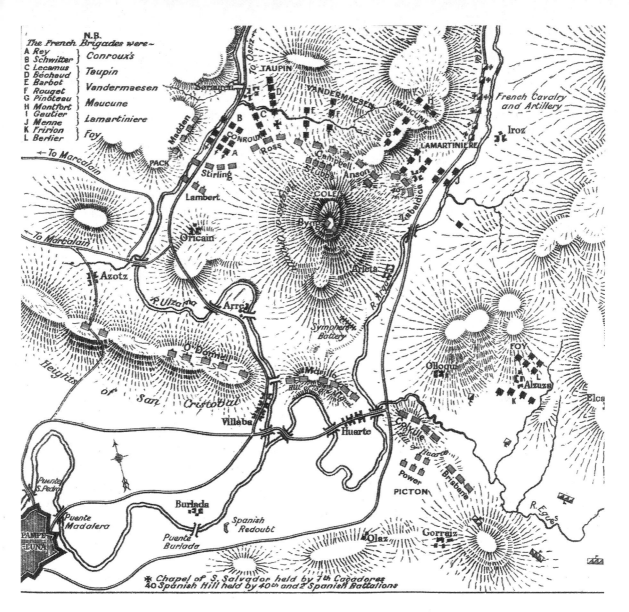

SORAUREN. JULY 28TH, AROUND 1.15 P.M.

the defiles of Zubietta leading round that mountain. But when Wellington reached Irueta, saw the reduced state of Stewart's division, and knew Picton had marched from Olague, he directed all the troops within his power upon Pampeluna, and to prevent mistakes indicated the valley of Lanz as the general line of movement. Of Picton's exact position, or of his intentions, nothing positive was known; but supposing him to have joined Cole at Linzoain, as indeed he had, Wellington judged their combined forces sufficient to check the enemy until assistance could reach them from the centre, or from Pampeluna, and he so advised Picton on the evening of the 26th.

MAJOR ARTHUR GRIFFITHS:
    27th July - The 6th, 7th, and Light Divisions were moving from St. Estevan, Echellar, and Vera respectively, towards Pampelona. It was a general retreat, very demoralising, and the confusion was greatly increased by vague rumours of terrible disasters everywhere. Picton, however, had turned, as Wellington expected, on the steep ridge of St. Christoval, and there assumed a strong position, which Cole, now under Picton's orders, rendered more secure by seizing some heights on his right. Soult, who was now up with his advanced troops, promptly decided he must assail

Picton at once in front and on both flanks.

Perhaps less voluble than Napier; but it must be the latter who tells of the dramatic and stimulating arrival on the field of the Duke, and the subsequent events dictated by his presence:

> While Soult was thus establishing a line of battle, Wellington, who had quitted Hill's quarters in the Bastan early on the 27th, crossed the great mountain spine into the valley of Lanz, without being able to learn anything of Picton's movements or position until he reached Ostiz, a few miles from Sauroren. There he found Long's brigade of light cavalry, placed to furnish posts of correspondence in the mountains, and from him heard that Picton had abandoned the heights of Linzoain: whereupon, leaving instructions to stop all the troops coming down the valley of Lanz until the state of affairs near Pampeluna could be ascertained, he made at racing speed for Sauroren. As he entered that village he saw Clausel's divisions moving along the crest of the mountain, and thus knew the allied troops in the valley of Lanz were intercepted; then pulling up his horse, he wrote on the parapet of the bridge at Sauroren fresh instructions to turn everything from that valley to the right by a cross-road, which led out of it to Marcalain and thence round the hills, to enter the valley again at Oricain, in rear of the position occupied by Cole. Lord Fitzroy Somerset, who had kept up with him, galloped with these orders out of Sauroren by one road, the French light cavalry simultaneously dashed in by another, and Wellington rode alone up the mountain.
>
> A Portuguese battalion on the left, first recognising him, raised a joyful cry, and soon the shrill clamour was taken up by the next regiments, swelling as it run along the line.
>
> Cole's position was the summit of a mountain mass, which filled all the space between the Guy and Lanz valleys, as far back as Huarte and Villalba. It was highest in the centre and well defined towards the enemy, yet the trace was irregular, the right being thrown back towards the village of Arletta so as to flank the great road, which was also swept by guns placed on a lower range behind.
>
> Overlooking Zabaldica and the Guy river, was the bulging hill vindicated by the Spaniards, a distinct but lower point on the right of the position. The left, also abating in height, was yet rugged and steep, overlooking the Lanz river, and Ross's brigade was posted on that side, having in front a Portuguese battalion, whose flank rested on a small chapel. Campbell was on the right of Ross. Anson was on the highest ground, partly behind, partly on the right of Campbell. Byng's brigade was on a second mass of hills in reserve, and the Spanish hill was further reinforced by a battalion of Portuguese.
>
> This front of battle was less than two miles, and well filled, its flanks being washed by the Lanz and the Guy; Wellington looked anxiously for his sixth division, then coming from Marcalain by a road which run behind his ridge beyond the Lanz and fell into that valley at Oricain, one mile in rear of Cole's left. It had been turned into that road from the higher part of the Lanz valley by Lord Fitzroy Somerset.

It must be mentioned that, on both sides, the heights on which the opposing armies were poised were steep, high and rugged, rocks massed on each other to stand out like castles, so difficult to approach and so difficult to assail that only the hardened veterans of the Peninsular would have dared such a trial.

NAPIER:

> One of Clausel's divisions already occupied Sauroren, and the other two were now posted on each side of that village; that on the right hand was ordered to send flankers to the ridge from whence Soult had made his observations, and upon signal to move down the valley, wheel to the left, and assail the rear of the allies while the other two divisions assailed their front: five thousand men would thus be enveloped by sixteen thousand, and Soult hoped to crush them notwithstanding the strength of ground. Meanwhile Reille's two divisions on the side of Zabaldica, were each to send a brigade against the Spanish hill, and connect the right of their attack with Clausel's left. The remaining brigades were to follow in support, the division beyond

the Guy was to keep Picton in check, and all were to throw themselves frankly into action."

First Battle of Sauroren

At midday on the 28th of July, the anniversary of the Talavera fight, the French gathered in masses at the foot of the position, and their skirmishers quickly spread over the face of the mountain, working upward like a conflagration; but the columns of attack were not all ready when Clausel's right-hand division, without awaiting the general signal of battle, threw out flankers on the ridge beyond the Lanz and pushed down the valley in one mass. With a rapid pace it turned Cole's left and was preparing to wheel up on his rear, when suddenly Madden's Portuguese brigade of the sixth division appeared on the crest of the ridge beyond the river, driving the flankers back and descending, as from the clouds, with a rattling fire upon the right and rear of the column; and not less suddenly the main body of that division, emerging from behind the same ridge near the village of Oricain, presented a line of battle across the front. It was the counter-stroke of Salamanca! The French were, while striving to encompass Cole's left, themselves encompassed; for two brigades of Cole's division instantly turned and smote them on the left, the Portuguese smote them on the right, and thus scathed on both flanks with fire, they were violently shocked and pushed back with a mighty force by the sixth division, yet not in flight, but fighting fiercely and strewing the ground with their enemies' bodies as well as with their own.

Clausel's second division, on the other side of Sauroren, seeing this dire conflict, with a hurried movement assailed the chapel height to draw off Cole's fire from the troops in the valley, and gallantly did the French soldiers throng up the craggy steep; yet the general unity of the attack was ruined; neither the third division nor Reille's brigades had yet received the signal, and their attacks were made irregularly, in succession, running from right to left as the necessity of aiding others became apparent. It was however a terrible battle and well fought. One column darting out of the village of Sauroren, silently, sternly, without firing a shot, worked up to the chapel under a tempest of bullets, which swept away whole ranks without abating the speed and power of the mass; the Portuguese there shrunk abashed, and that part of the position was won; soon however they rallied on Ross's British brigade, and the whole, running forward, charged the French with a loud shout and dashed them down the hill. Heavily stricken the latter were, yet undismayed, and they re-formed, and again ascended, to be again broken and overturned. But the other columns of attack now bore upwards through the smoke and flame with which the skirmishers covered the face of the mountain, and another Portuguese regiment, fighting on the right of Ross, yielded to their fury; thus a heavy body crowned the heights, and wheeling against Ross's exposed flank forced him back also, and his ground was instantly occupied by the enemies with whom he had been engaged in front. Now the fight raged close and desperate on the crest of the position, charge succeeding charge, each side yielding and advancing by turns. This astounding effort of French valour was however of no avail. Wellington brought Byng's brigade forward at a running pace, and calling his 27th and 48th British Regiments, from the higher ground in the centre, against the crowded masses, rolled them backward in disorder, and threw them, one after the other, violently down the mountain-side; yet with no child's play; the two British regiments had to fall upon the enemy three separate times with the bayonet, and lost more than half their own numbers.

During this battle on the mountain-top, the sixth division gained ground in the Lanz valley, and when it arrived on a front with the left of the victorious troops near the chapel, Wellington, seeing the momentary disorder of the enemy, ordered Madden's Portuguese brigade beyond the Lanz, which had never ceased its fire against the right flank of the French column, to assail the village of Sauroren in rear; but the state of the action in other parts and the exhaustion of the troops soon induced him to countermand this movement.

On the French left, Reille's brigades, connecting their right with Clausel's third division, had environed the Spanish hill and ascended it unchecked, at the moment when the fourth division was so hardly pressed from Sauroren; a Spanish regiment then gave way on the left of the 40th, but a Portuguese battalion, rushing forward, again covered the flank of that invincible regiment, which waited in stern silence until the French set their feet upon the broad summit. Scarcely did their glittering arms appear over the brow of the mountain when the charging British cry was heard, the fierce shock given, the French mass was broken to pieces and a tempest of bullets followed it down the mountain. Four times this assault was renewed, and the French officers were seen even to pull up their tired men by the belts, so fierce and resolute they were to win, but it was the labour of Sisyphus; the vehement shout and shock of the British soldier always prevailed, and at last, with thinned ranks, tired limbs, and fainting hearts, hopeless from repeated failures, the French were so abashed that three British companies sufficed to bear down a whole brigade.*

Such were the leading events of this sanguinary struggle, which Lord Wellington, fresh from the fight, with homely emphasis called "bludgeon work." Two generals and eighteen hundred men had been killed or wounded on the French side, following their official reports; a number far below the estimate made at the time by the allies, whose loss amounted to two thousand six hundred. These discrepancies between hostile calculations ever occur, and there is little wisdom in disputing where proof is unattainable; yet the numbers actually engaged were twenty-five thousand French and twelve thousand allies; hence, if the strength of the latter's position did not save them from greater loss, their steadfast courage is more to be admired.

The 29th the armies rested in position without firing a shot, and the wandering divisions on both sides were now entering the line.

*For this fact I had the authority of a French colonel of artillery.

Soult was now joined by D'Erlon's corps of 4 divisions of infantry and 2 of cavalry; thus encouraged he determined on a further attack on the 30th. However, Wellington had ideas of his own - Picton was to enter the Zubiri Valley and turn the French left while the 7th division swept over the hills beyond the Lanz river into Clausel's right; throughout Cole was constantly in action against Foy on the mountain between Zabaldica and Sorauren; the 6th Division reinforced by Byng's Brigade were to assault the village of Sorauren itself.

Napier takes up the story:

SECOND BATTLE OF SAUROREN.

Picton quickly gained the Val de Zubiri, and threw his skirmishers against Foy's left flank on the mountain, while on the other flank General Inglis, one of those veterans who purchase every step of promotion with their blood, advancing with only five hundred men of the seventh division, broke at one shock the two French regiments on the ridges covering Clausel's right, and drove them down into the valley of Lanz. He lost indeed one-third of his own men, but instantly spread the remainder in skirmishing order along the descent and opened a biting fire upon the flank of Conroux's division, which being in march up the valley from Sauroren, was now thrown into disorder by having two regiments thus suddenly tumbled upon it from the top of the mountain.

Foy's division was marching along the crest of the position between Zabaldica and Sauroren at the moment of this attack; but he was too far off to give aid, and his own light troops were engaged with Cole's skirmishers; moreover Inglis had been so sudden that before the evil was well perceived it was past remedy; for Wellington instantly pushed the sixth division under Pakenham to the left of Sauroren, and sent Byng headlong down from the chapel height against Maucune, who was in that village. This vigorous assault was simultaneously enforced from the other side of the Lanz by Madden's Portuguese, and the battery near the chapel sent its bullets crashing through the houses, or booming up the valley towards Conroux's column, which Inglis never ceased to vex.

The village and bridge of Sauroren and the straits beyond were soon covered with a pall of smoke, the musketry pealed frequent and loud, and the tumult and affray echoing from mountain to mountain filled all the valley. Byng with hard fighting carried Sauroren, fourteen hundred prisoners were made, and the two French divisions, being entirely broken, fled, partly up the valley towards Clausel's other divisions, partly up the original position, to seek refuge with Foy, who remained on the summit a helpless spectator of this rout. He rallied the fugitives in great numbers, but had soon to look to himself, for his own skirmishers were now driven up the mountain by Cole's men, and his left was infested by Picton's detachments. Thus pressed, he fell back along the hills separating the valley of Zubiri from that of Lanz, and the woods enabled him to effect his retreat without much loss; yet he dared not descend into either valley, and thinking himself entirely cut off, sent advice to Soult and went over the Great Spine into the Alduides by the pass of Urtiaga.

In fact, Foy's was the only division to escape, making their way back to France by a laborious succession of goat-tracks.

NAPIER:

> The allies lost nineteen hundred men killed, wounded, or taken in this and Hill's battle, and nearly twelve hundred were Portuguese for the soldiers of that nation bore the brunt of both fights. On the French side the loss was enormous. Conroux's and Maucune's divisions were completely disorganized. Eight thousand men under Foy were entirely separated from the main body, two thousand at the lowest computation were killed or wounded, many were dispersed in the woods and ravines, and three thousand prisoners were taken. Soult's fighting men were thus reduced to thirty-five thousand, of which fifteen thousand under Clausel and Reille were dispirited by defeat, and the whole in a critical situation, seeing that Hill's force, increased to fifteen thousand men by the junction of Morillo and Campbell, was in their front at Eguaros, and thirty thousand were on their rear in the valley of Lanz; for Picton, finding no enemies in the valley of Zubiri, had joined Cole on the heights.
>
> Soult was therefore completely isolated: he had indeed no resources save what his ability and courage could supply.
>
> His single line of retreat by Dona Maria was secure only as far as San Estevan, and from that town he could march up the Bidassoa to the Bastan, to regain France by the Col de Maya; or down the same river towards Vera by Sumbilla and Yanzi, from both of which roads branching off to the right over the mountains to Echallar: yet he might be intercepted on either side. The Col de Maya way was good, that down the Bidassoa was a long and terrible defile, so contracted about the bridges of Yanzi and Sumbilla that a few men only could march abreast. This then he had to dread. First, that Wellington by the pass of Vellate would reach the Bastan before him, and block the Maya passes. Second, that Graham would occupy the rocks of Yanzi and cut him off from Echallar. Then, confined to a narrow mountain way leading from San Estevan to Zagaramurdi, and far too rugged for wounded men and baggage, he would be followed by Hill, and perhaps headed at Urdax by Wellington.
>
> In this state, the first object being to get through Dona Maria, he commenced his retreat in the night of the 30th.

Making his name in India some thirty years later as commander of the East India Company's Army in the Mahratta War of 1843 and the two Sikh Wars of 1845/6 and 1848/9, Colonel Hugh Gough commanded the 87th Regiment of Foot (Keane's brigade, Colville's 3rd Division) present at Sorauren. Although they did not take any part in the fighting, the 34 year old Gough's account of the action is interesting:

> The Pyrenees are nearly wooded to their summit with very fine Beech, and are very grand indeed. This pass is that which Soult came lately through and which the Fourth Division abandoned, just as we came up to them; both Divisions then fell back to Huarte, the village we formerly were quartered in, close to Pampeluna, where Sir Thomas Picton took up a position, placing us, his own Division, on the right of the village, which he conceived the most assailable, the Fourth Division on the Left, supported by a Brigade of the 2nd and the Spaniards. The enemy pressed close after us, and we scarcely had got into position when their Columns made their appearance, but unfortunately (perhaps you will think otherways) for us, they attacked the Hills on which the Fourth Division were posted, leaving 7,000 Infantry and 2,500 Cavalry in front of us, so close that Colonel Duglas' guns frequently fired over them - a small rivulet only separated us. We every moment expected them, but that was not Soult's intention. During the night, the Enemy moved Columns to his Right, for the purpose of turning our left, which he would have done but for the providential arrival of the 6th division at the very critical moment. These attacks were very formidable as to numbers, but as to spirit miserable. This day they again attacked the

The Battle of Sorauren 1813. The landbridge over which Maucune and Reille attacked, and were then themselves hit in the flank by Anson.

hill twice, and were twice repulsed at the point of the Bayonet. Conceive how interesting this was to us, who could see every part of it and close to us. It was quite a show. Early the third morning, the Marquis came up to our hill. I was standing with Thos. Picton, who with Sir Stapleton Cotton, Generals Colville and Ponsonby, was with us the whole time. He appeared in the most wonderful good spirits, and shook Sir Thos. (who by the bye he has not been hitherto on good terms with) most heartily by the hand. It was this day supposed that Soult, finding himself foiled on the left, would have attacked the Right. We were therefore all prepared, but alas no such thing. The night passing, at daylight we saw the Enemy in full retreat, but supposing it to be manoeuvring we did not follow till 10 o'clock. Our Division then pushed forward, and we were in hopes we should have made up for lost time. He kept on the hills, and we were on the main road just below him, on his flank. We did not bring him into Action, altho' for two leagues we were within half a mile of his Columns. I will own I felt much disappointed as I think our Division might have done much more, had they either pushed in (as they latterly did) and got in the Enemy's Rear, or ascended the hill and attacked his flank. We however made him alter his point of Retreat. The whole business was grand to a degree and glorious. It is estimated that the Enemy's loss has been at least 15,000. He brought 45,000 into the country, and there are nine thousand still straggling amongst these Mountains.

Soult was forced to abandon his offensive and retreat to the French frontier, an outcome which could have been disastrous for the French had Wellington decided to press his full advantage, but preferred to complete the siege of San Sebastien and the blockade of Pamplona.

Contending Forces in the Pyrenees (actually engaged)

Allies:
Hill's Corps, including Morillo's Spaniards
Picton's (Colville's) 3rd Division.
Coles' 4th Division.
Pack's (later Packenham's) 6th Division
Dalhousie's 7th Division
Divisions averaging 6,500 each
Hill = 14,000 approximately
Total = 36,000 approximately
French:
Reille's corps, 3 divisions of 6 infantry   brigades, approximately 17,250
D'Erlon's corps, 3 divisions of 6 infantry   brigades, approximately 21,000
Clausel's corps, 3 divisions of 6 infantry   brigades, approximately 17,000
Total = 53,000 approx. 140 guns.

BRITIH LOSSES AT SORAUREN, 28 JULY			BRITISH LOSSES AT SECOND SORAUREN, 30 JULY	
2nd Division			2nd Division	
Byng's Brigade			Byng's Brigade	
1/3rd Foot	2		1/3rd Foot	30
1/57th Foot	63		1/57th Foot	37
1st Provisional Batt.	5		1st Provisional Batt.	64
Brigade Total	70		Brigade Total	131
3rd Division	No losses		3rd Division	
4th Division (Cole)			Brisbane's Brigade	
Anson's Brigade			1/45th Foot	8
3/27th Foot	254		5/60th Foot (4 companies)	31
1/40th Foot	129		74th Foot	39
1/48th Foot	135		1/88th Foot	1
2nd Provisional Batt.	20		Brigade Total	89
Ross's Brigade			Colville's Brigade	No Casualties
1/7th Foot	217		4th Division (Cole)	
1/20th Foot	108		Anson's Brigade	
1/23rd Foot	81		3/27th Foot	
1 company Brunswick-Oels	5		1/40th Foot	7
Divisional Total	949		1/48th Foot	–
6th Division (Pakenham)			2nd Provisional Batt.	6
Stirling's Brigade			Brigade Total	13
1/42nd Foot	22		Ross's Brigade	No Casualties
1/79th Foot	35		6th Division (Pakenham)	
1/91st Foot	112		Stirling's Brigade	
1 company 5/60th	5		1/42nd Foot	8
Lambert's Brigade			1/79th Foot	18
1/11th Foot	51		1/91st Foot	9
1/32nd Foot	24		Lambert's Brigade	
1/36th Foot	18		1/11th Foot	23
1/61st	62		1/32nd Foot	83
Divisional Total	949		1/36th Foot	26
Artillery	6		1/61st	13
General Staff	4		Divisional Total	130
			7th Division (Dalhousie)	
Total British	1,358		Barnes's Brigade	
Total Portuguese	1,102		1/6th Foot	7
General Total	2,460		3rd Provisional Batt.	3

Brunswick-Oels (9 companies) 17
Inglis's Brigade
51st Foot 24
68th Foot 23
1/82nd Foot 92
Chasseurs Britanniques 45
    Divisional Total 211
Artillery 9

Total British 583

PORTUGUESE LOSSES IN THE BATTLES OF THE PYRENEES

Da Costa's Brigade
2nd Line 200
14th Line 84
All at Buenza, July 30
A. Campbell's Brigade
2nd Line 114
14th Line 213
10th Cacadores 28
Almost all at two battles of Sorauren
Ashworth's Brigade (2nd Division)
6th Line 105
18th Line 150
6th Cacadores 62
All at Buenza, July 30

Lecor's Brigade (7th Division)
7th Line 4
19th Line 2
2nd Cacadores 58
Almost all at 2nd Sorauren, July 30
Madden's Brigade (6th Division)
8th Line 3
12th Line 269
9th Cacadores
Almost all at two battles of Sorauren
Power's Brigade (3rd Division)
9th Line 2
21st Line 14
11th Cacadores 6
Almost all at 2nd Sorauren, July 30
Stubb's Brigade (4th Division)
11th Line 142
23rd Line 50
7th Cacadores 121
Almost all at two battles of Sorauren

Total 1,732

A week later, Wellington (using rather terse language) described his ride to Larpent, his Judge-Advocate-General :

"At one time it was rather alarming, certainly, and a close run thing. When I came to the bridge of Sorauren I saw French on the hills on one side, and it was clear that we could make a stand on the other hill, in our position of the 28th, but I found that we could not keep Sorauren, as it was exposed to their fire and not to ours. I was obliged to write my orders accordingly at Sorauren, to be sent back instantly. For if they had not been dispatched back directly, by the way I had come, I must have sent them four leagues round, a quarter of an hour later. I stopped therefore to write accordingly, people saying to me all the time, "The French are coming!" "The French are coming!" I looked pretty sharp after them every now and then, till I had completed my orders, and then set off. I saw them just near the one end of the village as I went out of it at the other end. And then we took up our ground.'

WALKING THE AREA AND FIELD OF SORAUREN.

Leaving our base at Sare in the French Pyrenees, we crossed the border into Spain near Vera and, travelling at a speed far faster than the Duke's fine horse, moved south on the same road as used by him in 1813, through Almandoz - where he spent the night 26/27 July 1813 -and over the Pass at Velate. Here we branched off on a side road, taking us to the little village of Lizaso where, throughout the evening and night 26/27 July, 14,000 weary and hungry men of Pack's 6th division had tramped in, soaked to the skin by the thunderstorm that had been raging for hours. We pictured them, grousing as only the British soldier can truly do, stumbling around in the darkness, huddling together against walls and in alleys of this small Spanish village, where the old houses still cluster around the dominating church - it is possible to distinguish old from modern by the markedly contrasting roof styles. We laughed at the thought of the impact they must have had upon the amazed and stupefied locals!

THE BRIDGE AT SORAUREN THE HILL BEHIND ON WHICH THE CHAPELSTANDS AND THE BRITISH DEFENDED IS BEHIND US. WELLINGTON GALLOPED DOWN THE ROAD ON THE OTHER SIDE OF THE ULZANA RIVER, STOPPED AT THE OTHER END OF THE BRIDGE TO WRITE A THIRTEEN LINE DESPATCH TO MURRAY THE QMG AT ORTIZ, WHICH WAS TAKEN BY FITZROY SOMERSET BACK DOWN THE SAME ROAD. THEN WELLINGTON GALLOPED AWAY TOWARD US, WHILE THE FRENCH FORCES ENTERED THE VILLAGE JUST VISIBLE.

Aware that we were travelling on the same road as the Duke and Fitzroy Somerset (QMG Murray had been left at Lizaso) we hastened, as he did, to the little stone bridge over the river Ulzama at Sorauren, where we halted to savour the emotion of knowing we were standing on exactly the spot where stood the Duke as he unhurriedly wrote his message and despatched Somerset back to Lizaso with it. The Duke, aware that French light troops had entered the village to his left, had seen above him, crowning the rocky ridge, the red and brown tunics of British and Portugese. Our imaginations worked at full stretch, transforming the bare gorse-covered hillsides into the stage for the drama we knew had been played out there.

Owning no fine mount like that of the Duke's, it was hard going climbing the rough track leading up from the bridge to the east-west ridge - 2,000 feet high and 1 1/2 miles long - where, on the allied left, five brigades of Cole's Division were thrust well forward, the chapel at the end being garrisoned by the 7th Portugese Cacadores. It was these Portugese troops who, seeing the familiar figure of the Duke breasting the steep slope, had raised the echoing cry 'Douro! Douro!'. Alone on the hillside, and meriting no such greeting, we raised it ourselves - our dual cries, albeit somewhat breathless, resounded on the still warm air! By the time we reached the crest of Cole's Ridge, we had acquired a wholesome respect for any horse that could gallop up that slope. Regaining our breath in the ruins of the little chapel that had been held by the Portugese, we surveyed the rugged ridges and the mountainous terrain surrounding us on all sides.

It can be said, without fear of contradiction, that many among us - certainly the wargaming fraternity - probably learned more about the true nature of Peninsular warfare from that particular battle and terrain than from any other. We marvelled at the toughness of both British and French infantrymen who, in the blazing heat of a Spanish mid-Summer, could assail and assault over those semi-precipitous slopes, wearing overcoats, bearing heavy equipment and muskets.

In truth, the author recognizes Sorauren as a battle possessing so much interest and stimulation as to vie with the Coa, Roncesvalles, and Agincourt as being among the most evocative battlefields he has ever walked.

WARGAMING IN THE SORAUREN STYLE.

Stirring accounts of this battle by Fortescue, Oman, Weller and indeed William Napier, who wrote the stimulating story of the battle and is quoted in these pages, reveal just what an exciting affair it would be to wargame. Therefore, it is not without some shame that the author admits to having no notes of such a tabletop battle, nor indeed has any recollection of one being fought by him. Lame excuses can be offered, but the truth of the matter probably lays in the kindred difficulties of both constructing such terrain to realistically resemble the heights around Sorauren, and then persuading the little figures to stand up on its slopes!

THE SIEGE OF SAN SEBASTIAN 10 JULY - 31 AUGUST 1813.

Siege of San Sebastian 1813. This costly affair was summed up by Colonel Jones as "Thirty days open trenches, thirty days blockade, 3,500 officers and men killed or wounded, 70,831 rounds of ammunition expended."

After being defeated at Vitoria in June, the French rapidly retreated back into France, leaving Pamplona and San Sebastian garrisoned and soon under siege. The Duke's line of communication shifted from Lisbon to Santander and the superb small harbour of Pasajes east of San Sebastian - today a dreary conglomeration of large cranes, dusty coal-chutes and huge sheds - was used to bring down siege artillery in transports from Corunna, swiftly emplaced to begin battering San Sebastian.

Save a petty stand made against General Graham by Foy's Corps at Tolasa, the French made little or no resistance after Vitoria, and in July 1813, save for San Sebastian, Pamplona and a few other places, were completely driven out of Spain. Wellington, on leaving Portugal and driving the enemy across Spain, had abandoned his base at Lisbon, and San Sebastian was a suitable port at which food, stores and reinforcements coming from England could be landed, and direct communication maintained with Britain.

Major Arthur Griffiths described the town and the preparations for its investment :

San Sebastian is nowadays a most fashionable resort, and occupies the whole frontage of its spacious bay. In 1813 it was limited to the low peninsula running north and south, on which stood the small town surrounded by its fortifications. These defences to the landward or southern side of the isthmus were the more important, and consisted of a high rampart, 350 yards in length, at each end of which were half-bastions giving flanking fire along the ditch. In the centre of the rampart a bastion stood out to the front, and in front of that again was a more advanced fort, called a horn work, covered by a ditch and glacis. East and west of the town the only defence was a simple wall, indifferently flanked and unprotected by obstacles in front of it, for waters washed its base to the westward of those of the sea, to the eastward of the river Urumea, a tidal shallow stream that ebbed twice daily, leaving exposed a long, firm strand. The latter undoubtedly constituted the weakest part of the fortress, and it was within full view and easy reach of high land and commanding sandhills, the Chofres, on the far side of the river.

San Sebastian had a second and a third, an outer and an inner, line of defence. The first was the high ridge called San Bartolomeo, which crossed the isthmus at its neck; the other was the rocky height of the Monte Orgullo, or "Mountain of Pride," that rose steeply north of the town at the end of the peninsula. San Bartolomeo had been fortified directly the siege became imminent. A redoubt was constructed on the plateau connected with the convent buildings, and this redoubt was supported by a second made of casks nearer the town, and by stengthening the houses in the suburb just under the northern ridge of San Bartolomeo and on the inner side of the ridge.

Monte Orgullo was crowned by the castle of La Mota, a small enclosed fort with batteries on each flank, the whole raised on such an elevation as to command the town and the isthmus beyond. La Mota formed the citadel and key of the defence.

Rey set his garrison, which was now being strengthened by the arrival of fresh detachments, to work on the fortifications. It was now that the redoubt was built on San Bartolomeo; the bridge across the Urumea was burnt down; and as guns were received the batteries were armed and strengthened. When the siege actually began Rey could dispose of 76 pieces of artillery: 45 were in the main works, 13 on Monte Orgullo, 18 were held in reserve. The number of artillery men was insufficient, so detachments of infantry were instructed in gun drill. The garrison was without bomb-proof cover, and much exposed; so were the magazines.

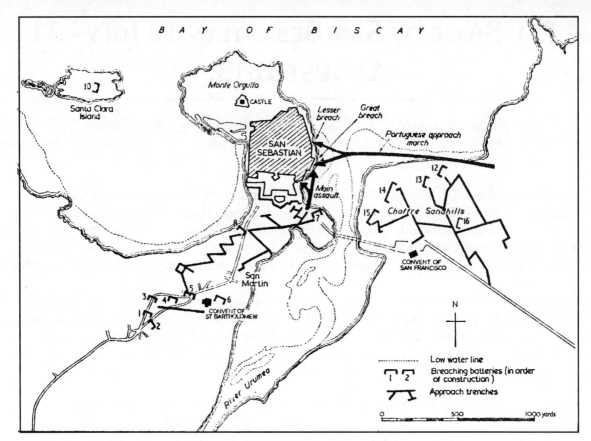

THE SIEGE OF SAN SEBASTIAN

Wellington, accompanied by his senior engineer officer, Major Smith, reconnoitred the place, July 12th, and with him concerted the plan of operations; but the conduct of the siege was given to Sir Thomas Graham, who had under his orders the 5th Division of British troops, two brigades of Portuguese, some bluejackets from H.M.S. Surveillante, and a party of sappers and miners, the first occasion on which these valuable soldiers were employed in a siege in Spain. The total force amounted to 10,000 men, being about three times the strength of the garrison. Forty pieces of artillery were available, part of them belonging to the battering-train prepared for Burgos, the whole train being under the command of Colonel Dickson, a favourite artillery officer of Wellington.

The weakest part of the defences - a point in the eastern wall of the town - was to be breached.

When the breach was formed, the assault was to be delivered, the assailants advancing at low water between the walls and the river. It soon became clear that the San Bartolomeo ridge must be wrested from the enemy, for its guns would have greatly harassed the attacking columns. The capture of San Bartolomeo was accordingly the first enterprise undertaken. It was bombarded, then attacked on the morning of July 17th by two columns, one of British, the other of Portuguese troops. The latter moved slowly. Colonel Cameron, leading the 9th and Royals, raced forward and charged with such impetuosity that the French were driven straight out of the redoubt. Down below in San Martin they rallied, but Cameron being reinforced the suburb was presently won. The cask redoubt beyond was next stormed, but without success. It was, however, taken a couple of nights later.

The fire from the breaching-batteries was continued without intermission, and effected great damage; the stone embrasures were destroyed, the guns dismounted, the walls shaken severely. The garrison, however, met the bombardment bravely, and laboured hard to repair damages or neutralise them. On the 22nd a breach which appeared to be practicable was formed. On the 23rd a second breach was commenced beyond the first. Our shells ignited some houses in the town, and a great conflagration was imminent, but it came to nothing beyond delaying the British attack, which had been fixed for the 24th.

258

Everything was ready for the last act in the siege. The storming party, 2,000 strong, was composed of General Hay's brigade of the 5th Division, for the first breach, while another battalion attacked the second. The whole of the stormers were to assemble in the foremost trench. The signal for the advance was to be the explosion of a mine on the left flank, designed by a young officer of engineers, Lieutenant Reid. On the 21st, while digging at a parallel, he had come upon a pipe four feet by three wide, which was actually the aqueduct conveying the water into the town. Reid had entered the mouth of this narrow opening and followed the passage right up to the counterscarp of the hornwork, where was stopped by a closed door. Returning to report, it was decided to form a mine at the end of the drain.

The postponement was unfortunate; the tide would have served well at daylight on the 24th; it was then at the lowest ebb, and the wide strand would have given ample space for the advancing columns. The troops assembled before daylight. The Royal Scots, under Major Frazer, intended to assail the great breach, supported by the 9th (Norfolk) Regiment and the 38th (South Staffordshire) Regiment, whose goal was the lesser breach beyond.

About 5 A.M. the column filed out of the trench on the signal given by the exploding mine. There were 300 hundred yards of the open to cover. The signal had not been heard by our batteries on the sand-hills, which fired upon our own men. The advance was very arduous, the ground most difficult, much narrowed between the wall and the waters, very slippery from the receding tide, which left the rocks covered with seaweed and here and there deep pools; moreover, the fortifications on the flanks were lined by sharpshooters, who kept up an effective fire. The first to reach the breach were Major Frazer of the Royal Scots and Lieutenant (afterwards Sir Harry) Jones, of the engineers; a few men closely followed, but in disorder, straggling and out of breath. On the far side down below was the yawning breach, filled with smoke and flames of the burning houses beyond. By this time a small handful of the most intrepid had gathered round their leaders, but quite two-thirds of the main column had turned aside on their road to the breach, and were engaged in a musketry battle with the enemy on the rampart.

The rear of the storming party was thus already in confusion, and the van would not advance. Frazer now was killed, so was Machel with the ladders; Jones was wounded and taken prisoner; the rest of the leading assailants were either slain or dispersed. The Colonels of the 38th and 9th, Greville and Cameron, and Captain Archimbeau, of the Royals, strove hard to encourage and urge on their men; but all were dispirited and in inextricable confusion, and now a hail of shot and shell fell upon them from the whole of the enemy's artillery, while continuous musketry fire, with showers of grape and hand-grenades, smote the struggling mass, which could neither advance nor retire, causing the most frightful slaughter.

According to the French account, at this last supreme moment, when defeat was unmistakable, "the bravest English rushed upon the French bayonets to find an honourable death; the rest sought safety in flight, still decimated by the furious fire, so that few escaped alive."

The attack had proved a failure, costly in valuable lives, of officers out of all proportion to men. Many reasons and some excuses were offered for the disaster; the most plausible were that the attack had been badly planned and feebly executed. Jones, in his "Sieges of Spain," says: "The efforts in the breach were certainly neither very obstinate nor very persevering," and he was an eyewitness. "No general or staff-officer went out of the trenches with the troops, and the isolated exertions of regimental officers failed."

The Siege Suspended

Lord Wellington went at once to San Sebastian and wished to renew the attack. But the besiegers were short of ammunition, which was daily expected from England, and he thought it better to await its arrival. Then momentous events followed elsewhere. Soult advanced and began the serious movements that produced the first set of the battles of the Pyrenees, and Wellington was peremptorily called away from San Sebastian. The siege was suspended for several weeks and converted into a blockade. Now the French, elated at their respite, were constantly alert, and being reinforced made many sallies. At the same time, under Rey's energetic impulse, the damaged defences were repaired and strengthened, the magazines were refilled, guns were remounted in the batteries.

The garrison had received materials and reinforcements by sea and were able to put 67 new pieces of artillery in position, in addition to repair-work. Although 850 men of the garrison had been killed or wounded since the commencement of the siege, there still remained 2,600 resolute veterans, ready to fight to the last. The allies battering-train numbered 117 pieces; however, Napier reported that "...by characteristic official negligence, this enormous armament brought with them only sufficient shot and shell for one day's consumption."

James Grant also wrote, about a hundred years ago, a highly detailed account of the storming attempts:

On the 24th of August, Lord Wellington began two batteries on the heights above San Bartolome, to breach the faces of the horn-work of San Juan and the end of the lofty curtain, which rose in gradation one above another, in the same line of shot; and two days later fifty-seven pieces of cannon opened with a general salvo, or volley, given in concert, and continued to fire with wondrous din and rapidity till evening.

The firing in time destroyed the revetment of the demi-bastion of San Juan, and nearly ruined the towers at the old breach, together with the wall connecting them, and on the 27th, a hundred soldiers in boats captured the islet of Santa Clara, with the loss of twenty-eight of their number. By the 29th it was found that the general firing had damaged the works of the city and castle alike, that the guns in both were nearly silenced; and as sixty-three pieces, of which twenty-nine threw shells or spherical case-shot, were now in play against them, the superiority of our cannonade was established.

About this time Captain Alexander Macdonald, of the Artillery, by voluntarily wading across the Urumea in the night, discovered that river to be fordable. He passed, daringly, close under the works to the breach, and returned. Hence, to save our guns from being spiked, in case the enemy made a sortie, the vents of those in the Chofre batteries were secured at night by iron plates and chains.

A false attack was ordered in the night, to make the enemy spring their mines, a most desperate service, undertaken by Lieutenant Macadam. The order was so suddenly issued that neither volunteers were asked nor rewards offered for it; but instantly some noble men of the Scots Royals leaped forth to court that which seemed instant death. With a rapid pace, and with loud shouts, in extended line, and firing rapidly, they rushed towards the breach, where the whole party perished save their leader, who was twice wounded, and survived to attain high rank in the service.

By the 30th the sea-front of the place was laid open, from the demi-bastion of San Juan to the most distant of the old breaches, a space of 500 feet; while another battery demolished the face of the San Juan, and the high curtain already mentioned as being above it. The whole of that quarter was now literally in ruins, for the San Bartolome batteries had broken the demi-bastion of the horn-work and swept away all the palisades. So Lord Wellington now resolved to order an assault for the next day at eleven o'clock, when the ebb-tide would leave full space between the horn-work and the water.

The French state of defence was still strong. Beyond the ruined sea-flank they had a counter-wall, lying parallel with the breach, loopholed for musketry and flanked by traverses. In front of this wall, and about the middle of the great breach, stood the tower of Las Hornos, beneath which was a secret mine, charged with twelve hundredweight of gunpowder. The streets were all trenched, and furnished with barricades or traverses, and in some places with mines. To support this system of defence, a sixteen-pounder at St. Elmo flanked the left of the breaches on the river face; a twelve and eighteen-pounder in the casemates of the cavalier swept the land face of San Juan; and many guns from other points could play on the advancing column. The governor and his garrison were full of courage and resolution.

Wellington now demanded fifty volunteers from fifteen different regiments of the 1st, 4th and light divisions, "men who could show other troops how to mount a breach," and instantly 750 gallant fellows responded to the appeal. The 5th division was brought to the trenches; and General Bradford, having offered the service of his Portuguese brigade, had a discretionary power to ford the Urumea and assail the farthest breach.

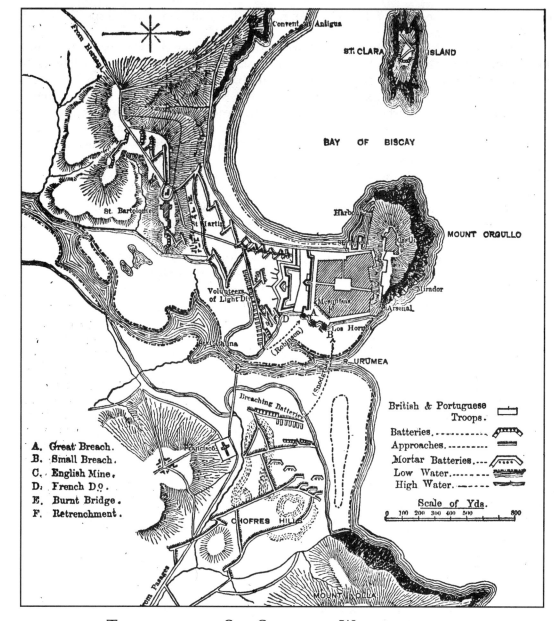

A. Great Breach.
B. Small Breach.
C. English Mine.
D. French D.o.
E. Burnt Bridge.
F. Retrenchment.

British & Portuguese Troops.
Batteries.
Approaches.
Mortar Batteries.
Low Water.
High Water.

Scale of Yds.
0   100   200   300   400   500   800

THE ASSAULT ON SAN SEBASTIAN. WEST IS THE TOP OF THE MAP.

Arthur Griffiths gives another account of this:

Wellington was prepared to take the risk while sparing no effort to succeed. His eagerness in this respect led him to do a grave injustice to the brave but unfortunate men who had been beaten back in the first attack. He would not again trust to the 5th Division alone, but he called for volunteers from the 1st, 4th and Light, asking for "men who could show others how to mount a breach"; and 750 under intrepid officers at once responded to the appeal. But the commander of the 5th Division, Sir James Leith, who had general charge of the assault, would not suffer his own men to be put aside by the volunteers, and gave the main attack to one of his own brigades. Some of the volunteers he distributed along the line of the trenches to keep down the enemy's fire, the rest were in reserve with Leith's second brigade, held to support the attacking columns.

JAMES GRANT:

Robinson's brigade was to assault in two columns, one at the old breach between the towers, the other at San Juan and the end of the high curtain. General Graham was to overlook the operations; and so the night of the 30th of August, the last that many were to spend on earth, closed over San Sebastian.

Heavily and loweringly the dawn of the 31st came in. A dense fog veiled every object, the little bay of San Sebastian, its shattered walls, the bed of the Urumea, and the sea to which it flows, till eight o'clock, when it began to disperse, and then the batteries opened, and again the boom of shot and the crash of exploding shells were heard; while Robinson's brigade, in light marching order, defiled out of the trenches, and made a rush at the breaches. Prior to this movement, twelve gallant men, under a heroic sergeant whose name neither despatch nor history has recorded, rushing to the front in advance of all, leaped on the covered way, to cut the saucisse of the enemy's mines. The latter were fired prematurely. The sergeant and those who followed him perished; while, with a mighty crash, the high sea-wall split, rose in the air, and with a thundering sound, fell upon the advancing column like an avalanche of masonry.

Only forty men were destroyed, the rush was scarcely checked, and over the fallen masses of the shattered wall, through dust and smoke, on went the forlorn hope. Grape, shells, and musketry were raining on them.

The ebbing tide had left a broad strand; the sun had dried the sea-weedy rocks, yet they still broke the ranks of the stormers, and the main breach was two hundred yards form them; and crowding to the river face, the French poured their musketry into the flank of the second column as it rushed along a few yards below them; while the batteries on Monte Orgullo and the St. Elmo sent showers of shot and shells upon them, the two pieces of the cavalier swept the breach at the San Juan, and a four-pounder in the horn-work poured grape shot into their rear.

Up, up, they scrambled into the breach, firing over each others' heads, and striding over the fast-falling wounded and dead, while the French musketry volleyed with deadly accuracy from the loopholed wall beyond. "In vain, the following multitude, covering the ascent, sought an entrance at every part; to advance was impossible, and the mass slowly sank downwards, yet remained stubborn and immovable on the lower part. There they were covered from the musketry in front; yet from several isolated points, especially the tower of Las Hornos, under which the great mine was placed, the French still struck them with small-arms, and the artillery from Monte Orgullo poured shell and grape without intermission." (Napier)

At the San Juan, the aspect of affairs was still worse. To reach the summit of the lofty curtain seemed practicable; and the effort to force a way there being constant and strenuous, the slaughter was proportionate, for the flanking traverse was manned by French grenadiers, who disdained to yield; the sixteen and eighteen-pounders swept the front face, and the musketry from the horn-work that of the river.

"The Royal Scots," states the Record of that Regiment, "commanded by Lieutenant-Colonel Barns, were directed to make their attack on the left of the second breach, and were supported by the 38th Regiment. The assault was made with great gallantry, some of the traverses of the semi-bastion were carried by the leading companies; but were retaken by the enemy. Nothing could exceed the bravery and steadiness of the troops employed at this point; and the enemy, observing the whole division in motion, sprung a mine on the top of the curtain; but the explosion was premature, and only a few of the leading men of the Royal Scots suffered from it. Yet, undismayed by the bursting mine and fierce opposition of the enemy, the Royal Scots pressed forward upon their adversaries and carried the coverlain."

During these assaults the British batteries kept up a constant counter-fire; and the reserves of the 5th division fed the attack until the left wing of the 9th Regiment only remained in the trenches. The 750 volunteers from the different corps, who had been with difficulty restrained in the parallel, were now vociferously demanding "why they had been brought there if they were not to lead the assault." And now these resolute, reckless, and gallant spirits, whose presence had so mortified General Leith, burst loose, officers and men. They swept like a whirlwind into the breaches; they swarmed up over the heaps of fallen masonry, the dead and the wounded: but on the crest the stream of fire and lead struck them down; rank after rank went up to totter and sink, and when the smoke melted into thin air, all were dead. In the works of General Graham, "no man outlived the attempt to gain the ridge."

Standing on the nearest of the Chofre batteries, he beheld this frightful destruction with a stern resolution to win at any cost. He, "the hero of Barossa," was a man to have put himself at the head of the last company, and died there sword in hand, rather than survive defeat.

Arthur Griffiths describes Graham's drastic course of action to break the deadlock:

In this desperate situation Sir Thomas Graham, having consulted with the chief of the artillery, determined to concentrate the fire of all our available guns upon the high curtain or rampart above the breached bastion. Forty-seven guns thus brought to bear cleared away the defenders; they did far more, for the gunners knew the exact range, and pitched their shell in the magazines, which speedily took light; explosion followed explosion, and a general conflagration broke out. Hundreds of the French defenders were destroyed.

JAMES GRANT:

When this unexpected storm of bullets first swept over the heads of our soldiers, some of the less experienced in war began to shout, "The batteries are firing on us; they are firing on the stormers!" But the veterans of the famous light division knew better, and, amid the very heat of this cannonade, had effected a secure lodgement amid the ruins of some houses within the rampart, and on the right flank of the great breach.

For half-an-hour the iron tempest rained on the summit of the shattered works, and on the houses in their rear, when a roar of French musketry again broke forth, showing that the defenders were unsubdued. About this time, the 13th Portuguese Regiment, under Major Snodgrass, and a detachment of the 24th, or Warwickshire Regiment, led by Colonel Macbean, entered the Urumea from the Chofres. The ford was deep, as the water rose so high that the men had to keep their cartridge-boxes out of it. When they were in the middle of the stream, which is there two hundred yards wide, a shower of grape from above made terrible havoc among them; many were killed, and more sank wounded, to drown miserably. But closing in, shoulder to shoulder, the survivors moved steadily and sternly on.

A second discharge swept through them with awful effect from front to rear; yet still they moved on, under a combined fire of cannon and musketry, booming, roaring, and flashing all at once from the castle, St. Elmo, and the Mirador. On landing, the Portuguese rushed against the third breach, while the party of the 24th reinforced those to whom the great breach was assigned.

Again the fighting grew desperate at all the points of attack; higher grew the heaps of slain, and bullets overtook the wounded as they crawled away for shelter. Once again the wedged mass of stormers, their eyes flashing, their faces pale with fury, their mouths black with the powder of bitten cartridges, sank to the foot of the ruins they were unable to capture. The living sought shelter from the leaden rain as best they could; and the dead and wounded lay so thickly together "that it could hardly be judged whether the hurt or unhurt were most numerous."

The tide was rising fast; the reserves were all engaged, and now no greater effort of strength or valour could be expected from our soldiers, whom fierce resistance had driven to the verge of madness. Yet fortune favoured them. A vast number of powder-barrels, live shells, and other combustible materials, accumulated in rear of one of the traverses, caught fire. A sheet of flame wrapped the whole of the lofty stone curtain; a succession of crashing explosions followed, and more than three hundred French grenadiers were destroyed, amid suffocating eddies of smoke. This decided the fate of San Sebastian.

Our stormers burst in at the first traverse; the French, bewildered by the terrible catastrophe, gave way for a moment, but only to rally again; and, with bayonet and butt-end, a close and desperate struggle ensued on the summit of the curtain. The tricolour on the cavalier was torn down by Lieutenant Richard Gethius, of the 11th Regiment; and, as the stormers increased in number every moment, the foe was driven back; the horn-work, the land front beneath the curtain, and the loopholed wall that faced the greater breach were all abandoned; and then the light division, from the French left, burst into the streets with furious cheers. The 13th Portuguese, at the small breach, also found entrance and mixed with them.

For five consecutive hours had this deadly work lasted about the shot-riven walls, yet the undaunted French commandant, even while the victors were pouring through the streets, still fought at his barricades, although his garrison was so reduced that even to retreat in rear of the line of defence separating the town from Monte Orgullo was difficult. It was thought that the latter might have been carried at once, had an officer of sufficient rank been at hand to direct the troops; but already three generals, Leith, Oswald, and Robinson, had fallen wounded in the trenches; Sir Richard Fletcher was killed, and Colonel Burgoyne, next in command of the Engineers, was wounded. The battalion officers were embarrassed for want of orders; and as a thunder-storm burst from the mountains with singular fury just as the place was carried, it added to the confusion of the time, and the opportunity was lost.

Fortified places are seldom carried by assault without the commission of great irregularities on the part of the victors; but on this occasion the British troops went beyond all that had occurred at Ciudad Rodrigo and Badajoz. Irritated by the fatigue and sufferings they had undergone for nearly six weeks, goaded by the memory of a former repulse, and burning for revenge, they poured, an armed and infuriated tide, through the streets. Wine and spirits were found in abundance. Some houses caught fire; the flames spread from street to street, till the whole town became involved in one general conflagration, and amid the most dreadful scenes occurred, for many while overcome by their own intemperance were burned to death. The shrieks of women, the wild shout of the drunkard, execrations in several languages, the groans of the wounded, and the prayers of the helpless, mingled with the crash of falling walls and the roar of flames.

A British staff-officer, being mistaken for a provost-marshal, narrowly escaped a volley of musketry; and a Portuguese adjutant, who, like him, had been seeking to repress the fury of the common rank and file, was butchered in the market-place, not suddenly, but deliberately. Yet amid all this outrages, there were not wanting traits of nobleness.

In the afternoon of that eventful day, two officers went to the great breach, to search among the dead who lay there so thick for the body of a missing friend. While employed in this melancholy task, a musket-ball suddenly whistled between their heads, and on looking round they saw a wounded Frenchman, with his musket just discharged. Exasperated by an attack so unprovoked, one of them called to a British soldier, and said, "Shoot that scoundrel."

The man addressed went up to the Frenchman, who, incapable of standing, reclined among the stones; he levelled his musket, but instantly "recovered" it, and, turning to the officer, said:

"Lord, sir, I can't shot a poor devil like that."

"The soldier," adds Lord Londonderry, "suffered nothing for his humanity, and the wounded Frenchman was kindly removed to the hospital."

The carnage in the breaches was appalling. Half of the volunteers perished, and the whole loss, since the renewal of the siege, exceeded 2,500 men and officers. "Among the last," says Napier, "may be mentioned Lieutenant John O'Connell, of the 43rd, in blood nearly related to the Agitator. He was gentle, amiable, and modest, and brave as man could be; and having been in several storming parties, here again sought in such dangerous service the promotion he had earned before without receiving, he found death."

During this siege, Thierry records that several of our pieces were discharged as many as nine thousand times, without experiencing any material damage. Their fire was so accurate that they threw shrapnel shells over the heads of the stormers, to sweep the summit of the great breach, and it was one of those shells which fired the combustibles in rear of the traverse, so fatally for the garrison.

Monte Orgullo was now to be attacked. It is steep and difficult of ascent, and just below the castle were four batteries, connected with masonry, thrown across its face; and from their extremities were ramps connected by redans, which led to the fortified convent of Santa Teresa. Towards the harbour and behind the mountain were sea-batteries; and had fresh troops been there, the war-worn besiegers would have found the capture difficult; but the garrison was greatly reduced. The engineers were all killed, the governor was wounded, as were 500 of his men. He had 1,300 fit for duty, with 500 prisoners to guard. He had only ten guns fit for service, and three of these faced the sea. There was little water in the place, and his soldiers had to lie on the naked rocks, exposed to our fire.

On the day after the assault, Lord Wellington arrived; and on the 3rd of September the governor was summoned. His resolution was yet unshaken, "and the vertical fire was continued day and night, the British prisoners suffering as well as the enemy; for the officer in the castle, irritated by the misery of the garrison, cruelly refused to let the unfortunate captives make trenches to cover themselves."

The French afterwards complained that their wounded and sick, placed in an empty magazine, on which a black flag was hoisted, were fired upon, although the British prisoners in their scarlet uniforms, were posted around it, to aid the claims of humanity.

New breaching batteries were commenced, and armed with guns, which at first were dragged through the Urumea in the night. Ammunition was scarce with the besieged, and contrary to Wellington's expectation, "the horrible vertical fire" subdued their energy; yet they still continued to resist till the 8th of September, when fifty-nine heavy pieces of cannon opened on them all at once, from the isle of Santa Clara, the isthmus, the horn-work, and the Chofres. In two hours the Mirador and the Queen's Battery were destroyed, the French fire extinguished, the whole hill furrowed up, and the little castle, crowded as it was with men, literally overlaid by a storm of descending shells; and now the governor surrendered.

With all the honours of war, his drums beating and colours flying, saluted by the British troops, this gallant French officer marched from the place he had defended so well, at the head of a garrison now reduced to one-third its original number; and thus, after sixty-three days of open trenches, terminated the siege of San Sebastian.

With reference to the survivors of the escalade, the colonel of the 52nd directed that "officers commanding companies will desire each non-commissioned officer and private of the storming party to wear a mark of distinction, the pattern of which may be seen at the adjutant's tent; and to acquaint them that it is the intention of the officers to give them a badge of merit, and to communicate this important service, lately performed, to the magistrates of their respective parishes."

BRITISH LOSSES AT THE STORM, AUGUST 31, 1813

5th Division	
Hay's Brigade	
3/1st Foot	194
1/9th Foot	166
1/38th Foot	135
Robinson's Brigade	
1/4th Foot	281
2/47th Foot	232
2/59th Foot	352
2 companies, Brunswick-Oels	15
Spry's Portuguese Brigade	
3rd Line	128
15th Line	197
8th Cacadores	83
Total 5th Division	1,783
1st Division Volunteers	
Guard's Brigade	122
K.G.L. Brigade	53
4th Division Volunteers	
Ross's Brigade	28
Anson's Brigade	28
Stubb's Portuguese	32
Light Division Volunteers	
Kempt's Brigade	29
Skerrett's Brigade	20
Cacadores	7
Bradford's Portuguese	
13th Line	73
24th Line	84
5th Cacadores	29
General staff	3
Artillery	16
Engineers & Sappers	20
General Total	2,376

Of whom British 1,696 and Portuguese 577. Killed 856, Wounded 1,416, Missing 44, a terrible proportion of killed to wounded.

STRENGTH OF THE GARRISON, AUGUST 15

Etat-Major	10
1st Line	201
22nd Line	404
34th Line	309
62nd Line	608
119th Line	178
Chasseurs des Montagnes	204
details of Various regiments	220
Gendarmes	8
Marines	21
Spanish Troops	18
Artillery	153
Engineers & Sappers	195
Non-combatant services	74
Total	2,698

BRITISH BATTLE HONOURS FOR THE STORMING OF SAN SEBASTIAN.
1st (Royal Scots) Regt. of Foot
4th (King's Own) Regt. of Foot
9th (East Norfolk) Regt. of Foot
59th (2nd Nottinghamshire) Regt. of Foot
38th (1st Staffordshire) Regt. of Foot
47th (Lancashire) Regt. of Foot

Rey held out for many days in the citadel while the town burned below; he was known to be employing tactics considered unacceptable for siege warfare. Wellington wrote of this to Graham on 5 September:

"I observe...that prisoners are kept in the yard of the magazine 'sans blindages' (without protection), and many have been killed and wounded by the fire directed against that building. I do not know that I have ever heard of such conduct, and the pretension founded upon it, viz., that we should not direct our fire against the place is too ridiculous.

I request you to send in to General Rey a protest against his keeping prisoners in the yard of this magazine 'sans blindages' and likewise against him making them work under fire."

EXPLORATION OF SAN SEBASTIAN AND ITS CASTLE.

Today, San Sebastian is a pleasant seaside town fronted by a picturesque bay; it is a fascinating mixture of narrow old streets and modern boulevards with smart shops and hotels. Most interesting is the Old Town below the castle, rebuilt after the siege, a maze of alleys and courts abounding in colourful bars and restaurants. In one street there are imposing houses each bearing an emblem denoting it to be the headquarters of a Dining Society, where exclusively male members prepare gourmet meals for leisurely ceremonious consumption; we were told that none of them had ever been known to help with the cooking at home!

It is an arduous climb to the very top of the castle on the summit of Mont Orgull, but the author has done it at least three times with varied groups of battlefield-walking comrades. On a well-remembered occasion, events of 1813 were described by an imperturbable David Chandler to a party vainly seeking shelter from a biting wind on the very top of Mont Orgull. On this occasion the small museum below was open, and we thawed-out while gazing at its interesting exhibits.

The effort is well worthwhile if only to see the panoramic view across the beautiful bay, but more important, because looking down from the lofty height it is easy to visualize the assault of 31 August 1813, that same day on which Soult chose to make his abortive attacks across the River Bidassoa, when Captain Dan Cadoux immortalised himself on the bridge at Vera. It is clear that the only feasible assault approach was over the low sandy isthmus bordering the front of the fortified town which was small and compact then, about 400 yards square, and some 600 yards from the mainland on a promontory bordered by the River Urumea on the east and a land-locked bay on its other sides; nestling around the foot of the lofty Monte Orgull, it had about 10,000 inhabitants. In 1813 it was encircled by a high wall backed by new earthworks, part being an older massive wall rising sheer from the river, which was fordable at low tide; above the town the fortified rocky mountain was crowned by an old castle. There are no traces of the walls today, but otherwise this part of the town is much the same; the castle is in good condition and houses an interesting military museum that was closed for repair on this occasion, but had been visited in the past when with the Military Historical Society party. From the castle high on the mountain the limits of the old town can be detected, having been rebuilt on the same site after being burned down in 1813; different architecture and roof-styles reveal where the old town ends and new town begins. The local museum in the old monastery of St. Elmo contains a large model of the town in the 18th century which confirms this.

At the time of the Battle of Vera, Wellington had his Headquarters at Lesaca, a few miles south and deeper into Spain. On two previous occasions with David Chandler and the Military Historical Society, we visited another of the Duke's H.Q.'s at Frenada on the Portuguese Frontier, where the inhabitants of the house, well aware of its historical significance, joyfully showed us over it, produced wine and encouraged uninhibited Anglo-Portuguese fraternisation. With this in mind optimistically we drove to Lesaca, where nothing indicated that the Duke had even been there, although we did find the squat tower pictured in Jac Weller's wonderful book *Wellington in the Peninsular*.

WARGAMING ASPECTS.

As has already been discussed in these pages, sieges do not make easy wargaming, whether in their execution or in the necessary construction of the besieged site - although both of these aspects present fascinating features, particularly to the sole wargamer aided by imagination and time. The equipment such as artillery is also diverse - it is recorded that at this particular siege the allies employed iron 24pdrs; 8inch brass howitzers; 68pdr iron carronades; iron 10inch mortars; 24pdrs landed from ships of war; and 18pdrs dragged with the army throughout the Peninsular!

THE DUKE OF WELLINGTON'S HEADQUARTERS IN THE PYRENEES IN 1814 WAS THIS CASTLE IN LESACA. THIS IS HOW IT APPEARS TODAY.

Nevertheless, the siege and taking of San Sebastian was a short sharp affair, well documented, and with relatively understandable methods of assault. Having said this, one has to simulate explosive mines in the breaches, fused shells rolling down on the attackers as they climbed out of the 20 feet deep ditch, and a unique occurrence which, to reproduce on the wargames table, would require specific rules and a lot of tolerance. This is, of course, Graham's ploy on seeing his men held-up by artillery and musketry fire from the walls, of having his own artillery re-open fire on those walls, aiming over the heads of his stormers; firing from about 1.200 yards distance, so accurate were the gun-crews that their missiles cleared the enemy from the walls without harming their own men a few feet below!

THE ACTIONS AT VERA ON 1 SEPTEMBER AND 7 OCTOBER AND THE CROSSING OF THE BIDASOA ON 7 OCTOBER 1813.

Serving in the Light Division at the time, Captain Cooke of the 43rd Regiment (Kempt's Brigade) described the three regiments of the Light Division in the Peninsular:

The 43rd were a gay set, the dandies of the army, the great encouragers of dramatic performances, dinner-parties, and balls, of which their headquarters was the pivot. The 52nd were highly gentlemenly men, of a steady aspect; they mixed little with other corps. But attended the theatricals of the 43rd with circumspect good humour and now and then relaxed but were soon again the 52nd. The Rifle Corps were skirmishers in every sense of the word, a sort of wild sportsmen, and up to every description of fun and good humour; nought came amiss; the very trees responded to their merriment, and scraps of their sarcastic rhymes passed current through all the camps and bivouacs.

Soult's second thrust was to despatch four divisions under Clausel to the gorge of the Bidassoa near Vera, where the Light Division had been stationed on the heights of Santa Barbara just to the south in case of such an eventuality. Increasingly as we traversed Peninsular War fields in Spain and Portugal, admiration for the famed Light Division became greater, so this is unashamedly a paean of praise for them, for those Light Bob's whose exploits on the Rhunes in the Battle of the Nivelle, described elsewhere in these pages, together with their almost legendary combats at Vera on 1st September and 7th October 1813 set a wargamer's blood tingling with excitement. Particularly the 95th Rifles, adorned with such immortal characters as riflemen Costello, Harris and Surtees, officers like Johnny Kincaid, Simmons and Harry Smith - men who gloried in the old Peninsular toast:

"Hurrah for the First in the Field and the Last out of it, the bloody fighting 95th!"

For truly, as Harry Smith wrote:

"The Light Division Gentlemen were proper saucy fellows!"

The cream of the Peninsular army was the Light Division, with their essential role of countering the French tirailleurs who skirmished ahead of their columns. Thoroughly trained, the British light infantry were able to operate in close order or as individuals in a manner far superior to the average French light infantryman, who frequently was only another conscript in a different uniform stuck out in front of the columns. Impressed by the skirmishing tactics of the Colonists during the American Revolution, Sir John Moore had invented completely new British infantry tactics when he created the Light Division at Shorncliffe, where Moore applied his theory that line and its fire-power, with the two-rank formation allowing a much wider musketry front with the same number of troops, was the most effective defence against column attack. Realising the need to break up French attacks before they could be pushed home, Moore armed his Light Division with rifles, which doubled the distance and accuracy of their fire-power. This weapon, coupled with first-class training in skirmishing, rapid movement and independent action made the riflemen of the Light Division the best infantry in the world. At this time the Light Division commanded by Major General C. Alten, was formed of:

"A" Brigade (Kempt's)
1st Bn. 43rd Foot
1/95th Foot
17th Portuguese Line Regiment.

"B" Brigade (Colborne's)
1st Bn. 52nd Foot
2nd Bn. 95th Rifles
1st and 3rd Portuguese Cacadores

The 95th and the Cacadores of the Light Division were all armed with the Baker Rifle which could be loaded and fired, from a lying down position if necessary, in 30 seconds but under battlefield conditions once per minute with an average misfire of one in every thirteen rounds.

The French attacks at Vera failed and Soult ordered Clausel to retire under cover of darkness and a fierce rainstorm, which caused the river to rise until there was six feet of water over the fords used by the French invaders earlier in the day. Trapped on the south bank was General Vandermaesen with his division and a brigade each from those of Taupin and Darmagnac - more than 10,000 men who would be overwhelmed if they did not re-cross before daybreak. Vandermaesen led them upstream to force a crossing of the bridge at Vera, and marched into one of those imperishable incidents that colour British military history.

The Battle of Vera took place on 7 October, but it had an overture on 1 September, after Soult had sent a strong force across the Bidasoa on 31 August which failed to achieve much and was forced to withdraw. During that day a severe storm caused the river suddenly to rise so that Vandermaesen's Division of Clausel's Corps found their sole crossing-place to be the bridge at Vera. George Simmons opens the story:

"Toward night it began to thunder and lighten (sic) horribly and poured with torrents of rain. I was on piquet and observed Johnny (the French) by the lightning's glare retracing his steps back on this horrid night. At 2 a.m. Johnny attacked a bridge where we had a piquet of Riflemen - two companies - who fought so handsomely that, with this small number, they checked them for an hour. A Captain of ours, Dan Cadoux, who stood upon the bridge rallying his men around him received several musket balls in his breast and fell like a soldier. Five officers of ours were wounded, and Lieutenant Llewellyn had his jaw shattered - all fought most heroically."

Harry Smith, who played a leading role in this affair, tells what subsequently occurred:

When the enemy put back our picquets in the morning, it was evidently their intention to possess themselves of the bridge, which was curiously placed as regard our line of picquets. Thus—

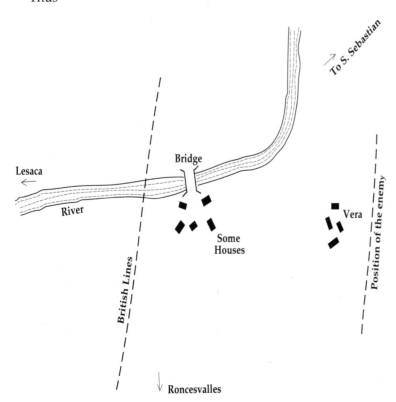

We did not occupy Vera, but withdrew on our own side of it, and I saw the enemy preparing to carry the houses near the bridge in the occupation of the 2nd Battalion Rifle Brigade. I said, "General Skerrett, unless we send down the 52nd Regiment in support, the enemy will drive back the Riflemen. They cannot hold those houses against the numbers prepared to attack. Our men will fight like devils expecting to be supported, and their loss, when driven out, will be very severe." He laughed (we were standing under a heavy fire exposed) and said, "Oh, is that your opinion?" I said—most impertinently, I admit— "And it will be yours in five minutes," for I was by no

269

means prepared to see the faith in support, which so many fights had established, destroyed, and our gallant fellows knocked over by a stupidity heretofore not exemplified. We had scarcely time to discuss the matter when down came a thundering French column with swarms of sharpshooters, and, as I predicted, drove our people out of the houses with one fell swoop, while my General would move nothing on their flank or rear to aid them. We lost many men and some officers, and the enemy possessed the houses, and consequently, for the moment, possessed the passage of the bridge. From its situation, however, it was impossible they could maintain it, unless they put us farther back by a renewed attack on our elevated position. So I said, "You see now what you have permitted, General, as we must retake these houses, which we ought never to have lost." He quietly said, "I believe you are right." I could stand this no longer, and I galloped up to Colonel Colborne, in command of that beautiful 52nd Regiment, now Lord Seaton, who was as angry as he soon saw I was. "Oh, sir, it is melancholy to see this. General Skerrett will do nothing; we must retake those houses. I told him what would happen." "I am glad of it, for I was angry with you." In two seconds we retook the houses, for the enemy, seeing our determination to hold them, was aware the nature of the ground would not enable him to do so unless he occupied the position we intended to defend, and his effort was as much as not to see whether we were in earnest, or whether, when attacked in force, we should retire. The houses were retaken, as I said, and the firing ceased the whole afternoon.

The evening came on very wet. We knew that the enemy had crossed the Bidassoa [31 Aug.], and that his retreat would be impossible from the swollen state of the river. We knew pretty well the Duke would shove him into the river if he could; this very bridge, therefore, was of the utmost importance, and no exertion should have been spared on our part so to occupy it after dark as to prevent the passage being seized. The rain was falling in torrents. I proposed that the whole of the 2nd Battalion Rifle Brigade should be posted in the houses, the bridge should be barricaded, and the 52nd Regiment should be close at hand in support. Skerrett positively laughed outright, ordered the whole Battalion into our position, but said, "You may leave a picquet of one officer and thirty men at the bridge." He was in the house on the heights he had previously occupied. I had a little memorandum-book in my pocket; I took it out for the first time in my life to note my General's orders. I read what he said, asking if that was his order. He said, "Yes, I have already told you so." I said most wickedly, "We shall repent this before daylight." He was callous to anything. I galloped down to the houses, ordered the Battalion to retire, and told my brother Tom, the Adjutant, to call to me a picquet of an officer and thirty men for the bridge. Every officer and soldier thought I was mad. Tom said, "Cadoux's company is for picquet." Up rode poor Cadoux, a noble soldier, who could scarcely believe what I said, but began to abuse me for not supporting them in the morning. I said, "Scold away, all true; but no fault of mine. But come, no time for jaw, the picquet!" Cadoux, noble fellow, says, "My company is so reduced this morning, I will stay with it if I may. There are about fifty men." I gladly consented, for I had great faith in Cadoux's ability and watchfulness, and I told him he might rest assured he would be attacked an hour or two before daylight. He said, "Most certainly I shall, and I will now strengthen myself, and block up the bridge as well as I can, and I will, if possible, hold the bridge until supported; so, when the attack commences, instantly send the whole Battalion to me, and, please God, I will keep the bridge." It was then dark, and I rode as fast as I could to tell Colborne, in whom we had all complete faith and confidence. He was astonished, and read my memorandum. We agreed that, so soon as the attack commenced, his Battalion should move down the heights on the flank of the 2nd Battalion Rifle Brigade, which would rush to support Cadoux, and thus we parted, I was as sulky as my hot nature would admit, knowing some disaster would befall my dear old Brigade heretofore so judiciously handled.

In the course of the night, as we were lying before the fire, I far from asleep, General Skerrett received a communication from General Aken to the purport "that the enemy were retiring over the swollen river; it was, therefore, to be apprehended he would before daylight endeavour to possess himself of the bridge; that every precaution must be taken to prevent him." I, now being reinforced in opinion, said, "Now, General, let me do so." As he was still as obstinate as ever, we were discussing the matter (I fear as far as I am concerned, very hotly) when the "En avant, en avant! L'Empereur recompensera le premier qu'avencera," was screeched into our very ears, and Cadoux's fire was as hot as ever fifty men's was on earth. "Now," says I, "General, who is right?" I knew what the troops would do. My only hope was that Cadoux could keep the bridge as he anticipated. The fire of the enemy was very severe, and the rushes of his columns most determined; still Cadoux's fire was from his post. Three successive times, with half his gallant band, did he charge and drive back the enemy over the bridge, the other half remaining in the houses as support. His hope and confidence in support and the importance of his position sustained him until a melancholy shot pierced his head, and he fell lifeless from his horse. A more gallant soul never left its mortal abode. His company at this critical moment were driven back; the French column and rear-guard crossed, and, by keeping near the bed of the river, succeeded in escaping, although the Riflemen were in support of poor Cadoux with as much rapidity as distance allowed, and daylight saw Colborne where he said he would be.

I was soon at the bridge. Such a scene of mortal strife from the fire of fifty men was never witnessed. The bridge was almost choked with the dead; the enemy's loss was enormous, and many of his men were drowned, and all his guns were left in the river a mile or two below the bridge. The number of dead was so great, the bodies were thrown into the rapid stream in the hope that the current would carry them, but many rocks impeded them, and when the river subsided, we had great cause to lament our precipitancy in hurling the bodies, for the stench soon after was awful. The Duke was awfully annoyed, as well he might be, but, as was his rule, never said anything when disaster could not be amended. I have never told my tale till now. Skerrett was a bilious fellow (a gallant Grenadier, I must readily avow), and I hope his annoyance so affected his liver it precipitated a step he had desired—as his father was just dead, and he was heir to an immense property—to retire home on sick leave. You may rely on it, I threw no impediment in his way, for when he was gone, Colonel Colborne was my Brigadier, whom we all regarded inferior to no one but the Duke. Many is the conversation he I have had over the lamentable affair which killed poor Cadoux. I really believe, had he survived, he would have held the bridge, although the enemy attacked it in desperation, and although each time the column was driven back, a few men in the dark succeeded in crossing, and these fellows, all practised soldiers, posted themselves under cover on the banks of the river below the bridge, and caused the loss our people sustained, that of noble Cadoux among the rest, with impunity. Cadoux's manner was effeminate, and, as a boy, I used to quiz him. He and I were, therefore, although not enemies, not friends, until the battle of Vittoria, when I saw him most conspicuous. He was ahead of me on his gallant war horse, which he took at Barossa with the holsters full of doubloons, as the story went. I was badly mounted that day, and my horse would not cross a brook which his was scrambling over. I leaped from my saddle over my horse's head (I was very active in those days), seized his horse by the tail, and I believe few, if any, were as soon in the middle of the Frenchmen's twelve guns as we were in support of the 7th Division. From that day we were comrades in every sense of the term, and I wept over his gallant remains with a bursting heart, as, with his Company who adored him, I consigned to the grave the last external appearance of Daniel Cadoux. His fame can never die.

An account derived from a colonel Thomas Smith, of whom no details are known, tells a rather different story, according to him -

Skerrett sent to desire Cadoux to evacuate his post. Cadoux refused, saying that he could hold it. At 2 a.m. the French made a rush, but Cadoux, by his fire from the bridge house, kept the head of the advancing column in check. Skerrett now peremptorily ordered Cadoux to leave the bridge-house. Cadoux could only comply, but remarked that "but few of his party would reach the camp." And as a matter of fact every officer present was either killed or wounded (Cadoux being killed), besides 11 sergeants and 48 rank and file out of a total strength of 100 men. Until the party left the bridge house, Cadoux had not lost a man except the double sentries on the bridge, who were killed in the rush made by the French. Accordingly, while Harry Smith in the text blames Skerrett for leaving Cadoux in an almost impossible position without support, Thomas Smith's charge against Skerrett is that he recalled Cadoux when he was well able to hold his own.

Bridges sometimes play vital roles in war. If the bridge at Arnhem, defended by Johnny Frost and his paratroopers in September 1944, was considered *A Bridge Too Far*, then the bridge at Vera 131 years earlier, held by Captain Dan Cadoux and a detachment of the 95th Rifles, may be said to have been *A Bridge Too Near*.

MAJOR ARTHUR GRIFFITHS:

We enter now upon the second great period in the Pyrenean conflict, when the initiative passed from Soult to Wellington, and the English general, at the head of the allied troops, invaded France.

All through September and into the first days of October the opposing armies remained inactive. Both sides were reorganising, replenishing, regaining strength. It was an especially trying time for Wellington and his troops, most of whom were still among the mountains, exposed to the wet and cold of an inclement autumn, while down below the fertile plains of France glittered in the warm sunshine, a veritable Promised Land. Duty was severe and unremitting, the outposts were ever on the alert, and a most stringent, irksome discipline was always maintained. The troops were discontented and lost heart; desertions became frequent; the provost-marshal was kept constantly busy; the halberds and the gallows found many victims. The forward move came not a day too soon, and was hailed with delight by all ranks as a prelude to brighter days.

All this time Wellington was being continually worried by the politicians to invade France; and so hasten the overthrow of Napoleon, now sorely pressed on every side. But the English general was reluctant to advance; the time was not yet ripe. Soult, undismayed, with abundant forces, stood based upon two fortresses, Bayonne and St. Jean Pied de Port, holding strongly-entrenched positions between them. Another French marshal, Suchet, was in Catalonia with an army of 60,000, ready to act against Wellington's flank and rear if he made any forward move. There was much to impose caution; yet the English general, yielding at length to the persistent pressure from home, resolved at least to place his left in a menacing attitude within the French territory. His right and centre, occupying the passes from Roncesvalles to Maya, were already well situated for attack, and it was on this side that Soult naturally looked for the next move. To deceive your enemy is one of the first and most important of all military maxims, and Wellington did everything to encourage Soult's idea, although he had no intention of so acting. He continually disquieted Soult with feints in this direction, while he was preparing serious operations in the other. His plan was to move by his left, to force the passage of the lower Bidassoa, to drive the French out of their entrenchments there, and at the same time move to the right, attack and, if possible, capture the Great Rhune mountain, a rocky peak rising some three thousand feet above the sea. This enterprise had been justly deemed by the historian to be "as daring and dangerous as any undertaken during the whole war." Let us now see how it was accomplished, briefly considering first the positions of the opposing armies.

Taking the French first form left to right, from Pied de Port to the sea: Foy was at that town and fortress, having, however, power to reinforce the right by the bridge of Cambo; D'Erlon stood next at Ainhoa, with an advance at Urdax and his right at the bridge of Amotz, on the Nivelle; then came Clausel, reaching as far as Serres on the same river, while redoubts covered his left front, and his right flank was behind the Great Rhune; and his right flank was behind the Great Rhune; finally, Reille occupied two long ridges that ran from the main chain of La Rhune towards the sea, one constituting the northern bank of the Bidassoa and rising sheer above the river's bed, the other in rear of it, and both crowned with many formidable earthworks. Behind all, about Ascain, was Villate in reserve and keeping up the connection between Reille and Clausel.

Wellington, on the other hand, kept his extreme right still at Roncesvalles, but with a preponderating weight towards his centre about Maya, where was Hill with the 2nd Division, having the 3rd a little to its left front. The 7th Division was at Echellar, with the 6th in support. More to the left was Giron's Spanish Division, backed up by the Light Division, and that again by the 4th, on the heights of Santa Barbara. Beyond Vera and on the farther or southern side of the Bidassoa were Longa's Spaniards, while the rest of the river was held by the 1st and 5th Divisions, with Freyre's Spaniards and two independent brigades, Aylmer's British and Wilson's Portuguese.

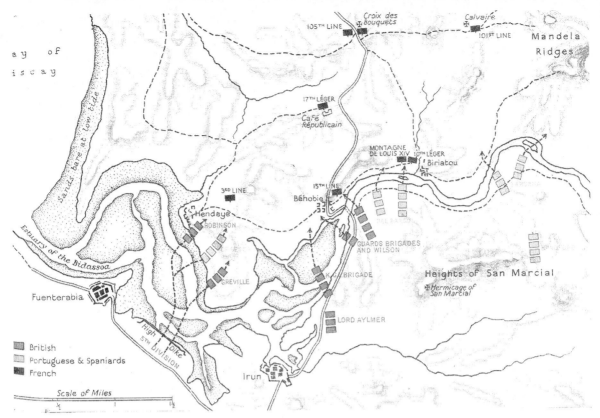

The following labels appear on the map:

Croix des Bouquets
105TH LINE
Calvaire
101ST LINE
Mandela Ridges
ay of iscay
17TH LÉGER
Café Republicain
MONTAGNE DE LOUIS XIV
10TH LÉGER
Biriatou
Sands bare at low tide
3RD LINE
15TH LINE
Béhobie
Estuary of the Bidassoa
Hendaye
ROBINSON
GUARDS BRIGADES AND WILSON
Heights of San Marcial
Hermitage of San Marcial
GREVILLE
K. BRIGADE
Fuenterabia
LORD AYLMER
British
Portuguese & Spaniards
French
High Dike 5TH DIVISION
Irun
Scale of Miles

THE PASSAGE OF THE BIDASOA

This was the plan of battle. Giron was to take the right of the Rhune mountain, with Alten next and in the centre, while Longa, crossing by the ford of Salinas and the bridge of Vera, was to assail the left. These troops numbered 20,000 in all, and they had much stiff climbing with hard fighting before them. Wellington held 24,000 more for a perhaps tougher job, the passage of the river lower down, where it was unbridged and where its few known fords were raked by artillery placed on purpose in entrenchments strongly garrisoned. But Wellington had heard of other fords, three of them secretly discovered near the mouth of the river; and it was on the existence of these that he based the main part of his hazardous operation. These last-named fords were only practicable at low water. The tide hereabouts rose and fell sixteen feet; but when quite out, it left broad sands firm for half a mile, good going, but in full view of the French positions on the northern shore. To cross so near the mouth of the river was deemed impossible, and the French were thus lulled into false security, never dreaming of attack on that side. They had in consequence established themselves most strongly about the centre, where the Bildox or Green Mountain overlooked the known fords. Soult was himself deceived. He had been warned by spies and deserters of the movement contemplated, yet he would not believe it, and his subordinate generals were as negligent as he was incredulous.

The 7th of October was the day fixed for the passage, and just before daylight a terrific storm burst over the French positions, which with tempest and darkness helped to cloak Wellington's movements. He had left all his tents standing, so as to further deceive the enemy; and his seven columns of attack, embracing a front of five miles, approached their several points of crossing without being observed. The 1st and 5th Divisions took the sands at the lowest fords, pointing the one towards the great redoubt of "Sans Culottes", to the right rear of the French position, the other towards Andaye, on the right flank. Both passed the river before a shot was fired; then the English signal went up, a rocket, fired from the steeple of Fuentarabia, the English guns began to play, and the remaining columns entered the water. Now the French awoke and gathered slowly, but all too tardily, to the defence. Their artillery in the nearest redoubts, the "Louis XIV," the "Cafe Republicain," and the "Croix de Bouquets," opened fire, and the struggle commenced.

273

The 1st British Division, with Halkett's Germans and Wilson's Portuguese, quickly drove the French out of the two first-named redoubts into the third, which was really the key to the position, and here the fight raged fiercely. Both sides brought up guns and troops in reinforcement, but the day was gained by Colonel Cameron at the head of the 9th Regiment, who charged with such astonishing courage and impetus that he carried all before him. Meanwhile Freyre with his Spaniards had gone against the Bildox and neighbouring heights, had gained them, and thus turned the French left; while the unopposed advance of the 5th Division towards the "Sans Culottes" equally compromised the French right. Reille, who was now in chief command, found himself beaten in the centre and menaced on both flanks. A precipitate retreat followed; only the arrival of Soult with some of Villatte's reserves saved the flight from degenerating into a disastrous rout.

On this lower side Wellington triumphed easily; his losses were trifling, his success extraordinary. Yet with less masterly skill in disposition, less unhesitating boldness in execution, this "stupendous operation," as Napier calls it, might have had a far different ending. Had Soult guessed Wellington's real design and prepared to meet it, he could have opposed him with 16,000 men securely posted and protected with artillery sufficient to resist, or greatly delay, the passage. Any prolonged check would have been fatal, "because in two hours the returning tide would have come with a swallowing flood upon the rear."

Yet again we have a description of a battle by one who played an active part in it - William Napier's regiment, the 43rd, were in Kempt's brigade of the Light Division., advancing with two battalions of Riflemen and the 17th Portuguese, up the Puerto de Vera. Here is his account of the action at Vera on 7 October 1813:

Before daybreak Giron descended with his Spaniards from the Ivantelly rocks, and Alten with the light division from Santa Barbara; the first to the gorge of the pass leading from Vera to Sarre, the last to the town of Vera, where he was joined by half of Longa's force.

One brigade, consisting of the 43rd, 17th Portuguese Regiment, and two battalions of British riflemen, were in columns on the right of Vera; the other brigade under Colonel Colborne, consisting of the 52nd, two battalions of Cacadores, and a third battalion of British riflemen, were on the left of that town: half of Longa's division was between these brigades, the other half, after crossing the ford of Salinas, drew up on Colborne's' left. The whole of the narrow vale of Vera was thus filled with troops ready to ascend the mountains; and General Cole, displaying his force to advantage on the heights of Santa Barbara, presented a formidable reserve.

Taupin's division guarded the enormous positions in front. His right was on the Bayonette, from whence a single slope descended to a small plain, two parts down the mountain. From this platform three distinct tongues shot into the valley below, each defended by an advanced post; the platform itself was secured by a star redoubt, behind which, about half-way up the single slope, there was a second retrenchment with abbatis. Another large redoubt and an unfinished breast-work on the superior crest completed the defence.

The Commissari, a continuation of the Bayonette towards the Great Rhune, had in front a profound gulf thickly wooded and filled with skirmishers; and between the gulf and another of the same nature, run the main road from Vera over the Puerto, piercing the centre of the French position. Ascending with short abrupt turns, this road was blocked at every uncovered point with abbatis and small retrenchments, each obstacle being commanded at half musket shot by small detachments placed on all the projecting parts overlooking the ascent. A regiment, entrenched above on the Puerto itself, connected the troops on the crest of the Bayonette and Commissari with those on a saddle-ridge, which joined those mountains with the Great Rhune, and was to be assailed by Giron.

Between Alten's right and Giron's left was an isolated advanced ridge called by the soldiers the Boar's back, the summit of which, half a mile long and rounded at each end, was occupied by four French companies. This huge cavalier, thrown as it were into the gulf on the allies' right of the road, covered the Puerto and the saddle-ridge; and though of mean height in comparison of the towering ranges behind, was yet so lofty, that a few warning-shots, fired from the summit

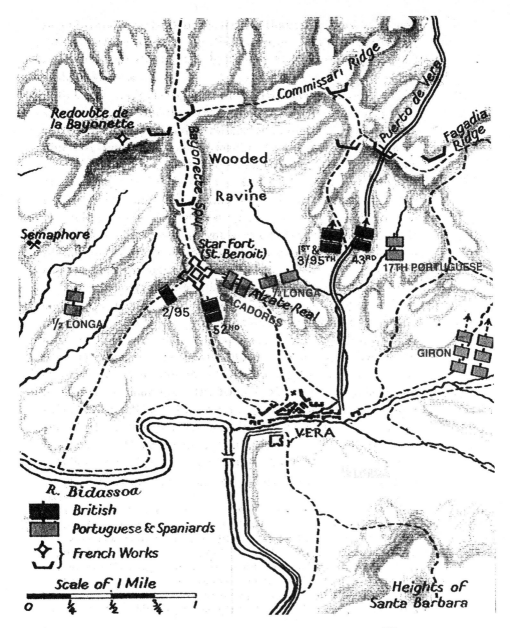

THE STORM OF THE FRENCH LINES ABOVE VERA

by the enemy, only reached the allies at it base with that slow singing sound which marks the dying force of a musket-ball. It was essential to take this Boar's back before the general attack commenced, and five companies of riflemen, supported by the 17th Portuguese, assailed it at the Vera end, while a battalion of Giron's Spaniards, preceded by a company of the 43rd, attacked it on the other. Meanwhile the French were in confusion.

Soon after seven o'clock a few cannon-shot from some mountain-guns, of which each side had a battery, were followed by the Spanish musketry on the right, and the next moment the Boar's back was simultaneously assailed at both ends. The riflemen on the Vera side ascended to a small pine-wood two-thirds up and there rested, but soon resumed their movement and with a scornful gallantry swept the French off the top, disdaining to use their rifles, save a few shots down the reverse side to show they were masters of the ridge. This had been the signal for the general attack. The Portuguese followed the victorious sharp-shooters; the 43rd, preceded by their own skirmishers and the remainder of the riflemen of the right wing, plunged into the rugged pass; Longa entered the gloomy wood of the ravine on their left; and beyond Longa, Colborne's brigade, moving by narrow paths, assailed the Bayonette. The 52nd took the middle tongue, the Cacadores and riflemen the two outermost, all bearing with a concentric movement against the star redoubt on the platform above. Longa's second brigade should have flanked the left of this attack with a wide skirting movement; but neither he nor his starved soldiers knew much of such warfare, and therefore quietly followed the riflemen in reserve.

Some of the best-known names in the famed Light Division took part in the action at Vera on 7 October 1813, Harry Smith, John Kincaid, George Simmons and Edward Costello among others. Captain John Kincaid wrote of October 7th in 'Adventures in the Rifle Brigade':

"...The 4th Division came up to support us, and we immediately marched down to the foot of the enemy's position, shook off our knapsacks before their faces, and went at them. The action commenced by five companies of our third battalion advancing, under Colonel Ross, to dislodge the enemy off a hill which they occupied in front of their entrenchments (Note: this was the Boar's or Hog's back) and never was there a movement more beautifully executed, for they walked quietly and steadily up, and swept them regularly off without firing a shot until the enemy had turned their back, when they served them out with a most destructive discharge. The movement excited the admiration of all who witnessed it, and added another to the already crowned wreath which adorned the name of that distinguished officer.
    At the first look of the enemy's position, it appeared as if our brigade had got the most difficult task to perform; but, as the capture of this hill showed us a way round the flank of their entrenchments, we carried one after the other, until we finally gained the summit, with very little loss. Our second brigade, however, were obliged to 'take the bull by the horns' on their side, and suffered more severely; but they rushed at everything with a determination that defied resistance, carrying redoubt after redoubt at the point of the bayonet, until they finally joined us on the summit of the mountain, with three hundred prisoners in their possession."

Harry Smith tells of a human incident that occurred at this stage of the battle, revealing that Juanita (the young 'Spanish Bride' he had met and married in Badajoz after the siege) was near at hand, as she was in almost every single military operation (including Waterloo) throughout their married life:

The 1st Cacadores, under poor Colonel Algeo, moved so as to threaten the enemy's left, and intercept or harass the retreat of the troops in the redoubt (which the noble 52nd were destined to carry at the point of the bayonet without one check), and the 2nd Battalion of the 95th and the 3rd Cacadores moved to the enemy's right of this redoubt for a similar purpose. This Battalion was fiercely opposed, but so soon as it succeeded in putting back the enemy, Colonel Colborne, at the head of the 52nd, and with an eye like a hawk's, saw the moment had arrived, and he gave the word "Forward." One rush put us in possession of the redoubt, and the Cacadores and 2nd Battalion 95th caused the enemy great loss in his retreat to the top of the pass where his great defence was made. The redoubt just carried was placed on the ridge of the ravine, and must be carried ere any advance could be made on the actual [position].
    In this attack poor Algeo was killed. He rode a chestnut horse marked precisely as my celebrated hunter and war-horse, "Old Chap," which I rode on that day. My wife was looking on the fight from the very cottage window we had occupied so long, barely without the range of musketry, and saw this horse gallop to the rear, dragging for some distance the body by the stirrup. The impulse of the moment caused her with one shriek to rush towards it, and so did anxiety and fright add to her speed that my servant for some time could not overtake her. The horse came on, when she soon recognized it was poor Algeo's charger, not mine, and fell senseless from emotion, but soon recovered, to express her gratitude to Almighty God.

NAPIER CONTINUES:
    Soon the open slopes were covered with men and with fire, and a confused sound of mingled shouts and musketry filled the deep hollows, from whence the white smoke came curling up from their gloomy recesses. The French, compared with their assailants, seemed few and

scattered on the mountain side, and Kempt's brigade fought its way without a check through all the retrenchments on the main pass, the skirmishers spreading wider as the depth of the ravines on each side lessened and melted into the high ridges. When half-way up an open platform gave a clear view over the Bayonette slopes, and all eyes were turned that way. Longa's right brigade, fighting in the gulf between, seemed labouring and over-matched; but beyond it, on the broad open space in front of the star-fort, Colborne's Cacadores and riflemen were seen to come out in small bodies from a forest which covered the three tongues of land up to the edge of the platform. Their fire was sharp, their pace rapid, and in a few moments they closed upon the redoubt in a mass; the 52nd were not then in sight, and the French, thinking from the dark clothing all were Portuguese, rushed in close order out of the entrenchment; they were numerous and very sudden, the rifle as a weapon is overmatched by the musket and bayonet, and this rough charge sent the scattered assailants back over the rocky edge of the descent. With shrill cries the French followed, but just then the 52nd soldiers appeared on the platform and raising their shout rushed forward; their red uniform and full career startled the hitherto adventurous French, they stopped short, wavered, turned, and fled to their entrenchment. The 52nd, following hard, entered the works with them, and then the riflemen and Cacadores, who had meanwhile rallied, passed it on both flanks; for a few moments everything was hidden by a dense volume of smoke, but again the British shout pealed high and the whole mass emerged on the other side, the French, now the fewer, flying, the others pursuing, until the second entrenchment, half-way up the parent slope, enabled the retreating troops to make another stand.

The exulting and approving cheers of Kempt's brigade then echoed along the mountain-side, and with renewed vigour the men continued to scale the craggy mountain, fighting their toilsome way to the top of the Puerto. Meanwhile Colborne, after having carried the second entrenchment above the star-fort, was brought to a check by the works on the crest of the mountain, from whence the French no only plied his troops with musketry at a great advantage but rolled huge stones down the steep. These works were well lined with men and strengthened by a large redoubt on the right, yet the defenders faltered, for their left flank was turned by Kempt, and the effects of Wellington's general combinations were then felt in another quarter.

Freyre's Spaniards, after carrying the Mandale mountain, had pushed to a road leading from the Bayonette to St. Jean de Luz, which was the line of retreat for Taupin's right wing. The Spaniards got there first, and Taupin, being thus cut off on that side, had to file his right under fire along the crest of the Bayonette to reach the Puerto de Vera road, where he joined his centre, but, so doing, lost a mountain-battery and three hundred men. These last were captured by Colborne in a remarkable manner. Accompanied by one of his staff and half-a-dozen riflemen, he crossed their march unexpectedly, and with his usual cool intrepidity ordered them to lay down their arms; an order which they, thinking themselves entirely cut off, obeyed.

Harry Smith, involved in the incident, tells what occurred:

we again advanced with a swarm of Riflemen in skirmishing order keeping up a murderous fire. Firing up a hill is far more destructive than firing down, as the balls in the latter case fly over. The 52nd Regiment, well in hand, with their bayonets sharp and glistening in the sun (for the afternoon was beautiful), were advanced under a most heavy fire, but, from the cause mentioned, it was not near so destructive as we expected. Still more to our astonishment, the enemy did not defend their well-constructed work as determinedly as we anticipated. Although they stood behind their parapets until we were in the act of leaping on them, they then gave way, and we were almost mixed together, till they precipitated themselves into a ravine, and fled down almost out of sight as if by magic.

On the opposite side of this ravine, a few of the Riflemen of General Kempt's Brigade were pushing forward with a noble fellow, Reid, of the Engineers, at their head. At the moment he did not know how full of the enemy the ravine was. Colonel Colborne and I were on horseback. We pushed on, a little madly, I admit, followed by those who could run fastest, until the ravine expanded and a whole column of French were visible, but we and Reid on the opposite side were rather ahead, while the enemy could not see from out the ravine. The few men who were there could not have resisted them, and certainly could not have cut them off, had they been aware.

Colonel Colborne, however, galloped up to the officer at the head of the column with the bearing of a man supported by 10,000, and said to the officer in French. "You are cut off. Lay down your arms." The officer, a fine soldier-like looking fellow, as cool as possible, says, presenting his sword to Colonel Colborne, "There, Monsieur, is a sword which has ever done its duty," and then ordered his men to lay down their arms. Colborne, with the presence of mind which stamps the character of a soldier, said, "Face your men to the left, and move out of the ravine." By this means the French soldiers were separated from their arms. At that moment there were up with Colborne myself, Winterbottom, Adjutant of the 52nd Regiment, my brother Tom, Adjutant of the 95th, and probably ten soldiers, and about as many with Reid on the opposite ridge. Reid wisely did not halt, but pushed forward, which added to the Frenchman's impression of our numbers, and Colborne turns to me, "Quick, Smith; what do you here? Get a few a men together, or we are yet in scrape." The French having moved from their arms, Colborne desired the officer commanding to order them to sit down. Our men were rapidly coming up and forming, and, when our strength permitted, we ordered the enemy to march out of the ravine, and there were 22 officers and 400 men.

NAPIER AGAIN:

During these events, the French skirmishers in the deep ravine between the two lines of attack, being feebly pushed by Longa's troops, retreated slowly, and getting amongst some rocks from whence there was no escape also surrendered to Kempt. Taupin's right and centre being then completely beaten fled down the side of the mountain, closely pursued until they rallied upon Vallatte's reserve, which was in order of battle on a ridge extending across the gorge of Olette, between Urogne and Ascain. The Bayonette, Commissari, and Puerto de Vera, were thus won after five hours' incessant fighting, and toiling, up their craggy sides. Nevertheless the battle was still maintained by the French troops on the summit of the Rhune.

Giron, after driving Conroux's advanced post from the gorge leading from Vera to Sarre, had pushed a battalion towards the head of the Great Rhune, and placed a reserve in the gorge to cover his rear from any counter-attack. When his left wing was free to move by the capture of the Boar's back, he fought his way up abreast with the British line until near the saddle-ridge, a little to the right of the Puerto; but there his men were arrested by a strong line of abbatis, from behind which two French regiments poured a heavy fire. An adventurer named Downie, then a Spanish general, exhorted them and they kept their ranks, yet did not advance; but there happened to be present an officer of the 43rd Regiment, named Havelock, who being a attached to Alten's staff had been sent to ascertain Giron's progress. His fiery temper could not brook the check. He took of his hat, called upon the Spaniards, and putting spurs to his horse at one bound cleared the abbatis and went headlong among the enemy. Then the soldiers, shouting for "El chica blanco"—"The fair boy," so they called him, for he was very young and had light hair,— with one shock broke through at the very moment the French centre was flying under the fire of Kempt's skirmishers from the Puerto on the left.

Giron's Spaniards fought hard to take the Greater Rhune, but were unsuccessful; however, next day the French evacuated the great mountain after being outflanked.

(Lieutenant-Colonel William Havelock was killed at Ramnuggur on 22 November 1848 during the 2nd Sikh War., when leading his regiment, the 14th Light Dragoons, in an impetuous charge across the sandy bed of a river.)

Among the most famous of all Riflemen, Sir Harry Smith (who became a Major-General gaining considerable successes both in India and Africa) was a proud gamecock of a man, well aware of his own status in military circles. In his autobiography he tells of an incident occurring at Vera:

Our Brigade was now commanded by Colonel Colborne, in whom we all had the most implicit confidence. I looked up to him as a man whose regard I hoped to deserve, and by whose knowledge and experience I desired to profit. He had more knowledge of ground, better understood the posting of picquets, consequently required fewer men on duty (he always strengthened every post by throwing obstacles—trees, stones, carts, etc.—on the road, to prevent a rush at night), knew better what the enemy were going to do, and more quickly anticipated his design than any officer; with that coolness and animation, under fire, no matter how hot, which marks a good huntsman when he finds his fox in his best country.

The French were now erecting works, upon a position by nature strong as one could well devise, for the purpose of defending the Pass of Vera, and every day Colonel Colborne and I took rides to look at them, with a pleasant reflexion that the stronger the works were, the greater the difficulty we should have in turning them out—an achievement we well knew in store for us. On Oct. 7, the Duke resolved to cross the Bidassoa, and push the enemy at once into his own country, San Sebastian having been taken. Now had arrived the time we long had anticipated of a regular tussle with our fortified friends on the heights of Vera. The Duke's dispatch, Oct 9, 1813, No. 837, tells the military glory of the exploit. My object is the record of anecdotes of myself and my friends. On the afternoon of the 7th, about two o'clock, we were formed for the attack, and so soon as the head of the 4th Division under that noble fellow, Sir Lowry Cole, appeared in sight, we received the command to move forward. We attacked on three different points. Advancing to the attack, Colborne, who had taken a liking to me as an active fellow, says, "Now, Smith, you see the heights above us?" "Well," I said, "I wish we were there." He laughed. "When we are," he says, "and you are not knocked over, you shall be a Brevet-Major, if my recommendation has any weight at head-quarters." Backed by the performance of our Brigade, next day off he posted to Lord Fitzroy Somerset, and came back as happy as a soldier ever is who served his comrade. "Well, Major Smith, give me your hand." I did, and my heart too (although not as a blushing bride). Kind-hearted Colonel Barnard heard of this, went to Lord Fitzroy Somerset, asking for the Brevet for one of his Captains, remarking that I should be made a Major over the heads of twenty in my own Regiment. This startling fact obliged Lord Fitzroy to lay the matter before the Duke, who, I am told, said, "A pity, by G—! Colborne and the Brigade are so anxious about it, and he deserves anything. If Smith will go and serve as Brigade-Major to another Brigade, I will give him the rank after the next battle." Colborne's mortification was so great that I banished mine altogether by way of alleviating his disappointment. There was such a demonstration of justice on the part of his Grace, and so did I love the fellows whose heads I should have jumped over, that, honestly and truly, I soon forgot the affair. Colborne said, "Go and serve with another Brigade." "No," says I, "dear Colonel, not to be made of Your rank. Here I will fight on happily, daily acquiring knowledge from your ability."

Colonel Sir John Colborne, later Baron Seaton and a Field-Marshal in the British Army, also commanded the 52nd at Waterloo where, in the late evening, took the decisive action - without orders, of laying his regiment on the flank of the huge Imperial Guard column, to pour in a fire so destructive that it caused the Guard to break and flee. During the 1830's he was Lieutenant-Governor of Upper Canada, where he crushed a revolt in 1838.

Troops Involved:

Allies :

The Light Division, two brigades, 8 battalions (3 of them Portuguese) = 5,484 men.

Longa's Spanish infantry division = 2,607 men.

Giron's two Spanish infantry divisions = 7,653 men.

French:

Clausel's Corps of 3 infantry divisions = 27,300 men.

Actually, all these forces did not take part in the battle; the figures of those participating were more likely to have been, Allies 6,500 and French 4,700.

The Passage of the Bidassoa, October 7, 1813

British Losses	
1st Division	
Howard's Brigade	
1st Coldstream	10
1/3rd Guards	11
Halkett's Brigade	
1st K.G.L. Line	8
2nd K.G.L. Line	9
5th K.G.L. Line	4
1st K.G.L. Light	74
2nd K.G.L. Light	43
5th Division	
Hay's Brigade	
3/1st Foot	20
1/9th Foot	82
1/38th Foot	20
Robinson's Brigade	
1/4th Foot	6
2/47th Foot	5
2/59th Foot	3
Light Division	
1/43rd Foot	19
1/52nd Foot	80
1/95th Rifles	10
2/95th Rifles	111
3/95th Rifles	22

Companies of Brunswick-Oels	
attached to 4th and 1st Divisions	32
Ditto, 5/60th	3
Artillery	1
British Total	573
Portuguese	242
Total	815

French Losses	
Reille's Wing:	
Maucune's Division	357
Boyer (later Lamartiniere)	97
Foy (detached)	–
Clausel's Centre:	
Conroux's Division	94
Maransin's Division	
(later Vandermaesen)	21
Taupin's Division	883
D'Erlon's Wing:	
Darmagnac's Division	203
Abbe's Division	20
Etat-Major	1
Total	1,676

Soult's Army at the Passage of the Bidassoa

State of October 1st, 1813

1st Division, Foy (8 battalions)	4,654	Detached at St. Jean-Pied-du-Port
2nd Division, Darmagnac (9 battalions)	4,447	In and about Ainhone
3rd Division, Abbe (8 battalions)	6,051	Front to west of Ainhone
4th Division, Conroux (9 battalions)	4,962	In and about Sare
5th Division, Maransin (9 battalions)	5,575	In and about Sare
6th Division, Daricau (7 battalions)	4,092	In reserve behind Ainhoue and Sare
7th Division, Maucune (8 battalions)	3,996	Lower Bidassoa as far as Biriatou
8th Division, Taupin (10 battalions)	4,778	Bayonette and Commissari Works
9th Division, Boyer (12 battalions)	6,515	Urrogne and Bordagain
Vilatte's Reserve (17 battalions)	8,018	Serres and Ascain
Total Infantry	*53,088*	

British Battle Honours for The Pyrenees.

14th (Duchess of York's Own) Regt. of (Light) Dragoons
2nd (Queen's Royal) Regt. of Foot
1st Bn. 3rd (East Kent) Regt. of Foot or the Buffs
1st Bn. 6th (1st Warwickshire) Regt. of Foot
1st Bn. 7th Regt. of Foot (or Royal Fuzileers)
1st Bn. 11th (North Devonshire) Regt. of Foot
20th (East Devonshire) Regt. of Foot
1st Bn. 23rd Regt. of Foot (or Royal Welsh Fuzileers)
2nd Bn. 24th (2nd Warwickshire) Regt. of Foot
2nd Bn. 27th (Inniskilling) Regt. of Foot
1st Bn. 28th (North Gloucestershire) Regt. of Foot

1st Bn. 61st (South Gloucestershire) Regt. of Foot
1st Bn. 36th (Herefordshire) Regt. of Foot
2nd Bn. 31st (Huntingdonshire) Regt. of Foot
1st Bn. 32nd (Cornwall) Regt. of Foot
2nd Bn. 34th (Cumberland) Regt. of Foot
1st Bn. 39th (Dorsetshire) Regt. of Foot
1st Bn. 40th (2nd Somersetshire) Regt. of Foot
1st Bn. 82nd Regt. of Foot (Prince of Wales's Volunteers)
1st Bn. 42nd (Royal Highland) Regt. of Foot
43rd (Monmouthshire Light Infantry) Regt.
52nd (Oxfordshire Light Infantry) Regt.
1st Bn. 45th (Nottinghamshire) Regt. of Foot
1st Bn. 48th (Northamptonshire) Regt. of Foot
2nd Bn. 58th (Rutlandshire) Regt. of Foot
2nd Bn. 66th (Berkshire) Regt. of Foot 1st Bn.
50th (West Kent) Regt. of Foot
51st (2nd Yorkshire, West Riding) Regt. (Light Infantry)
2nd Bn. 53rd (Shropshire) Regt. of Foot
1st Bn. 57th (West Middlesex) Regt. of Foot
5th Bn. 60th (Royal American) Regt. of Foot
68th (Durham) Regt. of Foot (Light Infantry)
1st Bn. 71st (Highland) Regt. of Foot (Light Infantry)
74th (Highland) Regt. of Foot
1st Bn. 92nd (Highland) Regt. of Foot
1st Bn. 79th Regt. of Foot (Cameron Highlanders)
1st Bn. 88th Regt. of Foot (or Connaught Rangers)
1st Bn. 91st Regt. of Foot
95th Regt. of Foot (or Rifle Corps)

Wellington to Earl Henry Bathurst, Secretary for War; 9th October: "My Lord, having deemed it expedient to cross the Bidasoa with the left of the Army, I have the pleasure to inform your Lordship that object was effected on the 7th instant. While this was going on upon the left, Major General Charles Baron Alten attacked, with the Light Division, the enemy's entrenchments in the Puerto de Vera, supported by the Spanish Division under Brigadier-General Longa...the Light Division took 22 officers and 400 prisoners..."

WALKING THE BATTLEFIELD OF VERA.

Crossing the Spanish Frontier at Hendaye, we drove along the side of the ravine in which flowed the River Bidassoa until we came to the village of Vera, where we lunched on an uninspiring Spanish Paella. Leaving the restaurant, we walked along the pavement-less street with huge trucks thundering past throwing up clouds of dust, so that we were glad to branch-off to the right, down a hedge-bordered track between houses that led to the banks of the River — and the bridge. Reaching deeply into the depths of imagination, we sought to transform the peaceful sunlit scene into a night of tumult, when musket-flashes lit up the scene and men's cries filled the air. We stood in the centre of the bridge, gazing at the commemorative plaque set in its wall, which read:

"To the Glory of God and in memory of Captain Daniel Cadoux and his gallant riflemen of the 2nd Battalion 95th (Rifle Brigade) who, on 1st September 1813, fell gloriously defending this bridge against the fierce attacks of a French Division - 'His fame can never die': Sir Harry Smith."

In Spanish, the wording is similar until the end, where it says -"...died defending this bridge...for the independence of Spain and allied to his heroic Spanish companions."

Despite the after-effects of the disastrous Paella-lunch, we managed to climb a high ridge on which lay the main French defence, the Star Redoubt. We knew where it was but could not

LOOKING STRAIGHT UP THE CENTRE SPUR OF BAYONETTE RIDGE AT VERA, UP WHICH COLBORNE'S 52ND FOOT ATTACKED. STAR FORT IS RIGHT BEHIND THE CENTRE CLUMP OF TREES.

actually find it because the whole area is now covered with a quite impenetrable forest of prickly conifers - however, we explored an extensive modern defence system without knowing whether it was mid-20th century French against possible invasion from Spain, or the reverse, or perhaps connected with the Spanish Civil War?

Gazing into the misty distance, we saw the battlefield of Vera spread out before us; immediately to the front was the two-miles long Bayonet Ridge, extending almost back into the village of Vera, and to our left was the unmistakable high-humped Hog's Back; all surmounted by the Lesser and Greater Rhunes on the skyline.

On another occasion, we did discover the Star Redoubt, its conifer-covering seemingly having been cut down; it needs imagination to achieve satisfaction because all that remains are shallow pits, about two feet deep, but covering sufficient ground in the right place to unmistakably be the Star Redoubt.

WARGAMING THE BATTLE OF VERA AND THE ACTION AT THE BRIDGE.

Pondering as to how Cadoux's defense of the bridge would go as a wargame, one immediately realises that it would only require relatively small numbers of figures, even if done on a one-to-one scale - because the sole French requirement will be that the number of men who would occupy an area about fifty yards long, four or five abreast. Rules would be so formulated as to allow packed groups of men to be halted and turned back, perhaps by grouping them into 'units' or 'formations', each having to take morale-checks on receiving casualties. The effect of single-shots from French soldiers who have gone into cover on the river-bank must also be considered.

It seemed to be a very promising wargame, with the objective of holding up a superior force for a set number of game-moves to secure victory.

The author cannot recall an actual re-fight of the field of Vera in his wargaming circles, but it was attempted by wargamer A. J. Mitchell, who set-up the Crossing of the Bidassoa and subsequent battle of Vera. His account is as follows:

Terrain built up with blocks of Polystyrene and a 'split level' table. All the main slopes were deemed to be steep enough to slow ascending troops to half speed. The general scale was agreed at 1mm = 1 yard. The town of Vera was represented by half a dozen houses (sufficient to hold two an a half battalions). The area covered was thus about right but the houses were all 10 to 12 times too tall!

Before the battle began the whole question of relative scales and vertical exaggeration had to be settled in terms of what was visible and what was not; to what extent could troops at the foot of very steep slopes claim to be below the angle to which gun barrels could be depressed; to what extent were troops on the top of a steep ridge protected from the fire of attacking formations just below the crest.

FORCES.

A limited choice was available and in the event Wellington settled for:
1st Division. 9 Infantry. Battalions (including 1 Brigade of Guards.)
Light Division. 6 Light or Rifle Battalions and 3 Portuguese Battalions
Spanish Division. 8 Infantry Battalions.
Two Independent British Brigades of three Battalions each.
Two Batteries of Horse Artillery, two Howitzer Batteries and two Field Artillery Batteries.
No Cavalry.

Soult decided on two divisions each consisting of 12 Battalions (including two light battalions each) plus 4 Battalions of the Guard (spirited back from the Russian front!). In addition he had four regiments of cavalry. In the Star redoubt he had two 24lb Howitzers and another in the emplacement on the Baionette ridge. In addition he had two batteries of Horse Artillery and two of Field Artillery.

SITUATION.

It was agreed that the British should all start on the far side of the Bidassoa, that they should have one move and that all moves after that should be simultaneous. A dice was thrown for visibility which for the initial British move was set at 12". This meant, in effect that on the British right they were immediately visible to the French troops in Vera, in the centre they were spotted from the Baionette but on the left they had a further screened move.

RULES.

Virtually standard with a few modifications particularly as to Morale.

DISPOSITIONS.

See the attached diagram. Soult confidently expected the Light Division to attack the Baionette from the centre with strong artillery support. He expected a strong diversion on his right flank and a weak demonstration on his left. Wellington intended the opposite in fact -a strong attack on each flank and a demonstration in the centre.

Move 1.

The Light Division waded across the Bidassoa on a front of two Battalions with four others following also in line, accompanied by the two batteries of Horse artillery.

Two batteries of Howitzers and one Field Battery immediately opposite the town of Vera began a systematic bombardment of the houses and breached five of them. The eight Spanish Battalions in column then assaulted the town. The Portuguese Brigade of the Light Division followed up the main street of the town.

Right Centre Aylmer's Independent Brigade attacked the French Light troops in the valley.

Left Centre Doyle's Independent Brigade attacked the Light troops the other side of the Baionette, in the valley. Their crossing was supported by a Field Battery.

On the Left the First Division crossed on a front of three battalions with the remainder of the Division in Column. The remaining battery of field artillery crossed behind the leading battalions.

The French sent their two Cavalry Regiments accompanied by 1 Battery of Horse Artillery in on the left and repeated the same manoeuvre on the right. For the rest, wherever British troops came within visibility they fired on them.

Move 2.

The British Light Division's leading battalions (with the two Horse Batteries) virtually destroyed the two cavalry regiments in the fire and melee. The French guns were overrun and spiked. The British lost only half a battalion. The Spaniards (whose morale factor only permitted them to attack when the odds were heavily in their favour and who could not support casualties of more than 40%) had, with the encouragement of British Staff Officers, cleared the town at the cost of 1 1/2 battalions. The French moved a Field Battery up to the head of the Main street (and having moved could not fire) and the leading Portuguese Battalion deployed and shot down the whole gun crew.

In the centre the French now deployed along the Baionette and on either side of the Star redoubt, together with the heavy Howitzers in their emplacements, proceeded to sweep the two Independent Brigades in the centre with heavy fire. On the British left the two French Cavalry Regiments supported by their Horse Artillery had met the concentrated fire of three British Battalions and one regiment had suffered over 60% casualties and fled, the other somewhat less badly mauled had retreated one move and fought the rest of the action dismounted as infantry. The Horse Artillery had elected to fire canister (three dice for casualties) in view of the short range but had thrown two ones - misses! They were however able to retreat to the cover of the farm buildings.

Move 3.

Soult was now rapidly moving troops from his centre to his threatened flanks particularly to his left where the formidable Light Division now made a double move after their two Horse Batteries had advanced and fired canister at the French wiping out another battalion completely and inflicting casualties on the remainder. The Portuguese now emerged from the town to overrun and spike the French Battery and then moved to the foot of the ridge. Their fire and that of Aylmer's Brigade cleared the valley of French Light troops. However, Aylmer's Brigade and Doyle's had each lost more than a battalion.

The French gunners in the redoubts now ranged further afield for targets and commenced to shell the Spaniards in Vera. Their morale fell with further casualties so that they evacuated the town and fled across the river. A long shot from the Star redoubt (a 6 on the dice) now hit the Duke and his Staff. The dice revealed them as all casualties and the command fell on Lord Hill but this necessitated a complete halt for two moves for the British (they stood their ground and fired, of course).

On the left the British had continued to advance and inflicted heavy casualties, shooting down the crew of the French Horse battery and scoring a 'Kill" (6 on the dice) on the Field battery with a lucky shot from their own Field guns.

Move 4 and 5.

Exchange of fire with casualties heavy on both ides but the advantage lay definitely with the British who had brought two howitzer batteries and a field battery across the river at Vera and were lobbing case up on the ridges. The Light Division (now deployed on a front of three battalions) were inflicting double casualties on the French Line and Guards units on the crest.

Move 6.

The French had now suffered 40% casualties and in turn were frozen for two moves. This was disastrous as the Batteries on the Baionette and in the Star redoubt were all out of shot and the supply train route now came under fire from the British riflemen. The Portuguese stormed the right hand ridge and moved toward the Star redoubt while the remnants of Aylmer's and Duncan's Brigades, (no more than a Battalion) stormed the Baionette. The right hand brigade of the first division now turned to their right and prepared to assault the left hand ridge. The remaining two Brigades battled on round the farmhouse driving in the French right.

Move 7.

Final assault on the French left with the British howitzers being brought right forward in support. On the right, the French remnants round the farm awaited the final attack. In the centre the French batteries, powerless to resist, were overrun. At this stage the French having suffered

284

60% casualties had, by the rules, to retreat, but the British had now suffered 40% and again had to pause for two moves so pursuit and complete annihilation of the enemy were denied to the victor.

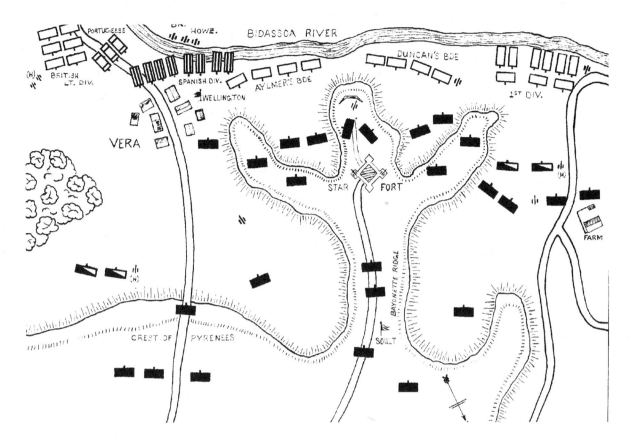

A.J.Mitchell's Vera Battlefield

Two and a half French battalions are out of sight in the houses.

A Southampton Wargame, inspired by the Terrain at Vera.

With the well-known undulating terrain of Vera in mind, a hypothetical battle was set-up which required tactical thought by both sides, and formed an ideal vehicle for the Light Division, as it reflected the type of operation best handled by this elite formation. The French were given a map formed of four wargames tables, set-out as in the diagram, the tables they occupied were 1. bisected by a river with three well-fortified bridges; and 2. a high ridge running the length of the table. To aid them, they were given orders from Marshal Soult, and spy's reports of Wellington's intentions. It seemed he intended attacking the bridges with his entire army, prefaced by a Light Division diversion towards the long ridge in the hope of drawing French defenders from the other area. The French refused to be drawn when the Light Division, supported by two squadrons of Light Dragoons and Ramsay's R.H.A. battery, advanced on the ridge; in fact, they pulled back and concentrated around a fortified village near their baseline.

After desultory fighting for about 20 game-moves, the Light Division who had suffered few casualties, withdrew from the ridge, and the French congratulated themselves on knowing a diversion when they saw one and were smug in the knowledge that they had not withdrawn any troops from the potential battle area on the next table. The smiles were wiped off their faces when they were told that the objective of the Light Division was to keep the French from the summit of the ridge, because from it a clear view could be obtained of the road over which

Wellington was moving his siege-train to batter the bridge-defences! The Lights had completely achieved their objective despite a tricky moment near the end when a message was received ordering them to prolong their operations for a further six moves as the siege-train was moving slower than expected - and at a time when overwhelming French cavalry were probing a flank and coming near the ridge-top!

The best of Wellington's Peninsular formations, the Light Division are obviously an elite group, but to grant the whole force such enhanced status might make them too strong so only the 95th are considered Elite, with all its privileges; the two British Line Infantry Battalions and the Portuguese are rated as normal Line troops. Armed with the Baker Rifle, formidable in the hands of such trained marksmen, the 95th and the Cacadores must be given increased fire-power, increased move-distance must be granted plus the faculty of open-order fighting in

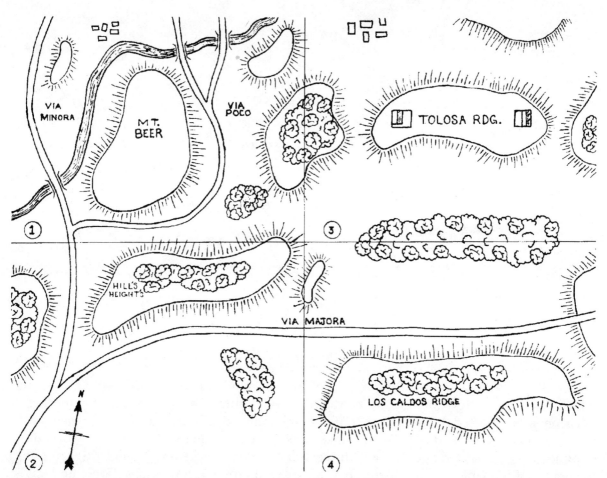

THE SOUTHAMPTON WARGAME TERRAIN. EACH SQUARE IS A WARGAMES TABLETOP.

woods and rough ground, where Line infantry would be in disorder; this is counter-balanced by a marked vulnerability if caught in the open - particularly by cavalry - when in open order. If your Napoleonic rules decree troops either moving or firing, the Light Infantry should be able to move half-distance and fire. And, of course, knowing they were an Elite formation, their morale - especially the 95th - will be sky-high. A noted light-infantry role was to pick-off enemy officers, this can be simulated by ruling that a dice is thrown for each casualty, all 1's and 2's are officers with subsequent effect upon their unit's morale.

THE BATTLE OF THE NIVELLE - 10 NOVEMBER 1813.

Captain John Kincaid of the Rifle Brigade - "A curious fact occurred in our regiment at this period. Prior to the action of the Nivelle, an owl had perched itself on the tent of one of our officers, Lieutenant Doyle. This officer was killed in the battle, and the owl afterwards was seen on Captain Duncan's tent. His brother officers quizzed him on the subject, by telling him he was the next on the list - a joke which Captain D. did not much relish, and it was prophetic, as he soon afterwards fell at Tarbes."

"The plains of France, so long overlooked from the towering crags of the Pyrenees, were to be the prize of battle; and the half-famished soldiers in their fury broke through the iron barrier erected by Soult as if it were but a screen of reeds."   (William Napier)

Wellington had now entered France, but was still in the Pyrenees. There were many reasons urging him forward, not the least being the clamour of the home-politicians; but the strongest argument was the necessities of his troops.

JAMES GRANT:

After the fall of San Sebastian, the hostile armies in Spain remained for some time inactive, or occupied principally in the task of strengthening their different positions, and preparing for further efforts at conquest. Meantime the troops suffered severely from the inclemency of the weather. While exposed on the bleak summits of the Pyrenees, some there were who cast fond and longing eyes upon the distant sea, "the high road to Old England," which the Highlanders of Hill's division hailed with three loud cheers when first they came in sight of it; others gazed with a different interest on the beautiful plains of Bearn, Gascony, and Languedoc, which stretched like a map at their feet; while the close vicinity of the watchful French outposts rendered the greatest vigilance necessary, and made the guard and picket duties most severe.

ARTHUR GRIFFITHS:

For Soult, after the passage of the Bidassoa, was more than ever limited upon a strict defensive, hoping, behind a strong line of fortifications, to revive the spirit of his troops. Since the loss of the Bidassoa he had taken up a more concentrated position between the Nive and the sea, and had strengthened it to the utmost with redoubts and forts and entrenched camps. These formidable works, hardly inferior to Wellington's celebrated lines of Torres Vedras, which had stopped Massena in Portugal in 1810, had been thrown up with incessant labour and at great expense; and they were strongly armed, and held by 60,000 men.
Soult's line of defence was in three great portions, the Right, Centre, and Left, all more or less inter-dependent, although each French commander had a special position assigned to him.
1.—The Right, under Reille, in front of St. Jean de Luz, was nearly impregnable in strong fortifications upon the lower ground, extending from the sea towards Ascain.
2.—The Centre, under Clausel, occupied a range of hills from Ascain to the bridge of Amotz, and as the Nivelle described a great curve behind him, both his flanks rested on that river. In front a brigade held the Lesser Rhune, and another the redoubts of St. Barbe and Grenada, both of which acted as advanced posts, covering his front and his entrenched camp at Sarre.
3.—The left, under D'Erlon, was beyond the Nivelle, on its right or northern bank, and between that river and the Nive, so that his flanks rested also on rivers. His right connected with Clausel at the bridge of Amotz, his left was on the Mondarrain mountain, and in between these he had two lines of defence—the first, and most forward, a continuation of the Mondarrain range; the second was a broad ridge farther to the rear, its right flank at Amotz, where it touched upon Clausel.

The moment so ardently desired arrived at length.

Early on the morning of the 7th of October the tents were struck, and under the cloud of a dark and stormy sky, the army descended from the heights, crossed the Bidassoa, and established itself, with opposition, on French territory; and the news of this movement—the invasion of the enemy's country—caused a thrill of triumph in the hearts of all at home. The continued inclemency of the weather and the wretched nature of the roads retarded the advance of the troops until the 10th of November, when, the last preparations having been made, the columns, 90,000 strong—of these 74,000 being British and Portuguese—with 95 guns, moved down the passes of the Pyrenees in silence, and halted each at its appointed post to await the dawn, ere making the final attack upon the various forces in front.

Soult's weakest point was between the Rhune mountains and the Nivelle, where the space, gradually narrowing as it approached the bridge of Amotz, was the most open and least fortified. Moving from the Puerto de Maya in the night, Hill was to attack D'Erlon's post. On Hill's left, Beresford was to hurl the 3rd division in all its strength against the redoubts at the bridge of Amotz. Farther to the left again, the 7th division, marching from the Echallar Pass, was to storm the Grenada Redoubt, pass the village of Sarre, and assail Clausel, abreast of the 3rd. Yet farther to the left, the 4th, from the slopes of the Greater Rhune was to rush upon St. Barbe. Beyond Sarre were Giron's Spaniards. All these other troops gained their respective stations so secretly in the night, that the enemy had no suspicion of their presence, although for several hours they were lying within half musket-range of the field-works. Towards dawn five or six cannon-shots, fired at random from some low ground near the sea, pealed through the darkened air; then the silence seemed to deepen, while quietly, with arms loaded, ammunition cast loose, and colours uncased, the Allies waited the sunrise, when three guns fired from the summit of Mount Atchulia were to be the signal for close battle.

The morning of the 10th of November dawned with unusual splendour on the rugged scenery of the Lower Pyrenees and the low range of hills that rise on the left of Nivelle, all bristling then with French bayonets, and covered by a network of their redoubts and intrenchments. As the first ray of the sun played on the green summit of the Atchulia, the three signal-guns pealed upon the air, and every man sprung to his arms; while, to their astonishment, from amid the hitherto silent hills the French of Soult saw the Allies rushing downward to the attack.

The light division came round the swelling flank of the Great Rhune, from the summit of which the mountain guns and two companies of our 43rd Light Infantry commenced the attack in one quarter, while the remainder of that gallant old regiment advanced against some high rocks, over which a biting fire of musketry was flashing; but the quick even run of the advancing line deceived the aim of the enemy, so few of our men fell, till the whole battalion reunited, and, after rushing over a half-mile of rough ground, threw themselves into lower works or cuttings, and there remained panting and breathless within pistol-shot of the enemy; and then, when their breath returned, they arose, and with a stern shout commenced the assault.

The defenders were quite as numerous as the assailants; "but strong and valiant in arms must the soldiers have been who stood in that hour before the veterans of the 43rd."

An officer of grenadiers alone ventured to withstand the headlong rush. On the high stone wall of the first redoubt—a veritable castle—he stood, exposing his tall and noble figure, hurling down stones with both hands, till a ball pierced his heart, and he fell dead, when his men, shrinking on each side, sought shelter among some rocks. Close and fierce was then the fight; bayonets flashed in the sun, and butt-ends were whirled in the air, to be whirled again covered with blood and brains, as man sought man, till the French were beaten, trod under foot, or literally turned by cold steel out of the redoubt, while our soldiers rushed to storm another, and another still beyond; and then, in an inconceivably short space, the white colours of the 43rd were seen flying in triumph in the morning breeze on the Donjon, as they named it. In twenty-six minutes they took this last redoubt, hurling 600 chosen veterans out of it, but losing 11 officers and 67 rank and file; while elsewhere the remainder of the light division cleared the whole Rhune."

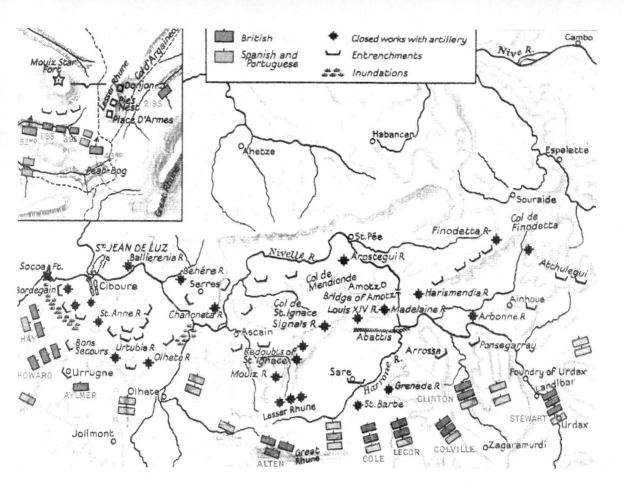

BATTLE OF THE NIVELLE

William Napier himself, whose classic writing on the Peninsular War is oft quoted in these pages, commanded the 43rd during this attack.

Captain John Kincaid was also there:

> Petite La Rhune was allotted to our division, as their first point of attack; and, accordingly, the 10th being the day fixed, we moved to our ground at midnight, on the 9th. The abrupt ridges in the neighbourhood enabled us to lodge ourselves, unperceived, within half-musket-shot of their piquets; and we had left every description of animal behind us in camp, in order that neither the barking of dogs nor the neighing of steeds should give indication of our intentions. Our signal of attack was to be a gun from Sir John Hope, who had now succeeded Sir Thomas Graham in the command of the left wing of the army.
>
> We stood to our arms at dawn of day, which was soon followed by the signal-gun; and each commanding officer, according to previous instructions, led gallantly off to his point of attack. The French must have been, no doubt, astonished to see such an armed force spring out of the ground almost under their noses; but they were, nevertheless, prepared behind their entrenchments, and caused us some loss in passing the short space between us: but the whole place was carried within the time required to walk over it; and, in less than half an hour from the commencement of the attack, it was in our possession, with all their tents left standing.
>
> Petite la Rhune was more of an outpost than a part of their position, the latter being a chain of stupendous mountains in its rear; so that while our battalion followed their skirmishers into the valley between, the remainder of our division were forming for the attack on the main position, and waiting for the co-operation of the other divisions, the thunder of whose artillery, echoing

289

along the valleys, proclaimed that they were engaged, far and wide, on both sides of us. About midday our division advanced to the grand attack on the most formidable-looking part of the whole of the enemy's position, and, much to our surprise, we carried it with more ease and less loss than the outpost in the morning, a circumstance which we could only account for by supposing that it had been defended by the same troops, and that they did not choose to sustain two hard beatings on the same day. The attack succeeded at every point; and, in the evening, we had the satisfaction of seeing the left wing of the army marching into St. Jean de Luz.

George Simmons relates a personal incident, confirmed by John Kincaid:

Colonel Barnard (of the Light Division) towards the end of the day's fighting, received a musket-ball in his right breast, which made him tumble from his horse; he fell upon the hilt of his sword and bruised his side very much. I was near him when he fell, and put my hand into his bosom to feel where the ball entered. I found his lungs had been wounded, as blood in quantities and air issued from the wound; some blood was passing from his mouth also. He in a most collected manner said, "Do you think I am dying? Did you ever see a man so wounded recover?" I observed, "Your wound is a very bad one, but there have been many instances of men recovering from such wounds, and your pulse does not indicate immediate dissolution." "Thank you," he exclaimed, "you give me hopes. If any man can recover, I know I shall." He was immediately bled very largely and taken by four men in a blanket to a farmhouse. After all was over, Sir James Kempt, who commanded the Brigade, sent for me, and said it was his wish, as well as that of all the officers, that I should go to the Colonel and stay with him a few days. My brother Joseph had been in the day's fight. I was anxious to find him. He soon turned up, as lucky as myself, without a wound.

I went to the house where the Colonel had been taken to and remained with him. Constructed a bearer, upon which the Colonel was placed and supported upon the shoulders of our band through the pass of Vera to that town. I remained with him night and day until every dangerous symptom was subdued, and having a good constitution, he speedily recovered, and on the 7th of December we rode to headquarters at St. Jean-de-Luz.

John Kincaid:
The enemy, seeing that they had shot an officer of rank, very maliciously kept up a heavy firing on the spot, while we were carrying him under the brow of the hill. The ball having passed through the lungs, he was spitting blood, and, at the moment, had every appearance of being in a dying state; but, to our joy and surprise, he, that day month, rode up to the battalion, when it was in action, near Bayonne; and, I need not add, that he was received with three hearty cheers.

Grant:
The same signal-guns which sent them against it had dispatched the 4th and 7th divisions against St. Barbe and Grenada; and while eighteen pieces of cannon heavily pounded the former, the troops advanced with ladders to the escalade. Creeping round, our skirmishers opened a fire in rear of the work; on this the French leaped out and fled, while Ross's battery of flying artillery, galloping to a rising ground in rear of the Grenada Redoubt, unlimbered, and by sheer dint of cannon-shot drove them from it. After that the 4th division, as related, won the village of Sarre and the heights beyond it, and advanced to the attack of Clausel.

Napier:
It was now eight o'clock, and to the troops posted on the Rhune a splendid spectacle was presented. On one hand, the ships of war sailing slowly to and fro were exchanging shots with the fort of Socoa; while Hope, menacing all the French lines in the low ground, sent the sound of a hundred pieces of artillery bellowing up the rocks. He was answered by nearly as many from the tops of the mountains, amid the smoke of which the summit of the great Atchulia glittered to the rising sun, while 50,000 men, rushing down its enormous slopes with ringing shouts, seemed to chase the receding shadows into the deep valley. The plains of France, so long overlooked from the towering crags of the Pyrenees, were to be the prize of battle; and the half-

famished soldiers, in their fury, were breaking through the iron barrier erected by Soult as if it were but a screen of reeds.

GRANT:

The most dense portion of the battle now raged over a space eight miles in length, yet its skirts spread wider still. Far away on the right, after a long and toilsome night march, Hill had got near the enemy at seven in the morning; yet the ground was so wild and rugged that eleven struck in the village spire of Ainhoe ere he, with three divisions, approached within cannon-shot of D'Erlon's second line, which was strengthened by redoubts, each containing 500 men. They were placed upon the summit of a high ridge, thickly clothed with brushwood and wild laurels, and were further covered by a rough ravine. At the head of the 6th division, General Clinton turned the flank of this ravine, and drove the enemy from their works at the bridge of Amotz. Defiling through this ravine came the blue masses of Hamilton's Portuguese, with the red-coats of the 2nd division—Hill's own—menacing the second and third redoubts on the ridge. These were instantly abandoned. A hutted camp was set on fire, and under the cloud of its smoke, the French in that quarter began to retreat towards San Pe, pursued by Clinton. Another division, forming the French left, began its retreat to Cambo, on the Nive.

It was the swift and fierce progress of our troops, advancing like a line of fire across a prairie, that rendered D'Erlon's fight on the right bank so feeble; for after the fall of San Barbe and Grenada, Conraux sought to defend the heights of Sarre, as we have shown, in vain; for while the 4th and 7th divisions carried those points amid prodigious slaughter, another captured the bridge of Amotz. The French were thus driven from all their works that covered the bridge on both sides of the Nivelle; and the division of Conraux, spreading from Sarre to Amotz, was swept away by superior numbers at every point.

In storming these various redoubts and works, there was an immense amount of close and deadly—even ferocious—close fighting; and when Conraux sank mortally wounded from his horse, his scattered troops retired; and the 3rd division, establishing itself between the bridge of Amotz and some works called the Redoubt of Louis XIV, caused D'Erlon to dread that he might be cut off; hence he fell back, and by doing so had his communication with Clausel's force cut off.

Firmly and bravely stood the latter for a time, covered by the Redoubt of Louis XIV, and eight field-guns; but Ross's flying battery soon silenced these, while our infantry stormed the redoubt itself, and bayoneted the whole garrison. Conraux's troops were still flying; those of General Marousin were hurled headlong into the deep ravines in their rear; ridge after ridge of glittering bayonets, with tricolours flying above them, seemed to melt away and disappear; but still Clausel, amid smoke, and blood, and dreadful slaughter, held his post.

A large body of conscripts, recently armed and recently clothed, with Taupin's division, forming his right, fighting nobly and desperately, he still thought he might dispute the victory. With the French 31st and 88th Regiments, he made several movements, and, aware that he could retreat by the bridge of Ascain, resolved to renew the already failing fight; but his plans failed, and he was swept away by our irresistible light division. The rout soon became general along all the lines; and, leaving 600 of their 88th Regiment to their fate, in a strong work called the Signal Redoubt, the French fled like flocks of sheep towards the different bridges of the Nivelle; for they were now being rapidly and sternly taught that for their years of splendid but unprincipled aggression, the days of retribution were come.

The formidable Signal Redoubt now alone barred the advance of the light division, though it had become valueless, when the whole lines of forts on its flanks were abandoned. Colborne approached it in front with the 52nd Regiment or Oxfordshire Light Infantry, and by other troops it was surrounded on every side. Colborne, an officer of great experience, knew that ere long the little garrison in the redoubt must capitulate, so he halted under the brow of a hill to save his men from its fire, when a staff-officer unknown, without order or warrant, directed him to advance. The gallant 52nd, led by Colborne on horseback, now rushed at the redoubt under a most severe fusilade, which three times drove them back. The intrepid Colborne now rode forward waving a white handkerchief, and assured the French commander that he was completely surrounded. On this he surrendered, with the loss of only one man killed; "but on the British side there fell 200 soldiers of a regiment never surpassed in arms since arms were first borne by men—victims to the presumptuous folly of a young staff-officer."

During this affair Clausel's other troops had crossed the Nivelle, pursued by the 3rd and 7th divisions. Soult was not present in any of these actions. On the first alarm he had hastened with his reserve of artillery and spare troops from St. Jean de Luz to Serres, and was now menacing Wellington's left flank by Ascain. A hard struggle with the column of Marousin, in which General Inglis was wounded, and the 51st and 68th Regiments of Light Infantry were seriously cut up, ended the battle in the centre; for darkness was coming on, and Clinton's troops, without food or rest, had been marching and fighting for four-and-twenty hours.

Ere night closed the whole line of the French intrenchments—the work of three months—was in our hands; and from mountain, ravine, and river they had been hurled in ruin and defeat, with the loss of 4,265 men and officers—including 1,400 prisoners—and one general slain. Fifty-five pieces of cannon were taken; while the Allies had three generals—Inglis, Kemp, and Byng—wounded, and lost 2,694 of all ranks.

In the morning the pitiless rain fell in torrents, drenching the bodies of the killed and wounded alike; and hundreds of the latter, who had been shrieking all night for water, turned their baked lips gratefully to the falling shower. Daylight showed Wellington that no attack would be made. Soult, perceiving that his line of defence was pierced in various directions, and that his communications with Bayonne were menaced, had retreated under cover of night, and was already far beyond the Nivelle and in full march towards the Adour.

WELLINGTON'S ARMY AT THE BATTLE OF THE NIVELLE

1st Division, (Howard)		**3rd Division, (Colville)**	
Maitland's Brigade		Brisbane's Brigade	
1st Guards, 1st Battalion	885	1/45th Foot	589
1st Guards, 3rd Battalion	785	74th Foot	640
Stopford's Brigade		1/88th Foot	809
1st Coldstream	918	5/60th Foot*	646
1st Scots Guards	1,124	Keane's Brigade	
Hinuber's Brigade		1/5th Foot	744
1st Line K.G.L.	658	2/83rd Foot	675
2nd Line K.G.L.	610	2/87th Foot	497
5th Line K.G.L.	582	94th Foot	428
1st Light K.G.L.	631	Power's Portuguese	
2nd Light K.G.L.	695	9th & 21st Line, 11th Cacadores	2,303
1st Division Total	6,898	*3rd Division Total*	7,334
2nd Division, (W. Stewart)		**4th Division, (Cole)**	
Walker's Brigade		W. Anson's Brigade	
1/50th Foot	494	3/27th Foot	631
1/71st Foot	621	1/40th Foot	657
1/92nd Foot	531	1/48th Foot	512
Byng's Brigade		2nd Prov. Batt (2nd & 2/53rd)	567
1/3rd Foot	794	Ross's Brigade	
1/57th Foot	678	1/7th Foot	700
1st Prov. Batt. (2/31st & 2/66th)	712	20th Foot	452
Pringle's Brigade		1/23rd Foot	647
1/28th Foot	733	Vasconcellos's Portuguese	
2/34th Foot	481	11th & 23rd Line, 7th Cacadores	2,419
1/39th Foot	723	*4th Division Total*	6,585
Ashworth's Portuguese			
6th & 18th Line, 6th Cacadores	2,713		
2nd Division Total	8,485		

5th Division, (Hay)
Greville's Brigade

3/1st Foot	390
1/9th Foot	623
1/38th Foot	443

Robinson's Brigade

1/4th Foot	512
2/47th Foot	345
2/59th Foot	475

De Regoa's Portuguese

3rd & 15th Line, 8th Cacadores	1,765
5th Division Total	*4,553*

6th Division, (Clinton)
Pack's Brigade

1/42nd Foot	814
1/79th Foot	711
1/91st Foot	636

Lambert's Brigade

1/11th Foot	596
1/32nd Foot	604
1/36th Foot	712
1/61st Foot	578

Douglas's Portuguese

8th & 12th Line, 9th Cacadores	2,067
6th Division Total	*6,718*

7th Division, (Le Cor)
Barnes's Brigade

1/6th Foot	882
3rd Prov. Batt (2/24 & 2/58)	534
Brunswick-Oels*	499

Inglis's Brigade

51st Foot	343
68th Foot	431
1/82nd Foot	636
Chasseurs Britanniques	417

Doyle's Portuguese

7th & 19th Line, 2nd Cacadores	2,326
7th Division Total	*6,068*

Light Division, (C. Alten)
Kempt's Brigade

1/43rd Foot	924
1/95th Foot	563
3/95th Foot	350

Colborne's Brigade

1/52nd Foot	928
2/95th Foot	526

Portuguese attached

17th Line, 1st & 3rd Cacadores	1,679
Light Division Total	*4,970*

Aylmer's Independent Brigade

76th Foot	611
2/84th Foot	754
85th Foot	565
	1,930

Hamilton's Division
Da Costa's Brigade

4th & 10th Line, 10th Cacadores	2,558

Buchan's Brigade

2nd & 14th Line	2,391

Wilson's Independent Brigade

1st & 16th Line, 4th Cacadores	2,185

Bradford's Independent Brigade

13th & 24th Line, 5th Cacadores	1,614

Gunners of 5 British Batteries	628
Gunners of 3 Portuguese	220

Grand Total, Anglo-Portuguese	63,140

Spanish Employed
Giron's Reserve of Andalusia

Virue's Division (6 batts.)	4,123
La Torre's Division (6 batts.)	3,530

Freire's 5th Army

Morillo's Division (6 batts.)	5,129
Longa's Division (5 batts.)	2,607
Del Barco's Division (8 batts.)	5,830
Barcena's Division (6 batts.)	4,154
Spanish Total	*25,373*
A total attacking force of three nations	88,513

Companies of the 5/60th and Brunswickers were detached to other divisions. These companies took most of the casualties, but the battalion strength and loss is shown under the parent brigade..

SOULT'S ARMY AT THE BATTLE OF THE NIVELLE

The regiments had one battalion each, save those marked (2) or (3)

1st Division, Foy	5,136
Fririon's Brigade: 6th Leger, 69th Line (2), 76th Line	
Berlier's Brigade: 36th (2), 39th, 65th (2) Line	
2nd Division, Darmagnac	4,705
Chasse's Brigade: 16th Leger, 8th, 28th (2) Line	
Gruardet's Brigade: 51st, 54th, 75th (2) Line	

3rd Division, Abbe	6,326
Boivin's Brigade: 27th Leger, 63rd, 64th (2) Line	
Maucomble's Brigade: 5th Leger, 94th (2), 95th Line	
4th Division, Conroux	5,399
Rey's Brigade: 12th Leger (2), 32nd (2), 43rd (2) Line	
Baurot's Brigade: 45th, 55th, 58th Line	
5th Division, Maransin	5,579
Barbot's Brigade: 4th Leger, 34th, 40th (2), 50th Line	
Rouget's Brigade: 27th, 59th, 130th (2) Line	
6th Division, Daricau	5,782
St. Pol's Brigade: 21st Leger, 24th, 96th Line	
Mocquery's Brigade: 28th Leger, 100th,103rd Line	
7th Division, Leval	4,539
Pinoteau's Brigade: 17th Leger, 3rd, 15th Line	
Montfort's Brigade: 16th Leger (2), 101st, 105th (2) Line	
8th Division, Taupin	4,889
Bechaud's Brigade: 9th Leger (2), 26th, 47th (2) Line	
Dein's Brigade: 31st Leger (3), 70th, 88th Line	
9th Division, Boyer	6,569
Boyer's Brigade: 2nd Leger (2), 32nd (2), 43rd (2) Line	
Gauthier's Brigade: 120th (3), 122nd (2) Line	
Reserve, Villatte	8,319
BrigadeJamin: 34th Leger (2), 66th, 82nd, 115th (2) Line	
Spanish Brigade (4), Italian Brigade (3), German Brigade (4)	
Artillery, 97 guns, Sappers, Etat-major, Gendarmerie and Train, say	4,200
Total in the field	61,443
Cavalry, all cantoned in the rear	6,788
Garrison of Bayonne	4,633

British and Portuguese Losses at the Nivelle

1st Division, (Howard)		Keane's Brigade	
Maitland's & Stopford's		1/5th Foot	130
Brigades of the Guards	10	2/83rd Foot	47
Hinuber's Brigade		2/87th Foot	103
1st, 2nd & 5th Line K.G.L.	74	94th Foot	75
1st & 2nd Light K.G.L.	109	Power's Portuguese	
1st Division Total	*198*	9th & 21st Line, 11th Cacadores	90
2nd Division, (W. Stewart)		*3rd Division Total*	*518*
Walker's Brigade	–	4th Division, (Cole)	
Byng's Brigade		W. Anson's Brigade	
1/3rd Foot	12	3/27th	65
1/57th Foot	62	1/40th	102
1st Prov. Batt. (2/31st & 2/66th)	54	1/48th Foot	71
Pringle's Brigade		2nd Prov. Batt (2nd & 2/53rd)	53
1/28th, 2/34th, 1/39th Foot	12	Ross's Brigade	
Ashworth's Portuguese		1/7th, 20th, 1/23rd Foot	24
6th & 18th Line, 6th Cacadores	11	Vasconcellos's Portuguese	
2nd Division Total	*151*	11th & 23rd Line, 7th Cacadores	24
3rd Division, (Colville)		*4th Division Total*	*339*
Brisbane's Brigade		5th Division, (Hay)	
1/45th, 74th, 1/88th, 5/60th Foot*	71	Greville's Brigade	
		3/1st , 1/9th, 1/38th Foot	16
		Robinson's Brigade	
		1/4th, 2/47th, 2/59th Foot	3

De Regoa's Portuguese
3rd & 15th Line, 8th Cacadores — 19
5th Division Total — *38*

6th Division, (Clinton)
Pack's Brigade
1/42nd, 1/79th, 1/91st Foot — 44
Lambert's Brigade
1/11th Foot — 12
1/32nd Foot — 50
1/36th Foot — 48
1/61st Foot — 49
Douglas's Portuguese
8th & 12th Line, 9th Cacadores — 59
6th Division Total — *262*

7th Division, (Le Cor)
Barnes's Brigade
1/6th, 3rd Prov.,Brunswick-Oels — 89
Inglis's Brigade
51st Foot — 92
68th Foot — 48
1/82nd Foot — 89
Chasseurs Britanniques — 19
Doyle's Portuguese
7th & 19th Line, 2nd Cacadores — 26
7th Division Total — *363*

Light Division, (C. Alten)
Kempt's Brigade
1/43rd Foot — 77
1/95th Foot — 52
3/95th Foot — 10
Colborne's Brigade
1/52nd Foot — 240
2/95th Foot — 34
Portuguese attached
17th Line, 1st & 3rd Cacadores — 38
Light Division Total — *451*

Aylmer's Independent Brigade
76th, 2/84th, 85th Foot — 22

Hamilton's Division
Da Costa's Brigade
4th & 10th Line,10th Cacadores — 90
Buchan's Brigade
2nd & 14th Line — 33
Bradford's Portuguese — –
Wilson's Portuguese — 18
General Staff — 5
Royal Artillery — 41
Royal Engineers — 1
13th Light Dragoons — 1

GENERAL TOTAL — 2,526

Spanish Loss, No returns, but approximately Army of Galicia and Longa 200 (Daricau & Villatte, who opposed them lost 190 - neither side exposed itself). Giron, 200 (never seriously engaged); Morillo, 20 (practically not engaged); Andrade's Brigade at Maya 400 (double Foy's loss). Something like 820 all told.

FRENCH LOSSES AT THE NIVELLE

Etat-Major	8
Conroux	997
Maransin	1,017
Taupin	941
Darmagnac	407
Abbe	199
Daricau	98
Boyer	189
Leval	114
Foy	220
Villatte's Reserve	92
Artillery	39
Total	*4,321*

BRITISH BATTLE HONOURS FOR THE NIVELLE.
2nd (Queen's Royal) Regt. of Foot
1st Bn. 3rd (East Kent) Regt. of Foot (The Buffs)
1st Bn. 5th (Northumberland) Regt. of Foot
1st Bn. 6th (1st Warwickshire) Regt. of Foot
1st Bn. 11th (North Devonshire) Regt. of Foot
1st Bn. 23rd Regt. of Foot (or Royal Welsh Fusiliers)
2nd Bn. 24th (2nd Warwickshire) Regt. of Foot
3rd Bn. 27th (Inniskilling) Regt. of Foot
1st Bn. 28th (North Gloucestershire) Regt. of Foot
1st Bn. 61st (South Gloucestershire) Regt. of Foot
1st Bn. 36th (Herefordshire) Regt. of Foot
2nd Bn. 31st (Huntingdonshire) Regt. of Foot
1st Bn. 32nd (Cornwall) Regt. of Foot
2nd Bn. 34th (Cumberland) Regt. of Foot

1st Bn. 39th (Dorsetshire) Regt. of Foot
1st Bn. 40th (2nd Somersetshire) Regt. of Foot
1st Bn. 82nd Regt. of Foot (or Prince of Wales's Volunteers)
1st Bn. 42nd (Royal Highland) Regt. of Foot
1st Bn. 43rd (Monmouthshire Light Infantry) Regt.
1st Bn. 52nd (Oxfordshire Light Infantry) Regt.
1st Bn. 45th (Nottinghamshire) Regt. of Foot
1st Bn. 48th (Northamptonshire) Regt. of Foot
2nd Bn. 58th (Rutlandshire) Regt. of Foot
2nd Bn. 66th (Berkshire) Regt. of Foot
51st (2nd Yorkshire, West Riding) Light Infantry Regt.
2nd Bn. 53rd (Shropshire) Regt. of Foot
1st Bn. 57th (West Middlesex) Regt. of Foot
5th Bn. 60th (Royal American) Regt. of Foot
68th (Durham Light Infantry) Regt.
74th (Highland) Regt. of Foot
79th Regt. of Foot (or Cameron Highlanders)
2nd Bn. 83rd Regt. of Foot
1st Bn. 87th (Prince of Wales's Own Irish) Regt. of Foot
1st Bn. 88th Regt. of Foot (or Connaught Rangers)
1st Bn. 94th Regt. of Foot
1st Bn. 91st Regt. of Foot
95th Regt. of Foot (or Rifle Corps)

"Hurrah for the first in the field, and the last out of it, the bloody fighting 95th!"
Old Peninsular Toast

WALKING THE FIELD OF THE BATTLE OF THE NIVELLE, OR ADVENTURES ON THE RHUNES.

Along with the field of Salamanca, the supreme nostalgia and yearning to return is centred on the Pyrenean slopes where was fought the Battle of the Nivelle in November 1813. There can be little in the way of battlefield-walking that approaches those grim rocky fortifications perched on the summit of the Lesser Rhune, nestling under the protective shadow of its big brother, the Greater Rhune. Three times has the author ascended the little rack-railway, and then tramped past herds of wild ponies, up the slope to where the Light Division lay-up during the night of 9/10 November 1813 - and three times has the all-enveloping mist rolled in from the sea and made descending a hazardous business! But what memories it conjures up!

The first occasion was in 1983, when invited to spend two weeks sharing a friend's bergerie (Shepherd's cottage) high in the Pyrenees above the French town of Sare. What follows is the author's account, written at the time.

In the Pyrenees the heat of high Summer had departed and Autumn was redly tinting the rolling hills and lush valley surrounding my friend's typically Basque cottage set down, desolate and sombre, in solitary glory in the middle of the battlefield of the Nivelle, fought on 10 November 1813. It presented a promising setting, for at the Bergerie everything was impressive, both visually and in the imagination - standing on a shelf of land seemingly cut out of the mountain side, I gazed across the valley to the forbidding heights of the Great Rhune, thrilling to the realization that across this very ground dashed the redcoats of Cole's 4th Division to attack the French strongholds of Signal and Louis XIV on the peaks a few yards behind the cottage.

Each night before next day's expedition we sat in the desolate stone-built bergerie, the rebuilt shepherd's hut bearing the impressive Basque name Guchaina Borda, set in a small oak wood high in the hills above the little Pyrenean village of Sare; around a book-piled table before a log-fire blazing and crackling in the open grate while the wind whistled outside. Next morning a perfunctory bachelor's breakfast of cornflakes and coffee, packed the car with books, binoculars, cameras and other essential paraphernalia, then the surging swoop down the steep winding mountain road to Sare 4 kms below. The local phlegmatic Basques had become accustomed to the crazy Anglais who fell like wolves on the fold in the small self-service store, buying long crusty loaves, sorting out cheese, pate and sausage as though choosing books in a library; emerging to juggle expertly with bottles of white and red local wine, tomatoes and a melon.

In a way that might be envied by the politician and those who attempt to forecast the future, the Historian is able to fly untrammelled on the Wings of Time, using Hindsight to carry him back and forth between major events and the occurrences leading to our following upon them. Thus, much of our Pyrenean Promenade was performed in reverse beginning with the Battle of the Nivelle on 11 November 1813, then the action at Vera on 7 October, Cadoux at the Vera bridge on 31 August, the twin battles of Maya and Roncesvalle on 25 July - which all led to the link between them, the two Battles of Sorauren on 28 and 30 July 1813, and the important side show at San Sebastian on 31 August. Eliminating guesswork and conjecture, such unconventional methods allowed fascinating insights into the thinking of Wellington and Soult, the opposing commanders. Truly it was turning to the end pages of the book to see how it all worked out! Being based in France meant that forays south into Spain were essentially full-day affairs and exploring the events of 1813 and centuries earlier at Roncesvalles allied to what was known already about the Battle of Maya, was no exception. Everything points to the fact that Wellington and the entire allied army learned much about fighting in some of the most difficult campaigning country in the world during those last weeks of the Peninsular War, which makes these battles so interesting and worthy of consideration. A bonus lays in the fact that the campaigning area in the South Pyrenees has hardly changed at all, one can still see - looking exactly as they looked to both Allied and French 172 years ago - the bridge and Hermitage Chapel at Sorauren, the Roman Road around the Altobiscar, the Chemin de Anglais at Maya, the Hog's Back above Vera, Cadoux's Bridge and much else.

In our chauvinistic latter-day journey back in Time, like Wellington and his French adversaries, we ranged far and wide over Northern Spain and the French Pyrenees, immaculately guided by the impressive works of Oman, Fortescue, Weller, Glover and others. Uniquely, we benefited from a series of far-from-coincidental circumstances - living in the area, my comrade's exceptional eye for military ground transposed battle accounts and maps onto the actual fields we walked; I saw it all with a wargamer's eye and a mind ceaselessly re-creating all I saw onto tabletop battlefields; essential preliminary research had been done, and we had the time to spend as much as a complete day on each field.

Next morning was hot and sunny so, dressed in lightweight shirts and shorts, we drove to the station at the foot of the Rhunes, from which the Emmett-like little rack-railway wound its patient way up to the summit 900 metres above, taking about 30 minutes to do so. At the halfway point, where the train halted to allow its descending comrade to pass at a junction on the single-track line, amid a barrage of puzzled but friendly hand-waving, we left the little wooden carriage and left the shelf of land bearing the tracks to begin climbing the steep slopes until reaching the valley between the Greater and Lesser Rhunes. Our only companions were herds of wild horses showily galloping and cavorting over the springy green carpet, but we did not feel alone as we knew we were marching in the tracks of the famous Light Division, that 1/95th, 2/95th and 3/95th, the 43rd, 52nd and Portuguese Cacadores had charged up these same slopes.

We halted here, sitting on rocky outcrops to study photo-copied pages of Oman, Weller, Glover, Napier and Fortescue and revise our knowledge of the battle fought over this very ground. Soult had fortified a naturally strong position with his right flank resting on the coast at St. Jean de Luz, posting there full divisions in the fortified villages and strongholds stretching east to Ascain. From there the most formidable part of the line extending to the massif of Mont

Monderrain (both sides considered the terrain to be impassible) was defended by only five divisions, although twice as long. In this section, the main bastion and anchor was the Lesser Rhune, a long rocky ridge crowned by three stone-built redoubts, a thousand feet lower than the Greater Rhune and separated from it by a sharply dipping ravine. From there a series of redoubts sited in depth extended the line to the River Nivelle at Amotz, with two large fortified positions, Signal and Louis XIV redoubts, covering the fortified village of Sare.

Wellington's plan was for General Hope with about a third of the Army to demonstrate against the defences running from the coast to Ascain; Hill with three divisions (26,000 men) was to attack on the far right east of the Nivelle, while Beresford with about the same numbers to attack between the Lesser Rhune and the western side of the Nivelle. Each force had two divisions of Spanish troops under command. The Light Division were to descend by night from the summit of the Greater Rhune, to lay in the saddle between the two ridges before attacking at daybreak, one force directly against the stone-built fortifications on the Lesser Rhune ridge, while the other swung left round the ridge to take the Mouiz Redoubt, covering the French line of retreat from these three positions. So rugged was the area that Wellington could get up in support only three small 3pdr mountain-guns.

Because it forms an excellent wargame in its own right, this part of the battle is given pride of place, beginning when the riflemen leapt up from the peat-bog where they had lain wrapped in their blankets, throughout the night, looking like '...lines of dirty sheep' to assault the three French stone-built forts, followed by formed battalions of Light Infantry, the 43rd and 52nd. The former, commanded by William Napier (later to write the classic history of the Peninsular Campaign) made straight for the redoubts, attacking them one after the other along the ridge - first Place d'Armes, then the Magpie's Nest, and finally the Donjon, while the 52nd swung round the flank to take the Mouiz position. Fighting desperately amid rocky crags, stone barriers, and the narrow ways between the positions, it was not until nearly 8 a.m. that the garrisons were driven out and sent in headlong retreat north-east into the valley of St. Ignace.

It was still hot and sunny when we rose to do our own personal assault on the Lesser Rhune, although to our left the world had begun to be blotted-out by an all-enveloping wall of opaque white mist, swirling swiftly in from the Bay of Biscay, to gobble-up the peat-bog in its more than walking-pace advance before overtaking and swallowing us in its chill and clammy coils. By the time we had clambered up the steep hillside to the first of the three French positions, it was difficult to discern one from the other; they were shaped to conform to the line of the ridge although their rock-ramparts were partly destroyed and now only a couple of feet high. Gingerly we climbed into the first of them—Place d'Armes, then into Magpie and finally the Donjon, all within a few yards of each other; we gazed out into the mist-enshrouded world, visualizing the storming Light Division coming up the grassy, rock-strewn slopes that fell away on both sides just as did the blue-coated French infantry awaiting the charge of green-jacketed riflemen, redcoated infantry and brown tunic'd Portuguese Cacadores. Although our own lightly clad bodies were now chilled by the mist, we decided to rest in the Donjon and take lunch - that almost legendary repast of the battlefield walker consisting of crusty French bread, cheese, pate, and a bottle of local wine. Firmly wedged upon the scattered stone of the now-ruined redoubt, we pondered on transferring this stirring-battle to the wargame table.

By the time lunch was ended, the temperature had dropped about 20 degrees and goosepimples like hens-eggs bespeckled our bare arms; we were quite alone imprisoned in a clinging white world, high up on a razor-edge ridge in the Pyrenees, amid roof-steep slopes, precipitous drops and numerous peat-bogs. The only possible way of getting down was by using a compass; by its aid we slithered cautiously across mountain sides, skirted rocky outcrops and obvious clumps of marsh grass until our lips muttered a prayer of thankfulness when reaching that narrow shelf of land cut into the mountain-side bearing the little railway track. Certainly we felt safer, but still very cold in our shorts and short-sleeved shirts, as we set abut walking down the Rhune on a very rough, rock covered path with tarred railway sleepers just the wrong distance apart to be comfortably walked upon. This five miles, two-hour walk became a major physical achievement that caused me to be thankful for the degree of fitness gained by running many miles along New Forest tracks. Also, it brought home the fact that these soldiers, both British and French, had all climbed up this rough terrain before they could fight their battle on the top of it!

In the author's experience, wargamers are friendly guys, always ready to help each other - so it was with no real surprise that a letter was received from Chris Russell (of Gloucester in England) who had heard of our adventures. He wrote:

> I have visited the area many times as it is only a brisk hour-and-a-half's climb from my Grandmother's house in Ascain. It is a very evocative place and I have passed many a happy afternoon pacing over that very path taken by the Light Division in their battle to gain these heights. I was pleasantly surprise to see that another wargamer had discovered this almost-lost place of History. However, as you did not mention the Mouiz Redoubt I can but assume you missed in it the enveloping fog, which would have been a great pity, for it is the most spectacular of the Peninsular War remains in the area. In fact, as far as I know, it is the only Napoleonic redoubt left standing anywhere, especially one that was involved in a battle over its possession.

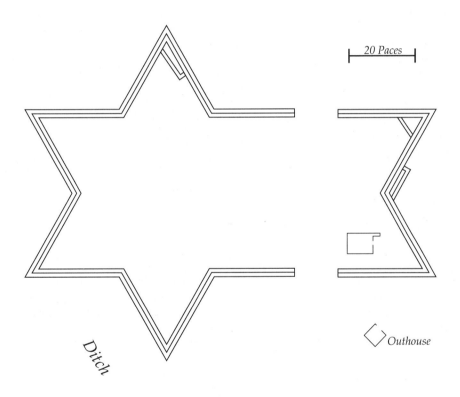

He was quite right, in that we did know of the Mouiz Redoubt and its general location in relation to the Donjon and the other fortifications, but did not dare venture down the steep, rock-strewn slopes because the fog-blanket made it rather hazardous.

Chris Russell continues:

If you had followed the slightly zig-zag mound of a ditch and earthwork, from the Donjon down the opposite side to the railway in the valley, for about 600 yards, you would have come to the star-shaped fortification.

If you are going to the area again (we were and we did what he suggested) I recommend the book 'Wellington: The Bidassoa and The Nivelle' by F. C. Beatson (published in the 1930's). It has an excellent map of the Rhune/Sare area, including your friends' house (the Bergerie, headquarters for the 1983 tour). This map shows the position of many other redoubts, most now being only discernible by their ditches, the walls probably having been dismantled and used by farmers to build their bergeries (including your friend's?)

Also useful are the Carte Touristique series of maps by the Institut Geographique National (of France) - No. 69 is the one for this area, but better scale maps are available that show several earthwork sites, including those from earlier battles along the Bidassoa. The area possesses a fair amount of history - there is an elegant Roman bridge at Ascain, and a Roman fort at Bayonne (or bits of it plus numerous Medieval additions) situated within the Vauban fortresses.

I have wargamed the battle for the Lesser Rhune, but found the British to be too strong for the French - of course, that could be the fault of the rules, or me, or both! Perhaps one day we can meet in the Bar Basque in St. Jean de Luz, and get out our toy soldiers - the French have always thought the British to be eccentric!

WARGAMING THE BATTLE OF THE NIVELLE.

Not for the first time came the realisation of how difficult it is to reproduce real heights and mountains in miniature, here they played such a vital part that the inclusion is vital, yet it is well known that little metal wargames figures are not very good at standing on steep slopes! The defenders must be given the benefits of the higher ground they historically occupied and attackers must be forced to ascend more slowly so that they must take increased volumes of fire. Perhaps varying contours can best be simulated by giving those ascending them varying rates of movement proportionate to the degree of slope they are climbing - thus, four degrees of gradient with the shortest move-distance for the steepest, and longest for the most gradual slopes. In other words, the slopes exist but mostly in the imagination, being given their true severity by rule-manipulation of move-distance. There was a high degree of surprise at the Battle of the Nivelle, always difficult to represent on the wargames table unless battling with amiable friends in a consensus-type game. It can be simulated by the use of maps marked before hand so that troop formations are not hastily altered to conform to some threatening move of the enemy; by using cards laid to represent formations, with an adequate number of 'false' cards that mean nothing - but it looks incredibly untidy and unrealistic! However, the more enlightened type of wargamer (and there must be some!) will agree with opponents that both sides accept surprise where it historically occurred, and react accordingly. As in all battles, every event did not occur simultaneously, so a Time-Chart is necessary, marked at relevant points to ensure that specific events take place only in their appropriate phase.

THE BATTLES OF THE NIVE - 9-13 DECEMBER 1813

During the Peninsular War there was a remarkable understanding between the outposts and sentries of the opposing armies. Napier tells a story which illustrates this:- "Lord Wellington, desirous to gain the top of a hill occupied by the enemy near Bayonne, ordered his escort of Riflemen to drive the French away, and seeing the soldiers stealing up too close, as he thought, called out to fire, but with a loud voice one of those veterans replied, No firing! Holding up the butt of his rifle towards the French, he tapped it in a peculiar way, and at the private signal, which meaned, We must have the hill for a short time, the French, who could not maintain, yet would not have relinquished it without a fight if they had been fired upon, quietly retired: yet this signal would never have been made if the post had been one capable of a permanent defence, so well did those veterans understand war and its proprieties."

Arthur Griffiths gives more information on this aspect of warfare, the courtesies being observed by the Allies, although aware that they were to attack on the following morning:

At the village of Cambo, on the Nive, the sentinels of the outlying pickets were so near each other that the French and British could converse at times, and, as if by tacit agreement, no shots were exchanged there. Daily the French drill-sergeants could be seen, cane in hand, drilling the conscripts, and the British used to crowd to the edge of the swollen river, to behold the novel sight of French regiments quietly on parade. The evening of the 8th of December proving a remarkably fine one, the French bands came to the edge of the stream at Cambo, on which the 71st and 92nd Highlanders were cantoned, and played many airs for their amusement. Other courtesies were interchanged by the officers; flasks of wine, bunches of fruit, and London and Paris newspapers were thrown across the stream. Military topics were strictly avoided by the officers of the adverse armies, who spent the evening laughing and jesting like friends, till recalled on each side by beat of drum when darkness came, and they separated to meet next morning sword in hand.

Early in December 1813 Wellington felt constrained to throw his army across the River Nive, to give himself access to the more fertile country beyond, in the awareness that this would mean heavy fighting as Soult's positions were strong and well chosen, as Napier reveals:

Bayonne, his base, being situated at the confluence of the Nive and the Adour rivers furnished bridges for the passage of both; and though weak in itself, was covered by Vauban's entrenched camp, which was exceedingly strong and not to be lightly attacked. In this camp Soult's right, under Reille, three divisions including Villatte's reserve, touched on the lower Adour, where there was a flotilla. His front was protected by inundations and a swamp, through which the royal coast road led to St. Jean de Luz, and along which fortified outposts extended to Anglet. On his left Clausel's three divisions extended to the Nive, being partly covered by the swamp, partly by a fortified house, partly by an artificial inundation spreading from the small bridge of Urdains to the Nive; and beyond these defences the country held by the allies was a deep clay, covered with small farm-houses and woods, very unfavourable for movement.

On the right of the Nive, Vauban's camp being continued to the upper Adour under the name of the "Front of Mousserolles," was held by D'Erlon's four divisions, with posts extending up the right bank of the Nive; that is to say, D'Armagnac fronted Ustaritz, and Foy was at Cambo. The communication with the left bank of the Nive was double; circuitous through Bayonne, direct by a bridge of boats. Moreover, after the battle of the Nivelle, Soult brought General Paris's division from St. Jean Pied de Port to Lahoussoa close under the Ursouia mountain, whence it communicated with Foy's left by the great road of St. Jean Pied de Port.

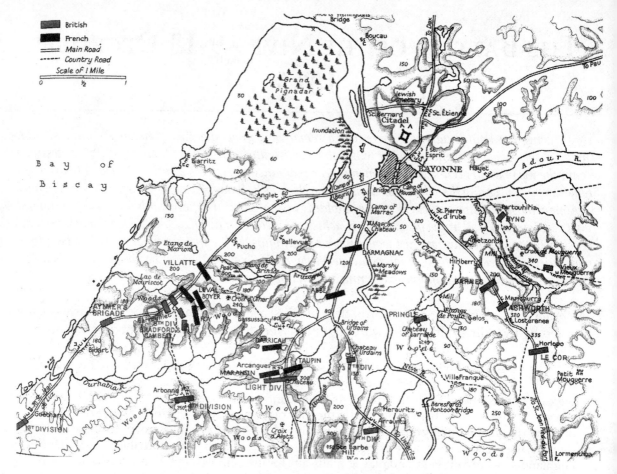

BATTLE OF THE NIVE, DECEMBER 10TH, 1813

Subsequently, beginning on 9 December, Hope and Alten with 24,000 men and 12 guns, set out to drive back the French advanced posts in front of their camp, between the Nive and the sea, thus keeping Soult in check while Beresford and Hill crossed the Nive - Beresford at Ustaritz with pontoons, Hill at Cambo and Larressore, by fords. Both generals were ordered to repair the standing bridges at those places, using materials prepared beforehand and carried with them. To cover Hill's movements on the right and to protect the valley of the Nive from General Paris, based at Lahoussoa who might have penetrated the rear of the army during the operations, Morillo's Spaniards were to cross at Itzassu.

Once in France, the Spanish troops began committing excesses, plundering and killing, causing French civilians to flee from the area. Wellington took immediate action, executing all caught in the act and then, despite reproaches and discontent of the Spanish generals, forced all formations, with the exception of Morillo's, to withdraw back into Spain. He disarmed Mina's mutinous battalions, placed Giron's Andulusians in the Bastan under O'Donnel, quartered Freyre's Galicians between Irun and Ernani, and sent Longa's force over the Ebro.

James Grant describes the operations:

A double bridge at Ustaritz, on the Nive, had been broken down, but an island which connected them was possessed by a detachment of our troops. Marshal Beresford had quietly laid his pontoons on the hither side in the night; and on the morning of the 9th a beacon suddenly flaring up on a height above Cambo gave the signal of action, and Colonel John Cameron threw himself into the river at the head of the 92nd Highlanders, which belonged to Hill's division. The latter forced the passage in three columns, above and below the river, but not without resistance, and the winter fords were so deep that some of the cavalry were drowned; and the French were strongly posted, especially at Halzou, where a deep and strong mill-race had to be crossed as well as the river, along the banks of which the red fire of the musketry sparkled out upon the gloom of the wintry dawn.

When the Highlanders were in the middle of the stream, Cameron's favourite piper was shot by his side. Stooping from his saddle, he strove to help him; but the man was swept away.

"Alas," cried he, "I would rather have lost twenty men that you!"

At this point Beresford drove back the column of D'Armagnac; but the swampy nature of the ground between the Nive and the high-road, by entangling the advance, gave the latter time to retreat, while Sir John Hope with his column, following the great road, drove in the pickets and ultimately established himself within three miles of Bayonne.

Murillo, with his Spaniards, forced the passage of the stream at the pretty village of Itzassu, and inaugurated the invasion of France by the murder of fifteen helpless peasants, among whom were some women and children.

Sir Rowland Hill placed a brigade of infantry at Urcurray, to cover the bridge of Cambo and to support the cavalry, which he had dispatched to scour the roads in front. With the rest of his troops he marched against the heights of Mouserolles, where D'Erlon was posted with four divisions. It was now one o'clock, and Soult, with a splendid staff, came galloping in from Bayonne to offer battle. A heavy cannonade took place, and a general skirmish along the front, but no general engagement, because the deep and adhesive mud of the roads retarded the rear of Hill's columns. However, the Portuguese of the 6th division drove the regiments of D'Armagnac, after a furious conflict, out of Villefranque about three in the afternoon, and a brigade was established in advance to connect Hill with Beresford.

Meanwhile, Hope had been fighting his way to the point he attained. Preceded by the fire of his guns, and the rattling shots of a long and thick line of skirmishers, in a great half-circle, his division had come sweeping through mud and mire, over field and hedge, through wood and vineyard, till one o'clock in the day, when he halted in front of Soult's intrenched camp, round which his "fiery crescent" closed, at which time his troops had been twenty-four hours under arms.

Such was the passage of the Nive, which was thus vigorously effected, with the loss only of 800 men on each side; but the fighting on the Nive was by no means over yet.

On the left the troops were placed in their old cantonments: the Guards, with the head-quarter staff and a large artillery force, occupied St. Jean de Luz; the 5th division, Lord Aylmer's independent brigade, and a corps of Portuguese were among the villages extending from thence to Bidart. In like manner, the light division re-established itself in Arcanques, and both from it and the 5th strong pickets were thrown forward to observe the roads, guard the defiles, and give due warning to the troops in reserve, should any movement be made by the enemy; but until ten o'clock in the day no alarm was given. Then, however, the pickets of the 5th and light divisions found themselves suddenly attacked by overwhelming numbers, and a furious contest began.

"We had dreamed of nothing else than a general action this morning," wrote an officer who was present, "and we found ourselves bearing the brunt of it before we could well very make up our minds as to the proximity of the enemy. Everything was accordingly done, every word spoken, and every movement made under the influence of that species of excitement which absolutely shuts out all ideas, except those which spring from the circumstances immediately about you; I mean, an apprehension lest your men shall give way, and an inexpressible eagerness to close with your adversary. Nor were sundry opportunities wanting of gratifying the last of these desires. We fought, at least where I was stationed, in a thick wood; and more than once it occurred that we fought hand to hand."

The attack in question was planned with skill, and executed with great daring. Soult, during the night of the 9th, had drawn every disposable bayonet from his intrenchments on the Nive, and passing them through Bayonne, advanced to assault the position of Sir John Hope at Arcanques. With loud yells and the rattle of close musketry, the French came on at a running pace upon the pickets of the light division. A cloud of their skirmishers, descending on the left flank, penetrated between the 43rd and 52nd Regiments. The attack was so strong, so rapid, and the foe so numerous, that to fall back on the church of Arcanques, across a common, seemed impossible; yet the pickets fell back steadily, firing into the very teeth of the enemy at pistol distance. During this, they had at times to run at full speed to gain the common before the enemy, who were constantly outflanking them; the paths were so muddy and narrow that no regular front could be formed, and the fire of the pursuing French was as close as their wild halloos and shouts of "Vive l'Empereur!" were incessant; but the moment the open ground in front of Arcanques was gained, the fugitives faced about, shoulder to shoulder, and opened a rolling fire which arrested the French at once.

Half a mile on the left of the 43rd was the Oxford Light Infantry, falling back towards the same ground, which it reached in good time. On the right, however, about a hundred men of the 43rd and our Rifles were intercepted and cut off. "The French were in a hollow road, and careless, never doubting that the officer of the 43rd, Ensign Campbell, a youth scarcely eighteen years of age, would surrender; but with a shout he broke into their column, sword in hand, and though the struggle was severe, and twenty of the 43rd and thirty riflemen with their officers remained prisoners, he reached the church."

Here at Arcanques, in the middle of a wood, is an ancient chateau which then belonged to the Mayor of Biarritz. It stands on the right of the high road, and a small lake lies on its left. D'Armagnac's division and D'Erlon's corps now came up, and opened a sharp fire of musketry. To secure their passage, one detachment rushed into the wood, while another bore upon the posts in the village, and at both points the fighting was desperate. The chateau was occupied by a battalion of the Rifles and another of the Portuguese. The church and its burial ground were garrisoned by the 43rd, supported by two mountain guns; their front being further protected by a thick copsewood, full of riflemen, and only to be turned by two hollow roads that lay one on each side of the bank or eminence on which the church is built.

Hot grew the skirmish and heavy the firing. The whole village of Arcanques and the woods were enveloped in smoke, above which the spire and the roof of the chateau were barely visible at times. And now Clausel came galloping forward with twelve pieces of cannon, which threw both shot and shell into the churchyard, at which 500 infantry made a rush, only to be hurled back by the terrible bayonets of the 43rd, whose white colours were waved in defiance above the church-yard wall. The cannonade, however, must have proved murderous, if our musketry had not compelled the gunners to draw their pieces under cover of a ridge, from whence their shot flew and wide of aim. The moment the firing lulled, forward came the French cannon again, and the shells were most destructive, till by dint of musket they were withdrawn again.

The sound of heavy firing at Arcanques soon gave an alarm to brigades that were in the rear; forming beside their cantonments, they moved rapidly and in excellent order to the scene of action. Groups of wounded men, pale, bleeding, and exhausted, and of captured prisoners, met them by the way.

"Push on, push on, or Arcanques will be lost!" was the incessant shout. At last the field of battle came in view, and while they were admiring and cheering the steadiness of "the handful of red-coats" that manned the church yard wall, the French cannon opened on themselves.

They pushed on, however, and were soon deployed into line. Then followed a sort of lull in the firing, as if Soult was pausing to consider how to act under such a change of circumstances. Then came another furious and bloody onset, made only to be repelled; and when darkness set in the hostile armies were precisely where they had been at two o'clock in the day; and both lay down beside their fires to await the coming morrow.

Of these events, Napier wrote:

It was not very severe, yet both French and English writers, misled perhaps by an inaccurate phrase in the public despatch, have represented it as a desperate attack by which the Light Division was driven into its entrenchments; whereas the piquets only were forced back, and there were no entrenchments save those made on the spur of the moment by the soldiers in the churchyard.

With Wellington's wings divided by the Nive, Soult resolved to fall upon one of them with his united force, part of this operation being the activities around Arcangues, the other consisted of attacks in the region of Barrouilhet. Here Reille's two divisions drove Campbell's Portuguese from Anglet, with Sparre's cavalry cutting down many of them.

Napier tells of the course of events:

The French infantry then assailed the position of Barrouilhet, but moving along a narrow ridge, confined on each flank by banks, only two brigades could get into action by the main road, and the rain had rendered all the bye-roads so deep that it was midday before their line of battle was filled. This delay saved the allies, for the attack here also was so unexpected that the first division and Lord Aylmer's brigade were at rest in St. Jean de Luz and Bidart when the action commenced, and the latter did not reach the position before eleven o'clock; the foot-guards did not march until after twelve, and only arrived at three o'clock when the fight was done; all the troops were exceedingly fatigued, only ten guns could be brought into play, and from some negligence part of the infantry were without ammunition.

Robinson's brigade of the fifth division first arrived to support Campbell and fight the battle. The French skirmishers had then spread along the whole valley, while their columns moved by the great road against the mayor's house on the platform of Barrouilhet, where the ground was thick of hedges and coppice-wood. A most confused fight took place. The assailants, cutting ways through the hedges, poured on in smaller or larger bodies as the openings allowed, and were immediately engaged, at some points successfully, at others beaten, and few knew what was going on to the right or left of where they stood. By degrees Reille engaged both his divisions, and some of Villatte's reserve also entered the fight, but then Bradford's Portuguese and Aylmer's brigade arrived on the allies' side, which enabled Greville's brigade of the fifth division, hitherto in reserve, to relieve Robinson's troops who had suffered severely, and he himself was dangerously wounded.

A notable action now happened with the 9th Regiment under Colonel Cameron. Posted on the extreme left of Greville's brigade, there was between it and Bradford's brigade a Portuguese battalion. Opposite the 9th was a coppice-wood possessed by the enemy, whose skirmishers were continually gathering in masses and rushing out as if to assail the regiment, and were as often driven back; but the ground was so broken that nothing could be seen on the flanks, and after some time Cameron, who had received no orders, heard a sudden firing along the main road close to his left. His adjutant, sent to look out, returned quickly to say a French regiment, which must have passed unseen in small bodies between the Portuguese battalion and the 9th, was rapidly filing into line on the rear. The 4th British Regiment was in column at a short distance, and its commander, Colonel Piper, was directed by Cameron to face about and fall on the French regiment; but he took a wrong direction, no firing followed, and the adjutant again hurried to the rear in observation. The 4th Regiment was not to be seen, and the enemy's line was then nearly formed, whereupon Cameron, leaving fifty men to answer the skirmishing fire, which now increased from the copse, faced about and marched against the new enemy, who was about his own strength. The French opened fire, slowly at first, but increasing vehemently as the distance lessened, until the 9th sprung forwards to charge; then the adverse line broke and fled by their flanks in disorder, those who made for their own right brushing the left of Greville's brigade and carrying off an officer of the Royals in their rush, yet the greatest number were made prisoners and Cameron having lost eighty men and officers resumed his old ground.

Eventually Clausel's inclinations to continue the battle were thwarted by Wellington rapidly moving the 3rd; 4th; 6th; and 7th Divisions, their dispositions checking Clausel and aborting Soult's attack at Barrouilhet.

NAPIER:
In this battle two generals and twelve hundred Anglo-Portuguese had been killed and wounded, three hundred made prisoners. The French had one general, Villatte, wounded, and lost two thousand men; and when the action terminated two regiments of Nassau with one of

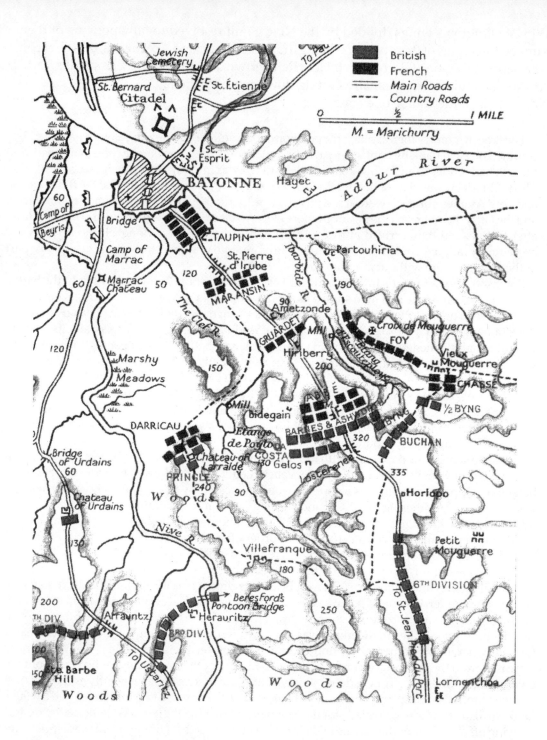

Frankfort came over to the allies. These men were not deserters. Their prince having abandoned Napoleon in Germany sent secret instructions to his troops to do so likewise, and in good time, for Napoleon's orders to disarm them reached Soult the next morning.

Next morning there was a thick fog.

NAPIER:

...at ten o'clock Lord Wellington, desirous to ascertain what Soult was doing, directed the 9th Regiment to skirmish beyond the tanks, but not to push the action if the French augmented their force. Cameron did so and the fight was becoming warm, when Colonel Delancy, a staff-officer, rashly directed the 9th to enter the village: an error sharply corrected. For the fog cleared up, and Soult, who had twenty-four thousand men at that point, seeing the 9th unsupported, made a counter-attack so strong and sudden that Cameron only saved his regiment with the aid of some Portuguese troops hastily brought up by Hope. The fighting then ceased and Wellington went to the right, leaving Hope with orders to drive back the French picquets and re-establish his own outposts.

Soult, hitherto seemingly undecided, was roused by this second insult. He ordered Daricau's division to attack the right of Barrouilhet in reply, while Boyer's division fell on by the main road between the tanks. The allies, unexpectant of battle, had dispersed to gather fuel, for the time was wet and cold, wherefore the French penetrated in all directions; they outflanked the right, they passed the tanks, seized the outhouses of the mayor's house and occupied the coppice in front of it; and though driven from the outbuildings by the Royals, the tumult was great and the coppice was filled with men of all nations intermixed and fighting in a perilous manner. Robinson's brigade was very hardly handled, the officer commanding it was wounded, a squadron of French cavalry again cut down some Portuguese near the wood; and on the right the colonel of the 84th having unwisely entered a hollow road, the French, having the banks, killed him and a great number of his men. However the 9th Regiment, posted on the main road, plied Boyer's flank with fire, the 85th Regiment came into action, and Hope, conspicuous from his gigantic stature and heroic courage, was seen wherever danger pressed, encouraging the troops: at one time he was in the midst of the enemy, his clothes were pierced with bullets and he was severely wounded in the ankle, yet he would not quit the field, and thus by his calm intrepidity restored the battle, and the French were beaten from Barrouilhet.

Rain again fell heavily during the night and although the morning broke fair, neither side seemed inclined to recommence hostilities. Then, at 10 o'clock, Soult imagining he was about to be attacked, reinforced his front causing Allied artillery to open fire, followed by the French guns and, for many hours, both sides fired continually without object, with casualties of about 400 a side because it died down."

George Simmons, in a letter to his father, told of a sad incident during the fighting:

On the 10th, my friends informed me that Marshal Soult advanced with a large force by the high road from Bayonne and formed up near Bassussarry, which is directly opposite the church and chateau of Archangues, and made an attack upon the left of our line. Lieutenant Hopwood and Sergeant Brotherwood were killed. A ball passed through both their heads, happening to be standing a little behind one another. They were both capital soldiers and were put in the same grave.

James Grant:

...the approach of darkness found both armies jaded and weary with four days of incessant exertion and fierce excitement, during which they had little leisure to eat, and yet less to cook.

The night of the 12th swelled the Nive; and the flood tore away the bridge of communication between the left and the right of the army on the right bank, under Sir Rowland Hill, who was thus isolated, and against whose solitary force Soult now poured his strength. Seven divisions of French infantry, mustering 35,000 bayonets, approached him in front; an eighth, under General Paris, and the cavalry of Pierre Soult, threatened his rear; and to meet all these in front, this gallant old Shropshire gentleman, whose kind heart made him the idol of the troops, had only 14,000 men in position, with fourteen guns; and to check those in his rear, only 4,000 Spaniards, and the cavalry of Sir Hussey Vivian.

The morning of the 13th of December dawned heavily. A thick mist overhung St. Pierre, and under its cover the Duke of Dalmatia formed his order of battle against Hill, whose position occupied a front of two miles. His left, composed of the 28th, the 34th, and 39th Regiments, under General Pringle, was posted on a well-wooded ridge, where stands the Chateau de Villefranque; it was separated from his centre by a small stream, that flowed through a deep marshy hollow.

The centre was on both sides of the highway, near the hamlet of St. Pierre, on a curved height studded with rocks and bushes. On the right were high and dense hedges, one of which covered part of the line, and was all but impassable. Here was posted the brigade of General Barnes; the

71st Highlanders being on the left, the 50th in the centre, and the 92nd Highlanders on the right.

The right wing, under Byng, was composed of the Buffs, the 57th, 31st, and 66th. Ashworth's Portuguese were posted in advance of the hamlet. Their skirmishers lay in a wood, and twelve pieces of cannon faced the road which led to the position of Soult, a range of counter heights one mile in front of St. Pierre. The ground between was broad, but so heavy and enclosed that infantry alone could act with effect.

As the gloomy December dawn stole in, the massed columns of the French could be seen dimly and darkly at times; they were quite shrouded in grey rolling vapour at others, and anon they loomed out large and distinctly, in their gray great-coats, with arms shouldered and bayonets fixed. They came on briskly; at half-past eight red musketry flashed out of the mist, and Hill's out-pickets were driven in. Then the morning sun burst forth, and the steel weapons of the adverse lines shone in light; while the rattling fire of the scattered skirmishers sparkled all along the valley, rolled up the green slopes on either flank, and the hoarse booming of forty pieces of cannon shook the heights were Hill was posted.

General Daricou's column was dispatched against that of General Pringle; D'Armagnac, marching by Old Moguerre, faced Byng; and Abbe assailed the centre, where the valiant old Sir William Stewart commanded; while Sir Rowland Hill took his station on a conspicuous eminence, from whence he could watch the whole progress of the battle.

General Abbe, a man of stern valour, dashed on with great vigour, and with the French light infantry gained ground so rapidly on the left flank of the Portuguese, that Stewart sent the 71st Highlanders and two cannon from St. Pierre to aid them.

The French, however, won a wood on their right, but were driven out of it by a wing of the 50th, which secured the flank of Stewart's position; but against him the whole fire of Soult's artillery was levelled, so the slaughter there was very great. Towards that point, Abbe pushed on with great intrepidity, though galled by flanking fires of musketry and a furious cannonade in front, and routed the Portuguese, together with the other wing of the 50th Regiment.

Barnes now brought on the Gordon Highlanders from the rear of St. Pierre, and so furious was their counter-attack, that they routed the whole of the French skirmishers, picking them out of their hiding-places by the bayonet, so they fled, leaving their column to meet the Highland charge, before which it wavered, broke, and fled. Abbe instantly replaced the fugitives by another column, while Soult redoubled the fire of his heavy guns on the heights; and a battery of horse artillery came galloping into the valley, along which it sent a plunging fire through the kilted ranks, which were torn up in a manner so horrible that they were compelled to give way, and retire in rear of St. Pierre. Cameron, their colonel, had his horse shot under him, and would have been bayoneted, but for the bravery and devotion of his foster-brother, Private Ewan Macmillan.

Matters were now seeming desperate. General Barnes was wounded; most of his staff and that of Stewart had been shot down. Overpowered by numbers, the light troops had been driven in, save the few who held the wood; the ground was strewn with mangled dead, or wretched wounded crawling in hundreds to the rear, while the leaden and iron storm swept over them. The French column of attack was steadily coming on; another launched on its right was already victorious, because the colonel of the 71st Highlanders—a regiment second to none in the annals of war—by some disgraceful mistake, ordered them to retire and abandon the Portuguese; while, on another part of the field, the colonel of the Buffs in the same manner abandoned his post to the soldiers of D'Armagnac.

During the fighting, Colonel Peacock who had returned to command the 71st after the death of Cadogan, their former Commanding Officer, had pusillanimously marched his men out the line of action. His second-in-command, Major Macdonald, realising that he was acting without orders, over-ruled him and marched the regiment back again. Peacock was later found by Wellington among the baggage-train; he was relieved of his command.

James Grant:

Fearing that all would be lost, Sir Rowland Hill came on the spur from the eminence, and led on the Buffs in person, and the reserves were brought into action; while the right wing of the 50th and Ashworth's cacadores still held the little wood with unflinching valour. This gave the shattered Gordon Highlanders time to re-form; and their gallant colonel, John Cameron, a worthy grandson of the great Cavalier Lochiel, once more led them down the road with pipes playing, their yellow colours flying, and their black plumes and green tartans waving on the wind, resolved to give the shock to whatever stood in their way.

"How gloriously did that regiment (the 92nd) come forth again to the charge," says Napier. "with the colours flying and its national music playing as if going to a review! This was to understand war. The man who in that moment, and immediately after a repulse, thought of such military pomp, was by nature a soldier."

"The 92nd," he continues, "was but a small clump compared with the dark mass in its front; and that mass seemed to stand firmly enough until an officer who rode at its head waved his sabre and ordered a retreat. This retrograde movement, for there was no panic or disorder, was produced partly by the gallant advance of the 92nd and the returning rush of the skirmishers, partly by the state of affairs on the right of the French column, where the 71st Highlanders, indignant at the conduct of their colonel, who was not a Highlander, had returned to the fight with such fierceness, and were so well aided by Lecor's Portuguese—Hill and Stewart in person leading the attack —that the hitherto victorious French were overthrown there also, at the very moment when the 92nd came with that brave show down the main road."

The Regimental Record states that on this day the latter corps "made four distinct charges with the bayonet, and lost 13 officers and 171 rank and file."

Daricou's division was now falling back in confusion before the brigade of Pringle, while Buchan's Portuguese regiment, on the extreme right, being detached by Hill to recapture the Moguerre ridge, rallied the 3rd Buffs at a happy moment; for D'Armagnac's first brigade was already fighting its way past Byng's flank at the stream, and was almost in rear of his line.

It was now twelve o'clock, and as the reserves were all engaged, the staff all killed or wounded, three of our generals badly hurt, and the divisions of Foy and Marousin were at hand to renew the fight in the centre, the Allies could not have continued it much longer, thinned and wasted as their ranks were by cannon and musketry.

At this crisis, the quick eye of Hill seeing Buchan's Portuguese fighting bravely at old Moguerre, and Byng holding his ground in the valley by the stream, drew the 57th from them to strengthen his centre; at the same time, the bridge of boats having been restored, the whole of our 6th division, which had been on the march since daybreak, with all their barrels glittering in the sun, appeared in order of battle, by contiguous battalions, on the ridge below St. Pierre. Other drums were heard, and other colours seen flying, as our 3rd and 4th divisions, and two brigades of the 7th, came hurrying on to take part in the battle.

With the first portion of these troops came Wellington in person, wearing a glazed cocked-hat, an oil-skin cape, and a telescope slung over his shoulder. From Barrouilhet he had hurried when first the sound of the cannon reached him; but he arrived only in time to witness the close of the strife—for the fierce crisis was past, and the glory of Sir Rowland was complete.

Soult, still indefatigable, made fresh demonstrations against the centre, but was repulsed; while at the same moment, Buchan, at the head of his Portuguese, hurled D'Armagnac headlong from the ridge of Moguerre. Massed columns of the enemy still continued to encumber the main road and fire from a hillock, till Byng was sent with two battalions against the latter, and some troops from the centre against the former. At this time the generals and staff were so cut down, that Colonel Currie, the aide-de-camp, could find no superior officer to whom to give the order. Hence he led the troops himself to the attack.

Both charges were successful, and two pieces of cannon were captured. The battle now dwindled down to a skirmish, amid which the French endeavoured to carry off their wounded and rally their stragglers; but at two o'clock Lord Wellington, to end the affair, ordered an advance of the whole line. The French then retreated, but still fighting nevertheless, and followed closely by the Allies, who plied them with musket-shot until darkness fell.

Soult's loss was certainly 3,000, making a total on the five days' fighting of 6,000 men, with two generals—Villatte and Maucomble.

Hill had three generals and 1,500 men killed and wounded; and our loss on he five days' fighting was 5,000 (including 500 prisoners); and five generals—Hope, Barnes, Ashworth, Lecor, and Robinson—were wounded.

Napier reported:

In this bloody action Soult had designed to employ seven divisions of infantry with one brigade of cavalry on the front, and one brigade of infantry with a division of cavalry on the rear; but the state of the roads and the narrow front did not permit more than five divisions to act, and only half of these were seriously engaged.

After this bloody finale the opposing armies went into Winter quarters; the Allies occupying cantonments, while the French withdrew behind the lines of Bayonne. Nothing of interest occurred until the middle of February, when the Spring weather returned.

BRITISH AND PORTUGUESE LOSSES

DECEMBER 9

(1) PASSAGE OF THE NIVE BY HILL'S CORPS

2nd Division	
Pringle's Brigade	67
Barnes's Brigade	6
Attached Companies 5/60th	14
6th Division	
Pack's Brigade	54
Lambert's Brigade	36
Douglas's Portuguese	117
Total	*294*

(2) COMBATS OF ANGLET AND BASSUSSARY BY HILL'S CORPS AND LIGHT DIVISION

Staff	3
1st Division	
Howard's Brigade	33
K.G.L. Brigade	70
5th Division	
Greville's Brigade	78
Robinson's Brigade	108
Light Division	34
Attached Companies Brunswickers	4
Artillery	6
Total	*336*

DECEMBER 10

(3) COMBAT OF ARCANGUES, LIGHT DIVISION

Kempt's Brigade	
1/43rd	32
1/95th	42
3/95th	23
Colborne's Brigade	
1/52nd	26
2/95th	15
Portuguese	
1st Cacadores	49
3rd Cacadores	26
17th Line	11
Total	*224*

(4) FIRST COMBAT OF BARROUILLET, HOPE'S CORPS

Staff	3
5th Division	
Greville's Brigade	
3/1st Foot	45
1/9th Foot	81
1/38th Foot	43
Robinson's Brigade	
1/4th Foot	56
2/47th Foot	115
2/59th Foot	74
2/84th Foot	94
Attached Companies Brunswickers	3
De Regoa's Brigade	
3rd Line	104
15th Line	134
8th Cacadores	34
Aylmer's Independent Brigade	
2/62nd Foot	1
76th Foot	16
85th Foot	13
A. Campbell's Brigade	
1st Line	140
16th Line	152
4th Cacadores	42
Bradford's Brigade	
13th Line	100
24th Line	118
5th Cacadores	123
Artillery	6
Total	*1,497*

DECEMBER 11

(5) SECOND COMBAT OF BARROUILLET AND ARCANGUES

5th Division	
Greville's Brigade	119
Robinson's Brigade	201
Attached Companies Brunswickers	3
Light Division	5
Total	*328*

Note: Portuguese Losses included in the December 10 Numbers

DECEMBER 12

(6) THIRD COMBAT OF BARROUILLET, AND
CAVALRY FIGHT AT HASPARREN

Guards Brigade, 1st Division	186
Artillery	8
5/60th	6
14th Light Dragoons (Hasparren)	7
Total	207

DECEMBER 13

(7) BATTLE OF ST. PIERRE D'IRRUBE

2nd Division

Barnes's Brigade

1/50th Foot	130
1/71st Foot	122
1/92nd Foot	185

Byng's Brigade

1/3rd Foot	86
1/57th Foot	128
1st Provisional Batt.	108

Pringle's Brigade

1/28th Foot	101
2/34th Foot	5
1/39th Foot	18
Attached Companies 5/60th	21

Ashworth's Portuguese

6th Line	199
18th Line	182
8th Cacadores	90

Le Cor's Division

Da Costa's Brigade

2nd Line	54
14th Line	133

Buchan's Brigade

4th Line	68
10th Line	68
10th Cacadores	44
General Staff	7
British Artillery	5
Portuguese Artillery	6
6th Division (9th Cacadores)	15
Total	1,784

Casualties, December 9th - 13th	4,671

SOULT'S ARMY AT THE NIVE

	Strength	Losses
1st Division, Foy	5,608	903
composition exactly as at the Nivelle		
2nd Division, Darmagnac	5,914	778
has received 2 batts. of 31st Leger from dissolved 8th Division		
3rd Division, Abbe	6,372	1,276
Baurot has replaced Boivin; composition exactly as at the Nivelle		
4th Division, Taupin (vice Conroux, killed)	6,098	197
composition exactly as at the Nivelle		
5th Division, Maransin	5,216	299
composition exactly as at the Nivelle		
6th Division, Daricau	5,519	869
has exchanged 24th Line for 119th Line		
7th Division, Leval	4,704	395
composition exactly as at the Nivelle		
8th Division *dissolved after the Nivelle*		
9th Division, Boyer	6,423	1,149
has received 24th Line, and 118th (3) Line, but surrendered 32nd and 43rd		
Reserve, Villatte	5,397	48
has lost its Italian brigade and 115th Line,		
but received the 9th Leger from dissolved 8th Division		
Brigade Paris:	3,881	–
10th (2), 81st (2), 114th, 117th, also 115th (2), taken from Villatte's Reserve		
Garrison of Bayonne:	8,801	–
increased by wrecks of dissolved 8th Division		
Artillery, Sappers, and Train (90 guns), say	2,000	33
TOTAL	65,933	5,947
Cavalry, all cantoned in the rear save 6 squadrons	7,788	

BRITISH BATTLE HONOURS FOR THE NIVE.

16th (the Queen's) Regt. of (Light) Dragoons
1st & 3rd Bns. 1st Regt. of Foot Guards
1st Bn. Coldstream Regt. of Foot Guards
1st Bn. 3rd Regt. of Foot Guards
3rd Bn. 1st (Royal Scots) Regt. of Foot
1st Bn. 3rd (East Kent) Regt of Foot (or the Buffs)
1st Bn. 4th (King's Own) Regt. of Foot
1st Bn. 9th (East Norfolk) Regt. of Foot
1st Bn. 11th (North Devonshire) Regt. of Foot
1st Bn. 28th (North Gloucestershire) Regt. of Foot
1st Bn. 61st (South Gloucestershire) Regt. of Foot
1st Bn. 36th (Herefordshire) Regt. of Foot
2nd Bn. 59th (2nd Nottinghamshire) Regt. of Foot
2nd Bn. 31st (Huntingdonshire) Regt. of Foot
1st Bn. 32nd (Cornwall) Regt. of Foot
76th Regt. of Foot
2nd Bn. 34th (Cumberland) Regt. of Foot
1st Bn. 38th (1st Staffordshire) Regt. of Foot
1st Bn. 39th (Dorsetshire) Regt. of Foot
1st Bn. 42nd (Royal Highland) Regt. of Foot
1st Bn. 43rd (Monmouthshire Light Infantry) Regt.
1st Bn. 52nd (Oxfordshire Light Infantry) Regt.
2nd Bn. 47th (Lancashire) Regt. of Foot
2nd Bn. 66th (Berkshire) Regt. of Foot
1st Bn. 50th (West Kent) Regt. of Foot
1st Bn. 57th (West Middlesex) Regt. of Foot
5th Bn. 60th (Royal American) Regt. of Foot
2nd Bn. 62nd (Wiltshire) Regt. of Foot
2nd Bn. 84th (York & Lancaster) Regt. of Foot
1st Bn. 71st (Highland) Regt. of Foot (Light Infantry)
1st Bn. 92nd (Highland) Regt. of Foot
1st Bn. 79th Regt. of Foot (or Cameron Highlanders)
1st Bn. 91st Regt. of Foot
85th Regt. of Foot (Bucks Volunteers) Light Infantry
95th Regt. of Foot (or Rifle Corps)

"It is agreed by French and British," says Napier, "that the battle of St. Pierre was one of the most desperate of the whole war. Wellington said he never saw a field so thickly strewn with dead; nor can the vigour of the combatants be well denied when 5,000 men were killed or wounded in three hours, upon a space of one mile square."

Yet it is strange that the name of this battle is not borne upon the colours of any regiment which was there engaged.

From George Simmons' Journal : "Lord Wellington galloped into the yard of our chateau soon after the attack had commenced (on 13 December) and demanded, with his usual quickness, what was to be seen? Sir James Kempt, who was spying at the action from an upper window, told him...and he (the Duke) galloped off to the scene of action. In the afternoon, when all was over, he called in again, on his return to headquarters, and told us - '...that it was the most glorious affair that he had ever seen; and that the enemy had absolutely left upwards of 5,000 men, killed and wounded, on the ground.'

Never a general to miss a chance, Soult noting that the Duke's forces were divided by the River Nive, decided to try and defeat each separately by refusing battle *west* of the river while hurling 60,000 men (9 infantry divisions, cavalry and 40 guns) against Hope to the East.

The battle that followed is ideal for tabletop re-creation, being a complete breakaway from the common practice of assembling two roughly equal armies opposite each other and setting-to in the usual style. It is a situation made up of two distinct actions, each involving well-disciplined forces skillfully withdrawing to strong positions, in the face of great numerical enemy superiority and hindered by terrain conditions forcing them to move on and around the two major roads running North-South. Directed at Wellington's bridge of boats at Urdain, four French infantry divisions advanced at dawn against Light Division picquets and outposts; in the running fight that followed in wooded valleys and enclosures, the battle-hardened and confident 95th Rifles, 43rd and 52nd Regiments supported each other by firing and running, then forming-up on every open area to throw back advancing French columns with rolling volley-fire. Finally they reached the ridge at Arcangues where they occupied the walled church and a chateau, against which French attacks sputtered out like waves against a sea-wall.

Quite unchanged and still marked by battle scars, the church at Arcangues is stimulating ground to tread, particularly if you happen to be among the few visitors who really know what happened - standing inside the little house of worship it all becomes clear. It is built in Basque style with two balconies above the nave; as the wall around the churchyard is lower than the nave, the 43rd were able to pack into the church and its yard to fire from *four* protected levels - the wall, the floor and both balconies. Their massed musketry so demoralised a French artillery battery 400 yards away that the gunners eventually abandoned their pieces - this should not be taken by ardent rule-compilers as giving the Brown Bess an effective range of 400 yards, because massed fire on a target as large as a battery meant that sufficient balls belaboured them as to disconcert the crews. Today, the open area fronting the church has been turned into the inevitable Basque pelota-court - some Sunday afternoon players having a knock-up found our comings-and-goings most curious.

The churchyard holds some interesting graves and memorials such as the large circular flat stone-bordered cross to Lieutenant Colonel William James of the 31st Regiment, killed on 12 December, probably when his regiment were part of Byng's Brigade on the extreme right of the Allied line in front of Croix de Mougerre hill east of the Nive. Also a number of tombs bearing obviously South American names, which confirmed aspects of the next phase of the battle, around the Mayor's House at Barrouillet, after the French advance down the great coast road had driven the Allied picquet line back three miles, between 9 and 10 a.m. The two Portuguese Independent Brigades, assailed by three French Infantry divisions, had been forced back to a line on either side of the road where they hastily loopholed Chateau Barrouillet (house of the Mayor of the small village of Biarritz) and were defending outbuildings, walls, hedges and a sunken road. The 5th Division came to their aid but could not make much impact as the position was not a strong one and the enemy had a three to two numerical advantage; then Aylmer's Brigade marched in from St. Jean de Luz.

Occasionally, when researching military history, one comes upon a detail of possibly little military consequence but so stimulating as to arouse wonder - our day was to be enlivened by such an occurrence! Earlier, local inhabitants in the small coastal town of Bidart had told us about a grave in their churchyard, of an English officer buried standing upright! Sure enough, there was a small square tomb surrounded by low railings, set against the church wall, with a stone recording the death on 10 December 1813 of Lieutenant Colonel Rickard (Richard?) Lloyd of the 84th (North Lancs) Regiment. Casualty lists for that day indicated him to be the only officer lost by the Regiment on the particular day, when they marched in from St. Jean de Luz as one of Aylmer's three British units. Consulting the abridged version of Napier's 'English

Battles and Sieges in the Peninsular' which we just happened to have with us, we found an account of how, in the confused fighting around the Mayor's house at Barrouillet, the Colonel commanding the 84th unwisely led his men into the sunken road where the French, lining the banks on either side promptly shot him down. Undoubtedly, this was the unfortunate officer, but how or why he was buried in the upright position remains a mystery.

At the junction of a busy motor-road stands the Mayor's house, set in extensive grounds surrounded by those same high walls loopholed so long ago; we looked through high wrought-iron gates but were unable to gain access to see a commemorative plaque said to be set in a wall of the house. Seemingly in the middle of the last century the owner of the house married an extremely wealthy Chilean lady which restored his flagging fortunes, and their descendants still live there, jealously guarding their privacy. The graves seen in Arcangues churchyard were those of the lady's South American servants and retainers.

On the night of 12 December a storm caused the Nive to rise and destroy the bridge of boats connecting Hill's 14,000 men and 12 guns east of the river with the rest of Wellington's forces on the west side. Taking advantage of this, Soult attacked Hill on the morning of the 13th, with 35,000 men in seven divisions; although the state of the roads and the narrow front allowed only five to engage, perhaps half of them seriously. Hill's three-mile front angled from the Nive on his left to the Adour on the right, where from the Croix de Mouguerre, a high ridge, the entire battlefield can be viewed. The centre, with the Bayonne-St. Jean Pied de Port road running through it, was the most open; the left was sodden ground and thick woods with stone-built Chateau Larralde on a defensive hill, where it stands unchanged today. It was a strong position, because of a couple of long and narrow millponds and marshy ground that limited attacks to three sectors only 400, 900 and 500 yards wide respectively, running from left to right.

The action on the river Nive, lasting from 9th to 13th December 1813 resulted in complete defeat for Marshal Soult, and the close investment of Bayonne south of the River Adour. Realising his army was too large to be revictualled and supplied with ammunition from the city's arsenals, the French commander moved East, away from Bayonne, countering Allied thrusts to force him to move even further and faster. History indicates Soult to be an experienced and competent commander, yet he was consistently defeated by Wellington in all manner of circumstances both defensive and offensive, which says a great deal for the Duke's military genius. Never the less, in 1917 - during the Great War and 103 years after the Peninsular War - the people of Bayonne publicly subscribed to a monument to Marshal Soult, a prominent landmark, the column is on the crest of the Croix de Mouguerre within sight of the city of Bayonne. It bears inscriptions and includes quotations by Napoleon (sent from St. Helena before he died in 1821) and Victor Hugo, glorifying this French commander; his twenty Peninsular War battles are enumerated although it is pertinent to remark that in only two of them could he claim to have been relatively successful! It also states he was defending with a numerically inferior force, whereas History informs he was attacking with a 3-1 superiority at St. Pierre, and lost 3,300 men to Hill's 1,775. Of this field, the Duke of Wellington later said he had never seen a battlefield on which the dead lay more thickly, more than 5,000 casualties in an hour on an area only one mile square.

Walking the battlefield of the Nive is very good for British ego -although, when reflecting on the calibres of the soldiers and their leaders, every Peninsular War battlefield encourages latent patriotism and chauvinism. It is hard to be upon such fields, peaceful as they are today, without walking tall!

WARGAMING THE BATTLES OF THE NIVE.

Stimulated by writing accounts of this tour and by recollections of walking the actual fields, recently we wargamed the Light Division's fighting withdrawal in the face of four French Divisions. Giving the elite Anglo-Portuguese formation certain advantages in the rules justified by their high standards of mobility and morale, it was proved in an unusual and fascinating encounter that it could be done - it reminded us of another immortal military legend that proved equally enjoyable to re-create, the retreat of the Light Division and Ramsay's Horse Artillery at Fuentes D'Onoro. The combat around the Mayor's house could provide the basis for a tabletop battle but, being confusing and episodic, must be well researched first. The second half of the Battle of Nive, known as the Battle of St. Pierre, provides a factor so often lacking in wargames - a definite objective. Circumstances decreed that Soult, with a numerical advantage of three to one, had four hours in which to defeat Hill before Wellington got reinforcements to the area. There is also an unusual and intriguing factor that can be built into the game arising from the two British Commanding Officers who lost their nerve and precipitated local disaster by retreating their battalions.

The practical use of Time in wargaming is often neglected, but can be made to play a vital part - as indeed it does in real life -thus, Soult had four hours in which to win his battle, realism is added to tabletop reconstructions by allowing the wargaming 'Soult' exactly that amount of real time to achieve his victory. Even more interesting as a means of solving the eternal problem of how long is a wargame day, is to mechanically 'doctor' an old clock so that its hands are made to move three hours or three times around the dial in an actual hour of time. Such a device produced by a professional clockmaker relative, has provided additional zest to many a Southampton wargame!

THE BATTLE OF ORTHEZ - 27 FEBRUARY 1814.

"...The only time the Duke ever was hit was at Orthez, by a spent ball, which struck him on the side and knocked him down. He and Alava were standing together, having both dismounted, and they were laughing at a Portuguese soldier who had passed by saying he was 'offendido' when the Duke was struck down. But he immediately rose and laughed all the more at being 'offendido' himself."
Lord Fitzroy Somerset, *Greville Memoirs.*

In mid-February 1814., striving to outflank the French line, Wellington began operations designed to lure, or drive, Soult from his position in and around Bayonne. Harry Smith tells how it all began:

...on the afternoon of the 26th February at Orthez, the Duke and his head-quarters came up. It was his intention to have fought the battle that afternoon, had the 3rd Division been able to reach its position in time. I heard the Duke say, "Very well, Murray, if the Division does not arrive in time, we must delay the attack till to-morrow. However, I must have a sleep." He folded his little white cloak round him, and lay down, saying, "Call me in time, Murray." Murray awoke the Duke, saying, "It is too late to-day, my Lord." "Very well, then, my orders for to-morrow hold good.

HARRY SMITH:

We remained in this position until the end of February, when we moved, reaching Orthez on the 26th. Here our Division had one of the sharpest skirmishes in a town which I ever saw. Orthez is situated on both sides of the Gave de Pau and has a bridge, which the enemy held with great jealousy.

At dark we withdrew all our posts out of Orthez but a picquet near the bridge in the town, and at daylight [27 Feb.] we crossed by a pontoon bridge below Orthez, and marched over difficult ground. We saw the enemy very strongly posted, both as regards the elevation and the nature of the ground, which was intersected by large banks and ditches, while the fences of the field were most admirably calculated for vigorous defence. As we were moving on the right of the 3rd Division, Sir Thomas Picton, who was ever ready to find fault with the Light, rode up to Colonel Barnard. "Who the devil are you?" knowing Barnard intimately. "We are the Light Division." "If you are the Light, sir, I wish you would move a little quicker," said in his most bitter and sarcastic tone. Barnard says very cool, "Alten commands. But the march of infantry is quick time, and you cannot accelerate the pace of the head of the column without doing an injury to the whole. Wherever the 3rd Division are, Sir Thomas, we will be in our places, depend on it."

We were soon engaged, but less for some time than the troops to our right and left. I never saw the French fight so hard as this day, and we were actually making no advance, when the Duke came up, and ordered the 52nd Regiment to form line and advance. The Battalion was upwards of seven hundred strong. It deployed into line like clockwork, and moved on, supported by clouds of sharpshooters. It was the most majestic advance I ever saw. The French, seeing this line advance so steadily, were appalled; their fire, which at first was terrific, gradually decreased as we neared. The Divisions on our right and left also moved on. The battle was won.

In this advance the 52nd suffered considerably. The present Duke of Richmond, then Lord March, a Captain in the corps, received a severe wound in the side; the ball still annoys him. The Duke himself also got a crack on his knee, which lamed him for several days. When Lord March lay on the ground after the attack, I went to bring up Maling, Surgeon of the 52nd Regiment. As soon as he arrived, to my horror, he poked his forefinger into the wound to trace the course of the ball. At this moment up rode Lord Fitzroy Somerset, and Lord March's brother, Lord George Lennox, awfully affected, believing the wound mortal. Lord March said, "Maling, tell me if I am mortally wounded, because I have something I wish to impart to George." Maling said, "If you will be quiet you will do very well." Maling did not think so. However, Lord March made a miraculous recovery. I never knew a finer young fellow, braver or cooler. We drove the enemy in great confusion before us. On this occasion, I literally lost a Battalion of my Brigade, the 1st Cacadores, for two days, they got so mixed with the 6th Division. The night I found them, after much diligence, I and my Brigadier, Barnard, got into a little sort of inn, kept by an old soldier disabled in Bonaparte's Italian campaigns. He did not require to be told the wants of a soldier, but from habit and sympathy turned to like a "good 'un" to cook us some dinner. As he was hard at work, he said to Barnard, "Ah, the French are not always victorious, and I see war is [not?] what it was when I served. The Cavalry give way first, then come the Artillery, and then follow the Infantry in disorder." He became in the course of the evening very eloquent over his own wine, and told us some very amusing stories. The next morning, when Barnard paid him for everything we had consumed, he was perfectly thunderstruck. I shall never forget his astonishment or his "Eh bien! monsieur, comme vous voulez."

Late-Victorian military historian and prolific writer James Grant tells the story of this penultimate battle of the Peninsular War, which cleared the way for the Allies to bite deep into France after being victorious in so many pitched battles, after storming so many strongholds, after driving all the armies France put into the field over deep and rapid rivers, across wide and fertile plains, through snowy sierras, and the savage passes of the Pyrenees.

The left wing of the Allies, intended for the investment of Bayonne, marched at one o'clock on the morning of the 23rd, driving the French outposts before them, and got their heavy guns into battery. The Adour was now to be spanned by a bridge of boats, 800 yards long; and this was achieved in presence of the French army under Soult. In the evening, when a company of the Coldstream and five of the 3rd or Scots Guards, had passed, two columns of the enemy deployed into line, fired a volley, and rushed on them, yelling, with bayonets fixed. The handful of Guards, however, being well posted on a ridge of sand, with their right flank resting on the river, their left towards the sea, the allied artillery from the other side sweeping the ground in their front (assisted by a discharge of those rockets in which Lieutenant-General Sir William Congreve had recently wrought such improvements that they now bear his name), the enemy were thrown into great disorder, and compelled to retire.

As only fifteen men in marching order could cross by the pontoons at a time, it was not until the evening of the following day that the whole of the 1st division and some of the cavalry were on the right bank. On the 26th another bridge was constructed below the town. The following evening, after a sharp skirmish, saw Bayonne blockaded by Sir John Hope, with the left wing, while the direct road to Bordeaux was now open by the bridge thrown across the Adour.

Lord Wellington, at the head of the corps of Hill and Beresford, made good the passage of the Gave d'Oleron at various points, and drove the enemy, with heavy loss, within the tete-du-pont of Peyreyhorade, which is defended by an ancient castle, flanked by two massive towers. By this the communications between Sauretarre and the Gave de Pau were threatened. Upon this Soult withdrew his troops from the former place, and took up a new and more formidable position on the other side of the river; but he was now completely out-generalled—isolated from Bayonne, he saw the road to Bordeaux threatened!

Having studied well the face of the country, however, he declined to accept the gage of battle which the eager Wellington was so anxious to deliver. He hovered for a time on the high road to Dax, a town on the left bank of the Adour, defended by old walls, flanked by towers. There the ground was sloping, as the road passed near a formidable hill, which was strengthened by the village of St. Boes, on which it rested. His position was a ridge partly bare and partly wooded, and is thus described:-

"In the centre was an open rounded hill, from whence long narrow tongues shot out towards the high road of Peyreyhorade on the left; on the right, by St. Boes, towards the church of Baights. The whole presented a concave front, covered with a marshy ravine, which was crossed by two shorter necks coming from the round hill in the centre. The road from Orthes to Dax passed behind the line to the village of St. Boes; and behind the centre a succession of undulating bare heathy hills trended for several miles to the rear. Behind the right the country was low and deep; but Orthes, receding from the river up the slope of a steep hill, was behind the left wing."

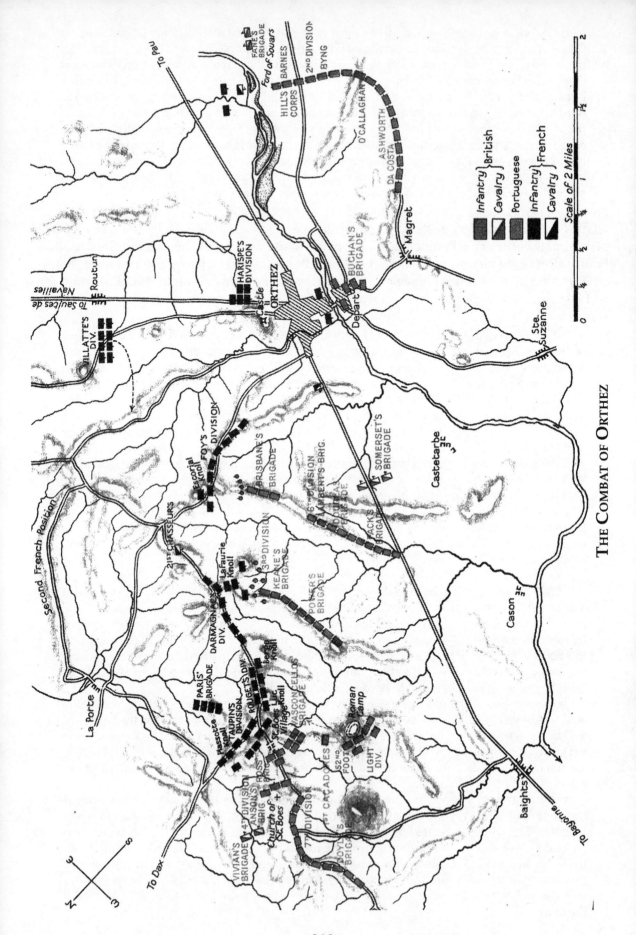

THE COMBAT OF ORTHEZ

Orthes, a little manufacturing town on the right bank of the Gave de Pau, had as yet no name in history, save that which it won during the religious wars of the sixteenth century, when the Huguenots put its garrison to the sword, and threw all the monks over the bridge into the river.

General Reille, with the divisions of Taupin, Roquet, and Pain, on the right, held the ground from St. Boes to the centre. The Comte D'Erlon, with those of Foy and D'Armagnac, was on Reille's left, extending along the ridge to the Peyreyhorade road—the second being in reserve. Villatte's division and the cavalry were posted above a village named Routun, on open hills covered with brown heath, from whence they overlooked the low country, and were in readiness to ride to the succour both of Reille and D'Erlon. Harispe occupied the town and lofty bridge of Orthes. He had there twelve guns; twelve more were upon the round hill in the centre of the position, to sweep the ground beyond St. Boes; and sixteen were in reserve on the road to Dax.

Such was the position of the French army when, a little after daybreak on the morning of the 27th of February, Wellington for more than an hour reconnoitred it with care and keenness from an old Roman camp, which crowned a hill nearly as lofty and as isolated as that which formed the centre of Soult's position. Then the camp, with its ancient mounds, was open, bare, and grassy; now it is covered by trees and vineyards.

Skirmishing and the exchange of cannon-shots had begun about daybreak on the allied right, and the French cavalry at times pushed their squadrons forward on each flank; but it was not until nine o'clock that Wellington ordered the real attack to commence. Advancing, and firing steadily as they advanced, the 3rd and 6th divisions won with difficulty the lower part of those ridges held by Foy, and sought to extend their left toward Soult's centre with a sharp fire of musketry. The main contest was, however, on the other flank, where Sir Lowry Cole, while keeping Anson's brigade of the 4th in reserve, assailed St. Boes at the head of Ross's corps and the Portuguese of Vasconcellos, his object being to cut a passage to the open ground beyond, and turn Soult's right flank.

Loudly rang the roar of battle there, and fierce and slaughtering was the struggle. Five times with the bayonet, led by their officers sword in hand, did the soldiers of the gallant Ross (who afterwards fell at New Orleans) break through the little vine-clad cottages, their gardens, and enclosures, and five times did he carry his portion of the battle into that open space beyond, to be five times hurled back over the dead and dying; for the French guns from the central hill swept them in front, and the reserve battery of sixteen guns on the Dax road tore through them from flank to flank with round shot and grape.

Sergeant Donaldson, of the Scots brigade, in his well-written little narrative, says, "The French made a most obstinate resistance at the point we had to carry, and kept up a severe cannonade on us, by which many of our men were decapitated in consequence of their firing chain shot."

And mingled with the din of the cannon and musketry in and about St. Boes were the yells of the French, the hurrahs of the British, the oaths, cries, prayers, and other exclamations of the Portuguese, as all mingled and grappled in wild melee together; till Taupin's supporting columns, pouring in a murderous fire, and lapping the flank with pestilent skirmishers, forced Cole's shattered regiments back from the open ground into St. Boes.

"It was in vain," says Napier, "that the Allies, with desperate valour, broke time after time through the narrow way, and strove to spread a front beyond. Ross fell dangerously wounded; and Taupin's troops, thickly clustered and well supported, defied every effort. Nor was Soult less happy on the other side. From the narrowness of the ground, the 3rd and 6th divisions could only engage a few men at once; hence no progress was made. One small detachment which Picton extended to his left, attempting to gain the smaller tongue jutting out from the central hill, was suddenly charged as it neared the summit by Foy, and driven down again in confusion, losing several prisoners."

For no less than three hours did that desperate combat continue on the side of St. Boes, and thickly lay the pale corpses there. Wellington sent a battalion of cacadores from the Roman camp to protect the right flank of Ross's shrinking brigade from the biting fire of the French skirmishers, which came in white spurts from every bush and wall; but this was of no avail, for already had their countrymen, under Vasconcellos, given way in utter disorder. The impetuous French came pouring on, with shouts of "Vive l'Empereur," and "Tue! Tue!" and the British troops retreated through St. Boes with extreme difficulty.

This happened at the very moment of Picton's repulse elsewhere; and Soult, who was seated on horseback on his central hill, the key to all his combinations, deeming that the hour of victory had come, smote his right thigh with exultation, and exclaimed, with reference to Wellington—

"At last I have him!"

"And it was no vain-glorious speech," says the great historian of the war; "the crisis seemed to justify the exultation. There was, however, a small black cloud rising just beneath, unheeded by the French commander, amid the thundering din and tumult that now shook the field of battle, but which soon burst with irresistible violence."

Wellington, seeing the great strength of St. Boes, suddenly changed his plan of battle.

Supporting Ross with Anson's brigade, which as yet had not fired a shot, he backed both the 7th division and Hussey Vivian's cavalry, thus establishing a heavy body toward the Dax road. He then ordered the 3rd and 6th divisions to be thrown in heavy columns upon the French left; and at the same moment sent down the Oxford Light Infantry from the Roman camp, with orders to cross the marsh in front, mount the French position, and assail the flank and rear of those troops who held our 4th division in play at St. Boes.

In obedience to this, the gallant Colborne led his regiment across the march under a scattering fire. The men in some places sank to their waists; yet, with stern resolution, quietly and steadily they struggled on, those veterans of one of the finest battalions of the light division, till they obtained firm footing and closed their ranks, at the very moment when Taupin, on the French right, was pushing with ardour through St. Boes, and when Foy and D'Armagnac, hitherto masters of their ground, were being assailed by the columns of the 3rd and 6th divisions.

With loud and ringing cheers, and a rolling fire of musketry, the men of the 52nd dashed to the front, all covered with mud and mire as they were, and getting in between Foy and Taupin, and cutting to pieces a French battalion in the fury of their advance, threw everything before them into disorder. General Bechaud was slain, Foy was dangerously wounded, and his troops, discouraged by this sudden storm, for the 52nd came like a thunderbolt from a quarter where no enemy was looked for, got into confusion; and the disorder spreading to the wing of Reille, he was forced to fall back and take up a new position. The narrow pass behind St. Boes was thus opened; and, seizing the critical moment, Wellington thrust through it the 4th and 7th divisions, with Vivian's cavalry and two battalions of artillery, and thus secured victory by spreading a front beyond.

On the other flank, the 3rd and 6th divisions had won D'Armagnac's ground, and established a battery of cannon on an eminence from whence the bullets made long and ghastly lines through those dense masses almost mobs, in which the French were wont to fight under Bonaparte—a trick in war, by which the rear pushed on the front—and though a squadron of gay chasseurs à cheval, in light green uniforms, with brass helmets, and dancing plumes of long horsehair, came *sabre a la main* down the Orthes road to charge their guns, they pushed their brave career too far. They got entangled in a hollow way; a shower of grape tore through them, and men and horses were alike destroyed.

The 3rd and 7th divisions now advanced, and the wings of the army were united.

On the heathy hills beyond the Dax road, Soult now concentrated his forces; and then, with the divisions of Pain, Roquet, Taupin, and D'Armagnac, he endeavoured to cover and rally Foy's disordered infantry. But his troubles were not yet over, and his foes were not all in front. When Wellington so suddenly changed his plan of attack, Hill, at the head of 12,000 men received orders to force the passage of the Gave, partly to prevent Harispe from falling upon the flank of the 6th division, and partly in the hope of a successful issue; and so it happened.

He forded the river above Souars, drove back the troops, and obtained possession of the heights above Gave, cut off the French from the Pau road, and turned the flank of those in Orthes; thus menacing Soult's only line of retreat by Sallespice, at the very time that the junction of wings was effected on the French position by the Allies.

On seeing that Hill's successful passage of the Gave rendered his whole position feeble, Soult gave orders for a general retreat along the whole line; but this movement was a matter of peril. The heath-clad eminences on which he was now fighting formed for some distance a succession of parallel positions, ending in a low green ridge, running rearward on a line with the St. Severs road. On the opposite side of the latter was a similar ridge, along which Sir Rowland Hill, judging by the sound of the firing how matters went with Soult, was rapidly bringing on his division.

The French yielded; and the Allies advanced step by step, with a terrible din of musketry and cannon, and the continued fall of many men on both sides. When the colours and glittering bayonets of Hill's division appeared upon the opposing ridge, and the danger of being cut off from Sallespice became imminent, the French retreat became more hurried and confused, and on perceiving this Hill quickened his pace. At last both sides were in motion double-quick; the mounted officers went at a canter, and ere long the pace of the infantry became a violent run. From the French ranks many men broke away in crowds, particularly conscripts, and rushed across the fields towards the fords of the Gave; a rush was made by the rest to gain the bridge of Sault de Nevailles, so that the whole country seemed to be covered by mobs of disorganised Frenchmen.

Among these our cavalry dashed forward in pursuit, and first fell upon a body which faced about, under General Harispe. This was at three in the afternoon, according to the Records of the 7th Hussars, a corps which charged more than once. In one charge, 300 men were sabred, and 2,000 threw down their arms in an enclosed field; 16 officers and 700 men were taken near Sault de Nevailles by the 7th alone, and the pursuit was continued to the Luy de Bearn, five miles from the field of battle.

So many fugitives threw away their muskets that, according to Donaldson's narrative, the road there was "almost impassable by the number of arms lying upon it. Near this place lay a sergeant of our light brigade, extended by the side of a French grenadier, their bayonets transfixed in each other, and both quite dead."

As darkness closed in, a corporal of the 94th Scots and a private of the 83rd, attracted by the piteous cries of a French officer, who lay wounded in a ditch, gave him some wine from a canteen, and while doing so found nestling in his cloak a stray English boy, four years old, whom he had picked up on the field; and two days after he was restored to his mother.

To all appearance the French army was now completely dispersed; yet it was not so. With the loss of only six guns, and less than 4,000 men killed, wounded, or taken, Soult had passed the Luy de Bearn; and that could not have been achieved by him so easily but that Wellington had been wounded by a musket-ball just above the thigh, which caused him to ride with difficulty and pain. The allied loss was 2,300; of these, fifty men and three officers were taken prisoners. Among the wounded were Wellington, Generals Ross, Walker, and the Earl of March. The latter Napier states, "had served on the head-quarter staff during the whole war without a hurt; but being made a captain in the 52nd, like a good soldier, joined his regiment the night before the battle, and a few hours afterwards was shot through the chest, thus learning by experience the difference between the labours and dangers of staff and regimental officers, which are generally in the inverse ratio to their promotions."

Having no position on which to rally, the discomfited Soult continued his retreat under cloud of night to St. Sever, destroying all the bridges in his rear. With daybreak, Wellington commenced a steady pursuit in three columns; one, in the centre, moved by the main road, the others on its right and left. At St. Sever he hoped to find the French still in confusion, but they were already beyond the river; the bridge had, like others, been destroyed, so the allied columns halted.

Soult now moved up the Adour, and sent General Clausel into the town of Aire, on the opposite side of the river, where his magazine and artillery park were stored up; and to capture or destroy these became the immediate object of Sir Rowland Hill. Moving in two columns, he came in sight of that place at three o'clock on the morning of the 2nd of March.

Aire, a little town of great antiquity, possessing the ruins of the castle of Alaric the Visigoth, is situated in a beautiful and fertile district, on the slope of a hill on the left bank of the Adour. Having with him two divisions of infantry, a brigade of cavalry, and some horse artillery, Hill did not expect much opposition; but Clausel awaited him in order of battle, with the divisions of Villatte and Harispe, flanked by some pieces of cannon.

These were in position on a steep ridge, which was high, and covered with wood, then in the early greenery of spring, on the right, where it overhung the Adour, but trended away on the left into flat table-land, across which lies the main road to Pau; hence his position, though strong, was far from secure. There was no retreat on the right, where the ravine was steep and rugged, with a deep mill-stream at the bottom; and he could easily be outflanked on the left. "Moreover, a branch of the Adour flowing behind Aire cut it off from Barcelona; and behind the left wing was the greater Lees, a river with steep banks and only one bridge."

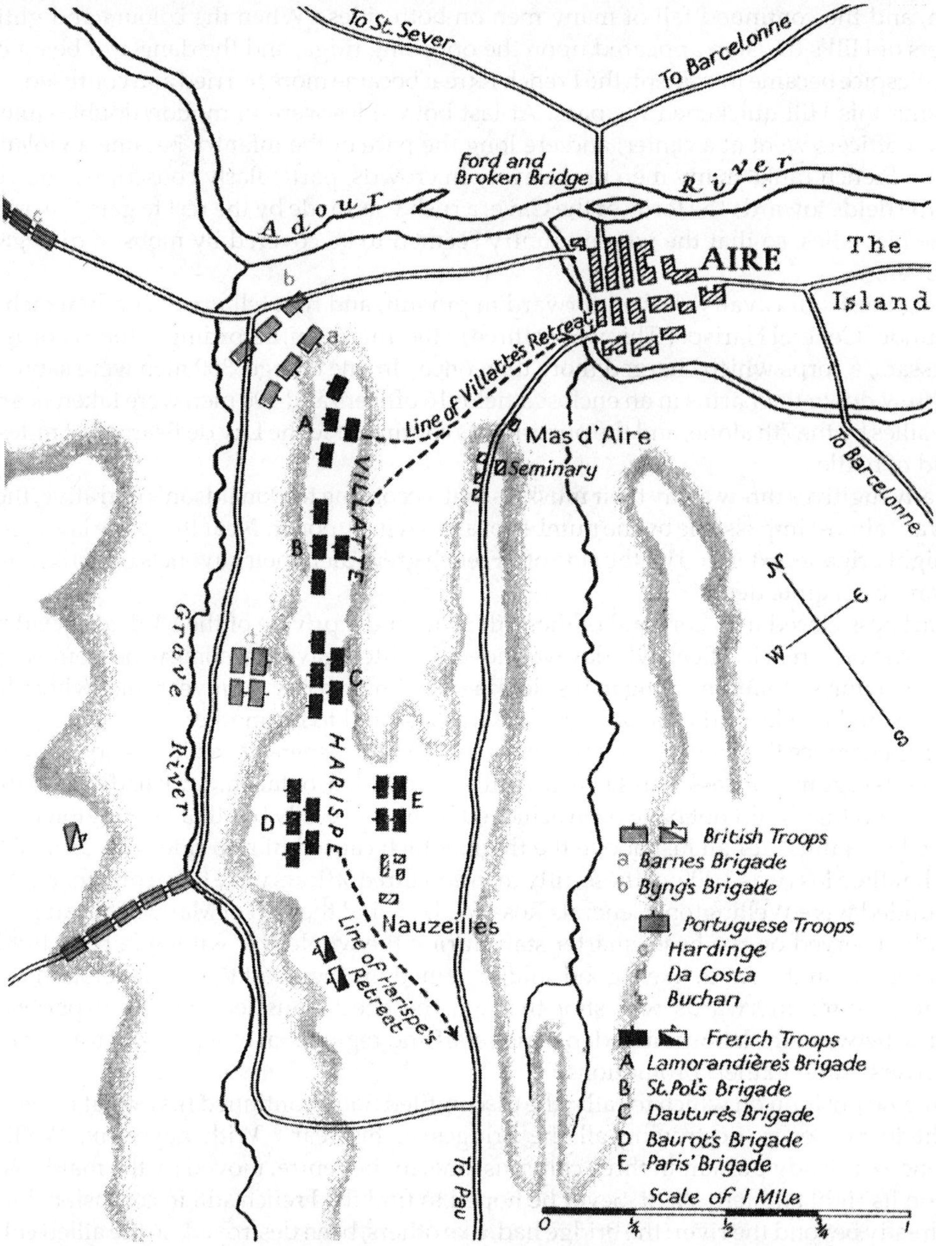
To St. Sever
To Barcelonne
Ford and
Broken Bridge
Adour River
AIRE
The Island
Line of Villatte's Retreat
Mas d'Aire
Seminary
To Barcelonne
VILLATTE
HARISPE
Grave River
Nauzeilles
Line of Harispe's Retreat
To Pau
N
E
W
S
British Troops
a Barnes Brigade
b Byng's Brigade
Portuguese Troops
c Hardinge
d Da Costa
e Buchan
French Troops
A Lamorandière's Brigade
B St. Pol's Brigade
C Dauture's Brigade
D Baurot's Brigade
E Paris' Brigade
Scale of 1 Mile
0
¼
½
¾
1

The Combat of Aire

Sir William Stewart—long familiarly known to the Scottish regiments as "Auld Grog Willie," from his kindness in giving them extra allowances of rum on the march—commenced the attack at the head of a British brigade on the French right; a Portuguese brigade, under Da Costa, assailed their centre; the other brigades followed in columns of march. Da Costa advanced up the wooded steep in a manner so slovenly, that at the summit, when his men were breathless and loose in hand, the French, under Harispe, met them with the bayonet with so furious a charge that they gave way and fled down the slope, while the other columns were still in motion, and when Stewart had actually won the greater height on the French right flank.

Sir William Stewart, on seeing the mishap of Da Costa's corps, dispatched the 50th Regiment and the 92nd Highlanders to his aid; and the fiery ardour with which these two corps came storming up the ridge restored the combat there, and by the vehemence of their assault the French were hurled back upon their reserves. Yet they rallied and renewed the action, only to be again broken and dispersed. Harispe was driven in rout towards the river Lees, and Villatte quite through the town of Aire, which was captured and kept by Colonel Cameron, at the head of the Highlanders.

The French lost many men; two generals, Dauture and Gasquet, were wounded, a colonel was killed, and 100 prisoners taken. All Harispe's conscripts threw away their arms and fled to their homes; while the cannon and magazines remained the prizes of Hill. Our loss was only two officers and 150 British soldiers.

The Portuguese loss was never stated.

The vigour with which the French fought at Aire showed that their courage was not lessened by the result of Orthes, though Soult's state was now most perilous. His losses in battle were heavy, his conscripts had fled, his veterans were dispersed, his officers were inspired by gloom and discontent, and all his magazines were taken.

The star of Napoleon was waning fast; the tide of war and fortune was setting steadily in against him. On the 12th of March, Marshal Beresford and the Duc d'Angouleme, with the 4th and 7th divisions of infantry and Vivian's cavalry, entered the ancient city of Bordeaux, where they were welcomed with every demonstration of joy, where already the white banner of the House of Bourbon had replaced the tricolour, and where Louis XVIII was formally proclaimed King of France.

WELLINGTON'S ARMY AT ORTHEZ

	STRENGTH	LOSSES
Cavalry		
Fane's Brigade	765	
13th Light Dragoons		9
14th Light Dragoons		2
Vivian's Brigade	989	
18th Hussars		–
1st Hussars K.G.L.		–
Somerset's Brigade	1,619	
7th Hussars		16
10th Hussars		1
15th Hussars		9
Total Cavalry	3,373	37
2nd Division (W. Stewart)		
Barnes's Brigade	2,013	
1/50th Foot		14
1/71st Foot		12
1/92nd Foot		3
Byng's Brigade	1,805	
1/3rd Foot		2
1/57th Foot		–
2/31st Foot		2
1/66th Foot		–
O'Callaghan's Brigade	1,664	
had no casualties		
Harding's Portuguese	2,298	
had no casualties		
Division Total	7,780	33
3rd Division (Picton)		
Brisbane's Brigade	2,491	
1/45th Foot		132
5/60th Foot		42
74th Foot		34
1/88th Foot		269
Keane's Brigade	2,006	
1/5th Foot		40
2/83rd Foot		58
2/87th Foot		109
94th Foot		15
Power's Portuguese	2,129	
9th Line		49
21st Line		37
11th Cacadores		23
Division Total	6,626	808
4th Division (Cole)		
Anson's Brigade	1,814	
3/27th Foot		6
1/40th Foot		5
1/48th Foot		14
2nd Provisional *absent*		
Ross's Brigade	1,753	
1/7th Foot		68
1/20th Foot		123
1/23rd Foot		88
Vasconcellos's Port.	2,385	
11th Line		148
23rd Line		122
7th Cacadores		25
Division Total	5,952	599
6th Division (Clinton)		
Pack's Brigade	1,415	
1/42nd Foot		60
1/91st Foot		12
1/79th Foot *absent*		
Lambert's Brigade	2,300	
1/61st Foot		7
1/32nd Foot		–
1/36th Foot		–
1/11th Foot		–

	Strength	Casualties
Douglas's Portuguese	1,856	
8th Line		9
12th Line		5
9th Cacadores		10
Division Total	5,571	103
7th Division (Walker)		
Gardiner's Brigade	1,865	
1/6th Foot		145
2/24th Foot		35
2/56th Foot		31
Brunswick-Oels		48
Inglis's Brigade	1,420	
68th Foot		31
1/82nd Foot		48
Chasseurs Britanniques		40
51st Foot *absent*		
Doyle's Portuguese	2,358	
7th Line		–
19th Line		–
2nd Cacadores		3
Division Total	5,648	371
Light Division (Alten)		
British Units	1,777	
1/43rd Foot *absent*		
1/52nd Foot		89
1/95th Rifles *absent*		
2/95th Rifles		–
3/95th Rifles		–
Portuguese units	1,703	
1st Cacadores		47
3rd Cacadores		26
17th Line		–
Division Total	3,480	162
Le Cor's Portuguese Division		
Da Costa's Brigade	2,109	
2nd Line		3
14th Line		–
Buchan's Brigade	2,356	
4th Line		1
10th Line		1
10th Cacadores		10
Division Total	4,465	15
6 British & 1 K.G.L. batteries and train	1,052	28
1 Portuguese battery	110	–
Artillery Total	1,162	28
Staff-corps, engineers & Wagon Train	350	8
Total, all ranks	44,402	2,174
of whom,		
British	26,798	1,645
Portuguese	17,604	529

British Battle Honours for Orthez

7th (Queen's Own) Regt. of (Light) Dragoons (Hussars)
13th Regt. of Light Dragoons
14th (Duchess of York's own) Regt. of (Light) Dragoons
1st Bn. 3rd (East Kent) Regt. of Foot (or the Buffs)
1st Bn. 5th (Northumberland) Regt. of Foot
1st Bn. 6th (1st Warwickshire) Regt. of Foot
1st Bn. 7th Regt. of Foot (or Royal Fuzileers)
1st Bn. 11th (North Devonshire) Regt. of Foot
20th (East Devonshire) Regt. of Foot
1st Bn. 23rd Regt. of Foot (or Royal Welsh Fuzileers)
2nd Bn. 24th (2nd Warwickshire) Regt. of Foot
3rd Bn. 27th (Inniskilling) Regt. of Foot
1st Bn. 28th (North Gloucestershire) Regt. of Foot
61st (South Gloucestershire) Regt. of Foot
1st Bn. 36th (Herefordshire) Regt. of Foot
2nd Bn. 31st (Huntingdonshire) Regt. of Foot
1st Bn. 32nd (Cornwall) Regt. of Foot
2nd Bn. 34th (Cumberland) Regt. of Foot
1st Bn. 39th (Dorsetshire) Regt. of Foot
1st Bn. 40th (2nd Somersetshire) Regt. of Foot
1st Bn. 82nd Regt. of Foot (or Prince of Wales's Volunteers)
1st Bn. 42nd (Royal Highland) Regt. of Foot
1st Bn. 52nd (Oxfordshire Light Infantry) Regt.
1st Bn. 45th (Nottinghamshire) Regt. of Foot
1st Bn. 48th (Northamptonshire) Regt. of Foot

2nd Bn. 58th (Rutlandshire) Regt. of Foot
2nd Bn. 66th (Berkshire) Regt. of Foot
1st Bn. 50th (West Kent) Regt. of Foot
51st (2nd Yorkshire, West Riding) Light Infantry Regt.
5th Bn. 60th (Royal American) Regt. of Foot
68th (Durham Light Infantry) Regt.
1st Bn. 71st (Highland) Light Infantry Regt.
1st Bn. 74th (Highland) Regt. of Foot
1st Bn. 92nd (Highland) Regt. of Foot
2nd Bn. 83rd Regt. of Foot
2nd Bn. 87th (Prince of Wales's Own Irish) Regt. of Foot
1st Bn. 88th Regt. of Foot (or Connaught Rangers)
94th Regt. of Foot
1st Bn. 91st Regt. of Foot
95th Regt. of Foot (or Rifle Corps)

Harry Smith wrote of his Spanish Wife, Juanita, whom he had married after the fall of Badajoz. Aged 16 at the time of the Battle of Orthez, she....

"....had ridden over the field of battle, and described it as covered with dead, dying, and wounded. She observed an extraordinary number of wounds in the head. These were due to the fact that, owing to the cover of the high banks before described, the head only was vulnerable or exposed. She saw one fine fellow of an Artillery-man with both his arms shot off, which he said occurred while he was ramming down the cartridge into his own gun. She offered him all she had in the eating or drinking way, but he most disdainfully refused all."

WALKING THE BATTLEFIELD OF ORTHEZ.

It is not at all difficult to follow the course of the battle in this area, as Orthez (at least, so far as the field is concerned) has changed very little over the years since it was fought. The fine old fortified bridge and the street leading to it, both scenes of fighting during the battle, are still there just as they were in 1814. The church of St. Boes still stands and is in regular use - there was a Sunday morning Service in progress when last the author explored the field. Standing alongside the building, one can view the exact area over which the 1/52nd charged, and further over, the ridge along which the Light Division attacked, towards the Roman Camp, which is well preserved.

On a spot some two miles north of the town of Orthez there is a monument commemorating the spot where French General Foy received his 14th wound. It was during this battle that, for the first and only time during the entire Peninsular War, Wellington received a wound, when a missile hitting his sword-hilt, drove it into his thigh and hip; he was unable to ride for some days - there is no monument to mark this occasion!

WARGAMING THE BATTLE OF ORTHEZ.

Orthez is a remarkable battle and worthy of research as the Allies, fighting in dashing style against a dispirited enemy, were numerically inferior yet drove their enemy from strong positions. It lends itself to re-creation on the wargames table, not only through being well-documented and fought over an easily reproducible terrain, but because of the scope it allows for rules affording a morale-edge to the Allies, together with enforced reaction-delays by the French to Wellington's moves, so reflecting his command-superiority.

THE BATTLE OF TOULOUSE - 10 APRIL 1814.

The battle of Toulouse [10 April] has been so often fought and refought, I shall only make two or three remarks. Sir Thomas Picton, as usual, attacked when he ought not, and lost men. The Spaniards made three attacks on a very important part of the enemy's position defended by a strong redoubt. The first was a very courageous though unsuccessful attack; the second, a most gallant, heavy, and persevering one, and had my dear old Light Division been pushed forward on the right of the Spaniards in place of remaining inactive, that attack of the Spaniards would have succeeded. I said so at the moment. The third attempt of the Spaniards was naturally, after two such repulses, a very poor one. At this period, about two o'clock in the afternoon, the Duke's Staff began to look grave, and all had some little disaster to report to His Grace, who says, "Ha, by God, this won't do; I must try something else."

This battle appeared to me then, and does the more I reflect on it, the only battle the Duke ever fought without a weight of attack and general support. It was no fault of the Duke's. There are fortunate days in war as in other things.   *Sir Harry Smith*

After Orthez, Soult retired towards Tarbes by the Toulouse road, Wellington in pursuit driving the enemy before him so that Soult was unable to halt or show front again until he had found shelter within the walls of Toulouse. There were innumerable small combats en route, as described by Harry Smith:

> We had also a sharp skirmish at Vic Begorre, but the brunt of it fell on the 3rd Division, where one of the most able officers got himself killed where he had no business to be—Major Sturgeon, of the Staff. I hold nothing to be more unsoldierlike than for officers well mounted to come galloping in among our skirmishers. The officers of companies have always some little exertion to restrain impetuosity, and your galloping gentlemen set our men wild sometimes. We Light Division, while ever conspicuous for undaunted bravery, prided ourselves upon destroying the enemy and preserving ourselves; for good, light troops, like deer-stalkers, may effect feats of heroism by stratagem, ability, and cool daring.
>
> At Tarbes [20 March] we fell in with the enemy, strongly posted, but evidently only a rearguard in force. The Duke made immediate dispositions to attack them, and so mixed up did we appear, that we concluded a large number of the enemy must be cut off. The Light Division, however, alone succeeded in getting up with them. Our three Battalions of the 95th were most sharply engaged. Three successive times the enemy, with greatly superior force, endeavoured to drive them off a hill, but the loss of the enemy from the fire of our Rifles was so great that one could not believe one's eyes. I certainly had never seen the dead lie so thick, nor ever did, except subsequently at Waterloo. Barnard even asked the Duke to ride over the hill and see the sight, which he consented to do, saying, "Well, Barnard, to please you, I will go, but I require no novel proof of the destructive fire of your Rifles."

There were other Light Division (Rifle Brigade) celebrities involved in the action at Tarbes, and for one of them, George Simmons, it was an unlucky occasion, described in his Journal:

> We were a considerable time in driving Johnny (the French) from all the strong ground whereon he was posted, but ultimately we succeeded. I never saw Frenchmen before so thick upon the ground; it was covered with dead bodies. Captain Duncan was killed; Lieutenant Colonel Norcott, three captains, and five lieutenants wounded, and a number of our poor fellows bit the dust towards evening, after having passed through the day's fight. A Frenchman took a long shot at me; the ball fractured my right knee-pan and knocked me down as if I had been struck with a sledge-hammer. Some others, seeing me down, fired several shots at me. My noble servant, Henry Short, as soon as he observed me, came running to me, and, with an oath, observed, "You shall not hit him again but through my body," and deliberately placed himself

in front of me. Colonel Barnard rode up, jumped off his horse, and showed me the greatest kindness.

The following morning I was moved into Tarbes in a cart.

Captain John Kincaid was also present:

On the morning of the 19th, while we were marching along the road, near the town of Tarbes, we saw what appeared to be a small piquet of the enemy, on the top of a hill to our left, looking down upon us, when a company of our second battalion was immediately sent to dislodge them. The enemy, however, increased in number, in proportion to those sent against them, until not only the whole of the second, but our own, and the third battalion were eventually brought into action; and still we had more than double our number opposed to us; but we, nevertheless, drove them from the field with great slaughter after a desperate struggle of a few minutes, in which we had eleven officers killed and wounded. As this fight was purely a rifle one, and took place within sight of the whole army, I may be justified in giving the following quotation from the author* of 'Twelve Years' Military Adventure', who was a spectator, and who, in allusion to this affair, says: 'Our rifles were immediately sent to dislodge the French from the hills on our left, and our battalion was sent to support them. Nothing could exceed the manner in which the ninety-fifth set about the business. ....Certainly I never saw such skirmishers as the ninety-fifth, now the rifle brigade. They could do the work much better and with infinitely less loss than any other of our best light troops. They possessed an individual boldness, a mutual understanding, and a quickness of eye, in taking advantage of the ground, which, taken altogether, I never saw equalled. They were, in fact, as much superior to the French voltigeurs, as the latter were to our skirmishers in general. As our regiment was often employed in supporting them, I think I am fairly qualified to speak of their merits.'

* This was Major John Blakiston; the full title of his book was "Twelve Years Military Adventures in Three-quarters of the Globe"

HARRY SMITH again:

We had at this time exceedingly wet weather. Notwithstanding the fulness of the Garonne, however, after a feint or two and some skilful demonstrations to deceive the enemy, the Duke succeeded [4 April] in throwing over the 3rd, 4th, and 6th Divisions with as much ease as he had previously overcome what seemed to others insurmountable difficulties. These Divisions were strongly posted under Marshal Beresford as a Tete du pont. They were barely established on the opposite side when such a torrent of rain fell, our bridge could not stem the flood. It was hauled to the shore, and, of course, our communication cut off. Marshal Beresford had every reason to apprehend an attack, for the enemy, being in his own country, possessed perfect information, and would know the moment the bridge was impassable. The Marshal wrote very strongly to the Duke, who was ferried over in a little boat with one or two of his Staff, while their horses swam across. His Grace quickly but narrowly examined the position, which was excellent, behind a very difficult ravine. "Beresford," said the Duke, "you are safe enough; two such armies as Soult's could make no impression on you. Be assured, he is too clever a General to attempt to drive you into the river." Our Division was immediately opposite the bridge, but on the left, or opposite bank, to the Marshal. The river soon subsided sufficiently to enable us to relay the bridge, and at daylight on the 10th of April the Light Division crossed, followed by the remainder of the army, except Lord Hill's corps, which was posted on the Pyrenees side of Toulouse. It was evidently the Duke's intention to attack Soult's position this day. Nor were we long on the march before each general officer had his point of rendezvous designated.

Our attacks were commenced by that of the 3rd Division; then came those of the Spaniards, in which the Light Division did not support as the 4th Division supported us at the heights of Vera. Thus, until the afternoon, we literally had done rather worse than nothing. The success of this battle is to be attributed mainly to the 4th and 6th Divisions, but I will ever assert that the second attack was most heavy and energetic, and would have succeeded if my dear old Division had

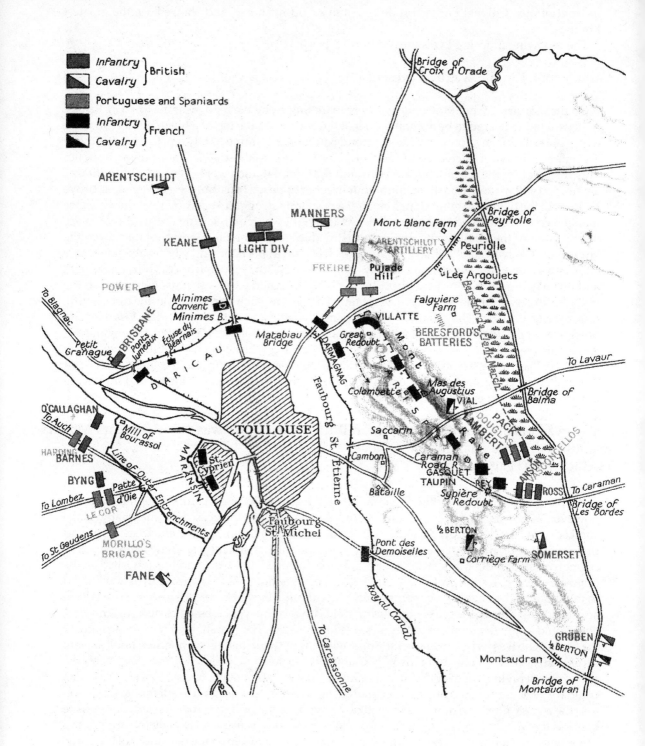

THE BATTLE OF TOULOUSE

been shoved up. As a whole, the French lost a great number of men and were thoroughly defeated. The French have now agitated a claim to the victory, which they are as much borne out in as they would be in claiming the victory at Waterloo.

But to the fight. The 4th and 6th Divisions were brought up in most gallant style, carrying redoubt after redoubt, which were ably defended by the enemy. It was the heaviest fighting I ever looked at, slow owing to the redoubts. The ground was gained step by step, and so was the battle of Toulouse. Our Cavalry lost a brilliant opportunity of distinguishing themselves and punishing the rearguard of the French.

Let the full story of this the last battle of the long Peninsular War, be told by faithful chronicler James Grant:

The ancient city of Toulouse, once the capital of Upper Languedoc, stands on the right bank of the Garonne, a point where it is navigable, though not broader than the Seine is at Paris. It had then about 50,000 inhabitants, and was enclosed by massive walls and towers of brick, the same material of which its streets and little squares are built. It is so situated as to be covered on three sides by water-courses—on the eastern and northern faces by the canal of Languedoc, and on its western front by the river. A suburb called the Faubourg de St. Cyprien occupies the left bank of the Garonne, also surrounded by a brick wall; and between it and the city was a bridge. The city itself stands on a peninsula, and, being accessible only from the south, constitutes a strong and extensive rallying-point for any army that might be compelled to act on the defensive. Strong though its ancient walls are, they are inadequate to withstand the missiles of modern warfare; thus Soult had resorted to every expedient to improve them. On its southern side little required to be done, for there lay the Faubourg St. Michael and the road that led to Narbonne, both so entirely covered by a bend of the river that no apprehensions for their safety could be entertained.

Selecting as his own position a formidable range of heights which lie between the canal of Languedoc and the river Ers, he strengthened it by redoubts and field-works wherever it seemed to be accessible, and there he resolved to abide battle once again. The ridge or range of heights had two distinct platforms, called the Calvinet and St. Sypiere. Between these the ground dipped, and through it ran two narrow roads that led to Toulouse, which could be seen beyond, with all its spires and towers.

The Calvinet platform he fortified on the left with two large redoubts, having open intrenchments in front. On the right were two other large forts, called the Colombette and the Tower of Augustine. St. Sypiere had also a redoubt bearing its own name, and another which was nameless. The whole line of the position was two miles long; and to attack its front it would be necessary to cross the Ers under fire, and advancing over ground naturally marshy, and now made almost impassable by artificial inundations, to storm the ridge with all its field-works. If the assailants succeeded in opening a passage with their bayonets between the fortified platforms, while battered by the guns of these, they would come upon other works bristling with guns and steel beyond, at Cambon and Sacarin; upon others, still beyond, at the suburbs of Guillemerie and Etienne; upon the canal; and, finally, upon the town itself, with its massive walls and great round flanking towers of dun-coloured brick.

Despite the amplitude of those defences, Wellington made his dispositions for an attack on the 10th of April. Sir Rowland Hill was to assail the Faubourg St. Cyprien, which General Reille held with the corps of Maransin and Taupin.

The 3rd and light divisions, with Don Manuel Freyre's Spaniards, were to move against the northern front of the position, where the division of Daricau lined the bank of the canal from its junction with the Garonne to the road of Alby. The two first-named divisions, supported by Bock's cavalry, were directly to menace the canal; Picton the bridge of Jumeaux, and the convent of the Minimes at the bridge of Matabiau. Alten was to connect him with Freyre's Spaniards; these, reinforced by the Portuguese artillery, were to storm a hill called Pugade, and then halt to cover the column of Beresford.

The latter, composed of the 4th and 6th divisions, with three batteries of guns, was to move round the hill of Pugade, along the low ground between Montrave and the river Ers, after which it was to wheel into line and advance against the platform of St. Sypiere. Freyre was then to attack the Calvinet with its redoubts; while Lord Edward Somerset's hussars and Vivian's dragoons were to keep by the banks of the Ers, lest the French cavalry, by the bridges of Bordes and Montaudron, might fall upon the head of Beresford's column.

Such were the plans formed by Wellington, after a careful study of the French position. He knew his troops, and the troops knew their general, and that what one planned skillfully the others would execute with valour and brilliance. So extensive a disposition for battle, embracing so many points of attack, could not be made without incurring many and serious risks. The extent of country covered by the troops was much greater than, in a military point of view, their numbers entitled them to occupy. In the second place, a sudden rise of the river might leave Hill's division dependent on their own exertions against the faubourg; and, thirdly, Beresford's march over the low ground between Montrave and the Ers might lure Soult down to assume the offensive and attack him.

At two o'clock on the morning of the 10th of April, while the people of Toulouse were sunk in slumber, and darkness shrouded the banks of the Garonne, the Ers, and the canal of Languedoc, a dark mass of armed men might have been seen defiling across the first of these by the bridge of Seilh. It was the gallant light division, in motion to take the initiative.

At six o'clock—after the sun was fairly up, and the waters of the Garonne were shining in its light, as they swept round the walls and spires of Toulouse, and away into the wooded landscape beyond—the whole allied army moved to the attack of the various points for which it had been detailed.

Picton and Alten, on the right, leading on a line of rolling fire, drove the French posts beyond the works covering the bridges on the canal. Freyre, marching at the head of his somberly-clad Spaniards, was severely cannonaded till he had passed a small stream, when the French commander at that point, in obedience to instructions from Soult, fell back on the Calvinet platform, leaving Freyre established on the Pugade hill, opposite the angle of the French position, which the Portuguese guns were now cannonading heavily.

Preceded by Somerset's hussars, Beresford moved from Croix d'Orade in three columns abreast, marching by the Pugade until he entered the low ground, which is described in the records of the 7th Hussars "as a dangerous route, through a deep marshy country, crossed and entangled with water-courses, and near the enemy's intrenched position;" but he left his guns behind, fearing to lose them in the morasses.

Beyond the Ers, on the left, Vivian's cavalry brigade, led by Colonel Arentschild, drove the French cavalry over the bridge of Bordes, which the leader of the latter destroyed with great difficulty. Our German hussars gained the bridge of Montaudran higher up; thus the two points from which Beresford might have been assailed were secured.

While these operations, involving the loss of many a life, were in progress, Freyre, from error or impatience, assailed the platform of Calvinet, at the head of 9,000 Spaniards, while Marshal Beresford's column was still on its march. The men of Freyre went on boldly enough for a time, the French musketry and great guns thinning their ranks at every pace; but, closing in upon their centre, the gaps made by death were filled by the living, until their right wing became exposed to a dreadful fire from the French at the bridge of Matabiou, and then, unable to endure it, the leading ranks sprang for shelter into a hollow road, twenty-five feet deep. The left wing and the second line gave way in disorder; the Cantabrian Fusiliers, under Colonel Leon de Sicilia, alone maintaining their ground, under the cover of a sheltering bank. "Then the French came leaping out of their works with loud cries, and, lining the edge of the hollow road, poured an incessant stream of shot upon the helpless crowds in the gulf below; while a battery from the Matabiou, constructed to rake the hollow, sent its bullets from flank to flank, hissing through the quivering mass of flesh and bones."

It is reported, says Lord Londonderry, that foreseeing what was about to happen, Lord Wellington turned to an officer near him, and said—

"Did you ever see nine thousand men run away?"

And when the officer replied in the negative, he added—

"Wait a minute, and you will see it now;" and while he spoke, the route of the Spaniards took place, and more than 1,500 of them were killed and wounded. The rest fled, and the country was covered with fugitives, who ran in wild disorder through the opened ranks of the light division, which had been brought from the position assigned it, and placed in reserve. When the last of the Spaniards was past, then the ranks were closed. Our red-coats moved to the front, "and in five minutes one British battalion had accomplished the object for which a whole Spanish division had struggled for half an hour in vain."

The fiery Picton, regardless of his orders, which, as his temper in battle was known, had been issued to him verbally and in writing, had turned his attack upon the bridge of Jumeaux from a false to a real one, and was repulsed, for the French works there were too high to be assailed without ladders, and could be approached only over open ground, swept by a withering fire. Thus he fell back with the loss of 400 men and officers. Among the latter Colonel Forbes, of the 45th was killed, and Major-General Brisbane was wounded. By these mishaps, the French maintained their ground as yet from the hill of Pugade to the edge of the Garonne, and the losses of the Allies were very great.

Beyond the river, Hill forced the exterior line of intrenchments, but the inner ones, more compact, more contracted, and more strongly fortified, he failed to storm, so the roar of musketry in that quarter subsided; but the din of "a prodigious cannonade was kept up along the whole French line, and by the Allies from St. Cyprien to where the artillery left by Beresford was, in concert with the guns on the Pugade, pouring shot incessantly against the Calvinet platform."

As yet our chances of victory depended on Beresford's attack, as, from the error of the gallant Picton, Wellington was left without reserves to enforce the decision, for the light division and the heavy cavalry alone remained in hand; but these were covering the fugitive Spaniards, and protecting the artillery employed to keep the enemy in check. The heavy brigade consisted of the 5th Dragoon Guards and the 3rd and 4th Dragoons, who saved the Portuguese guns from capture, and subsequently supported General Clinton's division.

The dispersion of the Spaniards, and the repulse of Picton, enabled Soult to draw 15,000 horse and foot from St. Cyprien for a counter-attack. With these he might have fallen upon Beresford's column, now fearfully reduced during its slow and painful march of two miles, through morasses and water-courses, sometimes in mass, sometimes in file, often under French musketry, and always that terrible cannonade, to which he had not a gun to reply.

Soult had seen this disastrous march, which left behind it corpses, torn, shattered, or disembowelled, or mutilated as only cannon-shot can mutilate, and ordered Taupin to advance to the attack; while Vial's cavalry descended to intercept retreat, and Bertou's horse assailed the flank from the bridge of Bordes.

Instead of attacking instantly, Taupin waited till Beresford had completed his flank movement, and deployed into line at the base of the heights. Then, with their customary yells, the dark masses of French infantry came pouring impetuously down the hill; but some well-fired rockets—the noise, the roaring hiss, and the dreadful aspect of which were all unknown to them—dismayed the men of Taupin, who almost immediately fell back. Meanwhile, with swords uplifted, Vial's cavalry came trotting to the attack; but Beresford's second and third lines instantly formed squares, the fire of which repulsed them.

Lambert's brigade of the 6th division, now pushing, won the summit of the platform. Taupin was killed by one shot, a general of brigade fell wounded by another; and, without a check, Lambert swept the platform, and pursued the enemy down the grassy slope on the other side. Covering this flight with Vial's cavalry, Soult sought to rally the fugitives, and sent a part of Travot's conscripts to the bridge of Demoiselles.

"This new order of battle required fresh dispositions for attack; but the indomitable courage of the British soldiers had decided the first great crisis of the fight, and was still buoyant. Lambert's brigade wheeled to its right across the platform; while Pack's Scotch brigade and Douglas's Portuguese, composing the second and third lines of the 6th division, formed on his right to march against the Colombette redoubts. Then, also, Arentschild's cavalry came down from the bridge of Montaudron, on the Ers river, round the south end of Montrave, when, in conjunction with the skirmishers of the 4th division, it again menaced the bridge of Demoiselles."

Thrown entirely on the defensive now, the French army were fighting on three sides of a square.

At half-past two the brigades of Pack and Douglas scrambled up the steep banks of the Lauvour road, under a wasting fire of cannon and musketry. They carried by storm all the French breastworks there, while two Highland regiments—the 42nd and 79th—carried by one wild rush the Colombette and Augustine redoubts. Though the French gave way before the impetuosity of the Highlanders, they came back with a reflux, for their reserves were strong, and, like a living sea, they surged about the redoubts where the two regiments were. Then they burst into the Colombette, and killed or wounded four-fifths of the 42nd, at the same time retaking the Augustine.

"Darkening the whole hill, flanked by clouds of cavalry, and covered by the fire of their redoubt, the enemy came down upon us like a torrent," says Lieutenant Malcolm, in his "Reminiscences," "their generals and field-officers riding in front and waving their hats amidst shouts of the multitude, resembling the roaring of the ocean. Our Highlanders, as if actuated by an instinctive impulse, took off their plumed bonnets, and, waving them in the air, returned their greeting with three loud cheers."

He adds that out of 500 men who came into action with the 42nd, scarcely ninety survived when the redoubt was retaken, as Napier states it was, by the 11th and 91st Argyleshire Regiment; yet so many of the Allies had fallen, that they appeared only as a thin line of skirmishers. The rallied Spaniards were again brought into action, and on the left, not less than on the right, the storm of war thickened fearfully around Soult. Bravely he stood it for a time, but at last confidence forsook his troops, and abandoning the whole range of heights, they retired into Toulouse, where Wellington resolved to keep them; and to accomplish this, a perfect command of the Garonne and the canal of Languedoc was necessary.

It was late ere the firing ended on the 10th; and thus closed the field of Toulouse, which some French writers call a victory. They had five generals and about 3,000 men killed or wounded, and lost one cannon; while the Allies lost 4,600 men and officers, 2,000 alone being Spaniards—a melancholy effusion of blood, and most inutile, for, as was afterwards discovered, by this time Bonaparte had abdicated, and a provisional government had been established in Paris.

On the 11th of April, Wellington hurried across the Garonne that he might ascertain the precise condition of Hill's division; and ordered a fresh distribution of ammunition to the infantry and artillery; and also that the pontoon bridge should be moved nearer to the town of Toulouse, on three sides of which he had established the army. But these arrangements were not completed in sufficient time to permit the renewal of active operations that day, although all was ready for a complete investment of the place upon the 12th, had Soult judged it expedient to abide the issue. But this he decided not to do, and on the preceding night he retreated in good order towards Carcassone, leaving to us in Toulouse Generals Harispe, Baurot, St. Hilaire, and 1,600 prisoners, with stores of all descriptions.

The Allies immediately marched in, and were hailed by all classes as deliverers, with every possible token of welcome. The white flag was hoisted on the churches; the bells were rung "Te Deum" chanted, and at night there was a general illumination.

SMITH:

The next day [11 March] various were the reports flying about camp as to peace, etc. In the afternoon I was posting a picquet, and in riding forward no nearer than usual to a French sentry, the fellow most deliberately fired at me. I took off my cocked hat and made him a low bow. The fellow, in place of reloading his musket, presented arms to me, evidently ashamed of what he had done.

Peace was soon made known. The French moved out of Toulouse, and we occupied it. (The most slippery pavement to ride over in Europe is that of the streets of Toulouse.) My Division was most comfortably cantoned in the suburbs. I and my wife, and two or three of my dear old Rifle comrades—Jack Molloy and young Johnstone (not the Rifle hero of Badajos and Ciudad Rodrigo, old Willie)—had a delightfully furnished chateau. We got a French cook, and were as extravagant and wanton in our ideas as lawless sailors just landed from a long cruise. The feeling of no war, no picquets, no alerts, no apprehension of being turned out, was so novel after six years' perpetual and vigilant war, it is impossible to describe the sensation.

Infantry
2nd Division (W. Stewart)
British Brigades of Barnes,

Byng & O'Callaghan	4,838
Harding's Portuguese	2,102
	6,940

3rd Division (Picton)
British Brigades of

Brisbane & Keane	3,157
Power's Portuguese	1,409
	4,566

4th Division (Cole)
British Brigades of

Ross & Anson	3,539
Vasconcellos's Portuguese	1,824
	5,363

6th Division (Clinton)
British Brigades of

Pack & Lambert	3,803
Douglas's Portuguese	1,890
	5,693

Light Division

British	2,799
Douglas's Portuguese	1,476
	4,275

Le Cor's Division
Brigades of

Buchan & Almeida	3,952

Total

Anglo-Portuguese Infantry	30,789
of which, British	18,136
Portuguese	12,653

Freire's Spaniards

Marcilla	3,959
Espeleta	3,576
Sappers, etc.	381
	7,916
Morillo's Spaniards	2,001
Total Infantry	40,706

Cavalry

C. Manner's Brigade	1,426
Bulow's Brigade	701
Fane's Brigade	816
Vivian's Brigade	939
Somerset's Brigade	1,717
Clifton's Brigade	891
Total Cavalry	6,490

Artillery

British	1,510
Portuguese	440
	1,950
Grand Total	49,146

2nd Division
Barnes's Brigade

1/50th Foot	12
1/71th Foot	16
1/92nd Foot	–

Byng's Brigade (No casualties)
O'Callaghan's Brigade

1/28th	31
2/34th	14
1/39th	5

Harding's Portuguese (No casualties)

Division Total	*78*

3rd Division
Brisbane's Brigade

1/45th Foot	93
5/60th Foot	62
74th Foot	113
1/88th Foot	86

Keane's Brigade

1/5th Foot	3
2/83th Foot	1
2/87th Foot	27
94th Foot	6

Power's Portuguese

9th Line	–
21st Line	20
11th Cacadores	23
Division Total	*434*

4th Division (Cole)
Anson's Brigade

3/27th Foot	106
1/40th Foot	86
1/48th Foot	48
2nd Provisional (2nd & 2/53rd)	33

Ross's Brigade

1/7th Foot	4
1/20th Foot	12
1/23rd Foot	8

Vasconcellos's Portuguese

11th Line	22
23rd Line	52
7th Cacadores	34
Division Total	*405*

6th Division (Clinton)
Pack's Brigade

1/42nd Foot	414
1/79th Foot	214
1/91st Foot	111

Lambert's Brigade

1/11th Foot	142
1/36th Foot	152
1/61st Foot	171

Douglas's Portuguese

8th Line	102
12th Line	173
9th Cacadores	41
Division Total	*1,520*

Light Division

British Units

1/43rd Foot	–
1/52nd Foot	5
1/95th Rifles	19
2/95th Rifles	–
3/95th Rifles	32

Portuguese units

1st Cacadores	35
3rd Cacadores	18
17th Line	5
Division Total	*114*

Le Cor's Division (No casualties)

Cavalry

Fane's Brigade (No casualties)

Vivian's Brigade

18th Hussars	–
1st Hussars K.G.L.	16

Somerset's Brigade

7th Hussars	–
10th Hussars	12
15th Hussars	4

C. Manner's Brigade

5th Dragoon Guards	4
3rd Dragoons	6
4th Dragoons	8

Clifton's Brigade (No casualties)

Bulow's Brigade (No casualties)

Total Cavalry	*50*
Horse Artillery	8
Field Artillery	11
K.G.L. Artillery	8
Portuguese Artillery	8
Artillery Total	*35*

of whom,

British	2,103
Portuguese	533
and, also Spanish	1,922
General Total	4,558

SOULT'S ARMY AT TOULOUSE

1st Division, Daricau

Fririon's Brigade: 6th Leger, 76th Line (1 batt. each), 69th Line (2 batts.)	1,840
Berlier's Brigade: 36th & 65th Line (2 batts. each), 39th Line (1 batt.)	1,999
	3,839

2nd Division, Darmagnac

Leseur's Brigade:31st Leger, 75th Line (2 batts. each), 51st Line (1 batt.)	2,387
Menne's Brigade: 118th & 120th Line (3 batts. each)	2,635
	5,022

4th Division, Taupin

Rey's Brigade: 12th Leger, 32nd & 43rd Line (2 batts. each)	3,039
Gasquet's Brigade: 118th & 120th Line (3 batts. each)	2,416
	5,455

5th Division, Maransin

Barbot's Brigade: 47th Line (2 batts.), 55th & 58th Line (1 batt. each)	2,045
Rouget's Brigade: 27th, 34th & 59th Line (1 batt. each)	1,672
	3,717

6th Division, Villatte

St. Pol's Brigade: 21st Leger, 86th, 96th & 100th Line (1 batt. each)	2,658
Lamorandiere's Brigade: 28th Leger, 103rd Line (1 batt. each), 119th Line (2 batts.)	1,951
	4,609

8th Division, Harispe

Dauture's Brigade: 9th Leger, 25th Leger, 34th Leger (2 batts. each)	2,198
Baurot's Brigade: 10th (2 batts.), 45th, 81st, 115th, 116th, 117th (1 each)	2,886
	5,084

Reserve Division, Travot

Brigades Pourailly & Vuillemont:conscript battalions of new levy	7,267
Total Infantry	34,993

Cavalry	
Berton's Brigade: 2nd Hussars, 13th & 21st Chasseurs	1,339
Vial's Brigade: 5th, 10th, 15th, 22nd Chasseurs	<u>1,361</u>
	2,700
Artillery & Train, and 2 companies pontoniers	3,603
Engineers & Sappers	541
Gendarmerie	206
General Total	42,048

Casualty figures in the French Official report were:
Killed 322, wounded 2,373, missing 541 + 3,236

British Battle Honours for Toulouse

5th (Princess Charlotte of Wales's) Regt. of Dragoon Guards
3rd (King's Own) Regt. of Dragoons
4th (Queen's Own) Regt. of Dragoons
13th Regt. of (Light) Dragoons
2nd (Queen's Royal) Regt. of Foot
1st Bn. 3rd (East Kent) Regt. of Foot (or the Buffs)
1st Bn. 5th (Northumberland) Regt. of Foot
1st Bn. 7th Regt. of Foot (or Royal Fuzileers)
1st Bn. 11th (North Devonshire) Regt. of Foot
1st Bn. 20th (East Devonshire) Regt. of Foot
1st Bn. 23rd Regt. of Foot (or Royal Welsh Fuzileers)
3rd Bn. 27th (Inniskilling) Regt. of Foot
1st Bn. 28th (North Gloucestershire) Regt. of Foot
1st Bn. 61st (South Gloucestershire) Regt. of Foot
1st Bn. 36th (Herefordshire) Regt. of Foot
1st Bn. 40th (2nd Somersetshire) Regt. of Foot
1st Bn. 42nd (Royal Highland) Regt. of Foot
1st Bn. 43rd (Monmouthshire Light Infantry) Regt.
1st Bn. 52nd (Oxfordshire Light Infantry) Regt.
1st Bn. 45th (Nottinghamshire) Regt. of Foot
1st Bn. 48th (Northamptonshire) Regt. of Foot
53rd (Shropshire) Regt. of Foot
5th Bn. 60th (Royal American) Regt. of Foot
74th (Highland) Regt. of Foot
1st Bn. 79th Regt. of Foot (or Cameron Highlanders)
2nd Bn. 83rd Regt. of Foot
2nd Bn. 87th (Prince of Wales's Own Irish) Regt. of Foot
1st Bn 88th Regt. of Foot (or Connaught Rangers)
94th Regt. of Foot
1st Bn. 91st Regt. of Foot
95th Regt. of Foot (or Rifle Corps)

Soult has been foully and falsely accused of fighting at Toulouse, knowing that the war was over, and the slander was repeated by Lord Aberdeen to the House of Lords, when the Marshal was Minister in France. The Duke of Wellington, with a generous warmth, instantly rose and truly declared that Soult did not know, and it was impossible he could know, of the Emperor's abdication when he fought the battle.
William Napier.

I was then off, to go round by head-quarters and to enter Toulouse with Lord Wellington. About eleven I arrived at the fortified entrance, and found, instead of the enemy behind the new works, the maire of the town, almost all the officers of the garde urbaine, a considerable number of national guard officers, deserters, etc., and about 200 smart but awkward men of the city guard, and a band of music, all with the white cockade, and a great crowd of citizens besides, all waiting with anxiety to receive Lord Wellington, and carry him in form to the mayorality. Unluckily, from some mismanagement and mistake, he went in at another entrance, and passed on, almost unknown.

The Private Journal of Judge-Advocate Larpent - Peninsular War.

It is not possible to walk the battlefield of Toulouse, as the town has changed completely in the intervening years, becoming immeasurably bigger so that it has pushed itself far beyond the old canal, and covered the Calvinet Ridge with a complex street system. The old walls were demolished many years ago, the only remaining remnants of them are in a suburb across the Garonne.

A WARGAMING SUBSTITUTE FOR THE BATTLE OF TOULOUSE.

Probably someone somewhere has refought this battle in miniature on a wargames table, but the author has no knowledge of such a venture. However, rather than conclude this book in such a defeatist spirit, a consolation is offered in the form of an account of a fictitious Peninsular battle, bearing a vague resemblance to the Toulouse action in that it is also an allied assault on a French-held town, albeit in Spain and not France. It seems to have been a good and satisfying game, fought and enjoyed as a solo wargame by Briton A. J. Mitchell, and, having it available, the author feels it is too good to completely omit. So, here you are - with any apologies that might be considered necessary!

THE ASSAULT ON TORRELANO.

Wargame table 10' by 4'. Ground scale 1/600. 1 figure = 30 men.

Situation: A combined British and Spanish force advancing from the South-West, South and South-East is to assault the French-held Spanish town of Torrelano standing at the confluence of the Maja and Mina rivers. A single main road runs northwards from the town and is the supply route of the French Army. (See map below)

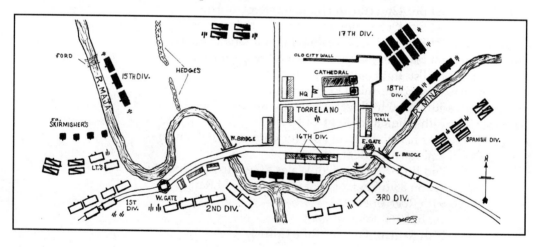

Forces: The total forces on either side are approximately equal.

French:
4 Infantry Divisions (each of 8 Infantry Bns and 1 Cavalry Regt.)
1 Cavalry Division of 8 Regiments (4 heavy and 4 light).
8 Batteries of Field Artillery.
2 Batteries of Howitzers.
2 Batteries of Horse Artillery.
1 Company of Sapeurs.
British:
3 Infantry Divisions of 9 Bns each.
Heavy Cavalry Brigade of 3 Regiments.

336

Light Cavalry Brigade of 3 Regiments.
1 Regiment of Household Cavalry and 1 Regiment of Brunswick Hussars in reserve.
6 Batteries of Field Artillery.
2 Batteries of Heavy Siege Howitzers.
2 Batteries of Horse Artillery.
1 Company of Engineers.
1 Spanish Division of 8 Infantry Bns and 5 Cavalry Regiments.
2 Spanish Batteries of Field Artillery.

Of the above the French have two Bns of Light Infantry per Division, the British have two Light Brigades (of high morale rating). The French 17th Division are elite veterans with a high morale rating. The British have one Brigade of Guards also of high morale rating. The remaining forces on both sides are of moderate morale with the exception of the Spanish troops who are below average.

Preliminary Moves:

First of all in the character of Marshal Soult I disposed of the French forces in the best defensive position I could devise, (See Map 1) bearing in mind the options open to Wellington.

Briefly 15th Division on the right were to defend the ford with one Bn of Light Infantry and one Cavalry Regiment on the far side of the Maja watching for a possible bridging operation further south. One Infantry Brigade was to be held in reserve lining the hedge until the British plans became clear. 16th Division were to garrison the main buildings in the town including the West gate and adjoining houses. The two Light Bns were to guard the north bank of the Mina as far as the East Bridge. The Cavalry Regiment was to scout on the southern bank. One battery of Howitzers was sited in the main square with an observation officer in the tower above the East gate. The other battery was to be entrenched by the Sapeurs in the bend of the Mina south of the East gate. 17th Division formed up in column were to be held in reserve by the North-East corner of the old town wall. 18th Division was to line the bank of the Mina from the East bridge North-Eastwards. 19th Cavalry Division together with the Horse Artillery were to be held to the North of the town on the Main Road - for possible use on either flank if the opportunity arose.

I now changed hats and in the character of Wellington drew up three separate plans with written orders for the first three moves in each case. They were -

(a) An all-out effort on the British left storming across the ford and bridging the river further south, while keeping up a steady pressure on the centre and right.

(b) A demonstration left and centre while two British and one Spanish Division smashed through on the British right on the Mina.

(c) Demonstrations only on the Left and Right while heavy assaults by three British Divisions crossed the West Bridge and a pontoon to be laid in the loop of the river between the Bridge and the West Gate, plus a crossing of the Mina between its confluence with the Maja and the East Bridge.

A dice throw decided Wellington's plan (c). The weather card was now drawn indicating a moderate south-westerly wind and heavy rain. Units firing into the wind suffered a 10% loss of accuracy. Cavalry and artillery were cut down to half-moves except on roads and any attempt to lay a pontoon over the swollen Maja was out. It could only be crossed at the Ford or the bridge. The Mina was fordable at a half-move with attack bonus lost except for Light Infantry.

Incident Cards were to be drawn at the commencement of moves 2, 4, 6, etc. Major deviations from original plans had to be decided by reference to a set of Situation Cards each containing at least two valid options.

Allied dispositions:

These were now made in accordance with the previously written plans except that as no bridging operations could take place the Engineers were detailed to accompany the assaulting troops with a view to blowing breaches in the walls of garrisoned houses in due course. With the Maja in full spate if Soult's Sapeurs could lay charges under the West Bridge and blow it if the West Gate position fell the British plan would be thrown into confusion. The Situation Card decision was that they should entrench the Howitzer Battery as ordered and then move to the bridge and prepare it for demolition.

On Wellington's left the two Brigades of Cavalry with the Horse Artillery and the Light Infantry Brigade from 1st Division were to demonstrate strongly in the direction of the ford. The remainder of 1st Division, one Guards Brigade and one Highland Brigade were after a preliminary bombardment by Siege and Field guns to force the West Gate and attempt to cross the bridge. They were to be supported by 2nd Division, one Brigade of which was to push into the loop of the river enfilading the French right. The Second Brigade was to follow 1st Division into the town, pushing up the Main Road while the third Brigade was to line the southern bank of the Maja as far as the confluence to give supporting fire. 3rd Division with its Light Brigade leading was to force the Mina from the confluence to the East Bridge. The Spanish Division had orders to demonstrate strongly towards the Mina above the East Bridge in order to draw in French Reserves, but not to attempt a crossing. (See Map 1).

Turn 1. British Cavalry on left swept aside French Cavalry patrols and Light Infantry, moving towards the ford taking minor casualties from French Artillery and Infantry fire. French Commander decided (Situation Card) to move his infantry across the ford and two Bns were so deployed, while the remaining three Bns formed up ready to cross.

British 1st and 2nd Divs moved into position for attack while concentrated artillery fire was directed against the West gate and adjoining houses. The Gate-house was penetrated by four salvos of 24pdr siege howitzers. (Dice throws of 6, 6, 5 & 4) The garrison (1/2 Bn) was all killed and the building on fire (Dice roll of 1). The fire spread to adjoining house (S.W. wind and dice throww of 1,2 or 3) and the garrison fled, being shot down as they ran. The second house was hit by three salvoes from Field Artillery and garrison killed (Dice throws 4, 4, 6). Troops in the fourth house now had to be morale tested and in the event surrendered to the advancing infantry (Dice throw 2).

Meanwhile the Light Bde of 2nd Division deployed along the south bank of the Mina firing into the flank of the French defenders causing heavy casualties. The Advancing 3rd Division threw the French Cavalry patrols back across the Mina where they prevented their own Infantry from firing effectively. The French Howitzers in the town square directed their fire onto the British columns however and caused moderate casualties to the Infantry and knocking out a Field Battery. (Dice throw of 5.)

The Spanish Division with its cavalry on the right advanced towards the Mina. French Commander having now sized up the situation decided (Situation Card) to strike hard at the weak Spanish Division and to roll them back. Orders to this effect were sent by ADC. Light Cavalry of 19th Cavalry Division ordered to move over to the left of 18th Div with a view to completing the rout of the Spaniards in due course. Orders also sent to 17th Div to prepare to strike south at the flank of the British 3rd Div.

Turn 2. British Cavalry on left in spite of orders made a 'runaway' charge against the French troops on the west bank of the Maja. (Incident Card) British Light Infantry eliminated the crews of the two artillery batteries on the East bank but lost one battalion from grape shot. Wellington on observing this incident, rather uncharacteristically (Situation Card), decided to exploit the temporary success with which it appeared to meet by sending his two regiments of reserve cavalry to join the attack.

Soult sent two Cavalry regiments of 19th Cavalry Div to reinforce the reserve position of 15th Division at the hedge, together with a battery of horse artillery. The remaining two cavalry regiments of the division with the other horsed battery were sent to assist in the defence of the west bridge, now threatened by two brigades of the 1st Div and one brigade of the 2nd Div moving through the ruins of the West gate. The other two Brigades of 2nd Div together with all the artillery of both Division now moved forward to the line of the burnt out houses ready to move into the loop of the river when the main British attack went forward.

French troops in Torrelano between the houses and the Mina suffered very heavy casualties (Dice throw of 4 & 6) and two of the houses behind them were set on fire by the remaining British Artillery on the south bank (Dice throw of 1, 2 or 3). The French Sapeurs entrenched the howitzer battery by the east gate and moved toward the threatened west bridge with the intention of demolishing it. Unfortunately a spark in the powder caused an explosion in the entrenched battery before it could fire and all the gun crews are killed. (Incident Card and dice throw of 1, 2 or 3)

The Spanish Division advanced cautiously toward the Mina.

Casualties at the end of the move: French 2 Cavalry regiments, 7 Infantry battalions and 2 Batteries; Allied 2 Cavalry regiments, 4 Infantry battalions, and 2 Artillery Batteries.

Turn 3. The British Cavalry action on the left threw one French Cavalry Regt and two French Infantry Bns into the river for the loss of 2 Cavalry Regts and 1 Bty Horse Arty. While the British regrouped their 'blown' horses the Light Infantry continued to fire with telling effect on the French Infantry on the far bank.

The weather was now normal. Ground drying rapidly— all moves normal but rivers still swollen and Maja impassable except at ford.

The three Guards Bns of 1st Div now assaulted the West Bridge and although the leading Bn was wiped out by fire from houses and the French Horse Artillery, the two remaining columns supported by the Highlanders and followed by the supporting Brigade of 2nd Div stormed the bridge hurling back the defenders and killing the garrison of two of the houses who have rashly sortied to join in the melee.

The remaining Brigades of 2nd Div were now in the loop of the river firing into the flank of 15th Div's reserve position along the hedge.

Two Brigades of 3rd division were now across the Mina, shooting down the unfortunate Sapeurs as they made for the bridge. The leading Light Infantry were into the town square and Soult hastily moved his H.Q. to the North side of the old town wall leaving nearly half his escort of Chasseurs as casualties. It was essential now for Soult to strike at the Spanish Div and attempt to roll up the British flank and accordingly the 18th Div now attacked across the Mina while the Cavalry came up on their left ready for the pursuit. Simultaneously the eight columns of 17th Division inclined to their left and moved south across their rear. In view of their higher morale and superior musketry the prospect for the French was good but both in the exchange of fire and the melee they did surprisingly badly. (A throw of two sixes for the Spaniards). The Spanish did not suffer sufficient casualties (40) to make them retreat automatically and the French recoiled across the river throwing the formations of 17th Division into confusion. There was one standstill move while cursing Staff Officers disentangled the troops. Spanish morale soared at this unexpected success (Morale factor increased from 3 to 4) but they did not follow up their victory by crossing the line particularly as the French cavalry was now forming up on the left of the shattered 18th Div.

Turn 4. On the left the British Light Infantry and the Cavalry forced the ford with the loss of 2 Cavalry Regts and one Bn of Infantry. The French were completely defeated in the melee but the British were unable to advance as they had outrun their supplies and had to wait two moves (Incident Card). British Infantry and Artillery in the loop of the river had now made the hedge position of the remnants of 5th Div untenable. The melee on the east side of the bridge resulted in the defeat of two French Infantry bns and two Cavalry Regts. The British losses had been heavy too but they had with the assistance of the Engineers breached and assaulted some of the houses. British 3rd Div had pushed into the square but fire from the French in the Town Hall and the Cathedral caused them heavy casualties. The Howitzer Bty in the Square had been put out of action. The Infantry and Artillery of the Spanish Div continued to pour fire into the struggling French troops of 18th Div and (Incident Card) one Bn of Hessians broke and ran.

The French losses now totaled 40% and they had to stand still for two moves (although able to fire) while Soult decided with the aid of the Situation Card whether to continue the fight or cut his losses.

Casualties: French 4 Cavalry Regts, 15 Infantry Bns, 5 Arty Batteries, Allied: 4 Cavalry Regts, 10 Infantry Bns, 3 Arty Batteries

Turns 5. & 6. As British troops pushed through the town threatening the rear of the French, and the 15th Division was forced to retreat northwards. Soult decided (Situation Card) to pull out the relatively untouched 17th Div rather than throw them into the town where they must eventually be trapped. Remnants of 18th Div withdrew their flank covered by the Cavalry. This was providential for the Spaniards whose casualties of nearly 50% brought them near to retreat. (Dice throw of 3) They did not follow up the retreating French. The remaining garrisons in the Town Hall and the Cathedral surrendered. (Dice throws of 2 & 2).

Turn 7. The British were now close to 40% casualties and were too widely dispersed to launch a concentrated attack on the retreating French 17th Div which withdrew in good order followed by the Cavalry and a few Bns of Infantry.

Summary:

The beauty of the solo wargame is that it focuses ones attentions on all ones mistakes. As Soult

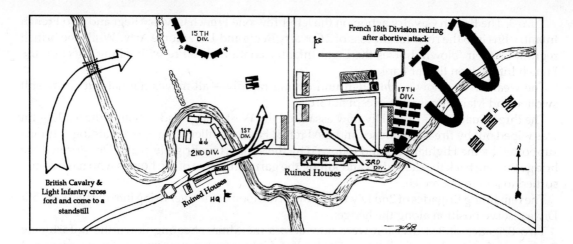

I had failed in my initial dispositions in that the 17th Division should have been kept in the Town and not left on the Left flank without adequate room to manoeuvre. The Cavalry should have been allocated to the two flanks and not held centrally. Too much reliance was placed on the West gate position which was in fact soon reduced by artillery fire (admittedly very lucky!)

On the British side the use of the unsupported Spanish Division on the vulnerable Right flank was an unjustified risk and could have been disastrous. For the rest the result was governed by the imponderable element of luck.

The Incident Cards referred to are all of a set-back nature but do not as a rule affect more than a single unit. Nevertheless the loss of the Howitzer Battery in move 2 had a decisive effect. Had it remained entrenched firing into the British troops crossing the Mina it could well have shattered the 3rd Div attack.

The Situation Cards need a word of explanation. A number of basic military situations for Attacking Troops and Defending Troops are tabulated and against each situation is listed two or more reasonable options. When a decision has to be made the appropriate card is referred to and a dice thrown for the choice of option. Examples are appended below:

Situation Card   Attacking
What was intended as a diversionary attack meets with unexpected success.
(a) Shift the whole emphasis of your attack to this point.
(b) Give the movement limited support in order to maintain pressure.
(c) Maintain your original plan and do not press the advantage further.

The dice decided Wellington to exercise option (b) on his left flank in move 2.

Situation Card   Defending
The enemy's main attack is being made at one point while a purely diversionary attack is made elsewhere.
(a) Move all your reserves to the enemy's weak point and counter-attack.
(b) Ignore the diversion and reinforce your defences against the enemy's main attack.
(c) Make no re-dispositions but appear to fall back before the diversionary attack in order to draw the enemy into an overstretched position.

The dice decided Soult to exercise option a.

Incidentally in order to prevent myself doing too much weighing of the pros and cons I limited myself to six minutes (with an audible timer) or each Commander-in-Chief, for each move which with well over 2,000 figures to shift left little time for careful cogitation.

The Sortie from Bayonne - 14 April 1814.

During the progress of the main army in the interior, General Hope had conducted the investment of Bayonne with all the unremitting vigilance that difficult operation required. He had gathered gabions and fascines and platforms, and was ready to attack the citadel, when rumours of the events at Paris reached him, yet indirectly and without any official character to warrant a formal communication to the garrison: he made them known indeed at the outposts, but to such irregular communications, which might be intended to deceive, the governor naturally paid little attention.
William Napier

While ostensibly the Battle of Toulouse was the final action of the Peninsular War, it went out with a roar rather than a whimper in a bloody and totally unnecessary anti-climatic action at Bayonne, where General Hope's besieging force had been left by Wellington. At Toulouse, immediately on hearing the news from Paris of Napoleon's abdication, the Duke had instantly transmitted the information to Hope at Bayonne.

James Grant:
...but his messenger arrived too late by a few days, for amid the dark hours of the morning of the 14th the French made a desperate sortie on the blockading force under Sir John Hope. With shouts and yells of "Vive l'Empereur!" 3,000 of them surprised the pickets, carried by one rush the church and village of St. Etienne, with the exception of one house, which was gallantly defended by Captain Forster, with a few of the 38th. They slew General Hay, took Colonel Townsend prisoner, and, bursting between the wings, threw the whole line into confusion. In the dark, friend could not be distinguished from foe. All was horror, all was wild carnage; bayonet clashing with bayonet. Vaguely guided by the red flashes of musketry and the tumultuous cries, which were heard on every side, the guns of the citadel sent shot and shell at random, till the flames of burning houses cast a lurid glare over all the scene.

The British centre was driven in; General Stopford fell wounded. General Hope, an officer of lofty stature and great bodily strength, came up with succours in the dark, and fell sword in hand among the enemy. Pierced by eight bullets, his horse sank under him; he was wounded and taken prisoner, with two of his staff, who were endeavouring to drag him from under his horse, during which process a British bullet struck his foot. Ultimately the lost ground was recovered, and the assailants were driven in with such slaughter that their own reports admit the loss of one general and more than 900 hundred men; while our loss was two generals and 830 other officers and men, including 200 taken with Sir John Hope.

William Napier:
At this time the fortified posts at St. Etienne were held by a brigade of the fifth division; from thence to the extreme right the Guards had charge of the line, one company being in St. Etienne itself; Hinuber's German brigade was encamped as a support to the left; the remainder of the first division was in the rear.

In this state, about one o'clock in the morning of the 14th, a deserter gave General Hay, who commanded the outposts that night, an exact account of a projected sally; the general could not speak French, and sent him to Hinuber, who interpreted the man's story to Hay, put his own troops under arms, and transmitted the intelligence to Hope. It would appear that Hay, perhaps disbelieving the man's story, took no additional precautions, and it is probable neither the German brigade nor the reserves of the Guards would have been under arms but for Hinuber. However, at three o'clock, the French, commencing with a false attack on the left of the Adour as a blind, poured suddenly out of the citadel to the number of three thousand combatants; they surprised the picquets, and with loud shouts, breaking through the chain of posts at various points, carried with one rush the church and the village of St. Etienne, with exception of a fortified house defended by Captain Forster of the 38th. Masters of every other part, and overbearing all before them, they drove picquets and supports in heaps along the Peyrehorade road, killed General Hay, took Colonel Townsend of the Guards prisoner, divided the wings of the investing troops, and, passing in rear of the right, threw the whole line into confusion. Then it was that Hinuber, having his Germans in hand, moved up to Etienne, rallied some of the fifth division, and being joined by a battalion of Bradford's Portuguese, bravely gave the counter-stroke to the enemy and regained the village and church.

On the right the combat was still more disastrous. Neither picquets nor reserves could sustain the fury of the assault, and the battle was most confused and terrible; for on both sides the troops, broken into small bodies by the inclosures, and unable to recover their order, came dashing together in the darkness, fighting often with the bayonet;—and sometimes friends encountered, sometimes foes—all was tumult and horror. The guns of the citadel, vaguely guided by the flashes of the musketry, sent their shot and shells booming at random through the lines of fight, while some gunboats, dropping down the river, opened their fire upon the flank of the supporting columns, which being put in motion by Hope on the first alarm were now coming up. One hundred pieces of artillery were thus in full play at once, the shells set fire to the fascine depots, and to several houses, the flames from which cast a horrid glare over the striving masses.

Amidst this confusion General Hope suddenly disappeared, none knew how or wherefore at the time. Afterwards it became known, that having brought up the reserves, he had pushed for St. Etienne by a hollow road behind the line of picquets; but the French were on both banks; he endeavoured to return, was wounded, and his horse, a large one, as was necessary to sustain the gigantic warrior, having received eight bullets fell on his leg. His staff had escaped from the defile, yet two of them, Captain Herries and Mr. Moore, nephew to Sir John Moore, returning, endeavoured to draw him from beneath the horse, but were both dangerously wounded and carried off with Hope, who was again badly hurt in the foot by an English bullet.

Light now beginning to break enabled the allies to act with more unity. The Germans were in possession of St. Etienne, the reserve brigades of the foot Guards, rallied in mass by General Howard, suddenly raised their shout, and running in upon the French drove them back to their works with such slaughter, that their own writers admit a loss of one general and more than nine hundred men. On the British side General Hay was killed, Stopford wounded, and the whole loss was eight hundred and thirty men and officers, of which more than two hundred, with the commander-in-chief were taken. Captain Forster's firm defence of the fortified house first, and next the ready gallantry with which Hinuber's Germans retook St. Etienne, had staved off a very terrible disaster.

A few days after this piteous event the convention made with Soult became known and hostilities ceased.

BRITISH LOSSES IN BAYONNE SORTIE OF APRIL 14, 1814

General Staff	8	5th Division (Hay's Brigade)	
1st Division		3/1st Foot	42
1st batt. 1st Foot Guards	7	1/9th Foot	10
3rd batt. 1st Foot Guards	58	1/35th Foot	9
1st Batt. Coldstream Guards	245	2/47th Foot	26
1st Batt. 3rd Guards	204	Company 5/60th	10
1st Light Batt. K.G.L.	28	Royal Artillery	4
2nd Light Batt. K.G.L.	90	Royal Engineers	2
1st Line Batt. K.G.L.	9	Portuguese (5th Cacadores	
5th Line Batt. K.G.L.	40	& 13th Line)	29
5th Line Batt. K.G.L.	22	*Grand Total*	838
Division Total	706		

The French loss was, killed 11 officers and 100 men, wounded 42 officers 736 men, missing 16 men, or in all 905. The regiment which suffered most was the 94th Line, which had 5 officers killed and 13 wounded out of 30 present. The apparent discrepancy between killed and wounded on the two sides—1 to 3 as against 1 to 7—is partly to be explained by the fact that the 233 British 'missing' were mostly wounded men, left on the ground when the pickets were driven in. (Oman)

From 'The Peninsular Veterans' by D. S. Richards (1975).

Following Wellington's victory at Toulouse and the capitulation of Bordeaux, General Thouvenot was officially notified of Napoleon's abdication and an armistice was signed. The affair which had cost the French 900 killed and wounded and the British very nearly 700 was at an end, but the suspicion and hostility between the two bodies was still very much alive. The end of hostilities was formally declared on April 27th and was marked by a ceremonious parade of Sir John Hope's troops and a general salute from the guns of the city. Even in this formality Thouvenot's men were able to demonstrate their mortification at Bonaparte's defeat, for the picquet guard afterwards told Lieutenant Gleig that the garrison's cannon had been crammed with sand and mud, presumably as an insult directed against the Bourbon authority to which they were forced to swear allegiance. British officers were obliged to enter the city two at a time with passports and in an atmosphere of bitter resentment they found that every friendly overture was met with haughty indifference by the Frenchmen. No longer did that unique camaraderie exist which once permitted George Gleig to wade across a disputed stream with his rod, whilst the opposing picquet watched his progress and offered advice as to where the best fishing was to be found.

The Lieutenant George Gleig mentioned was in the 85th Regiment and wrote 'The Subaltern' (1823)

WALKING THE AREA OF THE BAYONNE SALLY.

The citadel from which the French sallied out still exists and can be seen amid a housing estate, but only from the outside as now it houses a French Parachute Regiment. In the area is a monument, an imposing tall white column supported by carved eagles, flags, weapons and other French impedimenta of war; it bears the names of the French commanders of the town, and of officers who fell during the siege and the sortie. Both brigades of British Guards of the 1st Division lost numerous officers in this final action; they are buried on the outskirts of Bayonne. We knew of the cemeteries through the fortunate acquisition of a small booklet privately published about 150 years ago, detailing in text and engravings the dedicated work done by the sister of Captain Holbourne, one of the Guards officers who fell. Aided by an Englishman who lived in Bayonne, she had restored the two graveyards, had walls, railing, monuments and plaques erected, all still evident today. Overgrown and neglected, probably infrequently visited, they lay peacefully on French soil - one at the top of a field and the other in a wood, this one has a direction-board painted in blue and red - Guards colours - which may have been put-up by a Guards Old Comrades Association. The first contains, among others, the grave of Captain Holbourne, and a tablet commemorating a visit by Queen Victoria in 1889, seventy-five years after the battle and probably whilst she was staying at the popular Victorian watering-place, Biarritz which is nearby. Both cemeteries are railed enclosures with locked gates and within the second one - depicted in the booklet - is the stump of a tree surrounded by rusty railings, still embedded in it is the cannon-ball that originally felled it; in 1814 the Guards burial party fashioned it into a rough cross and carved their names on it.

The time has come to leave the fields of the Peninsular War - in France, Portugal and Spain; time to conclude our walking in the steps of Kings and Princes, Marshals, Dukes and Generals, and - to me always the most evocative - the Men-in-the-Ranks, be they the English yeomen who fought at Agincourt or the British infantryman of so many Peninsular fields. They were brave and spirited, yet humble men who so often had to pull from the fire the chestnuts of inadequate or over-confident commanders.

War being what it is, perhaps concluding with a quite unnecessary battle which cost the lives of many good soldiers, including two generals, is an appropriate place to sign-off.

WARGAMING THE SALLY FROM BAYONNE.

In their fullest sense sieges are infrequently tackled by wargamers; the inherent problems of reproducing all the besieged city and realistically assaulting it more than outweigh its many attractive and colourful features. However, adapting part of a siege is very workable, requiring not much more than a portion of wall, a gate or a sally-port at one end of the table and the main action on the remainder of the table in the manner of a normal wargame. Classical examples suitable for re-creation readily spring to mind - the attack on the Malakoff and the Russian sortie from Sebastopol to Inkerman in the Crimean War; the first relief of Lucknow when the relievers, too few to effect complete relief, became part of the garrison; the assaults on the beaches at Badajoz and Cuidad Rodrigo (where fell 'Black' Bob Craufurd, of Light Division fame); and the sortie from Bayonne. Sallies are made to disturb besiegers by destroying arduously dug parallels, or spiking troublesome siege-guns, or to secure food; Bayonne appears to have been the malevolent final gesture of a vengeful commander. For the wargamer these sorties bear the bonus of possessing definite and specific objectives - i.e. a gun has to be destroyed within a limited number of game-moves and the attackers have to return to their fortress. So perhaps we can view the sortie from Bayonne as an inspiration from which something can be salvaged, rather than a futile and wasteful operation.

In Conclusion

James Grant

The long and glorious war which he had waged in the Peninsula was thus brought to a close, and the troops looked forward with natural impatience to the day of embarkation for their homes, from which they had so long been absent.

All the French troops in the South were reorganised under Marshal Suchet; the Spaniards returned to Spain, and the Portuguese to Portugal. They separated from the British at Condom. "Acting always in concert with us, they were now little inferior to ourselves," writes a soldier of the Scots brigade; "a kind of friendship had thus arisen, and caused us to feel sorry at parting. On the morning this occurred, they were ranged upon the street, and saluted us as we passed, and their hearty 'vivas' and exclamations of regret evinced what they really felt; but scenes of a more affecting nature took place in Portuguese and Spanish women parting with the men of our army to whom they had attached themselves during the miserable state of their country—strict orders were given to prevent any of them proceeding farther."

The British infantry embarked at Bordeaux, some of them being bound for home, while others were destined for the colonies; at the same time marching through France, our war-worn cavalry took shipping at Boulogne.

Thus closed hostilities on land and sea between two gallant nations, who, with only one year's interruption, had been engaged in incessant warfare since 1793. "The war terminated, and with it," adds Napier, with just indignation, "all remembrance of the veterans' services. Yet those veterans had won nineteen pitched battles and innumerable combats; had made or sustained ten sieges, and taken four great fortresses; had thrice expelled the French from Portugal, and once from Spain; had penetrated France, and killed and wounded 200,000 of their enemies, leaving of their own number 40,000 whose bones whiten the plains and mountains of the Peninsula."

When the war medal was given to the surviving officers and soldiers of that army, tardily and grudgingly, in 1849—that army which its glorious leader proudly boasted "was the most perfect machine the world ever produced, and one with which he would have gone anywhere and done anything"—so busy had death been among them that there were alive on the 1st of May in that year only 20,369 claimants of all ranks.

Since then, time, war, and wounds, have fast thinned those veterans' ranks. A few years more, and the last of the Peninsular army will have crumbled into dust; but the memory of its glorious achievements will never be lost, but will endure for ever.   .

British Battle Honours for the Peninsula 1808-1814
1st Regt. of Life Guards
2nd Regt. of Life Guards
Royal Regt. of Horse Guards (Blues)
3rd (Prince of Wales's) Regt. of Dragoon Guards
4th (Royal Irish) Regt. of Dragoon Guards
5th (Princess Charlotte of Wales's) Regt. of Dragoon Guards
1st (Royal) Regt. of Dragoons
3rd (King's own) Regt. of Dragoons
4th (Queen's Own) Regt. of Dragoons
7th (Queen's Own) Regt. of (Light) Dragoons (Hussars)
9th Regt. of (Light) Dragoons
10th (Prince of Wales's Own Royal) Regt. of (Light) Dragoons (Hussars)
11th Regt. of (Light Dragoons)
12th (Prince of Wales's) Regt. of (Light) Dragoons
13th Regt. of (Light) Dragoons
14th (Duchess of York's Own) Regt. of (Light) Dragoons
15th (The King's) Regt. of (Light) Dragoons (Hussars)
16th (The Queen's) Regt. of (Light) Dragoons

18th Regt. of (Light) Dragoons (Hussars)
20th Regt. of (Light) Dragoons
1st Regt. of Foot Guards
Coldstream Regt. of Foot Guards
3rd Regt. of Foot Guards
3rd Bn. 1st (Royal Scots) Regt. of Foot
2nd (Queen's Royal) Regt. of Foot
3rd (East Kent) Regt. of Foot or the Buffs
4th (King's Own) Regt. of Foot
5th (Northumberland) Regt. of Foot
6th (1st Warwickshire) Regt. of Foot
7th Regt. of Foot (Royal Fuzileers)
9th (East Norfolk) Regt. of Foot
10th (North Lincolnshire) Regt. of Foot
11th (North Devonshire) Regt. of Foot
20th (East Devonshire) Regt. of Foot
23rd Regt. of Foot (Royal Welsh Fuzileers)
2nd Bn. 24th (2nd Warwickshire) Regt. of Foot
27th (Inniskilling) Regt. of Foot
28th (North Gloucestershire) Regt. of Foot
61st (South Gloucestershire) Regt. of Foot
29th (Worcestershire) Regt. of Foot
36th (Herefordshire) Regt. of Foot
2nd Bn. 30th (Cambridgeshire) Regt. of Foot
2nd Bn. 59th (2nd Nottinghamshire) Regt. of Foot
2nd Bn. 31st (Huntingdonshire) Regt. of Foot
32nd (Cornwall) Regt. of Foot
76th Regt. of Foot
2nd Bn. 34th (Cumberland) Regt. of Foot
37th (North Hampshire) Regt. of Foot
67th (South Hampshire) Regt. of Foot
38th (1st Staffordshire) Regt. of Foot
39th (Dorsetshire) Regt. of Foot
40th (2nd Somersetshire) Regt. of Foot
82nd Rest. of Foot (Prince of Wales's Volunteers)
42nd (Royal Highland) Regt. of Foot
43rd (Monmouthshire Light Infantry) Regt.
52nd (Oxfordshire Light Infantry) Regt.
44th (East Essex) Regt. of Foot
56th (West Essex) Regt. of Foot
45th (Nottinghamshire) Regt. of Foot
47th (Lancashire) Regt. of Foot
81st Regt. of Foot
48th (Northamptonshire) Regt. of Foot
58th (Rutlandshire) Regt. of Foot
66th (Berkshire) Regt. of Foot
50th (West Kent) Regt. of Foot
51st (2nd Yorkshire, West Riding) Regt. of Foot
2nd Bn. 53rd (Shropshire) Regt. of Foot
85th Regt. of Foot (Bucks Volunteers) (Light Infantry)
57th (West Middlesex) Regt. of Foot
77th (East Middlesex) Regt. of Foot
5th Bn. 60th (Royal American) Regt. of Foot
2nd Bn. 62nd (Wiltshire) Regt. of Foot
97th (Queen's Own) Regt. of Foot

2nd Bn. 84th (York and Lancaster) Regt. of Foot
68th (Durham) Regt. of Foot (Light Infantry)
71st (Highland) Regt. of Foot (Light Infantry)
74th (Highland) Regt. of Foot
92nd Regt. of Foot
79th Regt. of Foot (Cameron Highlanders)
83rd Regt. of Foot (2nd Bn.)
87th (Prince of Wales's Own Irish) Regt. of Foot
88th Regt. of Foot (Connaught Rangers)
94th Regt. of Foot
91st Regt. of Foot
93rd Regt. of Foot
95th Regt. of Foot (Rifle Corps)

"I don't know what effect these men will have upon the enemy, but, by God, they terrify me."
Wellington, on a draft of troops sent to him in Spain, 1809.

BIBLIOGRAPHY AND RECOMMENDED READING.

It would seem entirely fitting that this important section should be prefaced by the words of a leading British Military Historian - David Chandler (of the Royal Military Academy, Sandhurst) extolling the virtues of the greatest historian of the Peninsular War - William Napier,

Over the Centuries, the British Army has been served by some outstanding trios of brothers - the most remarkable of these, perhaps, being the three Napiers - Charles (1782-1853), William (1785-1860), and George (1794-1855). All three earned great distinction for gallantry in the Peninsula and became a legend for the number of wounds shared between them. In later life all three were knighted -Charles, the conqueror of Scind, became a Lt. General; George was appointed Governor of the Cape of Good Hope; but it was William, ultimately promoted full General, who left his mark most indelibly on posterity through his published works. Most notable of these was his famous chronicle of the Peninsular War, 1808-1814, of much of which he had been an eye-witness.

A friend persuaded him to undertake this task, which he began in 1823. Five years later the first volume was published and was at once acclaimed, and although his publisher refused to support a longer work, Napier was induced to continue the project at his own expense. By 1840, when the task was completed, six volumes had appeared. This famous 'History' established new standards in military historiography, and in many respects it has not been surpassed, for its subject, to the present day—although a number of factual errors and misinterpretations have been corrected over the years by such scholars as Sir John Fortescue and Sir Charles Oman, not to forget the modern American author, Mr. Jac Weller. No subsequent writer has ever surpassed the immediacy and colour of the narrative descriptions of events, and few have equalled the scope and comprehensiveness of this massive project. William Napier may justly be termed the father - and inspiration - of modern British military history.

The value of Napier's work was recently brought home to me once again during a battlefield tour to Northern Spain by the British Military Historical Society, which I was privileged to be invited to lead: our main purpose being to study on the actual terrain the campaigns of 1809, 1812 and 1813, and above all the battles of Talavera, Salamanca and Vitoria, and the sieges of Burgos. In anticipation this appeared rather a daunting venture; in retrospect, with a generally successful tour completed, I acknowledge how much I owed to my copy of the abridged version of Napier's magnum opus, namely his English Battles and Sieges in the Peninsula, inherited from my late father, which was my constant guide and companion throughout, equalled only in usefulness by the relevant atlas volumes of Fortescue's great History of the British Army. These sources, together with some excellent 1/25,000 maps of the battlefield areas kindly supplied by the Military History Service of the Spanish Army Ministry, and a few more recent studies of Wellington, provided me with my stock-in-trade. For the rest I depended upon my compass, shooting-stick, binoculars and native wits, sharpened by a dozen years of constant exposure to the enquiring minds of generations of officer cadets and young officers at Sandhurst.

It is fitting to let Napier have the final word. 'For the great captain who led the British troops so triumphantly,' runs part of the introductory notice to English Battles and Sieges, 'this record gives no measure of ability. To win victories was the least of his labours. Those who desire to know what an enormous political, financial and military pressure he sustained must seek the story in the original history from which this work has been extracted. For the soldiers it is no measure of their fortitude and endurance it records only their active courage.' Many of us may indeed be inveigled into making a reacquaintance with the larger work — how much better to take it as a treasured companion to the actual scenes of some of the great if blood-stained moments of British military history. The past can come very real on the actual ground, if properly studied and interpreted.

DAVID CHANDLER MA (OXON.), FRHISTS, FRGS.

The orders of battle in this book are based on those prepared by Charles Oman for his History of the Peninsular War, in seven volumes, which I highly recommend.

Most of the maps are those prepared by B. V. Darbyshire for Oman's History.

The direct quotations presented in these pages have been taken from the following books, all of which were first written and published from 80 to 172 years ago. Many of them have been long out of print, others republished by enterprising and perceptive publishers and thus made available to today's military historians and general readers.

Costello, Edward - The Peninsular and Waterloo Campaigns
Fortescue, The Hon. J.W. - A History of the British Army
Harris, John - The Recollections of Rifleman Harris
Kincaid, Captain Sir John - Adventures in the Rifle Brigade & Random Shots from a Rifleman
Napier, Sir William- English Battles and Sieges in the Peninsular
Oman, Charles - A History of the Peninsula War
Simmons, George - A British Rifleman
Smith, Sir Harry (Edited G.C. Moore-Smith) - The Autobiography of Lt-Gen Sir Harry Smith

The accounts and descriptions of the Battles and Sieges of the Peninsular War, written by a variety of authors, were taken from:

British Battles on Land and Sea- by James Grant.
Battles of the Nineteenth Century - by a number of authors, those relevant to this book being named in its Preface.
British Battles on Land and Sea- Edited by Field-Marshal Sir Evelyn Wood VC.
(Many of the accounts in Wood's book were reproduced from Battles of the Nineteenth Century.)

Generally available books on the Peninsular War (including old volumes previously listed and subsequently re-published).

Brett-James, A.- Wellington at War 1794-1815 (1961)
Brett-James, A - Edward Costello, Peninsular & Waterloo Campaigns (edt 1967)
Brett-James, A - Life in Wellington's Army (1972)
Bryant, Arthur - Jackets of Green (1972) (Collins)
Chandler, David - The Campaigns of Napoleon (1967) (Weidenfeld & Nicolson)
Chandler, David - Dictionary of the Napoleonic Wars (1979) (Arms & Armour Press)
Esdaile, Charles J.- The Spanish Army in the Peninsular War (1988) (Manchester U. P.)
Gates, David - The Spanish Ulcer (1986) (Allen and Unwin)
Glover, Michael - Wellington as Military Commander (1968) (Batsford)
Glover, Michael - The Peninsular War (1974) (David & Charles)
Glover, Michael - Legacy of Glory - Joseph of Spain (1973)

Glover, Michael - Wellington's Army in the Peninsula (1977) (David & Charles)
Haythornthwaite, Phillip - Weapons and Equipment of the Napoleonic Wars (1979) (Blandford)
Hibbert, Christopher - Corunna (1961)
Hibbert, Christopher - Recollections of Rifleman Harris (edt 1970)
Hibbert, Christopher - A Soldier of the 71st (edt 1976)
Kincaid, Sir John - Adventures in the Rifle Brigade (nd) (Maclaren)
Lawford, J. - Wellington's Peninsular Army (1973)
Lawford, J. & Peter Young - Wellington's Masterpiece - Salamanca (1973)
Longford, Lady- Wellington - The Years of the Sword (1971)
Napier, W.- English Battles and Sieges in thePeninsula (rpt 1973) (John Murray)
North, R.- Soldiers of the Peninsular War (1972)
Oman, Sir Charles - The History of the Peninsular War (rpt1970) (Greenhill Press)
Oman, Sir Charles - Sir John Moore (1953)
Oman, Sir Charles - Wellington's Army (rpt 1970) (Cambridge University Press)
Richards, D.S. - The Peninsular Veterans (1975) (McDonald & Janes)
Rogers, H.C.B. - Wellington's Army (1979) (Ian Allen)
Surtees, W.- Twenty-Five Years in the Rifle Brigade (rpt 1973) (Longmans)
Weller, Jac- Wellington in the Peninsula (1962) (Kaye & Ward)
Windrow, Martin & Embleton, Gerry - Military Dress of the Peninsular War (1974) (Ian Allen)

Books on the Peninsular War are legion - the Regimental Histories of every British Regiment (and the Royal Artillery) deal proudly and at length with their feats in Portugal and Spain during the momentous years 1808-1814.

The Greenhill Press (of Great Britain) are currently re-publishing a selection of classic, hitherto out-of-print, books on the Napoleonic period. Among them are :

Adventures with the Connaught Rangers - William Grattan
A British Rifleman (Journals & Correspondence during the Peninsula War) - George Simmons
A Boy in the Peninsular War- Robert Blakeney
In the Peninsular with a French Hussar - Albert Jean Michel de Rocca
The Peninsular Journal of Mag. Gen. Sir Benjamin D'Urban 1808 - 1817
Wellington's Army - Sir Charles Oman

Wargaming. The following books by Donald Featherstone contain material relating to the Peninsular War:

Advanced Wargames (1969)
Wargame Campaigns (1970)
Wargames Through the Ages vol.3 1792-1859 (1975)
Battle Notes for Wargamers (1973)
Battles with Model soldiers (1970 & 1980)
Solo Wargaming (1973)
Skirmish Wargames (1975)
Featherstone's Complete Wargaming (1989)
Wargaming in History - The Peninsular War (1991)

And don't forget...french bread, cheese, pate, and a bottle of the local wine.